TWO PTERODACTYLS TOGETHER WITH TOOTHED SEA-BIRDS

[Frontispiece

THE OUTLINE OF HISTORY

BEING A PLAIN HISTORY OF LIFE AND MANKIND

BY H. G. WELLS

Written with the advice and
: editorial help of :
Mr Ernest Barker
Sir H. H. Johnston
Sir E. Ray Lankester
and Professor Gilbert
Murray.

LONDON
GEORGE NEWNES LIMITED
SOUTHAMPTON ST. STRAND W.C.2

THE OUTLINE OF HISTORY

INTRODUCTION

" A philosophy of the history of the human race, worthy of its name, must begin with the heavens and descend to the earth, must be charged with the conviction that all existence is one—a single conception sustained from beginning to end upon one identical law."—FRIEDRICH RATZEL.

THIS *Outline of History* is an attempt to tell, truly and clearly, in one continuous narrative, the whole story of life and mankind so far as it is known to-day. It is written plainly for the general reader, but its aim goes beyond its use as merely interesting reading matter. There is a feeling abroad that the teaching of history considered as a part of general education is in an unsatisfactory condition, and particularly that the ordinary treatment of this " subject " by the class and teacher and examiner is too partial and narrow. But the desire to extend the general range of historical ideas is confronted by the argument that the available time for instruction is already consumed by that partial and narrow treatment, and that therefore, however desirable this extension of range may be, it is in practice impossible. If an Englishman, for example, has found the history of England quite enough for his powers of assimilation, then it seems hopeless to expect his sons and daughters to master universal history, if that is to consist of the history of England, plus the history of France, plus the history of Germany, plus the history of Russia, and so on. To which the only possible answer is that universal history is at once something more and something less

than the aggregate of the national histories to which we are accustomed, that it must be approached in a different spirit and dealt with in a different manner. This book seeks to justify that answer. It has been written primarily to show that *history as one whole* is amenable to a more broad and comprehensive handling than is the history of special nations and periods, a broader handling that will bring it within the normal limitations of time and energy set to the reading and education of an ordinary citizen. This outline deals with ages and races and nations, where the ordinary history deals with reigns and pedigrees and campaigns; but it will not be found to be more crowded with names and dates nor more difficult to follow and understand. History is no exception amongst the sciences; as the gaps fill in, the outline simplifies; as the outlook broadens, the clustering multitude of details dissolves into general laws. And many topics of quite primary interest to mankind, the first appearance and the growth of scientific knowledge for example, and its effects upon human life, the elaboration of the ideas of money and credit, or the story of the origins and spread and influence of Christianity, which must be treated fragmentarily or by elaborate digressions in any partial history,

I

arise and flow completely and naturally in one general record of the world in which we live.

The need for a common knowledge of the general facts of human history throughout the world has become very evident during the tragic happenings of the last few years. Swifter means of communication have brought all men very close to one another for good or for evil. War becomes a universal disaster, blind and monstrously destructive; it bombs the baby in its cradle and sinks the food-ships that cater for the non-combatant and the neutral. There can be no peace now, we realize, but a common peace in all the world; no prosperity but a general prosperity. But *there can be no common peace and prosperity without common historical ideas.* Without such ideas to hold them together in harmonious co-operation, with nothing but narrow, selfish, and conflicting nationalist tradditions, races and peoples are bound to drift towards conflict and destruction. This truth, which was apparent to that great philosopher Kant a century or more ago—it is the gist of his tract upon universal peace—is now plain to the man in the street. Our internal policies and our economic and social ideas are profoundly vitiated at present by wrong and fantastic ideas of the origin and historical relationship of social classes. A sense of history as the common adventure of all mankind is as necessary for peace within as it is for peace between the nations.

Such are the views of history that this *Outline* seeks to realize. It is an attempt to tell how our present state of affairs, this distressed and multifarious human life about us, arose in the course of vast ages and out of the inanimate clash of matter, and to estimate the quality and amount and range of the hopes with which it now faces its destiny. It is one experimental contribution to a great and urgently necessary educational reformation, which must ultimately restore universal history, revised, corrected, and brought up to date, to its proper place and use as the backbone of a general education. We say " restore," because all the great cultures

of the world hitherto, Judaism and Christianity in the Bible, Islam in the Koran, have used some sort of cosmogony and world history as a basis. It may indeed be argued that without such a basis any true binding culture of men is inconceivable. Without it we are a chaos.[1]

Remarkably few sketches of universal history by one single author have been written. One book that has influenced the writer very strongly is Winwood Reade's *Martyrdom of Man*. This *dates*, as people say, nowadays, and it has a fine gloom of its own, but it is still an extraordinarily inspiring presentation of human history as one consistent process. Mr. F. S. Marvin's *Living Past* is also an admirable summary of human progress. America has recently produced two well-illustrated and up-to-date class books, Breasted's *Ancient Times* and Robinson's *Medieval and Modern Times*, which together give a very good idea of the story of mankind since the beginning of human societies. There are, moreover, quite a number of nominally Universal Histories in existence, but they are really not histories at all, they are encyclopedias of history; they lack the unity of presentation attainable only when the whole subject has been passed through one single mind. These universal histories are compilations, assemblies of separate national or regional histories by different hands, the parts being necessarily unequal in merit and authority and disproportionate one to another. Several such universal histories in thirty or forty volumes or so, adorned with allegorical title pages and illustrated by folding maps and plans of Noah's Ark, Solomon's Temple, and the Tower of Babel, were produced for the libraries of gentlemen in the eighteenth century. Helmolt's *World History*, in eight massive volumes, is a modern compilation of the same sort, very useful for reference and richly illustrated, but far better in its parts than as a whole. *The Encyclopedia Britannica* contains, of course, a complete encyclopedia of history within

[1] See upon this an excellent pamphlet by F. J. Gould, *History, the Supreme Subject in the Instruction of the Young* (Watts & Co.).

itself, and is the most modern of all such collections. F. Ratzel's *History of Mankind*, in spite of the promise of its title, is mainly a natural history of man, though it is rich with suggestions upon the nature and development of civilization. That publication and Miss Ellen Churchill Semple's *Influence of Geographical Environment*, based on Ratzel's work, are quoted in this *Outline*, and have had considerable influence upon its plan. F. Ratzel would indeed have been the ideal author for such a book as our present one. Unfortunately neither he nor any other ideal author was available.

The writer will offer no apology for making this experiment. His disqualifications are manifest. But such work needs to be done by as many people as possible, he was free to make his contribution, and he was greatly attracted by the task. He has read sedulously and made the utmost use of all the help he could obtain. There is not a chapter that has not been examined by some more competent person than himself and very carefully revised. He has particularly to thank his friends Sir E. Ray Lankester, Sir H. H. Johnston, Professor Gilbert Murray, and Mr. Ernest Barker for much counsel and direction and editorial help. Sir Richard Gregory, Professor J. L. Myres, Professor W. S. Culbertson of Harvard, Dr. Singer of Oxford, Mr. Philip Guedalla, Mr. L. Cranmer Byng, and Sir Denison Ross have all to be thanked for help, either by reading parts of the MS. or by answering questions and giving advice. But of course none of these generous helpers are to be held responsible for the judgements, tone, arrangement, or writing of this *Outline*. In the relative importance of the parts, in the moral and political implications of the story, the final decision has necessarily fallen to the writer. The problem of illustrations was a very difficult one for him, for he had had no previous experience in the production of an illustrated book. In Mr. J. F. Horrabin he has had the good fortune to find not only an illustrator but a collaborator. Mr. Horrabin has spared no pains to make his work informative and exact. His maps and drawings are a part of the text, the most vital and decorative part. Some of them, the hypothetical maps, for example, of the western world at the end of the last glacial age, during the " pluvial age " and 12,000 years ago, represent the reading and inquiry of many laborious days.

And here the writer owes a word of thanks to that living index of printed books, Mr. J. F. Cox of the London Library. He would also like to acknowledge here the help he has received from Mrs. Wells. Without her labour in typing and re-typing the drafts of the various chapters as they have been revised and amended, in checking references, finding suitable quotations, hunting up illustrations, and keeping in order the whole mass of material for this history, and without her constant help and watchful criticism, its completion would have been impossible.

H. G. WELLS.

Book I

THE MAKING OF OUR WORLD

I

THE EARTH IN SPACE AND TIME

THE earth on which we live is a spinning globe. Vast though it seems to us, it is a mere speck of matter in the greater vastness of space.

Space is, for the most part, emptiness. At great intervals there are in this emptiness flaring centres of heat and light, the " fixed stars." They are all moving about in space, notwithstanding that they are called fixed stars, but for a long time men did not realize their motion. They are so vast and at such tremendous distances that their motion is not perceived. Only in the course of many thousands of years is it appreciable. These fixed stars are so far off that, for all their immensity, they seem to be, even when we look at them through the most powerful telescopes, mere points of light, brighter or less bright. A few, however, when we turn a telescope upon them, are seen to be whirls and clouds of shining vapour which we call nebulæ. They are so far off that a movement of millions of miles would be imperceptible.

One star, however, is so near to us that it is like a great ball of flame. This one is the sun. The sun is itself in its nature like a fixed star, but it differs from the other fixed stars in appearance because it is beyond comparison nearer than they are; and because it is nearer men have been able to learn something of its nature. Its mean distance from the earth is ninety-three million miles. It is a mass of flaming matter, having a diameter of 866,000 miles. Its bulk is a million and a quarter times the bulk of our earth.

These are difficult figures for the imagination. If a bullet fired from a Maxim gun at the sun kept its muzzle velocity unimpaired, it would take seven years to reach the sun. And yet we say the sun is near, measured by the scale of the stars. If the earth were a small ball, one inch in diameter, the sun would be a globe of nine feet diameter; it would fill a small bedroom. It is spinning round on its axis, but since it is an incandescent fluid, its polar regions do not travel with the same velocity as its equator, the surface of which rotates in about twenty-five days. The surface visible to us consists of clouds of incandescent metallic vapour. At what lies below we can only guess. So hot is the sun's atmosphere that iron, nickel, copper, and tin are present in it in a gaseous state. About it at great distances circle not only our earth, but certain kindred bodies called the planets. These shine in the sky because they reflect the light of the sun; they are near enough for us to note their movements quite easily. Night by night their positions change with regard to the fixed stars.

It is well to understand how empty space is. If, as we have said, the sun were a ball nine feet across, our earth would, in proportion, be the size of a one-inch ball, and at a distance of 330 yards from the sun. The moon would be a speck the size of a small pea, twenty inches from the earth. Nearer to the sun than the earth would be two other very similar specks, the planets Mercury and Venus, at a distance of rather more than a hundred and two hundred yards respectively. Beyond the earth would come the planets Mars, Jupiter, Saturn, Uranus, and Neptune, at distances of 500, 850, 3,000, 6,300, and 10,000 yards respectively. There would also be a certain number of very much smaller specks, flying about amongst these planets, more particularly a number called the asteroids circling between Mars and Jupiter, and occasionally a little puff of more or less luminous vapour and dust would drift into the system from the almost limitless emptiness beyond. Such a puff is what we call a comet. *All the rest of the space about us and around us and for unfathomable distances beyond is cold, lifeless, and void.* The nearest fixed star to us, *on this minute scale*, be it remembered, of the earth as a one-inch ball, and the moon a little pea, would be over 40,000 miles away.

The science that tells of these things and how men have come to know about them is Astronomy, and to books of astronomy the reader must go to learn more about the sun and stars. The science and description of the world on which we live are called respectively Geology and Geography.

The diameter of our world is a little under 8,000 miles. Its surface is rough, the more projecting parts of the roughness are mountains, and in the hollows of its surface there is a film of water, the oceans and seas. This film of water is about five miles thick at its deepest part—that is to say, the deepest oceans have a depth of five miles. This is very little in comparison with the bulk of the world.

About this sphere is a thin covering of air, the atmosphere. As we ascend in a balloon or go up a mountain from the level of the sea-shore the air is continually less dense, until at last it becomes so thin that it cannot support life. At a height of twenty miles there is scarcely any air at all—not one hundredth part of the density of air at the surface of the sea. The highest point to which a bird can fly is about four miles up—the condor, it is said, can struggle up to that; but most small birds and insects which are carried up by aeroplanes or balloons drop off insensible at a much lower level, and the greatest height to which any mountaineer has ever climbed is under five miles. Men have flown in aeroplanes to a height of over four miles, and balloons with men in them have reached very nearly seven miles, but at the cost of considerable physical suffering. Small experimental balloons, containing not men, but recording instruments, have gone as high as twenty-two miles.

It is in the upper few hundred feet of the crust of the earth, in the sea, and in the lower levels of the air below four miles that life is found. We do not know of any life at all except in these films of air and water upon our planet. So far as we know, all the rest of space is as yet without life. Scientific men have discussed the possibility of life, or of some process of a similar kind, occurring upon such kindred bodies as the planets Venus and Mars. But they point merely to questionable possibilities.

Astronomers and geologists and those who study physics have been able to tell us something. of the origin and history of the earth. They consider that, vast ages ago, the sun was a spinning, flaring mass of matter, not yet concentrated into a compact centre of heat and light, considerably larger than it is now, and spinning very much faster, and that as it whirled, a series of fragments detached themselves from it, which became the planets. Our earth is one of these planets. The flaring mass that was the material of the earth broke as it spun into two masses, a larger, the earth itself, and a smaller, which is now the dead, still moon. Astronomers give us convincing reasons for supposing that sun and earth and moon and all that system were then whirling about at a speed much greater than the speed at which they are moving to-day, and that at first our earth was a flaming thing upon which no life could live. The way in which they have reached these conclusions is by a very beautiful and interesting series of observations and reasoning, too long and elaborate for us to deal with here. But they oblige us to believe that the sun, incandescent though it is, is now much cooler than it was, and that it spins more slowly now than it did, and that it continues to cool and slow down. And they also show that the rate at which the earth spins is diminishing and continues to diminish—that is to say, that our day is growing longer and longer, and that the heat at the centre of the earth wastes slowly. There was a time when the day was not a half and not a third of what it is to-day; when a blazing hot sun, much greater than it is now, must have moved visibly— had there been an eye to mark it—from its rise to its setting across the skies. There will be a time when the day will be as long as a year is now, and the cooling sun, shorn of its beams, will hang motionless in the heavens.

It must have been in days of a much hotter sun, a far swifter day and night, high tides, great heat, tremendous storms and earthquakes, that life, of which we are a part, began upon the world. The moon also was nearer and brighter in those days and had a changing face.[1]

[1] For a convenient recent discussion of the origin of the earth and its early history before the seas were precipitated and sedimentation began, the student should consult Professor Burrell's contribution to the Yale lectures, *The Evolution of the Earth and its Inhabitants* (1918), edited by President Lull.

II

THE RECORD OF THE ROCKS

§ 1

WE do not know how life began upon the earth.[1] Biologists, that is to say, students of life, have made guesses about these beginnings, but we will not discuss them here. Let us only **The First** note that they all agree that life **Living** began where the tides of those swift **Things.** days spread and receded over the steaming beaches of mud and sand.

The atmosphere was much denser then, usually great cloud masses obscured the sun, frequent storms darkened the heavens. The

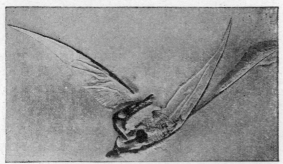

Natural History Museum Photograph.

AN EXCEPTIONALLY PLAIN PAGE IN THE RECORD OF THE ROCKS.

The remains of a Pterodactyl embedded in fine sandstone. The actual animal is shown in the large coloured illustration.

land of those days, upheaved by violent volcanic forces, was a barren land, without vegetation, without soil. The almost incessant rain-storms swept down upon it, and rivers

[1] But although we know nothing of the origin of life, there are many guesses, and some, in the light of modern physiological and chemical science, are quite plausible guesses. Here in this history of life we are doing our best to give only known and established facts in the broadest way, and to reduce the speculative element that must necessarily enter into our account to a minimum. The reader who is curious upon this question of life's beginning will find a very good summary of current suggestions done by Professor L. L. Woodruff in President Lull's excellent compilation *The Evolution of the Earth* (Yale University Press, 1918). Professor H. F. Osborne's *Origin and Evolution of Life* is also a very vigorous and suggestive book upon this subject, but it demands a fair knowledge of physics and chemistry in the reader.

and torrents carried great loads of sediment out to sea, to become muds that hardened later into slates and shales, and sands that became sandstones. The geologists have studied the whole accumulation of these sediments as it remains to-day, from those of the earliest ages to the most recent. Of course the oldest deposits are the most distorted and changed and worn, and in them there is now no certain trace to be found of life at all. Probably the earliest forms of life were small and soft, leaving no evidence of their existence behind them. It was only when some of these living things developed skeletons and shells of lime and such-like hard material that they left fossil vestiges after they died, and so put themselves on record for examination.

The literature of geology is very largely an account of the fossils that are found in the rocks, and of the order in which layers after layers of rocks follow one another. The very oldest rocks must have been formed before there was any sea at all, when the earth was too hot for a sea to exist, and when the water that is now sea was an atmosphere of steam mixed with the air. Its higher levels were dense with clouds, from which a hot rain fell towards the rocks below, to be converted again into steam long before it reached their incandescence. Below this steam atmosphere the molten world-stuff solidified as the first rocks. These first rocks must have solidified as a cake over glowing liquid material beneath, much as cooling lava does. They must have appeared first as crusts and clinkers. They must have been constantly remelted and recrystallized before any thickness of them became permanently solid. The name of Fundamental Gneiss is given to a great underlying system of crystalline rocks which probably formed age by age as this hot youth of the world drew to its close. The scenery of the world in the days when the Fundamental Gneiss was formed must have been more like the interior of a furnace than anything else to be found upon earth at the present time.

After long ages the steam in the atmosphere began also to condense and fall right down to earth, pouring at last over these warm primordial rocks in rivulets of hot water and gathering in depressions as pools and lakes and the first seas. Into those seas the streams that poured over the rocks brought with them dust and particles to form a sediment, and this sediment accumulated in layers, or as geologists call them, *strata*, and formed the first Sedimentary Rocks. Those earliest sedimentary rocks sank into depressions and were covered by others; they were bent, tilted up, and torn by great volcanic disturbances and by tidal strains that swept through the rocky crust of the earth. We find these first sedimentary rocks still coming to the surface of the land here and there, either not covered by later strata or exposed after vast ages of concealment by the wearing off of the rock that covered them later—there are great surfaces of them in Canada especially; they are cleft and bent, partially remelted, recrystallized, hardened and compressed, but recognizable for what they are. And they contain no single certain trace of life at all. They are frequently called *Azoic* (lifeless) Rocks. But since in some of these earliest sedimentary rocks a substance called graphite (black lead) occurs, and also red and black oxide of iron, and since it is asserted that these substances need the activity of living things for their production, which may or may not be the case, some geologists prefer to call these earliest sedimentary rocks *Archæozoic* (primordial life). They suppose that the first life was soft living matter that had no shells or skeletons or any such structure that could remain as a recognizable fossil after its death, and that its chemical influence caused the deposition of graphite and iron oxide. This is pure guessing, of course, and there is at least an equal probability that in the time of formation of the Azoic Rocks, life had not yet begun.

Long ago there were found in certain of these ancient first-formed rocks in Canada, curious striped masses, and thin layers of white and green mineral substance which Sir William Dawson considered were fossil vestiges, the walls or coverings of some very simple sort of living thing which has now vanished from the earth.

He called these markings *Eozoon Canadense* (the Canadian dawn-animal). There has been much discussion and controversy over this Eozoon, but to-day it is agreed that Eozoon is nothing more than a crystalline marking. Mixed minerals will often intercrystallize in blobs or branching shapes that are very suggestive of simple plant or animal forms. Any one who has made a lead tree in his schooldays,

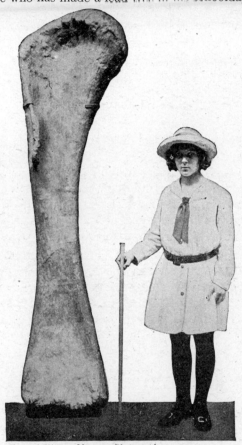

Natural History Museum Photograph.

ANOTHER PLAIN ITEM IN THE RECORD OF THE ROCKS.

The thigh bone of a *Gigantosaurus*, one of the greatest dinosaurs. The lady holds a yard measure in her hand.

or lit those queer indoor fireworks known as serpents' eggs, which unfold like a long snake, or who has seen the curious markings often found in quartz crystals, or noted the tree-like pattern on old stone-ware beer mugs, will realize how closely non-living matter can sometimes mock the shapes of living things.

Overlying or overlapping these Azoic or Archæozoic rocks come others, manifestly also very ancient and worn, which do contain traces of life. These first traces are of the very simplest description; they are the vestiges of simple plants called algæ, or traces like the tracks made by worms in the sea mud. There are also the skeletons of the microscopic creatures called Radiolaria. This second series of rocks is called the Proterozoic (beginning of life) series, and marks a long age in the world's history. Lying over and above the Proterozoic rocks is a third series, which is found to contain a considerable number and variety of traces of living things. First comes the evidence of a diversity of shell-fish, crabs, and such-like crawling things, worms, seaweeds, and the like; then of a multitude of fishes and of the beginnings of land plants and land creatures. These rocks are called the Palæozoic (ancient life) rocks. They mark a vast era, during which life was slowly spreading, increasing, and developing in the seas of our world. Through long ages, through the earliest Palæozoic time, it was no more than a proliferation of such swimming and creeping things in the water. There were creatures called trilobites;

they were crawling things like big sea woodlice that were probably related to the American king-crab of to-day. There were also sea-scorpions, the prefects of that early world. The individuals of certain species of these were nine feet long. These were the very highest sorts of life. There were abundant different sorts of an order of shellfish called brachiopods. There were plant animals, rooted and joined together like plants, and loose weeds that waved in the waters.

It was not a display of life to excite our imaginations. There was nothing that ran or flew or even swam swiftly or skilfully. Except for the size of some of the creatures, it was not very different from, and rather less various than, the kind of life a student would gather from any summer-time ditch nowadays for microscopic examination. Such was the life of the shallow seas through a hundred million years or more in the early Palæozoic period. The land during that time was apparently absolutely barren. We find no trace nor hint of land life. Everything that lived in those days lived under water for most or all of its life.

Lifeless bare rock: no moss nor lichen.

Intertidal green scum

No vertebrated animals

Life in the Early Palæozoic

J.F.H.

DIAGRAM OF LIFE IN THE EARLY PALÆOZOIC WORLD.

Between the formation of these Lower Palæo-zoic rocks in which the sea scorpion and tri-lobite ruled, and our own time, there have inter-vened almost immeasurable ages, represented by layers and masses of sedimentary rocks. There are first the Upper Palæozoic Rocks, and above these the geologists distinguish two great divisions. Next above the Palæozoic

(It is, we may note, the practice of many geologists to make a break between the rest of the Cainozoic system of rocks and those which contain traces of humanity, which latter are cut off as a separate system under the name of Quaternary. But that, as we shall see, is rather like taking the last page of a book, which is really the conclusion of the last chapter,

RESTORATION OF EARLY PALÆOZOIC LIFE.
Note its general resemblance, except for size, to the microscopic summer ditchwater life of to-day.

come the Mesozoic (middle life) rocks, a second vast system of fossil-bearing rocks, representing perhaps a hundred millions of swift years, and containing a wonderful array of fossil remains, bones of giant reptiles and the like, which we will presently describe ; and above these again are the Cainozoic (recent life) rocks, a third great volume in the history of life, an unfinished volume of which the sand and mud that was carried out to sea yesterday by the rivers of the world, to bury the bones and scales and bodies and tracks that will become at last fossils of the things of to-day, constitute the last written leaf.

and making a separate chapter of it and calling it the last chapter.)

These markings and fossils in the rocks and the rocks themselves are our first historical documents. The history of life that men have puzzled out, and are still puzzling out from them is called the Record of the Rocks. By studying this record men are slowly piecing together a story of life's beginnings, and of the beginnings of our kind, of which our ancestors a century or so ago had no suspicion. But when we call these rocks and the fossils a record and a history, it must not be supposed that there

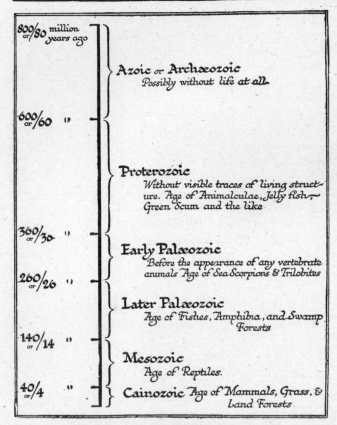

800/80 million
or/ years ago

Azoic or Archæozoic
Possibly without life at all

600/60 "
or/

Proterozoic
Without visible traces of living struct-
ure. Age of Animalculae, Jelly fish,
Green Scum and the like

360/36 "
or/

Early Palæozoic
Before the appearance of any vertebrate
animals Age of Sea Scorpions & Trilobites

260/26 "
or/

Later Palæozoic
Age of Fishes, Amphibia, and Swamp
Forests

140/14 "
or/

Mesozoic
Age of Reptiles.

40/4 "
or/
Cainozoic Age of Mammals, Grass, &
Land Forests

THIS IS A NOTEWORTHY DIAGRAM.

It gives the extreme estimates of the age of our
earth and the proportionate length of the main divisions
of its history. So vast is the time this line represents
that even on the lowest estimate the whole duration of
recorded history from earliest Egypt to our own day
would be but an almost imperceptible scrap of the last
division. Note the vast slowness with which life has
developed. Note, too, that for more than half of the
world's age there are no certain evidences of life at all.

is any sign of an orderly keeping of a record.
It is merely that whatever happens leaves
some trace, if only we are intelligent enough to
detect the meaning of that trace. Nor are the
rocks of the world in orderly layers one above
the other, convenient for men to read. They
are not like the books and pages of a library.
They are torn, disrupted, interrupted, flung
about, defaced, like a carelessly arranged office
after it has experienced in succession a bom-
bardment, a hostile military occupation, looting,
an earthquake, riots, and a fire. And so it is
that for countless generations this Record of the
Rocks lay unsuspected beneath the feet of men.
Fossils were discussed at Alexandria by Eratosthenes and others in the third century B.C., a
discussion which is summarised in Strabo's
Geography (? 20–10 B.C.). They were known to
the Latin poet Ovid, but he did not understand
their nature. He thought they were the first
rude efforts of creative power. They were
noted by Arabic writers in the tenth century.
Leonardo da Vinci, who lived so recently as the
opening of the sixteenth century (1452—1519),
was one of the first Europeans to grasp the real

significance of fossils,[1] and it has been only
within the last century and a half that man
has begun the serious and sustained deciphering
of these long-neglected early pages of his
world's history.

§ 2

Speculations about geological time vary
enormously. Estimates of the age of the oldest
rocks by geologists and astronomers
starting from different standpoints
have varied between 1,600,000,000,
and 25,000,000. The lowest estimate was
made by Lord Kelvin in 1867. Professor
Huxley guessed at 400,000,000 years. There
is a summary of views and the grounds
upon which the estimates have been made in
Osborne's *Origin and Evolution of Life*; he
inclines to the moderate total of 100,000,000.
It must be clearly understood by the reader
how sketchy and provisional all these time
estimates are. They rest nearly always upon

How Old is the World ?

[1] There is a discussion of fossils in the Holkham
Hall Leonardo MS.

theoretical assumptions of the slenderest kind. That the period of time has been vast, that it is to be counted by scores and possibly by hundreds of millions of years, is the utmost that can be said with certainty in the matter. It is quite open to the reader to divide every number in the appended time diagram by ten or multiply it by two ; no one can gainsay him. Of the relative amount of time as between one age and another we have, however, stronger evidence ; if the reader cuts down the 800,000,000 we have given here to 400,000,000, then he must reduce the 40,000,000 of the Cainozoic to 20,000,000. And be it noted that whatever the total sum may be, most geologists are in agreement that *half or more than half of the whole of geological time had passed before life had developed to the Later Palæozoic level.* The reader reading quickly through these opening chapters may be apt to think of them as a mere swift prelude of preparation to the apparently much longer history that follows, but in reality that subsequent history is longer only because it is more detailed and more interesting to us. It looms larger in perspective. For ages that stagger the imagination this earth spun hot and lifeless, and again for ages of equal vastness it held no life above the level of the animalculæ in a drop of ditchwater.

Not only is Space from the point of view of life and humanity empty, but Time is empty also. Life is like a little glow, scarcely kindled yet, in these void immensities.

III

NATURAL SELECTION AND THE CHANGES OF SPECIES

NOW here it will be well to put plainly certain general facts about this new thing, *life*, that was creeping in the shallow waters and intertidal muds of the early Palæozoic period, and which is perhaps confined to our planet alone in all the immensity of space.

Life differs from all things whatever that are without life in certain general aspects. There are the most wonderful differences among living things to-day, but all living things past and present agree in possessing *a certain power of growth* ; all living things *take nourishment*, all living things *move about* as they feed and grow, though the movement may be no more than the spread of roots through the soil or of branches in the air. Moreover, living things reproduce ; they give rise to other living things, either by growing and then dividing or by means of seeds or spores or eggs or other ways of producing young. *Reproduction* is a characteristic of life.

No living thing goes on living for ever. There seems to be *a limit of growth* for every kind of living thing. Among very small and simple living things, such as that microscopic blob of living matter the *Amœba*, an individual may grow and then divide completely into two new individuals, which again may divide in their turn. Many other microscopic creatures live actively for a time, grow, and then become quiet and inactive, enclose themselves in an outer covering and break up wholly into a number of still smaller things, spores, which are released and scattered and again grow into the likeness of their parent. Among more complex creatures the reproduction is not usually such simple division, though division does occur even in the case of many creatures big enough to be visible to the unassisted eye. But the rule with almost all larger beings is that the individual grows up to a certain limit of size. Then, before it becomes unwieldy, its growth declines and stops. As it reaches its full size it *matures*, it begins to produce young, which are either born alive or hatched from eggs. But all of its body does not produce young. Only a special part does that. After the individual has lived and produced offspring for some time, it ages and dies. It does so by a sort of necessity. There is a practical limit to its life as well as to its growth. These things are as true of plants as they are of animals. And they are not true of things that do not live. Non-living things, such as crystals, grow, but they have no set limits of growth or size, they *do not move of their own accord* and there is *no stir within them.* Crystals once formed may last unchanged for millions of years. There is *no reproduction* for any non-living thing.

that slight difference. It is hard for us to see individuality in butterflies because we do not observe them very closely, but it is easy for us to see it in men. All the men and women in the world now are descended from the men and women of A.D. 1800, but not one of us now is exactly the same as one of that vanished generation. And what is true of men and butterflies is true of every sort of living thing, of plants as of animals. Every species changes all its individualities in each generation. That is as true of all the minute creatures that swarmed

DIAGRAM OF LIFE IN THE LATER PALÆOZOIC AGE.

Life is creeping out of the water. An insect, like a dragon-fly, is shown. There were amphibia like gigantic newts and salamanders, and even primitive reptiles in these swamps, as the larger illustration shows.

This growth and dying and reproduction of living things leads to some very wonderful consequences. The young which a living thing produces are either directly, or after some intermediate stages and changes (such as the changes of a caterpillar and butterfly), like the parent living thing. But they are never exactly like it or like each other. There is always a slight difference, which we speak of as *individuality.* A thousand butterflies this year may produce two or three thousand next year ; these latter will look to us almost exactly like their predecessors, but each one will have just

and reproduced and died in the Archæozoic and Proterozoic seas, as it is of men to-day.

Every species of living things is continually dying and being born again, as a multitude of fresh individuals.

Consider, then, what must happen to a new-born generation of living things of any species. Some of the individuals will be stronger or sturdier or better suited to succeed in life in some way than the rest, many individuals will be weaker or less suited. In particular single cases any sort of luck or accident may occur, but *on the whole* the better equipped individuals will live and grow up and reproduce themselves and the weaker will *as a rule* go under. The latter will be less able to get food, to fight their enemies and pull through. So that in each generation there is as it were a picking over of a species, a picking out of most of the weak or unsuitable and a preference for the strong and suitable. This process is called *Natural Selection* or the *Survival of the Fittest.*[1]

It follows, therefore, from the fact that living things grow and breed and die, that every species, so long as the conditions under which it lives remain the same, becomes more and more perfectly fitted to those conditions in every generation.

But now suppose those conditions change, then the sort of individual that used to succeed may now fail to succeed and a sort of individual that could not get on at all under the old conditions may now find its opportunity. These species will change, therefore, generation by generation; the old sort of individual that used to prosper and dominate will fail and die out and the new sort of individual will become the rule,—until the general character of the species changes.

Suppose, for example, there is some little furry whitey-brown animal living in a bitterly cold land which is usually under snow. Such individuals as have the thickest, whitest fur will be least hurt by the cold, less seen by their enemies, and less conspicuous as they seek their prey. The fur of this species will thicken and its whiteness increase with every generation, until there is no advantage in carrying any more fur.

Imagine now a change of climate that brings warmth into the land, sweeps away the snows, makes white creatures glaringly visible during the greater part of the year and thick fur an encumbrance. Then every individual with a touch of brown in its colouring and a thinner fur will find itself at an advantage, and very white and heavy fur will be a handicap. There will be a weeding out of the white in favour of the brown in each generation. If this change of climate come about too quickly, it may of course exterminate the species altogether; but if it come about gradually, the species, although

[1] It might be called with more exactness the *Survival of the Fitter.*

it may have a hard time, may yet be able to change itself and adapt itself generation by generation. This change and adaptation is called the *Modification of Species.*

Perhaps this change of climate does not occur all over the lands inhabited by the species; maybe it occurs only on one side of some great arm of the sea or some great mountain range or such-like divide, and not on the other. A warm ocean current like the Gulf Stream may be deflected, and flow so as to warm one side of the barrier, leaving the other still cold. Then on the cold side this species will still be going on to its utmost possible furriness and whiteness and on the other side it will be modifying towards brownness and a thinner coat. At the same time there will probably be other changes going on; a difference in the paws perhaps, because one half of the species will be frequently scratching through snow for its food, while the other will be scampering over brown earth. Probably also the difference of climate will mean differences in the sort of food available, and that may produce differences in the teeth and the digestive organs. And there may be changes in the sweat and oil glands of the skin due to the changes in the fur, and these will affect the excretory organs and all the internal chemistry of the body. And so through all the structure of the creature. A time will come when the two separated varieties of this formerly single species will become so unlike each other as to be recognizably different species. Such a splitting up of a species in the course of generations into two or more species is called the *Differentiation of Species.*

And it should be clear to the reader that given these elemental facts of life, given growth and death and reproduction with individual variation in a world that changes, life *must* change in this way, modification and differentiation *must* occur, old species *must* disappear, and new ones appear. We have chosen for our instance here a familiar sort of animal, but what is true of furry beasts in snow and ice is true of all life, and equally true of the soft jellies and simple beginnings that flowed and crawled for hundreds of millions of years between the tidal levels and in the shallow, warm waters of the Proterozoic seas.

The early life of the early world, when the

ANIMAL LIFE OF THE LATER PALÆOZOIC.

blazing sun rose and set in only a quarter of the time it now takes, when the warm seas poured in great tides over the sandy and muddy shores of the rocky lands and the air was full of clouds and steam, must have been modified and varied and species must have developed at a great pace. Life was probably as swift and short as the days and years; the generations, which natural selection picked over, followed one another in rapid succession.

Natural selection is a slower process with man than with any other creature. It takes twenty years or more before an ordinary human being in Western Europe grows up and reproduces. In the case of most animals the new generation is on trial in a year or less. With such simple and lowly beings, however, as first appeared in the primordial seas, growth and reproduction was probably a matter of a few brief hours or even of a few brief minutes. Modification and differentiation of species must accordingly have been very rapid, and life had already developed a very great variety of widely contrasted forms before it began to leave traces in the rocks. The Record of the Rocks does not begin, therefore, with any group of closely related forms from which all subsequent and existing creatures are descended. It begins in the midst of the game, with nearly every main division of the animal kingdom already represented. Plants are already plants, and animals animals. The curtain rises on a drama in the sea that has already begun, and has been

going on for some time. The brachiopods are discovered already in their shells, accepting and consuming much the same sort of food that

Australian Lung-fish breathing air. After Dean.

A TRANSITION TYPE BETWEEN WATER VERTEBRATA AND LAND VERTEBRATA.

oysters and mussels do now; the great water scorpions crawl among the seaweeds, the trilobites roll up into balls and unroll and scuttle away. In that ancient mud and among those early weeds there was probably as rich and abundant and active a life of infusoria and the like as one finds in a drop of ditch-water to-day. In the ocean waters too, down to the utmost downward limit to which light could filter, then as now, there was an abundance of minute and translucent, and in many cases phosphorescent, beings.

But though the ocean and intertidal waters already swarmed with life, the land above the high-tide line was still, so far as we can guess, a stony wilderness without a trace of life.

IV

THE INVASION OF THE DRY LAND BY LIFE

§ I

WHEREVER the shore line ran there was life, and that life went on in and by and with water as its home, its medium, and its fundamental necessity. The first jelly-like beginnings of life must have perished whenever they got out of the water, as jelly-fish dry up and perish on our beaches to-day. Drying up was the fatal thing for life in those days, against which at first it had no protection.

Life and Water.

But in a world of rain-pools and shallow seas and tides, any variation that enabled a living thing to hold out and keep its moisture during hours of low tide or drought met with every encouragement in the circumstances of the time. There must have been a constant risk of stranding. And, on the other hand, life had to keep rather near the shore and beaches in the shallows because it had need of air (dissolved of course in the water) and light.

No creature can breathe, no creature can digest its food, without water. We talk of

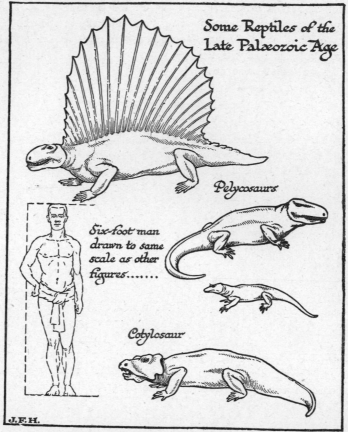

SOME OF THE EARLIEST REPTILES.

breathing air, but what all living things really do is to breathe oxygen dissolved in water. The air we ourselves breathe must first be dissolved in the moisture in our lungs ; and all our food must be liquefied before it can be assimilated. Water-living creatures which are always under water, wave the freely exposed gills by which they breathe in that water, and extract the air dissolved in it. But any creature that is to be exposed for any time out of the water, must have its body and its breathing apparatus protected from drying up. Before the seaweeds could creep up out of the Early Palæozoic seas into the intertidal line of the beach, they had to develop a tougher outer skin to hold their moisture. Before the ancestor of the sea scorpion could survive being left by the tide it had to develop its casing and armour. The trilobites probably developed their tough covering and rolled up into balls, far less as a protection against each other and any other enemies they may have possessed, than as a

precaution against drying. And when presently, as we ascend the Palæozoic rocks, the fish appear, first of all the backboned or vertebrated animals, it is evident that a number of them are already adapted by the protection of their gills by gill covers and by a sort of primitive lung swimming-bladder, to face the same risk of temporary stranding.

Now the weeds and plants that were adapting themselves to intertidal conditions were also bringing themselves into a region of brighter light, and light is very necessary and precious to all plants. Any development of structure that would stiffen them and hold them up to the light, so that instead of crumpling and flopping when the waters receded, they would stand up outspread, was a great advantage. And so we find them developing fibre and support and the beginning of *woody fibre* in them. The early plants reproduced by soft spores, or half-animal " gametes," that were released in water, were distributed by water and could

PLESIOSAURS ON A MESOZOIC BEACH

16]

only germinate under water. The early plants were tied, and most lowly plants to-day are tied, by the conditions of their life cycle, to water. But here again there was a great advantage to be got by the development of some protection of the spores from drought that would enable reproduction to occur without submergence. So soon as a species could do that, it could live and reproduce and spread above the high-water mark, bathed in light and out of reach of the beating and distress of the waves. The main classificatory divisions of the larger plants mark stages in the release of plant life from the necessity of submergence by the development of woody support and of a method of reproduction that is more and more defiant of drying up. The lower plants are still the prisoner attendants of water. The lower mosses must live in damp, and even the development of the spore of the ferns demands at certain stages extreme wetness. The highest plants have carried freedom from water so far that they can live and reproduce if only there is some moisture in the soil below them. They have solved their problem of living out of water altogether.

The essentials of that problem were worked out through the vast æons of the Proterozoic Age and the early Palæozoic Age by nature's method of experiment and trial. Then slowly, but in great abundance, a variety of new plants began to swarm away from the sea and over the lower lands, still keeping to swamp and lagoon and water-course as they spread.

§ 2

And after the plants came the animal life. There is no sort of land animal in the world, as there is no sort of land plant, whose
The Earliest Animals. structure is not primarily that of a water-inhabiting being which has been adapted through the modification and differentiation of species to life out of the water. This adaptation is attained in various ways. In the case of the land scorpion the gill-plates of the primitive sea scorpion are sunken into the body so as to make the lung-books secure from rapid evaporation. The gills of crustaceans, such as the crabs which run about in the air, are protected by the gill-cover ex-

tensions of the back shell or carapace. The ancestors of the insects developed a system of air pouches and air tubes, the tracheal tubes, which carry the air all over the body before it is dissolved. In the case of the vertebrated land animals, the gills of the ancestral fish were first supplemented and then replaced by a bag-like growth from the throat, the primitive lung swimming-bladder. To this day there survive certain mudfish which enable us to understand very clearly the method by which the vertebrated land animals worked their way out of the water. These creatures (e.g. the African lung fish) are found in tropical regions in which there is a rainy full season and a dry season, during which the rivers become mere ditches of baked mud. During the rainy season these fish swim about and breathe by gills like any other fish. As the waters of the river evaporate, these fish bury themselves in the mud, their gills go out of action, and the creature keeps itself alive until the waters return by swallowing air, which passes into its swimming-bladder. The Australian lung fish, when it is caught by the drying up of the river in stagnant pools, and the water has become deaerated and foul, rises to the surface and gulps air. A newt in a pond does exactly the same thing. These creatures still remain at the transition stage, the stage at which the ancestors of the higher vertebrated animals were released from their restriction to an under-water life.

The amphibia (frogs, newts, tritons, etc.) still show in their life history all the stages in the process of this liberation. They are still dependent on water for their reproduction; their eggs must be laid in sunlit water, and there they must develop. The young tadpole has branching external gills that wave in the water; then a gill cover grows back over them and forms a gill chamber. Then, as the creature's legs appear and its tail is absorbed, it begins to use its lungs, and its gills dwindle and vanish. The adult frog can live all the rest of its days in the air, but it can be drowned if it is kept steadfastly below water. When we come to the reptile, however, we find an egg which is protected from evaporation by a tough egg case, and this egg produces young which breathe by lungs from the very moment of hatching. The reptile is on all fours with the seeding plant in its freedom from the necessity to pass any stage of its life cycle in water.

The later Palæolithic Rocks of the northern hemisphere give us the materials for a series of pictures of this slow spreading of life over the land. Geographically, all round the northern half of the world it was an age of lagoons and shallow seas very favourable to this invasion. The new plants, now that they had acquired the power to live this new aerial life, developed with an extraordinary richness and variety.

There were as yet no flowering plants of any sort,[1] no grasses nor trees that shed their leaves in winter;[2] the first "flora" consisted of great tree ferns, gigantic equisetums, cycad ferns, and kindred vegetation. Many of these plants took the form of huge-stemmed trees, of which great multitudes of trunks survive fossilized to this day. Some of these trees were over a hundred feet high, of orders and classes now vanished from the world. They stood with their stems in the water, in which no doubt there was a thick tangle of soft mosses and green slime and fungoid growths that left few plain vestiges behind them. The abundant remains of these first swamp forests constitute the main coal measures of the world of to-day.

[1] Phanerogams.   [2] Deciduous trees.

Amidst this luxuriant primitive vegetation crawled and glided and flew the first insects. They were rigid-winged, four-winged creatures, often very big, some of them having wings measuring a foot in length. There were numerous dragon flies—one found in the Belgian coal-measures had a wing span of twenty-nine inches ! There were also a great variety of flying cock-roaches. Scorpions abounded, and a number of early spiders, which, however, had no spinnerets for web making. Land snails appeared. So too did the first-known step of our own ancestry upon land, the amphibia. As we ascend the higher levels of the Later Palæozoic record, we find the process of air adaptation has gone as far as the appearance of true reptiles amidst the abundant and various amphibia.

The land life of the Upper Palæozoic Age was the life of a green swamp forest without flowers or birds or the noises of modern insects. There were no big land beasts at all ; wallowing amphibia and primitive reptiles were the very highest creatures that life had so far produced. Whatever land lay away from the water or high above the water was still altogether barren and lifeless. But steadfastly, generation by generation, life was creeping away from the shallow sea-water of its beginning.

V

CHANGES IN THE WORLD'S CLIMATE

§ 1

THE Record of the Rocks is like a great book that has been carelessly misused. All its pages are torn, worn, and defaced, and many are altogether missing. The outline of the story that we sketch here has been **Why Life** pieced together slowly and painfully **must change** in an investigation that is still in-**continually.** complete and still in progress. The Carboniferous Rocks, the "coal-measures," give us a vision of the first great expansion of life over the wet lowlands. Then come the torn pages known as the Permian Rocks (which count as the last of the palæozoic), that preserve very little for us of the land vestiges of their age.

Only after a long interval of time does the history spread out generously again.

It must be borne in mind that great changes of climate have always been in progress, that have sometimes stimulated and sometimes checked life. Every species of living thing is always adapting itself more and more closely to its conditions. And conditions are always changing. There is no finality in adaptation. There is a continuing urgency towards fresh change.

About these changes of climate some explanations are necessary here. They are not regular changes ; they are slow fluctuations between heat and cold. The reader must not think that because the sun and earth were once incandescent, the climatic history of the world is a simple story of cooling down. The centre of the earth is certainly very hot to this day, but we feel nothing of that internal heat at the surface; the internal heat, except for volcanoes and hot springs, has not been perceptible at the surface since first the rocks grew solid. Even in the Azoic or Archæozoic Age there are traces in ice-worn rocks and the like of periods of intense cold. Such cold waves have always been going on everywhere, alternately with warmer conditions. And there have been periods of great wetness and periods of great dryness throughout the earth.

A complete account of the causes of these great climatic fluctuations has still to be worked out, but we may perhaps point out some of the chief of them.[1] Prominent among them is the fact that the earth does not spin in a perfect circle round the sun. Its path or orbit

[1] See Sir R. Ball's *Causes of the Great Ice Age,* and Dr. Croll's *Climate and Time.* These are sound books to read still, but the reader will find many of their conclusions modified in Wright's *The Quaternary Ice Age,* which is a quarter of a century more recent.

is like a hoop that is distorted; it is, roughly speaking, elliptical (ovo-elliptical), and the sun is nearer to one end of the ellipse than the other. It is at a point which is a focus of the ellipse. And the shape of this orbit never remains the same. It is slowly distorted by the attractions of the other planets, for ages it may be nearly circular, for ages it is more or less elliptical. As the ellipse becomes most nearly circular, then the focus becomes most nearly the centre. When the orbit becomes most elliptical, then the position of the sun becomes most remote from the middle or, to use the astronomer's phrase, most eccentric. When the orbit is most nearly circular, then it must be manifest that all the year round the earth must be getting much the same amount of heat from the sun; when the orbit is most distorted, then there will be a season in each year when the earth is nearest the sun (this phase is called *Perihelion*) and getting a great deal of heat comparatively, and a season when it will be at its furthest from the sun (*Aphelion*) and getting very little warmth. A planet at *aphelion* is travelling its slowest, and its fastest at *perihelion*; so that the hot

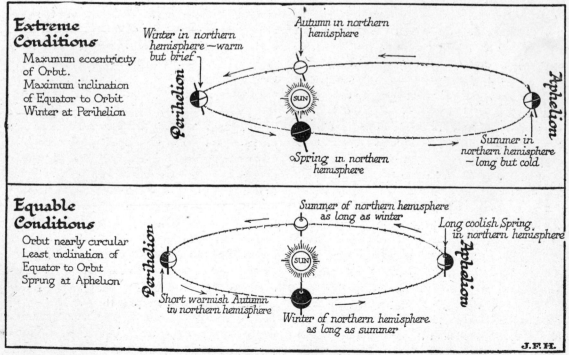

DIAGRAM TO ILLUSTRATE ONE SET OF CAUSES, THE ASTRONOMICAL VARIATIONS, WHICH MAKE THE CLIMATE OF THE WORLD CHANGE SLOWLY BUT CONTINUOUSLY.

It does not change in regular periods. It fluctuates irregularly through vast ages. As the world climate changes, life must change too or perish.

part of its year will last for a much less time than the cold part of its year. (Sir Robert Ball calculated that the greatest difference possible between the seasons was thirty-three days.) During ages when the orbit is most nearly circular there will therefore be least extremes of climate, and when the orbit is at its greatest eccentricity, there will be an age of cold with great extremes of seasonal temperature. These *changes in the orbit of the earth* are due to the varying pull of all the planets, and Sir Robert Ball declared himself unable to calculate any regular cycle of orbital change, but Professor G. H. Darwin maintained that it is possible to make out a kind of cycle between greatest and least eccentricity of about 200,000 years.

But this change in the shape of the orbit is only one cause of the change of the world's climate. There are many others that have to be considered with it. As most people know, the change in the seasons is due to the fact that the equator of the earth is inclined at an angle to the plane of its orbit. If the earth stood up straight in its orbit, so that its equator was in the plane of its orbit, there would be no change in the seasons at all. The sun would always be overhead at the equator, and the day and night would each be exactly twelve hours long throughout the year everywhere. It is this inclination which causes the difference in the seasons and the unequal length of the day in summer and winter. There is, according to Laplace, a possible variation of three degrees (from 22° 6′ to 24° 50′) in this inclination of the equator to the orbit, and when this is at a maximum, the difference between summer and winter is at its greatest. Great importance has been attached to this variation in the inclination of the equator to the orbit by Dr. Croll in his book *Climate and Time*. At present the angle is 23° 27′. Manifestly when the angle is at its least, the world's climate, other things being equal, will be most equable.

And as a third important factor there is what is called the *precession of the equinoxes*. This is a slow wabble of the pole of the spinning earth that takes 25,000 odd years. Any one who watches a spinning top as it "sleeps," will see its axis making a slow circular movement, exactly after the fashion of this circling movement of the earth's axis. The north pole, therefore, does not always point to the same north point among the stars; its pointing traces out a circle in the heavens every 25,000 years.

Now, there will be times when the earth is at its extreme of aphelion or of perihelion, when one hemisphere will be most turned to the sun in its midsummer position and the other most turned away at its midwinter position. And as the precession of the equinoxes goes on, a time will come when the summer-winter position will come not at aphelion and perihelion, but at the half-way points between them. When the summer of one hemisphere happens at perihelion and the winter at aphelion, it will be clear that the summer of the other hemisphere will happen at aphelion and its winter at perihelion. One hemisphere will have a short hot summer and a very cold winter, and the other a long cold summer and a briefer warmish winter. But when the summer-winter positions come at the half-way point of the orbit, and it is the spring of one hemisphere and the autumn of the other that is at aphelion or perihelion, there will not be the same wide difference between the climate of the two hemispheres.

Here are three wavering systems of change all going on independently of each other; the precession of the equinoxes, the change in the obliquity of the equator to the orbit, and the changes in the eccentricity of the orbit. Each system tends by itself to produce periods of equability and periods of greater climatic contrast. And all these systems of change interplay with each other. When it happens that at the same time the orbit is most nearly circular, the equator is at its least inclination from the plane of the earth's orbit, and the spring and autumn are at perihelion and aphelion, then all these causes will be conspiring to make climate warm and uniform; there will be least difference of summer and winter. When, on the other hand, the orbit is in its most eccentric stage of deformation, when also the equator is most tilted up and when further the summer and winter are at aphelion and perihelion, then climates will be at their extremest and winter at its bitterest. There will be great accumulations of ice and snow in winter; the heat of the brief hot summer will be partly reflected back into space by the white snow, and it will be unequal to the task of melting all the winter's ice before the earth spins away once more towards its chilly aphelion. The earth will accumulate cold so long as this conspiracy of extreme conditions continues.

So our earth's climate changes and wavers perpetually as these three systems of influence come together with a common tendency towards warmth or severity, or as they contradict and cancel each other.

We can trace in the Record of the Rocks an irregular series of changes due to the interplay of these influences; there have been great ages when the separate rhythms of these three systems kept them out of agreement and the atmosphere was temperate, ages of world-wide warmth, and other ages when they seemed to concentrate bitterly to their utmost extremity, to freeze out and inflict the utmost stresses and hardship upon life.

And in accordance we find from the record in the rocks that there have been long periods of expansion and multiplication when life flowed and abounded and varied, and harsh ages when there was a great weeding out and disappearance of species, genera, and classes, and the learning of stern lessons by all that survived. Such a propitious conjunction it must have been that gave the age of luxuriant low-grade growth of the coal measures; such an adverse series of circumstances that chilled the closing æons of the Palæolithic time.

It is probable that the warm spells have been long relatively to the cold ages. Our world to-day seems to be emerging with fluctuations from a prolonged phase of adversity and extreme conditions. Half a million years ahead it may be a winterless world with trees and vegetation even in the polar circles. At present we have no certainty in such a forecast, but later on, as knowledge increases, it may be possible to reckon with more precision, so that our race will make its plans thousands of years ahead to meet the coming changes.

§ 2

Another entirely different cause of changes in the general climate of the earth may be due to variations in the heat of the sun. We do **The Sun a Steadfast Star.** not yet understand what causes the heat of the sun or what sustains that undying fire. It is possible that in the past there have been periods of greater and lesser intensity. About that we know nothing; human experience has been too short; and so far we have been able to find no evidence on this matter in the geological record. On the whole, scientific men are inclined to believe that the sun has blazed with a general steadfastness throughout geological time. It may have been cooling slowly, but, speaking upon the scale of things astronomical, it has certainly not cooled very much.

§ 3

A third great group of causes influencing climate are to be found in the forces within the **Changes from within the Earth.** world itself. Throughout the long history of the earth there has been a continuous wearing down of the hills and mountains by frost and rain and a carrying out of their material to become sedimentary rocks under the seas. There has been a continuous process of wearing down the land and filling up the seas, by which the seas, as they became shallower, must have spread more and more over the land. The reverse process, a process of crumpling and upheaval, has also been in progress, but less regularly. The forces of upheaval have been spasmodic; the forces of wearing down continuous. For long ages there has been comparatively little volcanic upheaval, and then have come periods in which vast mountain chains have been thrust up and the whole outline of land and sea changed. Such a time was the opening stage of the Cainozoic period, in which the Alps, the Himalayas, and the Andes were all thrust up from the sea-level to far beyond their present elevations, and the main outlines of the existing geography of the world were drawn.

Now, a time of high mountains and deep seas would mean a larger dry land surface for the world, and a more restricted sea surface, and a time of low lands would mean a time of wider and shallower seas. High mountains precipitate moisture from the atmosphere and hold it out of circulation as snow and glaciers, while

Natural History Museum Photograph.

THE BONES OF A VERY INTERESTING EARLY MESOZOIC REPTILE, *PAREIOSAURUS.*

It belonged to a group, the Theriomorphous reptiles, whose skeletons show many features that also distinguish mammalian skeletons. The mammals, including ourselves, must be descended from very similar reptilian creatures.

smaller oceans mean a lesser area for surface evaporation. Other things being equal, lowland stages of the world's history would be ages of more general atmospheric moisture than periods of relatively greater height of the mountains and greater depth of the seas. But even small increases in the amount of moisture in the air have a powerful influence upon the transmission of radiant heat through that air. The sun's heat will pass much more freely through dry air than through moist air, and so a greater amount of heat would reach the land surfaces of the globe under the conditions of extremes of elevation and depth, than during the periods of relative lowness and shallowness. Dry phases in the history of the earth mean, therefore, hot days. But they also mean cold nights, because for the same reason that the heat comes abundantly to the earth, it will be abundantly radiated away. Moist phases mean, on the other hand, cooler days and warmer nights. The same principle applies to the seasons, and so a phase of great elevations and depressions of the surface would also be another contributory factor on the side of extreme climatic conditions.

And a stage of greater elevation and depression would intensify its extreme conditions by the gradual accumulation of ice caps upon the polar regions and upon the more elevated mountain masses. This accumulation would be at the expense of the sea, whose surface would thus be further shrunken in comparison with the land.

Here then is another set of varying influences that will play in with and help or check the influence of the astronomical variations stated in §1 and §2. There are other more localized forces at work into which we cannot go in any detail here, but which will be familiar to the student of the elements of physical geography; the influence of great ocean currents in carrying warmth from equatorial to more temperate latitudes; the interference of mountain chains with the moisture borne by prevalent winds and the like. As in the slow processes of nature these currents are deflected or the mountain chains worn down or displaced by fresh upheavals, the climate over great areas will be changed and all the conditions of life changed with it. Under the incessant slow variations of these astronomical, telluric, and geographical influences life has no rest. As its conditions change it must change or perish.

§ 4

And while we are enumerating the forces that change climate and the conditions of terrestrial life, we may perhaps look ahead a little and add a fourth set of influences, at first unimportant in the history of the world so far as the land surface is concerned, but becoming more important

Life may control Change.

after the age of Reptiles, to which we shall proceed in our next chapter. These are the effects produced upon climate by life itself. Particularly great is the influence of vegetation, and especially that of forests. Every tree is continually transpiring water vapour into the air; the amount of water evaporated in summer by a lake surface is far less than the amount evaporated by the same area of beech forest. As in the later Mesozoic and the Cainozoic Age, great forests spread over the world, and their action in keeping the air moist and mitigating and stabilizing climate by keeping the summer cool and the winter mild must have become more and more important. Moreover, forests accumulate and protect soil and so prepare the possibility of agricultural life.

Water-weeds again may accumulate to choke and deflect rivers, flood and convert great areas into marshes, and so lead to the destruction of forests or the replacement of grass-lands by boggy wildernesses.

Finally, with the appearance of human communities, came what is perhaps the most powerful of all living influences upon climate. By fire and plough and axe man alters his world. By destroying forests and by irrigation man has already affected the climate of great regions of the world's surface. The destruction of forests makes the seasons more extreme; this has happened, for instance, in the north-eastern states of the United States of America. Moreover, the soil is no longer protected from the scour of rain, and is washed away, leaving only barren rock beneath. This has happened in Spain and Dalmatia and, some thousands of years earlier, in South Arabia. By irrigation, on the other hand, man restores the desert to life and mitigates climate. This process is going on in North-west India and Australia. In the future, by making such operations world-wide and systematic, man may be able to control climate to an extent that as yet we can only guess at.

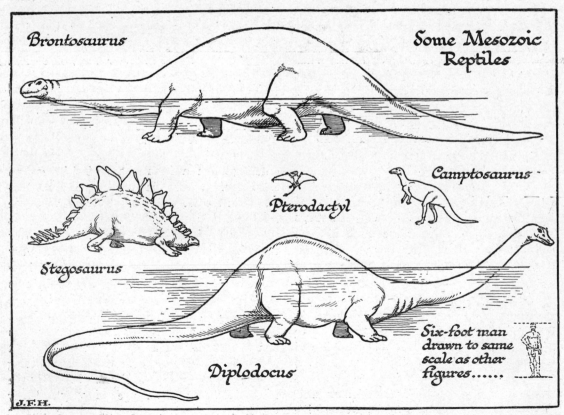

Brontosaurus

Some Mesozoic Reptiles

Stegosaurus

Pterodactyl

Camptosaurus

Diplodocus

Six-foot man drawn to same scale as other figures......

J.F.H.

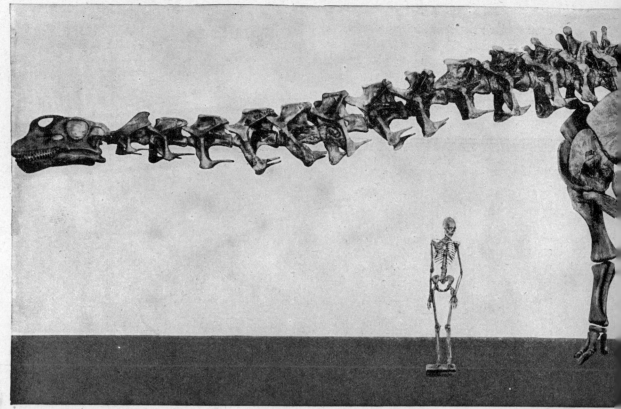

Reproduced by permission of the American Museum of Natural History.   THE ACTUAL SKELETON OF *BRONTOSAURUS*

VI

THE AGE OF REPTILES

§ 1

WE know that for hundreds of thousands of years the wetness and warmth, the shallow lagoon conditions that made possible the vast accumulations of vegetable matter which, compressed and mummified,[1] are now coal, prevailed over most of the world. There were some cold intervals, it is true; but they did not last long enough to destroy the growths. Then that long age of luxuriant low-grade vegetation drew to its end, and for a time life on the earth seems to have undergone a period of world-wide bleakness.

When the story resumes again, we find life

The Age of Lowland Life.

[1] Dr. Mary Stopes, *Monograph on the Constitution of Coal.*

entering upon a fresh phase of richness and expansion. Vegetation has made great advances in the art of living out of water. While the Palæozoic plants of the coal measures probably grew with swamp water flowing over their roots, the Mesozoic flora from its very outset included palm-like cycads and low-ground conifers that were distinctly land plants growing on soil above the water level. The lower levels of the Mesozoic land were no doubt covered by great fern brakes and shrubby bush and a kind of jungle growth of trees. But there were as yet no grass, no small flowering plants, no turf nor greensward. Probably the Mesozoic was not an age of very brightly coloured vegetation. It must have had a flora green in the wet season and brown and purple in the dry. There were no gay flowers,

COMPARED WITH A HUMAN SKELETON.

no bright autumn tints before the fall of the leaf, because there was as yet no fall of the leaf. And beyond the lower levels the world was still barren, still unclothed, still exposed without any mitigation to the wear and tear of the wind and rain.

When one speaks of conifers in the Mesozoic, the reader must not think of the pines and firs that clothe the high mountain slopes of our time. He must think of low-growing ever-greens. The mountains were still as bare and lifeless as ever. The only colour effects among the mountains were the colour effects of naked rock, such colours as make the landscape of Colorado so marvellous to-day.

Amidst this spreading vegetation of the lower plains the reptiles were increasing mightily in multitude and variety. They were now in many cases absolutely land animals. There are numerous anatomical points of distinction between a reptile and an amphibian; they held good between such reptiles and amphibians as prevailed in the carboniferous time of the Upper

Palæozoic; but the fundamental difference between reptiles and amphibia which matters in this history is that the amphibian must go back to the water to lay its eggs, and that in the early stages of its life it must live in and under water. The reptile, on the other hand, has cut out all the tadpole stages from its life-cycle, or, to be more exact, its tadpole stages are got through before the young leave the egg case. The reptile has come out of the water altogether. Some had gone back to it again, just as the hippopotamus and the otter among mammals have gone back, but that is a further extension of the story to which we cannot give much attention in this *Outline*.

In the Palæozoic period, as we have said, life had not spread beyond the swampy river valleys and the borders of sea lagoons and the like; but in the Mesozoic, life was growing ever more accustomed to the thinner medium of the air, was sweeping boldly up over the plains and towards the hill-sides. It is well for the student of human history and the human future to note that. If a disembodied intelligence with no knowledge of the future had come to earth and studied life during the early Palæozoic age, he might very reasonably have concluded that life was absolutely confined to the water, and that it could never spread over the land. It found a way. In the Later Palæozoic Period that visitant might have been equally sure that life could not go beyond the edge of a swamp. The Mesozoic Period would still have found him setting bounds to life far

of them began to balance themselves on tail and hindlegs, rather as the kangaroos do now, in order to release the fore limbs for grasping food. The bones of one notable division of reptiles which retained a quadrupedal habit, a division of which many remains have been found in South African and Russian Early Mesozoic deposits, display a number of characters which approach those of the mammalian skeleton, and because of this resemblance to the mammals (beasts) this division is called

ANOTHER RESTORATION OF A STEGOSAUR.

more limited than the bounds that are set to-day. And so to-day, though we mark how life and man are still limited to five miles of air and a depth of perhaps a mile or so of sea, we must not conclude from that present limitation that life, through man, may not presently spread out and up and down to a range of living as yet inconceivable.

The earliest known reptiles were beasts with great bellies and not very powerful legs, very like their kindred amphibia, wallowing as the crocodile wallows to this day; but in the Mesozoic they soon began to stand up and go stoutly on all fours, and several great sections

the *Theriomorpha* (beastlike). Another division was the crocodile branch, and another developed towards the tortoises and turtles. The *Plesiosaurs* and *Ichthyosaurs* were two groups which have left no living representatives; they were huge reptiles returning to a whale-like life in the sea. *Pliosaurus*, one of the largest plesiosaurs, measured thirty feet from snout to tail tip—of which half was neck. The *Mosasaurs* were a third group of great porpoise-like marine lizards. But the largest and most diversified group of these Mesozoic reptiles was the group we have spoken of as kangaroo like, the *Dinosaurs*, many of which attained enormous

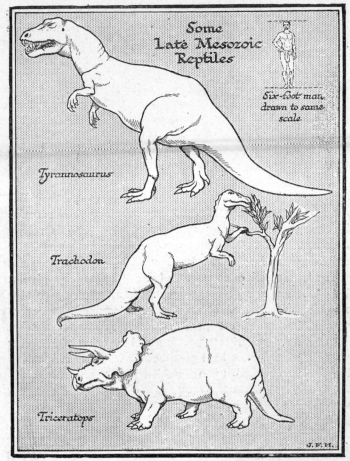

Some Late Mesozoic Reptiles

Six-foot man drawn to same scale

Tyrannosaurus

Trachodon

Triceratops

J.F.H.

rocks in East Africa, was still more colossal. It measured well over a hundred feet! These greater monsters had legs, and they are usually figured as standing up on them; but it is very doubtful if they could have supported their weight in this way, out of water. Buoyed up by water or mud, they may have got along. Another noteworthy type we have figured is the *Triceratops*. There were also a number of great flesh-eaters who preyed upon these herbivores. Of these, *Tyrannosaurus* seems almost the last word in "frightfulness" among living things. Some species of this genus measured forty feet from snout to tail. Apparently it carried this vast body kangaroo fashion on its tail and hindlegs. Probably it reared itself up. Some authorities even suppose that it leapt through the air. If so, it possessed muscles of a quite miraculous quality. A leaping elephant would be a far less astounding idea. Much more probably it waded half submerged in pursuit of the herbivorous river saurians.

proportions. In bigness these greater *Dinosaurs* have never been exceeded, although the sea can still show in the whales creatures as great. Some of these, and the largest among them, were herbivorous animals; they browsed on the rushy vegetation and among the ferns and bushes, or they stood up and grasped trees with their fore-legs while they devoured the foliage. Among the browsers, for example, were the *Diplodocus carnegii*, which measured eighty-four feet in length, and the *Atlantosaurus*. The *Gigantosaurus*, disinterred by a German expedition in 1912 from

Natural History Museum Photograph.

THE ACTUAL SKELETON OF *TRICERATOPS* UPON WHICH THE FIGURE IN THE PRECEDING ILLUSTRATION IS BASED.

§ 2

One special development of the dinosaurian type of reptile was a light hopping, climbing group of creatures which developed a bat-like web between the fifth finger and the side of the body, which was used in gliding from tree to tree after the fashion of the flying squirrels. These bat-lizards were the *Pterodactyls*. They are often described as *flying* reptiles, and pictures are drawn of Mesozoic scenery in which they are seen soaring and swooping about. But their breastbone has no keel such as the breastbone of a bird has for the attachment of muscles strong enough for flying. At the most they fluttered. They must have had a grotesque resemblance to heraldic dragons, and they played the part of bat-like birds in the Mesozoic jungles. But bird-like though they were, they were not birds nor the ancestors of birds. The structure of their wings was altogether different from that of birds. The structure of their wings was that of a hand with one long finger and a web;

Flying Dragons.

the wing of a bird is like an arm with feathers projecting from its hind edge. And these Pterodactyls had no feathers.

§ 3

Far less prevalent at this time were certain other truly bird-like creatures, of which the earlier sorts also hopped and clambered and the later sorts skimmed and flew. These were at first—by all the standards of classification—Reptiles. They developed into true birds as they developed wings and as their reptilian scales became long and complicated, fronds rather than scales, and so at last, by much spreading and splitting, feathers. Feathers are the distinctive covering of birds, and they give a power of resisting heat and cold far greater than that of any other integumentary covering except perhaps the thickest fur. At a very early stage this novel covering of feathers, this new heat-proof contrivance that life had chanced upon, enabled many species of birds

The First Birds.

ANOTHER RESTORATION OF *TRICERATOPS*.

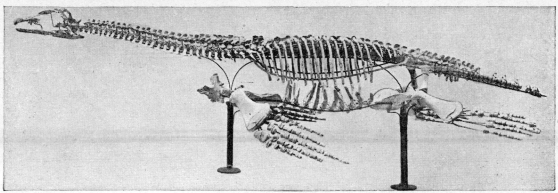

Natural History Museum Photograph.

THE ACTUAL SKELETON OF A PLESIOSAUR UPON WHICH THE LARGE COLOURED
ILLUSTRATION IS BASED.

to invade a province for which the pterodactyl was ill equipped. They took to sea fishing—if indeed they did not begin with it—and spread to the north and south polewards beyond the temperature limits set to the true reptiles. The earliest birds seem to have been carnivorous divers and water birds. To this day some of the most primitive bird forms are found among the sea birds of the Arctic and Antarctic seas, and it is among these sea birds that zoologists still find lingering traces of teeth, which have otherwise vanished completely from the beak of the bird.

The earliest known bird (the *Archæopteryx*) had no beak; it had a row of teeth in a jaw like a reptile's. It had three claws at the forward corner of its wing. Its tail too was peculiar. All modern birds have their tail feathers set in a short compact bony rump; the *Archæopteryx* had a long bony tail with a row of feathers along each side.

§ 4

This great period of Mesozoic life, this second volume of the book of life, is indeed an amazing story of reptilian life proliferating and developing. But the most striking thing of all the story remains to be told. Right up to the latest Mesozoic Rocks we find all these reptilian orders we have enumerated still flourishing unchallenged. There is no hint of an enemy or competitor to them in the relics we find of their world. Then the record is broken. We do not know how long a time the break represents; many pages may be missing here, pages that may

An Age of Hardship and Death.

represent some great cataclysmal climatic change. When next we find abundant traces of the land plants and the land animals of the earth, this great multitude of reptile species had gone. For the most part they have left no descendants. They have been "wiped out." The pterodactyls have gone absolutely, of the plesiosaurs and ichthyosaurs none are alive; the mosasaurs have gone; of the lizards a few small forms remain, the iguana is the largest; all the multitude and diversity of the dinosaurs have vanished. Only the crocodiles and the turtles and tortoises carry on in any quantity into Cainozoic times. The place of all these types in the picture that the Cainozoic fossils presently unfold to us is taken by other animals not closely related to the Mesozoic reptiles and certainly not descended from any of their ruling types. A new kind of life is in possession of the world.

This apparently abrupt ending up of the reptiles is, beyond all question, the most striking revolution in the whole history of the earth before the coming of mankind. It is probably connected with the close of a vast period of equable warm conditions and the onset of a new austerer age, in which the winters were bitterer and the summers brief but hot. The Mesozoic life, animal and vegetable alike, was adapted to warm conditions and capable of little resistance to cold. The new life, on the other hand, was before all things capable of resisting great changes of temperature.

Whatever it was that led to the extinction of the Mesozoic reptiles, it was probably some very far-reaching change indeed, for the life of the seas did at the same time undergo a similar catastrophic alteration. The crescendo and ending of the Reptiles on land was paralleled by the crescendo and ending of the Ammonites, a division of creatures like squids with coiled shells which swarmed in those ancient seas. All through the rocky record of this Mesozoic period there is a vast multitude and variety of these coiled shells; there are hundreds of species, and towards the end of the Mesozoic period they increased in diversity and produced exaggerated types. When the record resumes these too have gone. So far as the reptiles are concerned, people may perhaps be inclined to argue that they were exterminated because the Mammals that replaced them, competed with them, and were more fitted to survive; but nothing of the sort can be true of the Ammonites, because to this day their place has not been taken. Simply they are gone. Unknown conditions made it possible for them to live in the Mesozoic seas, and then some unknown change made life impossible for them. Only one genus of Ammonite survives to-day of all that vast variety, the Pearly Nautilus. It is found, it is to be noted, in the warm waters of the Indian and Pacific Oceans.[1]

And as for the Mammals competing with and ousting the less fit reptiles, a struggle of which people talk at times, there is not a scrap of evidence of any such direct competition. To judge by the Record of the Rocks as we know it to-day, there is much more reason for believing that first the reptiles in some inexplicable way perished, and then that later on, after a very hard time for all life upon the earth, the mammals, as conditions became more genial again, developed and spread to fill the vacant world.

[1] See article "Cephalopoda" in the *Encyclopædia Britannica* for its anatomy.

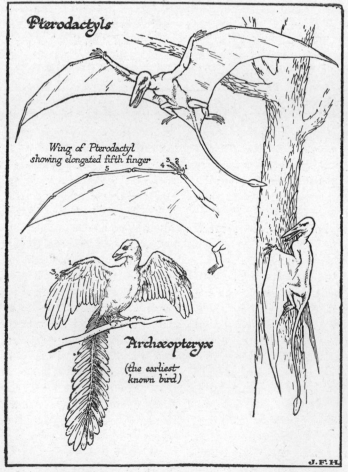

RESTORATION OF PTERODACTYLS AND EARLY BIRDS BASED ON SUCH FOSSIL REMAINS AS WE HAVE SHOWN IN OUR FIRST ILLUSTRATION.

§ 5

Were there mammals in the Mesozoic period?

This is a question not yet to be answered precisely. Patiently and steadily the geologists **The First Appearance of Fur and Feathers.** gather fresh evidence and reason out completer conclusions. At any time some new deposit may reveal fossils that will illuminate this question. Certainly either mammals, or the ancestors of the mammals, must have lived throughout the Mesozoic period. In the very opening chapter of the Mesozoic volume of the Record there were those Theriomorphous Reptiles to which we have already alluded, and in the later Mesozoic a number of small jaw-bones are found, entirely mammalian in character. But there is not a scrap, not a bone, to suggest that there lived any Mesozoic Mammal which could look a dinosaur in the face. The Mesozoic mammals or mammal-like reptiles, for we do not know clearly which they were, seem to have been all obscure little beasts of the size of mice and rats, more like a down-trodden order of reptiles than a distinct class; probably they still laid eggs and were developing only slowly their distinctive covering of hair. They lived away from big waters, and perhaps in the desolate uplands, as marmots do now; probably they lived there beyond the pursuit of the carnivorous dinosaurs. Some perhaps went on all fours, some chiefly went on their hind-legs and clambered with their fore limbs. They became fossils only so occasionally that chance has not yet revealed a single complete skeleton in the whole vast record of the Mesozoic rocks by which to check these guesses.

These little Theriomorphs, these ancestral mammals, developed hair. Hairs, like feathers, are long and elaborately specialized scales. Hair is perhaps the clue to the salvation of the early mammals. Living lives upon the margin of existence, away from the marshes and the warmth, they developed an outer

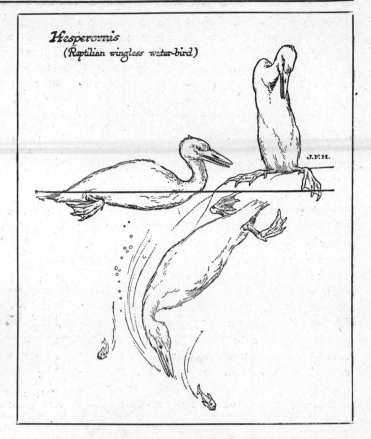

Hesperornis
(*Reptilian wingless water-bird*)

J.F.H.

covering only second in its warmth-holding (or heat-resisting) powers to the down and feathers of the Arctic sea-birds. And so they held out through the age of hardship between the Mesozoic and Cainozoic ages, to which most of the true reptiles succumbed.

All the main characteristics of this flora and sea and land fauna that came to an end with the end of the Mesozoic age were such as were adapted to an equable climate and to shallow and swampy regions. But in the case of their Cainozoic successors, both hair and feathers gave *a power of resistance to variable temperatures* such as no reptile possessed, and with it they gave a range far greater than any animal had hitherto attained.

The range of life of the Lower Palæozoic Period was confined to warm water.

The range of life of the Upper Palæozoic Period was confined to warm water or to warm swamps and wet ground.

The range of life of the Mesozoic Period as we know it was confined to water and fairly low-lying valley regions under equable conditions.

Meanwhile in each of these periods there were types involuntarily extending the range of life beyond the limits prevailing in that period; and when ages of extreme conditions prevailed, it was these marginal types which survived to inherit the depopulated world.

That perhaps is the most general statement we can make about the story of the geological record; it is a story of widening range. Classes, genera, and species of animals appear and disappear, but the range widens. It widens always. Life has never had so great a range as it has to-day. Life to-day, in the form of man, goes higher in the air than any other creature has ever done, his geographical range is from pole to pole, he goes under the water in submarines, he sounds the cold, lifeless darkness of the deepest seas, he burrows into virgin levels of the rocks, and in thought and knowledge he pierces to the centre of the earth and reaches out to the uttermost star. Yet in all the relics of the Mesozoic time we find no certain memorials of his ancestry. His ancestors, like the ancestors of all the kindred mammals, must have been creatures so rare, so obscure, and so remote that they have left scarcely a trace amidst the abundant vestiges of the monsters that wallowed rejoicing in the steamy air and lush vegetation of the Mesozoic lagoons, or crawled or hopped or fluttered over the great river plains of that time.[1]

[1] And here the genius of a great humorous artist (E. T. Reed) obliges us to add a footnote to clear away a common misconception. He was the creator of a series of fantastic pictures, *Prehistoric Peeps*, which have had a deserved and immense vogue, and it was his whim to represent primitive men as engaged in an unending wild struggle with great Plesiosaurs and the like. His fantasy has become a common belief. As a matter of fact, millions of years elapsed between the vanishing of the last great Mesozoic reptile and the first appearance of man upon this earth. Early man had as contemporaries some monstrous animals, as we shall note, but not these extreme monsters.

In these six opening chapters we have been much indebted, in addition to the books already named in the text or in footnotes, to Ray Lankester's *Extinct Animals*, Osborn's *Age of Mammals*, Jukes Browne's, Lyell's and Pirsson and Schuchert's text-books of geology, and the collections and catalogues of the Natural History Museum at South Kensington. H. R. Knipe's admirably illustrated *From Nebula to Man* and his *Evolution in the Past* have also been very useful and suggestive.

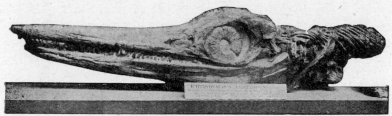

Natural History Museum Photograph.

AN EXTINCT LORD OF CREATION.
Head of a Mesozoic *Ichthyosaur*. Note the extraordinary circle of bone round the eye.

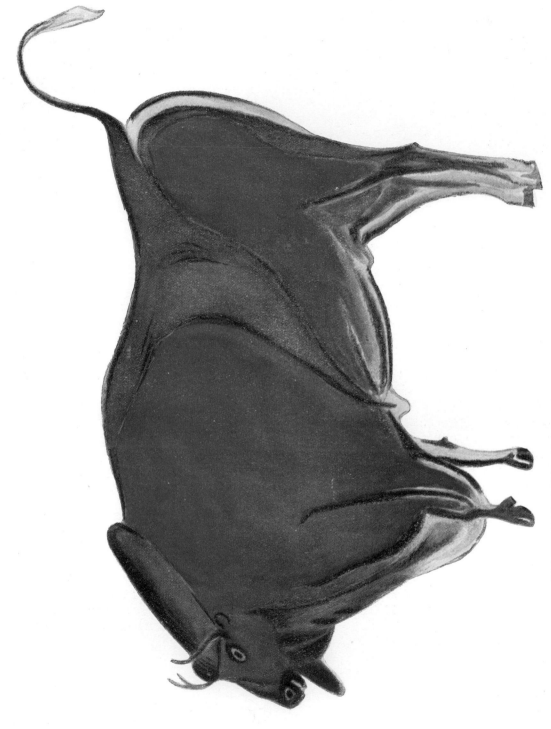

PALÆOLITHIC PAINTING OF A BISON FROM THE ALTAMIRA CAVE

331

VII

THE AGE OF MAMMALS

§ I

THE third great division of the geological record, the Cainozoic, opens with a world already physically very like the world we live in to-day. Probably the day was at first still perceptibly shorter, but the scenery had become very modern **A New Age** in its character. Climate was, of **of Life.** course, undergoing, age by age, its incessant and irregular variations; lands that are temperate to-day have passed, since the Cainozoic age began, through phases of great warmth, intense cold, and extreme dryness; but the landscape, if it altered, altered to nothing that cannot still be paralleled to-day in some part of the world or other. In the place of the cycads sequoias, and strange conifers of the Mesozoic, the plant names that now appear in the lists of fossils include birch, beech, holly, tulip trees, ivy, sweet gum, breadfruit trees. Flowers have developed concurrently with bees and butterflies. Palms are now very important. Such plants had already been in evidence in the later levels of the (American Cretaceous) Mesozoic, but now they dominate the scene altogether. Grass is becoming a great fact in the world. Certain grasses too had appeared in the later Mesozoic, but only with the Cainozoic period came grass plains and turf spreading wide over a world that was once barren stone.

The period opened with a long phase of considerable warmth; then the world cooled. And in the opening of this third part of the record, this Cainozoic period, a gigantic crumpling of the earth's crust and an upheaval of mountain ranges was in progress. The Alps, the Andes, the Himalayas, are all Cainozoic mountain ranges; the background of an early Cainozoic scene to be typical should display an active volcano or so. It must have been an age of great earthquakes.

Geologists make certain main divisions of

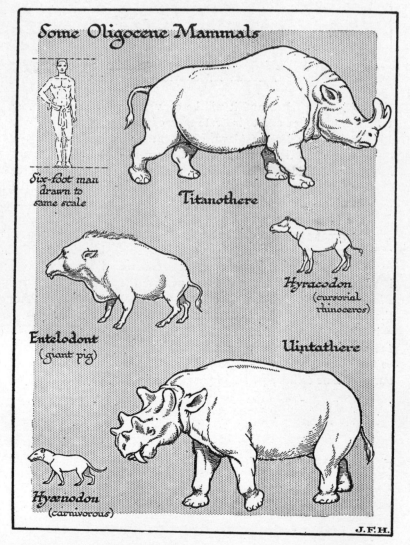

Some Oligocene Mammals

Six-foot man drawn to same scale

Titanothere

Hyracodon (cursorial rhinoceros)

Entelodont (giant pig)

Uintathere

Hyænodon (carnivorous)

J.F.H.

ANOTHER RESTORATION OF A TITANOTHERE (EARLY CAINOZOIC).

the Cainozoic period, and it will be convenient to name them here and to indicate their climate. First comes the *Eocene* (dawn of recent life), an age of exceptional warmth in the world's history, subdivided into an older and newer Eocene ; then the *Oligocene* (but little of recent life), in which the climate was still equable. The *Miocene* (with living species still in a minority) was the great age of mountain building, and the general temperature was falling. In the *Pliocene* (more living than extinct species), climate is very much at its present phase ; but with the *Pleistocene* (a great majority of living species) there sets in a long period of extreme conditions —it is the Great Ice Age. Glaciers spread from the poles towards the equator, until England to the Thames is covered in ice. Thereafter to our own time comes a period of partial recovery.

§ 2

In the forests and following the grass over the Eocene plains there appeared for the first **Tradition** time a variety and abundance of **comes into** mammals. Before we proceed to **the World.** any description of these mammals, it may be well to note in general terms what a mammal is.

From the appearance of the vertebrated animals in the Lower Palæolithic Age, when the fish first swarmed out into the sea, there has been a steady progressive development of vertebrated creatures. A fish is a vertebrated animal that breathes by gills and can live only in water. An amphibian may be described as a fish that has added to its gill-breathing the power of breathing air with its swimming bladder in adult life, and that has also developed limbs with five toes to them in place of the fins of a fish. A tadpole is for a time a fish, which becomes a land creature with limbs and toes as it develops. A reptile is a further stage of detachment ; it is an amphibian that is no longer amphibious ; it passes through its tadpole stage, its fish stage, that is—in an egg. From the beginning it must breathe in air ; it can never breathe under water as a tadpole can do. Now, a modern mammal is really a sort of reptile that has developed a peculiarly effective protective covering, hair ; and that also retains its eggs in the body until they hatch so that it brings forth living young (viviparous), and even after birth it cares for them and feeds them by its mammæ for a longer or shorter period. Some reptiles, some vipers for example, are viviparous, but none stand by their young as the real mammals do. Both the birds and the mammals, which escaped whatever destructive forces made an end to the Mesozoic reptiles, and which survived to dominate the Cainozoic world, have these two things in common : first, a far more effective protection against changes of temperature than any other variation of the reptile type ever produced, and, secondly, a peculiar care for their eggs, the bird by incubation and the mammal by retention, and a disposition to look after the young for a certain period after hatching or birth. There is by comparison the greatest carelessness about offspring in the reptile.

Hair was evidently the earliest distinction of the mammals from the rest of the reptiles. It is doubtful if the particular Theriodont reptiles who were developing hair in the early Mesozoic were viviparous. Two mammals survive to this day which not only do not suckle their young, but which lay eggs, the *Ornithorhynchus* and the *Echidna*, and in the Eocene there are a number of allied forms. They were the survivors of what was probably a much larger number and variety of small egg-laying hairy creatures, hairy reptiles, hoppers, climbers, and runners, which included the Mesozoic ancestors of all existing mammals up to and including man.

Now we may put the essential facts about mammalian reproduction in another way. *The mammal is a family animal.* And the family habit involved the possibility of a new sort of continuity of experience in the world. Compare the completely closed-in life of an in- dividual lizard with the life of even a quite lowly mammal of almost any kind. The former has no mental continuity with anything be- yond itself ; it is a little self-contained globe of experience that serves its purpose and ends ; but the latter " picks up " from its mother, and " hands on " to its offspring. All the mammals, except for the two genera we have named, had already before the lower Eocene age arrived at this stage of pre-adult dependence and imitation. They were all more or less imitative in youth and capable of a certain modicum of education ; they all, as a part of their development, received a certain amount of care and example and even direction from

their mother. This is as true of the hyæna and rhinoceros as it is of the dog or man ; the difference of educability is enormous, but the fact of protection and educability in the young stage is undeniable. So far as the vertebrated animals go, these new mammals, with their viviparous, young-protecting disposition, and these new birds, with their incubating, young- protecting disposition, introduce at the opening of the Cainozoic period a new thing into the expanding story of life, namely, social associa- tion, the addition to hard and inflexible instinct of *tradition*, and the nervous organisa- tion necessary to receive tradition.

All the innovations that come into the history of life begin very humbly. The supply of blood-vessels in the swimming bladder of the mudfish in the lower Palæozoic torrent-river, that enabled it to pull through a season of drought, would have seemed at that time to that bodiless visitant to our planet we have already imagined, a very unimportant side fact in that ancient world of great sharks and plated fishes, sea-scorpions, and coral reefs and sea- weed ; but it opened the narrow way by which the land vertebrates arose to predominance. The mudfish would have seemed then a poor refugee from the too crowded and aggressive life of the sea. But once lungs were launched into the world, every line of descent that had lungs went on improving them. So too in the upper Palæozoic, the fact that some of the Amphibia were losing their " amphibious- ness " by a retardation of hatching of their eggs, would have appeared a mere response to the distressful dangers that threatened the young tadpole. Yet that prepared the conquest of the dry land for the triumphant multitude of the Mesozoic reptiles. It opened a new direction towards a free and vigorous land-life along which all the reptilian animals moved. And this viviparous, young-tending training that the ancestral mammalia underwent during that age of inferiority and hardship for them, set going in the world a new continuity of perception, of which even man to-day only begins to appreciate the significance.

§ 3

A number of types of mammal already ap- pear in the Eocene. Some are differentiating in

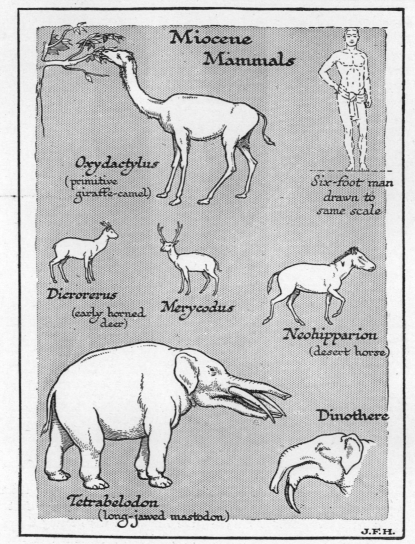

Miocene Mammals

Oxydactylus
(primitive giraffe-camel)

Six-foot man drawn to same scale

Dicrorerus
(early horned deer)

Merycodus

Neohipparion
(desert horse)

Dinothere

Tetrabelodon
(long-jawed mastodon)

J.F.H.

one direction, and some in another, some are perfecting themselves as herbivorous quad-rupeds, some leap and climb among the trees, some turn back to the water to swim, but all types are un-consciously exploiting and developing the brain which is the instrument of this new power of acquisition and educability. In the Eocene rocks are found small early predecessors of the horse (Eohippus), tiny camels, pigs, early tapirs, early hedgehogs, monkeys and lemurs, oppossums and carnivores. Now, all these were more or less ancestral to living forms, and all have brains relatively much smaller than their living representatives. There is, for instance, an early rhinoceros, *Titanotherium*, with a brain not one tenth the size of that of

An Age of Brain Growth.

the existing rhinoceros. The latter is by no means a perfect type of the attentive and sub-missive student, but even so it is ten times more observant and teachable than its pre-decessor. This sort of thing is true of all the orders and families that survive until to-day. All the Cainozoic mammals were doing this one thing in common under the urgency of a common necessity; they were all growing brain. It was a parallel advance. In the same order or family to-day, the brain is usually from six to ten times what it was in the Eocene ancestor.

Grass was now spreading over the world, and with this extension arose some huge gram-inivorous brutes of which no representative survives to-day. Such were the Uintatheres and the Titanotheres. And in pursuit of such beasts came great swarms of primitive dogs, some as big as bears, and the first cats, one in particular (*Smilodon*), a small fierce-looking creature with knife-like canines, the first sabre-toothed tiger, which was to develop into greater things. American deposits in the Miocene display a great variety of camels, giraffe camels with long necks, gazelle camels, llamas, and true camels. North America, throughout most of the Cainozoic period, appears to have been in open and easy continuation with Asia, and when at last the glaciers of the Great Ice Age, and then the Bering Straits, came to separate the two great continental regions, the last camels were left in the old world and the llamas in the new.

In the Eocene the first ancestors of the elephants appear in northern Africa as snouted creatures ; the elephant's trunk dawned on the world in the Miocene.

One group of creatures is of peculiar interest in a history that is mainly to be the story of mankind. We find fossils in the Eocene of monkeys and lemurs, but of one particular creature we have as yet not a single bone. It was a lemur-like creature that clambered about the trees and ran, and probably ran well, on its hindlegs upon the ground. It was small-brained by our present standards, but it had clever hands with which it handled fruits and beat nuts upon the rocks and perhaps caught up sticks and stones to smite its fellows. It was our ancestor.

§ 4

Slowly through vast intervals of time the spinning world circled about the sun, and slowly The World its orbit, which may have been grows hard nearly circular during the equable again. days of the early Eocene, was drawn by the attraction of the circling outer planets into a more elliptical form. Its axis of rotation, which had always heeled over to the plane of its orbit, as the mast of a yacht under sail heels over to the level of the water, heeled over by imperceptible degrees a little more and a little more. And each year its summer point shifted a little further from perihelion round its path. These were small changes to happen to a one-inch ball, circling at a distance of 330 yards from a flaming sun nine feet across, in the course of a few million years. They were changes an immortal astronomer in Neptune, watching the earth from age to age, would have found almost imperceptible. But from the point of view of the surviving mammalian life of the Miocene, they mattered pro-

ANOTHER RESTORATION OF AN EARLY ELEPHANTINE FORM (MIOCENE).

foundly. Age by age the winters grew on the whole colder and harder and a few hours longer relatively to the summers in a thousand years ; age by age the summers grew briefer. On an average the winter snow lay a little later in the spring in each century, and the glaciers in the northern mountains gained an inch this year, receded half an inch next, came on again a few inches. . . .

The Record of the Rocks tells of the increasing chill. The Pliocene was a temperate time, and many of the warmth-loving plants and animals had gone. Then, rather less deliberately, some feet or some inches every year, the ice came on.

An arctic fauna, musk ox, woolly mammoth, woolly rhinoceros, lemming, ushers in the Pleistocene. Over North America, and Europe and Asia alike, the ice advanced. For thousands of years it advanced, and then for thousands of years it receded, to advance again. Europe down to the Baltic shores, Britain down to the Thames, North America down to New England, and more centrally as far south as Ohio, lay for ages under the glaciers. Enormous volumes of water were withdrawn from the ocean and locked up in those stupendous ice caps so as to cause a world-wide change in the relative levels of land and sea. Vast areas were exposed that are now again sea bottom.

The world to-day is still coming slowly out of the last of four great waves of cold. And it is amidst this crescendo and diminuendo of frost and snow that we first recognize forms that are like the forms of men. The Age of Mammals culminated in ice and hardship and man.

§ 5

Time guesses about the periods of the great age of cold are still vague, but we will follow H. F. Osborn in accepting as our guides the estimates of

Chronology of the Ice Age.

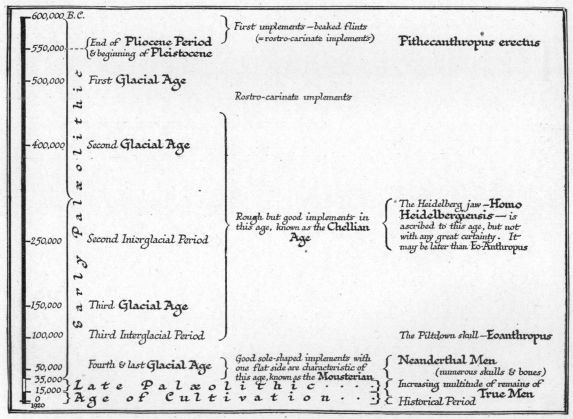

TIME DIAGRAM OF THE GLACIAL AGES.

The reader should compare this diagram carefully with our first time diagram, Chapter II, § 2. That diagram, if it were on the same scale as this one, would be between 44 and 440 feet long.

Albrecht Penck[1] and C. A. Reeds.[2] These give the

Pleistocene Age.
{
FIRST GLACIAL AGE as at its maximum about 500,000 years ago.
First Interglacial Period.
SECOND GLACIAL AGE maximum 400,000 years ago.
Second Interglacial Period.
THIRD GLACIAL AGE maximum 150,000 years ago.
Third Interglacial Period.
}

[1] *Die Alpen in Eiszeitalters,* vol. iii.
[2] "Graphic Projection of Pleistocene," "Climatic Oscillations," in *Bulletin of Geological Soc. Am.,* vol. **xxvi.**

Pleistocene Age (cont.)
{
FOURTH AND LAST GLACIAL AGE maximum 50,000 years ago.
A Period of temperate climate. The amelioration set in perhaps 35,000 years ago.
}

With some subsequent fluctuations. Remains of bog oaks, for example, which grew two or three thousand years ago, are found in Scotland at latitudes in which not even a stunted oak will grow at the present time.

BOOK II
THE MAKING OF MAN

VIII
THE ANCESTRY OF MAN[3]

§ I

THE origin of man is still very obscure. It is commonly asserted that he is "descended" from some man-like ape such as the chimpanzee, the orang-utang, or the gorilla, but that of course is as reasonable as saying that I am "descended" from some Hottentot or Esquimau as young or younger than myself.

Man descended from a Walking Ape. Others, alive to this objection, say that man is descended from the common ancestor of the chimpanzee, the orang-utang, and the gorilla. Some "anthropologists" have even indulged in a speculation whether mankind may not have a double or treble origin : the negro being descended from a gorilla-like ancestor, the Chinese from a chimpanzee-like ancestor, and so on. These are very fanciful ideas. Reasons have recently been given for

[3] In this and the next chapters the writer has used Osborn's *Men of the Old Stone Age,* Sollas' *Ancient Hunters,* Dr. Keith's *Antiquity of Man,* W. B. Wright's *The Quaternary Ice Age,* Worthington Smith's *Man, the Primeval Savage,* F. Wood Jones' *Arboreal Man,* H. G. F. Spurrell's *Modern Man and his Forerunners,* O. T. Mason's *Origins of Invention,* Parkyn's *History of Prehistoric Art,* Salomon Reinach's *Repertoire de l'Art Quaternaire,* and various of the papers in Ray Lankester's *Science from an Easy Chair.*

doubting whether man is nearly so close to the great apes as was formerly supposed.

Of course if one puts the skeleton of a man and the skeleton of a gorilla side by side, their general resemblance is so great that it is easy to jump to the conclusion that the former is derived from such a type as the latter by a process of brain growth and general refinement. But if one examines closely into one or two differences, the gap widens. The particular difference upon which stress is laid is the foot. Man walks on his toe and his heel ; his great toe is his chief lever in walking, as the reader may see for himself if he examines his own footprints on the bathroom floor and notes where the pressure falls as the footprints become fainter. His great toe is the king of his toes.

Among all the apes and monkeys, the only group that have their great toes developed on anything like the same fashion as man are some of the lemurs. The baboon walks on his hind-legs it is true, but he walks on a flat foot and all his toes, using his middle toe as his chief throw off, much as the bear does. And the three great apes all walk on the outer side of the foot, never touching the ground with the great toes at all, in an entirely different manner

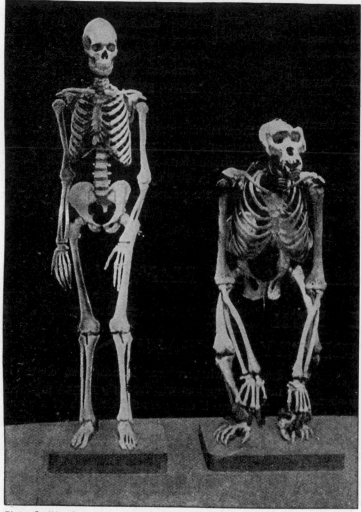

Photo: Gambier, Bolton
THE SKELETONS OF MAN AND GORILLA SHOWING THE CONTRAST OF THE GROUND AND ARBOREAL TYPES OF LIMB AND BUILD.

is to be noted that he does not swim naturally; he has to learn to swim, and that seems to point to a long-standing separation from rivers and lakes and the sea. Almost certainly that ancestor was a smaller and slighter creature than its human descendants. Conceivably the human ancestor at the opening of the Cainozoic period was something rather like a running lemur, living chiefly on the ground, hiding among rocks rather than trees. It could still climb trees well and hold things between its great toe and its second toe (as the Japanese can to this day), but it was already coming down to the ground again from a still remoter, a Mesozoic arboreal ancestry. It is quite understandable that such a creature would very rarely die in water in such circumstances as to leave bones to become fossilized.

It must always be borne in mind that among its many other imperfections the Geological Record necessarily contains abundant traces only of water or marsh creatures or of creatures easily and frequently drowned. The same reasons that make any traces of the ancestors of the mammals rare and relatively unprocurable in the Mesozoic rocks, probably make the traces of possible human ancestors rare and rela-

from the walking of man. They learnt to walk on their hindlegs at a different school, it would seem, and under different conditions from those under which man became erect. The walking habit of man may not be the same thing as the walking habit of the great apes; it may be a parallelism and not a common inheritance.

The great apes are forest dwellers; their walking even now is incidental; they are at their happiest among trees. But man walks so well and runs so swiftly as to suggest a very long ancestry upon the ground. Also, he does not climb well now; he climbs with caution and hesitation. His ancestors may have been running creatures for long ages. Moreover, it

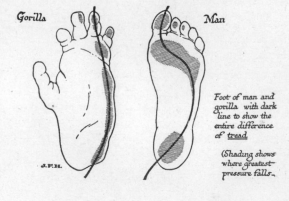

Foot of man and gorilla with dark line to show the entire difference of tread

(Shading shows where greatest pressure falls.

tively unprocurable in the Cainozoic rocks. Such knowledge as we have of the earliest men, for example, is almost entirely got from a few caves, into which they went and in which they left their traces. Until the hard Pleistocene times they lived and died in the open, and their bodies were consumed or decayed altogether.

But it is well to bear in mind also that the record of the rocks has still to be thoroughly examined. It has been studied only for a few generations, and by only a few men in each generation. Most men have been too busy making war, making profits out of their neighbours, toiling at work that machinery could do for them in a tenth of the time, or simply playing about, to give any attention to these more interesting things. There may be, there probably are, thousands of deposits still untouched containing countless fragments and vestiges of man and his progenitors. In Asia particularly, in India or the East Indies, there may be hidden the most illuminating clues. What we know to-day of early men is the merest scrap of what will presently be known.

The apes and monkeys already appear to have been differentiated at the beginning of the Cainozoic Age, and there are a number of Oligocene and Miocene apes whose relations to one another and to the human line have still to be made out. Among these we may mention *Dryopithecus* of the Miocene Age, with a very human-looking jaw. In the Siwalik Hills of northern India remains of some very interesting apes have been found, of which *Sivapithecus* and *Palæopithecus* were possibly related closely to the human ancestor. Possibly these animals already used implements. Charles Darwin represents baboons as opening nuts by breaking them with stones, using stakes to prize up rocks in the hunt for insects, and striking blows with sticks and stones.[1] The chimpanzee makes itself a sort of tree hut by intertwining branches. Stones apparently chipped for use have been found in strata of Oligocene Age at Boncelles in Belgium. Possibly the implement-using disposition was already present in that running lemuroid ancestry from which we are descended.

[1] Darwin's *Descent of Man.*

POSSIBLE APPEARANCE OF THE SUB-MAN *PITHECANTHROPUS.*
The face, jaws, and teeth are mere guess-work (see text).

§ 2

Among the earliest evidences of some creature, either human or at least more man-like than any living ape upon earth, are a number of flints and stones very roughly chipped and shaped so as to be held in the hand. These were probably used as hand-axes. These early implements ("Eoliths") are often so crude and simple that there was for a long time a controversy whether they were to be regarded as natural or artificial productions.[2] The date of the earliest of them is put by geologists as Pliocene— that is to say, *before the First Glacial Age.* They occur also throughout the First Interglacial period. We know of no bones or other remains in Europe or America of the quasi-human beings of half a million years ago, who made and used these implements. They used them to hammer with, perhaps they used them to

First Traces of Man-like Creatures.

[2] Among the earlier pioneers of the latter view was Mr. Harrison, a grocer of Ightham in Kent, one of those modest and devoted observers to whom British geology owes so much. At first his "Eoliths" were flouted and derided by archæologists, but to-day he has the scientific world with him in the recognition of the quasi-human origin of many of his specimens. With him we must honour Mr. W. J. Lewis Abbott, a jeweller of St. Leonards, whose intimate knowledge of stone structure has been of the utmost value in these discussions. See "Occ. Papers," No. 4, of the Royal Anthpl. Inst., for a description by Sir E. R. Lankester of one of the better formed of these early implements.

fight with, and perhaps they used bits of wood for similar purposes.[1]

But at Trinil, in Java, in strata which are said to correspond either to the latter Pliocene or to the American and European First Ice Age, there have been found some scattered bones of a creature, such as the makers of these early implements may have been. The top of a skull, some teeth, and a thigh-bone have been found. The skull shows a brain-case about half-way in size between that of the chimpanzee and man, but the thigh-bone is that of a creature as well adapted to standing and running as a man, and as free, therefore, to use its hands. The creature was not a man, nor was it an arboreal ape like the chimpanzee. It was a walking ape. It has been named by naturalists *Pithecanthropus erectus* (the walking ape-man). We cannot say that it is a direct human ancestor, but we may guess that the creatures who scattered these first stone tools over the world must have been closely similar and kindred, and that our ancestor was a beast of like kind. This little trayful of bony fragments from Trinil is, at present, apart from stone implements, the oldest relic of early humanity, or of the close blood relations of early humanity, that is known.

While these early men or " sub-men " were running about Europe four or five hundred thousand years ago, there were mammoths, rhinoceroses, a huge hippopotamus, a giant beaver, and a bison and wild cattle in their world. There were also wild horses, and the sabre-toothed tiger still abounded, a creature with canine teeth so greatly developed that it could not have eaten meat after the fashion of a lion or tiger, its sabres must have prevented it from biting ; it must have leapt upon its prey and hung on until its victim died from exhaustion, and then probably it sucked the blood. There are no traces of lions or tigers at that time in Europe, but there were bears, otters, wolves, and a wild boar. It may be that the early sub-man played jackal to the sabre-toothed tiger, and finished up the bodies the latter had done with.

[1] Some writers suppose that a Wood and Shell age preceded the earliest Stone Age. South Sea Islanders, Negroes, and Bushmen still make use of wood and the sharp-edged shells of land and water molluscs as implements.

A RHINOCEROS CONTEMPORARY WITH THE PRE-MEN.

THE MAMMOTH A CONTEMPORARY OF EARLY MAN.

§ 3

After this first glimpse of something at least sub-human in the record of geology, there is **The Heidelberg Sub-man.** not another fragment of human or man-like bone yet known from that record for an interval of hundreds of thousands of years. It is not until we reach deposits which are stated to be of the Second Interglacial period, 200,000 years later, 200,000 or 250,000 years ago, that another little scrap of bone comes to hand. Then we find a jaw-bone.

This jaw-bone was found in a sandpit near Heidelberg, at a depth of eighty feet from the surface,[1] and it is not the jaw-bone of a man as we understand man, but it is man-like in every respect, except that it has absolutely no trace of a chin; it is more massive than a man's, and its narrowness behind could not, it is thought, have given the tongue sufficient play for articulate speech. It is not an ape's jaw-bone; the teeth are human. This jaw-bone has been variously named *Homo Heidelbergensis* and *Palæoanthropus Heidelbergensis*, according to the estimate formed of its humanity or sub-humanity by various authorities. It lived in

[1] Sollas' *Ancient Hunters*, p. 40.

a world not remotely unlike the world of the still earlier sub-man of the first implements; the deposits in which it is found show that there were elephants, horses, rhinoceroses, bison, a moose, and so forth with it in the world, but the sabre-toothed tiger was dying out and the lion was spreading over Europe. The instruments of this period (known as the Chellian period) are a very considerable advance upon those of the Pliocene Age.

§ 4

We must turn over the Record for, it may be, another 100,000 years for the next remains **The Piltdown Sub-man.** of anything human or sub-human. Then in the Third Interglacial period, which may have begun 100,000 years ago and lasted 50,000 years,[2] the smashed pieces of a whole skull turn up. After all the vast lapse of time between this and the remote First Glacial period, the human creature has learnt only very slight improvements upon the primitive stone tools; and the bony remains discovered at Piltdown in Sussex display a

[2] We follow Penck.

creature still ascending only very gradually from the sub-human.

The first scraps of this skull were found in an excavation for road gravel in Sussex. Bit by bit other fragments of this skull were hunted out from the quarry heaps until most of it could be pieced together. It is a thick skull, thicker than that of any living race of men, and it has a brain capacity intermediate between that of Pithecanthropus and man. This creature has been named *Eoanthropus*, the dawn man. In the same gravel-pits were found teeth of rhinoceros, hippopotamus, and the leg-bone of a deer with marks upon it that may be cuts.

There was also a jaw-bone among these scattered remains, which was at first assumed naturally enough to belong to *Eoanthropus*, but which it was afterwards suggested was probably that of a chimpanzee. It is extraordinarily like that of a chimpanzee, but Dr. Keith, one of the greatest authorities in these questions, assigns it, after an exhaustive analysis in his *Antiquity of Man* (1915), to the skull with which it is found. It is, as a jaw-bone, far less human in character than the jaw of the much more ancient *Homo Heidelbergensis*, but the teeth are in some respects more like those of living men.

Dr. Keith, swayed by the jaw-bone, does not think that *Eoanthropus*, in spite of its name, is a creature in the direct ancestry of man. Much less is it an intermediate form between the Heidelberg man and the Neanderthal man we shall presently describe. It was only related to the true ancestor of man as the orang is related to the chimpanzee. It was one of a number of sub-human running apes of more than ape-like intelligence, and if it was not on the line royal, it was at any rate a very close collateral.

After this glimpse of a skull, the Record for very many centuries gives nothing but flint implements, which improve steadily in quality. A very characteristic form is shaped like a sole, with one flat side stricken off at one blow and the other side worked. The archæologists, as the Record continues, are presently able to distinguish scrapers, borers, knives, darts, throwing stones, and the like. Progress is now more rapid ; in a few centuries the shape of the hand-axe shows distinct and recognizable improvements. And then comes quite a number of remains. The Fourth Glacial Age is rising towards its maximum. Man is taking to caves and leaving vestiges there ; at Krapina in Croatia, at Neanderthal near Düsseldorf, at Spy, human remains have been found, skulls and bones of a creature that is certainly

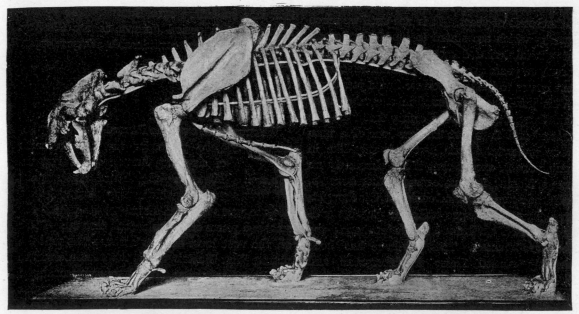

SKELETON OF THE SABRE-TOOTHED TIGER, A CONTEMPORARY OF THE SUB-MEN, BUT NOT APPARENTLY OF THE EARLY TRUE MEN.

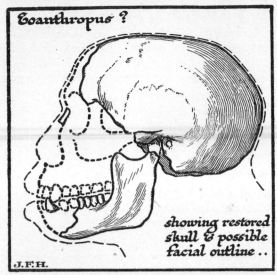

Eoanthropus ?

showing restored skull & possible facial outline ..

J.F.H.

DIAGRAM TO ILLUSTRATE THE RIDDLE OF THE PILTDOWN SUB-MAN.

the question in a familiar and luminous manner. It will enable the reader to gauge the extent and quality of the evidence that we possess at present upon the nature of these early human and sub-human animals. Upon these fragile Piltdown fragments alone more than a hundred books, pamphlets, and papers have been written. They are guarded more carefully from theft and wilful damage than the most precious jewels, and in the museum cases one sees only carefully executed *fac-similes.*

"As to the Piltdown jaw-bone, the best study of it is that by Smith Woodward, who first described it and the canine found later. The jaw is imperfect in front, but has the broad, flat symphysis of the Apes. G. S. Miller, an American anthropologist, has made a very good comparison of it with a chimpanzee's jaw, and concludes that it is a chimpanzee's. (His latest paper is in the *Am. Jour. of Phys. Anthrop.* vol. i., no. 1.) The one point in the

a man. Somewhere between 100,000 and 50,000 years ago, if not earlier, appeared *Homo Neanderthalensis* (also called *Homo antiquus* and *Homo primigenius*), a quite passable human being. His thumb was not quite equal in flexibility and usefulness to a human thumb, he stooped forward and could not hold his head erect, as all living men do, he was chinless and perhaps incapable of speech, there were curious differences about the enamel and the roots of his teeth from those of all living men, he was very thick-set, he was, indeed, not quite of the human species ; but there is no dispute about his attribution to the genus *Homo.* He was certainly not descended from Eoanthropus, but his jaw-bone is so like the Heidelberg jaw-bone, as to make it possible that *Homo Heidelbergensis,* a thousand centuries before him, was of his blood and race.

§ 5

The Riddle of the Piltdown Remains. Upon this question of the Piltdown jaw-bone, it may be of interest to quote here a letter to the writer from Sir Ray Lankester, discussing

Early Pleistocene Animals contemporary with earliest Man [before Homo Sapiens]

Hairy Mammoth

Heidelberg Man

Six-foot man drawn to same scale

Reindeer

Sabre-tooth Tiger

Musk Ox

Wild Horse

Woolly Rhinoceros

J.F.H.

Piltdown jaw itself against chimpanzee identification is the smooth, flat, worn surface of the molars. This is a *human* character, and is due to lateral movement of the jaw, and hence rubbing down of the tubercles of the molars. This is not worth much. But the serious question is, are we to associate this jaw with the cranium found close by it? If so, it is certainly not chimpanzee nor close to the Apes, but decidedly hominid. Two other small fragments of crania and a few more teeth have been found in the gravel two miles from Piltdown, which agree with the Piltdown cranium in having superciliary ridges fairly strong for a human skull, but not anything like the great superciliary ridges of Apes. The fact one has to face is this: here you have an imperfect cranium, very thick-walled and of small cubical contents (1,100 or so), but much larger in that respect than any ape's. A few yards distant from it in the same layer of gravel is found a jaw-bone having rather large pointed canines, a flat, broad symphysis, and other points about the inner face of the ramus and ridges which resemble those of the chimpanzee. Which is the more likely: (*a*) that these two novel fragments tending apewards from man were parts of the same individual; or (*b*), that the sweeping of the Wealden valley has brought there together a half-jaw and a broken cranium *both* more ape-like in character than any known human corresponding bits, and yet derived from two separate anthropoid beasts, one (the jaw) more simian, and the other (the cranium) much less so? As to the probabilities, we must remember that this patch of gravel at Piltdown, clearly and definitely, is a wash-up of remains of various later tertiary and post-tertiary deposits. It contains fragments of Miocene mastodon and rhinoceros teeth. These latter differ entirely in mineral character from the Eoanthropus jaw and the cranium. But (and this needs re-examination and *chemical* analysis) the Piltdown jaw and the Piltdown cranium do not seem to me to be quite alike in their mineral condition. The jaw is more deeply iron-stained, and, I should say (but not confidently), harder than the cranium. Now, it is easy to attribute too much importance to that difference, since in a patch of iron-stained gravel, such as that at Piltdown, the soaking of water and iron salts into bones embedded may be much greater in one spot than in another only a yard off, or a few inches deeper!

"So I think we are stumped and baffled! The most prudent way is to keep the jaw and the cranium apart in all argument about them. On the other hand, on the principle that hypotheses are not to be multiplied beyond necessity, there is a case for regarding the two—jaw and cranium —as having been parts of one beast—or man."

To which Sir H. H. Johnston adds: "Against the chimpanzee hypothesis it must be borne in mind that so far no living chimpanzee or fossil chimpanzee-like remains have been found nearer England than north equatorial Africa or Northwest India, and no remains of great apes at all nearer than Southern France and the upper Rhine—and those widely different from the *Eoanthropus* jaw."

IX

THE NEANDERTHAL MEN, AN EXTINCT RACE
(The Early Palæolithic Age [1])

§ 1

IN the time of the Third Interglacial period the outline of Europe and western Asia was very different from what it is to-day. Vast areas to the west and north-west which are now under the Atlantic waters were then dry land; the Irish sea and the North Sea were river valleys. Over these northern areas

The World 50,000 Years Ago.

there spread and receded and spread again a

[1] Three phases of human history before the knowledge and use of metals are often distinguished. First there is the so-called Eolithic Age (dawn of stone implements), then the Palæolithic Age (old stone implements), and finally an age in which the implements are skilfully made and frequently well finished and polished (Neolithic Age). The Palæolithic Period is further divided into an earlier (sub-human) and a later (fully human) period. We shall comment on these divisions later.

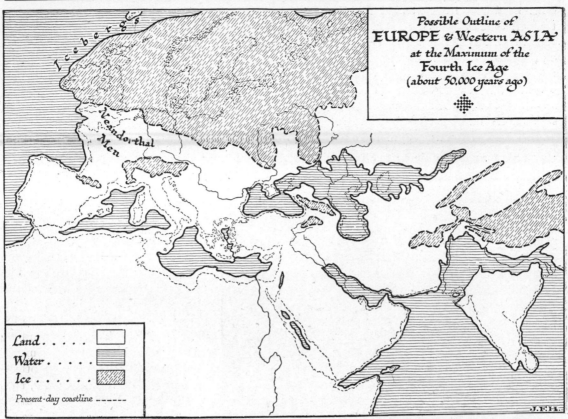

THIS MAP REPRESENTS THE PRESENT STATE OF OUR KNOWLEDGE OF THE GEOGRAPHY OF EUROPE
AND WESTERN ASIA AT A PERIOD WHICH WE GUESS TO BE ABOUT 50,000 YEARS AGO.
Much of this map is of course speculative, but its broad outlines must be fairly like those of the world in which men first became men.

great ice cap such as covers central Greenland to-day (see Map, herewith). This vast ice cap, which covered both polar regions of the earth, withdrew huge masses of water from the ocean, and the sea-level consequently fell, exposing great areas of land that are now submerged again. The Mediterranean area was probably a great valley below the general sea-level, containing two inland seas cut off from the general ocean. The climate of this Mediterranean basin was perhaps cold temperate, and the region of the Sahara to the south was not then a desert of baked rock and blown sand, but a well-watered and fertile country. Between the ice sheets to the north and the Alps and Mediterranean valley to the south stretched a bleak wilderness whose climate changed from harshness to a mild kindliness and then hardened again for the Fourth Glacial Age.

Across this wilderness, which is now the great plain of Europe, wandered a various fauna. At first there were hippopotami, rhinoceroses, mammoths, and elephants. The sabre-toothed tiger was diminishing towards extinction. Then, as the air chilled, the hippopotamus, and then other warmth-loving creatures, ceased to come so far north, and the sabre-toothed tiger disappeared altogether. The woolly mammoth, the woolly rhinoceros, the musk ox, the bison, the aurochs, and the reindeer became prevalent, and the temperate vegetation gave place to plants of a more arctic type. The glaciers spread southward to the maximum of the Fourth Glacial Age (about 50,000 years ago), and then receded again. In the earlier phase, the Third Interglacial period, a certain number of small family groups of men (*Homo Neanderthalensis*) and probably of sub-men (*Eoanthropus*) wandered over the land, leaving nothing but their flint implements to witness to their presence. They probably used a multitude and variety of wooden implements also; they had probably learnt much about the shapes of objects and the use of different shapes from wood, knowledge which they afterwards applied to stone; but none of this wooden material has survived; we can only speculate about its forms and uses. As the weather hardened to its maximum of severity, the Neanderthal men, already it would seem acquainted with the use of fire, began to seek shelter under rock ledges and in caves— and so leave remains behind them. Hitherto they had been accustomed to squat in the open

A GUESS AT THE APPEARANCE OF *HOMO NEANDERTHALENSIS*.

about the fire, and near their water supply. But they were sufficiently intelligent to adapt themselves to the new and harder conditions. (As for the sub-men, they seem to have succumbed to the stresses of this Fourth Glacial Age altogether. At any rate, the rudest type of Palæolithic implements presently disappears.)

Not merely man was taking to the caves. This period also had a cave lion, a cave bear, and a cave hyæna. These creatures had to be

driven out of the caves and kept out of the caves in which these early men wanted to squat and hide; and no doubt fire was an effective method of eviction and protection. Probably early men did not go deeply into the caves, because they had no means of lighting their recesses. They got in far enough to be out of the weather, and stored wood and food in odd corners. Perhaps they barricaded the cave mouths. Their only available light for going deeply into the caverns would be torches.

What did these Neanderthal men hunt? Their only possible weapons for killing such giant creatures as the mammoth or the cave bear, or even the reindeer, were spears of wood, wooden clubs, and those big pieces of flint they left behind them, the Chellian and Moustierian implements; and probably their usual quarry was smaller game. But they did certainly eat the flesh of the big beasts when they had a chance, and perhaps they followed them when sick or when wounded by combats, or took advantage of them when they were bogged or in trouble with ice or water. (The Labrador Indians still kill the caribou with spears at awkward river crossings.) At Dewlish, in Dorset, an artificial trench has been found which is supposed to have been a Palæolithic trap for elephants.[1] We know that the Neanderthalers partly ate their kill where it fell; but they brought back the big marrow bones to the cave to crack and eat at leisure, because few ribs and vertebræ are found in the caves, but great quantities of cracked and split long bones. They used skins to wrap about them, and the women probably dressed the skins.

We know also that they were right-handed like modern men, because the left side of the brain (which serves the right side of the body) is bigger than the right. But while the back parts of the brain which deal with sight and

[1] Osmond Fisher, quoted in Wright's *Quaternary Ice Age*.

OUR NEANDERTHALOID ANCESTOR (NOT A NEANDERTHAL MAN, BUT A
PARALLEL SPECIES)

touch and the energy of the body are well developed, the front parts, which are connected with thought and speech, are comparatively small. It was as big a brain as ours, but different. This species of *Homo* had certainly a very different mentality from ours ; its individuals were not merely simpler and lower than we are, they were on another line. It may be they did not speak at all, or very sparingly. They had nothing that we should call a language.

§ 2

In Worthington Smith's *Man the Primeval Savage* there is a very vividly written descrip-

The Daily Life of the First Men. tion of early Palæolithic life, from which much of the following account is borrowed. In the original, Mr. Worthington Smith assumes a more extensive social life, a larger community, and a more definite division of labour among its members than is altogether justifiable in the face of such subsequent writings as J. J. Atkinson's memorable essay on Primal Law.[1] For the little tribe Mr. Worthington Smith described, there has been substituted, therefore, a family group under the leadership of one Old Man, and the suggestions of Mr. Atkinson as to the behaviour of the Old Man have been worked into the sketch.

Mr. Worthington Smith describes a squatting-place near a stream, because primitive man, having no pots or other vessels, must needs have kept close to a water supply, and with some chalk cliffs adjacent from which flints could be got to work. The air was bleak, and the fire was of great importance, because fires once out were not easily relit in those days. When not required to blaze it was probably banked down with ashes. The most probable way in which fires were started was by hacking a bit of iron pyrites with a flint amidst dry dead leaves ; concretions of iron pyrites and flints are found together in England where the gault and chalk approach each other.[2] The little group of people would be squatting about amidst a litter of fern, moss, and such-like dry material.

[1] *Social Origins*, by Andrew Lang, and *Primal Law*, by J. J. Atkinson. (Longmans, 1903.)

[2] This first origin of fire was suggested by Sir John Lubbock (*Prehistoric Times*), and Ludwig Hopf, in *The Human Species*, says that " Flints and pieces of pyrites are found in close proximity in palæolithic settlements near the remains of mammoths."

Some of the women and children would need to be continually gathering fuel to keep up the fires. It would be a tradition that had grown up. The young would imitate their elders in this task. Perhaps there would be rude wind shelters of boughs on one side of the encampment.

The Old Man, the father and master of the group, would perhaps be engaged in hammering

ANOTHER ESSAY IN THE RESTORATION OF
HOMO NEANDERTHALENSIS.

flints beside the fire. The children would imitate him and learn to use the sharpened fragments. Probably some of the women would hunt good flints ; they would fish them out of the chalk with sticks and bring them to the squatting-place.

There would be skins about. It seems probable that at a very early time primitive men took to using skins. Probably they were wrapped about the children, and used to lie upon when the ground was damp and cold. A woman would perhaps be preparing a skin. The inside of the skin would be well scraped free of superfluous flesh with trimmed flints, and then strained and pulled and pegged out flat on the grass, and dried in the rays of the sun.

Away from the fire other members of the family group prowl in search of food, but at night they all gather closely round the fire and build it up, for it is their protection against the wandering bear and such-like beasts of prey. The Old

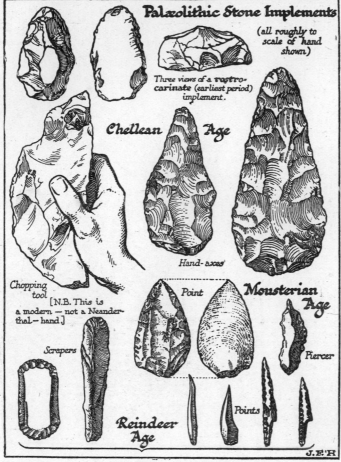

Palæolithic Stone Implements

(all roughly to scale of hand shown)

Three views of a rostro-carinate (earliest period) implement.

Chellean   Age

Hand-axes

Chopping tool [N.B. This is a modern — not a Neander-thal — hand.]

Point   Mousterian Age

Scrapers

Piercer

Reindeer Age   Points

J.F.H

EARLY STONE IMPLEMENTS.

The Mousterian Age implements, and all above it, are those of Neanderthal men or, possibly in the case of the rostro-carinates, of sub-men. The lower row (Reindeer Age) are the work of true men. The student should compare this diagram with the time diagram attached to Chapter VII, § 6.

Man is the only fully adult male in the little group. There are women, boys and girls, but so soon as the boys are big enough to rouse the Old Man's jealousy, he will fall foul of them and either drive them off or kill them. Some girls may perhaps go off with these exiles, or two or three of these youths may keep together for a time, wandering until they come upon some other group, from which they may try to steal a mate. Then they would probably fall out among themselves. Some day, when he is forty years old perhaps or even older, and his teeth are worn down and his energy abating, some younger male will stand up to the old man and kill him and reign in his stead. There is probably short shrift for the old at the squatting-place. So soon as they grow weak and bad-tempered, trouble and death come upon them.

What did they eat at the squatting-place?

"Primeval man is commonly described as a hunter of the great hairy mammoth, of the bear, and the lion, but it is in the highest degree improbable that the human savage ever hunted animals much larger than the hare, the rabbit, and the rat. Man was probably the hunted rather than the hunter.

"The primeval savage was both herbivorous and carnivorous. He had for food hazel-nuts, beech-nuts, sweet chestnuts, earth-nuts, and acorns. He had crab-apples, wild pears, wild cherries, wild goose-berries, bullaces, sorbs, sloes, black-berries, yewberries, hips and haws, watercress, fungi, the larger and softer leaf-buds, Nostoc (the vegetable substance called 'fallen stars' by countryfolk), the fleshy, juicy, asparagus-like rhizomes or subterranean stems of the *Labiatæ* and like plants, as well as other delicacies of the vegetable kingdom. He had birds' eggs, young birds, and the honey and honeycomb of wild bees. He had newts, snails, and frogs—the two latter delicacies are still highly esteemed in Normandy and Brittany. He had fish, dead and alive, and fresh-water mussels; he could easily catch fish with his hands and paddle and dive for and trap them. By the seaside he would have fish, mollusca, and seaweed. He would have many of the larger birds and smaller mammals, which he could easily secure by throwing stones and sticks, or by setting simple snares. He would have the snake, the slow-worm, and the cray-fish. He would have various grubs and insects, the large larvæ of beetles and various caterpillars. The taste for caterpillars still survives in China, where they are sold in dried bundles in the markets. A chief and highly nourishing object of food would doubtlessly be bones smashed up into a stiff and gritty paste.

"A fact of great importance is this—primeval man would not be particular about having his flesh food over-fresh. He would constantly find it in a dead state, and, if semi-putrid, he would relish it none the less—the taste for high or half-putrid game still survives. If driven by hunger and hard pressed, he would perhaps sometimes eat his weaker companions or unhealthy children who happened to be feeble or unsightly or burthensome. The larger animals in a weak and dying state would no doubt be much sought for ; when these were not forthcoming, dead and half-rotten examples would be made to suffice. An unpleasant odour would not be objected to ; it is not objected to now in many continental hotels.

"The savages sat huddled close together round their fire, with fruits, bones, and half-putrid flesh. We can imagine the old man and his women twitching the skin of their shoulders, brows, and muzzles as they were annoyed or bitten by flies or other insects. We can imagine the large human nostrils, indicative of keen scent, giving rapidly repeated sniffs at the foul meat before it was consumed ; the bad odour of the meat, and the various other disgusting odours belonging to a haunt of savages, being not in the least disapproved.

"Man at that time was not a *degraded* animal, for he had never been higher ; he was therefore an exalted animal, and, low as we esteem him now, he yet represented the highest stage of development of the animal kingdom of his time."

That is at least an acceptable sketch of a Neanderthal squatting-place. But before extinction overtook them, even the Neanderthalers learnt much and went far.

Whatever the older Palæolithic men did with their dead, there is reason to suppose that the later *Homo Neanderthalensis* buried some individuals at least with respect and ceremony. One of the best-known Neanderthal skeletons is that of a youth who apparently had been deliberately interred. He had been placed in a sleeping posture, head on the right forearm. The head lay on a number of flint fragments carefully piled together " pillow fashion." A big hand-axe lay near his head, and around him were numerous charred and split ox bones, as though there had been a feast or an offering.

To this appearance of burial during the later Neanderthal age we shall return later, when we are considering the ideas that were inside the heads of primitive men.

This sort of men may have wandered, squatted about their fires, and died in Europe for a period extending over 100,000 years, if we assume, that is, that the Heidelberg jaw-bone belongs to a member of the species, a period so vast that all the subsequent history of our race becomes a thing of yesterday. Along its own line this species of men was accumulating a dim tradition, and working out its limited

AUSTRALIA & the Western Pacific in the Glacial Age (The 100-fathom line as coastline..)

While the waters were held up in the Polar Ice Caps, the sea-level was low enough to enable Palæolithic Man to reach Tasmania.

possibilities. Its thick skull imprisoned its brain, and to the end it was low-browed and brutish.

§ 3

When the Dutch discovered Tasmania, they found a detached human race not very greatly **The Last Palæolithic Men.** advanced beyond this Lower Palæolithic stage. But over most of the world the Lower Palæolithic culture had developed into a more complicated and higher life twenty or thirty thousand years ago. The Tasmanians were not racially Neanderthalers ;[1] their brain-cases, their neck-bones, their jaws and teeth, show that ; they had no

[1] But compare Sollas' *Ancient Hunters.*

Neanderthal affinities ; they were of the same species as ourselves. There can be little doubt that throughout the hundreds of centuries during which the scattered little groups of Neanderthal men were all that represented men in Europe, real men, of our own species, in some other part of the world, were working their way along parallel lines from much the same stage as the Neanderthalers ended at, and which the Tasmanians preserved, to a higher level of power and achievement. The Tas-

manians, living under unstimulating conditions, remote from any other human competition or example, lagged behind the rest of the human brotherhood.[1]

About 200 centuries ago or earlier, real men of our own species, if not of our own race, came drifting into the European area.

[1] What is known of the Tasmanian Old Stone men is to be found in Roth and Butler's *Aborigines of Tasmania*. See also footnote on the Tasmanian language to Chapter XIII.

X

THE LATER POSTGLACIAL PALÆOLITHIC MEN, THE FIRST TRUE MEN
(Later Palæolithic Age)

§ 1

THE Neanderthal type of man prevailed in Europe at least for tens of thousands of years. For ages that make all history seem a thing of yesterday, these nearly human creatures prevailed. **The coming of Men like Ourselves.** If the Heidelberg jaw was that of a Neanderthaler, and if there is no error in the estimate of the age of that jaw, then the Neanderthal Race lasted out for more than 200,000 years ! Finally, between 40,000 and 25,000 years ago, as the Fourth Glacial Age softened towards more temperate conditions (see Map on p. 53), a different human type came upon the scene, and, it would seem, exterminated *Homo Neanderthalensis*.[2] This new

type was probably developed in South Asia or North Africa, or in lands now submerged in the Mediterranean basin, and, as more remains are collected and evidence accumulates, men will learn more of their early stages. At present we can only guess where and how, through the slow ages, parallel with the Neanderthal cousin, these first *true men* arose out of some more ape-like progenitor. For hundreds of centuries they were acquiring skill of hand and limb, and power and bulk of brain, in that still unknown environment. They were already far above the Neanderthal level of achievement and intelligence, when first they come into our ken, and they had already split into two or more very distinctive races.

[2] The opinion that the Neanderthal race (*Homo Neanderthalensis*) is an extinct species which did not interbreed with the true men (*Homo sapiens*) is held by Professor Osborne, and it is the view to which the writer inclines and to which he has pointed in the treatment of this section ; but it is only fair to the reader to note that many writers do not share this view. They write and speak of living " Neanderthalers " in contemporary populations. One observer has written in the past of such types in the west of Ireland ; another has observed them in Greece. These so-called " living Neanderthalers " have neither the peculiarities of neck, thumb, nor teeth that distinguish the Neanderthal race of pre-men. The cheek teeth of true men, for instance, have what we call fangs, long fangs ; the Neanderthaler's cheek tooth is a *more complicated and specialized* cheek tooth, a long tooth with short fangs, and his canine teeth were *less* marked,

less like dog-teeth, than ours. Nothing could show more clearly that he was on a different line of development. We must remember that so far only Western Europe has been properly explored for Palæolithic remains, and that practically all we know of the Neanderthal species comes from that area (see Map, p. 47). No doubt the ancestor of *Homo sapiens* (which species includes the Tasmanians) was a very similar and parallel creature to *Homo Neanderthalensis*. And we are not so far from that ancestor as to have eliminated not indeed " Neanderthal," but " Neanderthaloid " types. The existence of such types no more proves that the Neanderthal species, the makers of the Chellian and Mousterian implements, interbred with *Homo sapiens* in the European area than do monkey-faced people testify to an interbreeding with monkeys ; or people with faces like horses, that there is an equine strain in our population.

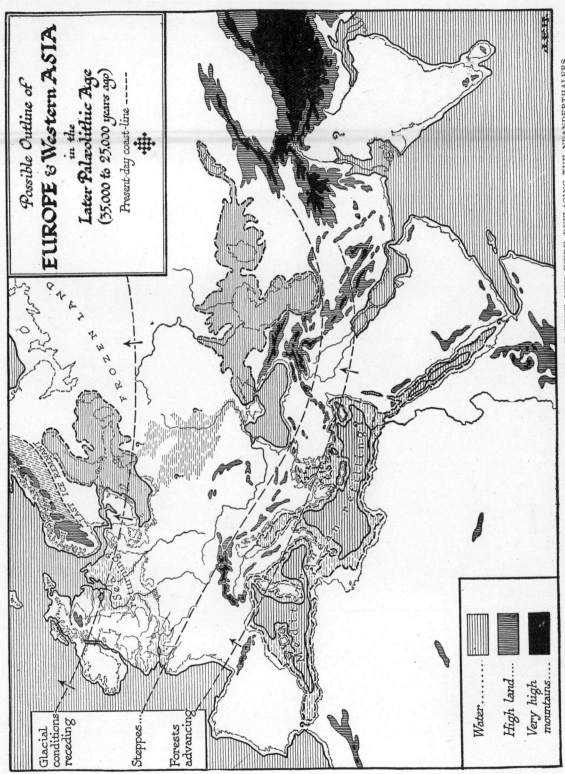

Possible Outline of
EUROPE & Western ASIA
in the
Later Palaeolithic Age
(35,000 to 25,000 years ago)

Present-day coast-line ------

FROZEN LAND

LAST ICE REMNANT

Severius? returning

Glacial conditions receding

Steppes......

Forests advancing

Water.......
High land.....
Very high mountains......

MAP SHOWING EUROPE AND WESTERN ASIA ABOUT THE TIME WHEN THE TRUE MEN WERE REPLACING THE NEANDERTHALERS IN WESTERN EUROPE.

Cromagnon Man

J.F.H.

These new-comers did not migrate into Europe in the strict sense of the word, but rather, as century by century the climate ameliorated, they followed the food and plants to which they were accustomed, as those spread into the new realms that opened to them. The ice was receding, vegetation was increasing, big game of all sorts was becoming more abundant. Steppe-like conditions, conditions of pasture and shrub, were bringing with them vast herds of wild horse. Ethnologists (students of race) class these new human races in one same species as ourselves, and with all human races subsequent to them, under one common specific name of *Homo Sapiens*. They had quite human brain-cases and hands. Their teeth and their necks were anatomically as ours are.

Now, here again, with every desire to be plain and explicit with the reader, we have still to trouble him with qualified statements and notes of interrogation. There is now an enormous literature about these earliest true men, the men of the Later Palæozoic Age, and it is still for the general reader a very confusing literature indeed. It is confusing because it is still confused at the source. We know of two distinct sorts of skeletal remains in this period, the first of these known as the Cro-Magnon race, and the second the Grimaldi race ; but the great bulk of the human traces and appliances we find are either without human bones or with insufficient bones for us to define their associated physical type. There may have

been many more distinct races than these two. There may have been intermediate types. In the grotto of Cro-Magnon it was that complete skeletons of one main type of these Newer Palæolithic men, these true men, were first found, and so it is that they are spoken of as Cro-Magnards.

These Cro-Magnards were a tall people with very broad faces, prominent noses, and, all things considered, astonishingly big brains. The brain capacity of the woman in the Cro-Magnon cave exceeded that of the average male to-day. Her head had been smashed by a heavy blow. There were also in the same cave with her the complete skeleton of an older man, nearly six feet high, the fragments of a child's skeleton, and the skeletons of two young men. There were also flint implements and perforated sea-shells, used no doubt as ornaments. Such is one sample of the earliest true men. But at the Grimaldi cave, near Mentone, were discovered two skeletons also of the later Palæolithic Period, but of a widely contrasted type, with negroid characteristics that point rather to the negroid type. There can be no doubt that we have to deal in this period with at least two and probably more highly divergent races of true men. They may have overlapped in time, or Cro-Magnards may have followed the Grimaldi race, and either or both may have been contemporaries with the late Neanderthal men. Various authorities have very strong opinions upon these points, but they are, at most, opinions. The whole story is further fogged at present by our inability to distinguish, in the absence of skeletons, which race has been at work in any particular case. In what follows the reader will ask of this or that particular statement, " Yes, but is this the Cro-Magnard or the Grimaldi man or some other that you are writing about ? " To which in most cases the honest answer is, " As yet we do not know." Confessedly our account of the newer Palæolithic is a jumbled account. There are probably two or three concurrent and only roughly similar histories of these newer Palæolithic men as yet, inextricably mixed up together. Some authorities appear to favour the Cro-Magnards unduly and to dismiss the Grimaldi people with as little as possible of the record.

The appearance of these truly human Post

glacial Palæolithic peoples was certainly an enormous leap forward in the history of mankind. Both of these main races had a human fore-brain, a human hand, an intelligence very like our own. They dispossessed *Homo Neander-thalensis* from his caverns and his stone quarries. And they agreed with modern ethnologists, it would seem, in regarding him as a different species. Unlike most savage conquerors, who take the women of the defeated side for their own and interbreed with them, it would seem that the true men would have nothing to do with the Neanderthal race, women or men. There is no trace of any intermixture between the races, in spite of the fact that the new-comers, being also flint users, were establishing themselves in the very same spots that their predecessors had occupied. We know very little of the appearance of the Neanderthal man, but this absence of intermixture seems to suggest an extreme hairiness, an ugliness, or a repulsive strangeness in his appearance over and above his low forehead, his beetle brows, his ape neck, and his inferior stature. Or he—and she—may have been too fierce to tame. Says Sir Harry Johnston, in a survey of the rise of modern man in his *Views and Reviews* : " The dim racial remembrance of such gorilla-like monsters, with cunning brains, shambling gait, hairy bodies, strong teeth, and possibly can-nibalistic tendencies, may be the germ of the ogre in folklore. . . ."

These true men of the Palæolithic Age, who replace the Neanderthalers, were coming into a milder climate, and although they used the caves and shelters of their predecessors, they lived largely in the open. They were hunting peoples, and some or all of them appear to have hunted the mammoth and the wild horse as well as the reindeer, bison, and aurochs. They ate much horse. At a great open-air camp at Solutré, where they seem to have had annual gatherings for many centuries, it is estimated that there are the bones of 100,000 horses, besides reindeer, mammoth, and bison bones. They probably followed herds of horses, the little bearded ponies of that age, as these moved after pasture. They hung about on the flanks of the herd, and became very wise about its habits and dispositions. A large part of these men's lives must have been spent in watching animals.

Whether they tamed and domesticated the horse is still an open question. Perhaps they learnt to do so by degrees as the centuries passed. At any rate, we find late Palæolithic drawings of horses with marks about the heads that are strongly suggestive of bridles, and there exists a carving of a horse's head showing what is perhaps a rope of twisted skin or tendon. But even if they tamed the horse, it is still more doubtful whether they rode it or had much use for it when it was tamed. The horse they knew was a wild pony with a beard under its chin, not up to carrying a man for any distance. It is improbable that these men had yet learnt the rather unnatural use of animal's milk as food. If they tamed the horse at last, it was the only animal they seem to have tamed. They had no dogs, and they had little to do with any sort of domesticated sheep or cattle.

It greatly aids us to realize their common humanity that these earliest true men could draw. Both races, it would seem, drew astonish-ingly well. They were by all standards savages, but they were artistic savages. They drew better than any of their successors down to the beginnings of history. They drew and painted on the cliffs and cave walls that they had wrested from the Neanderthal men. And the surviving drawings come to the ethnologist, puzzling over bones and scraps, with the effect of a plain message shining through guesswork and darkness. They drew on bones and antlers ; they carved little figures.

These later Palæolithic people not only drew remarkably well for our information, and with an increasing skill as the centuries passed, but they have also left us other information about their lives in their graves. They buried. They buried their dead, often with ornaments, weapons, and food ; they used a lot of colour in the burial, and evidently painted the body. From that one may infer that they painted their bodies during life. Paint was a big fact in their lives. They were inveterate painters ; they used black, brown, red, yellow, and white pigments, and the pigments they used endure to this day in the caves of France and Spain. Of all modern races, none have shown so pictorial a disposition ; the nearest approach to it has been among the American Indians.

These drawings and paintings of the later

Palæolithic people went on through a long period of time, and present wide fluctuations in artistic merit. We give here some early sketches, from which we learn of the interest taken by these early men in the bison, horse, ibex, cave bear, and reindeer. In its early stages the drawing is often primitive like the drawings of clever children; quadrupeds are usually drawn with one hindleg and one foreleg, as children draw them to this day. The legs on

Reindeer Age Articles (drawn to differing scales)

Harpoons of reindeer horn

(Azilian—pierced for thong)

Pebble cup or mortar

Bone points

Bone needles

Arrow straighteners

(reindeer horn)

Australian natives' method of using throwing-stick or spear-thrower

Throwing-stick (reindeer horn)

J.F.H.

the other side were too much for the artist's technique. Possibly the first drawings began as children's drawings begin, out of idle scratchings. The savage scratched with a flint on a smooth rock surface, and was reminded of some line or gesture. But their solid carvings are at least as old as their first pictures. The earlier drawings betray a complete incapacity to group animals. As the centuries progressed, more skilful artists appeared. The representation of beasts became at last astonishingly

vivid and like. At the crest of their artistic time, eighteen or twenty thousand years ago, there were Palæolithic men who could draw as well as most modern European artists. They rarely drew themselves. The vast majority of their drawings represent animals. The mammoth and the horse are among the commonest themes. Some of the people, whether Grimaldi people or Cro-Magnon people, also made little ivory and soapstone statuettes, and among these are some very fat female figures. These latter suggest the physique of Grimaldi rather than of Cro-Magnon artists. They are like Bushmen women. The human sculpture of the earlier times inclined to caricature, and generally such human figures as they represent are far below the animal studies in vigour and veracity.

Later on there was more grace and less coarseness in the human representations. One little ivory head discovered is that of a girl with an elaborate coiffure. These people at a later stage also scratched and engraved designs on ivory and bone. Some of the most interesting groups of figures are carved very curiously round bone, and especially round rods of deer bone, so that it is impossible to see the entire design altogether. Figures have also been found modelled in clay, although no Palæolithic people made any use of pottery.

Many of the paintings are found in the depths of unlit caves. They are often difficult of access. The artists must have employed lamps to do their work, and shallow soapstone lamps in which fat could have been burnt have been found. Whether the seeing of these cavern paintings was in some way ceremonial or under what circumstances they were seen, we are now altogether at a loss to imagine.

§ 2

Archæologists distinguish at present three chief stages in the history of these newer Palæolithic men, and we must name these stages here. But it may be as well to note at the same time that it is a matter of the utmost **Subdivisions of the Later Palæolithic.** difficulty to distinguish which of two deposits in different places is the older or newer. We may very well be dealing with the work of more or less contemporary and different races when we think we are dealing with successive ones. We are dealing, the reader must bear in mind, with little disconnected patches of material, a few score altogether. The earliest stage usually distinguished by the experts is the *Aurignacean*; it is characterized by very well-made flint instruments, and by a rapid development of art and more particularly of statuettes and wall paintings. The most esteemed of the painted caves is ascribed to the latter part of this the first of the three subdivisions of the newer Palæolithic. The second subdivision of this period is called the *Solutrian*, and is distinguished particularly by the quality and beauty of its stone implements; some of its razor-like blades are only equalled and not surpassed by the very best of the Neolithic work. They are of course unpolished, but the best specimens are as thin as steel blades and almost as sharp. Finally, it would seem, came the *Magdalenian* stage, in which the horse and reindeer were dwindling in numbers and the red deer coming into Europe.[1] The stone implements are smaller, and there is a great quantity of bone harpoons, spearheads, needles, and the like. The hunters of the third and last stage of the later Palæolithic Age appear to have supplemented the diminishing food supply by fishing. The characteristic art of the period consists of deep reliefs done upon bone and line engraving upon bone. It is to this period that the designs drawn round bones belong, and it has been suggested that these designs upon round bones were used to print

coloured designs upon leather. Some of the workmanship on bone was extraordinarily fine. Parkyn quotes from de Mortillet, about the Reindeer Age (Magdalenian) bone needles, that they " are much superior to those of later, even historical, times, down to the Renaissance. The Romans, for example, never had needles comparable to those of the Magdalenian epoch."

It is quite impossible at present to guess at

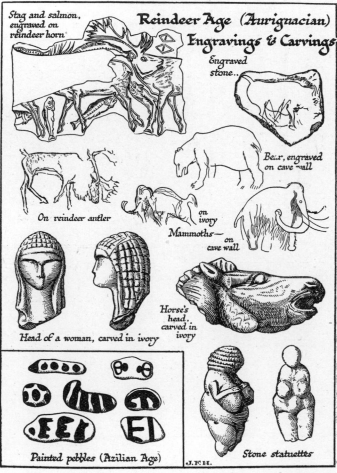

Stag and salmon, engraved on reindeer horn

Reindeer Age (Aurignacian) Engravings & Carvings

Engraved stone..

Bear, engraved on cave wall

On reindeer antler

on ivory

Mammoths— on cave wall

Head of a woman, carved in ivory

Horse's head.. carved in ivory

Painted pebbles (Azilian Age)

J.F.H.

Stone statuettes

the relative lengths of these ages. We are not even positive about their relative relationship. Each lasted perhaps for two or three or more thousand years, as long a time as the whole period from Moses to our own day.

At last it would seem that circumstances began to turn altogether against these hunting Newer Palæolithic peoples who had flourished for so long in Europe. They disappeared. New kinds of men appeared in Europe, replacing them. These latter seem to have brought in

[1] So Osborn in his *Men of the Old Stone Age*. But see Wright's *Quaternary Ice Age* for a different view of the Magdalenian Age.

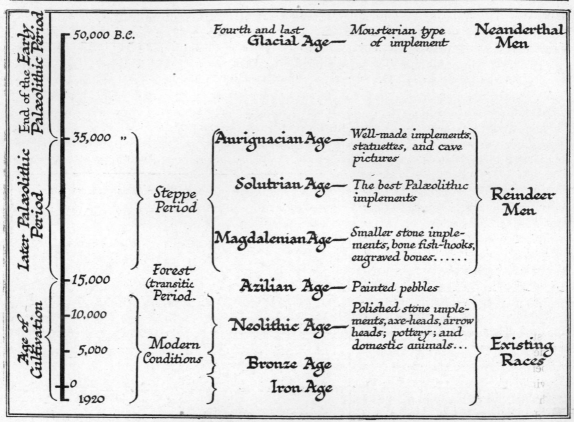

TIME DIAGRAM SHOWING THE ESTIMATED DURATION OF THE TRUE HUMAN PERIODS.
This time diagram again is on a larger scale than its predecessors. The time diagram to Chapter VII, p. 38, if it were on this scale would be nearly 4 feet long, and the diagram of the whole of geological time (Chap. II, § 2), between 486 and 4,860 feet long.

bow and arrows; they had domesticated animals and cultivated the soil. A new way of living, the Neolithic way of living, spread over the European area; and the life of the Reindeer Age and of the races of Reindeer men, the Later Palæolithic men, after a reign vastly greater than the time between ourselves and the very earliest beginnings of recorded history, passed off the European stage.

§ 3

There is a disposition on the part of many writers to exaggerate the intellectual and physical qualities of these later Palæolithic men and make a wonder of them.[1] Collectively considered, these people had remarkable gifts, but a little reflection will show they had almost as remarkable deficiencies. The tremendous

The Earliest True Men were Splendid Savages.

[1] See, for example, H. G. F. Spurrell, *Modern Man and his Forerunners*, end of Chapter III.

advance they display upon their Neanderthalian predecessors and their special artistic gift must not blind us to their very obvious limitations. For all the quantity of their brains, the quality was narrow and special. They had vivid perceptions, an acute sense of animal form, they had the real artist's impulse to render; so far they were fully grown human beings. But that disposition to paint and draw is shown to-day by the Bushmen, by Californian Indians, and by Australian black fellows; it is not a mark of all-round high intellectual quality. The cumulative effect of their drawings and paintings is very great, but we must not make the mistake of crowding all these achievements together in our minds as though they had suddenly flashed out upon the world in a brief interval of time, or as though they were all the achievements of one people. These races of Reindeer men were in undisturbed possession of Western Europe for a period at least four times as long as the interval between ourselves and Moses, and through all that immense time they were free to develop and vary their life to its utmost possibilities. Their art constitutes their one claim to be accounted more than common savages.

They were in close contact with animals, but they never seemed to have got to terms with any animal unless it was the horse. They had no dogs. They had no properly domesticated animals at all. They watched and drew and killed and ate. They do not seem to have cooked their food. Perhaps they scorched and grilled it, but they could not have done much more, because they had no cooking implements. Although they had clay available, and although there are several Palæolithic clay figures on record, they had *no pottery*. Although they had a great variety of flint and bone implements, they never rose to the possibilities of using timber for permanent shelters or such-like structures. They never made hafted axes or the like that would enable them to deal with timber. There is a suggestion in some of the drawings of a fence of stakes in which a mammoth seems to be entangled. But here we may be dealing with superimposed scratchings. They had *no buildings*. It is not even certain that they had tents or huts. They may have had simple skin tents. Some of the drawings seem to suggest as much. It is doubtful if they knew of the bow. They left no good arrowheads behind them. Certain of their implements are said to be " arrow-straighteners " by distinguished authorities, but that is about as much evidence as we have of arrows. They may have used sharpened sticks as arrows. They had *no cultivation* of grain or vegetables of any sort. Their women were probably squaws, smaller than the men ; the earlier statuettes represent them as grossly fat, almost as the Bushmen women are often fat to-day. (But this may not be true of the Cro-Magnards.)

They clothed themselves, it would seem, in skins, if they clothed themselves at all. These skins they prepared with skill and elaboration, and towards the end of the age they used bone needles, no doubt to sew these pelts. One may guess pretty safely that they painted these skins, and it has even been supposed, printed off designs upon them from bone cylinders.

But their garments were mere wraps ; there are no clasps or catches to be found. They do not seem to have used grass or such-like fibre for textiles. Their statuettes are naked. They were, in fact, except for a fur wrap in cold weather, naked painted savages.

These hunters lived on open steppes for a hundred centuries or so, five times the length of the Christian era. They were, perhaps, overtaken by the growth of the European forests, as the climate became milder and damper. When the wild horse and the reindeer diminished in Europe, and a newer type of human culture, with a greater power over food supply, a greater tenacity of settlement, and probably a larger social organization, arose, the Reindeer Men had to learn fresh ways of living or disappear. How far they learnt and mingled their strain with the new European populations, and how far they went under we cannot yet guess. Opinions differ widely. Wright lays much stress on the " great hiatus " between the Palæolithic and Neolithic remains, while Osborn traces the likeness of the former in several living populations. In the region of the Doubs and of the Dordogne in France, many individuals are to be met with to this day with skulls of the "Cro-Magnon" type. Apparently the Grimaldi type of men has disappeared altogether from Europe. Whether the Cro-Magnon type of men mingled completely with the Neolithic peoples, or whether they remained distinct and held their own in favourable localities to the north and west, following the reindeer over Siberia and towards America, which at that time was continuous with Siberia, or whether they disappeared altogether from the world, is a matter that can be only speculated about at present. There is not enough evidence for a judgment. Possibly they mingled to a certain extent. There is little to prevent our believing that they survived without much intermixture for a long time in north Asia, that " pockets " of them remained here and there in Europe, that there is a streak of their blood in most European peoples to-day, and that there is a much stronger streak, if not a predominant strain, in the Mongolian and American races.[1]

[1] Upon this question W. J. Sollas' *Ancient Hunters* is very full and suggestive.

LATER PALÆOLITHIC PAINTING OF A BOAR.

§ 4

It was about 12,000 or fewer years ago that, with the spread of forests and a great change **Hunters give place to Herdsmen.** of the fauna, the long prevalence of the hunting life in Europe drew to its end. Reindeer vanished. Changing conditions frequently bring with them new diseases. There may have been prehistoric pestilences. For many centuries there may have been no men in Britain or Central Europe (Wright). For a time there were in Southern Europe drifting communities of some little known people who are called the Azilians. They may have been transition generations; they may have been a different race. We do not know. Some authorities incline to the view that the Azilians were the first wave of a race which, as we shall see later, has played a great part in populating Europe, the dark-white or Mediterranean or Iberian race. These Azilian people have left behind them a multitude of pebbles, roughly daubed with markings of an unknown purport (see illus. p. 57). The use or significance of these Azilian pebbles is still a profound mystery. Was this some sort of token writing? Were they counters in some game? Did the Azilians play with these pebbles or tell a story with them, as imaginative children will do with bits of wood and stone nowadays? At present we are unable to cope with any of these questions.

We will not deal here with the other various peoples who left their scanty traces in the world during the close of the New Palæolithic period, the spread of the forests where formerly there had been steppes, and the wane of the hunters, some 10,000 or 12,000 years ago. We will go on to describe the new sort of human community that was now spreading over the northern hemisphere, whose appearance marks what is called the *Neolithic Age*. The map of the world was assuming something like its present outlines, the landscape and the flora and fauna were taking on their existing characteristics. The prevailing animals in the spreading woods of Europe were the royal stag, the great ox, and the bison; the mammoth and the musk ox had gone. The great ox, or aurochs, is now extinct, but it survived in the German forests up to the time of the Roman Empire. It was never domesticated.[1] It stood eleven feet high at the shoulder, as high as an elephant. There were still lions in the Balkan peninsula, and they remained there until about 1,000 or 1,200 B.C. The lions of Würtemberg and South Germany in those days were twice the size of the modern lion. South Russia and Central Asia were thickly wooded then, and there were elephants in Mesopotamia and Syria,

[1] But our domestic cattle are derived from some form of aurochs—probably from some lesser Central Asiatic variety.—H. H. J.

and a fauna in Algeria that was tropical African in character.

Hitherto men in Europe had never gone further north than the Baltic Sea or the English midlands, but now Ireland, the Scandinavian peninsula, and perhaps Great Russia were becoming possible regions for human occupation. There are no Palæolithic remains in Sweden or Norway, nor in Ireland or Scotland. Man, when he entered these countries, was

have allowed them to wander across the land that is now cut by Bering Straits, and so reach the American continent. They spread thence southward, age by age. When they reached South America, they found the giant sloth (the *Megatherium*), the glyptodon, and many other extinct creatures, still flourishing. The glyptodon was a monstrous South American armadillo, and a human skeleton has been found by Roth buried beneath its huge tortoise-like shell.[2]

A Reindeer Age Masterpiece

Painting in four colours (Cave of Altamira, Spain)

apparently already at the Neolithic stage of social development.

§ 5

Nor is there any convincing evidence of man in America before the end of the Pleistocene.[1] The same relaxation of the climate **No Sub-Men in America.** that permitted the retreat of the reindeer hunters into Russia and Siberia, as the Neolithic tribes advanced, may

All the human remains in America, even the earliest, it is to be noted, are of an Amer-Indian character. In America there does not seem to have been any preceding races of sub-men. Man was fully man when he entered America. The old world was the nursery of the sub-races of mankind.

[1] "The various finds of human remains in North America for which the geological antiquity has been claimed have been thus briefly passed under review. In every instance where enough of the bones is preserved for comparison, the evidence bears witness against the geological antiquity of the remains and for their close affinity to or identity with the modern Indian." (Smithsonian Institute. Bureau of American Ethnology, Bulletin 33. Dr. Hrdlicka.)

But J. Deniker quotes evidence to show that eoliths and early palæoliths have been found in America. See his compact but full summary of the evidence and views for and against in his *Races of Man*, pp. 510, 511.

[2] "Questioned by some authorities," says J. Deniker in *The Races of Man.*

XI

NEOLITHIC MAN IN EUROPE

§ 1

THE Neolithic phase of human affairs began in Europe about 10,000 or 12,000 years ago. But probably men had reached the Neolithic stage elsewhere some thousands of years earlier. Neolithic men came slowly into Europe from the south or south-east as the reindeer and the open steppes gave way to forest and modern European conditions.

The Age of Cultivation begins.

The Neolithic stage in culture is characterized by : (1) the presence of polished stone implements, and in particular the stone *axe*, which was perforated so as to be the more effectually fastened to a wooden handle, and which was probably used rather for working wood than in conflict. There are also abundant arrow heads. The fact that some implements are polished does not preclude the presence of great quantities of implements of unpolished stone. But there are differences in the make between even the unpolished tools of the Neolithic and of the Palæolithic Period. (2) The beginning of a sort of agriculture, and the use of plants and seeds. But at first there are abundant evidences that hunting was still of great importance in the Neolithic Age. Neolithic man did not at first sit down to his agriculture. He took snatch crops. He settled later. (3) Pottery and proper cooking. The horse is no longer eaten. (4) Domesticated animals. The dog appears very early. The Neolithic man had domesticated cattle, sheep, goats, and pigs. He was a huntsman turned herdsman of the herds he once hunted.[1] (5) Plaiting and weaving.

These Neolithic people probably " migrated " into Europe, in the same way that the Reindeer Men had migrated before them ; that is to say, generation by generation and century by century, as the climate changed, they spread after their accustomed food. They were not " nomads." Nomadism, like civilization, had still to be developed. At present we are quite un-

able to estimate how far the Neolithic peoples were newcomers, and how far their arts were developed or acquired by the descendants of some of the hunters and fishers of the Later Palæolithic Age.

Whatever our conclusions in that matter, this much we may say with certainty ; there is no great break, no further sweeping away of one kind of man and replacement by another kind between the appearance of the Neolithic way of living and our own time. There are invasions, conquests, extensive emigrations and intermixtures, but the races as a whole carry on and continue to adapt themselves to the areas into which they began to settle in the opening of the Neolithic Age. The Neolithic men of Europe were white men ancestral to the modern Europeans. They may have been of a darker complexion than many of their descendants ; of that we cannot speak with certainty. But there is no real break in culture from their time onward until we reach the age of coal, steam, and power-driven machinery that began in the eighteenth century.

After a long time gold, the first known of the metals, appears among the bone ornaments with jet and amber. Irish Neolithic remains are particularly rich in gold. Then, perhaps 6,000 or 7,000 years ago in Europe, Neolithic people began to use copper in certain centres, making out of it implements of much the same pattern as their stone ones. They cast the copper in moulds made to the shape of the stone implements. Possibly they first found native copper and hammered it into shape.[2] Later— we will not venture upon figures—men had found out how to get copper from its ore. Perhaps, as Lord Avebury suggested, they discovered the secret of smelting by the chance putting of lumps of copper ore among the ordinary stones with which they built the fire pits they used for cooking. In China, Hungary, Cornwall, and elsewhere copper ore

[1] See Peisker, *Cambridge Medieval History*, Vol. I, for some interesting views upon domestication.—E. B.

[2] Native copper is still found to-day in Italy, Hungary, Cornwall, and many other places.

and tinstone occur in the same veins; it is a very common association, and so, rather through dirtiness than skill, the ancient smelters, it may be, hit upon the harder and better bronze, which is an alloy of copper and tin.[1] Bronze is not only harder than copper, but the mixture of tin and copper is more fusible and easier to reduce. The so-called "pure copper" implements usually contain a small proportion of tin, and there are no tin implements known, nor very much evidence to show, that early men knew of tin as a separate metal.[2][3] The plant of a prehistoric copper smelter has been found in Spain, and the material of bronze foundries in various localities. The method of smelting revealed by these finds carries out Lord Avebury's suggestion. In India, where zinc and copper ore occur together, brass (which is an alloy of the two metals) was similarly hit upon.

Finally, perhaps as early as 3,000 years ago in Europe, and even earlier in Asia Minor, men began to smelt iron. Once smelting was known to men, there is no great marvel in the finding of iron. They smelted iron by blowing up a charcoal fire, and wrought it by heating and hammering. They produced it at first in comparatively small pieces[4]; its appearance worked a revolution in weapons and implements; but it did not suffice to change the general character of men's surroundings. Much the same daily life that was being led by the more settled Neolithic men 10,000 years ago, was being led by peasants in out-of-the-way places all over

Europe at the beginning of the eighteenth century.

People talk of the Stone Age, the Bronze Age, and the Iron Age in Europe, but it is misleading to put these ages as if they were of equal importance in history. Much truer is it to say that there was:

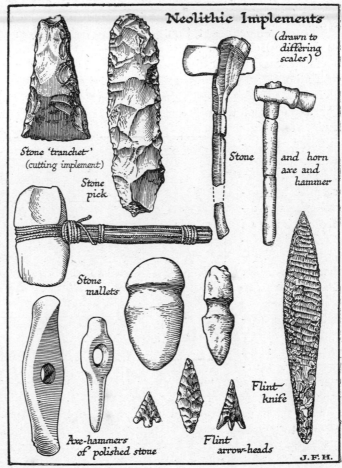

Neolithic Implements (drawn to differing scales)

Stone 'tranchet' (cutting implement)

Stone pick

Stone mallets

Stone and horn axe and hammer

Axe-hammers of polished stone

Flint arrow-heads

Flint knife

J. F. H.

(1) An *Early Palæolithic Age*, of vast duration; (2) a *Later Palæolithic Age*, that lasted not a tithe of the time; and (3) the *Age of Cultivation*, the age of the white men in Europe, which began 10,000 or at most 12,000 years ago, of

[1] This view of the origin of bronze is that of Dr Gowland, *The Metals in Antiquity* (Huxley Lecture 1912). But Lord Avebury quotes the verbal opinion of the late Lord Swansea against this view, and sets it aside without further argument.

[2] Ridgeway (*Early Age of Greece*) says a lump of tin has been found in the Swiss pile-dwelling deposits.

[3] Tin was known as a foreign import in Egypt under the XVIIIth Dynasty: there is (rare) Mycenæan tin, and there are (probably later, but not clearly dated) tin objects in the Caucasus. But it is very difficult to distinguish tin from antimony. There is a good deal

of Cyprus bronze which contains antimony; a good deal which seems to be tin is antimony—the ancients trying to get tin, but actually getting antimony and thinking it was tin.—J. L. M.

[4] In connection with iron, note the distinction of ornamental and useful iron. Ornamental iron, a rarity, perhaps meteoric, as jewellery or magical stuff, occurs in East Europe sporadically in the time of the XVIIIth Dynasty. This must be distinguished from the copious useful iron which appears in Greece much later from the North.—J. L. M.

which the Neolithic Period was the beginning, and which is still going on.

§ 2

We do not know yet the region in which the ancestors of the white and whitish Neolithic peoples worked their way up from the Palæolithic stage of human development. Probably it was somewhere about **South** Western Asia, or in some region now submerged beneath the Mediterranean Sea or the Indian Ocean, that, while the Neanderthal men still lived their hard lives in the bleak climate of a glaciated Europe, the ancestors of the white men developed the rude arts of *their* Later Palæolithic period. But they do not seem to have developed the artistic skill of their more northerly kindred, the European Later Palæolithic races. And through the hundred centuries or so while Reindeer men were living under comparatively unprogressive conditions upon the steppes of France, Germany, and Spain, these more-favoured and progressive people to the south were mastering agriculture, learning to develop their appliances, taming the dog, domesticating cattle, and, as the climate to the north mitigated and the equatorial climate grew more tropical, spreading northward. All these early chapters of our story have yet to be disinterred. They will probably be found in Asia Minor, Persia, Arabia, India, or North Africa, or beneath the Mediterranean waters. Twelve thousand years ago, or thereabouts—we are still too early for anything but the roughest chronology—Neolithic peoples were scattered all over Europe, North Africa, and Asia.

Where did Neolithic Culture arise ?

§ 3

It will be of interest here to give a brief account of the life of the European Neolithic people before the appearance of metals. We get our light upon that life from various sources.

Everyday Neolithic Life.

They scattered their refuse about, and in some places (*e.g.* on the Danish coast) it accumulated in great heaps, known as the kitchen-middens. They buried some of their people, but not the common herd, with great care and distinction, and made huge heaps of earth over their sepulchres ; these heaps are the barrows or dolmens which contribute a feature to the European, Indian, and American scenery in many districts to this day. In connection with these mounds, or independently of them, they set up great stones (megaliths), either singly or in groups, of which Stonehenge in Wiltshire and Carnac in Brittany are among the best-known examples. In various places their villages are still traceable.

Restoration of a Lake Dwelling

(after a drawing in Déchelette's "Manuel d'Archéologie")

One fruitful source of knowledge about Neolithic life comes from Switzerland, and was first revealed by the very dry winter of 1854, when the water level of one of the lakes, sinking to an unheard-of lowness, revealed the foundations of prehistoric pile dwellings of the Neolithic and early Bronze Ages, built out over the water after the fashion of similar homes that exist to-day in Celebes and elsewhere. Not only were the timbers of those ancient platforms preserved, but a great multitude of wooden, bone, stone, and earthenware utensils and ornaments, remains of food and the like, were found in the peaty accumulations below them. Even pieces of net and garments have been recovered. Similar lake dwellings existed in Scotland, Ireland, and elsewhere—there are well-known remains at Glastonbury in Somersetshire ; in Ireland lake dwellings were inhabited from prehistoric times up to the days when O'Neil of Tyrone was fighting against the English before the plantation of Scotch colonists

LION HUNTERS OF THE EUROPEAN BRONZE AGE

This picture is based on a representation of a lion hunt inlaid upon the blade of a dagger found at Mycenæ

to replace the Irish in Ulster. These lake villages had considerable defensive value, and there was a sanitary advantage in living over flowing water.

Probably these Neolithic Swiss pile dwellings did not shelter the largest communities that existed in those days. They were the homes of small patriarchal groups. Elsewhere upon fertile plains and in more open country there were probably already much larger assemblies of homes than in those mountain valleys. There are traces of such a large community of families

Neolithic people who accumulated the shell mounds, the kitchen middens, of the Danish and Scotch coasts. The latter may have been as early as 10,000 B.C. or earlier; the lake dwellings were probably occupied continuously from 5,000 or 4,000 B.C. down almost to historic times. Those early kitchen-midden people were among the most barbaric of Neolithic peoples, their stone axes were rough, and they had no domesticated animal except the dog. The lake-dwellers, on the other hand, had, in addition to the dog, which was of a medium-sized breed,

Pottery from Lake Dwellings

J.F.H.

in Wiltshire in England, for example; the remains of the stone circle of Avebury near Silbury mound were once the "finest megalithic ruin in Europe."[1] It consisted of two circles of stones surrounded by a larger circle and a ditch, and covering altogether twenty-eight and a half acres. From it two avenues of stones, each a mile and a half long, ran west and south on either side of Silbury Hill. The dimensions of this centre of a faith and a social life now forgotten altogether by men indicate the concerted efforts and interests of a very large number of people, widely scattered though they may have been over the west and south and centre of England. Possibly they assembled at some particular season of the year in a primitive sort of fair. The whole community "lent a hand" in building the mounds and hauling the stones. The Swiss pile-dwellers, on the contrary, seem to have lived in practically self-contained villages.

These lake-village people were considerably more advanced in methods and knowledge, and probably much later in time than the early

[1] Lord Avebury.

oxen, goats, and sheep. Later on, as they were approaching the Bronze Age, they got swine. The remains of cattle and goats prevail in their débris, and, having regard to the climate and country about them, it seems probable that these beasts were sheltered in the buildings upon the piles in winter, and that fodder was stored for them. Probably the beasts lived in the same houses with the people, as the men and beasts do now in Swiss chalets. The people in the houses possibly milked the cows and goats, and milk perhaps played as important a part in their economy as it does in that of the mountain Swiss of to-day. But of that we are not sure at present. Milk is not a natural food for adults; it must have seemed queer stuff to take at first; and it may have been only after much breeding that a continuous supply of milk was secured from cows and goats. Some people think that the use of milk, cheese, butter, and other milk products came later into human life when men became nomadic. The writer is, however, disposed to give the Neolithic men credit for having discovered milking. The milk,

5

MODERN LAKE DWELLINGS IN BORNEO.
The Swiss Lake Dwellings of 5,000 B.C. did not differ materially from these.

if they did use it (and, no doubt, in that case sour curdled milk also, but not well-made cheese and butter), they must have kept in earthenware pots, for they had pottery, though it was roughly hand-made pottery and not the shapely product of the potter's wheel. They eked out this food supply by hunting. They killed and ate red deer and roe deer, bison and wild boar. And they ate the fox, a rather high-flavoured meat, and not what any one would eat in a world of plenty. Oddly enough, they do not seem to have eaten the hare, although it was available as food. They are supposed to have avoided eating it, as some savages are said to avoid eating it to this day, because they feared that the flesh of so timid a creature might make them, by a sort of infection, cowardly.

Of their agricultural methods we know very little. No ploughs and no hoes have been found. They were of wood and have perished. Neolithic men cultivated and ate wheat, barley, and millet, but they knew nothing of oats or rye. Their grain they roasted, ground between stones and stored in pots, to be eaten when needed. And they made exceedingly solid and heavy bread, because round flat slabs of it have been got out of these deposits. Apparently they had no yeast. If they had no yeast, then they had no fermented drink. One sort of barley that they had is the sort that was cultivated by the ancient Greeks, Romans, and Egyptians, and they also had an Egyptian sort of wheat, showing that their ancestors had brought or derived this cultivation from the south. At present wheat is nowhere found wild in all the world, and according to De Candolle it has been spread by man throughout the world from a centre of diffusion in south-western Asia. Somewhere in that part of the world then, the wild wheat grew originally. When the lake dwellers sowed their little patches of wheat in Switzerland, they were already following the immemorial practice of mankind. The seed must have been brought age by age from that distant centre of diffusion. In the ancestral lands of the south-east men had already been sowing wheat perhaps for thousands of years.[1] Those lake dwellers also ate peas, and crab-apples—the only apples that then existed in the world. Cultivation and selection had not yet produced the apple of to-day.

They dressed chiefly in skins, but they also made a rough cloth of flax. Fragments of that flaxen cloth have been discovered. Their nets were made of flax; they had as yet no knowledge of hemp and hempen rope. With the coming of bronze, their pins and ornaments increased in number. There is reason to believe they set great store upon their hair, wearing it in large shocks with pins of bone and afterwards of metal. To judge from the absence of realistic

[1] All Old World peoples who had entered upon the Neolithic stage grew and ate wheat, but the American Indians must have developed agriculture independently in America after their separation from the Old World populations. They never had wheat. Their cultivation was maize, Indian corn, a New World grain.

carvings or engravings or paintings, they either did not decorate their garments or decorated them with plaids, spots, interlacing designs, or similar conventional ornament. Before the coming of bronze there is no evidence of stools or tables; the Neolithic people probably squatted on their clay floors. There were no cats in these lake dwellings; no mice or rats had yet adapted themselves to human dwellings; the cluck of the hen was not as yet added to the sounds of human life, nor the domestic egg to its diet.[1]

The chief tool and weapon of Neolithic man was his axe; his next the bow and arrow. His arrow heads were of flint, beautifully made, and he lashed them tightly to their shafts. Probably he prepared the ground for his sowing with a pole, or a pole upon which he had stuck a stag's horn. Fish he hooked or harpooned. These implements no doubt stood about in the interior of the house, from the walls of which hung his fowling-nets. On the floor, which was of clay or trodden cow-dung (after the fashion of hut floors in India to-day), stood pots and jars and woven baskets containing grain, milk, and such-like food. Some of the pots and pans hung by rope loops to the walls. At one end of the room, and helping to keep it warm in winter by their animal heat, stabled the beasts. The children took the cows and goats out to graze, and brought them in at night before the wolves and bears came prowling.

Since Neolithic man had the bow, he probably also had stringed instruments, for the rhythmic twanging of a bow-string seems almost inevitably to lead to that. He also had earthenware drums across which skins were stretched; perhaps also he made drums by stretching skins over hollow tree stems.[2] We do not know when

man began to sing, but evidently he was making music, and since he had words, songs were no doubt being made. To begin with, perhaps, he just let his voice loose as one may hear Italian peasants now behind their ploughs singing songs without words. After dark in the winter he sat in his house and talked and sang and made implements by touch rather than sight. His lighting must have been poor, and chiefly firelight, but there was probably always

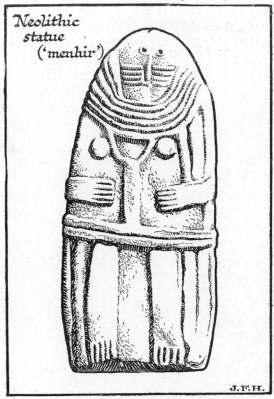

A CARVED STATUE ("MENHIR") OF THE NEOLITHIC PERIOD—A CONTRAST TO THE FREEDOM AND VIGOUR OF THE PALÆOLITHIC DRAWINGS AND CARVINGS ILLUSTRATED PREVIOUSLY.

some fire in the village, summer or winter. Fire was too troublesome to make for men to be willing to let it out readily. Sometimes a great disaster happened to those pile villages, the fire got free, and they were burnt out. The Swiss deposits contain clear evidence of such catastrophes.

All this we gather from the remains of the Swiss pile dwellings, and such was the character of the human life that spread over Europe, coming from the south and from the east with the forests as, 10,000 or 12,000 years ago, the reindeer and the Reindeer men passed away.

---

[1] Poultry and hens' eggs were late additions to the human cuisine, in spite of the large part they now play in our dietary. The hen is not mentioned in the Old Testament nor by Homer. Up to about 1500 B.C. the only fowls in the world were jungle denizens in India and Burmah. The crowing of jungle cocks is noted by Glasfurd in his admirable accounts of tiger shooting as the invariable preliminary of dawn in the Indian jungle. Probably poultry were first domesticated in Burmah. They got to China, according to the records, only about 1100 B.C. They reached Greece via Persia before the time of Socrates. In the New Testament the crowing of the cock reproaches Peter for his desertion of the Master.

[2] Later Palæolithic bone whistles are known. One may guess that reed pipes were an early invention.

It is evident that we have here a way of life already separated by a great gap of thousands of years of invention from its original Palæolithic stage. The steps by which it rose from that condition we can only guess at. From being a hunter hovering upon the outskirts of flocks and herds of wild cattle and sheep, and from being a co-hunter with the dog, man by insensible degrees may have developed a sense of proprietorship in the beasts and struck up a friendship with his canine competitor. He learnt to turn the cattle when they wandered too far ; he brought his better brain to bear to guide them to fresh pasture. He hemmed the beasts into valleys and enclosures where he could be sure to find them again. He fed them when primitive people in any part of the world, it is accompanied by a human sacrifice or by some ceremony which may be interpreted as the mitigation and vestige of an ancient sacrificial custom. This is the theme of Sir J. G. Frazer's *Golden Bough*. From this it has been supposed that the first sowings were in connection with the burial of a human being, either through wild grain being put with the dead body as food or through the scattering of grain over the body. It may be argued that there is only one reason why man should have disturbed the surface of the earth before he took to agriculture, and that was to bury his dead ; and in order to bury a dead body and make a mound over it, it was probably necessary for

Photo : Photochrom Co., Ltd.

MEGALITHIC REMAINS AT STONEHENGE (BRONZE AGE).

they starved, and so slowly he tamed them. Perhaps his agriculture began with the storage of fodder. He reaped, no doubt, before he sowed. The Palæolithic ancestor away in that unknown land of origin to the south-east first supplemented the precarious meat supply of the hunter by eating roots and fruits and wild grains. Man storing graminiferous grasses for his cattle might easily come to beat out the grain for himself.

§ 4

How did man learn to sow in order that he might reap ?

How did Sowing begin ? We may hesitate here to guess at the answer to that question. But a very great deal has been made of the fact that wherever sowing occurs among him to disturb the surface over a considerable area. Neolithic man's chief apparatus for mound-making consisted of picks of deer's horn and shovels of their shoulder-blades, and with this he would have found great difficulty in making a deep excavation. Nor do we find such excavations beside the barrows. Instead of going down into tough sub-soil, the mound-makers probably scraped up some of the surface soil and carried it to the mound. All this seems probable, and it gives just that wide area of bared and turned-over earth upon which an eared grass, such as barley, millet, or primitive wheat, might have seeded and grown. Moreover, the mound-makers, being busy with the mound, would not have time to hunt meat, and if they were accustomed to store and eat wild grain, they would be likely to scatter grain,

Photo: E. N. A.

MEGALITHIC REMAINS AT CARNAC (BRONZE AGE).

and the grain would be blown by the wind out of their rude vessels, over the area they were disturbing. And if they were bringing up seed in any quantity in baskets and pots to bury with the corpse, some of it might easily blow and be scattered over the fresh earth. Returning later to the region of the mound, they would discover an exceptionally vigorous growth of food grain, and it would be a natural thing to associate it with the buried person, and regard it as a consequence of his death and burial. He had given them back the grain they gave him increased a hundredfold.

At any rate, there is apparently all over the world a traceable association in ancient ceremonial and in the minds of barbaric people between the death and burial of a person and the ploughing and sowing of grain. From this it is assumed that there was once a world-wide persuasion that it was necessary that some one should be buried before a crop could be sown, and that out of this persuasion arose a practice and tradition of human sacrifice at seedtime, which has produced profound effects in the religious development of the race. We state these considerations here merely as suggestions that have been made of the way in which the association of seedtime and sacrifice arose. They are, at the best, speculations; they have a considerable vogue at the present time, and

we have to note them, but we have neither the space nor the time here to examine them at length. The valuable accumulation of suggestions due to the industry and ingenuity of Sir J. G. Frazer still await a thorough critical examination, and to his works the reader must go for the indefatigable expansion of this idea.

§ 5

All these early beginnings must have taken place far back in time, and in regions of the world that have still to be effectively explored by the archæologists. They were probably going on in Asia or Africa, in what is now the bed of the Mediterranean, or in the region of the Indian Ocean while the Reindeer man was developing his art in Europe. The Neolithic men who drifted over Europe and Western Asia 12,000 or 10,000 years ago were long past these beginnings; they were already close, a few thousand years, to the dawn of written tradition and the remembered history of mankind. Without any very great shock or break, bronze came at last into human life, giving a great advantage in warfare to those tribes who first obtained it. Written history had already begun before weapons of iron came into Europe to supersede bronze.

Already in those days a sort of primitive trade had sprung up. Bronze and bronze weapons,

Primitive Trade.

and such rare and hard stones as jade, gold because of its plastic and ornamental possibilities, and skins and flax-net and cloth, were being swapped and stolen and passed from hand to hand over great stretches of country. Salt also was probably being traded. On a meat dietary men can live without salt, but grain-consuming people need it just as herbivorous animals need it. Hopf says that bitter tribal wars have been carried on by the desert tribes of the Soudan in recent years for the possession of the salt deposits between Fezzan and Murzuk. To begin with, barter, blackmail, tribute, and robbery by violence passed into each other by insensible degrees. Men got what they wanted by such means as they could.[1]

§ 6

So far we have been telling of a history without events, a history of ages and periods and stages in development. But before we conclude this portion of the human story, we must record what was probably an event of primary importance and at first perhaps of tragic importance to developing mankind, and that was the breaking in of the Atlantic waters to the great Mediterranean valley.

The Flooding of the Mediterranean Valley.

[1] In addition to authorities already cited, we have used for this and the following chapters Lord Avebury's *Prehistoric Times*, Schrader and Jevons' *Prehistoric Antiquities of the Aryan Peoples*, and A. H. Keane's *Man Past and Present*.

The reader must keep in mind that we are endeavouring to give him plain statements that he can take hold of comfortably. But both in the matter of our time charts and the three maps we have given of prehistoric geography there is much speculative matter. We have dated the last Glacial Age and the appearance of the true men as about 40,000 and 35,000 years ago. Please bear that " about " in mind. The truth may be 60,000 or 20,000. But it is no good saying " a very long time " or " ages " ago, because then the reader will not know whether we mean centuries or millions of years. And similarly in these maps we give, they represent not the truth, but something like the truth. The outline of the land was " some such outline." There were such seas and such land masses. But both Mr. Horrabin, who has drawn these maps, and I, who have incited him to do so, have preferred to err on the timid side.[2] We are not geologists enough to launch out into original research in these matters, and so we have stuck to the 40-fathom line and the recent deposits as our guides for our post-glacial map and for the map of 10,000 to 12,000 B.C. But in one matter we have gone beyond these guides. It is practically certain that at the end of the last Glacial Age the Mediterranean was a couple of land-locked sea basins, not connected—or only connected

[2] Among other books we have used Jukes Browne's *Building of the British Isles*.

SILBURY HILL, A BRONZE AGE MOUND.

by a torrential overflow river. The eastern basin was the fresher; it was fed by the Nile, the " Adriatic " river, the " Red-Sea " river, and perhaps by a river that poured down amidst the mountains that are now the Greek Archipelago from the very much bigger Sea of Central Asia that then existed. Almost certainly human beings, and possibly even Neolithic men, wandered over that now lost land.

The reasons for believing this are very good and plain. To this day the Mediterranean is a sea of evaporation. The rivers that flow into it do not make up for the evaporation from its surface. There is a constant current of water pouring into the Mediterranean from the Atlantic, and another current streaming in from the Bosphorus and Black Sea. For the Black Sea gets more water than it needs from all the big rivers that flow into it; it is an overflowing sea, while the Mediterranean is a thirsty sea. From which it must be plain that when the Mediterranean was cut off both from the Atlantic Ocean and the Black Sea it must have been a shrinking sea with its waters sinking to a much lower level than those of the ocean outside. This is the case of the Caspian Sea to-day. Still more so is it the case with the Dead Sea.

But if this reasoning is sound, then where to-day roll the blue waters of the Mediterranean there must once have been great areas of land, and land with a very agreeable climate. This was probably the case during the last Glacial Age, and we do not know how near it was to our time when the change occurred that brought back the ocean waters into the Mediterranean basin. Certainly there must have been Grimaldi people, and perhaps even Azilian and Neolithic people going about in the valleys and forests of these regions that are now submerged. The Neolithic Dark Whites, the people of the Mediterranean race, may have gone far towards the beginnings of settlement and civilization in that great lost Mediterranean Valley.

Mr. W. B. Wright [1] gives us some very stimulating suggestions here. He suggests that in the Mediterranean basin there were two lakes, " one a fresh-water lake, in the eastern depression, which drained into the other in the western depression. It is interesting to think what must have happened when the ocean level rose once more as a result of the dissipation of the ice-

[1] *The Quaternary Ice Age.*

sheets, and its waters began to pour over into the Mediterranean area. The inflow, small at first, must have ultimately increased to enormous dimensions, as the channel was slowly lowered by erosion and the ocean level slowly rose. If there were any unconsolidated materials on the sill of the Strait, the result must have been a genuine debacle, and if we consider the length of time which even an enormous torrent would take to fill such a basin as that of the Mediterranean, we must conclude that this result was likely to have been attained in any case. Now, this may seem all the wildest speculation, but it is not entirely so, for if we examine a submarine contour map of the Straits of Gibraltar, we find there is an enormous valley running up from the Mediterranean deep, right through the Straits, and trenching some distance out on to the Atlantic shelf. This valley or gorge is probably the work of the inflowing waters of the ocean at the termination of the period of interior drainage."

This refilling of the Mediterranean, which by the rough chronology we are employing in this book may have happened somewhen between 30,000 and 10,000 A.D., must have been one of the greatest single events in the pre-history of our race. If the later date is the truer, then, as the reader will see plainly enough after reading the next two chapters, the crude beginnings of civilization, the first lake dwellings and the first cultivation, were probably round that eastern Levantine lake into which there flowed not only the Nile, but the two great rivers that are now the Adriatic and the Red Sea. Suddenly the ocean waters began to break through over the westward hills and to pour in upon these primitive peoples—the lake that had been their home and friend, became their enemy; its waters rose and never abated; their settlements were submerged; the waters pursued them in their flight. Day by day and year by year the waters spread up the valleys and drove mankind before them. Many must have been surrounded and caught by the continually rising salt flood. It knew no check; it came faster and faster; it rose over the tree-tops, over the hills, until it had filled the whole basin of the present Mediterranean and until it lapped the mountain cliffs of Arabia and Africa. Far away, long before the dawn of history, this catastrophe occurred.

XII

EARLY THOUGHT

§ 1

BEFORE we go on to tell how 6,000 or 7,000 years ago men began to gather into the first towns and to develop something more than the loose-knit tribes that had hitherto been their highest political association, something must be said about Primitive Philosophy. the things that were going on inside these brains of which we have traced the growth and development through a period of 500,000 years from the Pithecanthropus stage.

What was man thinking about himself and about the world in those remote days ?

At first he thought very little about anything but immediate things. At first he was busy thinking such things as : " Here is a bear ; what shall I do ? " Or " There is a squirrel ; how can I get it ? " Until language had developed to some extent there could have been little thinking beyond the range of actual experience, for language is the instrument of thought as book-keeping is the instrument of business. It records and fixes and enables thought to get on to more and more complex ideas. It is the hand of the mind to hold and keep. Primordial man, before he could talk, probably saw very vividly, mimicked very cleverly, gestured, laughed, danced, and lived, without much speculation about whence he came or why he lived. He feared the dark, no doubt, and thunderstorms and big animals and queer things and whatever he dreamt about, and no doubt he did things to propitiate what he feared or to change his luck and please the imaginary powers in rock and beast and river. He made no clear distinction between animate and inanimate things ; if a stick hurt him, he kicked it ; if the river foamed and flooded, he thought it was hostile. His thought was probably very much at the level of a bright little contemporary boy of four or five. He had the same subtle unreasonableness of transition and the same limitations. But since he had little or no speech he would do little to pass on the fancies that came to him, and develop any tradition or concerted acts about them.

The drawings even of Late Palæolithic man do not suggest that he paid any attention to sun or moon or stars or trees. He was preoccupied only with animals and men. Probably he took day and night, sun and stars, trees and mountains, as being in the nature of things—as a child takes its meal times and its nursery staircase for granted. So far as we can judge, he drew no fantasies, no ghosts or anything of that sort. The Reindeer Men's drawings are fearless familiar things, with no hint about them of any religious or occult feelings. There is scarcely anything that we can suppose to be a religious or mystical symbol at all in his productions. No doubt he had a certain amount of what is called *fetishism* in his life ; he did things we should now think unreasonable to produce desired ends, for that is all fetishism amounts to ; it is only incorrect science based on guess-work or false analogy, and entirely different in its nature from religion. No doubt he was excited by his dreams, and his dreams mixed up at times in his mind with his waking impressions and puzzled him. Since he buried his dead, and since even the later Neanderthal men seem to have buried their dead, and apparently with food and weapons, it has been argued that he had a belief in a future life. But it is just as reasonable to suppose that early men buried their dead because they doubted if they were dead, which is not the same thing as believing them to have immortal spirits, and that their belief in their continuing vitality was reinforced by dreams of the departed. They may have ascribed a sort of were-wolf existence to the dead, and wished to propitiate them.

The Reindeer Man, we feel, was too intelligent and too like ourselves not to have had some speech, but quite probably it was not very serviceable for anything beyond direct statement or matter of fact narrative. He lived in a larger community than the Neanderthaler, but how large we do not know. Except when game is swarming, hunting communities must not keep together in large bodies or they will starve. The Indians who depend upon the caribou in Labrador must be living under circumstances rather like those of the Reindeer Men. They scatter in small family groups, as the caribou scatter; but when the deer collect for the seasonal migration, the Indians also collect. That is the time for trade and feasts and marriages. The simplest American Indian is 10,000 years more sophisticated than the Reindeer Man, but probably that sort of gathering and dispersal was also the way of Reindeer Men. At Solutré in France there are traces of a great camping and feasting-place. There was no doubt an exchange of news there, but one may doubt if there was anything like an exchange of ideas. One sees no scope in such a life for theology or philosophy or superstition or speculation. Fears, yes; but unsystematic fears; fancies and freaks of the imagination, but personal and transitory freaks and fancies.

Perhaps there was a certain power of suggestion in these encounters. A fear really felt needs few words for its transmission; a value set upon something may be very simply conveyed.

In these questions of primitive thought and religion, we must remember that the lowly and savage peoples of to-day probably throw very little light on the mental state of men before the days of fully developed language. Primordial man could have had little or no tradition before the development of speech. All savage and primitive peoples of to-day, on the contrary, are soaked in tradition—the tradition of thousands of generations. They may have weapons like their remote ancestors and methods like them, but what were slight and shallow impressions on the minds of their predecessors are now deep and intricate grooves worn throughout the intervening centuries generation by generation.

§ 2

Certain very fundamental things there may have been in men's minds long before the coming of speech. Chief among these must have been fear of the Old Man of the tribe. The young of the primitive squatting-place grew up under that fear. Objects associated with him were probably forbidden. Every one was forbidden to touch his spear or to sit in his place, just as to-day little boys must not touch father's pipe or sit in his chair. He was probably the master of all the women. The youths of the little community had to remember that. The idea of *something forbidden*, the idea of things being, as it is called, *tabu*, not to be touched, not to be looked at, may thus have got well into the human mind at a very early stage indeed. J. J. Atkinson, in an ingenious analysis of these primitive tabus which are found among savage peoples all over the world, the tabus that separate brother and sister, the tabus that make a man

The Old Man in Religion.

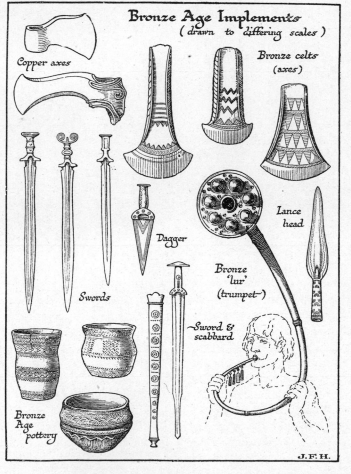

Bronze Age Implements
(drawn to differing scales)

Copper axes

Bronze celts
(axes)

Swords

Dagger

Bronze 'lur' (trumpet)

Lance head

Sword & scabbard

Bronze Age pottery

J.F.H.

run and hide from his step-mother, traces them to such a fundamental cause as this.[1] Only by respecting this primal law could the young male hope to escape the Old Man's wrath. And the Old Man must have been an actor in many a primordial nightmare. A disposition to propitiate him even after he was dead is quite understandable. One was not sure that he *was* dead. He might only be asleep or shamming. Long after an Old Man was dead, when there was nothing to represent him but a mound and a megalith, the women would convey to their children how awful and wonderful he was. And being still a terror to his own little tribe, it was easy to go on to hoping that he would be a terror to other and hostile people. In his life he had fought for his tribe, even if he had bullied it. Why not when he was dead? One sees that the Old Man idea was an idea very natural to the primitive mind and capable of great development.

§ 3

Another idea probably arose early out of the mysterious visitation of infectious diseases, and that was the idea of uncleanness and of being accurst. From that, too, there may have come an idea of avoiding particular places and persons, and persons in particular phases of health. Here was the root of another set of tabus. Then man, from the very dawn of his mental life, may have had a feeling of the sinister about places and things. Animals, who dread traps, have that feeling. A tiger will abandon its usual jungle route at the sight of a few threads of cotton.[2] Like most young animals, young human beings are easily made fearful of this or that by their nurses and seniors. Here is another set of ideas, ideas of repulsion and avoidance that sprang up almost inevitably in men.

Fear and Hope in Religion.

As soon as speech began to develop, it must have got to work upon such fundamental feelings and begun to systematize them, and keep them in mind. By talking together men would reinforce each other's fears, and establish a common tradition of tabus of things forbidden

and of things unclean. With the idea of uncleanness would come ideas of cleansing and of removing a curse. The cleansing would be conducted through the advice and with the aid of wise old men or wise old women, and in such cleansing would lie the germ of the earliest priestcraft and witchcraft.

Speech from the first would be a powerful supplement to the merely imitative education and to the education of cuffs and blows conducted by a speechless parent. Mothers would tell their young and scold their young. As speech developed, men would find they had experiences and persuasions that gave them or seemed to give them power. They would make secrets of these things. There is a double streak in the human mind, a streak of cunning secretiveness and a streak perhaps of later origin that makes us all anxious to tell and astonish and impress each other. Many people make secrets in order to have secrets to tell. These secrets of early men they would convey to younger, more impressionable people, more or less honestly and impressively in some process of initiation. Moreover, the pedagogic spirit overflows in the human mind; most people like " telling other people not to." Extensive arbitrary prohibitions for the boys, for the girls, for the women, also probably came very early into human history.

Then the idea of the sinister has for its correlative the idea of the propitious, and from that to the idea of making things propitious by ceremonies is an easy step.

§ 4

Out of such ideas and a jumble of kindred ones grew the first quasi-religious elements in human life. With every development of speech it became possible to intensify and develop the tradition of tabus and restraints and ceremonies. There is not a savage or barbaric race to-day that is not held in a net of such tradition. And with the coming of the primitive herdsman there would be a considerable broadening out of all this sort of practice. Things hitherto unheeded would be found of importance in human affairs. Neolithic man was nomadic in a different spirit from the mere daylight drift after food of the primordial hunter. He was a herdsman, upon

Stars and the Seasons.

---

[1] J. J. Atkinson's *Primal Law.*
[2] Glasfurd's *Rifle and Romance in the Indian Jungle,* 1915.

whose mind a sense of direction and the lie of the land had been forced. He watched his flock by night as well as by day. The sun by day and presently the stars by night helped to guide his migrations ; he began to find after many ages that the stars are steadier guides than the sun. He would begin to note particular stars and star groups, and to distinguish any individual thing was, for primitive man, to believe it individualized and personal. He would begin to think of the chief stars as persons, very shining and dignified and trustworthy persons looking at him like bright eyes in the night. His primitive tillage strengthened his sense of the seasons. Particular stars ruled his heavens when seedtime was due. The beginnings of agriculture were in the sub-tropical zone, or even nearer the equator, where stars of the first magnitude shine with a splen-dour unknown in more temperate latitudes.

And Neolithic man was counting, and falling under the spell of numbers. There are savage languages that have no word for any number above five. Some peoples cannot go above two. But Neolithic man in the lands of his origin in Asia and Africa even more than in Europe was already counting his accumulating possessions. He was beginning to use tallies, and wondering at the triangularity of three and the squareness of four, and why some quantities like twelve were easy to divide in all sorts of ways, and others, like thirteen, impossible. Twelve be-came a noble, generous, and familiar number to him, and thirteen rather an outcast and dis-reputable one.

Probably man began reckoning time by the clock of the full and new moons. Moonlight is an important thing to herdsmen who no longer merely hunt their herds, but watch and guard them. Moonlight too, was, per-haps, his time for love-making, as indeed it may have been for primordial man and the lemur-ape ancestor before him. But from the phases of the moon, as his tillage increased, man's attitude would go on to the greater cycle of the seasons. Pri-mordial man probably only drifted before the winter as the days grew cold. Neolithic man knew surely that the winter would come,

and stored his fodder and presently his grain. He had to fix a seedtime, a propitious seedtime, or his sowing was a failure. The earliest re-corded reckoning is by moons and by generations of men. The former seems to be the case in the Book of Genesis, where, if one reads the great ages of the patriarchs who lived before the flood as lunar months instead of years, Methusaleh and the others are reduced to a credible length of life. But with agriculture began the difficult task of squaring the lunar month with the solar year ; a task which has left its scars on our calendar to-day. Easter shifts uneasily from year to year, to the great discomfort of holiday-makers ; it is now inconveniently early and now late in the season because of this ancient refer-ence of time to the moon.

And when men began to move with set inten-tion from place to place with their animal and other possessions, then they would begin to develop the idea of other places in which they were not, and to think of what might be in those other places. And in any valley where they lingered for a time, they would, remembering how they got there, ask, " How did this or that other thing get here ? " They would begin to wonder what was beyond the mountains, and where the sun went when it set, and what was above the clouds.

§ 5

The capacity for telling things increased with their vocabulary. The simple individual

Story-telling and Myth-making. fancies, the unsystematic fetish tricks and fundamental tabus of Palæo-lithic man began to be handed on and made into a more consistent system. Men began to tell stories about themselves,

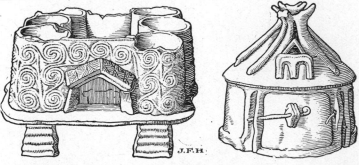

Hut urns, the first probably representing a lake-dwelling. After Lubbock

about the tribe, about its tabus and why they had to be, about the world and the why for the world. A tribal mind came into existence, a tradition. Palæolithic man was certainly more of a free individualist, more of an artist, as well as more of a savage, than Neolithic man. Neolithic man was coming under prescription; he could be trained from his youth and told to do things and not to do things; he was not so free to form independent ideas of his own about things. He had thoughts given to him; he was

	EUROPE	EGYPT	MESOPOTAMIA
18,000 B.C.	Steppe Period	Men entering upon Neolithic stage Agriculture beginning	
15,000 " "	Reindeer men going Forest (transition) Period		
13,000 " "	Azilian		
10,000 " "	Neolithic men spreading into Europe		
8,000 " "	First lake dwellings		Sumerian civilization dawns Bronze
6,000 " "			Nippur & Eridu
5,000 " "		First Dynasty The Pyramids	First Sumerian writing
4,000 " "			
3000 " "	Bronze		
2,000 " "	Spreading of Aryan system of languages		Sargon I
1,000 " "	Iron		Iron
320 " "	Alexander the Great		
50 " "	Julius Caesar		
A.D.	Christian Era		
1919 "			

TIME DIAGRAM SHOWING THE GENERAL DURATION OF THE NEOLITHIC PERIOD IN WHICH EARLY THOUGHT DEVELOPED.

By this scale the diagram on p. 38 of the period since the earliest subhuman traces would be 8 feet long, and the diagram of geological time (ch. ii. § 2) somewhere between 1,000 and 10,000 feet.

under a new power of suggestion. And to have more words and to attend more to words is not simply to increase mental power; words themselves are powerful things and dangerous things. Palæolithic man's words, perhaps, were chiefly just names. He used them for what they were. But Neolithic man was thinking about these words, he was thinking about a number of things with a great deal of verbal confusion, and getting to some odd conclusions. In speech he had woven a net to bind his race together,

but also it was a net about his feet. Man was binding himself into new and larger and more efficient combinations indeed, but at a price. One of the most notable things about the Neolithic Age is the total absence of that free direct artistic impulse which was the supreme quality of later Palæolithic man. We find much industry, much skill, polished implements, pottery with conventional designs, co-operation upon all sorts of things, but no evidence of personal creativeness.[1] Self-suppression is beginning for men. Man has entered upon the long and tortuous and difficult path towards a life for the common good, with all its sacrifice of personal impulse, which he is still treading to-day.

Certain things appear in the mythology of mankind again and again. Neolithic man was enormously impressed by serpents—and he no longer took the sun for granted. Nearly everywhere that Neolithic culture went, there went a disposition to associate the sun and the serpent in decoration and worship. This primitive serpent worship spread ultimately far beyond the regions where the snake is of serious practical importance in human life.

§ 6

With the beginnings of agriculture a fresh set of ideas arose in men's minds.

Complex Origins of Religion.

We have already indicated how easily and naturally men may have come to associate the idea of sowing with a burial. Sir J. G. Frazer has pursued the development of this association in the human mind, linking up with it the conception of special sacrificial persons who are killed at seedtime, the conception of a specially purified class of people to kill these sacrifices, the first priests, and the conception of a *sacrament*, a ceremonial

[1] Ludwig Hopf, in *The Human Species*, calls the later Palæolithic art "masculine" and the Neolithic "feminine." The pottery was made by women, he says, and that accounts for it. But the arrowheads were made by men, and there was nothing to prevent Neolithic men from taking scraps of bone or slabs of rock and carving them—had they dared. We suggest they did not dare to do so.

feast in which the tribe eats portions of the body of the victim in order to share in the sacrificial benefits.

Out of all these factors, out of the Old Man tradition, out of the desire to escape infection and uncleanness, out of the desire for power and success through magic, out of the sacrificial tradition of seedtime, and out of a number of like beliefs and mental experiments and mis-conceptions, a complex something was growing up in the lives of men which was beginning to bind them together mentally and emotionally in a common life and action. This something we may call *religion* (Lat. *religare*, to bind [1]). It was not a simple or logical something, it was a tangle of ideas about commanding beings and spirits, about gods, about all sorts of " musts " and " must-nots." Like all other human mat-ters, religion has grown. It must be clear from what has gone before that primitive man—much less his ancestral apes and his ancestral Mesozoic mammals—could have had no idea of God or Religion ; only very slowly did his brain and his powers of comprehension become capable of such general conceptions. Religion is some-thing that has grown up with and through human association, and God has been and is still being discovered by man.

This book is not a theological book, and it is not for us to embark upon theological discussion ; but it is a part, a necessary and central part, of the history of man to describe the dawn and development of his religious ideas and their influence upon his activities. All these factors we have noted must have contributed to this development, and various writers have laid most stress upon one or other of them. Sir J. G. Frazer we have already noted as the leading student of the derivation of sacraments from magic sacrifices. Grant Allen, in his *Evolution of the Idea of God*, laid stress chiefly on the posthumous worship of the " Old Man." Sir E. B. Tylor (*Primitive Culture*) gave his atten-tion mainly to the disposition of primitive man to ascribe a soul to every object animate and inanimate. Mr. A. E. Crawley, in *The Tree of Life*, has called attention to other centres of impulse and emotion, and particularly to sex as a

source of deep excitement. The thing we have to bear in mind is that Neolithic man was still mentally undeveloped, he could be confused and illogical to a degree quite impossible to an educated modern person. Conflicting and con-tradictory ideas could lie in his mind without challenging one another ; now one thing ruled his thoughts intensely and vividly and now another ; his fears, his acts, were still discon-nected as children's are.

Confusedly under the stimulus of the need and possibility of co-operation and a combined life, Neolithic mankind was feeling out for guidance and knowledge. Men were becoming aware that personally they needed protection and direction, cleansing from impurity, power beyond their own strength. Confusedly in response to that demand, bold men, wise men, shrewd and cun-ning men were arising to become magicians, priests, chiefs, and kings. They are not to be thought of as cheats or usurpers of power, nor the rest of mankind as their dupes. All men are mixed in their motives ; a hundred things move men to seek ascendancy over other men, but not all such motives are base or bad. The magicians usually believed more or less in their own magic, the priests in their ceremonies, the chiefs in their right. The history of mankind henceforth is a history of more or less blind endeavours to conceive a common purpose in relation to which all men may live happily, and to create and develop a common consciousness and a common stock of knowledge which may serve and illuminate that purpose. In a vast variety of forms this appearance of kings and priests and magic men was happening all over the world under Neolithic conditions. Every-where mankind was seeking where knowledge and mastery and magic power might reside ; everywhere individual men were willing, hon-estly or dishonestly, to rule, to direct, or to be the magic beings who would reconcile the con-fusions of the community.

In many ways the simplicity, directness, and detachment of a later Palæolithic rock-painter appeal more to modern sympathies than does the state of mind of these Neolithic men, full of the fear of some ancient Old Man who had developed into a tribal God, obsessed by ideas of sacrificial propitiation and magic murder. No doubt the reindeer hunter was a ruthless

[1] But Cicero says relegere, " *to read over*," and the " binding " by those who accept *religare* is often written of as being merely the binding of a vow.

hunter and a combative and passionate creature, but he killed for reasons we can still understand ; Neolithic man, under the sway of talk and a confused thought process, killed on theory, he killed for monstrous and now incredible ideas, he killed those he loved through fear and under direction. Those Neolithic men not only made human sacrifices at seedtime ; there is every reason to suppose they sacrificed wives and slaves at the burial of their chieftains ; they killed men, women, and children whenever they were under adversity and thought the gods were athirst. They practised infanticide.[1] All these things passed on into the Bronze Age.

Hitherto a social consciousness had been asleep and not even dreaming in human history. Before it awakened it produced nightmares.

Away beyond the dawn of history, 3,000 or 4,000 years ago, one thinks of the Wiltshire

[1] Bateman, *Ten Years' Digging in Celtic and Saxon Gravehills*, quoted by Lord Avebury in *Prehistoric Times*, p. 176.

uplands in the twilight of a midsummer day's morning. The torches pale in the growing light. One has a dim apprehension of a procession through the avenue of stone, of priests, perhaps fantastically dressed with skins and horns and horrible painted masks—not the robed and bearded dignitaries our artists represent the Druids to have been—of chiefs in skins adorned with necklaces of teeth and bearing spears and axes, their great heads of hair held up with pins of bone, of women in skins or flaxen robes, of a great peering crowd of shock-headed men and naked children. They have assembled from many distant places ; the ground between the avenues and Silbury Hill is dotted with their encampments. A certain festive cheerfulness prevails. And amidst the throng march the appointed human victims, submissive, helpless, staring towards the distant smoking altar at which they are to die. . . . To that had life progressed 3,000 or 4,000 years ago from its starting-place in the slime of the tidal beaches.

XIII

THE RACES OF MANKIND

§ 1

IT is necessary now to discuss very plainly what is meant by a phrase, used often very carelessly, " The Races of Mankind."

It must be evident from what has already been explained in Chapter III that **Is Mankind still differentiating ?** man, so widely spread and subjected therefore to great differences of climate, consuming very different food in different regions, attacked by different enemies, must always have been undergoing considerable local modification and differentiation. Man, like every other species of living thing, has constantly been tending to differentiate into several species ; wherever a body of men has been cut off, in islands or oceans or by deserts or mountains, from the rest of humanity, it must have begun very soon to develop special characteristics, specially adapted to the local conditions. But, on the other hand, man is usually a wandering and enterprising animal, for whom there exist few insurmountable barriers. Men imitate men, fight and conquer them, interbreed, one people with another. Concurrently for thousands of years there have been two sets of forces at work, one tending to separate men into a multitude of local varieties, and another to remix and blend these varieties together before a separate species has been established.

These two sets of forces may have fluctuated in this relative effect in the past. Palæolithic man, for instance, may have been more of a wanderer, he may have drifted about over a much greater area, than later Neolithic man ; he was less fixed to any sort of home or lair, he was tied by fewer possessions. Being a hunter, he was obliged to follow the migrations of his ordinary quarry. A few bad seasons may have shifted him hundreds of miles. He may therefore have mixed very widely and developed few varieties over the greater part of the world.

The appearance of agriculture tended to tie those communities of mankind that took it up to the region in which it was most conveniently

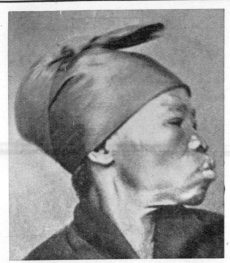

BUSHWOMAN FROM NEAR THE LOWER
ORANGE RIVER.

BUSHMAN FROM NORTHERN
CAPE COLONY.

carried on, and so to favour differentiation. Mixing or differentiation are not dependent upon a higher or lower stage of civilization; many savage tribes wander now for hundreds of miles; many English villagers in the eighteenth century, on the other hand, had never been more than eight or ten miles from their villages, they nor their fathers nor grandfathers before them. Hunting peoples often have enormous range. The Labrador country, for instance, is inhabited by a few thousand Indians,[1] who follow the one great herd of caribou as it wanders yearly north and then south again in pursuit of food. This mere handful of people covers a territory as large as France.

It carries out this suggestion, that Palæolithic man ranged widely and was distributed thinly indeed, but uniformly, throughout the world, that the Palæolithic remains we find are everywhere astonishingly uniform. To quote Sir John Evans,[2] "The implements in distant lands are so identical in form and character with the British specimens that they might have been manufactured by the same hands. . . . On the banks of the Nile, many hundreds of feet above its present level, implements of the European types have been discovered; while in Somaliland, in an ancient river-valley at a great elevation above the sea, Sir H. W. Seton-Karr has collected a large number of implements formed

[1] *Cabot in Labrador*, by Grenfell and others. Macmillan, New York.

[2] Quoted in *Ency. Brit.*, vol. ix. p. 850.

of flint and quartzite, which, judging from their form and character, might have been dug out of the drift-deposits of the Somme and the Seine, the Thames or the ancient Solent."

Phases of spreading and intermixture have probably alternated with phases of settlement and specialization in the history of mankind. But up to a few hundred years ago it is probable that since the days of the Palæolithic Age at least mankind has on the whole been differentiating. The species has differentiated in that period into a very great number of varieties, many of which have reblended with others, which have spread and undergone further differentiation or become extinct. Wherever there has been a strongly marked local difference of conditions and a check upon intermixture, there one is almost obliged to assume a variety of mankind must have appeared. Of such local varieties there must have been a great multitude.

In one remote corner of the world, Tasmania, a little cut-off population of people remained in the early Palæolithic stage until the discovery of that island by the Dutch in 1642. They are now, unhappily, extinct. The last Tasmanian died in 1877. They may have been cut off from the rest of mankind for 15,000 or 20,000 or 25,000 years.

But among the numerous obstacles and interruptions to intermixture there have been certain main barriers, such as the Atlantic Ocean, the highlands, once higher, and the now vanished seas of Central Asia and the

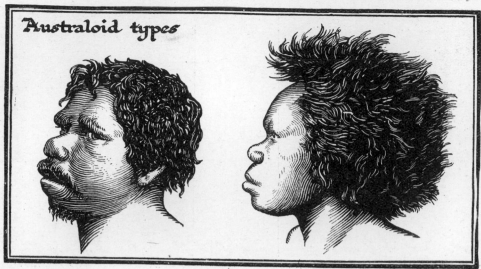

Australoid types

like, which have cut off great groups of varieties from other great groups of varieties over long periods of time. These separated groups of varieties developed very early certain broad resemblances and differences. Most of the varieties of men in Eastern Asia and America, but not all, have now this in common, that they have yellowish buff skins, straight black hair, and often high cheek-bones. Most of the native peoples of Africa south of the Sahara, but not all, have black or blackish skins, flat noses, thick lips, and frizzy hair. In North and Western Europe a great number of peoples have fairer hair, blue eyes, and ruddy complexions ; and about the Mediterranean there is a prevalence of white-skinned peoples with dark eyes and black hair. The black hair of many of these dark whites is straight, but never so strong and waveless as the hair of the yellow peoples. It is straighter in the east than in the west. In Southern India we find brownish and darker peoples with straight black hair. In scattered islands and in Papua and New Guinea we find another series of black and brownish peoples of a more lowly type with frizzy hair.

But it must be borne in mind that these are very loose-fitting generalizations. Some of the areas and isolated pockets of mankind in the Asiatic area may have been under conditions more like those in the European area ; some of the African areas are of a more Asiatic and less distinctively African type. We find a wavy-haired, fairish, hairy-skinned race, the Ainu, in Japan. They are more like the Europeans in their facial type than the surrounding yellow Japanese. They may be a drifted patch of the whites or they may be a quite distinct people. We find primitive black people in the Andaman Islands far away from Australia and far away from Africa. These are the " Asiatic " negroids. There is little or no proof that all black people derive from one origin, but only that they have lived for vast periods under similar conditions. We must not assume that human beings in the eastern Asiatic area were all differentiating in one direction and all the human beings in Africa in another. There were great currents of tendency, it is true, but there were also backwaters, eddies, admixtures, readmixtures, and leakages from one main area to the other. A coloured map of the world to show the races would not present just four great areas of colour ; it would have to be dabbed over with a multitude of tints and intermediate shades, simple here, mixed and overlapping there.

In the early Neolithic Period in Europe—it may be 10,000 or 12,000 years ago or so—man was differentiating all over the world, and he had already differentiated into a number of varieties, but he has never differentiated into different *species*. A "species," we must remember, in biological language is distinguished from a "variety" by the fact that varieties can interbreed, while species either do not do so or produce offspring which, like mules, are sterile. All mankind can interbreed freely, can learn to understand the same speech, can adapt itself to co-operation. And in the present age, man is

A NEOLITHIC CATASTROPHE

The charred remains of several such burnings out are to be found in the Swiss Lake Dwelling deposits

probably no longer undergoing differentiation at all. Readmixture is now a far stronger force than differentiation. Men mingle more and more. Mankind from the view of a biologist is an animal species in a state of arrested differentiation and possible re-admixture.

Negro types

Asia there are, and have been for many thousand years, white peoples, the CAUCASIANS, sub-divided into two or three sub-divisions, the northern blonds, an alleged inter-mediate race about which many authorities are doubtful, and the southern dark whites; over Eastern Asia and America a second group of races prevail, the MONGO-LIANS, generally with yellow skins, straight black hair, and sturdy bodies; over Africa the NEGROES, and in the region of Aus-tralia and New Guinea the black, squat, primitive AUSTRALOIDS. These are convenient terms, provided the student bears in mind that they are not exactly defined terms. They represent only the common characteristics of certain main groups of races; they leave out a number of little peoples who belong properly to none of these divisions, and they disregard the perpetual mixing where the main groups overlap.

§ 2

It is only in the last fifty or sixty years that the varieties of men came to be regarded in this light, as a tangle of differentiations recently arrested or still in progress.

The Main Races of Mankind.

Before that time students of man-kind, influenced, consciously or unconsciously, by the story of Noah and the Ark and his three sons, Shem, Ham, and Japhet, were inclined to classify men into three or four great races, and they were disposed to regard these races as having always been separate things, descended from originally separate an-cestors. They ignored the great possibilities of blended races and of special local isolations and variations. The classification has varied con-siderably, but there has been rather too much readiness to assume that mankind *must* be com-pletely divisible into three or four main groups. Ethnologists (students of race) have fallen into grievous disputes about a multitude of minor peoples, as to whether they were of this or that primary race or "mixed," or strayed early forms, or what not. But all races are more or less mixed. There are, no doubt, four main groups, but each is a miscellany, and there are little groups that will not go into any of the four main divisions.

Subject to these reservations, when it is clearly understood that when we speak of these main divisions we mean not simple and pure races, but groups of races, then they have a certain convenience in discussion. Over the European and Mediterranean area and Western

§ 3

Whether the Caucasian race is to be divided into two or three main subdivisions depends

Was there an Alpine Race?

upon the classificatory value to be attached to certain differences in the skeleton and particularly to the shape of the skull. The student in his further reading will meet with constant references to round-skulled (Brachycephalic) and long-skulled peoples (Dolichocephalic). No skull looked at from above is completely round, but some skulls (the dolichocephalic) are much more oblong than others; when the width of a skull is four-fifths or more than its length from back to front, that skull is called brachy-cephalic; when the width is less than four-fifths of the length, the skull is dolichocephalic. While some ethnologists regard the difference between brachycephaly and dolichocephaly as a

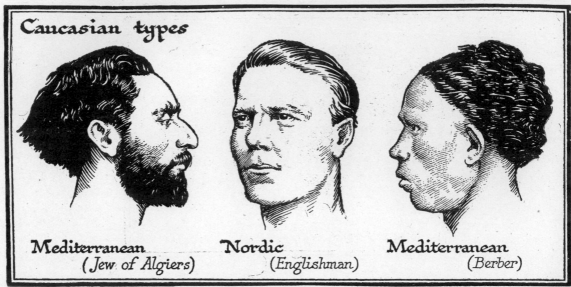

Caucasian types

Mediterranean
(*Jew of Algiers*)

Nordic
(*Englishman*)

Mediterranean
(*Berber*)

difference of quite primary importance, another school—which the writer must confess has entirely captured his convictions—dismisses this as a quite secondary distinction. It seems probable that the skull shapes of a people may under special circumstances vary in comparatively few generations.[1] We do not know what influences alter the shape of the skull, just as we do not know why people of British descent in the Darling region of Australia ("Corn-

[1] The skull shape of the Lombards, says Flinders Petrie, changed from dolichocephalic to brachycephalic in a few hundred years. See his Huxley Lecture for 1906, *Migrations*, published by the *Anthropological Institute*. Ripley is the great authority on the other side.

stalks") grow exceptionally tall, or why in New England their jaw-bones seem to become slighter and their teeth in consequence rather crowded. Even in Neolithic times dolichocephalic and brachycephalic skulls are found in the same group of remains and often buried together, and that is true of most peoples to-day. Some peoples, such as the mountain people of Central Europe, have more brachycephalic individuals per cent. than others; some, as the Scandinavians, are more prevalently dolichocephalic. In Neolithic Britain and in Scandinavia the earliest barrows (= tomb mounds) are long grave-shaped barrows and the late ones round, and the skulls found in the former are

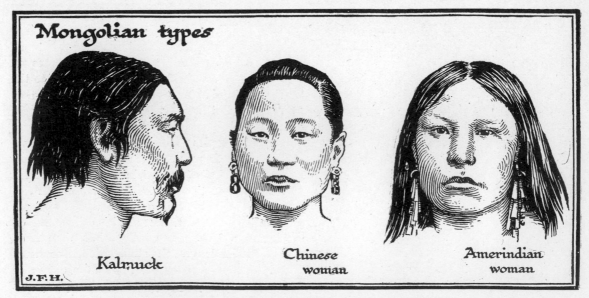

Mongolian types

Kalmuck

Chinese
woman

Amerindian
woman

J.F.H.

usually dolichocephalic and in the latter most frequently brachycephalic. This points perhaps to a succession of races in Western Europe in the Neolithic Period (see Chapter XLV), but it may also point to changes of diet, habit, or climate.

But it is this study of skull shapes which has led many ethnologists to divide the Caucasian race, not as it was divided by Huxley, into two, the northern *blonds* and the Mediterranean and North African *dark whites* or brunets, but into three. They split his blonds into two classes. They distinguish a northern European type, blond and dolichocephalic, the Nordic; a Mediterranean or Iberian race, Huxley's dark whites, which is dark-haired and dolichocephalic, and between these two they descry this third race, their brachycephalic race, the Alpine race. The opposite school would treat the alleged Alpine race simply as a number of local brachycephalic varieties of Nordic or Iberian peoples. The Iberian peoples were the Neolithic people of the long barrows, and seem at first to have pervaded most of Europe and Western Asia.

§ 4

This Mediterranean or Iberian race certainly had a wider range in early times, and was a less specialized and distinctive race than the Nordic. It is very hard to define its southward boundaries from the Negro, or to mark off its early traces in Central Asia from those of early Dravidians or Mongolians. Wilfred Scawen Blunt [1] says that Huxley " had long suspected a common origin of the Egyptians and the Dravidians of India, perhaps a long belt of brown-skinned men from India to Spain in very early days." Across France and Great Britain these dark-white Iberian or Mediterranean people were ousted by a round-barrow-making "Alpine" or Alpine-Nordic race, and the dawn of history in Europe sees them being pressed westward and southward everywhere by the expansion of the fairer northern peoples.

It is possible that this " belt " of Huxley's of dark-white and brown-skinned men, this race of brunet-brown folk, ultimately spread even further than India ; that they reached to the

The Brunet Peoples.

[1] *My Diaries*, under date of July 25, 1894.

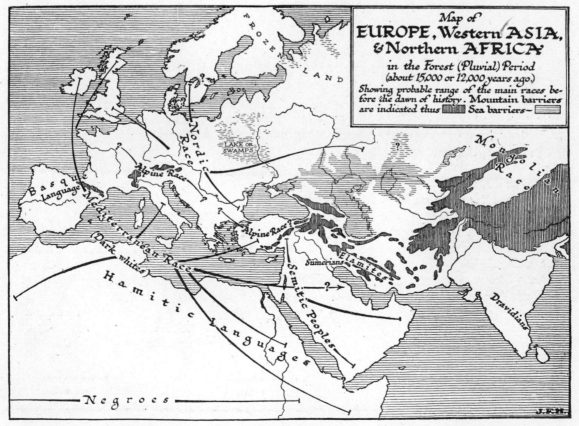

Map of EUROPE, Western ASIA, & Northern AFRICA in the Forest (Pluvial) Period (about 15,000 or 12,000 years ago.) Showing probable range of the main races before the dawn of history. Mountain barriers are indicated thus ▦ Sea barriers ▭

shores of the Pacific, and that they were everywhere the original possessors of the Neolithic culture and the beginners of what we call civilization. The Nordic and the Mongolian peoples may have been but north-western and north-eastern branches from this more fundamental stem. Or the Nordic race may have been a branch, while the Mongolian, like the Negro, may have been another equal and distinct stem with which the brunet-browns met and mingled in South China.

At some period in human history (see Elliot Smith's *Migrations of Early Culture*) there seems to have been a primitive Neolithic culture very widely distributed in the world which had a group of features so curious and so unlikely to have been independently developed in different regions of the earth, as to compel us to believe that it was in effect one culture. It reached through all the regions inhabited by the brunet Mediterranean race, and beyond through India, Further India, up the Pacific coast of China, and it spread at last across the Pacific and to Mexico and Peru. It was a coastal culture not reaching deeply inland. (Here again we cover the ground of Huxley's "belt of brown-skinned men," and extend it far to the east across the stepping-stones of Polynesia. There are, we may note, some very striking resemblances between early Japanese pottery and so forth and similar Peruvian productions.) This peculiar culture, which Elliot Smith calls the *heliolithic* culture, included

many or all of the following odd practices : (1) circumcision, (2) the very queer custom of sending the *father* to bed when a child is born, known as the *couvade*, (3) the practice of massage, (4) the making of mummies, (5) megalithic monuments [1] (*e.g.* Stonehenge), (6) artificial deformation of the heads of the young by bandages, (7) tattooing, (8) religious association of the sun and the serpent, and (9) the use of the symbol known as the swastika (see figure) for good luck. (The swastika is found in Palæolithic bone drawings.) Elliot Smith traces these practices in a sort of constellation all over this great Mediterranean-India Ocean-Pacific area. Where one occurs, most of the others occur. But this constellation of practices does not crop up in the primitive homes of Nordic or Mongolian peoples, nor do they extend southward much beyond equatorial Africa. For thousands of years, from 15,000 to 1,000 B.C., such a heliolithic Neolithic culture and its brownish possessors may have been oozing round the world through the warmer regions of the world. And its region of origin may have been, as Elliot Smith suggests, the Mediterranean and North-African region. It must have been spreading up the Pacific Coast and across the island stepping-stones to America, long after it had been forgotten in its areas of origin. But the reader must bear in mind that all this is still highly speculative matter.

[1] Megalithic monuments have been made quite recently by primitive Indian peoples.

The Swastika

XIV

THE LANGUAGES OF MANKIND

§ 1

IT is improbable that there was ever such a thing as a common human language. We know nothing of the language of Palæolithic man ; we do not even know whether Palæolithic man talked freely.

No one Primitive Language. We know that Palæolithic man had a keen sense of form and attitude, because of his drawings ; and it has been suggested that he communicated his ideas very largely by gesture. Probably such words as the earlier men used were largely cries of alarm or passion or names for concrete things, and in many cases they were probably imitative sounds made by or associated with the things named.[1]

The first languages were probably small collections of such words ; they consisted of interjections and nouns. Probably the nouns were said in different intonations to convey different meanings. If Palæolithic man had a word for " horse " or " bear," he probably showed by tone or gesture whether he meant " bear is coming," " bear is going," " bear is to be hunted," " dead bear," " bear has been here," " bear did this," and so on. Only very slowly did the human mind develop methods of indicating action and relationship in a formal manner. Modern languages contain many thousands of words, but the earlier languages could have consisted only of a few hundred. It is said that even modern European peasants can get along with something less than a thousand words, and it is quite conceivable that so late as the Early Neolithic Period that was the limit of the available vocabulary. Probably men did not indulge in those days in conversation or description. For narrative purposes they danced and acted rather than told. They had no method of counting beyond a method of indicating two by a dual number, and some way of expressing many. The growth of speech was at first a very slow process indeed, and grammatical forms and the expression of abstract ideas may have come very late in human history, perhaps only 400 or 500 generations ago.

§ 2

The students of languages (philologists) tell us that they are unable to trace with certainty any common features in all the languages of mankind. They cannot even find any elements common to all the Caucasian languages. They find over great areas groups of languages which have similar root words and similar ways of expressing the same idea, but then they find in other areas languages which appear to be dissimilar down to their fundamental structure, which express action and relation by entirely dissimilar devices, and have an altogether different grammatical scheme.[2] One great group of languages, for example, now covers nearly all Europe and stretches out to India ; it includes English, French, German, Spanish, Italian, Greek, Russian, Armenian, Persian, and various Indian tongues. It is called the Indo-European or ARYAN family. The same fundamental roots, the same grammatical ideas, are traceable through all this family. Compare, for example, English *father, mother*, Gothic *fadar, moutar*, German *vater, mutter*, Latin *pater, mater*, Greek *pater, meter*, French *père, mère*, Armenian *hair, mair*, Sanscrit *pitar, matar*, etc., etc. In a similar manner the Aryan languages ring the changes on a great number of fundamental words, *f* in the Germanic languages becoming *p* in Latin, and so on. They follow a law of variation called Grimm's Law. These languages are not different things, they are variations of one thing. The people who use these languages think in the same way.

At one time in the remote past, in the Neolithic Age, that is to say, 6,000[3] years or more

The Aryan Languages.

---

[1] Sir Arthur Evans suggests that in America sign-language arose before speech, because the sign-language is common to all Indians in North America, whereas the languages are different. See his *Anthropology and the Classics.*—G. M.

[2] See article " Grammar " in the *Encyclopædia Britannica*.

[3] Sir H. H. Johnston gives this estimate in his *Comparative Study of the Bantu and Semi-Bantu Languages*.

Photo : Anderson.

NORDIC FEMALE TYPE IDEALIZED BY AN
ARTIST OF THAT RACE (GREEK).

Photo : Alinari.

NORDIC MALE TYPE IDEALIZED BY AN ARTIST
OF THAT RACE (GREEK).

ago, there may have been one simple original speech from which all these Aryan languages have differentiated. Somewhere between Central Europe and Western Asia there must have wandered a number of tribes sufficiently intermingled to develop and use one tongue. It is convenient here to call them the Aryan peoples. Sir H. H. Johnston has called them "Aryan Russians." They belonged mostly to the Caucasian group of races and to the blond and northern subdivision of the group, to the Nordic race that is.

Here one must sound a note of warning. There was a time when the philologists were disposed to confuse languages and races, and to suppose that people who once all spoke the same tongue must be all of the same blood. That, however, is not the case, as the reader will understand if he will think of the negroes of the United States who now all speak English, or of the Irish, who—except for purposes of political demonstration—no longer speak the old Erse language but English, or of the Cornish people, who have lost their ancient Celtic speech. But what a common language does do, is to show that a common intercourse has existed, and the possibility of intermixture ; and if it does not point to a common origin, it points at least to a common future.

But even this original Aryan language, which was a spoken speech perhaps 4,000 or 3,000 B.C., was by no means a *primordial* language or the

language of a savage race. Its speakers were in or past the Neolithic stage of civilization. It had grammatical forms and verbal devices of some complexity. The vanished methods of expression of the later Palæolithic peoples, of the Azilians, or of the early Neolithic kitchen-midden people for instance, were probably much simpler than the most elementary form of Aryan.

Probably the Aryan group of languages became distinct in a wide region of which the Danube, Dnieper, Don, and Volga were the main rivers, a region that extended eastward beyond the Ural mountains north of the Caspian Sea. The area over which the Aryan speakers roamed probably did not for a long time reach to the Atlantic or to the south of the Black Sea beyond Asia Minor. There was no effectual separation of Europe from Asia then at the Bosphorus.[1] The Danube flowed eastward to a great sea that extended across the Volga region of South-eastern Russia right into Turkestan, and included the Black, Caspian, and Aral Seas of to-day. Perhaps it sent out arms to the Arctic Ocean. It must have been a pretty effectual barrier between the Aryan speakers and the people in North-eastern Asia. South of this sea stretched a continuous shore from the Balkans to Afghanistan.[2] North-west of it a region of swamps and lagoons reached to the Baltic.

[1] Greek—ox-ford.
[2] Ratzel (quoted in the *Ency. Brit.*, art. " Caspian ")

Mediterranean, but the fundamental differences of the primary Aryan and primary Semitic languages oblige us to believe that in early Neolithic times, before the historical period, there must for thousands of years have been an almost complete separation of the Aryan-speaking and the Semitic-speaking peoples. The latter seem to have lived either in South Arabia or in North-east Africa. In the opening centuries of the Neolithic Age the original Aryan speakers and the original Semitic speakers were probably living, so to speak, in different worlds with a minimum of intercourse. Racially, it would seem, they had a remote common origin; both Aryan speakers and Semites are classed as Caucasians; but while the original Aryan speakers seem to have been of Nordic race, the original Semites were rather of the Mediterranean type.

§ 4

Philologists speak with less unanimity of a third group of languages, the HAMITIC, which **The Hamitic Languages.** some declare to be distinct from, and others allied to, the Semitic.

The weight of opinion inclines now towards the idea of some primordial connection of these two groups. The Hamitic group is certainly a much wider and more various language group than the Semitic or the Aryan,

Photo: Mansell.
SEMITIC MALE TYPE, BY A SEMITIC ARTIST (ASSYRIAN).

§ 3

Next to Aryan, philologists distinguish another group of languages which seem to have been **The Semitic Languages.** made quite separately from the Aryan languages, the Semitic. Hebrew and Arabic are kindred, but they seem to have even a different set of root words from the Aryan tongues; they express their ideas of relationship in a different way; the fundamental ideas of their grammars are generally different. They were in all probability made by human communities quite out of touch with the Aryans, separately and independently. Hebrew, Arabic, Abyssinian, ancient Assyrian, ancient Phœnician, and a number of associated tongues are put together, therefore, as being derived from a second primary language, which is called the SEMITIC. In the very beginnings of recorded history we find Aryan-speaking peoples and Semitic-speaking peoples carrying on the liveliest intercourse of war and trade round and about the eastern end of the

Photo: Mansell.
SEMITIC FEMALE TYPE, BY A SEMITIC ARTIST (ASSYRIAN).

Photo: Mansell.

TWO HAMITIC TYPES (AN OFFICIAL AT THE COURT OF THOTHMES I. AND HIS WIFE),
RENDERED BY AN ARTIST OF HAMITIC RACE.

and the Semitic tongues are more of a family, have more of a common likeness, than the Aryan. The Semitic languages may have arisen as some specialized proto-Hamitic group, just as the birds arose from a special group of reptiles (Chap. IV.). It is a tempting speculation, but one for which there is really no basis of justifying fact, to suppose that the rude primordial ancestor group of the Aryan tongues branched off from the proto-Hamitic speech forms at some still earlier date than the separation and specialization of Semitic. The Hamitic speakers to-day, like the Semitic speakers, are mainly of the Mediterranean Caucasian race. Among the Hamitic languages are the ancient Egyptian and Coptic, the Berber languages (of the mountain people of North Africa, the Masked Tuaregs, and other such peoples), and what are called the Ethiopic group of African languages in Eastern Africa, including the speech of the Gallas and the Somalis. The general grouping of these various tongues suggests that they originated over some great area to the west, as the primitive Semitic may have arisen to the east, of the Red Sea divide. That divide was probably much more effective in Pleistocene times; the sea extended across to the west of the Isthmus of Suez, and a great part of Lower Egypt was under water. Long before the dawn of history, however, Asia and Africa had joined at Suez, and these two language systems were in contact in that region. And if Asia and Africa were separated then at Suez, they may, on the other hand, have been joined by way of Arabia and Abyssinia.

These Hamitic languages may have radiated from a centre on the African coast of the Mediterranean, and they may have extended over the then existing land connections very widely into Western Europe.

All these three great groups of languages, it may be noted, the Aryan, Semitic, and Hamitic, have one feature in common which they do not share with any other language, and that is grammatical gender; but whether that has much weight as evidence of a remote common origin of Aryan, Semitic, and Hamitic, is a question for the philologist rather than for the general student. It does not affect the clear evidence of a very long and very ancient pre-historic separation of the speakers of these three diverse groups of tongues.

The bulk of the Semitic and Hamitic-speaking peoples are put by ethnologists with the Aryans among the Caucasian group of races. They are " white."

§ 5

Across to the north-east of the Aryan and Semitic areas there must once have spread a **The Ural Altaic Languages.** further distinct language system which is now represented by a group of languages known as the TURANIAN, or URAL-ALTAIC group. This includes the Lappish of Lapland and the Samoyed speech of Siberia, the Finnish language, Magyar, Turkish or Tartar, Manchu and Mongol; it has not as a group been so exhaustively studied by European philologists, and there is insufficient evidence yet whether it does or does not include the Korean and Japanese languages. (A Japanese writer, Mr. K. Hirai, has attempted to show that Japanese and Aryan may have had a common parent tongue.[1])

§ 6

A fifth region of language formation was South-eastern Asia, where there still prevails a group of languages consisting of **The Chinese Languages.** monosyllables without any inflections, in which the tone used in uttering a word determines its meaning. This may be called the Chinese or MONOSYLLABIC group, and it includes Chinese, Burmese, Siamese, and Tibetan. The difference between any of these Chinese tongues and the more western language is profound. In the Pekinese form of Chinese there are only about 420 primary monosyllables, and consequently each of these has to do duty for a great number of things, and the different meanings are indicated either by the context or by saying the word in a distinctive tone. The relations of these words to each other are expressed by quite different methods from the Aryan methods; Chinese grammar is a thing different in nature from English grammar; it is a separate and different invention. Many writers declare there is no Chinese grammar at all, and that is true if we mean by grammar anything in the European sense of inflections and concords. Consequently any such

[1] *Encyclopædia Britannica,* article " Japan."

thing as a literal translation from Chinese into English is an impossibility. The very method of the thought is different.[2] Their philosophy remains still largely a sealed book to the European on this account and vice versa, because of the different nature of the expressions.

§ 7

In addition the following other great language families are distinguished by the philologist. All **Other Language Groups.** the American-Indian languages, which vary widely among themselves, are separable from any Old World group. Here we may lump them together not so much as a family as a miscellany.[3] There is one great group of languages in Africa, from a little way north of the equator, to its southern extremity, the BANTU, and in addition a complex of other languages across the centre of the continent about which we will not trouble here.[4] There are also two

[2] The four characters indicating " Affairs query imperative old," placed in that order, for example, represent " Why walk in the ancient ways ? " The Chinaman gives the bare cores of his meaning; the Englishman gets to it by a bold metaphor. He may be talking of conservatism in cooking or in book-binding, but he will say : " Why walk in the ancient ways ? " Mr. Arthur Waley, in the interesting essay on Chinese thought and poetry which precedes his book, *170 Chinese Poems* (Constable, 1918), makes it clear how in these fields Chinese thought is kept practical and restricted by the limitations upon metaphor the linguistic structure of Chinese imposes. See also Hirst, *Ancient History of China,* ch. vii.

[3] See Farrand, *The American Nation,* and E. S. Payne, *History of the New World called America,* and note footnote to § 1 of this chapter.

[4] These are discussed compactly, but with very special knowledge, by Sir Harry Johnston in his little book on *The Opening up of Africa,* in the Home University Library. The student who finds this subject of philological history interesting, should

Photo : Mansell.
HAMITIC TYPE, BY AN ARTIST OF THAT RACE
(Pharaoh of the XVIIIth Dynasty).

probably separate groups, the DRAVIDIAN in South India, and the MALAY-POLYNESIAN stretched over Polynesia, and also now including Indian tongues.

Now it seems reasonable to conclude from these fundamental differences that about the time when men were passing from the Palæolithic to Neolithic conditions, and beginning to form rather larger communities than the family

American, and Chinese-speaking tribes and families, wandering over their several areas of hunting and pasture, all at very much the same stage of culture, and each developing its linguistic instrument in its own way. Probably each of these original tribes was not more numerous altogether than the Indians in Hudson's Bay Territory to-day. Agriculture was barely beginning, and until agriculture made a denser population possible men may have been almost as rare as the great apes have always been.

In addition to these early Neolithic tribes, there must have been various varieties of still more primitive forest folk in Africa and in India. Central Africa, from the Upper Nile, was then a vast forest, impenetrable to ordinary human life, a forest of which the Congo forests of to-day are the last shrunken remains.

Possibly the spread of men of a race higher than primitive Australoids into the East Indies,[1] and the development of the languages of the Malay-Polynesian type came later in time than the origination of these other language groups.

The language divisions of the philologist do tally, it is manifest, in a broad sort of way with the main race classes of the ethnologist, and they carry out the same idea of age-long separations between great divisions of mankind. In the Glacial Age, ice, or at least a climate too severe for the free spreading of peoples, extended from the north pole into Central Europe and across Russia and Siberia to the great table-

MONGOLIAN TYPE IDEALIZED BY A *CHINESE* ARTIST.

herd, when they were beginning to tell each other long stories and argue and exchange ideas, human beings were distributed about the world in a number of areas which communicated very little with each other. They were separated by oceans, seas, thick forests, deserts or mountains from one another. There may have been in that remote time, it may be 10,000 years ago or more, Aryan, Semitic, Hamitic, Turanian,

read the introduction to the same writer's *Comparative Study of the Bantu and Semi-Bantu Languages.*

lands of Central Asia. After the last Glacial Age, this cold north mitigated its severities very slowly, and was for long without any other population than the wandering hunters who spread eastward and across Behring Straits. North and Central Europe and Asia did not become sufficiently temperate for agriculture until quite recent times, times that is within

[1] The Polynesians appear to be a later eastward extension of the dark whites or brown peoples. See again § 4 of chap. xiii.

the limit of 12,000 or possibly even 10,000 years, and a dense forest period intervened between the age of the hunter and the agricultural clearings.

This forest period was also a very wet period. It has been called the Pluvial or Lacustrine Age; the rain or pond period. It has to be remembered that the outlines of the land of the world have changed greatly even in the last hundred centuries. Across European Russia, from the Baltic to the Caspian Sea, as the ice receded there certainly spread much water and many impassable swamps; the Caspian Sea and the Sea of Aral and parts of the Desert of Turkestan, are the vestiges of a great extent of sea that reached far up to the Volga Valley and sent an arm westward to join the Black Sea. Mountain barriers much higher than they are now, and the arm of the sea that is now the region of the Indus, completed the separation of the early Caucasian races from the Mongolians and the Dravidians, and made the broad racial differentiation of those groups possible.

Again the blown-sand Desert of Sahara—it is not a dried-up sea, but a wind desert, and was once fertile and rich in life—becoming more and more dry and sandy, cut the Caucasians off from the sparse primitive Negro population in the central forest region of Africa.

The Persian Gulf extended very far to the north of its present head, and combined with the Syrian desert to cut off the Semitic peoples from the eastern areas, while on the other hand the south of Arabia, much more fertile than it is now, may have reached across what is now the Gulf of Aden towards Abyssinia and Somaliland. The Mediterranean and Red Sea were probably still joined at Suez. The Himalayas and the higher and vaster massif of Central Asia and the northward extension of the Bay of Bengal up to the present Ganges valley divided off the Dravidians from the Mon-

golians, and the Gobi system of seas and lakes which presently became the Gobi desert, and the great system of mountain chains which follow one another across Asia from the centre to the north-east, split the Mongolian races into the Chinese and the Ural-Altaic language groups.

Behring Strait, when this came into existence, before or after the Pluvial Period, isolated the Amer-Indians.

These ancient separations must have remained

MONGOLIAN TYPE IDEALIZED BY A JAPANESE ARTIST.

effectual well into Neolithic times. The barriers between Africa, Asia, and Europe were lowered or bridged by that time, but mixing had not gone far. The practical separation of the west from Dravidian India and China continued indeed down almost into historical times; but the Semite, the Hamite, and the Aryan were already in close contact and vigorous reaction again in the very dawn of history.

We are not suggesting here, be it noted, that these ancient separations were absolute separations, but that they were effectual enough at least to prevent any great intermixture of blood or any great intermixture of speech in those days of man's social beginnings. There was, nevertheless, some amount of meeting and exchange even then, some drift of knowledge that spread the crude patterns and use of various implements, and the seeds of a primitive agriculture about the world.

§ 8

The fundamental tongues of these nine main language groups we have noted were not by Submerged any means all the human speech and Lost beginnings of the Neolithic Age. Languages. There may have been other, and possibly many other, ineffective centres of speech which were afterwards overrun by the speakers of still surviving tongues, and of elementary languages which faded out. We find strange little patches of speech still in the world which do not seem to be connected with any other language about them. Sometimes, however, an exhaustive inquiry seems to affiliate these disconnected patches, seems to open out to us tantalizing glimpses of some simpler, wider, and more fundamental and universal form of human speech. One language group that has been keenly discussed is the Basque group of dialects. The Basques live now on the north and south slopes of the Pyrenees; they number perhaps 600,000 altogether in Europe, and to this day they are a very sturdy and independent-spirited people. Their language, as it exists to-day, is a fully developed one. But it is developed upon lines absolutely different from those of the Aryan languages about it. Basque newspapers have been published in the Argentine and in the United States to supply groups of prosperous emigrants. The earliest " French " settlers in Canada were Basque, and Basque names are frequent among the French Canadians to this day. Ancient remains point to a much wider distribution of the Basque speech and people over Spain. For a long time this Basque language was a profound perplexity to scholars,

and its structural character led to the suggestion that it might be related to some Amer-Indian tongue. A. H. Keane, in *Man Past and Present*, assembles reasons for linking it—though remotely—with the Berber language of North Africa, and through the Berber with the general body of Hamitic languages, but this relationship is questioned by other philologists. They find Basque more akin to certain similarly stranded vestiges of speech found in the Caucasian Mountains, and they are disposed to regard it as a last surviving member, much changed and specialized, of a once very widely extended group of pre-Hamitic languages, otherwise extinct, spoken chiefly by peoples of that Mediterranean race (round-barrow men) which once occupied most of Western and Southern Europe and Western Asia.

It is quite possible that over Western and Southern Europe language groups extended 10,000 years ago that have completely vanished before Aryan tongues. Later on we shall note in passing the possibility of three lost language groups represented by (1) Ancient Cretan, Lydian, and the like (though these may have belonged, says Sir H. H. Johnston, to the " Basque—Caucasian—Dravidian (!) group "), (2) Sumerian, and (3) Elamite. The suggestion has been made—it is a mere guess—that ancient Sumerian may have been a linking language between the early Basque-Caucasian and early Mongolian groups. If this is true, then we have in this " Basque-Caucasian-Dravidian-Sumerian-Mongolian " group a still more ancient and more ancestral system of speech than the fundamental Hamitic. We have the speech of the " heliolithic " culture.

The Hottentot language is said to have affinities with the Hamitic tongues, from which it is separated by the whole breadth of Bantu-speaking Central Africa. A Hottentot-like language with Bushman affinities is still spoken in equatorial East Africa, and this strengthens the idea that the whole of East Africa was once Hamitic-speaking. The Bantu languages and peoples spread, in comparatively recent times, from some centre of origin in West Central Africa and cut off the Hottentots from the other Hamitic peoples. But it is at least equally probable that the Hottentot is a separate language group.

Among other remote and isolated little patches of language are the Papuan speech of New Guinea and the native Australian. The now extinct Tasmanian language is but little known. What we do know of it is in support of what we have guessed about the comparative speechlessness of Palæolithic man.

We may quote a passage from Hutchinson's *Living Races of Mankind* upon this matter :—

" The language of the natives is irretrievably lost, only imperfect indications of its structure and a small proportion of its words having been preserved. In the absence of sibilants and some other features, their dialects resembled the Australian, but were of ruder, of less developed structure, and so imperfect that, according to Joseph Milligan, our best authority on the subject, they observed no settled order or arrangement of words in the construction of their sentences, but conveyed in a supplementary fashion by tone, manner, and gesture those modifications of meaning which we express by mood, tense, number, etc. Abstract terms were rare ; for

every variety of gum-tree or wattle-tree there was a name, but no word for " tree " in general, nor for qualities such as hard, soft, warm, cold, long, short, round, etc. Anything hard was " like a stone," anything round " like the moon," and so on, usually suiting the action to the word and confirming by some sign the meaning to be understood."

§ 9

In reading this chapter it is well to remember how laborious and difficult are the tasks of **How Languages may be related.** comparative philology, and how necessary it is to understand the qualifications and limitations that are to be put upon its conclusions. The Aryan group of languages is much better understood than any other, for the simple reason that it has been more familiar and accessible to European science. The other groups have been less thoroughly investigated, because so far they have not been studied exhaustively by men accustomed to use them, and whose minds are set in the key of their structure. Even the

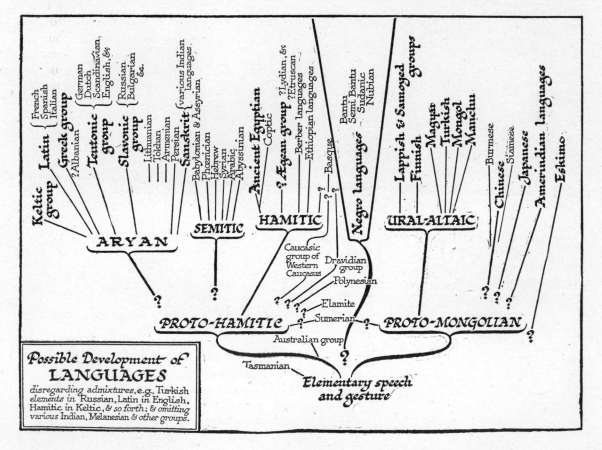

Possible Development of **LANGUAGES** disregarding admixtures, e.g. Turkish elements in Russian, Latin in English, Hamitic in Keltic, & so forth; & omitting various Indian, Melanesian & other groups.

Semitic languages have been approached at a disadvantage because few Jews think in Hebrew. But a time is fast approaching when Japanese, Chinese, Arabic, and Indian philologists will come to the rescue in these matters, and good reason may be found for revising much that has been said above about the native American, Ural-Altaic, primitive Chinese, and Polynesian groups of tongues.

The writer has amused himself by sketching a fanciful diagram of possible relationships of the various language groups, and he gives that here. It may be useful to the reader by holding together in his mind the broad classification here made, but he must remember that it is drawn without authority, as a mere suggestion of the possible course of linguistic evolution.

Book III

THE DAWN OF HISTORY

XV

THE ARYAN-SPEAKING PEOPLES IN PREHISTORIC TIMES

§ 1

WE have spoken of the Aryan language as probably arising in the region of the Danube and South Russia and spreading from that region of origin. We say "probably," because it is by no means certainly proved that that was the centre; there have been vast discussions upon this point and wide divergences of opinion. We give the prevalent view. As it spread widely, Aryan began to differentiate into a number of subordinate languages. To the west and south it encountered the Basque language, which was then widely spread in Spain, and also possibly various Hamitic Mediterranean languages.

The Spreading of the Aryan-Speakers.

The Neolithic Mediterranean race, the Iberian race, was distributed over Great Britain, Ireland, France, Spain, North Africa, South Italy, and, in a more civilized state, Greece and Asia Minor. It was probably closely related to the Egyptian. To judge by its European vestiges it was a rather small human type, generally with an oval face and a long head. It buried its chiefs and important people in megalithic chambers—*i.e.* made of big stones—covered over by great mounds of earth; and these mounds of earth, being much longer than they are broad, are spoken of as the long barrows. These people

sheltered at times in caves, and also buried some of their dead therein; and from the traces of charred, broken, and cut human bones, including the bones of children, it is inferred that they were cannibals. These short dark Iberian tribes (and the Basques also if they were a different race) were thrust back westward, and conquered and enslaved by slowly advancing waves of a taller and fairer Aryan-speaking people, coming southward and westward through Central Europe, who are spoken of as the Kelts. Only the Basque resisted the conquering Aryan speech. Gradually these Keltic-speakers made their way to the Atlantic, and all that now remains of the Iberians is mixed into the Keltic population. There is a certain sort of short dark Welshman, and certain types of Irishmen, who are probably Iberians by race. The modern Portuguese are also largely of Iberian blood.

The Kelts spoke a language, Keltic,[1] which was also in its turn to differentiate into the language of Gaul, Welsh, Breton, Scotch Gaelic, Erse (the native Irish language), and other tongues. They buried the ashes of their chiefs and important people in round barrows. While

[1] "The Keltic group of languages of which it has been said that they combined an Aryan vocabulary with a Berber (or Iberian) grammar." Sir Harry Johnston. See also Sir John Rhys, *The Welsh People.*

these Nordic Kelts were spreading westward, other Nordic Aryan peoples were pressing down upon the dark white Mediterranean race in the Italian and Greek peninsulas, and developing the Latin and Greek groups of tongues. Certain other Aryan tribes were drifting towards the Baltic and across into Scandinavia, speaking varieties of the Aryan which became ancient Norse—the parent of Swedish, Danish, Norwegian, and Icelandic—Gothic, and Low and High German.

While the primitive Aryan speech was thus spreading and breaking up into daughter languages to the west, it was also spreading and breaking up to the east. North of the Carpathians and the Black Sea, Aryan-speaking tribes were increasing and spreading and using a distinctive dialect called Slavonian, from which came Russian, Serbian, Polish, Bulgarian, and other tongues ; other variations of Aryan distributed over Asia Minor and Persia were also being individualized as Armenian and Indo-Iranian, the parent of Sanscrit and Persian. In this book we have used the word Aryan for all this family of languages, but the term Indo-European is sometimes used for the entire family, and "Aryan" itself restricted in a narrower sense to the Indo-Iranian speech.[1] This Indo-Iranian speech was destined to split later into a number of languages, including Persian and Sanscrit, the latter being the language of certain tribes of fair-complexioned Aryan speakers who pushed eastward into India somewhen between 3,000 and 1,000 B.C. and conquered dark Dravidian peoples who were then in possession of that land.

§ 2

What sort of life did these prehistoric Aryans lead, these Nordic Aryans who were the chief ancestors of most Europeans and most white Americans and European colonists of to-day, as well as

Primitive
Aryan
Life.

of the Armenians,[2] Persians, and high-caste Hindus ?

In answering that question we are able to resort to a new source of knowledge in addition to the dug-up remains and vestiges upon which we have had to rely in the case of Palæolithic man. We have language. By careful study of the Aryan languages it has been found possible to deduce a number of conclusions about the life of these Aryan peoples 5,000 or 4,000 years ago. All these languages have a common resemblance, as each, as we have already explained, rings the changes upon a number of common roots. When we find the same root word running through all or most of these tongues, it seems reasonable to conclude that the thing that root word signifies must have been known to the common ancestors. Of course, if they have *exactly the same word* in their languages, this may not be the case ; it may be the new name of a new thing or of a new idea that has spread over the world quite recently. "Gas," for instance, is a word that was made by Van Helmont, a Dutch chemist, about 1625, and has spread into most civilized tongues, and "tobacco" again is an American-Indian word which followed the introduction of smoking almost everywhere. But if the same word turns up in a number of languages, and *if it follows the characteristic modifications of each language*, we may feel sure that it has been in that language, and a part of that language, since the beginning, suffering the same changes with the rest of it. We know, for example, that the words for waggon and wheel run in this fashion through the Aryan tongues, and so we are able to conclude that the primitive Aryans, the more purely Nordic Aryans, had waggons, though it would seem from the absence of any common roots for spokes, rim, or axle that their wheels were not wheelwright's wheels with spokes, but made of the trunks of trees shaped out with an axe between the ends.

These primitive waggons were drawn by oxen. The primitive Aryans did not ride or drive horses ; they had very little to do with horses. The Reindeer men were a horse-people, but the Neolithic Aryans were a cow-people. They ate beef, not horse ; and after many ages they began

[1] See Schrader (translated by Jevons), *Prehistoric Antiquities of the Aryan Peoples*, p. 404. But though the word Aryan was undoubtedly in its original application the name only of the Indo-Iranian people, it has been used in modern discussion for more than half a century in the wider sense. A word was badly wanted for that purpose, and "Aryan" was taken ; failing "Aryan" we should be obliged to fall back on "Indo-Germanic" or "Indo-European," terms equally open to objection and ugly and clumsy to employ.

[2] But these may have been an originally Semitic people who learnt an Aryan speech.

this use of draught cattle. They reckoned wealth by cows. They wandered, following pasture, and "trekking" their goods, as the South African Boers do, in ox-waggons, though of course their waggons were much clumsier than any to be found in the world to-day. They probably ranged over very wide areas. They were migratory, but not in the strict sense of the word "nomadic"; they moved in a slower, clumsier fashion than did the later, more specialized nomadic peoples. They were forest and parkland people without horses. They were developing a migratory life out of the more settled "forest clearing" life of the earlier Neolithic period. Changes of climate which were replacing forest by pasture, and the accidental burning of forests by fire may have assisted this development.

When these early "Aryans" came to big rivers or open water, they built boats, at first hollow tree trunks and then skin-covered frameworks of lighter wood. Before history began there was already some Aryan canoe-traffic across the British Channel and in the Baltic, and also among the Greek islands. But the Aryans, as we shall see later, were probably not the first peoples to take to the sea.

We have already described the sort of home the primitive Aryan occupied and his household life, so far as the remains of the Swiss pile-dwellings enable us to describe these things. Mostly his houses were of too flimsy a sort, probably of wattle and mud, to have survived, and possibly he left them and trekked on for very slight reasons. The Aryan peoples burnt their dead, a custom they still preserve in India, but their predecessors, the long-barrow people, the Iberians, buried their dead in a sitting position. In some ancient Aryan burial mounds (round barrows) the urns containing the ashes of the departed are shaped like houses, and these represent rounded huts with thatched roofs.

The grazing of the primitive Aryan was far more important to him than his agriculture. At first he cultivated with a rough wooden hoe; then, after he had found out the use of cattle for draught purposes, he began real ploughing with oxen, using at first a suitably bent tree bough as his plough. His first cultivation before that came about must have been rather in the form of garden patches near the house buildings than

of fields. Most of the land his tribe occupied was common land on which the cattle grazed together.

He never used stone for building houses until upon the very verge of history. Over Europe, wherever the glaciers of the Ice Age extended, he found great stones scattered, the great stones that glaciers bring with them; and with these he piled up tombs for his illustrious dead, or possibly built such primitive temples as Stonehenge or Carnac.[1] But there are no evidences of any use of stone as a habitation for the living.

His social life was growing. Man was now living in clans and tribal communities. These clans and communities clashed; they took each other's grazing land, they sought to rob each other; there began a new thing in human life, *war*. For war is not a primeval thing; it has not been in this world for more than 20,000 years. To this day very primitive peoples, such as the Australian black-fellows, do not understand war. The Palæolithic Age was an age of fights and murder, no doubt, but not of the organized collective fighting of numbers of men.[2] But now men could talk together and group themselves under leaders, and they found a need of centres where they could come together with their cattle in time of raids and danger. They began to make camps with walls of earth and palisades, many of which are still to be traced in the history-worn contours of the European scenery. The leaders under whom men fought in war were often the same men as the sacrificial purifiers who were their early priests.

The knowledge of bronze spread late in Europe. Neolithic man had been making his slow advances age by age for 7,000 or 8,000 years before the metals came. By that time his social life had developed so that there were men of various occupations and men and women of different ranks in the community. There were men who worked wood and leather, potters and carvers. The women span and wove and embroidered. There were chiefs and families that were distinguished as leaderly and noble; and man varied the monotony of his herding

---

[1] Unless these temples were the work of the preceding long-barrow people.
[2] On this point see Perry. *An Ethnological Study of Warfare*, vol. lxi. Mem. Manchester Lit. and Phil. Soc.—G. M.

THE PYRAMIDS AS THEY ARE TO-DAY.

From a photograph by the Photochrom Co. Ld.

and wandering, he consecrated undertakings and celebrated triumphs, held funeral assemblies, and distinguished the traditional seasons of the year, by *feasts*. His meats we have already glanced at; but somewhen between 10,000 B.C. and the broadening separation of the Aryan peoples towards 2,000 or 1,000 B.C., mankind discovered fermentation, and began to brew intoxicating drinks. He made these of honey, of barley, and, as the Aryan tribes spread southward, of the grape. And he got merry and drunken. Whether he first used yeast to make his bread light or to ferment his drink we do not know.

At his feasts there were individuals with a gift for "playing the fool," who did so no doubt to win the laughter of their friends,[1] but there was also another sort of men, of great importance in their time, and still more important to the historian, certain singers of songs and stories, the bards or rhapsodists. These *bards* existed among all the Aryan-speaking peoples; they were a consequence of and a further factor in that development of spoken language which was the chief of all the human advances made in Neolithic times. They chanted or recited stories of the past, or stories of the living

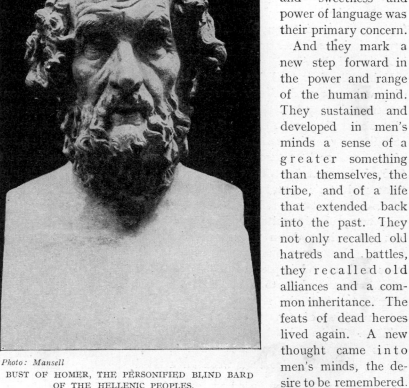

Photo: Mansell

BUST OF HOMER, THE PERSONIFIED BLIND BARD OF THE HELLENIC PEOPLES.

chief and his people; they told other stories that they invented; they memorized jokes and catches. They found and seized upon and improved the rhythms, rhymes, alliterations, and such-like possibilities latent in language; they probably did much to elaborate and fix grammatical forms. They were the first great artists of the ear, as the later Aurignacian rock painters were the first great artists of the eye and hand. No doubt they used much gesture; probably they learnt appropriate gestures when they learnt their songs; but the order and sweetness and power of language was their primary concern.

And they mark a new step forward in the power and range of the human mind. They sustained and developed in men's minds a sense of a greater something than themselves, the tribe, and of a life that extended back into the past. They not only recalled old hatreds and battles, they recalled old alliances and a common inheritance. The feats of dead heroes lived again. A new thought came into men's minds, the desire to be remembered. Men began to live in thought before they were born and after they were dead.

Like most human things, this bardic tradition grew first slowly and then more rapidly. By the time bronze was coming into Europe there was not an Aryan people that had not a profession and training of bards. In their hands language became as beautiful as it is ever likely to be. These bards were living books, man-histories, guardians and makers of a new and more powerful tradition in human life. Every Aryan people

[1] Fools, I think, were not wits, but deformed idiots, whom the company teased and laughed at. Certainly so in Roman and mediæval times. They do not occur in the Hellenic Age, except at courts in Asia Minor; but they must have been present in pre-Hellenic kingdoms; cf. end of *Iliad I*, where the gods laugh consumedly not at Hephaestus' wit, but at his lameness. The idealized Fool of Shakespeare is, like the idealized Hermit of the romances, the invention of later days.—G. M.

had its long poetical records thus handed down, its sagas (Teutonic), its epics (Greek), its vedas (Old Sanscrit). The earliest Aryan people were essentially a people of the voice. The recitation seems to have predominated even in those ceremonial and dramatic dances and that " dressing-up " which among most human races have also served for the transmission of tradition.[1]

At that time there was no writing, and when first the art of writing crept into Europe, as we shall tell later, it must have seemed far too slow, clumsy, and lifeless a method of record for men to trouble very much about writing down these glowing and beautiful treasures of the memory. Writing was at first kept for accounts and exact records. The bards and rhapsodists flourished for long after the introduction of writing. They survived, indeed, in Europe as the minstrels into the Middle Ages.

Unhappily their tradition had not the fixity of a written record. They amended and re-constructed, they had their fashions and their phases of negligence. Accordingly we have now only the very much altered and revised vestiges of that spoken literature of prehistoric times. One of the most interesting and informing of these prehistoric compositions of the Aryans survives in the Greek *Iliad*. An early form of *Iliad* was probably recited by 1,000 B.C., but it was not written down until perhaps 700 or 600 B.C. Many men must have had to do with it as authors and improvers, but later Greek tradition ascribed it to a blind bard named Homer, to whom also is ascribed the *Odyssey*, a composition of a very different spirit and outlook. To be a bard was naturally a blind man's occupation.[2] The Slavs called all bards *sliepac*, which was also their word for a blind man. The original recited version of the *Iliad* was older than that of the *Odyssey*. " The *Iliad* as a complete poem is older than the *Odyssey*, though the material of the *Odyssey*, being largely undatable folk-lore, is older than any of the historical material in the *Iliad*." [3] Both epics were probably written over and rewritten by some poet of a later date, in much the same manner that Lord Tennyson, the poet laureate of Queen Victoria, in his *Idylls of the King*, wrote over the *Morte d'Arthur* (which was itself a writing over by Sir Thomas Malory, *circ.* 1450, of pre-existing legends), making the speeches and sentiments and the characters more in accordance with those of his own time. But the events of the *Iliad* and the *Odyssey*, the way of living they describe, the spirit of the acts recorded, belong to the closing centuries of the prehistoric age. These sagas, epics, and vedas do supply, in addition to archæology and philology, a third source of information about those vanished times.

Here, for example, is the concluding passage of the *Iliad*, describing very exactly the making of a prehistoric barrow. (We have taken here Chapman's rhymed translation, correcting certain words with the help of the prose version of Lang, Leaf, and Myers.)

" . . . Thus oxen, mules, in waggons straight they put,
Went forth, and an unmeasur'd pile of sylvan matter cut ;
Nine days employ'd in carriage, but when the tenth morn shin'd
On wretched mortals, then they brought the bravest of his kind
Forth to be burned. Troy swam in tears. Upon the pile's most height
They laid the body, and gave fire. All day it burn'd, all night.
But when th' elev'nth morn let on earth her rosy fingers shine,
The people flock'd about the pile, and first with gleaming wine
Quench'd all the flames. His brothers then, and friends, the snowy bones
Gather'd into an urn of gold, still pouring out their moans.
Then wrapt they in soft purple veils the rich urn, digg'd a pit,
Grav'd it, built up the grave with stones, and quickly piled on it
A barrow. . . .
. . . The barrow heap'd once, all the town
In Jove-nurs'd Priam's Court partook a sumptuous fun'ral feast,
And so horse-taming Hector's rites gave up his soul to rest."

---

[1] The Aryans developed their languages and their ballads and epics between 10,0co B.C. and the historical period. Very much later in time, probably within the last 3,000 years, the nomadic Mongolian peoples of Asia began to develop their Ural-Altaic speech, under similar conditions, by similar poetic uses. Later we shall note the presence of bards at the court of Attila the Hun.—H. G. W.

[2] It is suggested in the text that blind men became bards : Myres says that bards were (artificially) blinded to stop them from going elsewhere—the tribe wanted to keep them. The poetic touch is that " the Muses " blind the poet. Not a bit of it. (Homer, being a blind bard, describes things by sound—the twanging arrow, the far-thundering sea, the noise of the chariot going through the gate. He is audile, not visual.)—E. B.

[3] G. M.

There remains also an old English saga, *Beowulf*, made long before the English had crossed from Germany into England, which winds up with a similar burial. The preparation of a pyre is first described. It is hung round with shields and coats of mail. The body is brought and the pyre fired, and then for ten days the warriors built a mighty mound to be seen afar by the traveller on sea or land. *Beowulf*, which is at least a thousand years later than the *Iliad*, is also interesting because one

COMBAT BETWEEN MENELAUS AND HECTOR
(IN THE *ILIAD*).

From a platter ascribed to the end of the seventh century in the British Museum. This is probably the earliest known vase bearing a Greek inscription. Greek writing was just beginning. Note the Swastika.

of the main adventures in it is the looting of the treasures of a barrow already ancient in those days.

§ 3

The Greek epics reveal the early Greeks with no knowledge of iron, without writing, and

Early Aryan Daily Life. before any Greek-founded cities existed in the land into which they had evidently come quite recently as conquerors. They were spreading southward from the Aryan region of origin. They seem to have been a fair people, newcomers in Greece, newcomers to a land that had been held hitherto by a darker people, people who are now supposed to have belonged to a dark white "aboriginal" race, a "Mediterranean" people allied to those Iberians whom the Kelts pressed westward, and to the Hamitic white people of North Africa.

Let us, at the risk of a slight repetition, be perfectly clear upon one point. The *Iliad* does not give us the primitive neolithic life of that Aryan region of origin; it gives us that life already well on the move towards a new state of affairs. The primitive neolithic way of living, with its tame and domesticated animals, its pottery and cooking, and its patches of rude cultivation, we have sketched in Chapter XI. We have already discussed in § 4 of Chapter XIII the probability of a widespread *heliolithic* culture. Between 15,000 and 6,000 B.C. the neolithic way of living had spread with the forests and abundant vegetation of the Pluvial Period, over the greater part of the old world, from the Niger to the Hwang-ho and from Ireland to the south of India. Now, as the climate of great portions of the earth was swinging towards drier and more open conditions again, the primitive neolithic life was developing along two divergent directions. One was towards a more wandering life, towards at last a constantly migratory life in pursuit of pasture, which is called NOMADISM; the other, in certain sunlit river valleys, was towards a water-treasuring life of irrigation, in which men gathered into the first towns and made the first CIVILIZATION. The nature and development of civilization we shall consider more fully in the next chapter, but here we have to note that the Greeks, as the *Iliad* presents them, are neither simple neolithic nomads, innocent of civilization, nor are they civilized men. They are primitive nomads in an excited state, because they have just come upon civilization, and regard it as an opportunity for war and loot.[1] So far they are exceptional and not representative. But our interest in them in this chapter is not in their distinctively Greek and predatory aspect, but in what they reveal of the ordinary northward life from which they are coming.

These early Greeks of the *Iliad* are sturdy fighters, but without discipline—their battles

[1] The *Iliad* describes what Chadwick calls a Heroic Age: i.e. a time when the barbarians or nomads are breaking up an old civilization. Men are led by chiefs, who live by plunder and conquest and make themselves kingdoms. The tribe is broken up; instead comes the comitatus of casual men who attach themselves to a particular chief, as Phœnix or Patroclus to Achilles. Religion is broken up, being by origin local. Hence there is almost no religion in the *Iliad* or the *Nibelungenlied*. Almost no magic. No family life. Tremendous booty, and *la carrière ouverte aux talents* with a vengeance.—G. M.

are a confusion of single combats. They have horses, but no cavalry; they use the horse, which is a comparatively recent addition to Aryan resources, to drag a rude fighting chariot into battle. The horse is still novel enough to be something of a terror in itself. For ordinary draught purposes, as in the quotation from the *Iliad* we have just made, oxen were employed.

The only priests of these Aryans are the keepers of shrines and sacred places. There are chiefs, who are heads of families and who also perform sacrifices, but there does not seem

Horses & chariots —
(from an archaic Greek vase)

to be much mystery or sacramental feeling in their religion. When the Greeks go to war, these heads and elders meet in council and appoint a king, whose powers are very loosely defined. There are no laws, but only customs; and no exact standards of conduct.

The social life of the early Greeks centred about the households of these leading men. There were no doubt huts for herds and the like, and outlying farm buildings; but the hall of the chief was a comprehensive centre, to which everyone went to feast, to hear the bards, to take part in games and exercises. The primitive craftsmen were gathered there. About it were cowsheds and stabling and such-like offices. Unimportant people slept about anywhere as retainers did in the medieval castles and as people still do in Indian households. Except for quite personal possessions, there was still an air of patriarchal communism about the tribe. The tribe, or the chief as the head of the tribe, owned the grazing lands; forest and rivers were the wild.

The Aryan civilization seems, and indeed all early communities seem, to have been without the little separate households that make up the mass of the population in Western Europe or America to-day. The tribe was a big family; the nation a group of tribal families; a household often contained hundreds of people. Human society began, just as herds and droves begin among animals, by the family delaying its breaking up. Nowadays the lions in East Africa are apparently becoming social animals in this way, by the young keeping with the mother after they are fully grown, and hunting in a group. Hitherto the lion has been much more of a solitary beast. If men and women do not cling to their families nowadays as much as they did, it is because the state and the community supply now safety and help and facilities that were once only possible in the family group.

In the Hindu community of to-day these great households of the earlier stages of human society are still to be found. Mr. Bhupendranath Basu has recently described a typical Hindu household.[1] It is an Aryan household refined and made gentle after thousands of years of civilization, but its social structure is the same as that of the households of which the Aryan epics tell.

"The joint family system," he said, "has descended to us from time immemorial, the Aryan patriarchal system of old still holding sway in India. The structure, though ancient, remains full of life. The joint family is a co-operative corporation, in which men and women have a well-defined place. At the head of the corporation is the senior member of the family, generally the eldest male member, but in his absence, the senior female member often assumes control (cp. Penelope in the *Odyssey*).

"All able-bodied members must contribute their labour and earnings, whether of personal skill or agriculture and trade, to the common stock; weaker members, widows, orphans, and destitute relations, all must be maintained and supported; sons, nephews, brothers, cousins, all must be treated equally, for any undue preference is apt to break up the family. We

[1] *Some Aspects of Hindu Life in India.* Paper read to the Royal Society of Arts, Nov. 28, 1918.

have no word for cousins—they are either brothers or sisters, and we do not know what are cousins two degrees removed. The children of a first cousin are your nephews and nieces, just the same as the children of your brothers and sisters. A man can no more marry a cousin, however removed, than he can marry his own sister, except in certain parts of Madras, where a man may marry his maternal uncle's daughter. The family affections, the family ties, are always very strong, and therefore the maintenance of an equal standard among so many members is not so difficult as it may appear at first sight. Moreover, life is very simple. Until recently shoes were not in general use at home, but sandals without any leather fastenings. I have known of a well-to-do middle-class family of several brothers and cousins who had two or three pairs of leather shoes between them, these shoes being only used when they had occasion to go out, and the same practice is still followed in the case of the more expensive garments, like shawls, which last for generations, and with their age are treated with loving care, as having been used by ancestors of revered memory.

"The joint family remains together sometimes for several generations, until it becomes too unwieldy, when it breaks up into smaller families, and you thus see whole villages peopled by members of the same clan. I have said that the family is a co-operative society, and it may be likened to a small state, and is kept in its place by strong discipline based on love and obedience. You see nearly every day the younger members coming to the head of the family and taking the dust of his feet as a token of benediction; whenever they go on an enterprise, they take his leave and carry his blessing. . . . There are many bonds which bind the family together—the bonds of sympathy, of common pleasures, of common sorrows; when a death occurs, all the members go into mourning; when there is a birth or a wedding, the whole family rejoices. Then above all is the family deity, some image of Vishnu, the preserver; his place is in a separate room, generally known as the room of God, or in well-to-do families in a temple attached to the house, where the family performs its daily worship. There is a sense of personal attachment between

this image of the deity and the family, for the image generally comes down from past generations, often miraculously acquired by a pious ancestor at some remote time. . . . With the household gods is intimately associated the family priest. . . . The Hindu priest is a part of the family life of his flock, between whom and himself the tie has existed for many generations. The priest is not generally a man of much learning; he knows, however, the traditions of his faith. . . . He is not a very heavy burden, for he is satisfied with little—a few handfuls of rice, a few home-grown bananas or vegetables, a little unrefined sugar made in the village, and sometimes a few pieces of copper are all that is needed. . . . A picture of our family life would be incomplete without the household servants. A female servant is known as the ' jhi,' or daughter, in Bengal—she is like the daughter of the house; she calls the master and the mistress father and mother, and the young men and women of the family brothers and sisters. She participates in the life of the family; she goes to the holy places along with her mistress, for she could not go alone, and generally she spends her life with the family of her adoption; her children are looked after by the family. The treatment of men servants is very similar. These servants, men and women, are generally people of the humbler castes, but a sense of personal attachment grows up between them and the members of the family, and as they get on in years they are affectionately called by the younger members elder brothers, uncles, aunts, etc. . . . In a well-to-do house there is always a resident teacher, who instructs the children of the family as well as other boys of the village; there is no expensive school building, but room is found in some veranda or shed in the courtyard for the children and their teacher, and into this school low-caste boys are freely admitted. These indigenous schools were not of a very high order, but they supplied an agency of instruction for the masses which was probably not available in many other countries. . . .

" With Hindu life is bound up its traditional duty of hospitality. It is the duty of a householder to offer a meal to any stranger who may come before midday and ask for one; the mistress of the house does not sit down to her meal until every member is fed, and, as some-times her food is all that is left, she does not take her meal until well after midday lest a hungry stranger should come and claim one."...

We have been tempted to quote Mr. Basu at some length, because here we do get to some-thing like a living understanding of the type of household which has prevailed in human com-munities since neolithic days, which still prevails to-day in India, China, and the Far East, but which in the west is rapidly giving ground before a state and municipal organization of education and a large-scale industrialism within which an amount of individual detachment and freedom is possible, such as these great house-holds never knew. . . .

But let us return now to the history preserved for us in the Aryan epics.

The *Rig Veda*, the chief of the old Sanscrit epics, tells a very similar story to that under-lying the *Iliad*, the story of a fair, beef-eating people—only later did they become vegetarians —coming down from Persia into the plain of North India and conquering their way slowly towards the Indus. From the Indus they spread over India, but as they spread they acquired much from the dark Dravidians they con-quered, and they seem to have lost their bardic

tradition. The vedas, says Mr. Basu, were transmitted chiefly in the households by the women. . . .

The oral literature of the Keltic peoples who pressed westward has not been preserved so completely as that of the Greeks or Indians; it was written down many centuries later, and so, like the barbaric, primitive English *Beowulf*, has lost any clear evidence of a period of migra-tion into the lands of an antecedent people. If the pre-Aryans figure in it at all, it is as the fairy folk of the Irish stories. Ireland, most cut off of all the Keltic-speaking communities, retained to the latest date its primitive Aryan life; and the *Táin*, the Irish *Iliad*, describes a cattle-keeping life in which war chariots are still used, and war dogs also, and the heads of the slain are carried off slung round the horses' necks. The *Táin* is the story of a cattle raid. Here too the same social order appears as in the *Iliad*; the chiefs sit and feast in great halls, they build halls for themselves, there is singing and story-telling by the bards, and drinking and intoxication.[1] Priests are not very much in evidence, but there is a sort of medicine man, who deals in spells and prophecy.

[1] No Greek heroes, in Homer or the heroic tradition, ever get drunk. In the comic tradition they do, and of course centaurs and barbarians do.—G. M.

XVI

THE FIRST CIVILIZATIONS

§ 1

WHEN the Aryan way of speech and life was beginning to spread to the east and west of the region in which it began, and breaking up as it spread into a number of languages and nations, con-siderable communities of much more civilized men were already in exist-ence in Egypt and in Mesopotamia, and probably also in China and in (still purely Dravidian) India. Our story has overshot itself in its account of the Aryans and of their slow progress from early Neolithic conditions to the heroic barbarism of the Bronze Age. We must now go back. Such a Keltic (or pre-Keltic) gathering as we sketched at Avebury

Early Cities and Early Nomads.

would have happened about 2,000 B.C., and the building of the barrow for Hector as the *Iliad* describes it, 1,300 B.C. or even later. It is perhaps natural for a European writer writing primarily for English-reading students to over-run his subject in this way. No great harm is done if the student does clearly grasp that there has been an overlap.

Here then we take up the main thread of human history again. We must hark back to 6,000 B.C. or even earlier. But although we shall go back so far, the people we shall describe are people already in some respects beyond the neolithic Aryans of three thousand years later, more particularly in their social organization and their material welfare. While in Central

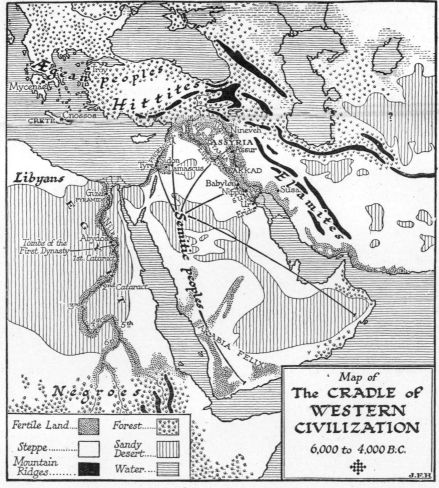

Map of
The CRADLE of
WESTERN
CIVILIZATION
6,000 to 4,000 B.C.

Fertile Land.... Forest......

Steppe.......... Sandy Desert.....

Mountain Ridges........ Water....

Europe and Central Asia the primitive Neolithic way of life was becoming more migratory and developing into nomadism, here it is becoming more settled and localized. It was long doubtful whether we were to consider Mesopotamia or Egypt the earlier scene of the two parallel beginnings of settled communities living in towns. By 4,000 B.C., in both these regions of the earth, such communities existed, and had been going on for a very considerable time. The excavations of the American expedition[1] at Nippur have unearthed evidence of a city community existing there at least as early as 5,000 B.C., and probably as early as 6,000 B.C., an earlier date than anything we know of in Egypt. It is to be remembered that it is only in the Euphrates–Tigris district that wheat has ever been found growing wild. It may be that from Mesopotamia as a centre the cultiva-

[1] Babylonian expedition of the University of Pennsylvania.

tion of wheat spread over the entire eastern hemisphere. Or it may be that wheat grew wild in some regions now submerged. But cultivation is not civilization ; the growing of wheat had spread from the Atlantic to the Pacific with the distribution of the Neolithic culture by perhaps 10,000 or 9,000 B.C. Civilization is something more than the occasional, seasonal growing of wheat. It is the settlement of men upon an area continuously cultivated and possessed, who live in buildings continuously inhabited. For a long time civilization may quite possibly have developed in Mesopotamia without any relations with the parallel beginnings in Egypt. The two beginnings may have been quite independent. Or they may have had a common origin in the region of the Mediterranean, the Red Sea, and Southern Arabia.

The first condition necessary to a real settling down of Neolithic men, as distinguished from a mere temporary settlement among abundant food, was of course a trustworthy all-the-year-round supply of water, fodder for the animals, food for themselves, and building material for their homes. There had to be everything they could need at any season, and no want that would tempt them to wander further. This was a possible state of affairs, no doubt, in many European and Asiatic valleys ; and in many such valleys, as in the case of the Swiss lake-dwellings, men settled from a very early date indeed; but nowhere, of any countries now known to us, were these favourable conditions found upon such a scale, and nowhere did they hold good so surely year in and year out as in Egypt and in the country between the upper waters of the Euphrates and Tigris and the Persian Gulf.[1] Here was a constant water supply under enduring sunlight ; trustworthy harvests year by year ; in Mesopotamia wheat grew wild and yielded, says Herodotus, two hundred-fold to the sower ; Pliny says that it was cut twice and afterwards yielded good fodder for sheep ; there were abundant palms and many sorts of fruits ; and as for building material, in Egypt there was clay and easily worked stone, and in Mesopotamia a clay that becomes a brick in the sunshine. In such countries men would cease to wander and settle down almost un-awares ; they would multiply and discover themselves numerous and by their numbers safe from any casual assailant. They multi-plied, producing a denser human population than the earth had ever known before ; their houses became more substantial, wild beasts were exterminated over great areas, the security of life increased so that ordinary men went about in the towns and fields without encumber-ing themselves with weapons, and among them-selves, at least, they became peaceful peoples. Men took root as man had never taken root before.

But in the less fertile and more seasonal lands outside these favoured areas, there

[1] We shall use " Mesopotamia " here loosely for the Euphrates-Tigris country generally. Strictly, of course, as its name indicates, Mesopotamia (mid-rivers) means only the country *between* those two great rivers. That country in the fork was probably very marshy and unhealthy in early times (Sayce), until it was drained by man, and the early cities grew up west of the Euphrates and east of the Tigris. Probably these rivers then flowed separately into the Persian Gulf.

developed on the other hand a thinner, more active population of peoples, the primitive nomadic peoples. In contrast with the settled folk, the agriculturists, these nomads lived freely and dangerously. They were in com-parison lean and hungry men. Their herding was still blended with hunting ; they fought constantly for their pastures with hostile families. The discoveries in the elaboration of implements and the use of metals made by the settled peoples spread to them and improved their weapons. They followed the settled folk from Neolithic phase to Bronze phase. It is possible that in the case of iron, the first users were nomadic. They became more warlike with better arms, and more capable of rapid movements with the improvement of their transport. One must not think of a nomadic stage as a predecessor of a settled stage in human affairs. To begin with, man was a slow drifter, following food. Then one sort of men began to settle down, and another sort became more distinctly nomadic. The settled sort began to rely more and more upon grain for food ; the nomad began to make a greater use of milk for food. He bred his cows for milk. The two ways of life specialized in opposite directions. It was inevitable that nomad folk and the settled folk should clash, that the nomads should seem hard barbarians to the settled peoples, and the settled people soft and effeminate and very good plunder to the nomad peoples. Along the fringes of the developing civilizations there must have been a constant raiding and bickering between hardy nomad tribes and mountain tribes and the more numerous and less warlike peoples in the towns and villages.

For the most part this was a mere raiding of the borders. The settled folk had the weight of numbers on their side ; the herdsmen might raid and loot, but they could not stay. That sort of mutual friction might go on for many generations. But ever and again we find some leader or some tribe amidst the disorder of free and independent nomads, powerful enough to force a sort of unity upon its kindred tribes, and then woe betide the nearest civilization. Down pour the united nomads on the unwarlike, unarmed plains, and there ensues a war of con-quest. Instead of carrying off the booty, the conquerors settle down on the conquered land, which becomes all booty for them ; the villagers and townsmen are reduced to servitude and tribute-paying, they become hewers of wood and drawers of water, and the leaders of the nomads become kings and princes, masters and aristocrats. They too settle down, they learn many of the arts and refinements of the conquered, they cease to be lean and hungry, but for many generations they retain traces of their old nomadic habits, they hunt and indulge in open-air sports, they drive and race chariots, they regard work, especially agricultural work, as the lot of an inferior race and class.

This in a thousand variations has been one of the main stories in history for the last seventy centuries or more. In the first history that we can clearly decipher we find already in all the civilized regions a distinction between a non-working ruler class and the working mass of the population. And we find too that after some generations, the aristocrat, having settled down, begins to respect the arts and refinements and law-abidingness of settlement, and to lose something of his original hardihood. He intermarries, he patches up a sort of toleration between conqueror and conquered ; he exchanges religious ideas and learns the lessons upon which soil and climate insist. He becomes

a part of the civilization he has captured. And as he does so, events gather towards a fresh invasion by the free adventurers of the outer world.[1]

§ 2A

This alternation of settlement, conquest, refinement, fresh conquest, refinement, is particularly to be noted in the region of the Euphrates and Tigris, which lay open in every direction to great areas which are not arid enough to be complete deserts, but which were not fertile enough to support civilized population. Perhaps the earliest people to form real cities in this part of the world, or indeed in any part of the world,

The Riddle of the Sumerians.

[1] My friend, Colonel Lawrence, tells me that the movement among the Arabs is somewhat as follows : (1) the sessile village cultivators are pushed out by over-population into the desert—very reluctantly ; (2) they wander in the desert for a thousand years or so—as a stick pushed into the water gets carried about for a long way ; (3) they are pushed again out of the desert, back again into sessile life, by starvation—very reluctantly (they have learned to love the desert) ; and when they come back into sessile life they are on the other side – *i.e.* having started in West Arabia, they land in Mesopotamia. Thus they wander a thousand years or so, and end up thousands of miles from where they started.—E. B.

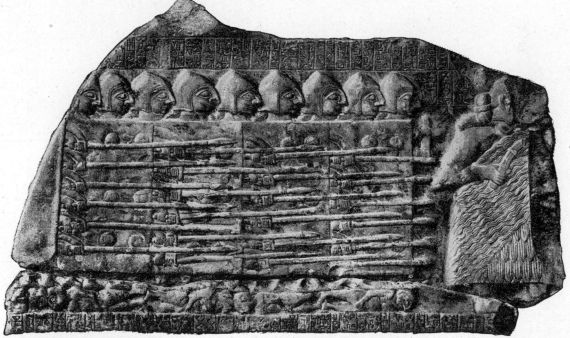

A VERY EARLY SUMERIAN STONE CARVING SHOWING SUMERIAN WARRIORS.
Above the heads of the figures note the cuneiform inscription.

Photo. Mansell.

THIS DELIGHTFULLY ARCHAIC SUMERIAN STATUE
REPRESENTS SOME UNKNOWN PERSONAGE OF THE
SUMERIAN CITY OF LAGASH.

were a people of mysterious origin called the
Sumerians. They were neither Semites nor
Aryans, and whence they came we do not know.
Whether they were dark whites of Iberian or
Dravidian affinities is less certainly to be denied.[1]
They used a kind of writing which they scratched
upon clay, and their language has been de-

ciphered.[2] It was a language more like the
unclassified Caucasic language groups than any
others that now exist. These languages may
be connected with Basque, and may represent
what was once a widespread group extending
from Spain and Western Europe to Eastern
India, and reaching southwards to Central
Africa. These people shaved their heads and
wore simple tunic-like garments of wool. They
settled first on the lower courses of the great
river and not very far from the Persian Gulf,
which in those days ran up for a hundred and
thirty miles[3] and more beyond its present head.
They fertilized their fields by letting water run
through irrigation trenches, and they gradually
became very skilful hydraulic engineers ; they
had cattle, asses, sheep, and goats, but no
horses ; and their collections of mud huts grew
into towns ; and their religion raised up tower-
like temple buildings.

Clay, dried in the sun, was a very great fact
in the lives of these people. This lower country
of the Euphrates-Tigris valleys had little or no
stone. They built of brick, they made
pottery and earthenware images, and they
drew and presently wrote upon thin tile-like
cakes of clay. They do not seem to have had
paper or to have used parchment. Their books
and memoranda, even their letters, were
potsherds.

At Nippur they built a great tower of brick to
their chief god, El-lil (Enlil), the memory of which
is supposed to be preserved in the story of
the Tower of Babel. They seem to have been
divided up into city states, which warred among
themselves and maintained for many centuries
their military capacity. Their soldiers carried
long spears and shields, and fought in close

[1] Sir H. H. Johnston is inclined to believe that a
common late Neolithic and early bronze culture spread
widely in this primitive world. He links the Dravidian
languages of India—some of which group are to be
found in Beluchistan and the eastern fringe of
Persia—with certain languages in the Caucasian
Mountains, and these again with Basque. He would
bring the Sumerians, the early Cretans, and the early
peoples of Asia Minor into this early " brown " or dark
white culture before the Aryans, Semites, or Hamites
developed their language cultures and thrust across
this band of primordial civilization. He connects
these " class and prefix " languages with the creation
of the African Bantu, but that is a speculation beyond
the scope of this present work. A series of articles on
this subject by the Rev. W. Crabtree will be found in
the *Journal of the African Society*. The connection

of Sumerian and Bantu was first suggested by Sir
Richard Burton in 1885. These views are in complete
accordance with Elliot Smith's suggestion of a widespread heliolithic culture already dealt with in chap.
xiii, § 4.—H. G. W.

[2] Excavations conducted at Eridu by Capt. R. Camp-
bell Thompson during the recent war have revealed an
early Neolithic agricultural stage, before the invention
of writing or the use of bronze, beneath the earliest
Sumerian foundations. The crops were cut by sickles
of earthenware. Capt. Thompson thinks that these
pre-Sumerian people were not of Sumerian race, but
proto-Elamites. Entirely similar Neolithic remains
have been found at Susa, once the chief city of Elam.

[3] Sayce, in *Babylonian and Assyrian Life*, estimates
that in 6,500 B.C. Eridu was on the seacoast.

formation. Sumerians conquered Sumerians. Sumeria remained unconquered by any stranger race for a very long period of time indeed. They developed their civilization, their writing, and their shipping, through a period that may be as long as the whole period from the days of Moses to the present time.

The first of all known empires was that founded by the high priest of the god of the Sumerian city of Erech. It reached, says an inscription at Nippur, from the Lower (Persian Gulf) to the Upper (Mediterranean or Red ?) Sea. Among the mud heaps of the Euphrates-Tigris valley the record of that vast period of history, that first half of the Age of Cultivation, is buried. There rose the first temples and the first priest-rulers that we know of among mankind.

§ 2B

Upon the western edge of this country appeared nomadic tribes of Semitic-speaking The Empire peoples who traded, raided, and of Sargon fought with the Sumerians for many the First. generations. Then arose at last a great leader among these Semites, Sargon (2,750 B.C.),[1] who united them, and not only conquered the Sumerians, but extended his rule from beyond the Persian Gulf on the east to the Mediterranean on the west. His own people were called the Akkadians and his empire is called the Sumerian Akkadian empire. It endured for over two hundred years.

But though the Semites conquered and gave a king to the Sumerian cities, it was the Sumerian civilization which prevailed over the simpler Semitic culture. The newcomers learnt the Sumerian writing (the " cuneiform " writing) and the Sumerian language ; they set up no Semitic writing of their own. The Sumerian language became for these barbarians the language of knowledge and power, as Latin was the language of knowledge and power among the barbaric peoples of the middle ages in Europe. This Sumerian learning had a very great vitality. It was destined to survive through a long series of conquests and

[1] Authorities vary upon this date. Some put back Sargon I to 3,750 B.C. This latter was his traditional date based on Babylonian records.

changes that now began in the valley of the two rivers.

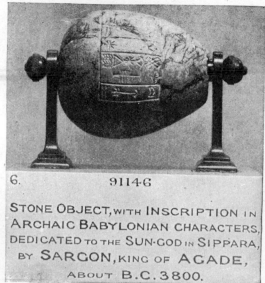

6.   9114G

STONE OBJECT, WITH INSCRIPTION IN ARCHAIC BABYLONIAN CHARACTERS, DEDICATED TO THE SUN-GOD IN SIPPARA, BY SARGON, KING OF AGADE, ABOUT B.C. 3800.

Photo: Mansell.

THE CONQUERING SEMITES, WHO HAD NO WRITING, ADOPTED THAT OF THE SUMERIANS.

The British Museum inscription gives the earlier date to Sargon (see footnote 1).

§ 2C

As the people of the Sumerian Akkadian empire lost their political and military vigour, The Empire fresh inundations of a warlike of Ham- people began from the east, the murabi. Elamites,[2] while from the west came the Semitic Amorites, pinching the Sumerian Akkadian empire between them. The Amorites settled in what was at first a small up-river town, named Babylon ; and after a hundred years of warfare became masters of all Mesopotamia under a great king, Hammurabi (2,100 B.C.), who founded the first Babylonian empire.

Again came peace and security and a decline in aggressive prowess, and in another hundred years fresh nomads from the east were invading Babylonia, bringing with them the horse and the war chariot, and setting up their own king in Babylon. . . .

[2] Of unknown language and race, " neither Sumerians nor Semites," says Sayce. Their central city was Susa. Their archæology is still largely an unworked mine. They are believed by some, says Sir H. H. Johnston, to have been negroid in type. There is a strong negroid strain in the modern people of Elam.

Photo : Mansell.

ASSYRIAN SOLDIERS AND LED HORSES (TIME OF SARDANAPALUS).

§ 2D

Higher up the Tigris, above the clay lands and with easy supplies of workable stone, a **The Assyrians and their Empire.** Semitic people, the Assyrians, while the Sumerians were still unconquered by the Semites, were settling about a number of cities of which Assur and Nineveh were the chief. Their peculiar physiognomy, the long nose and thick lips, was very like that of the commoner type of Polish Jew to-day. They wore great beards and ringletted long hair, tall caps and long robes. They were constantly engaged in mutual raiding with the Hittites to the west; they were conquered by Sargon I and became free again; a certain Tushratta, King of Mitanni, to the north-west, captured and held their capital, Nineveh, for a time; they intrigued with Egypt against Babylon and were in the pay of Egypt ; they developed the military art to a very high pitch, and became mighty raiders and exacters of tribute; and at last, adopting the horse and the war chariot, they settled accounts for a time with the Hittites, and then, under Tiglath Pileser I, conquered Babylon for themselves (about 1,100 B.C.[1]). But their hold on the lower, older, and more civilized land was not secure, and

[1] For most of these dates here Winckler in *Helmolt's World History* has been followed.

Nineveh, the stone city, remained their capital. For many centuries power swayed between Nineveh and Babylon, and sometimes it was an Assyrian and sometimes a Babylonian who claimed to be " king of the world."

For four centuries Assyria was restrained from expansion towards Egypt by a fresh northward thrust and settlement of another group of Semitic peoples, the Arameans, whose chief city was Damascus, and whose descendants are the Syrians of to-day. (There is, we may note, no connection whatever between the words Assyrian and Syrian. It is an accidental similarity.) Across these Syrians the Assyrian kings fought for power and expansion south-westward. In 745 B.C. arose another Tiglath Pileser, Tiglath Pileser III, the Tiglath Pileser of the Bible.[2] He not only directed the transfer of the Israelites to Media (the " Lost Ten Tribes " whose ultimate fate has exercised so many curious minds), but he conquered and ruled Babylon, so founding what historians know as the New Assyrian Empire. His son, Shalmaneser IV,[3] died during the siege of Samaria, and was succeeded by a usurper, who, no doubt to flatter Babylonian susceptibilities, took the ancient Akkadian Sumerian name of

[2] II. Kings xv. 29, and xvi. 7 *et seq.*
[3] II. Kings xvii. 3.

Sargon, Sargon II. He seems to have armed the Assyrian forces for the first time with iron weapons. It was probably Sargon II who actually carried out the deportation of the Ten Tribes.

Such shiftings about of population became a very distinctive part of the political methods of the Assyrian new empire. Whole nations who were difficult to control in their native country would be shifted *en masse* to unaccustomed regions and amidst strange neighbours, where their only hope of survival would lie in obedience to the supreme power.

Sargon's son, Sennacherib, led the Assyrian hosts to the borders of Egypt. There Sennacherib's army was smitten by a pestilence, a disaster described in the nineteenth chapter of the Second Book of Kings.

" And it came to pass that night, that the angel of the Lord went out, and smote in the camp of the Assyrians an hundred fourscore and five thousand : and when they arose early in the morning, behold, they were all dead corpses. So Sennacherib king of Assyria departed, and went and returned, and dwelt at Nineveh." [1]

Sennacherib's grandson, Assurbanipal (called by the Greeks Sardanapalus), did succeed in conquering and for a time holding lower Egypt.

§ 2E

The Assyrian empire lasted only a hundred and fifty years after Sargon II. Fresh nomadic Semites coming from the southeast, the Chaldeans, assisted by two Aryan peoples from the north, the Medes and Persians, combined against it, and took Nineveh in 606 B.C.

The Chaldean Empire.

The Chaldean Empire, with its capital at Babylon (Second Babylonian Empire), lasted under Nebuchadnezzar the Great (Nebuchadnezzar II) and his successors until 539 B.C.,

[1] To be murdered by his sons.

Photo : Mansell.

SARDANAPALUS FEASTS WITH A QUEEN.

SARDANAPALUS HUNTS.
This illustration is continuous with the next.

Sumerians give place to Aryan rulers, Medes and Persians appear in the place of the Elamites, the Aryan Persian language dominates the empire until the Aryan Greek ousts it from official life. Meanwhile the plough does its work year by year, the harvests are gathered, the builders build as they are told, the tradesmen work and acquire fresh devices ; the knowledge of writing spreads, novel things, the horse and wheeled vehicles and iron, are introduced and become part of the permanent inheritance of mankind ; the volume of trade upon sea and desert increases, men's ideas widen, and knowledge grows. There are set-backs, massacres, pestilence ; but the story is, on the whole, one of enlargement. For four thousand years this new thing, civilization, which had set its root into the soil of the two rivers, grew as a tree grows ; now losing a limb, now stripped by a storm, but always growing and resuming its growth. After four thousand years the warriors and conquerors were still going to and fro over this growing thing they did not under-

when it collapsed before the attack of Cyrus, the founder of the Persian power. . . .

So the story goes on. In 330 B.C., as we shall tell later in some detail, a Greek conqueror, Alexander the Great, is looking on the murdered body of the last of the Persian rulers.

The story of the Tigris and Euphrates civilizations, of which we have given as yet only the bare outline, is a story of conquest following after conquest, and each conquest replaces old rulers and ruling classes by new ; races like the Sumerian and the Elamite are swallowed up, their languages vanish, they interbreed and are lost, the Assyrian melts away into Chaldean and Syrian, the Hittites become Aryanized and lose distinction, the Semites who swallowed up the

ASSYRIAN SCULPTURE OF LIONS SLAIN BY SARDANAPALUS.

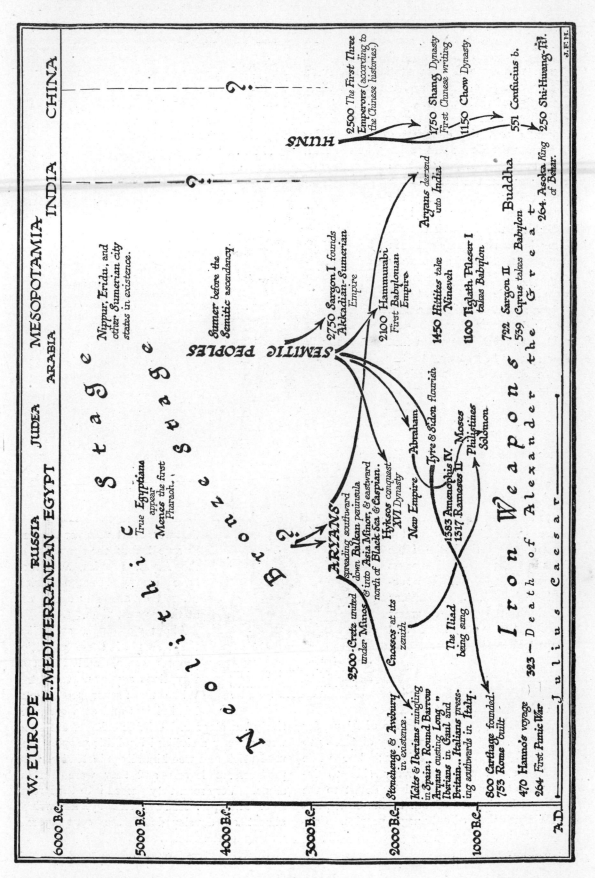

W. EUROPE   RUSSIA   JUDEA   MESOPOTAMIA
E. MEDITERRANEAN   EGYPT   ARABIA   INDIA   CHINA

J.F.H.

6000 B.C.

Neolithic Stage

5000 B.C.

True Egyptians appear
Menes the first Pharaoh.

Nippur, Eridu, and other Sumerian city states in existence.

4000 B.C.

Bronze Stage

?

Sumer before the Semitic ascendancy.

3000 B.C.

ARYANS

SEMITIC PEOPLES

2750 Sargon I founds Akkadian-Sumerian Empire

2500 - Crete united under Minos.

ARYANS spreading southward down Balkan peninsula & into Asia Minor, & eastward north of Black Sea & Caspian.

Hyksos conquest
XVI Dynasty

2100 Hammurabi First Babylonian Empire

2500 The First Three Emperors (according to the Chinese histories).

2000 B.C.

Knossos at its zenith

New Empire

Abraham

Tyre & Sidon flourish

1450 Hittites take Nineveh

Aryans descend into India

1750 Shang Dynasty First Chinese writing

1150 Chow Dynasty

Stonehenge & Avebury in existence.

Kelts & Iberians mingling in Spain; Round Barrow Aryans ousting Long "Iberians in Gaul and Britain... Italians pressing southwards in Italy.

The Iliad being sung

1383 Amenophis IV.
1517 Ramases II.

Moses
Philistines
Solomon.

1100 Tiglath Pileser I takes Babylon

HUNS

1000 B.C.

800 Carthage founded.
753 Rome built

Iron Weapons

722 Sargon II
539 Cyrus takes Babylon

Buddha

551 Confucius b.

470 Hanno's voyage
264 First Punic War

323 — Death of Alexander the Great

264. Asoka King of Behar.

250 Shi-Huang-Ti.

A.D.

Julius Caesar

111

stand, but men had now (330 B.C.) got iron, horses, writing and computation, money, a greater variety of foods and textiles, a wider knowledge of their world.

The time that elapsed between the empire of Sargon I and the conquest of Babylon by Alexander the Great was as long, be it noted, at the least estimate, as the time from Alexander the Great to the present day. And before the time of Sargon, men had been settled in the Sumerian land, living in towns, worshipping in temples, following an orderly Neolithic agricultural life in an organized community for at least as long again. "Eridu, Lagash, Ur, Uruk, Larsa, have already an immemorial past when first they appear in history." [1]

One of the most difficult things for both the writer and student of history is to sustain the sense of these time intervals and prevent these ages becoming shortened by perspective in his imagination. Half the duration of human civilization and the keys to all its chief institutions are to be found *before* Sargon I. Moreover, the reader cannot too often compare the scale of the dates in these latter fuller pages of man's history with the succession of countless generations to which the time diagrams given with Chapter X and Chapter II bear witness.

§ 3

The story of the Nile valley from the dawn of its traceable

The Early History of Egypt. history until the time of Alexander the Great is not very dissimilar to that of Babylonia; but while Babylonia lay open on every side to invasion, Egypt was protected by desert to the west and by desert and sea to the east, while to the south she had only negro peoples. Consequently her history is less broken by the in-

[1] Winckler (Craig), *History of Babylonia and Assyria.*

vasions of strange races than is the history of Assyria and Babylon, and until towards the eighth century B.C., when she fell under an Ethiopian dynasty, whenever a conqueror did come into her story, he came in from Asia by way of the Isthmus of Suez.

The Stone Age remains in Egypt are of very uncertain date; there are Palæolithic and then Neolithic remains. It is not certain whether the Neolithic pastoral people who left those remains were the direct ancestors of the later Egyptians. In many respects they differed entirely from their successors. They buried their dead, but before they buried them they cut up the bodies and apparently ate portions of the flesh. They seem to have done this out of a feeling of reverence for the departed; the dead were "eaten with honour" according to the phrase of Mr. Flinders Petrie. It may have been that the survivors hoped to retain thereby some vestige of the strength and virtue that had died. Traces of similar savage customs have been found in the long barrows that were scattered over Western Europe before the spreading of the Aryan peoples, and they have pervaded negro Africa, where they are only dying out at the present time.

About 5,000 B.C., or earlier, the traces of these primitive peoples cease, and the true Egyptians appear on the scene. While the former people were hut builders and at a comparatively low stage of Neolithic culture, the latter were already a civilized Neolithic people; they used brick and wood buildings instead of their predecessors' hovels, and they were working stone. Very soon they passed into the Bronze Age. They possessed a system of picture writing almost as developed as the contemporary writings of the Sumerians, but quite different in character. Possibly there was an irruption from

Photo: Mansell.

EARLY FIGURE OF THE EGYPTIAN HIPPOPOTAMUS GODDESS.

THE HEAD OF AN EARLY EGYPTIAN (FOURTH DYNASTY), COLOURED LIMESTONE
STATUE OF A GREAT LADY, THE PRINCESS NEFERT, WHO LIVED NEARLY SIX
THOUSAND YEARS AGO.

Photo: Bonfils.

PYRAMID OF SAKHARAH, THE OLDEST PYRAMID, BUILT LONG BEFORE THE GREAT PYRAMIDS
OF THE FOURTH DYNASTY.

Southern Arabia by way of Aden, of a fresh people, who came into upper Egypt and descended slowly towards the delta of the Nile. Dr. Wallis Budge writes of them as "conquerors from the East." It is tempting to think of their coming originally from the already long-established civilization of Sumeria. But their gods and their ways, like their picture writing, were very different from the Sumerian. One of the earliest known figures of a deity is that of a hippopotamus goddess, and so very distinctively African.[1]

The clay of the Nile is not so fine and plastic as the Sumerian clay, and the Egyptians made no use of it for writing. But they early resorted to strips of the papyrus reed fastened together, from whose name comes our word "paper."

The broad outline of the history of Egypt is simpler than the history of Mesopotamia. It has long been the custom to divide the rulers of Egypt into a succession of Dynasties, and in speaking of the periods of Egyptian history it is usual to speak of the first, fourth, fourteenth, and so on, Dynasty. The Egyptians were ultimately conquered by the Persians after their establishment in Babylon, and when finally Egypt fell to Alexander the Great in 332 B.C., it was Dynasty XXXI that came to an end. In that long history of over 4,000 years, a much longer period than that between the career of Alexander the Great and the present day, certain broad phases of development may be noted here. There was a phase known as the "old kingdom," which culminated in the IVth Dynasty; this Dynasty marks a period of wealth and splendour, and its monarchs were obsessed by such a passion for making monuments for themselves as no men have ever before or since had a chance to display and gratify. It was Cheops [2] and Chephren and Mycerinus of this IVth Dynasty who raised the vast piles of the great and the second and the

[1] "The original home or centre of development of this 'Dynastic' Egyptian type seems to have been in Southern or South-western Arabia. This region of South-western and Southern Arabia, ten to fifteen thousand years ago, was probably an even better favoured province than it is at the present day, when it still bears the Roman designation of Arabia Felix—so much of the rest of this gaunt, lava-covered, sand-strewn peninsula being decidedly 'infelix.' It has high mountains, a certain degree of rainfall on them, and was anciently clothed in rich forests before the camels, goats, and sheep of Neolithic and Bronze Age man nibbled away much of this verdure. Above all there grew trees oozing with delicious-scented resins or gums. These, when civilization dawned on the world, became very precious and an offering of sweet savour to the civilized man's gods, because so grateful to his own nostrils" (*Africa*, by Sir H. H. Johnston).

[2] 3,733 B.C., Wallis Budge.

third pyramids at Gizeh. These unmeaning sepulchral piles, of an almost incredible vastness,[1] erected in an age when engineering science had scarcely begun, exhausted the resources of Egypt through three long reigns, and left her wasted as if by a war.

The story of Egypt from the IVth to the XVth Dynasty is a story of conflicts between alternative capitals and competing religions, of separations into several kingdoms and reunions. It is, so to speak, an internal history. Here we can name only one of that long series of

Hammurabi founded was flourishing, but the exact correspondences of dates between early Egypt and Babylonia are still very doubtful. Only after a long period of servitude did a popular uprising expel these foreigners again.

After the war of liberation (*circa* 1,600 B.C.) there followed a period of great prosperity in Egypt, *the New Empire*. Egypt became a great and united military state, and pushed her expeditions at last as far as the Euphrates, and so the age-long struggle between the Egyptian and Babylonian-Assyrian power began.

THE ARRIVAL OF A TRIBE OF SEMITIC NOMADS IN EGYPT, ABOUT THE YEAR 1,895 B.C.
Ancient Egyptian wall-painting in a tomb near Beni Hassan, Middle Egypt.

Pharaohs, Pepi II, who reigned ninety years, the longest reign in history, and left a great abundance of inscriptions and buildings. At last there happened to Egypt what happened so frequently to the civilizations of Mesopotamia. Egypt was conquered by nomadic Semites, who founded a " shepherd " dynasty, the Hyksos (XVIth), which was finally expelled by native Egyptians. This invasion probably happened while that first Babylonian Empire which

[1] The great pyramid is 450 feet high and its side 700 feet long. It is calculated (says Wallis Budge) to weigh 4,883,000 tons. All this stone was lugged into place chiefly by human muscle.

For a time Egypt was an ascendant power. Thothmes III[2] and his son Amenophis III

[2] There are variants to these names, and to most Egyptian names, for few self-respecting Egyptologists will tolerate the spelling of their colleagues. One may find, for instance, Thethmosis, Thoutmosis, Tahutmes, Thutmose, or Tethmosis; Amunothph, Amenhotep, or Amenothes. A pleasing variation is to break up the name, as, for instance, Amen Hetep. This particular little constellation of variants is given here not only because it is amusing, but because it is desirable that the reader should know such variations exist. For most names the rule of this book has been to follow whatever usage has established itself in English literature, regardless of the possible contemporary pronunciation. Amenophis, for example, has been so written

(XVIIIth Dynasty) ruled from Ethiopia to the Euphrates in the fifteenth century B.C. For various reasons these names stand out with unusual distinctness in the Egyptian record. They were great builders, and left many monuments and inscriptions. Amenophis III founded Luxor, and added greatly to Karnak. At Tel-el-Amarna a mass of letters has been found, the royal correspondence with Babylonian and Hittite and other monarchs, including that Tushratta who took Nineveh, throwing a flood of light upon the political and social affairs of this particular age. Of Amenophis IV we shall have more to tell later, but of one, the most extraordinary and able of Egyptian monarchs, Queen Hatasu, the aunt and stepmother of Thotmes III, we have no space to tell. She is represented upon her monuments in masculine garb, and with a long beard as a symbol of wisdom.

Thereafter there was a brief Syrian conquest of Egypt, a series of changing dynasties, among which we may note the XIXth, which included Rameses II, a great builder of temples, who reigned seventy-seven years (about 1,317 to 1,250 B.C.), and who is supposed by some to have been the Pharaoh of Moses, and the XXIInd, which included Shishak, who plundered Solomon's temple (*circa* 930 B.C.). An Ethiopian conqueror from the Upper Nile founded the XXVth Dynasty, a foreign dynasty, which went down (670 B.C.) before the new Assyrian Empire created by Tiglath Pileser III, Sargon II, and Sennacherib, of which we have already made mention.

The days of any Egyptian predominance over foreign nations was drawing to an end. For a time under Psammetichus I of the XXVIth Dynasty (664–610 B.C.) native rule was restored, and Necho II recovered for a time the old Egyptian possessions in Syria up to the Euphrates while the Medes and Chaldeans were attacking Nineveh. From those gains Necho II was routed out again after the fall of Nineveh

in English books for two centuries. It came into the language by indirect routes, but it is now as fairly established as is Damascus as the English name of a Syrian town. Nevertheless, there are limits to this classicism. The writer, after some vacillation, has abandoned Oliver Goldsmith and Dr. Johnson in the case of " Peisistratus " and " Keltic," which were formerly spelt " Pisistratus " and " Celtic."

and the Assyrians by Nebuchadnezzar II, the great Chaldean king, the Nebuchadnezzar of the Bible. The Jews, who had been the allies of Necho II, were taken into captivity by Nebuchadnezzar to Babylon.

When, in the sixth century B.C., Chaldea fell to the Persians, Egypt followed suit, a

Photo: Mansell.
VERY EARLY BRONZE FIGURE REPRESENTING I-EM-HETEP, THE ARCHITECT OF THE EARLIEST PYRAMID.

rebellion later made Egypt independent once more for sixty years, and in 332 B.C. she welcomed Alexander the Great as her conqueror, to be ruled thereafter by foreigners, first by Greeks, then by Romans, then in succession by Arabs, Turks, and British, until the present day.

Such briefly is the history of Egypt from its beginnings ; a history first of isolation and then of increasing entanglement with the affairs of other nations, as increasing facilities of communication drew the peoples of the world into closer and closer interaction.

§ 4

The history we need to tell here of India is simpler even than this brief record of Egypt. **The Early Civilization of India.** Somewhere about the time of Hammurabi or later, a branch of the Aryan-speaking people who then occupied North Persia and Afghanistan, pushed down the north-west passes into India. They conquered their way until they prevailed over all the darker populations of North India, and spread their rule or influence over the whole peninsula. They never achieved any unity in India ; their history is a history of warring kings and republics. The Persian empire, in the days of its expansion after the capture of Babylon, pushed its boundaries beyond the Indus, and later Alexander the Great marched as far as the border of the desert that separates the Punjab from the Ganges valley. But with this bare statement we will for a time leave the history of India.

§ 5

Meanwhile, as this triple system of White **The Early History of China.** Man civilization developed in India and in the lands about the meeting-places of Asia, Africa, and Europe, another and quite distinct civilization was developing and spreading out either from the then fertile but now dry and desolate valley of the Tarim

CHEOPS.

or from the upper valley of the Yellow River (the Hwang-ho), down the course of the Hwang-ho, and into the valley of the Yang-tsze-kiang. We know practically nothing as yet of the archæology of China, we do not know anything of the Stone Age in that part of the world, and at present our ideas of the early history of this civilization are derived almost entirely from the Chinese literature. It has evidently been from the first and throughout a Mongolian civilization. Until after the time of Alexander the Great there are no traces of any Aryan or Semitic, much less of Hamitic influence. All such influences were still in another world, separated by mountains, deserts, and wild nomadic tribes until that time. The Chinese seem to have made their civilization spontaneously and unassisted. Some recent writers suppose indeed a connection with ancient Sumeria. Of course both China and Sumeria arose on the basis of the almost world-wide early Neolithic culture, but the Tarim valley and the lower Euphrates are separated by such vast obstacles of mountain and desert as to forbid the idea of any migration or interchange of peoples who had once settled down.

But though the civilization of China is wholly Mongolian (as we have defined Mongolian), it does not follow that the northern roots are the only ones from which it grew. We Europeans know very little as yet of the ethnology and pre-history of southern China. There the Chinese mingle with such kindred peoples as the Siamese and Burmese, and seem to bridge over towards the darker Dravidian peoples and towards the Malays. It is quite probable, indeed it is highly probable, that there were southern as well as northern beginnings of a civilization, and that the Chinese civilization that comes into history 2,000 years B.C. is the result of a long process of prehistoric minglings and interchange between a southern and a northern culture. The southern Chinese played perhaps the rôle towards the northern Chinese that the Hamites or Sumerians played to the Aryan and Semitic peoples in the west, or that the settled Dravidians played towards the Aryans in India. But so little is known as yet of this attractive chapter in pre-history, that we cannot dwell upon it further here.

The chief foreigners mentioned in the early annals of China were a Ural-Altaic people on the north-east frontier, the Huns, against whom certain of the earlier emperors made war. In the account of the first " Three Emperors " history has been sacrificed to moral edification. Those incredibly model and exemplary beings are alleged to have reigned about 2,500 B.C. Before that time the history of China is evidently altogether mythological.

There follows upon these first three emperors a series of dynasties, of whom the account becomes more and more exact and convincing as they become more recent. China has to tell a long history of border warfare and of graver struggles between the settled and nomad peoples. To begin with, China, like Sumer and like Egypt, was a land of city states. The government was at first a government of numerous kings ; they became loosely feudal under an emperor, as the Egyptians did ; and then later, as with the Egyptians, came a centralizing empire. Shang (1,750 to 1,125 B.C.) and Chow (1,125 to 250 B.C.) are named as being the two great dynasties of the feudal period. Bronze vessels of these earlier dynasties, beautiful, splendid, and with a distinctive style of their own, still exist, and there can be no doubt of the existence of a high state of culture even before the days of Shang.

It is perhaps a sense of symmetry that made the later historians of Egypt and China talk of the earlier phases of their national history as being under dynasties comparable to the

Photo: Mansell.

EARLY EGYPTIAN PAINTED CARVING.

dynasties of the later empires, and of such early "Emperors" as Menes (in Egypt) or the First Three Emperors (in China). The early dynasties exercised far less centralized powers than the later ones. Such unity as China possessed under the Shang Dynasty was a religious rather than an effective political union. The "Son of Heaven" offered sacrifices for all the Chinese. There was a common script, a common civilization, and a common enemy in the Huns of the north-western borders.

The last of the Shang Dynasty was a cruel and foolish monarch who burnt himself alive (1,125 B.C.) in his palace after a decisive defeat by Wu Wang, the founder of the Chow Dynasty. Wu Wang seems to have been helped by the Huns or by allies among the Huns as well as by a popular revolt.

Photo : Mansell.
HEAD OF COLOSSAL STATUE OF THOTHMES III, FROM KARNAK.

that between the eighth and fourth centuries B.C. "there were in the Hoang-ho and Yang-tse valleys no less than five or six thousand small states with about a dozen powerful states dominating over them." The land was subjected to perpetual warfare ("Age of Confusion"). In the sixth century B.C. the great powers in conflict were Tsi and Tsin, which were northern Hoang-ho states, and Tso, which was a vigorous, aggressive power in the Yangtse valley. A confederation against Tso laid the foundation for a league that kept the peace for a hundred years; the league subdued and incorporated Tso and made a general treaty of disarmament. It became the foundation of a new pacific empire.

The knowledge of iron entered China at some unknown date, but iron weapons began to be commonly used only about 500 B.C., that is to say, two or three hundred years or more after this had become customary in Assyria, Egypt, and Europe. Iron was probably introduced from the north into China by the Huns.

For a time China remained loosely united under the Chow emperors, as loosely united as was Christendom under the popes in the Middle Ages ; the Chow emperors had become the traditional high priests of the land in the place of the Shang Dynasty and claimed a sort of overlordship in Chinese affairs, but gradually the loose ties of usage and sentiment that held the empire together lost their hold upon men's minds. Hunnish peoples to the north and west took on the Chinese civilization without acquiring a sense of its unity. Feudal princes began to regard themselves as independent. Mr. Liang-chi-Chao,[1] one of the Chinese representatives at the Paris Conference of 1919, states

[1] *China and the League of Nations,* a pamphlet by Mr. Liang-Chi-Chao. (Pekin Leader Office.)

The last rulers of the Chow Dynasty were ousted by the kings of Tsin, the latter seized upon the sacred sacrificial bronze tripods, and so were able to take over the imperial duty of offering sacrifices to Heaven. In this manner was the Tsin dynasty established. It ruled with far more vigour and effect than any previous family. Shi-Hwang-ti of this dynasty is called by Chinese historians "the first universal emperor," and his reign is usually taken to mark the end of feudal and divided China. He seems to have played the unifying rôle in the east that Alexander the Great might have played in the west, but he lived longer, and the unity he made (or restored) was comparatively permanent, while the empire of Alexander the Great fell to pieces, as we shall tell, at his death. Shi-Hwang-ti, among other feats in the direction of common effort, organized the building of the Great Wall of China against the Huns. A civil war followed close upon his reign, and ended in the establishment of the Han Dynasty. Under this Han Dynasty the empire grew greatly beyond its original two river valleys, the Huns were effectively restrained, and the Chinese penetrated westward until they began to learn at last of civilized races and civilizations other than their own.

By 100 B.C. the Chinese had heard of India, their power had spread across Tibet and into Western Turkestan, and they were trading by camel caravans with Persia and the western world. So much for the present must suffice for our account of China. We shall return to the distinctive characters of its civilization later.

§ 6

And in these thousands of years during which man was making his way step by step from **While the** nomadic savagery to civilization **Civilizations** at these old-world centres, what **were growing.** was happening in the rest of the world? In Central and Southern Africa the negro was making a slower progress, and that, it would seem, under the stimulus of invasion by whiter tribes from the Mediterranean regions, bringing with them in succession cultivation and the use of metals. These white men came to the black by two routes : across the Sahara to the west as Berbers and Tuaregs and the like, to mix with the negro and create such quasi-white races as the Fulas ; and also by way of the Nile, where the Baganda (= Ganda-folk) of Uganda, for example, may possibly be of remote white origin. The African forests were denser then, and spread eastward and northward from the Upper Nile.

The islands of Oceania, three thousand years ago, were probably still only inhabited here and there by stranded patches of Palæolithic Australoids, who had wandered thither in those immemorial ages when there was a land bridge by way of the East Indies to Australia. The spreading of the heliolithic peoples by sea going canoes into the islands of the Pacific came much later in the history of man. Still later did they reach Madagascar. The beauty of New Zealand also was as yet wasted upon mankind ; its highest living creatures were a great ostrich-like bird, the moa, now extinct, and the little kiwi which has feathers like coarse hair and the merest rudiment of wings.

In North America a group of Mongoloid tribes were now cut off altogether from the old world.

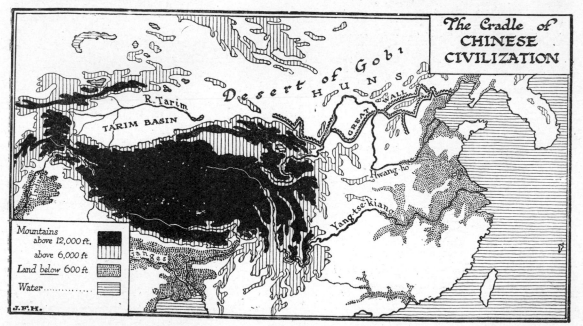

The Cradle of CHINESE CIVILIZATION

Mountains
above 12,000 ft.
above 6,000 ft.
Land below 600 ft.
Water

They were spreading slowly southward, hunting the innumerable bison of the plains. They had still to learn for themselves the secrets of a separate agriculture based on maize, and in South America to tame the lama to their service, and so build up in Mexico and Peru two civilizations roughly parallel in their nature to that of Sumer, but different in many respects, and later by six or seven thousand years. . . .

When men reached the southern extremity of America, the *Megatherium*, the giant sloth, and the *Glyptodon*, the giant armadillo, were still living. . . .

There is a considerable imaginative appeal in the obscure story of the early American civilizations. It was almost certainly an almost entirely separate development ; there is very little evidence of any immigrants bringing later arts or traditions from either Asia or Europe after the palæolithic, or at latest the heliolithic phase. These peoples got to the use of bronze and copper, but not to the use of iron ; they had gold and silver ; and their stonework, their pottery, weaving, and dyeing were carried to a very high level. In all these things the American product resembles the old-world product *generally*, but always it has characteristics that are all its own. The American civilizations had picture-writing of a primitive sort, but it never developed even to the pitch of the earliest Egyptian hieroglyphics. In Yucatan only was there a kind of script, the Maya writing, but it was used simply for keeping a calendar. In Peru the beginnings of writing were superseded by a curious and complicated method of keeping records by means of knots tied upon strings of various colours and shapes. It is said that even laws and orders could be conveyed by this code. These string bundles were called *quipus*, but though *quipus* are still to be found in collections, the art of reading them is altogether lost. The Peruvians also got to making maps and the use of counting-frames. "But with all this there was no means of handing on knowledge and experience from one generation to another, nor was anything done to fix and summarize these intellectual possessions, which are the basis of literature and science."[1] When the Spaniards came to America, the Mexicans knew nothing of the Peruvians nor the Peruvians of the Mexicans. Intercourse had not begun. The Mexicans had never heard of the potato, which was a principal article of Peruvian diet. In 5,000 B.C. the Sumerians and Egyptians probably knew as little of one another. America was 6,000 years behind the Old World.

CHRONOLOGICAL NOTE

Here we would call the reader's attention to the chronological diagram on page 111. By the scale of this diagram, the one given on page 58 would be 44 inches long, that on page 38, 44 feet, and the diagram of the whole of geological time on p. 10 between a mile and ten miles long.

[1] F. Ratzel, *History of Mankind.*

XVII

SEA PEOPLES AND TRADING PEOPLES

§ I

THE first boats were made very early by riverside peoples. They were no more than trees and floating wood, used to assist the very imperfect natural swimming powers of men. Then came the hollowing out of the trees, and then, with the development of tools and a primitive carpentry, the building of boats. Men in Egypt and Mesopotamia also developed very early a type of basketwork boat, caulked with bitumen. Such was the "ark of bulrushes" in which Moses was hidden by his mother. A kindred sort of vessel grew up by the use of skins and hides expanded upon a wicker framework. To this day cow-hide wicker boats (coracles) are used upon the west coast of Ireland, where there is plenty of cattle and a poverty of big trees. They are also used on the Euphrates, and they were until recently employed in South Wales. Inflated skins may have preceded the coracle, and are still used on the Euphrates. In the valleys of the great rivers, boats must early have become an important means of communication; and it seems natural to suppose that it was from the mouths of the great rivers that man, already in a reasonably seaworthy vessel, first ventured out upon what must have seemed to him then the trackless and homeless sea.

No doubt he ventured at first as a fisherman, having learnt the elements of seacraft in creeks and lagoons. Men may have navigated boats upon the Levantine lake before the refilling of the Mediterranean by the Atlantic waters. Possibly the first men to paddle out into salt water were Sumerians, coming out from the Euphrates and Tigris, which in 7,000 B.C. fell by separate mouths into the Persian Gulf. The Sumerian city of Eridu, which stood at the head of the Persian Gulf (from which it is now separated by a hundred and thirty miles of alluvium [1]), had ships upon the sea very early indeed. We find evidence of a fully developed sea life six thousand years ago in the eastern end of the Mediterranean, and possibly at that time also there were canoes on the seas among the islands of the nearer East Indies.

Very soon the seafaring men must have realized the peculiar freedom and opportunities the ship gave them. They could get away to islands; no chief nor king could pursue a boat or ship with any certainty; every captain was a king. The seamen would find it easy to make nests upon islands and in strong positions on the mainland. There they could harbour, there they could carry on a certain agriculture and fishery; but their speciality and their main business was, of course, the expeditions across the sea. That was not usually a trading expedition; it was much more frequently a piratical raid. From what we know of mankind, we are bound to conclude that the first sailors plundered when they could, and traded when they had to.

[1] Sayce.

Boats on the Nile, about 2500 B.C   [From Torr's "Ancient Ships".]

Because it developed in the comparatively warm and tranquil waters of the eastern Mediterranean, the Red Sea, the Persian Gulf, and the western horn of the Indian Ocean, the shipping of the ancient world retained throughout certain characteristics that make it differ very widely from the ocean-going sailing shipping, with its vast spread of canvas, of the last four hundred years. "The Mediterranean," says Mr. Torr,[1] "is a sea where a vessel with

And that practice may really have ceased before 2,500 B.C., despite the testimony of monuments of that date; for in monuments dating from about 1,250 B.C., crews are represented unmistakably rowing with their faces towards the stern and yet grasping their oars in the attitude of paddling, so that even then Egyptian artists mechanically followed the turn of the hieroglyph to which their hands were accustomed. In these reliefs there are

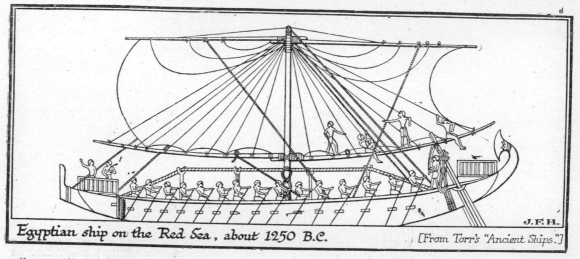

Egyptian ship on the Red Sea, about 1250 B.C.   [From Torr's "Ancient Ships."]

sails may lie becalmed for days together, while a vessel with oars would easily be traversing the smooth waters, with coasts and islands everywhere at hand to give her shelter in case of storm. In that sea, therefore, oars became the characteristic instruments of navigation, and the arrangement of oars the chief problem in shipbuilding. And so long as the Mediterranean nations dominated Western Europe, vessels of the southern type were built upon the northern coasts, though there generally was wind enough here for sails and too much wave for oars. . . . The art of rowing can first be discerned upon the Nile. Boats with oars are represented in the earliest pictorial monuments of Egypt, dating from about 2,500 B.C.; and although some crews are paddling with their faces towards the bow, others are rowing with their faces towards the stern. The paddling is certainly the older practice, for the hieroglyph *chen* depicts two arms grasping an oar in the attitude of paddling, and the hieroglyphs were invented in the earliest ages.

[1] Cecil Torr, *Ancient Ships*

twenty rowers on the boats on the Nile, and thirty on the ships on the Red Sea; but in the earliest reliefs the number varies considerably, and seems dependent on the amount of space at the sculptor's disposal."

The Aryan peoples came late to the sea. The earliest ships on the sea were either Sumerian or Hamitic; the Semitic peoples followed close upon these pioneers. Along the eastern end of the Mediterranean, the Phœnicians, a Semitic people, set up a string of independent harbour towns of which Acre, Tyre, and Sidon were the chief; and later they pushed their voyages westward and founded Carthage in North Africa and Utica. Possibly Phœnician keels were already in the Mediterranean by 2,000 B.C. Both Tyre and Sidon were originally on islands, and so easily defensible against a land raid. But before we go on to the marine exploits of this, the first great sea-going race, we must note a very remarkable and curious nest of early sea people whose remains have recently been discovered in Crete.[2]

[2] See Evans' *Prehistoric Tombs of Cnossos*.

§ 2

These early Cretans were of unknown race, but probably of a race akin to the Iberians of Spain and Western Europe and the dark whites of Asia Minor and North Africa, and their language is unknown. This race lived not only in Crete, but in Cyprus, Greece, Asia Minor, Sicily, and South Italy. It was a civilized people for long ages before the fair Aryan Greeks spread southward through Macedonia. At Cnossos, in Crete, there have been found the most astonishing ruins and remains, and Cnossos, therefore, is apt to overshadow the rest of these settlements in people's imaginations, but it is well to bear in mind that though Cnossos was no doubt a chief city of this Ægean civilization, these "Ægeans" had in the fullness of their time many cities and a wide range. Possibly, all that we know of them now are but the vestiges of a far more extensive Neolithic civilization which is now submerged under the waters of the Mediterranean.

At Cnossos there are Neolithic remains as old or older than any of the pre-dynastic remains of Egypt. The Bronze Age began in Crete as soon as it did in Egypt, and there have been vases found by Flinders Petrie in Egypt and referred by him to the Ist Dynasty, which he declared to be importations from Crete. Stone vessels have been found in Crete of forms characteristic of the IVth (pyramid-building) Dynasty, and there can be no doubt that there was a vigorous trade between Crete and Egypt in the time of the XIIth Dynasty. This continued until about 1,000 B.C. It is clear that this island civilization arising upon the soil of Crete is at least as old as the Egyptian, and that it was already launched upon the sea as early as 4,000 B.C.

The great days of Crete were not so early as this. It was only about 2,500 B.C. that the island appears to have been unified under one ruler. Then began an age of peace and prosperity unexampled in the history of the ancient world. Secure from invasion, living in a delightful climate, trading with every civilized community in the world, the Cretans were free to develop all the arts and amenities of life.

The Ægean Cities before History.

Photo: Mansell.

B.C. 668. A SHIP OF THE KING OF TYRE IN THE ARABIAN GULF (ASSYRIAN STONE CARVING).

This Cnossos was not so much a town as the vast palace of the king and his people. It was not even fortified. The kings, it would seem, were called Minos always, as the kings of Egypt were all called Pharaoh; the king of Cnossos figures in the early legends of the Greeks as King Minos, who lived in the Labyrinth, who kept there a horrible monster, half man, half bull, the Minotaur, and levied a tribute of youths and maidens from the Athenians. Those

It is the custom nowadays to make a sort of wonder of these achievements of the Cretans, as though they were a people of incredible artistic ability living in the dawn of civilization. But their great time was long past that dawn; as late as 2,000 B.C. It took them many centuries to reach their best in art and skill, and their art and luxury are by no means so great a wonder if we reflect that for 3,000 years they were immune from invasion, that for a

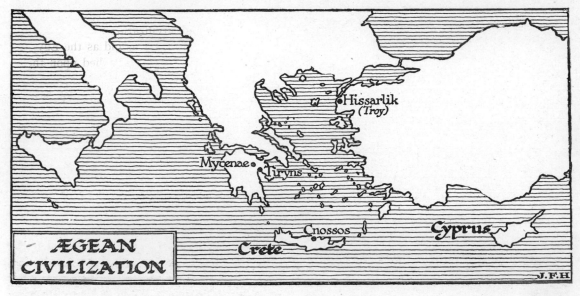

AEGEAN CIVILIZATION

stories are a part of Greek literature, and have always been known, but it is only in the last few decades that the excavations at Cnossos have revealed how close these legends were to the reality. The Cretan labyrinth was a building as stately, complex, and luxurious as any in the ancient world. Among other details we find waterpipes, bathrooms, and the like conveniences, such as have hitherto been regarded as among the latest refinements of modern life. The pottery, the textile manufactures, the sculpture and painting of these people, their gem and ivory work, their metal and inlaid work, is as admirable as any that mankind has produced. They were much given to festivals and shows, and, in particular, they were addicted to bull-fights and gymnastic entertainments. Their female costume became astonishingly " modern " in style; their women wore corsets and flounced dresses. They had a system of writing which has not yet been deciphered.

thousand years they were at peace. Century after century their artizans could perfect their skill and their men and women refine upon refinement. Wherever men of almost any race have been comparatively safe in this fashion for such a length of time, they have developed much artistic beauty. Given the opportunity, all races are artistic. Greek legend has it that it was in Crete that Dædalus attempted to make the first flying machine. Dædalus (= cunning artificer) was a sort of personified summary of mechanical skill. It is curious to speculate what germ of fact lies behind him and those waxen wings that, according to the legend, melted and plunged his son Icarus in the sea.

There came at last a change in the condition of the lives of these Cretans, for other peoples, the Greeks and the Phœnicians, were also coming out with powerful fleets upon the seas. We do not know what led to the disaster nor who inflicted it; but somewhen about 1,400

B.C. Cnossos was sacked and burnt, and though the Cretan life struggled on there rather lamely for another four centuries, there came at last a final blow about 1,000 B.C. (that is to say, in the days of the Assyrian ascendancy in the East). The palace at Cnossos was destroyed, and never rebuilt nor reinhabited. Possibly this was done by the ships of those new-comers into the Mediterranean, the barbaric Greeks, a group of Aryan tribes, who may have wiped out Cnossos as they wiped out the city of Troy. The legend of Theseus tells of such a raid. He entered the Labyrinth (which may have been the Cnossos Palace) by the aid of Ariadne, the daughter of Minos, and slew the Minotaur.

The *Iliad* makes it clear that destruction came upon Troy because the Trojans stole Greek women. Modern writers, with modern ideas in their heads, have tried to make out that the Greeks assailed Troy in order to secure a trade route or some such fine-spun commercial advantage. If so, the authors of the *Iliad* hid the motives of their characters very skilfully. It would be about as reasonable to say that the Homeric Greeks went to war with the Trojans in order to be well ahead with a station on the Berlin to Bagdad railway. The Homeric Greeks were a healthy barbaric Aryan people, with very poor ideas about trade and "trade routes"; they went to war with the Trojans because they were thoroughly annoyed about this stealing of women. It is fairly clear from the Minos legend and from the evidence of the Cnossos remains, that the Cretans kidnapped or stole youths and maidens to be slaves, bull-fighters, athletes, and perhaps sacrifices. They traded fairly with the Egyptians, but it may be they did not realize the gathering strength of the Greek barbarians; they "traded" violently with them, and so brought sword and flame upon themselves.[1]

Another great sea people were the Phœnicians.

[1] This is, I think, too dogmatic about Helen. True, raids on women were a real cause of war, but they were also a very favourite *ficelle* of fiction. A war with Troy might easily arise by the carrying off of a woman. But why was Troy destroyed six several times? It looks to me as if there was some strong motive for building just there, and an equally strong motive for great confederacies destroying the city when built.—G. M.

Photo: Maraghiannie.

RUINS OF THE GREAT CRETAN CITY-PALACE.

BEAUTIFULLY WORKED CRETAN GOLD CUP, SHOWING A BULL-FIGHT.

They were great seamen because they were great traders. Their colony of Carthage (founded before 800 B.C. by Tyre) became at last greater than any of the older Phœnician cities, but already before 1,500 B.C. both Sidon and Tyre had settlements upon the African coast. Carthage was comparatively inaccessible to the Assyrian and Babylonian hosts, and, profiting greatly by the long siege of Tyre by Nebuchadnezzar II, became the greatest maritime power the world had hitherto seen. She claimed the Western Mediterranean as her own, and seized every ship she could catch west of Sardinia. Roman writers accuse her of great cruelties. She fought the Greeks for Sicily, and later (in the second century B.C.) she fought the Romans. Alexander the Great formed plans for her conquest; but he died, as we shall tell later, before he could carry them out.

§ 3

At her zenith Carthage probably had the hitherto unheard-of population of a million. This population was largely indus-

The First Voyages of Exploration. trial, and her woven goods were universally famous. As well as a coasting trade, she had a considerable land trade with Central Africa,[1] and she sold negro slaves, ivory, metals, precious stones, and the like, to all the Mediterranean people; she worked Spanish copper mines, and her ships went out into the Atlantic and coasted along Portugal and France northward as far as the Cassiterides (the Scilly Isles, or Cornwall, in England) to get tin. About 520 B.C. a certain Hanno made a voyage that is still one of the most notable in the world. This Hanno, if we may trust the *Periplus of Hanno*, the Greek translation of his account which still survives, followed the African coast southward from the Straits of Gibraltar as far as the confines of Liberia. He had sixty big ships, and his main task was to found or reinforce certain Carthaginian stations upon the Morocco coast. Then he pushed southward. He founded a settlement in the Rio de Oro (on Kerne or Herne Island), and sailed on past the Senegal river. The voyagers passed on for seven days beyond the Gambia, and landed upon some island beyond. This they left in a panic, because, although the day was silent with the silence of the tropical forest, at night they heard the sound of flutes, drums, and gongs, and the sky was red with the blaze of the bush fires. The coast country for the rest of the voyage was one blaze of fire, from the burning of the bush. Streams of fire ran down the hills into the sea, and at length a blaze arose so loftily that it touched the skies. Three

[1] There were no domesticated camels in Africa until after the Persian conquest of Egypt. This must have greatly restricted the desert routes. (See Bunbury, *History of Ancient Geography*, note to Chap. VIII.) But the Sahara desert of 3,000 or 2,000 years ago was less parched and sterile than it is to-day. From rock engravings we may deduce the theory that the desert was crossed from oasis to oasis by riding oxen and by ox-carts: perhaps, also, on horses and asses. The camel as a beast of transport was seemingly not introduced into North Africa till the Arab invasions of the seventh century A.D. The fossil remains of camels are found in Algeria, and wild camels may have lingered in the wastes of the Sahara and Somaliland till the domesticated camel was introduced. The Nubian wild ass also seems to have extended its range to the Sahara.—H. H. J.

days further brought them to an island containing a lake (? Sherbro Island). In this lake was another island (? Macaulay Island), and on this were wild, hairy men and women, "whom the interpreters called gorilla." The Carthaginians, having caught some of the females of these "gorillas"—they were probably chimpanzees—turned back and eventually deposited the skins of their captives—who had proved impossibly violent guests to entertain on board ship—in the Temple of Juno.

A still more wonderful Phœnician sea voyage, long doubted, but now supported by some archæological evidence, is related by Herodotus, who declares that the Pharaoh Necho of the XXVIth Dynasty commissioned some Phœnicians to attempt the circumnavigation of Africa, and that starting from the Gulf of Suez southward, they did finally come back through the Mediterranean to the Nile delta. They took nearly three years to complete their voyage. Each year they landed, and sowed and harvested a crop of wheat before going on.

§ 4

The great trading cities of the Phœnicians are the most striking of the early manifestations of the peculiar and characteristic gift of the Semitic peoples to mankind, trade and exchange.[1] While the Semitic Phœnician peoples were spreading themselves upon the seas, another kindred

Early Traders.

[1] There was Sumerian trade organized round temples before the Semites got into Babylonia. See Hall and King, *Archæological Discoveries in Western Asia.*—E. B.

Photos: "British School at Athens."

CHINA FIGURE FROM CNOSSOS, A VOTARY OF THE SNAKE GODDESS.
NOTE THE CORSET AND FLOUNCES.

Semitic people, the Arameans, whose occupation of Damascus we have already noted, were developing the caravan routes of the Arabian and Persian deserts, and becoming the chief trading people of Western Asia. The Semitic peoples, earlier civilized than the Aryan, have always shown, and still show to-day, a far greater sense of quality and quantity in marketable goods than the latter; it is to their need of account-keeping that the development of alphabetical writing is to be ascribed, and it is to them that most of the great advances in computation are due. Our modern numerals

Photo: Mansell.

BRONZE LION WEIGHT (FROM ABYDOS), WITH PHŒNICIAN INSCRIPTION: "FOUND CORRECT BY THE COMMISSIONER FOR MONEY."

are Arabic; our arithmetic and algebra are essentially Semitic sciences.

The Semitic peoples, we may point out here, are to this day *counting peoples* strong in their sense of equivalents and reparation. The moral teaching of the Hebrews was saturated by such ideas. "With what measure ye mete, the same shall be meted unto you." Other races and peoples have imagined diverse and fitful and marvellous gods, but it was the trading Semites who first began to think of God as a Righteous Dealer, whose promises were kept, who failed not the humblest creditor, and called to account every spurious act.

The trade that was going on in the ancient world before the sixth or seventh century B.C. was almost entirely a barter trade. There was little or no credit or coined money. The ordinary standard of value with the early Aryans was cattle, as it still is with the Zulus and Kaffirs to-day. In the *Iliad*, the respective

values of two shields are stated in head of cattle, and the Roman word for moneys, *pecunia*, is derived from *pecus*, cattle. Cattle as money had this advantage; it did not need to be carried from one owner to another, and if it needed attention and food, at any rate it bred. But it was inconvenient for ship or caravan transit. Many other substances have at various times been found convenient as a standard; tobacco was once legal tender in the colonial days in North America, and in West Africa fines are paid and bargains made in bottles of trade gin. The early Asiatic trade included metals; and weighed lumps of metal, since they were in general demand and were convenient for hoarding and storage, costing nothing for fodder and needing small house-room, soon asserted their superiority over cattle and sheep. Iron, which seems to have been first reduced from its ores by the Hittites, was, to begin with, a rare and much-desired substance. It is stated by Aristotle to have supplied the first currency. In the collection of letters found at Tel-el-Amarna, addressed to and from Amenophis III (already mentioned) and his successor Amenophis IV, one from a Hittite king promises iron as a most precious gift. Gold, then as now, was the most precious, and therefore most portable, security. In early Egypt silver was almost as rare as gold until after the XVIIIth Dynasty. Later the general standard of value in the Eastern world became silver, measured by weight.

To begin with, metals were handed about in ingots and weighed at each transaction. Then they were stamped to indicate their fineness and guarantee their purity. The first recorded coins were minted about 600 B.C. in Lydia, a gold-producing country in the west of Asia Minor. The first-known gold coins were minted in Lydia by Crœsus, whose name has become a proverb for wealth; he was conquered, as we shall tell later, by that same Cyrus the Persian who took Babylon in 539 B.C. But

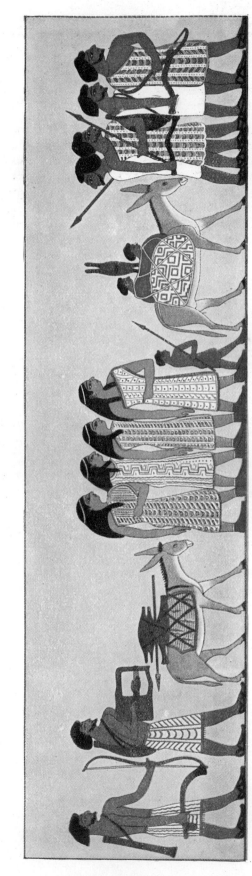

PAINTING FROM A TOMB IN MIDDLE EGYPT SHOWING A TRIBE OF SEMITIC NOMADS WITH THEIR WEAPONS
AND GEAR IN EGYPT. ABOUT 1,800–2,000 B.C.

129]

very probably coined money had been used in Babylonia before that time. The "sealed shekel," a stamped piece of silver, came very near to being a coin. The promise to pay so much silver or gold on "leather" (= parchment) with the seal of some established firm is probably as old or older than coinage. The Carthaginians used such "leather money." We know very little of the way in which small traffic was conducted. Common people, who in those ancient times were in dependent positions, seem to have had no money at all; they did their business by barter. Early Egyptian paintings show this going on.[1]

§ 5

When one realizes the absence of small money or of any conveniently portable means of exchange in the pre-Alexandrian world, one perceives how impossible was private travel in those days.[2] The first "inns"—no doubt a sort of caravanserai—are commonly said to have come into existence in Lydia in the third or fourth century B.C. That, however, is too late a date. They are certainly older than that. There is good evidence of them at least as early as the sixth century. Æschylus twice mentions inns. His word is "all-receiver," or "all-receiving house."[3] Private travellers must have been fairly common in the Greek world, including its colonies, by his time. But such

Early Travellers.

private travel was a comparatively new thing then. The early historians Hecatæus and Herodotus travelled widely. "I suspect," says Professor Gilbert Murray, "that this sort of travel 'for Historie' or 'for discovery' was rather a Greek invention. Solon is supposed to have practised it; and even Lycurgus." . . . The earlier travellers were traders travelling in a caravan or in a shipload, and carrying their goods and their minas and shekels of metal or gems or bales of fine stuff with them, or government officials travelling with letters of introduction and a proper retinue. Possibly there were a few mendicants, and, in some restricted regions, religious pilgrims.

That earlier world before 600 B.C. was one in which a lonely "stranger" was a rare and suspected and endangered being. He might suffer horrible cruelties, for there was little law to protect such as he. Few individuals strayed therefore. One lived and died attached and tied to some patriarchal tribe, if one was a nomad, or to some great household if one was civilized, or to one of the big temple establishments which we will presently discuss. Or one was a herded slave. One knew nothing, except for a few monstrous legends, of the rest of the world in which one lived. We know more to-day, indeed, of the world of 600 B.C. than any single living being knew at that time. We map it out, see it as a whole in relation to past and future. We begin to learn precisely what was going on at the same time in Egypt and Spain and Medea and India and China. We can share in imagination, not only the wonder of Hanno's sailors, but of the men who lit the warning beacons on the shore. We know that those "mountains flaming to the sky" were only the customary burning of the dry grass at that season of the year. Year by year, more and more rapidly, our common knowledge increases. In the years to come men will understand still more of those lives in the past, until perhaps they will understand them altogether.

[1] The earliest coinage of the west coast of Asia Minor was in electrum, a mixture of gold and silver, and there is an interesting controversy as to whether the first issues were stamped by cities, temples, or private bankers.—P. G.

[2] Small change was in existence before the time of Alexander. The Athenians had a range of exceedingly small silver coins running almost down to the size of a pinhead, which were generally carried in the mouth; a character in Aristophanes was suddenly assaulted, and swallowed his change in consequence.—P. G.

[3] There is an inn-keeper in Aristophanes, but it may be inferred from the circumstance that she is represented as letting lodgings in hell, that the early inn left much to be desired.—P. G.

XVIII

WRITING

§ 1

Picture Writing.

IN the five preceding chapters (XIII to XVII) we have sketched in broad outline the development of the chief human communities from the primitive beginnings of the heliolithic culture to the great historical kingdoms and empires in the sixth century B.C. We must now study a little more closely the general process of social change, the growth of human ideas, and the elaboration of human relationships that was going on during these ages between 10,000 B.C. and 500 B.C. What we have done so far is to draw the map and name the chief kings and empires, to define the relations in time and space of Babylonia, Assyria, Egypt, Phœnicia, Cnossos, and the like ; we come now to the real business of history, which is to get down below these outer forms to the thoughts and lives of individual men.

By far the most important thing that was going on during those fifty or sixty centuries of social development was the invention of writing and its gradual progress to importance in human affairs. It was a new instrument for the human mind, an enormous enlargement of its range of action, a new means of continuity. We have seen how in later Palæolithic and early Neolithic times the elaboration of articulate speech gave men a mental handhold for consecutive thought, and a vast enlargement of their powers of co-operation. For a time this new acquirement seems to have overshadowed their earlier achievement of drawing, and possibly it checked the use of gesture. But drawing presently reappeared again, for record, for signs, for the joy of drawing. Before real writing came picture-writing, such as is still practised by the Amerindians, the Bushmen, and savage and barbaric people in all parts of the world. It is essentially a drawing of things and acts, helped out by heraldic indications of proper names, and by strokes and dots to represent days and distances and such-like quantitative ideas.

Quite kindred to such picture-writing is the pictograph that one finds still in use to-day in international railway time-tables upon the continent of Europe, where a little black sign of a cup indicates a stand-up buffet for light refreshments ; a crossed knife and fork, a restaurant ; a little steamboat, a transfer to a steamboat ; and a postillion's horn, a diligence. Similar signs are used in the well-known Michelin guides for automobilists in Europe, to show a post-office (envelope) or a telephone (telephone receiver). The quality of hotels is shown by an inn with one, two, three, or four gables, and so forth. Similarly, the roads of Europe are

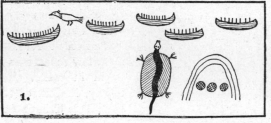

SPECIMENS OF AMERICAN INDIAN PICTURE-WRITING
(after Schoolcraft).

No 1, painted on a rock on the shore of Lake Superior, records an expedition across the lake, in which five canoes took part. The upright strokes in each indicate the number of the crew, and the bird represents a chief, "The Kingfisher." The three circles (suns) under the arch (of heaven) indicate that the voyage lasted three days, and the tortoise, a symbol of land, denotes a safe arrival. No. 2 is a petition sent to the United States Congress by a group of Indian tribes, asking for fishing rights in certain small lakes. The tribes are represented by their totems, martens, bear, manfish and catfish, led by the crane. Lines running from the heart and eye of each animal to the heart and eye of the crane denote that they are all of one mind ; and a line runs from the eye of the crane to the lakes, shown in the crude little " map " in the lower left-hand corner.

marked with wayside signs representing a gate, to indicate a level crossing ahead, a sinuous bend for a dangerous curve, and the like. From such pictographic signs to the first elements of Chinese writing is not a very long stretch.

In Chinese writing there are still traceable a number of pictographs. Most are now difficult to recognize. A mouth was originally written as a mouth-shaped hole, and is now, for convenience of brushwork, squared; a child, originally a recognizable little mannikin, is now a hasty wriggle and a cross; the sun, originally a large circle with a dot in the centre, has been converted, for the sake of convenience of combination, into a crossed oblong, which is easier to make with a brush. By combining these pictographs, a second order of ideas is expressed. For example, the pictograph for mouth combined with pictograph for vapour expressed "words." [1]

From such combinations one passes to what are called *ideograms*: the sign for "words" and the sign for "tongue" combine to make "speech"; the sign for "roof" and the sign for "pig" make "home"—for in the early domestic economy of China the pig was as important as it used to be in Ireland. But, as we have already noted earlier, the Chinese language consists of a comparatively few elementary monosyllabic sounds, which are all used in a great variety of meanings, and the Chinese soon discovered that a number of these *pictographs* and *ideographs* could be used also to express other ideas, not so conveniently pictured, but having the same sound. Characters so used are called *phonograms*. For example, the word *fang* meant not only "square," but "a place," "spinning," "fragrant," "inquire," and several other meanings according to the context. But while a square is easy to draw, most of the other meanings are undrawable. How can one draw "fragrant" or "inquire"? The Chinese, therefore, took the same sign for all these meanings of "fang," but added to each of them another distinctive sign, the determinative, to show what sort of *fang* was intended. A "place" was indicated by the same sign as for "square" (*fang*) and the determinative sign for "earth"; "spinning"

[1] See the *Encyclopædia Brit.*, Article *China*, p. 218.

by the sign for *fang* and the sign for "silk"; "inquire" by the sign for *fang*, and the sign for "words," and so on.

One may perhaps make this development of pictographs, ideograms, and phonograms a little clearer by taking an analogous case in English. Suppose we were making up a sort of picture-writing in English, then it would be very natural to use a square with a slanting line to suggest a lid, for the word and thing *box*. That would be a pictograph. But now suppose we had a round sign for money, and suppose

VERY EARLY SUMERIAN CUNEIFORM
(perhaps 4,500 B.C.).
The pictorial quality is still quite plain.

we put this sign inside the box sign, that would do for "cash-box" or "treasury." That would be an ideogram. But the word "box" is used for other things than boxes. There is the box shrub which gives us box-wood. It would be hard to draw a recognizable box-tree distinct from other trees, but it is quite easy to put our sign "box," and add our sign for shrub as a determinative to determine that it is that sort of box and not a common box that we want to express. And then there is "box," the verb, meaning to fight with fists. Here, again, we need a determinative; we might add the two crossed swords, a sign which is used very often upon maps to denote a battle. A box at a theatre needs yet another determina-

BASALT WEIGHT FOR TWO-THIRDS OF A MANEH AND ONE SHEKEL, SHOWING THE LATER, MUCH MORE ABSTRACT, CUNEIFORM WRITING.

The trilingual inscription in Persian, Median, and Babylonian, records the name of Darius, the son of Hystaspes, the Achamenian, about 520 B.C.

tive, and so we go on, through a long series of phonograms.

Now it is manifest that here in the Chinese writing is a very peculiar and complex system of sign-writing. A very great number of characters have to be learnt and the mind habituated to their use. The power it possesses to carry ideas and discussion is still ungauged by western standards, but we may doubt whether with this instrument it will ever be possible to establish such a wide, common mentality as the simpler and swifter alphabets of the western civilizations permit. In China it created a special reading-class, the mandarins, who were also the ruling and official class. Their necessary concentration upon words and classical forms, rather than upon ideas and realities, seems, in spite of her comparative peacefulness and the very high individual intellectual quality of her people, to have greatly hampered the social and economic development of China. Probably it is the complexity of her speech and writing, more than any other imaginable cause, that has made China to-day politically, socially, and individually a vast pool of backward people rather than the foremost power in the whole world.

§ 2

But while the Chinese mind thus made for itself an instrument which is probably too elaborate in structure, too laborious in use, and too inflexible in its form to meet the modern need for simple, swift, exact, and lucid communications, the growing civilizations of the west were working

Syllable Writing.

out the problem of a written record upon rather different and, on the whole, more advantageous lines. They did not seek to improve their script to make it swift and easy, but circumstances conspired to make it so. The Sumerian picture-writing, which had to be done upon clay and with little styles, which made curved marks with difficulty and inaccurately, rapidly degenerated by a conventionalized dabbing down of wedged-shaped marks (cuneiform = wedge-shaped) into almost unrecognizable hints of the shapes intended. It helped the Sumerians greatly to learn to write, that they had to draw so badly. They got very soon to the Chinese pictographs, ideographs, and phonograms, and beyond them.

Most people know a sort of puzzle called a rebus. It is a way of representing words by pictures, not of the things the words represent, but by the pictures of other things having a similar sound. For example, two gates and a head is a rebus for Gateshead; a little streamlet (beck), a crowned monarch, and a ham, Beckingham. The Sumerian language was a language well adapted to this sort of representation. It was apparently a language of often quite vast polysyllables, made up of very distinct inalterable syllables; and many of the syllables taken separately were the names of concrete things. So that this cuneiform writing developed very readily into a syllabic way of writing, in which each sign conveys a syllable just as each act in a charade conveys a syllable. When presently the Semites conquered Sumeria, they adapted the syllabic system to their own speech, and so this writing became entirely a sign-for-a-sound writing. It was so used by the Assyrians and by the Chaldeans. But it was not a letter-writing, it was a syllable-writing. This cuneiform script prevailed for long ages over Assyria, Babylonia, and the Near East generally; there are vestiges of it in some of the letters of our alphabet to-day.

§ 3

But, meanwhile, in Egypt and upon the Mediterranean coast another system of writing grew up. Its beginnings are probably to be found in the priestly picture-writing (hieroglyphics) of the Egyptians, which also in the usual way became

Alphabet Writing.

partly a sound-sign system. As we see it on the Egyptian monuments, the hieroglyphic writing consists of decorative but stiff and elaborate forms, but for such purpose as letter-writing and the keeping of recipes and the like, the Egyptian priests used a much simplified and flowing form of these characters, the *hieratic script*. Side by side with this hieratic script rose another, probably also derivative from the hieroglyphs, a script now lost to us, which was taken over by various non-Egyptian peoples in the Mediterranean, the Phœnicians, Libyans, Lydians, Cretans, and Celt-Iberians, and used for business purposes. Possibly a few letters were borrowed from the later cuneiform. In the hands of these foreigners this writing was, so to speak, cut off from its roots; it lost all but a few traces of its early pictorial character. It ceased to be pictographic or ideographic; it became simply a pure sound-sign system, an *alphabet*. There were a number of such alphabets in the Mediterranean differing widely from each other.[1] It may be noted that the Phœnician alphabet (and perhaps others) omitted

vowels. Possibly they pronounced their consonants very hard and had rather indeterminate vowels, as is said to be still the case with tribes of South Arabia. Quite probably, too, the Phœnicians used their alphabet at first not so much for writing as for single initial letters in their business accounts and tallies. One of these Mediterranean alphabets reached the Greeks, long after the time of the *Iliad*, who presently set to work to make it express the clear and beautiful sounds of their own highly developed Aryan speech. It consisted at first of consonants, and the Greeks added the vowels. They began to write for record, to help and fix their bardic tradition. . . .

§ 4

The Place of Writing in Human Life. So it was by a series of very natural steps that writing grew out of the life of man. At first and for long ages it was the interest and the secret of only a few people in a special class, a mere accessory to the record of pictures. But there were certain very manifest advantages, quite apart from the increased expressiveness

[1] The Libyan alphabet survived in North Africa until a century ago, and was still used then for correspondence. It was supposed to be extinct, but in 1897 Sir Arthur Evans and J. L. Myres saw what looked like ancient Cretan lettering on some dyed skins from the Sahara in the bazaar at Tripoli. It was the ancient alphabet still in use for commercial signs.—E. B.

Photo: Bonfils.

FIGURES FROM AN EGYPTIAN TOMB, SHOWING THE STIFF HIEROGLYPHIC PICTURE-WRITING.

of mood and qualification, to be gained by making writing a little less plain than straightforward pictures, and in conventionalizing and codifying it. One of these was that so messages might be sent understandable by the sender and receiver, but not plain to the uninitiated. Another was that so one might put down various matters and help one's memory and the memory of one's friends, without giving away too much to the common herd. Among some of the earliest Egyptian writings, for example, are medical recipes and magic formulæ. Accounts, letters, recipes, name lists, itineraries; these were the earliest of written documents. Then, as the art of writing and reading spread, came that odd desire, that pathetic desire so common among human beings, to astonish some strange and remote person by writing down something striking, some secret one knew, some strange thought, or even one's name, so that long after one had gone one's way, it might strike upon the sight and mind of another reader. Even in Sumeria men scratched on walls, and all that remains to us of the ancient world, its rocks, its buildings, is plastered thickly with the names and the boasting of those foremost among human advertisers, its kings. Perhaps half the early inscriptions in that ancient world are of this nature, if, that is, we group with the name-writing and boasting the epitaphs, which were probably, in many cases, prearranged by the deceased.

For long the desire for crude self-assertion of the name-scrawling sort and the love of secret understandings kept writing within a narrow scope; but that other, more truly social desire in men, the desire to *tell*, was also at work. The profounder possibilities of writing, the possibilities of a vast extension and definition and settlement of knowledge and tradition, only grew apparent after long ages. But it will be interesting at this point and in this connection to recapitulate certain elemental facts about life, upon which we laid stress in our earlier chapters, because they illuminate not only the huge value of writing in the whole field of man's history, but also the rôle it is likely to play in his future.

1. Life had at first, it must be remembered, only a discontinuous repetition of consciousness, as the old died and the young were born.

Such a creature as a reptile has in its brain a capacity for experience, but when the individual dies, its experience dies with it. Most of its motives are purely instinctive, and all the mental life that it has is the result of heredity (birth inheritance).

2. But ordinary mammals have added to pure instinct *tradition*, a tradition of experience imparted by the imitated example of the mother, and in the case of such mentally developed animals as dogs, cats, or apes, by a sort of mute precept also. For example, the mother cat chastises her young for misbehaviour. So do mother apes and baboons.

3. Primitive man added to his powers of transmitting experience, representative art and speech. Pictorial and sculptured record and *verbal tradition* began.

Verbal tradition was developed to its highest possibility by the bards. They did much to make language what it is to the world to-day.

4. With the invention of writing, which developed out of pictorial record, human tradition was able to become fuller and much more exact. Verbal tradition, which had hitherto changed from age to age, began to be fixed. Men separated by hundreds of miles could now communicate their thoughts. An increasing number of human beings began to share a common written knowledge and a common sense of a past and a future. Human thinking became a larger operation in which hundreds of minds in different places and in different ages could react upon one another; it became a process constantly more continuous and sustained. . . .

5. For hundreds of generations the full power of writing was not revealed to the world, because for a long time the idea of multiplying writings by taking prints of a first copy did not become effective. The only way of multiplying writings was by copying one copy at a time, and this made books costly and rare. Moreover, the tendency to keep things secret, to make a cult and mystery of them, and so to gain an advantage over the generality of men, has always been very strong in men's minds. It is only nowadays that the great masses of mankind are learning to read, and reaching out towards the treasures of knowledge and thought already stored in books.

Nevertheless, from the first writings onward a new sort of tradition, an enduring and immortal tradition, began in the minds of men. Mankind and life grows thereafter more and more distinctly conscious of itself and its world. It is a thin streak of steadfast intellectual life we trace in history, at first in a world of tumultuous ignorance and forgetfulness; it is like a mere line of light coming through the chink of an opening door into a darkened room; but slowly it widens, it grows. At last came a time in the history of Europe when the door, at the push of the printer, began to open more rapidly. Knowledge flared up, and as it flared it ceased to be the privilege of a favoured minority. For us now that door swings wider, and the light behind grows brighter. Misty it is still, glowing through clouds of dust and reek.

The door is not half open; the light is but a light new lit. Our world to-day is only in the beginning of knowledge.

XIX

GODS AND STARS, PRIESTS AND KINGS

§ 1

WE have already told what there is to tell of the social life of the Aryan tribes when they were settling down to the **Nomadic and Settled Religion.** beginnings of civilized life; we have seen how they were associated in great households, grouped together under tribal leaders, who made a sort of informal aristocracy rather like that of the sixth form and prefects in an English boys' school; we have considered the rôle of the bards in the creation of an oral tradition, and we have glanced at their not very complex religious ideas. We may note one or two points of difference from the equivalent life of the nomadic Semites.

Like the early Aryan life, it was a life in a sort of family-tribe household. But it had differences due originally perhaps to the warmer, drier climate. Though both groups of races had cattle and sheep, the Aryans were rather herdsmen, the Semites, shepherds. The

Photo: Mansell.
EGYPTIAN ICHNEUMON GODDESS SYMBOL.

Semites had no long winter evenings and no bardic singing. They never sat in hall. They have consequently no epics. They had stories, camp-fire stories, but not verbally beautified story recitations. The Semite also was more polygamous than the Aryan, his women less self-assertive,[1] and the tendency of his government more patriarchal. The head of the household or the tribe was less of a leader and more of a master, more like the Palæolithic Old Man. And the Semitic nomads were closer to the earlier civilizations, a thing that fitted in with their greater aptitude for trade and counting. But the religion of the nomadic Semite was as little organized as the religion of the Aryan. In either case the leading man performed most of the functions of the priest. The Aryan gods were little more than a kind of magical super-prince; they were

[1] The Sumerians allowed much more freedom and authority to women than the Semites. They had priestess-queens, and one of their great divinities was a goddess, Ishtar.

supposed to sit in hall together, and to talk and make scenes with one another under Jupiter or Thor. The early Semitic gods, on the other hand, were thought of as tribal patriarchs. As peoples develop towards nomadism, they seem to lose even such primitive religion and magic as their Neolithic ancestors professed. Nomadism cuts men off from fixed temples and intense local associations; they take a broader and simpler view of the world. They tend towards religious simplification.

We write here of the nomadic peoples, the Aryan herdsmen and Semitic shepherds, and we write in the most general terms. They had their undercurrent of fables and superstitions, their phases of fear and abjection and sacrificial fury. These people were people like ourselves, with brains as busy and moody and inconsistent, and with even less training and discipline. It is absurd to suppose—as so many writers about early religion do seem to suppose—that their religious notions can be reduced to the consistent logical development of some one simple idea. We have already glanced, in Chapter XII, at the elements of religion that must have arisen necessarily in the minds of those early peoples. But for most of the twenty-four hours these nomads were busy upon other things, and there is no sign that their houses, their daily routines, their ordinary acts, were dominated or their social order shaped, by any ideas that we should now call religious. As yet life and its ideas were too elementary for that.

But directly we turn our attention to these new accumulations of human beings that are beginning in Egypt and Mesopotamia, we find that one of the most conspicuous objects in every city is a temple or a group of temples. In some cases there arises beside it in these regions a royal palace, but as often the temple towers over the palace. This presence of the temple is equally true of the Phœnician cities and of the Greek and Roman as they arise. The palace of Cnossos, with its signs of comfort and pleasure-seeking, and the kindred cities of the Ægean peoples, include religious shrines, but in Crete there are also temples standing apart from the palatial city-households. All over the ancient civilized world we find them; wherever primitive civilization set its foot in Africa, Europe, or Western Asia, a temple arose, and where the civilization is most ancient, in Egypt and in Sumer, there the temple is most in evidence. When Hanno reached what he thought was the most westerly point of Africa, he set up a temple to Hercules. We have, in fact, come now to a new stage in the history of mankind, the temple stage.

§ 2

In all these temples there was a shrine; dominating the shrine there was commonly a great figure usually of some monstrous half-animal form, before which stood an altar for sacrifices. This figure was either regarded as the god or as the image or symbol of the god, for whose worship the temple existed. And connected with the temple there were a number, and often a considerable number, of priests or priestesses, and temple servants, generally wearing a distinctive costume and forming an important part of the city population. They belonged to no household, as did the simple priest of the primitive Aryan; they made up a new kind of household of their own. They were a caste and a class apart, attracting intelligent recruits from the general population.

The Priest comes into History.

The primary duty of this priesthood was concerned with the worship of and the sacrifices to the god of the temple. And these things were done, not at any time, but at particular times and seasons. There has come into the life of man with his herding and agriculture a sense of a difference between the parts of the year and of a difference between day and day. Men were beginning to work—and to need days of rest. The temple, by its festivals, kept count. The temple in the ancient city was like the clock and calendar upon a writing-desk.

But it was a centre of other functions. It was in the early temples that the records and tallies of events were kept and that writing began. And there was knowledge there. The people went to the temple not only *en masse* for festivals, but individually for help. The early priests were also doctors and magicians. In the earliest temples we already find those little offerings for some private and particular

COLONNADE ACROSS COURT OF AMENOPHIS III.   LUXOR TEMPLE, THEBES.

Set
Egyptian god of
darkness.

Anubis
a darkness god.

Typhon
wife of Anubis, also
known as the Terrible One.

The cheerful
Bes.

J.F.H.

end, which are still made in the chapels of catholic churches to-day, *ex votos*, little models of hearts relieved and limbs restored, acknowledgment of prayers answered and accepted vows.

It is clear that here we have that comparatively unimportant element in the life of the early nomad, the medicine-man, the shrine-keeper, and the memorist, developed, with the development of the community, and as a part of the development of the community from barbarism to civilized settlement, into something of very much greater importance. And it is equally evident that those primitive fears of (and hopes of help from) strange beings, the desire to propitiate unknown forces, the primitive desire for cleansing and the primitive craving for power and knowledge have all contributed to crystallize out this new social fact of the temple.

The temple was accumulated by complex necessities, it grew from many roots and needs, and the god that dominated the temple was the creation of many imaginations and made up of all sort of impulses, ideas, and half ideas. Here there was a god in which one sort of idea predominated, and there another. It is necessary to lay some stress upon this confusion and variety of origin in gods, because there is a very great literature now in existence upon religious origins, in which a number of writers insist, some on this leading idea and some on that—we have noted several in our Chapter XII on " Early Thought "—as though it were the only idea. Professor Max Müller in his time, for example, harped perpetually on the idea of sun stories and sun worship. He would have had us think that early man never had lusts or fears, cravings for power, nightmares or fantasies, but that he meditated perpetually on the beneficent source of light and life in the sky. Now dawn and sunset are very moving facts in the daily life, but they are only two among many. Early men, three or four hundred generations ago, had brains very like our own. The fancies of our childhood and youth are perhaps the best clue we have to the ground-stuff of early religion, and any one who can recall those early mental experiences, will understand very easily the vagueness, the monstrosity, and the incoherent variety of the first gods. There were sun gods, no doubt, early in the history of temples, but there were also hippopotamus gods and hawk gods ; there were cow deities, there were monstrous male and female gods, there were gods of terror and gods of an adorable quaintness, there were gods who were nothing but lumps of meteoric stone that had fallen amazingly out of the sky, and gods who were mere natural stones that had chanced to have a queer and impressive shape. Some gods, like Marduk of Babylon and the Baal (= the Lord) of the Phœnicians, Canaanites, and the like, were quite probably at bottom just legendary wonder beings, such as little boys will invent for themselves to-day. The early Semites, it is said, as soon as they thought of a god, invented a wife for him; most of the Egyptian and Babylonian gods were married. But the gods of the nomadic Semites had not this marrying disposition. Children were less eagerly sought by the inhabitants of the food-grudging steppes.

Even more natural than to require a wife for a god is to give him a house to live in to which offerings can be brought. Of this house the knowing man, the magician, would naturally become the custodian. A certain seclusion, a certain aloofness, would add greatly to the prestige of the god. The steps by which the early temple and the early priesthood developed so soon as an agricultural population settled and increased are all quite natural and understandable, up to the stage of the long temple with the image, shrine and altar at one end and the long nave in which the worshippers stood. And this temple, because it had records and secrets, because it was a centre of power, advice, and instruction, because it sought and attracted imaginative and clever people for its service, naturally became a sort of brain in the growing community. The attitude of the common people who tilled the fields and herded the beasts towards the temple would remain simple and credulous. There, rarely seen and so imaginatively enhanced, lived the god whose approval gave prosperity, whose anger meant misfortune; he could be propitiated by little presents and the help of his servants could be obtained. He was wonderful, and of such power and knowledge that it did not do to be disrespectful to him even in one's thoughts. Within the priesthood, however, a certain amount of thinking went on at a rather higher level than that.

§ 3

And now we have to note a very interesting fact about the chief temples of Egypt and, so

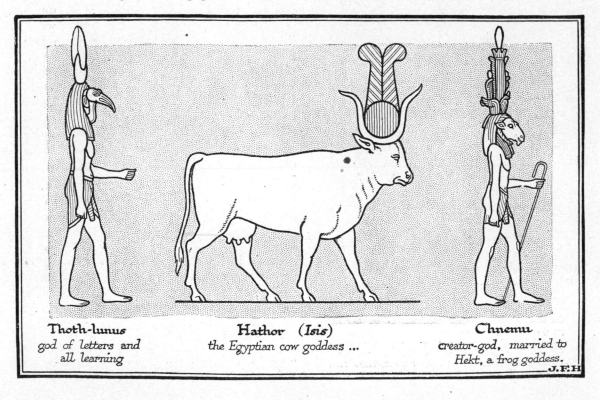

Thoth-lunus
god of letters and
all learning

Hathor (Isis)
the Egyptian cow goddess ...

Chnemu
creator-god, married to
Hekt, a frog goddess.

J.F.H

far as we know—because the ruins are not so distinct—of Babylonia, and that is **Priests and the Stars.[1]** that they are "oriented"—that is to say, that the same sort of temple

[1] See Johnson's *Byeways of British Archæology.*

Photo: Mansell.

2,200(?) B.C., BASALT STELE, ARCHAIC BABYLONIAN TEXT OF THE CODE OF LAWS DRAWN UP BY HAMMURABI. THE KING SEEN RECEIVING THE LAWS FROM THE SUN-GOD.

is built so that the shrine and entrance always face in the same direction.[2] In Babylonian temples this was most often due east, facing the sunrise on March 21st and September 21st, the equinoxes; and it is to be noted that it was at the spring equinox that the Euphrates and Tigris came down in flood. The Pyramids of Gizeh are also oriented east and west, and the Sphinx faces due east, but very many of the Egyptian temples to the south of the delta of the Nile do not point due east, but to the point where the sun rises at the longest day—and in Egypt the inundation comes close to that date. Others, however, pointed nearly northward, and others again pointed to the rising of the star Sirius or to the rising-point of other conspicuous stars. The fact of orientation links up with the fact that there early arose a close association between various gods and the sun and various fixed stars. Whatever the mass of people outside were thinking, the priests of the temples were beginning to link the movements of those heavenly bodies with the power in the shrine. They were thinking about the gods they served and thinking new meanings into them. They were brooding upon the mystery of the stars. It was very natural for them to suppose that these shining bodies, so irregularly distributed and circling so solemnly and silently, must be charged with portents to mankind.

Among other things, this orientation of the temples served to fix and help the great annual festival of the New Year. On one morning in the year, and one morning alone, in a temple oriented to the rising-place of the sun at Midsummer Day, the sun's first rays would smite down through the gloom of the temple and the long alley of the temple pillars, and light up the god above the altar and irradiate him with glory. The narrow, darkened structure of the ancient temples seems to be deliberately planned for such an effect. No doubt the people were gathered in the darkness before the dawn; in the darkness there was chanting and perhaps the offering of sacrifices; the god alone stood mute and invisible. Prayers and invocations

[2] Many Christian churches, almost all, indeed, built between the fifth century and the Renaissance, are oriented to the east. St. Peter's at Rome is oriented east and west.

would be made. Then upon the eyes of the worshippers, sensitized by the darkness, as the sun rose behind them, the god would suddenly shine.

So, at least, one explanation of orientation is found by such students of orientation as Sir Norman Lockyer.[1] Not only is orientation apparent in most of the temples of Egypt, Assyria, Babylonia, and the east, it is found in the Greek temples ; Stonehenge is oriented to the midsummer sunrise, and so are most of the megalithic circles of Europe ; the Temple of Heaven in Pekin is oriented to midwinter. In the days of the Chinese Empire, up to a few years ago, one of the most important of all the duties of the Emperor of China was to sacrifice and pray in this temple upon midwinter's day for a propitious year.

The Egyptian priests had mapped out the stars into the constellations, and divided up the zodiac into twelve signs by 3,000 B.C. . . .

§ 4

This clear evidence of astronomical inquiry and of a development of astronomical ideas is **Priests and the Dawn of Learning.** the most obvious, but only the most obvious evidence of the very considerable intellectual activities that went on within the temple precincts in ancient times. There is a curious disposition among many modern writers to deprecate priesthoods and to speak of priests as though they had always been impostors and tricksters, preying upon the simplicity of mankind. But, indeed, they were for long the only writing class, the only reading public, the only learned and the only thinkers ; they were all the professional classes of the time. You could have no intellectual life at all, you could not get access to literature or any knowledge except through the priesthood. The temples were not only observatories and libraries and clinics, they were museums and treasure-houses. The original *Periplus* of Hanno hung in one temple in Carthage, skins of his " gorillas " were hung and treasured in another. Whatever there was of abiding worth in the life of the community sheltered there. Herodotus, the early Greek historian (485—425 B.C.), collected most of his

[1] In his *Dawn of Astronomy.*

material from the priests of the countries in which he travelled, and it is evident they met him generously and put their very considerable resources completely at his disposal. Outside the temples the world was still a world of blankly illiterate and unspeculative human beings, living from day to day entirely for themselves. Moreover, there is little evidence that the commonality felt cheated by the priests,

A CUNEIFORM LETTER FROM TUSHRATTA TO AMENOPHIS III.

or had anything but trust and affection for the early priesthoods. Even the great conquerors of later times were anxious to keep themselves upon the right side of the priests of the nations and cities whose obedience they desired, because of the immense popular influence of these priests.

No doubt there were great differences between temple and temple and cult and cult in the spirit and quality of the priesthood. Some probably were cruel, some vicious and greedy, many dull and doctrinaire, stupid with tradition, but it has to be kept in mind that there were distinct limits to the degeneracy or inefficiency of a priesthood. It had to keep its grip upon the general mind. It could not go beyond what people would stand—either towards the darkness or towards the light. Its authority rested, in the end, on the persuasion that its activities were propitious.

its people together for war, but its traditionalism and all its methods unfit it for military control. Against the enemy without, a priest-led people is feeble.

Moreover, a priest is a man vowed, trained, and consecrated, a man belonging to a special corps, and necessarily with an intense *esprit de corps*. He has given up his life to his temple and his god. This is a very excellent thing for the internal vigour of his own priesthood, his own temple. He lives or dies for the honour

Photo: Mansell.
ASSURBANIPAL=SARDANAPALUS, THE MOST SCHOLARLY OF THE GREAT LINE OF ASSYRIAN MONARCHS.

§ 5 [1]

It is clear that the earliest civilized governments were essentially priestly governments. It was not kings and captains who **King against Priest.** first set men to the plough and a settled life. It was the ideas of the gods and plenty, working with the acquiescence of common men. The early rulers of Sumer we know were all priests, kings only because they were chief priests. And priestly government had its own weaknesses as well as its peculiar deep-rooted strength. The power of a priesthood is a power over their own people alone. It is a subjugation through mysterious fears and hopes. The priesthood can gather

[1] Legrain's *Le Temps des Rois d'Ur* (Bibliothèque de l'École des Hautes Études) was useful here.

of his particular god. But in the next town or village is another temple with another god. It is his constant preoccupation to keep his people from that god. Religious cults and priesthoods are sectarian by nature; they will convert, they will overcome, but they will never coalesce. Our first perceptions of events in Sumer, in the dim uncertain light before history began, is of priests and gods in conflict; until the Sumerians were conquered by the Semites they were never united; and the same incurable conflict of priesthoods scars all the temple ruins of Egypt. It was impossible that it could have been otherwise, having regard to the elements out of which religion arose.

It was out of those two main weaknesses of all priesthoods, namely, the incapacity for efficient military leadership and their inevitable jealousy of all other religious cults, that the power of secular kingship arose. The foreign enemy either prevailed and set up a king over the people, or the priesthoods who would not give way to each other set up a common fighting captain, who retained more or less power in peace time. First, in relation to other cities, this secular king developed a group of officials about him and began, in relation to military organization, to take a share in the priestly administration of the people's affairs. So, growing out of priestcraft and beside the priest, the protagonist of the priest, the king, appears upon the stage of human history, and a very large amount of the subsequent experiences of mankind is only to be understood as an elaboration, complication, and distortion of the struggle, unconscious or deliberate, between these two systems of human control, the temple and the palace. And it was in the original centres of civilization that this antagonism was most completely developed. The Aryan peoples never passed through a phase of temple rule on their way to civilization ; they came to civilization late ; they found that drama already half-played. If any exception is to be made to that statement among the Aryans, it must be the Western Kelts who made, if indeed it was they who made, such open temples as Stonehenge.[1] Most of the Aryan peoples took over the ideas of both temple and kingship, when those ideas were already elaborately developed, from the more civilized Hamitic or Semitic people they conquered.

The greater importance of the gods and the

CHEPHREN

priests in the earlier history of the Mesopotamian civilization is very apparent, but gradually the palace won its way until it was at last in a position to struggle definitely for the supreme power. At first, in the story, the palace is ignorant and friendless in the face of the temple ; the priests alone read, the priests alone know, the people are afraid of them. But in the dissensions of the various cults comes the opportunity of the palace. From other cities, from among captives, from defeated or suppressed religious cults, the palace gets men who also can read and who can do magic things.[2] The court also becomes a centre of writing and record ; the king thinks for himself and becomes politic. Traders and foreigners drift to the court, and if the king has not the full records and the finished scholarship of the priests, he has a wider and fresher first-hand knowledge of many things. The priest comes into the temple when he is very young ; he passes many years as a neophyte ; the path of learning the clumsy letters of primitive times is slow and toilsome ; he becomes erudite and prejudiced rather than a man of the world. Some of the more active-minded young priests may even cast envious eyes at the king's service. There are many complications and variations in this ages-long drama of the struggle going on beneath the outward conflicts of priest and king, between the made man and the born man, between learning and originality, between established knowledge and settled usage on the one hand, and creative will and imagination on the other. It is not always, as we shall find later, the priest who is the conservative and unimaginative antagonist. Sometimes a king struggles against narrow and obstructive priesthoods ; sometimes

[1] Most authorities are agreed that Stonehenge was erected before any invasion of Aryan Kelts took place. —H. H. J.

[2] Cp. Moses and the Egyptian Magicians.

priesthoods uphold the standards of civilization against savage, egotistical, or reactionary kings.

One or two outstanding facts and incidents of the early stages of this fundamental struggle in political affairs are all that we can note here between 4,000 B.C. and the days of Alexander.

Rameses III as Osiris — between the goddesses Nephthys and Isis..

Relief on the cover of the sarcophagus (at Cambridge).   After Sharpe.

SARCOPHAGUS OF RAMESES III.

Inscription (round the edges of cover) as far as decipherable :—
" Osiris, King of Upper and Lower Egypt, lord of the two countries . . . son of the Sun, beloved of the gods, lord of diadems, Rameses, prince of Heliopolis, triumphant ! Thou art in the condition of a god, thou shalt arise as Usr, there is no enemy to thee, I give to thee triumph among them. . . ."
BUDGE, *Catalogue, Egyptian Collection, Fitzwilliam Museum, Cambridge*

§ 6

In the early days of Sumeria and Akkadia the city-kings were priests and medicine-men

How Bel-Marduk struggled against the Kings. rather than kings, and it was only when foreign conquerors sought to establish their hold in relation to existing institutions that the distinction of priest and king became definite. But the god of the priests remained as the real overlord of the land and of priest and king alike. He was the universal landlord; the wealth and authority of his temples and establishments outshone those of the king. Especially was this the case within the city walls.

Hammurabi, the founder of the first Babylonian empire, is one of the earlier monarchs whom we find taking a firm grip upon the affairs of the community. He does it with the utmost politeness to the gods. In an inscription recording his irrigation work in Sumeria and Akkadia, he begins : " When Anu and Bel entrusted me with the rule of Sumer and Akkad——." We possess a code of laws made by this same Hammurabi—it is the earliest known code of law—and at the head of this code we see the figure of Hammurabi receiving the law from its nominal promulgator, the god Shamash.

An act of great political importance in the conquest of any city was the carrying off of its god to become a subordinate in the temple of its conqueror. This was far more important than the subjugation of king by king. Merodach, the Babylonian Jupiter, was carried off by the Elamites, and Babylon did not feel independent until its return. But sometimes a conqueror was afraid of the god he had conquered. In the collection of letters addressed to Amenophis III and IV at Tel-Amarna in Egypt, to which allusion has already been made, is one from a certain king, Tushratta, King of Mitani, who has conquered Assyria and taken the statue of the goddess Ishtar. Apparently he has sent this statue into Egypt, partly to acknowledge the overlordship of Amenophis, but partly because he fears her anger. (Winckler.) In the Bible is related (Sam. i. v. 1) how the Ark of the Covenant of the God of the Hebrews was carried off by the Philistines, as a token of conquest, into the temple of the fish god, Dagon, at Ashdod, and how Dagon fell down and was broken, and how the people of Ashdod were smitten with disease. In the latter story, particularly, the gods and priests fill the scene ; there is no king in evidence at all.

Right through the history of the Babylonian and Assyrian empires no monarch seems to have felt his tenure of power secure in Babylon until he had " taken the hand of Bel "—that is to say, that he had been adopted by the priesthood of " Bel " as the god's son and representative. As our knowledge of Assyrian and Babylonian history grows clearer, it becomes plainer that the politics of that world, the

GIANT ROCK-HEWN STATUES OF RAMESES II (CIRCA 1,317-1,250 B.C.) AT ABU
SIMBEL IN NUBIA.

From a photograph by Underwood & Underwood.

revolutions, usurpations, changes of dynasty, intrigues with foreign powers, turned largely upon issues between the great wealthy priesthoods and the growing but still inadequate power of the monarchy. The king relied on his army, and this was usually a mercenary army of foreigners, speedily mutinous if there was no pay or plunder, and easily bribed. We have already noted the name of Sennacherib, the son of Sargon II, among the monarchs of the Assyrian empire. Sennacherib was involved in a violent quarrel with the priesthood of Babylon; he never " took the hand of Bel "; and, finally, struck at that power by destroying altogether the holy part of the city of Babylon (691 B.C.) and removing the statue of Bel-Marduk to Assyria. He was assassinated by one of his sons, and his successor, Esar-haddon (his son, but not the son who was his assassin), found it expedient to restore Bel-Marduk and rebuild his temple, and make his peace with the god.[1]

Assurbanipal (Greek, Sardanapalus), the son of this Esar-haddon, is a particularly interesting figure from this point of view of the relationship of priesthood and king. His father's reconciliation with the priests of Bel-Marduk went so far that Sardanapalus was given a Babylonian instead of a military Assyrian education. He became a great collector of the clay documents of the past, and his library, which has been unearthed, is now the most precious source of historical material in the world. But he also

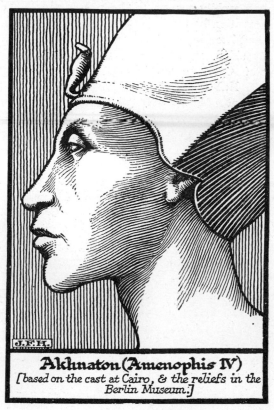

Akhnaton (Amenophis IV)
[based on the cast at Cairo, & the reliefs in the Berlin Museum.]

kept his grip on the Assyrian army; he made a temporary conquest of Egypt, suppressed a rebellion in Babylon, and carried out a number of successful expeditions. But, as we have already told in Chapter XVI, he was almost the last of the Assyrian monarchs. The Aryan tribes, who knew more of war than of priestcraft, and particularly the Scythians, the Medes and Persians, had long been pressing upon Assyria from the north and north-east. The Medes and Persians formed an alliance with the nomadic Semitic Chaldeans of the south for the joint undoing of Assyria. Nineveh, the Assyrian capital, fell to these Aryans in 606 B.C.

Sixty-seven years after the taking of Nineveh by the Aryans, which left Babylonia to the Semitic Chaldeans, the last monarch of the Chaldean Empire (the Second Babylonian Empire), Nabonidus, the father of Belshazzar, was overthrown by Cyrus, the Persian. This Nabonidus, again, was a highly educated monarch, who brought far too much intelligence and imagination and not enough of the short range wisdom of this world to affairs of state. He conducted antiquarian researches, and to his researches it is that we owe the date of 3,750 B.C., assigned to Sargon I and still accepted by many authorities. He was proud of this determination, and left inscriptions to record it. It is clear he was a religious innovator; he built and rearranged temples and attempted to centralize religion in Babylon by bringing a number of local gods to the temple of Bel-Marduk. No doubt he realized the weakness and disunion of his empire due to these conflicting cults, and had some conception of unification in his mind.

[1] According to Winckler, Sargon II, unlike his son, was pro-priest, and his usurpation of the throne was the result of an intrigue of the Babylonian priests against the feudal Assyrian military system of Tiglath Pileser III.

10

Events were marching too rapidly for any such development. His innovation had manifestly raised the suspicion and hostility of the priesthood of Bel. They sided with the Persians. "The soldiers of Cyrus entered Babylon without fighting." Nabonidus was taken prisoner, and Persian sentinels were set at the gates of the temple of Bel, " where the services continued without intermission."

Cyrus did, in fact, set up the Persian Empire in Babylon with the blessing of Bel-Marduk. He gratified the conservative instincts of the priests by packing off the local gods back to their ancestral temples. He also restored the Jews to Jerusalem.[1] These were merely matters of immediate policy to him. But in bringing in the irreligious Aryans, the ancient priesthood was paying too highly for the continuation of its temple services. It would have been wiser to have dealt with the innovations of Nabonidus, that earnest heretic, to have listened to his ideas, and to have met the needs of a changing world. Cyrus entered Babylon 539 B.C.; by 521 B.C. Babylon was in insurrection again, and in 520 B.C. another Persian monarch, Darius, was pulling down her walls. Within two hundred years the life had altogether gone out of those venerable rituals of Bel-Marduk, and the temple of Bel-Marduk was being used by builders as a quarry.

§ 7[2]

The story of priest and king in Egypt is similar to, but by no means parallel with, that of Babylonia. The kings of Sumeria and Assyria were priests who had become kings; they were secularized priests. The Pharaoh of Egypt does not appear to have followed precisely that line. Already in the very oldest records the Pharaoh has a power and importance exceeding that of any priest. He is, in fact, a god, and more than either priest or king. We do not know how he got to that position. No monarch of Sumeria or Babylonia or Assyria could have induced his people to do for him what the great pyramid-building Pharaohs of the IVth Dynasty

The God Kings of Egypt.

made their people do in those vast erections. The earlier Pharaohs were not improbably regarded as incarnations of the dominant god. The falcon god Horus sits behind the head of the great statue of Chephren. So late a monarch as Rameses III (XIXth Dynasty) is represented upon his sarcophagus (now at Cambridge) bearing the distinctive symbols of the three great gods of the Egyptian system.[3] He carries the two sceptres of Osiris, the god of Day and Resurrection; upon his head are horns of the cow goddess Hathor, and also the sun ball and feathers of Ammon Ra. He is not merely wearing the symbols of these gods as a devout Babylonian might wear the symbols of Bel-Marduk; he is these three gods in one.

The student will find much more in Sir J. G. Frazer's Golden Bough about the ancient use of human beings as well as statues to represent gods. Here we have merely to point to an apparent difference of idea between the Asiatic and African monarchies in this respect.

We find also a number of sculptures and paintings to enforce the idea that the Pharaohs were the actual sons of gods. The divine fathering and birth of Amenophis III, for instance (of the XVIIIth Dynasty), is displayed in extraordinary detail in a series of sculptures at Luxor. Moreover, it was held that the Pharaohs, being of so divine a strain, could not marry common clay, and, consequently, they were accustomed to marry blood relations within the degrees of consanguinity now prohibited, even marrying their sisters.

The struggle between palace and temple came into Egyptian history, therefore, at a different angle from that at which it came into Babylonia. Nevertheless, it came in. Professor Maspero (in his New Light on Ancient Egypt) gives a very interesting account of the struggle of Amenophis IV with the priesthoods, and particularly with priests of the great god, Ammon Ra, Lord of Karnak. The mother of Amenophis IV was not of the race of Pharaoh; it would seem that his father, Amenophis III, made a love match with a subject, a beautiful Syrian named Tii, and Professor Maspero finds in the possible opposition to and annoyance of this queen by the priests of Ammon Ra

[1] See the last two verses of the Second Book of Chronicles and Ezra, ch. i.

[2] A book of the utmost interest and value here is Breasted's Religion and Thought in Ancient Egypt.

[3] See S. Sharpe's Egyptian Mythology and Egyptian Christianity.

the beginnings of the quarrel. She may, he thinks, have inspired her son with a fanatical hatred of Ammon Ra. But Amenophis IV may have had a wider view. Like the Babylonian Nabonidus, who lived a thousand years later, he may have had in mind the problem of moral unity in his empire. We have already noted that Amenophis III ruled from Ethiopia to the Euphrates,

Photo: The Photochrom Co. Ld.

KARNAK: COLONNADE OF THE GRAND TEMPLE.

him as the creature of his mother's hatred of Ammon and the uxorious spouse of a beautiful wife. Certainly he loved his wife very passionately; he showed her great honour —Egypt honoured women, and was ruled at different times by several queens—and he was sculptured in one instance with his wife seated upon his knees, and in another in the act of

and that the store of letters to himself and his son found at Tel Amarna show a very wide range of interest and influence. At any rate, Amenophis IV set himself to close all the Egyptian and Syrian temples, to put an end to all sectarian worship throughout his dominions, and to establish everywhere the worship of one god, Aton, the solar disk. He left his capital, Thebes, which was even more the city of Ammon Ra than later Babylon was the city of Bel-Marduk, and set up his capital at Tel Amarna; he altered his name from "Amenophis," which consecrated him to Ammon (Amen) to "Akhnaton," the Sun's Glory; and he held his own against all the priesthoods of his empire for eighteen years and died a Pharaoh.

Opinions upon Amenophis IV or Akhnaton, differ very widely. There are those who regard

kissing her in a chariot; but men who live under the sway of their womenkind do not sustain and extend great empires in the face of the bitter hostility of the most influential organized bodies in their realm. Others write of him as a "gloomy fanatic." Matrimonial bliss is rare in the cases of gloomy fanatics. It is much more reasonable to regard him as the Pharaoh who refused to be a god. It is not simply his religious policy and his frank display of natural affection that seems to mark a strong and very original personality. His æsthetic ideas were his own. He refused to have his portrait conventionalized into the customary smooth beauty of the Pharaoh god, and his face looks out at us across an interval of thirty-four centuries, a man amidst ranks of divine insipidities.

A reign of eighteen years was not long enough

for the revolution he contemplated, and his son-in-law who succeeded him went back to Thebes and made his peace with Ammon Ra.

To the very end of the story the divinity of kings haunted the Egyptian mind, and infected the thoughts of intellectually healthier races. When Alexander the Great reached Babylon, the prestige of Bel-Marduk was already far gone in decay, but in Egypt, Ammon Ra was still god enough to make a snob of the conquering Grecian. The priests of Ammon Ra, about the time of the XVIIIth or XIXth Dynasty (*circa* 1,400 B.C.), had set up in an oasis of the desert a temple and oracle. Here was an image of the god which could speak, move its head, and accept or reject scrolls of inquiry. This oracle was still flourishing in 332 B.C. The young master of the world, it is related, made a special journey to visit it ; he came into the sanctuary, and the image advanced out of the darkness at the back to meet him. There was an impressive exchange of salutations. Some such formula as this must have been used (says Professor Maspero) : " Come, son of my loins, who loves me so that I give thee the royalty of Ra and the royalty of Horus ! I give thee valiance, I give thee to hold all countries and all religions under thy feet ; I give thee to strike all the peoples united together with thy arm ! "

So it was that the priests of Egypt conquered their conqueror, and an Aryan monarch first became a god. . . .[1]

§ 8

The struggle of priest and king in China cannot be discussed here at any length. It was different again, as in Egypt it was different from Babylonia, but we find the same effort on the part of the ruler to break up tradition because it divides up the people. The Chinese Emperor, the " Son of Heaven," was himself a high-priest, and his chief duty was sacrificial ; in the more disorderly phases of Chinese history he ceases to rule and continues only to sacrifice. The literary class was detached from the priestly class at an early date. It became a bureaucratic body serving the local kings and rulers. That is a fundamental difference between the history of China and any Western history. While Alexander was overrunning Western Asia, China, under the last priest-emperors of the Chow Dynasty, was sinking into a state of great disorder. Each province clung to its separate nationality and traditions, and the Huns spread from province to province. The King of T'sin (who came about eighty years after Alexander the Great), impressed by the mischief tradition was doing in the land, resolved to destroy the entire Chinese literature, and his son, Shi Hwang-ti, the " first universal Emperor," made a strenuous attempt to seek out and destroy all the existing classics.[2] They vanished while he ruled, and he ruled without tradition, and welded China into a unity that endured for some centuries ; but when he had passed, the hidden books crept out again. China remained united, though not under his descendants, but after a civil war under a fresh dynasty, the Han Dynasty (206 B.C.). The first Han monarch continued the campaign of Shi-Hwang-ti against the *literati*, but his successor made his peace with them and restored the texts of the classics.

Shi Hwang-ti destroys the Books.

[1] Many authorities regard Alexander as a man with the ideas of a pushful nineteenth-century (A.D.) monarch, and consider this visit to Jupiter Ammon as a masterstroke of policy. He was, we are asked to believe, deliberately and cynically acquiring divinity as a " unifying idea." The writer is totally unable to accept anything of the sort. For a discussion of the question, see Ferguson's *Greek Imperialism*.

[2] " His reforming zeal made him unpopular with the upper classes. Schoolmen and pedants held up to the admiration of the people the heroes of the feudal times and the advantages of the system they administered. Seeing in this propaganda danger to the state, Shi Hwang-ti determined to break once and for all with the past. To this end he ordered the destruction of all books having reference to the past history of the empire, and many scholars were put to death for failing in obedience to it."—The late Sir R. K. Douglas in the *Encyclopædia Brit.*, article *China*.

Photo: Mansell.

AGRICULTURAL WORK IN EGYPT AND GENTLEMAN'S CHARIOT (above).

XX

SERFS, SLAVES, SOCIAL CLASSES, AND FREE INDIVIDUALS

§ 1

WE have been sketching in the last four chapters the growth of civilized states out of the primitive Neolithic agriculture that began in Mesopotamia perhaps 15,000, perhaps 20,000, years ago. It was at first horticulture rather than agriculture ; it was done with the hoe before the plough, and at first it was quite supplementary to the sheep, goat, and cattle tending that made the " living " of the family tribe. We have traced the broad outlines of the development in regions of exceptional fruitfulness of the first settled village communities into more populous towns and cities, and the growth of the village shrine and the village medicine-man into the city temple and the city priesthood. We have noted the beginnings of organized war, first as a bickering between villages, and then as a more disciplined struggle between the priest-king

The Common Man in Ancient Times.

and god of one city and those of another. Our story has passed on rapidly from the first indications of conquest and empire in Sumer, perhaps 6,000 or 7,000 B.C., to the spectacle of great empires growing up, with roads and armies, with inscriptions and written documents, with educated priesthoods and kings and rulers sustained by a tradition already ancient. We have traced in broad outline the appearance and conflicts and replacements of these empires of the great rivers. We have directed attention, in particular, to the evidence of a development of still wider political ideas as we find it betrayed by the actions and utterances of such men as Nabonidus and Amenophis IV. It has been an outline of the accumulations of human experience for ten or fifteen thousand years, a vast space of time in comparison with all subsequent history, but a brief period when we measure it against the succession of endless generations that intervenes between us and the first rude flint-using human creatures of the Pleistocene dawn. But for these last four chapters we have been writing almost entirely not about mankind generally, but only about the men who thought, the men who could draw and read and write, the men who were altering their world. Beneath their activities what was the life of the mute multitude ?

The life of the common man was, of course, affected and changed by these things, just as the lives of the domestic animals and the face of the cultivated country were changed ; but for the most part it was a change suffered and not a change in which the common man upon the land had any voice or will. Reading and writing were not yet for the likes of him. He went on cultivating his patch, loving his wife and children, beating his dog and tending his beasts, grumbling at hard times, fearing the magic of the priests and the power of the gods, desiring little more except to be left alone by the powers above him. So he was in 10,000 B.C. ; so he was, unchanged in nature and outlook, in the time of Alexander the Great ; so over the greater part of the world he remains to-day. He got rather better tools, better seeds, better methods, a slightly sounder house, he sold his

produce in a more organized market as civilization progressed. A certain freedom and a certain equality passed out of human life when men ceased to wander. Men paid in liberty for safety, shelter, and regular meals. By imperceptible degrees the common man found the patch he cultivated was not his own ; it belonged to the god ; and he had to pay a fraction of his produce to the god. Or the god had given it to the king, who exacted his rent and tax. Or the king had given it to an official, who was the lord of the common man. And sometimes the god or the king or the noble had work to be done, and then the common man had to leave his patch and work for his master.

How far the patch he cultivated was his own was never very clear to him. In ancient Assyria the land seems to have been held as a sort of freehold and the occupier paid taxes ; in Babylonia the land was the god's, and he permitted the cultivator to work thereon. In Egypt the temples or Pharaoh-the-god or the nobles under Pharaoh were the owners and rent receivers. But the cultivator was not a slave ; he was a peasant, and only bound to the land in so far that there was nothing else for him to do but cultivate, and nowhere else for him to go. He

TOMB PICTURE SHOWING SCRIBE INSPECTING CATTLE ON AN EGYPTIAN RANCH.

lived in a village or town, and went out to his work. The village, to begin with, was often merely a big household of related people under a patriarch headman, the early town a group of householders under its elders. There was no process of enslavement as civilization grew, but the headmen and leaderly men grew in power and authority, and the common men did not keep pace with them, and fell into a tradition of dependence and subordination.

On the whole, the common men were probably well content to live under lord or king or god and obey their bidding. It was safer. It was easier. All animals —and man is no exception—begin life as dependents. Most men never shake themselves loose from the desire for leading and protection.[1]

§ 2

The earlier wars did not involve remote or prolonged campaigns, and they were waged
The Earliest Slaves.
by levies of the common people. But war brought in a new source of possessions, plunder; and a new social factor, the captive. In the earlier, simpler days of war, the captive man was kept only to be tortured or sacrificed to the victorious god; the captive women and children were assimilated into the tribe. But later many captives were spared as slaves because they had exceptional gifts or peculiar arts. It would be the kings and captains who would take these slaves at first, and it would speedily become apparent to them that these men were

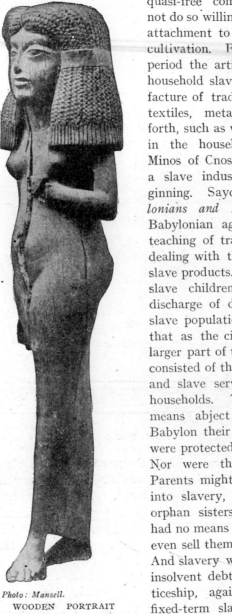

Photo: Mansell.
WOODEN PORTRAIT FIGURE OF A LADY, 1,500 B.C.

much more their own than were the peasant cultivators and common men of their own race.[2] The slave could be commanded to do all sorts of things for his master that the quasi-free common man would not do so willingly because of his attachment to his own patch of cultivation. From a very early period the artificer was often a household slave, and the manufacture of trade goods, pottery, textiles, metal ware, and so forth, such as went on vigorously in the household city of the Minos of Cnossos, was probably a slave industry from the beginning. Sayce, in his *Babylonians and Assyrians*,[3] quotes Babylonian agreements for the teaching of trades to slaves, and dealing with the exploitation of slave products. Slaves produced slave children, enslavement in discharge of debts added to the slave population; it is probable that as the cities grew larger, a larger part of the new population consisted of these slave artificers and slave servants in the large households. They were by no means abject slaves; in later Babylon their lives and property were protected by elaborate laws. Nor were they all outlanders. Parents might sell their children into slavery, and brothers their orphan sisters. Free men who had no means of livelihood would even sell themselves into slavery. And slavery was the fate of the insolvent debtor. Craft apprenticeship, again, was a sort of fixed-term slavery. Out of the slave population, by a converse process, arose the freed-man and freed-woman, who worked for wages and had

[1] There were literary expressions of social discontent in Egypt before 2,000 B.C. See " Social Forces and Religion " in Breasted's *Religion and Thought in Ancient Egypt* from some of the earliest complaints of the common man under the ancient civilizations.

[2] The student should compare with this J. J. Atkinson's account (in his *Primal Law*) of the significance of marriage by capture and his theory of the origin of marriage.

[3] See also his shorter *Social Life of the Babylonians and Assyrians*.

still more definite individual rights. Since in Babylon slaves could themselves own property, many slaves saved up and bought themselves. Probably the town slave was often better off and practically as free as the cultivator of the soil, and as the rural population increased, its sons and daughters came to mix with and swell the growing ranks of artificers, some bound, some free.

As the extent and complexity of government increased, the number of households multiplied. Under the king's household grew up the households of his great ministers and officials, under the temple grew up the personal households of temple functionaries; it is not difficult to realize how houses and patches of land would

in huge earthenware jars.) Upon this gathering mixture of more or less free and detached people would live other people, traders, merchants, small dealers, catering for their needs. Sayce (*op. cit.*) gives the particulars of an agreement for the setting up and stocking of a tavern and beerhouse, for example. The passer-by, the man who happened to be about, had come into existence.

But another and far less kindly sort of slavery also arose in the old civilization, and that was gang slavery. If it did not figure very largely in the cities, it was very much in evidence elsewhere. The king was, to begin with, the chief *entrepreneur*. He made the canals and organized the irrigation (*e.g.* Hammurabi's

BRAWL AMONG BOATMEN.
From the tomb of Ptah-hetep (Maspero).   Pyramid Age.

become more and more distinctly the property of the occupiers, and more and more definitely alienated from the original owner-god. The earlier empires in Egypt and China both passed into a feudal stage, in which families, originally official, became for a time independent noble families. In the later stages of Babylonian civilization we find an increasing propertied class of people appearing in the social structure, neither slaves nor peasants nor priests nor officials, but widows and descendants of such people, or successful traders and the like, and all *masterless* folk. Traders came in from the outside. Babylon was full of Aramean traders, who had great establishments, with slaves, freed-men, employees of all sorts. (Their book-keeping was a serious undertaking. It involved storing a great multitude of earthenware tablets

enterprises noted in the previous chapter). He exploited mines. He seems (at Cnossos, *e.g.*) to have organized manufactures for export. The Pharaohs of the Ist Dynasty were already working the copper and turquoise mines in the peninsula of Sinai. For many such purposes gangs of captives were cheaper and far more controllable than levies of the king's own people. From an early period, too, captives may have tugged the oars of the galleys, though Torr (*Ancient Ships*) notes that up to the age of Pericles (450 B.C.) the free Athenians were not above this task. And the monarch also found slaves convenient for his military expeditions. They were uprooted men; they did not fret to go home, because they had no homes to go to. The Pharaohs hunted slaves in Nubia, in order to have black troops for their Syrian

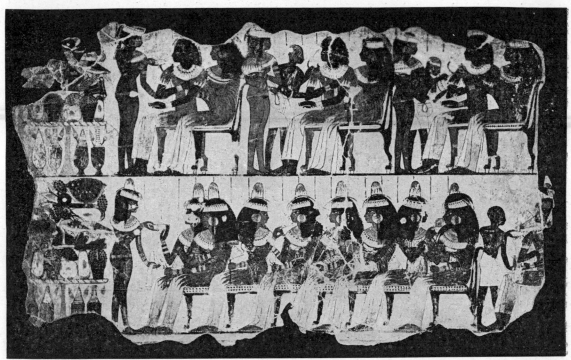

Photo: Mansell.

A FASHIONABLE ENTERTAINMENT IN EGYPT, SLAVES IN ATTENDANCE.

expeditions. Closely allied to such slave troops were the mercenary barbaric troops the monarchs caught into their service, not by positive compulsion, but by the bribes of food and plunder and under the pressure of need. As the old civilization developed, these mercenary armies replaced the national levies of the old order more and more, and servile gang labour became a more and more important and significant factor in the economic system. From mines and canal and wall building, the servile gang spread into cultivation. Nobles and temples adopted the gang-slave system for their works. Plantation gangs began to oust the patch cultivation of the labourer-serf in the case of some staple products. . . .

§ 3

So, in a few paragraphs, we trace the development of the simple social structure of the early

The First "Independent" Persons. Sumerian cities to the complex city crowds, the multitude of individuals varying in race, tradition, education, and function, varying in wealth, freedom, authority, and usefulness, in the great cities of the last thousand years B.C.

The most notable thing of all is the gradual increase amidst this heterogeneous multitude of what we may call *free individuals*, detached persons who are neither priests, nor kings, nor officials, nor serfs, nor slaves, who are under no great pressure to work, who have time to read and inquire. They appear side by side with the development of social security and private property. Coined money and monetary reckoning developed. The operations of the Arameans and such-like Semitic trading people led to the organization of credit and monetary security. In the earlier days almost the only property, except a few movables, consisted of rights in land and in houses; later, one could deposit and lend securities, could go away and return to find one's property faithfully held and secure. Towards the middle of the period of the Persian Empire there lived one free individual, Herodotus, who has a great interest for us because he was among the first writers of critical and intelligent history, as distinguished from a mere priestly or court chronicle. It is worth while to glance here very briefly at the circumstances of his life. Later on we shall quote from his history.

We have already noted the conquest of Babylonia by the Aryan Persians under Cyrus in 539 B.C. We have noted, further, that the Persian Empire spread into Egypt, where its hold was precarious; and it extended also over Asia Minor. Herodotus was born about 484 B.C. in a Greek city of Asia Minor, Halicarnassus, which was under the overlordship of the Persians, and directly under the rule of a political boss or tyrant. There is no sign that he was obliged either to work for a living or spend very much time in the administration of his property. We do not know the particulars of his affairs, but it is clear that in this minor Greek city, under foreign rule, he was able to obtain and read and study manuscripts of nearly everything that had been written in the Greek language before his time. He travelled, so far as one can gather, with freedom and comfort about the Greek archipelagoes; he stayed wherever he wanted to stay, and he seems to have found comfortable accommodation; he went to Babylon and to Susa, the new capital the Persians had set up in Babylonia to the east of the Tigris; he toured along the coast of the Black Sea, and accumulated a considerable amount of knowledge about the Scythians, the Aryan people who were then distributed over South Russia; he went to the south of Italy, explored the antiquities of Tyre, coasted Palestine, landed at Gaza, and made a long stay in Egypt. He went about Egypt looking at temples and monuments and gathering information. We know not only from him, but from other evidence, that in those days the older temples and the pyramids (which were already nearly three thousand years old) were visited by strings of tourists, a special sort of priests acting as guides. The inscriptions the sightseers scribbled upon the walls remain to this day, and many of them have been deciphered and published.

As his knowledge accumulated, he conceived the idea of writing a great history of the attempts of Persia to subdue Greece. But in order to introduce that history he composed an account of the past of Greece, Persia, Assyria, Babylonia, Egypt, Scythia, and of the geography and peoples of those countries. He then set himself, it is said, to make his history known among his friends in Halicarnassus by reciting it to them, but they failed to appreciate it; and he then betook himself to Athens, the most flourishing of all Greek cities at that time. There his work was received with applause. We find him in the centre of a brilliant circle of intelligent and active-minded people, and the city authorities voted him a reward of ten talents (a sum of money equivalent to £2,400) in recognition of his literary achievement. . . .

But we will not complete the biography of this most interesting man, nor will we enter into any criticism of his garrulous, marvel-telling, and most entertaining history. It is a book to which all intelligent readers come sooner or later, abounding as it does in illuminating errors and Boswellian charm. We give these particulars here simply to show that in the fifth century B.C. a new factor was already evident in human affairs. Reading and writing had already long escaped from the temple precincts and the ranks of the court scribes. Record was no longer confined to court and temple. A new sort of people, these people of leisure and independent means, were asking questions, exchanging knowledge and views, and developing ideas. So beneath the march of armies and the policies of monarchs, and above the common lives of illiterate and incurious men, we note the beginnings of what is becoming at last nowadays a dominant power in human affairs, the *free intelligence of mankind*.

Of that free intelligence we shall have more to say when in a subsequent chapter we discuss the Greeks.

§ 4

We may summarize the discussion of the last two chapters here by making a list of the chief elements in this complicated accumulation of human beings which made up the later Babylonian and Egyptian civilizations of from two thousand five hundred to three thousand years ago. These elements grew up and became distinct one from another in the great river valleys of the world in the course of five or six thousand years. They developed mental dispositions and traditions and attitudes of thought one to another. The civilization in which we live to-day is simply carrying on and still further developing and working out and

Social Classes Three Thousand Years Ago.

rearranging these relationships. This is the world from which we inherit. It is only by the attentive study of their origins that we can detach ourselves from the prejudices and immediate ideas of the particular class to which we may belong, and begin to understand the social and political questions of our own time.

(1) First, then, came the priesthood, *the temple system*, which was the nucleus and the guiding intelligence about which the primitive civilizations grew. It was still in these later days a great power in the world, the chief repository of knowledge and tradition, an influence over the lives of every one, and a binding force to hold the community

agents, captains, and guards. Many of his officials, particularly his provincial officials, had great subordinate establishments, and were constantly tending to become independent. The nobility of the old river valley civilizations arose out of the court system. It was, therefore, a different thing in its origins from the nobility of the early Aryans, which was a republican nobility of elders and leading men.

(3) At the base of the social pyramid was the large and most necessary class in the community, *the tillers of the soil*. Their status varied from age to age and in different lands ; they were free peasants paying taxes, or serfs of the god, or serfs or tenants of king or noble,

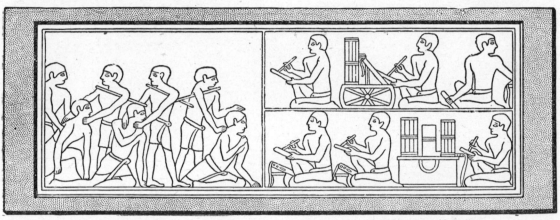

EGYPTIAN PEASANTS SEIZED FOR NON-PAYMENT OF TAXES. (Pyramid Age.)

together. But it was no longer all-powerful, because its nature made it conservative and inadaptable. It no longer monopolized knowledge nor initiated fresh ideas. Learning had already leaked out to other less pledged and controlled people, who thought for themselves. About the temple system were grouped its priests and priestesses, its scribes, its physicians, its magicians, its lay brethren, treasurers, managers, directors, and the like. It owned great properties and often hoarded huge treasures.

(2) Over against the priesthood, and originally arising out of it, was the *court system*, headed by a king or a " king of kings," who was in later Assyria and Babylonia a sort of captain and lay controller of affairs, and in Egypt a god-man, who had released himself from the control of his priests. About the monarch were accumulated his scribes, counsellors, record keepers,

or of a private owner, paying him a rent ; in most cases tax or rent was paid in produce. In the states of the river valleys they were high cultivators, cultivating comparatively small holdings ; they lived together for safety in villages, and had a common interest in maintaining their irrigation channels and a sense of community in their village life. The cultivation of the soil is an exacting occupation ; the seasons and the harvest sunsets will not wait for men ; children can be utilized at an early age, and so the cultivator class is generally a poorly educated, close-toiling class, superstitious by reason of ignorance and the uncertainty of the seasons, ill-informed and easily put upon. It is capable at times of great passive resistance, but it has no purpose in its round but crops and crops, to keep out of debt and hoard against bad times. So it has remained to our own days over the greater part of Europe and Asia.

Foot soldier

Brewer

Servant carrying baggage

Musician

STATUETTES FROM MIDDLE CLASS EGYPTIAN TOMBS, SHOWING LOW-CLASS SOCIAL TYPES IN THE ANCIENT COMMUNITIES.

(4) Differing widely in origin and quality from the tillers of the soil were *the artisan class*. At first, this was probably in part a town-slave class, in part it consisted of peasants who had specialized upon a craft. But in developing an art and mystery of its own, a technique that had to be learnt before it could be practised, each sort of craft probably developed a certain independence and a certain sense of community of its own. The artisans were able to get together and discuss their affairs more readily than the toilers on the land, and they were able to form guilds to restrict output, maintain rates of pay, and protect their common interest.

(5) As the power of the Babylonian rulers spread out beyond the original areas of good husbandry into grazing regions and less fertile districts, a class of *herdsmen* came into existence. In the case of Babylonia these were nomadic Semites, the Bedouwin, like the Bedouwin of to-day. They probably grazed their flocks over great areas much as the sheep ranchers of California do.[1] They were paid and esteemed much more highly than the husbandmen.

(6) The first *merchants* in the world were shipowners, like the people of Tyre and Cnossos, or nomads who carried and traded goods as they wandered between one area of primitive civilization and another. In the Babylonian and Assyrian world the traders were predominantly

[1] See Mary Austin, *The Flock*.

the Semitic Arameans, the ancestors of the modern Syrians. They became a distinct factor in the life of the community ; they formed great households of their own. Usury developed largely in the last thousand years B.C. Traders needed accommodation ; cultivators wished to anticipate their crops. Sayce (*op cit.*) gives an account of the Babylonian banking-house of Egibi, which lasted through several generations and outlived the Chaldean Empire.

(7) A class of *small retailers*, one must suppose, came into existence with the complication of society during the later days of the first empires, but it was not probably of any great importance. It is difficult to understand how there could be much active retailing without small change, and there is little evidence of small change to be found either in Egypt or Mesopotamia.[2] Shekels and half-shekels of silver, weighing something between a quarter and half an ounce, are the lightest weights of stamped metal of which we find mention.

(8) A growing class of *independent property owners*.

(9) As the amenities of life increased, there grew up in the court, temples, and prosperous private houses a class of *domestic servants*,

[2] J. L. M. says this is the view of a Londoner. In a village or small town where everyone knows everyone, long credits are possible with barter. In Asia Minor there is much reckoning with quite imaginary money of account.

slaves or freed slaves, or young peasants taken into the household.

(10) *Gang workers.*—These were prisoners of war or debt slaves, or impressed or deported men.

(11) *Mercenary soldiers.*—These also were often captives or impressed men Sometimes they were enlisted from friendly foreign populations in which the military spirit still prevailed.

(12) *Seamen.*

In modern political and economic discussions we are apt to talk rather glibly of "labour." Much has been made of the *solidarity of labour* and its sense of community. · It is well to note that in these first civilizations, what we speak of as "labour" is represented by five distinct classes dissimilar in origin, traditions, and outlook—namely, classes 3, 4, 5, 9, 10, and the oar-tugging part of 12. The "solidarity of labour" is, we shall find when we come to study the mechanical revolution of the nineteenth century A.D., a new idea and a new possibility in human affairs.

§ 5

Let us, before we leave this discussion of the social classes that were developing in these first **Classes hardening into Castes.** civilizations, devote a little attention to their fixity. How far did they stand aloof from each other, and how far did they intermingle? So far as the classes we have counted as 9, 10, 11, and 12 go, the servants, the gang labourers and slaves, the gang soldiers, and, to a lesser extent, the sailors, or at any rate the galley rowers among the sailors, they were largely recruited classes, they did not readily and easily form homes, they were not distinctively breeding classes; they were probably replenished generation after generation by captives, by the failures of other classes, and especially from the failures of the class of small retailers, and by persuasion and impressment from among the cultivators. But so far as the sailors go, we have to distinguish between the mere rower and the navigating and shipowning seamen of such ports as Tyre and Sidon. The shipowners pass, no doubt, by insensible gradations into the mercantile class, but the navigators must have made a peculiar community in the great seaports, having homes there and handing on the

secrets of seacraft to their sons. The eighth class we have distinguished was certainly a precarious class, continually increased by the accession of the heirs and dependents, the widows and retired members of the wealthy and powerful, and continually diminished by the deaths or speculative losses of these people and the dispersal of their properties. The priests and priestesses too, so far as all this world west of India went, were not a very reproductive class; many priesthoods were celibate, and that class, too, may also be counted as a recruited class. Nor are servants, as a rule, reproductive. They live in the households of other people; they do not have households and rear large families of their own. This leaves us as the really vital classes of the ancient civilized community:

(*a*) The royal and aristocratic class, officials, military officers, and the like;

(*b*) The mercantile class;

(*c*) The town artisans; ·

(*d*) The cultivators of the soil; and

(*e*) The herdsmen.

Each of these classes reared its own children in its own fashion, and so naturally kept itself more or less continuously distinct from the others. General education was not organized in those ancient states, education was mainly a household matter (as it is still in many parts of India to-day), and so it was natural and necessary for the sons to follow in the footsteps of their father and to marry women accustomed to their own sort of household. Except during times of great political disturbance therefore, there would be a natural and continuous separation of classes; which would not, however, prevent exceptional individuals from intermarrying or passing from one class to another. Poor aristocrats would marry rich members of the mercantile class; ambitious herdsmen, artisans, or sailors would become rich merchants. So far as one can gather, that was the general state of affairs in both Egypt and Babylonia. The idea was formerly entertained that in Egypt there was a fixity of classes, but this appears to be a misconception due to a misreading of Herodotus. The only exclusive class in Egypt which did not intermarry was, as in England to-day, the semi-divine royal family.

. At various points in the social system there were probably developments of exclusiveness, an actual barring out of interlopers. Artisans of particular crafts possessing secrets, for example, have among all races and in all ages tended to develop guild organizations restricting the practice of their craft and the marriage of members outside their guild.

Photo: Mansell.

STATUE OF A SCRIBE, 3,500 B.C.

(*a*) Knights, the military and official caste, with heraldic coats-of-arms ;

(*b* and *c*) The Bürgerstand, the merchants, shipping people, and artisans; and

(*d*) The Bauernstand, the cultivating serfs or peasants.

Mediæval Germany went as far as any of the Western heirs of the first great civilizations to-

Conquering people have also, and especially when there were marked physical differences of race, been disposed to keep themselves aloof from the conquered peoples, and have developed an aristocratic exclusiveness. Such organizations of restriction upon free intercourse have come and gone in great variety in the history of all long-standing civilizations. The natural boundaries of function were always there, but sometimes they have been drawn sharply and laid stress upon, and sometimes they have been made little of. There has been a general tendency among the Aryan peoples to distinguish noble (patrician) from common (plebeian) families ; the traces of it are evident throughout the literature and life of Europe to-day, and it has received a picturesque enforcement in the " science " of heraldry. This tradition is still active even in democratic America. Germany, the most methodical of European countries, had in the Middle Ages a very clear conception of the fixity of such distinctions. Below the princes (who themselves constituted an exclusive class which did not marry beneath itself) there were the :

wards a fixation of classes. The idea is far less congenial both to the English-speaking people and to the French and Italians, who, by a sort of instinct, favour a free movement from class to class. Such exclusive ideas began at first among, and were promoted chiefly by, the upper classes, but it is a natural response and a natural Nemesis to such ideas that the mass of the excluded should presently range themselves in antagonism to their superiors. It was in Germany, as we shall see in the concluding chapters of this story, that the conception of a natural and necessary conflict, " the class war," between the miscellaneous multitudes of the disinherited (" the class-conscious proletariat." of the Marxist) and the rulers and merchants first arose. It was an idea more acceptable to the German mind than to the British or French. . . . But before we come to that conflict, we must traverse a long history of many centuries.

§ 6

If now we turn eastward from this main development of civilization in the world between Central Asia and the Atlantic, to the social development of India in the 2,000 years next before the Christian era, we find certain broad and very interesting differences. The first of these is that we find such a fixity of classes in process of establishment as no other part of the world can present. This fixity of classes is known to Europeans as the institution of *caste* ; [1] its origins are still in complete obscurity, but it was certainly well rooted in the Ganges valley before the days of Alexander the Great. It is a complicated horizontal division of the social structure into classes or castes, the members of which may neither eat nor intermarry with persons of a lower caste under penalty of becoming outcasts, and who may also " lose caste " for various ceremonial negligences and defilements. By losing caste a man does not sink to a lower caste ; he becomes outcast. The various subdivisions of caste are very complex ; many are practically trade organizations. Each caste has its local organization which maintains discipline, distributes various charities, looks after its own poor, protects the common interests of its members, and examines the credentials of newcomers from other districts. (There is little to check the pretensions of a travelling Hindu to be of a higher caste than is legitimately his.) Originally, the four main castes seem to have been:

Caste in India.

The Brahmins—the priests and teachers;

The Kshatriyas—the warriors;

The Vaisya—herdsmen, merchants, money-lenders, and land-owners;

The Sudras;

And, outside the castes, the Pariahs.

But these primary divisions have long been superseded by the disappearance of the second and third primary castes, and the subdivision of the Brahmins and Sudras into a multitude of minor castes, all exclusive, each holding its members to one definite way of living and one group of associates.

Next to this extraordinary fission and complication of the social body we have to note that the Brahmins, the priests and teachers of the Indian world, unlike so many Western priesthoods, are a reproductive and exclusive class, taking no recruits from any other social stratum.

[1] From *casta*, a word of Portuguese origin ; the Indian word is *varna*, colour.

Whatever may have been the original incentive to this extensive fixation of class in India, there can be little doubt of the rôle played by the Brahmins as the custodians of tradition and the only teachers of the people in sustaining it. By some it is supposed that the first three of the four original castes, known also as the " twice born," were the descendants of the Vedic Aryan conquerors of India, who established these hard-and-fast separations to prevent racial mixing with the conquered Sudras and Pariahs. The Sudras are represented as a previous wave of northern conquerors, and the Pariahs are the original Dravidian inhabitants of India. But these speculations are not universally accepted, and it is, perhaps, rather the case that the uniform conditions of life in the Ganges valley throughout long centuries served to stereotype a difference of classes that have never had the same steadfastness of definition under the more various and variable conditions of the greater world to the west.

However caste arose, there can be no doubt of its extraordinary hold upon the Indian mind. In the sixth century B.C. arose Gautama, the great teacher of Buddhism, proclaiming, " As the four streams that flow into the Ganges lose their names as soon as they mingle their waters in the holy river, so all who believe in Buddha cease to be Brahmins, Kshatriyas, Vaisyas, and Sudras." His teaching prevailed in India for some centuries ; it spread over China, Tibet, Japan, Burmah, Ceylon, Turkestan, Manchuria ; it is to-day the religion of one-third of the human race, but it was finally defeated and driven out of Indian life by the vitality and persistence of the Brahmins and of their caste ideas. . . .

§ 7

In China we find a social system travelling along yet another, and only a very roughly parallel line to that followed by the Indian and Western civilizations. The Chinese civilization even more than the Hindu is organized for peace, and the warrior plays a small part in its social scheme. As in the Indian civilization, the leading class is an intellectual one ; less priestly than the Brahmin and more official. But unlike the Brahmins, the mandarins, who are the literate

The System of the Mandarins.

men of China, are not a caste; one is not a mandarin by birth, but by education; they are drawn by education and examination from all classes of the community, and the son of a mandarin has no prescriptive right to succeed his father. As a consequence of these differences, while the Brahmins of India are, as a class, ignorant even of their own sacred books, mentally slack, and full of a pretentious as-

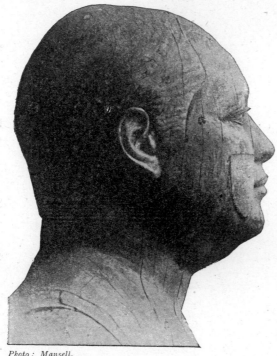

Photo : Mansell.

AN EGYPTIAN OFFICIAL OF THE IVTH DYNASTY. (From a wood carving.)

surance, the Chinese mandarin has the energy that comes from hard mental work. But since his education so far has been almost entirely a scholarly study of the classical Chinese literature, his influence has been entirely conservative. Before the days of Alexander the Great, China had already formed itself and set its feet in the way in which it was still walking in the year 1900 A.D. Invaders and dynasties had come and gone, but the routine of life of the yellow civilization remained unchanged.

The traditional Chinese social system recognized four main classes below the priest-emperor.

(*a*) The literary class, which was equivalent partly to the officials of the Western world and partly to its teachers and clerics.

(*b*) The mercantile class.

(*c*) The artisans.

(*d*) The cultivators of the land.

But since from the earliest times it has been the Chinese way to divide the landed possessions of a man among all his sons, there has never been in Chinese history any class of great landowners, renting their land to tenants, such as most other countries have displayed. The Chinese land has always been cut up into small holdings, which are chiefly freeholds, and cultivated intensively. There are landlords in China who own one or a few farms and rent them to tenants, but there are no great, permanent estates. When a patch of land, by repeated division, is too small to sustain a man, it is sold to some prospering neighbour, and the former owner drifts to some one of the great towns of China to join the mass of wage-earning workers there. In China, for many centuries, there have been these masses of town population with scarcely any property at all, men neither serfs nor slaves, but held to their daily work by their utter impecuniousness. From such masses it is that the soldiers needed by the Chinese government are recruited, and also such gang labour as has been needed for the making of canals, the building of walls, and the like has been drawn.[1] The war captive and the slave class play a smaller part in Chinese history than in any more westerly record of these ages before the Christian era.

One fact, we may note, is common to all these three stories of developing social structure, and that is the immense power exercised by the educated class in the early stages before the crown or the commonalty began to read and, consequently, to think for itself. In India, by reason of their exclusiveness, the Brahmins, the educated class, retain their influence to this day; over the masses of China, along entirely

[1] The Grand Canal of China, the longer portion of which was made in the third century B.C., has a total length of nearly 900 miles. "Between Su-chow and Chin-kiang the canal is often 100 feet wide, and its sides are, in many places, faced with stone. It is spanned by fine stone bridges, and near its banks are many memorial arches and lofty pagodas." The Great Wall of China, which was begun also in the third century B.C., was built originally to defend China against the Huns. It is about 1,500 miles long; its average height is between 20 and 30 feet, and every 200 yards there are towers 40 feet high.

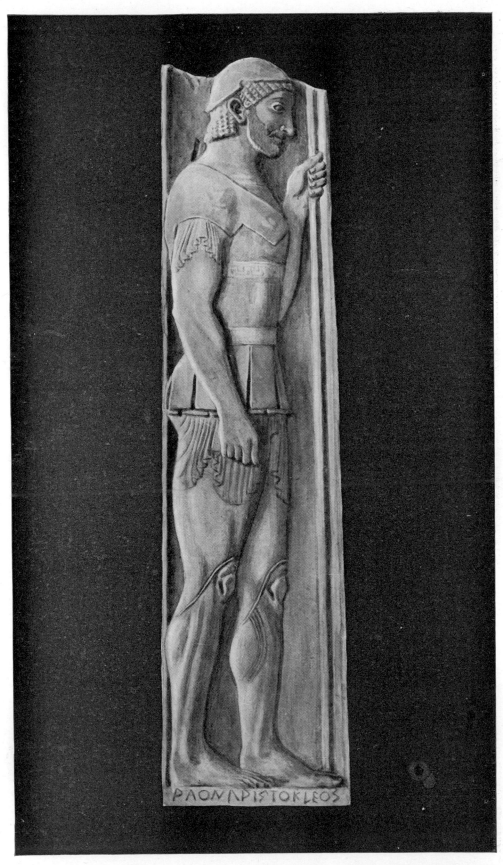

ATHENIAN FOOT SOLDIER, FROM A MONUMENT FOUND NEAR MARATHON.

From a photograph by Alinari.

different lines and because of the complexities of the written language, the mandarinate has prevailed. The diversity of race and tradition in the more various and eventful world of the West has delayed, and perhaps arrested for ever, any parallel organization of the specially intellectual elements of society into a class ascendancy. In the Western world, as we have already noted, education early " slopped over," and soaked away out of the control of any special class ; it escaped from the limitation of castes and priesthoods and traditions into the general life of the community. Writing and reading had been simplified down to a point when it was no longer possible to make a cult and mystery of them. It may be due to the peculiar elaboration and difficulty of the Chinese characters, rather than to any racial difference, that the same thing did not happen to the same extent in China.

§ 8

In these last six chapters we have traced in outline the whole process by which, in the course of 5,000 or 6,000 years—

A Summary of Five Thousand Years. that is to say, in something between 150 and 200 generations—mankind passed from the stage of early Neolithic husbandry, in which the primitive skin-clad family tribe reaped and stored in their rude mud huts the wild-growing fodder and grain-bearing grasses with sickles of stone, to the days of the fourth century B.C., when all round the shores of the Mediterranean and up the Nile, and across Asia to India, and again over the great alluvial areas of China, spread the fields of human cultivation and busy cities, great temples, and the coming and going of human commerce. Galleys and lateen-sailed ships entered and left crowded harbours, and made their careful way from headland to headland and from headland to island, keeping always close to the land. Across the deserts of Africa and Arabia and through Turkestan toiled the caravans with their remote trade ; silk was already coming from China, ivory from Central Africa, and tin from Britain to the centres of this new life in the world. Men had learnt to weave fine linen [1] and delicate fabrics

[1] Damascus was already making Damask, and " Damascening " steel.

of coloured wool ; they could bleach and dye ; they had iron as well as copper, bronze, silver, and gold ; they had made the most beautiful pottery and porcelain ; there was hardly a variety of precious stone in the world that they had not found and cut and polished ; they could read and write ; divert the course of rivers, pile pyramids, and make walls a thousand miles long. The fifty or sixty centuries in which all this had to be achieved may seem a long time in comparison with the threescore and ten years of a single human life, but it is utterly inconsiderable in comparison with the stretches of geological time. Measuring backward from these Alexandrian cities to the days of the first stone implements, the *rostro-carinate* implements of the Pliocene Age, gives us an extent of time fully a hundred times as long.

We have tried in this account, and with the help of maps and figures and time charts, to give a just idea of the order and shape of these fifty or sixty centuries. Our business is with that outline. We have named but a few names ; though henceforth the names must increase in number. But the content of this outline that we have drawn here in a few diagrams and charts cannot but touch the imagination. If only we could look closelier, we should see through all these sixty centuries a procession of lives more and more akin in their fashion to our own. We have shown how the naked Palæolithic savage gave place to the Neolithic cultivator, a type of man still to be found in the backward places of the world. We have given an illustration of Sumerian soldiers copied from a carved stone that was set up long before the days when the Semitic Sargon I conquered the land. Day by day some busy brownish man carved those figures, and, no doubt, whistled as he carved. In those days the plain of the Egyptian delta was crowded with gangs of swarthy workmen unloading the stone that had come down the Nile to add a fresh course to the current pyramid. One might paint a thousand scenes from those ages : of some hawker merchant in Egypt spreading his stock of Babylonish garments before the eyes of some pretty, rich lady ; of a miscellaneous crowd swarming between the pylons to some temple festival at Thebes ; of an excited, dark-eyed audience of Cretans, like the Spaniards of to-day, watching a bull-fight, with the bull-fighters in trousers and tightly girded, exactly like any contemporary bull-fighter ; of children learning their cuneiform signs—at Nippur the clay exercise tiles of a school have been found ; of a woman with a sick husband at home slipping into some great temple in Carthage to make a vow for his recovery. Or perhaps it is a wild Greek, skin-clad and armed with a bronze axe, standing motionless on some Illyrian mountain crest, struck with amazement at his first vision of a many-oared Cretan galley crawling like some great insect across the amethystine mirror of the Adriatic Sea. He went home to tell his folk a strange story of a monster, Briareus with his hundred arms. Of millions of such stitches in each of these 200 generations is the fabric of this history woven. But unless they mark the presence of some primary seam or join, we cannot pause now to examine any of these stitches.

Book IV

JUDEA, GREECE AND INDIA

XXI

THE HEBREW SCRIPTURES AND THE PROPHETS [1]

§ 1

WE are now in a position to place in their proper relationship to this general outline of human history the Israelites, and the most remarkable collection of ancient documents in the world, that collection which is known to all Christian peoples as the Old Testament. We find in these documents the most interesting and valuable lights upon the development of civilization, and the clearest indications of a new spirit that was coming into human affairs during the struggles of Egypt and Assyria for predominance in the world of men.

The Place of the Israelites in History.

All the books that constitute the Old Testament were certainly in existence, and in very much their present form, at latest by the year 100 B.C. They were probably already recognized as sacred writings in the time of Alexander the Great (330 B.C.), and known and read with the utmost respect a hundred years before his time. At that time some of them were of comparatively recent composition ; others were already of very considerable antiquity. They were the sacred literature of a people, the Jews, who, except for a small remnant of common people, had recently been deported to Babylonia from their own country in 587 B.C. by Nebuchad-nezzar II, the Chaldean. They had returned to their city, Jerusalem, and had rebuilt their temple there under the auspices of Cyrus, that Persian conqueror who, we have already noted, in 539 B.C. overthrew Nabonidus, the last of the Chaldean rulers in Babylon. The Babylonian Captivity had lasted about fifty years, and many authorities are of opinion that there was a considerable admixture during that period both of race and ideas with the Babylonians.

The position of the land of Judæa and of Jerusalem, its capital, is a peculiar one. The country is a band-shaped strip between the Mediterranean to the west and the desert beyond the Jordan to the east ; through it lies the natural high road between the Hittites, Syria, Assyria, and Babylonia to the north and Egypt to the south. It was a country pre-destined, therefore, to a stormy history. Across it Egypt, and whatever power was ascendant in the north, fought for empire ; against its people they fought for a trade route. It had itself neither the area, the agricultural possi-bilities, nor the mineral wealth to be important.

[1] *The Encyclopædia Biblica* has been of great use here.

The story of its people that these scriptures have preserved runs like a commentary to the greater history of the two systems of civilization to the north and south and of the sea peoples to the west.

These scriptures consist of a number of different elements. The first five books, the *Pentateuch*, were early regarded with peculiar respect. They begin in the form of a universal history with a double account of the Creation of the world and mankind, of the early life of the race, and of a great Flood by which, except for certain favoured individuals, mankind was destroyed. Excavations have revealed Babylonian versions of both the Creation story and the Flood story of prior date to the restoration of the Jews, and it is therefore argued by Biblical critics that these opening chapters were acquired by the Jews during their captivity. They constitute the first ten chapters of Genesis. There follows a history of the fathers and founders of the Hebrew nation, Abraham, Isaac, and Jacob. They are presented as patriarchal Bedouwin chiefs, living the life of nomadic shepherds in the country between Babylonia and Egypt. The existing Biblical account is said by the critics to be made up out of several pre-existing versions; but whatever its origins, the story, as we have it to-day, is full of colour and vitality. What is called Palestine to-day was at that time the land of Canaan, inhabited by a Semitic people called the Canaanites, closely related to the Phœnicians who founded Tyre and Sidon, and to the Amorites who took Babylon and, under Hammurabi, founded the first Babylonian Empire. The Canaanites were a settled folk in the days—which were perhaps contemporary with the days of Hammurabi—when Abraham's flocks and herds passed through the land. The God of Abraham, says the Bible narrative, promised this smiling land of pros-

perous cities to him and to his children. To the book of Genesis the reader must go to read how Abraham, being childless, doubted this promise, and of the births of Ishmael and Isaac. And in Genesis, too, he will find the lives of Isaac and Jacob, whose name was changed to Israel, and of the twelve sons of Israel; and how in the days of a great famine they went down into Egypt. With that, Genesis, the first book of the Pentateuch, ends. The next book, Exodus, is concerned with the story of Moses.

The story of the settlement and slavery of the children of Israel in Egypt is a difficult one. There is an Egyptian record of a settle-

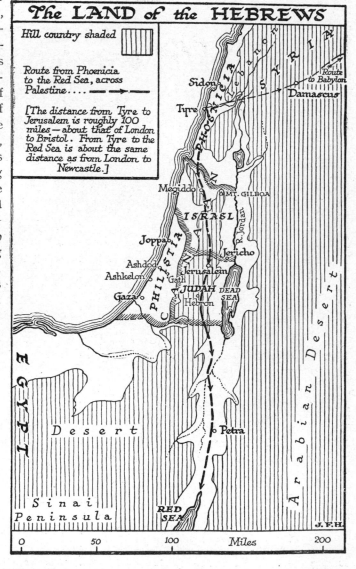

Photo: Mansell.

TRIBUTE OF JEHU, KING OF ISRAEL: TRIBUTE BEARERS WITH VESSELS AND FRUITS.

ment of certain Semitic peoples in the land of Goshen by the Pharaoh Rameses II, and it is stated that they were drawn into Egypt by want of food. But of the life and career of Moses there is no Egyptian record at all ; there is no account of any plagues of Egypt or of any Pharaoh who was drowned in the Red Sea. There is much about the story of Moses that has a mythical flavour, and one of the most remarkable incidents in it, his concealment by his mother in an ark of bulrushes, has also been found in an ancient Sumerian inscription made at least a thousand years before his time by that Sargon I who founded the ancient Akkadian-Sumerian Empire. It runs:

" Sargon, the powerful king, the king of Akkadia am I, my mother was poor, my father I knew not ; the brother of my father lived in the mountains. . . . My mother, who was poor, secretly gave birth to me ; she placed me in a *basket of reeds*, she shut up the mouth of it with bitumen, she abandoned me to the river, which did not overwhelm me. The river bore me away and brought me to Akki the irrigator. Akki the irrigator received me in the goodness of his heart. Akki the irrigator reared me to boyhood. Akki the irrigator made me a

gardener. My service as a gardener was pleasing unto Istar and I became king."

This is perplexing. Still more perplexing is the discovery of a clay tablet written by the Egyptian governors of a city in Canaan to the Pharaoh Amenophis IV, who came in the XVIIIth Dynasty before Rameses II, apparently mentioning the Hebrews by name and declaring that they are overrunning Canaan. Manifestly, if the Hebrews were conquering Canaan in the time of the XVIIIth Dynasty, they could not have been made captive and oppressed, before they conquered Canaan, by Rameses II of the XIXth Dynasty. But it is quite understandable that the Exodus story, written long after the events it narrates, may have concentrated and simplified, and perhaps personified and symbolized, what was really a long and complicated history of tribal invasions. One Hebrew tribe may have drifted down into Egypt and become enslaved, while the others were already attacking the outlying Canaanite cities. It is even possible that the land of the captivity was not Egypt (Hebrew, Misraim), but Misrim in the north of Arabia, on the other side of the Red Sea. These questions are discussed fully and acutely in the *Encyclopædia*

Biblica (articles *Moses* and *Exodus*), to which the curious reader must be referred.[1]

Two other books of the Pentateuch, Deuteronomy and Leviticus, are concerned with the Law and the priestly rules. The book of Numbers takes up the wanderings of the Israelites in the desert and their invasion of Canaan.

Whatever the true particulars of the Hebrew invasion of Canaan may be, there can be no doubt that the country they invaded had changed very greatly since the days of the legendary promise, made centuries before, to Abraham. Then it seems to have been largely a Semitic land, with many prosperous trading cities. But great waves of strange peoples had washed along this coast. We have already told how the dark Iberian or Mediterranean peoples of Italy and Greece, the peoples of that Ægean civilization which culminated at Cnossos, were being assailed by the southward movement of Aryan-speaking races, such as the Italians and Greeks, and how Cnossos was sacked about 1,400 B.C., and destroyed altogether about 1,000 B.C. It is now evident that the people of these Ægean seaports were crossing the sea in search of securer land nests. They invaded the Egyptian delta and the African coast to the west, they formed alliances with the Hittites and other Aryan or Aryanized races. This happened after the time of Rameses II, in the time of Rameses III. Egyptian monuments record great sea fights, and also a march of these people along the coast of Palestine towards Egypt. Their transport was in the ox-carts characteristic of the Aryan tribes, and it is clear that these Cretans were acting in alliance with some early Aryan invaders. No connected narrative of these conflicts that went on between 1,300 B.C. and 1,000 B.C. has yet been made out, but it is evident from the Bible narrative, that when the Hebrews under Joshua pursued their slow subjugation of the promised land, they came against a new people, the Philistines, unknown to Abraham, who were settling along the coast in a series of cities of which Gaza, Gath, Ashdod, Ascalon, and Joppa became the chief, who were really, like the Hebrews, newcomers, and probably chiefly these Cretans from the sea and from the north. The invasion,

therefore, that began as an attack upon the Canaanites, speedily became a long and not very successful struggle for the coveted and promised land with these much more formidable newcomers, the Philistines.

It cannot be said that the promised land was ever completely in the grasp of the Hebrews. Following after the Pentateuch in the Bible come the books of Joshua, Judges, Ruth (a digression), Samuel I and II, and Kings I and II, with Chronicles repeating with variation much of the matter of Samuel II and Kings; there is a growing flavour of reality in most of this latter history, and in these books we find the Philistines steadfastly in possession of the fertile lowlands of the south, and the Canaanites and Phœnicians holding out against the Israelites in the north. The first triumphs of Joshua are not repeated. Judges I and II are a melancholy catalogue of failures. The people lose heart. They desert the worship of their own god Jehovah,[2] and worship Baal and Ashtaroth (= Bel and Ishtar). They mixed

[1] See also G. B. Gray, *A Critical Introduction to the Old Testament.*

[2] So this name should be spelt in English. It is now the fashion among the learned and among the sceptical to spell it Yahwe or Jahveh or Jahve, or in some such fashion. There is a justification for this in the fact that at first only the consonants were written in Hebrew, and then, for reasons into which we will not enter here, the wrong vowels were inserted in this name. But ever since the days of Tyndale's Bible, Jehovah has been established in English literature as the name of the God of Israel, and it is not to be lightly altered. There is at present a deplorable tendency to strange spelling among historians. Attention has already been called to the confusion that is being accumulated in people's minds by the variable spelling of Egyptologists, but the tendency is now almost universal among historical writers. In an otherwise admirable little book, *The Opening-up of Africa*, by Sir H. H. Johnston, for example, one finds him spelling Saul as Sha'ul, and Solomon as Shelomoh; Jerusalem becomes Yerusalim and the Hebrews, Habiru or Ibrim. Historians do not realize how the mind of the general reader is distressed and discouraged by these constantly fluctuating attempts to achieve phonetic exactitude. This treatment of old forms has much the same effect as the dazzle-painting of ships that went on during the submarine warfare. It is dazzle-spelling. The ordinary educated man is so confused that he fails altogether to recognize even his oldest friends under their modern disguises. He loses his way in the story hopelessly. The old events occur to novel names in unfamiliar places. He conceives a disgust for history in which no record seems to tally with any other record. Still more maddening and confusing is the variable spelling of Chinese names.

their race with the Philistines, with the Hittites, and so forth, and became, as they have always subsequently been, a racially mixed people. Under a series of wise men and heroes they wage a generally unsuccessful and never very united warfare against their enemies. In succession they are conquered by the Moabites, the Canaanites, the Midianites, and the Philistines. The story of these conflicts, of Gideon and of Samson and the other heroes who now and then cast a gleam of hope upon

This was a real pitched battle in which the Israelites lost 30,000 (!) men. They had previously suffered a reverse and lost 4,000 men, and then they brought out their most sacred symbol, the Ark of the Covenant of God.

"And when the ark of the covenant of the Lord came into the camp, all Israel shouted with a great shout, so that the earth rang again. And when the Philistines heard the noise of the shout, they said, 'What meaneth the noise of this great shout in the camp of the Hebrews?'

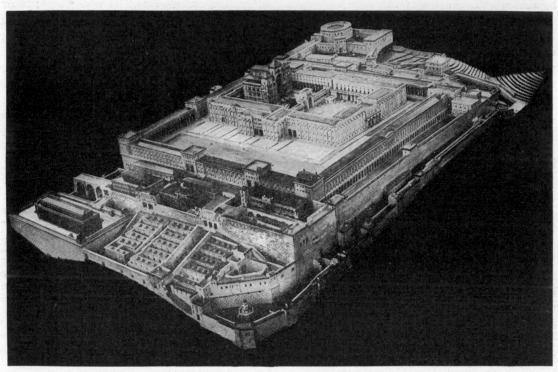

THIS IS THE PHOTOGRAPH OF A MODEL RESTORATION OF SOLOMON'S TEMPLE.
It is a very exaggerated and glorified restoration. The only justifiable thing in it is the central temple, and that is done on the maximum scale of 44 inches to the cubit. All the splendid galleries round about it are *imaginary*. The true walls were probably rough piled stone.

the distresses of Israel, is told in the book of Judges. In the first book of Samuel is told the story of their great disaster at Ebenezer in the days when Eli was judge.

A large part of the popular indifference to Chinese history may be due to the impossibility of holding on to the thread of a story in which one narrator talks of T'sin and another of Sin, and both forms mix themselves with Chin and T'chin. A boldly Europeanized name, such as Confucius, is far more readily grasped. Modern writers in their zeal for phonetics seem to have lost their sense of proportion. It is of far more importance not merely to civilization, but to the welfare, respect, and endowment of historians, that the general community should form clear and sound ideas of

And they understood, that the ark of the Lord was come into the camp. And the Philistines were afraid, for they said, 'God is come into the camp.' And they said, 'Woe unto us!

historical processes, than that it should pronounce the name Jehovah exactly as this or that learned gentleman believes it was pronounced by the Hebrews of the days of Ezra. A day may come in the future for one final, conclusive reform in the spelling of historical names. Meanwhile, it will probably save school teachers of history from endless confusion and muddle if they adhere firmly to the time-established spelling. Yet we have attempted no pedantic classicalism. The reader will find Peisistratus for Goldsmith's Pisistratus and Habsburg has replaced the older Hapsburg.

for there hath not been such a thing heretofore. Woe unto us! who shall deliver us out of the hand of these mighty Gods? these are the Gods that smote the Egyptians with all the plagues in the wilderness. Be strong, and quit yourselves like men, O ye Philistines, that ye be not servants unto the Hebrews, as they have been to you: quit yourselves like men, and fight.'

"And the Philistines fought, and Israel was smitten, and they fled every man into his tent:

of this tumult?' And the man came in hastily, and told Eli. Now Eli was ninety and eight years old; and his eyes were dim, that he could not see. And the man said unto Eli, 'I am he that came out of the army, and I fled to day out of the army.' And he said, 'What is there done, my son?' And the messenger answered and said, 'Israel is fled before the Philistines, and there hath been also a great slaughter among the people, and thy two sons also, Hophni and Phinehas, are dead. and the ark of God is

MODEL OF THE TEMPLE AREA TO-DAY, SHOWING THE MOSQUE OF OMAR, ONCE A CHRISTIAN CHURCH, UPON THE SITE OF THE TEMPLE.
This model covers a much larger area than the preceding one.

and there was a very great slaughter; for there fell of Israel thirty thousand [1] footmen. And the ark of God was taken; and the two sons of Eli, Hophni and Phinehas, were slain.

"And there ran a man of Benjamin out of the army, and came to Shiloh the same day with his clothes rent, and with earth upon his head. And when he came, lo, Eli sat upon a seat by the wayside watching: for his heart trembled for the ark of God. And when the man came into the city, and told it, all the city cried out. And when Eli heard the noise of the crying, he said, 'What meaneth the noise

[1] Figures certainly exaggerated.—G. M.

taken.' And it came to pass when he made mention of the ark of God, that Eli fell from off the seat backward by the side of the gate, and his neck brake, and he died: for he was an old man, and heavy. And he had judged Israel forty years.

"And his daughter in law, Phinehas' wife, was with child, near to be delivered: and when she heard the tidings that the ark of God was taken, and that her father in law and her husband were dead, she bowed herself and travailed: for her pains came upon her. And about the time of her death the women that stood by her said unto her, 'Fear not; for thou hast born a son! But she answered not, neither did she regard it. And she named the child I-chabod,[1] saying, 'The glory is departed from Israel': because the ark of God was taken, and because of her father in law and her husband.'' (1 Sam., chap. iv.)

The successor of Eli and the last of the Judges was Samuel, and at the end of his rule came an event in the history of Israel which paralleled and was suggested by the experience of the greater nations around. A king arose. We are told in vivid language the plain issue between the more ancient rule of priestcraft and the newer fashion in human affairs. It is impossible to avoid a second quotation.

" Then all the elders of Israel gathered themselves together, and came to Samuel unto Ramah, and said unto him: 'Behold, thou art old, and thy sons walk not in thy ways: now make us a king to judge us like all the nations.'

" But the thing displeased Samuel, when they said, 'Give us a king to judge us.' And

[1] That is, where is the glory?

Samuel prayed unto the Lord. And the Lord said unto Samuel, 'Hearken unto the voice of the people in all that they say unto thee: for they have not rejected thee, but they have rejected me, that I should not reign over them. According to all the works which they have done since the day that I brought them up out of Egypt even unto this day, wherewith they have forsaken me, and served other gods, so do they also unto thee. Now therefore hearken unto their voice: howbeit yet protest solemnly unto them, and shew them the manner of the king that shall reign over them.'

" And Samuel told all the words of the Lord unto the people that asked of him a king. And he said, 'This will be the manner of the king that shall reign over you: He will take your sons, and appoint them for himself, for his chariots, and to be his horsemen; and some shall run before his chariots. And he will appoint him captains over thousands, and captains over fifties; and will set them to ear his ground, and to reap his harvest, and to make

Photo: American Colony, Jerusalem.

THE CEDARS OF LEBANON TO-DAY.

his instruments of war, and instruments of his chariots. And he will take your daughters to be confectioners, and to be cooks, and to be bakers. And he will take your fields, and your vineyards, and your oliveyards, even the best of them, and give them to his servants. And he will take the tenth of your seed, and of your vineyards, and give to his officers, and to his servants. And he will take your menservants, and your maidservants, and your goodliest young men, and your asses, and put them to his work. He will take the tenth of your sheep: and ye shall be his servants. And ye shall cry out in that day because of your king which ye shall have chosen you; and the Lord will not hear you in that day.'

"Nevertheless the people refused to obey the voice of Samuel; and they said, 'Nay; but we will have a king over us; that we also may be like all the nations; and that our king may judge us, and go out before us, and fight our battles.'" (1 Sam., chap. viii.)

§ 2

But the nature and position of their land was against the Hebrews, and their first king Saul was no more successful than their judges. The long intrigues of the adventurer David against Saul are told in the rest of the first book of Samuel, and the end of Saul was utter defeat upon Mount Gilboa. His army was overwhelmed by the Philistine archers.

Saul, David, and Solomon.

"And it came to pass on the morrow, when the Philistines came to strip the slain, that they found Saul and his three sons fallen in mount Gilboa. And they cut off his head, and stripped off his armour, and sent into the land of the Philistines round about, to publish it in the house of their idols, and among the people. And they put his armour in the house of Ashtaroth: and they fastened his body to the wall of Beth-shan." (1 Sam., chap. xxxi.)

David (990 B.C. roughly) was more politic and successful than his predecessor, and he seems to have placed himself under the protection of Hiram, King of Tyre. He married Michal, the daughter of Saul, but there was no love between them. The marriage was an attempt to legitimate his position. She hated and insulted him—he had hung her sons—and

he kept her a close captive (2 Sam. vi). But the Phœnician alliance sustained him, and was the essential element in the greatness of his son Solomon.

The first book of Kings begins with the reign of King Solomon (960 B.C. roughly). The most interesting thing in that story, from the point of view of the general historian, is the relationship of Solomon to the national religion and the priesthood, and his dealings with the tabernacle, the priest Zadok, and the prophet Nathan.

The opening of Solomon's reign is as bloody as his father's. The last recorded speech of David's arranges for the murder of Shimei; his last recorded word is " blood." " But his hoar head bring thou down to the grave with blood," he says, pointing out that though old Shimei is protected by David's vow to the Lord so long as David lives, there is nothing to bind Solomon in that matter. Solomon proceeds to murder his brother, who has sought the throne but quailed and made submission. He then deals freely with his brother's party. The weak hold of religion upon the racially and mentally confused Hebrews at that time is shown by the ease with which he replaces the hostile chief priest by his own adherent Zadok, and still more strikingly by the murder of Joab by Benaiah, Solomon's chief ruffian, in the Tabernacle, while the victim is claiming sanctuary and holding to the very horns of Jehovah's altar. Then Solomon sets to work, in what was for that time a thoroughly modern spirit, to recast the religion of his people. He continues the alliance with Hiram, King of Sidon, who uses Solomon's kingdom as a high road by which to reach and build shipping upon the Red Sea, and a hitherto unheard-of wealth accumulates in Jerusalem as a result of this partnership. Gang labour appears in Israel; Solomon sends relays of men to cut cedarwood in Lebanon under Hiram, and organizes a service of porters through the land. (There is much in all this to remind the reader of the relations of some Central African chief to a European trading concern.) Solomon then builds a palace for himself, and a temple not nearly as big for Jehovah. Hitherto, the Ark of the Covenant, the divine symbol of these ancient Hebrews, had abode in a large tent, which had been shifted from one high

Photo : Mansell.

SHALMANESER RECEIVING TRIBUTE AND AMBASSADOR OF JEHU, KING OF ISRAEL.

place to another, and sacrifices had been offered to the God of Israel upon a number of different high places. Now the ark is brought in to the golden splendours of the inner chamber of a temple of cedar-sheathed stone, and put between two great winged figures of gilded olivewood, and sacrifices are henceforth to be made only upon the altar before it.

This centralizing innovation will remind the reader of both Akhnaton and Nabonidus. Such things as this are done successfully only when the prestige and tradition and learning of the priestly order has sunken to a very low level.

"And he appointed, according to the order of David his father, the courses of the priests to their service, and the Levites to their charges, to praise and minister before the priests, as the duty of every day required ; the porters also by their courses at every gate ; for so had David the man of God commanded. And they departed not from the commandment of the king unto the priests and Levites concerning any matter, or concerning the treasures."

Neither Solomon's establishment of the worship of Jehovah in Jerusalem upon this new footing, nor his vision of and conversation with his God at the opening of his reign, stood in the way of his developing a sort of theological flirtatiousness in his declining years. He married widely, if only for reasons of state and splendour, and he entertained his numerous wives by sacrificing to their national deities, to the Sidonian goddess Ashtaroth (Ishtar), to Chemosh (a Moabitish god), to Moloch, and so forth. The Bible account of Solomon does, in fact, show us a king and a confused people, both superstitious and mentally unstable, in no way more religious than any other people of the surrounding world.

A point of considerable interest in the story of Solomon, because it marks a phase in Egyptian affairs, is his marriage to a daughter of Pharaoh. This must have been one of the Pharaohs of the XXIst Dynasty. In the great days of Amenophis III, as the Tel Amarna letters witness, Pharaoh could condescend to receive a Babylonian princess into his harem, but he refused absolutely to grant so divine a creature as an Egyptian princess in marriage to the Babylonian monarch. It points to the steady decline of Egyptian prestige that now, three centuries later, such a petty monarch as Solomon could wed on equal terms with an Egyptian princess. There was, however, a revival with the next Egyptian dynasty (XXII) ; and the Pharaoh Shishak, the founder, taking advantage of the cleavage between Israel and Judah, which had been developing through the reigns of both David and Solomon, took Jerusalem and looted the all-too-brief splendours both of the new temple and of the king's house.

Shishak seems also to have subjugated Philistia. From this time onward it is to be noted that the Philistines fade in importance. They had already lost their Cretan language and adopted that of the Semites they had conquered, and although their cities remain more or less independent, they merge gradually into the general Semitic life of Palestine.

There is evidence that the original rude but convincing narrative of Solomon's rule, of his various murders, of his association with Hiram, of his palace and temple building, and the extravagances that weakened and finally tore his kingdom in twain, has been subjected to extensive interpolations and expansions by a later writer, anxious to exaggerate his prosperity and glorify his wisdom. It is not the place here to deal with the criticism of Bible origins, but it is a matter of ordinary common sense rather than of scholarship to note the manifest reality and veracity of the main substance of the account of David and Solomon, an account explaining sometimes and justifying sometimes, but nevertheless relating facts, even the harshest facts, as only a contemporary or almost contemporary writer, convinced that they cannot be concealed, would relate them, and then to remark the sudden lapse into adulation when the inserted passages occur. It is a striking tribute to the power of the written assertion over realities in men's minds that this Bible narrative has imposed, not only upon the Christian, but upon the Moslim world, the belief that King Solomon was not only one of the most magnificent, but one of the wisest of men. Yet the first book of Kings tells in detail his utmost splendours, and beside the beauty and wonder of the buildings and organizations of such great monarchs as Thotmes III or Rameses II or half a dozen other Pharaohs, or of Sargon II or Sardanapalus or Nebuchadnezzar the Great, they are trivial. His temple measured internally was twenty cubits broad, about 35 feet [1]—that is, the breadth of a small villa residence—and sixty cubits, say, 100 feet, long. And as for his wisdom and statescraft, one need go no further than the Bible to see that Solomon was a mere helper in the wide-reaching schemes of the trader-king Hiram, and his kingdom a pawn between Phœnicia and Egypt.

[1] Estimates of the cubit vary. The greatest is 44 inches. This would extend the width to seventy-odd feet.

His importance was due largely to the temporary enfeeblement of Egypt, which encouraged the ambition of the Phœnician and made it necessary to propitiate the holder of the key to an alternate trade route to the East. To his own people Solomon was a wasteful and oppressive monarch, and already before his death his kingdom was splitting, visibly to all men.

With the reign of King Solomon the brief glory of the Hebrews ends ; the northern and richer section of his kingdom, long oppressed by taxation to sustain his splendours, breaks off from Jerusalem to become the separate kingdom of Israel, and this split ruptures that linking connection between Sidon and the Red Sea by which Solomon's gleam of wealth was possible. There is no more wealth in Hebrew history. Jerusalem remains the capital of one tribe, the tribe of Judah, the capital of a land of barren hills, cut off by Philistia from the sea and surrounded by enemies.

The tale of wars, of religious conflicts, of usurpations, assassinations, and of fratricidal murders to secure the throne goes on for three centuries. It is a tale frankly barbaric. Israel wars with Judah and the neighbouring states ; forms alliances first with one and then with the other. The power of Aramean Syria burns like a baleful star over the affairs of the Hebrews, and then there rises behind it the great and growing power of the last Assyrian empire. For three centuries the life of the Hebrews was like the life of a man who insists upon living in the middle of a busy thoroughfare, and is consequently being run over constantly by omnibuses and motor-lorries.

" Pul " (apparently the same person as Tiglath Pileser III) is the first Assyrian monarch to appear upon the Hebrew horizon, and Menahem buys him off with a thousand talents of silver (738 B.C.). But the power of Assyria is heading straight for the now aged and decadent land of Egypt, and the line of attack lies through Judea ; Tiglath Pileser III returns and Shalmaneser follows in his steps, the King of Israel intrigues for help with Egypt, that " broken reed," and in 721 B.C., as we have already noted, his kingdom is swept off into captivity and utterly lost to history. The same fate hung over Judah, but for a little while it was averted. The fate of Sennacherib's

Photo: Mansell.
PART OF A LARGE TERRA-COTTA TABLET, WITH INSCRIPTION OF TIGLATH-PILESER III, KING OF ASSYRIA, RECORDING CONQUESTS AND BUILDING OPERATIONS.
Among the tributary kings, " Ahaz, King of Judah," is mentioned.

army in the reign of King Hezekiah (701 B.C.), and how he was murdered by his sons (II. Kings xix. 37), we have already mentioned. The subsequent subjugation of Egypt by Assyria finds no mention in Holy Writ, but it is clear that before the reign of Sennacherib, King Hezekiah had carried on a diplomatic correspondence with Babylon (700 B.C.), which was in revolt against Sargon II of Assyria. There followed the conquest of Egypt by Esarhaddon, and then for a time Assyria was occupied with her own troubles; the Scythians and Medes and Persians were pressing her on the north, and Babylon was in insurrection. As we have already noted, Egypt, relieved for a time from Assyrian pressure, entered upon a phase of revival, first under Psammetichus and then under Necho II.

Again the little country in between made mistakes in its alliances. But on neither side was there safety. Josiah opposed Necho, and was slain at the battle of Megiddo (608 B.C.). The king of Judah became an Egyptian tribu-tary. Then when Necho, after pushing as far as the Euphrates, fell before Nebuchadnezzar II, Judah fell with him (604 B.C.). Nebuchadnezzar, after a trial of three puppet kings, carried off the greater part of the people into captivity in Babylon (586 B.C.), and the rest, after a rising and a massacre of Babylonian officials, took refuge from the vengeance of Chaldea in Egypt.

"And all the vessels of the house of God, great and small, and the treasures of the house of the Lord, and the treasures of the king, and of his princes; all these he brought to Babylon. And they burnt the house of God and brake down the wall of Jerusalem, and burnt all the palaces thereof with fire, and destroyed all the goodly vessels thereof. And them that had escaped from the sword carried he away to Babylon; where they were servants to him and his sons until the reign of the kingdom of Persia." [1]

So the four centuries of Hebrew kingship

[1] II. Chron. xxxvi. 18, 19, 20.

comes to its end. From first to last it was a mere incident in the larger and greater history of Egypt, Syria, Assyria, and Phœnicia. But out of it there were now to arise moral and intellectual consequences of primary importance to all mankind.

§ 3

The Jews who returned, after an interval of more than two generations, to Jerusalem from Babylonia in the time of Cyrus were a very different people from the warring Baal worshippers and Jehovah worshippers, the sacrificers in the high places and sacrificers at Jerusalem of the kingdoms of Israel and Judah. The plain fact of the Bible narrative is that the Jews went to Babylon barbarians and came back civilized. They went a confused and divided multitude, with no national self-consciousness; they came back with an intense and exclusive national spirit. They went with no common literature generally known to them, for it was only about forty years before the captivity that king Josiah is said to have discovered "a book of the law" in the temple (II. Kings xxii.), and, besides that, there is not a hint in the record of any reading of books; and they returned with most of their material for the Old Testament. It is manifest that, relieved of their bickering and murderous kings, restrained from politics and in the intellectually stimulating atmosphere of that Babylonian world, the Jewish mind made a great step forward during the captivity.

The Jews a People of Mixed Origins.

It was an age of historical inquiry and learning in Babylonia. The Babylonian influences that had made Sardanapalus collect a great library of ancient writings in Nineveh were still at work. We have already told how Nabonidus was so preoccupied with antiquarian research as to neglect the defence of his kingdom against Cyrus. Everything, therefore, contributed to set the exiled Jews inquiring into their own history, and they found an inspiring leader in the prophet Ezekiel. From such hidden and forgotten records as they had with them, genealogies, contemporary histories of David, Solomon, and their other kings, legends and traditions, they made out and amplified their own story, and told it to Babylon and themselves. The story of the Creation and the Flood,

much of the story of Moses, much of Samson, were probably incorporated from Babylonian sources. When they returned to Jerusalem, only the Pentateuch had been put together into one book, but the grouping of the rest of the historical books was bound to follow.

The rest of their literature remained for some centuries as separate books, to which a very variable amount of respect was paid. Some of the later books are frankly post-captivity compositions. Over all this literature were thrown certain leading ideas. There was an idea, which even these books themselves gainsay in detail, that all the people were pure-blooded children of Abraham; there was next an idea of a promise made by Jehovah to Abraham that he would exalt the Jewish race above all other races; and, thirdly, there was the belief first of all that Jehovah was the greatest and most powerful of tribal gods, and then that he was a god above all other gods, and at last that he was the only true god. The Jews became convinced at last, as a people, that they were the chosen people of the one God of all the earth.

And arising very naturally out of these three ideas, was a fourth, the idea of a coming leader, a saviour, a Messiah who would realize the long-postponed promises of Jehovah.

This welding together of the Jews into one tradition-cemented people in the course of the "seventy years" is the first instance in history of the new power of the written word in human affairs. It was a mental consolidation that did much more than unite the people who returned to Jerusalem under Ezra and Nehemiah. This idea of belonging to a chosen race predestined to pre-eminence was a very attractive one. It possessed also those Jews who remained in Babylonia. Its literature reached the Jews now established in Egypt. It affected the mixed people who had been placed in Samaria, the old capital of the kings of Israel when the ten tribes were deported to Medea. It inspired a great number of Babylonians and the like to claim Abraham as their father, and thrust their company upon the returning Jews. Ammonites and Moabites became adherents. The book of Nehemiah is full of the distress occasioned by this invasion of the privileges of the chosen. The Jews were already a people dispersed in many lands and cities, when their minds and hopes were unified and they became an exclusive people. But at first their exclusiveness is merely to preserve soundness of doctrine and worship, warned by such lamentable lapses as those of King Solomon. To genuine proselytes of whatever race, Judaism long held out welcoming arms.

To Phœnicians after the falls of Tyre and Carthage, conversion to Judaism must have been particularly easy and attractive. Their language was closely akin to Hebrew. It is possible that the great majority of African and Spanish Jews are really of Phœnician origin. There were also great Arabian accessions. In South Russia, as we shall note later, there were even Mongolian Jews.

§ 4·

The historical books from Genesis to Nehemiah, upon which the idea of the promise to the chosen people had been imposed later, were no doubt the backbone of Jewish mental unity, but they by no means complete the Hebrew literature from which finally the Bible was made up. Of such books as Job, said to be

The Importance of the Hebrew Prophets.

an imitation of Greek tragedy, the Song of Solomon, the Psalms, Proverbs, and others, there is no time to write in this *Outline*, but it is necessary to deal with the books known as "the Prophets" with some fullness. For those books are almost the earliest and certainly the best evidence of the appearance of a new kind of leading in human affairs.[1]

These prophets are not a new class in the community; they are of the most various origins—Ezekiel was of the priestly caste and of priestly sympathies, and Amos was a shepherd; but they have this in common, that they bring into life a religious force outside the sacrifices and formalities of priesthood and temple. The earlier prophets seem most like the earlier priests, they are oracular, they give advice and foretell events; it is quite possible that at first, in the days when there were many high places in the land and religious ideas were comparatively unsettled, there was no great distinction between priest and prophet. The prophets danced, it would seem, somewhat

[1] For early Egyptian anticipations of the idea of a Messiah and of the prophetic style, see Breasted's *Development of Religion and Thought in Ancient Egypt.* A very good book on the Hebrew prophets is W. A. C. Allen's *Old Testament Prophets.*

Photo: Mansell.

A GENERAL VIEW OF TYRE.

after the Dervish fashion, and uttered oracles. Generally, it would seem, they wore a distinctive mantle of rough goatskin. They kept up the nomadic tradition as against the "new ways" of the settlement. But after the building of the temple and the organization of the priesthood, the prophetic type remains over and outside the formal religious scheme. They were probably always more or less of an annoyance to the priests. They became informal advisers upon public affairs, denouncers of sin and strange practices, " self-constituted," as we should say, having no sanction but an inner light. " Now the word of the Lord came unto "—so and so ; that is the formula.

In the latter and most troubled days of the kingdom of Judah, as Egypt, North Arabia, Assyria, and then Babylonia closed like a vice upon the land, these prophets became very significant and powerful. Their appeal was to anxious and fearful minds, and at first their exhortation was chiefly towards repentance, the pulling down of this or that high place, the restoration of worship in Jerusalem, or the like. But through some of the prophecies there runs already a note like the note of what we call nowadays a " social reformer." The rich are " grinding the faces of the poor " ; the luxurious are consuming the children's bread ; influential and wealthy people make friends with and imitate the splendours and vices of foreigners, and sacrifice the common people to these new fashions ; and this is hateful to Jehovah, who will certainly punish the land.

But with the broadening of ideas that came with the Captivity, the tenour of prophecy broadens and changes. The jealous pettiness that disfigures the earlier tribal ideas of God give place to a new idea of a god of universal righteousness. It is clear that the increase and influence of prophets was not confined to the Jewish people ; it was something that was going on in those days all over the Semitic world. The breaking down of nations and kingdoms to form the great and changing empires of that age, the smashing up of cults and priesthoods, the mutual discrediting of temple by temple in their rivalries and disputes – all these influences were releasing men's minds to a freer and wider religious outlook. The temples had accumulated great stores of golden vessels and

lost their hold upon the imaginations of men. It is difficult to estimate whether, amidst these constant wars, life had become more uncertain and unhappy than it had ever been before, but there can be no doubt that men had become more conscious of its miseries and insecurities. Except for the weak and the women, there remained little comfort or assurance in the sacrifices, ritual, and formal devotions of the temples. Such was the world to which the later prophets of Israel began to talk of the One God, and of a Promise that some day the world should come to peace and unity and happiness. This great God that men were now discovering lived in a temple " not made with hands, eternal in the heavens." [1] There can be little doubt of a great body of such thought and utterance in Babylonia, Egypt, and throughout the Semitic east. The prophetic books of the Bible can be but specimens of the prophesyings of that time. . . .

We have already drawn attention to the gradual escape of writing and knowledge from their original limitation to the priesthood and the temple precincts, from the shell in which they were first developed and cherished. We have taken Herodotus as an interesting specimen of what we have called the free intelligence of mankind. Now here we are dealing with a similar overflow of moral ideas into the general community. The Hebrew prophets, and the steady expansion of their ideas towards one God in all the world, is a parallel development of the free conscience of mankind. From this time onward there runs through human thought, now weakly and obscurely, now gathering power, the idea of one rule in the world, and of a promise and possibility of an active and splendid peace and happiness in human affairs. From being a temple religion of the old type, the Jewish religion becomes, to a large extent, a prophetic and creative religion of a new type. Prophet succeeds prophet. Later on, as we shall tell, there was born a prophet of unprecedented power, Jesus, whose followers founded the great universal religion of Christianity. Still later

[1] The reader should compare the splendour of I. Kings viii. 27, which is clearly a later interpolation, with the gross materialism of II. Chron. v. 13, 14, and the ideas underlying the patched and altered chap. vii. of Sam. ii.

Mahommed, another prophet, appears in Arabia and founds Islam. In spite of very distinctive features of their own, these two teachers do in a manner arise out of, and in succession to these Jewish prophets. It is not the place of the historian to discuss the truth and falsity of religion, but it is his business to record the appearance of great constructive ideas. Two thousand four hundred years ago, and six or seven or eight thousand years after the walls of the first Sumerian cities arose, the ideas of the moral unity of mankind and of a world peace had come into the world.[1]

[1] Fletcher H. Swift's *Education in Ancient Israel from Earliest Times to* A.D. 70 is an interesting account of the way in which the Jewish religion, because it was a literature-sustained religion, led to the first efforts to provide elementary education for *all* the children in the community.

XXII

THE GREEKS AND THE PERSIANS[2]

§ 1

AND now our history must go back again to those Aryan-speaking peoples of whose early beginnings we have given an account in Chapters XIV and XV. We must, for the sake of precision, repeat here two warnings we have already given the reader: first, that we use the word Aryan in its widest sense, to express all the early peoples who spoke languages of the "Indo-Germanic" or "Indo-European" group; and, secondly, that when we use the word Aryan we do not imply any racial purity.

The Hellenic Peoples.

The original speakers of the fundamental Aryan language, 2,000 or 3,000 years B.C., were probably a specialized and distinctive Nordic race of fair white men, accustomed to forests and cattle, who wandered east of the Rhine and through the forests of the Danube valley, the Balkan peninsula, Asia Minor, and eastward to the north and west of the great Central Asian Sea; but very early they had encountered and mixed themselves extensively, and as they spread they continued to mix themselves with other races, with races of uncertain affinities in Asia Minor and with Iberian and Mediterranean peoples of the dark-haired white race. For instance, the Aryans, spreading and pressing westward in successive waves of Keltic-speaking peoples through Gaul and Britain and Ireland, mixed more and more with Iberian races, and were affected more and more by that Iberian blood and their speech by the characteristics of the language their Keltic tongue superseded. Other waves of Keltic peoples washed with diminishing force into Spain and Portugal, where to this day the pre-Keltic strain is altogether dominant, although the languages spoken are Aryan. Northward, in Europe, the Aryan peoples were spreading into hitherto uninhabited country, and so remaining racially more purely Nordic blonds. They had already reached Scandinavia many centuries B.C.

From their original range of wandering, other Aryan tribes spread to the north as well as to the south of the Black Sea, and ultimately, as these seas shrank and made way for them, to the north and east of the Caspian, and so began to come into conflict with and mix also with Mongolian peoples of the Ural-Altaic linguistic group, the horse-keeping people of the grassy steppes of Central Asia. From these Mongolian races the Aryans seem to have acquired the use of the horse for riding and warfare. There were three or four prehistoric varieties or subspecies of horse in Europe and Asia, but it was the steppe or semi-desert lands that first gave horses of a build adapted to other than food uses.[3] All these peoples, it must be understood, shifted their ground rapidly, a succession of bad seasons might drive them many hundreds of miles, and it is only in a very rough and provisional manner that their "beats" can now be indicated. Every summer they went north, every winter they swung south again. This annual swing covered sometimes hundreds of miles. On our maps, for the sake of sim-

[2] Ridgeway's *Early History of Greece* has been used here, and Gilbert Murray's *Rise of the Greek Epic*.

[3] Roger Pocock's *Horses* is a good and readable book on these questions.

SOLDIERS OF THE PERSIAN BODY GUARD, FROM A FRIEZE OF GLAZED TILES
IN THE AUDIENCE HALL OF DARIUS AT SUSA.

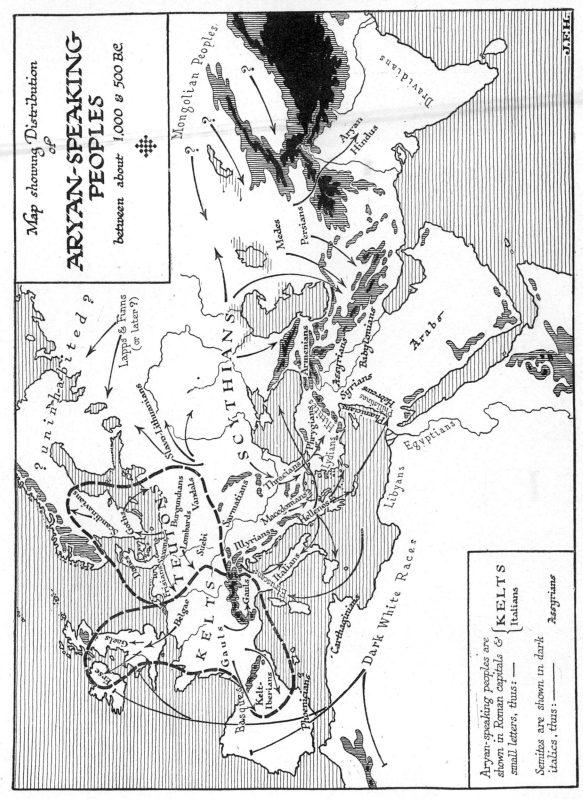

Map showing Distribution of **ARYAN-SPEAKING PEOPLES** between about 1,000 & 500 B.C.

Mongolian Peoples

Dravidians

Aryan Hindus

Medes

Persians

Scythians

? uninhabited ?

Lapps & Funns (or later ?)

Slavo-Lithuanians

Armenians

Assyrians

Babylonians

Arabs

Syrians

Hebrews

Phrygians

Lydians

Phoenicians

Philistines

Egyptians

Teutons

Goths

Frisians

Saxons

Belgae

Suebi

Lombards

Burgundians

Vandals

Illyrians

Thracians

Macedonians

Hellenes

Sarmatians

Libyans

Scandinavians

Kelts

Gauls

Etruscans

Italians

Gaels

Erse

Basques

Kelt-Iberians

Carthaginians

Dark White Races

Aryan-speaking peoples are shown in Roman capitals & small letters, thus: —— { **KELTS** Italians

Semites are shown in dark italics, thus: —— *Assyrians*

12   177

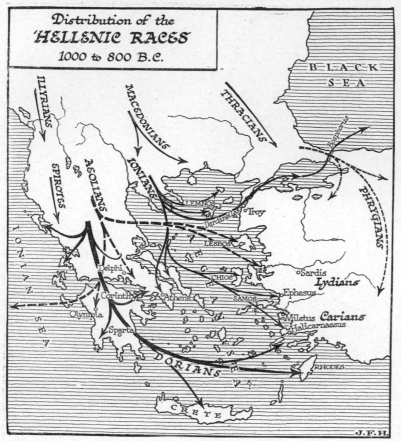

Distribution of the HELLENIC RACES 1000 to 800 B.C.

intermixing freely—to the great confusion of historians. They seem, for instance, to have broken up and assimilated the Hittite civilization, which was probably pre-Aryan in its origin. They were, perhaps, not so far advanced along the nomadic line as the Scythians of the great plains.

The general characteristics of the original Aryan peoples we have already discussed in Chapter XV. They were a forest people, not a steppe people, and, consequently, wasteful of wood; they were a cattle people and not a horse people. The Greeks appear in the dim light before the dawn of history (say, 1,500 B.C.), as one of the wandering imperfectly nomadic Aryan peoples who were gradually extending the range of their pasturage southward into the Balkan peninsula and coming into conflict and mixing with that preceding Ægean civilization of which Cnossos was the crown.

In the Homeric poems these Greek tribes speak one common language, and a common tradition upheld by the epic poems keeps them together in a loose unity; they call their various tribes by a common name, *Hellenes*. They probably came in successive waves. Three main variations of the ancient Greek speech are distinguished; the Ionic, the Æolic, and the Doric. There was a great variety of dialects in Greece, almost every city having its own output of literature. The Doric apparently constituted the last and most powerful wave of the migration. These Hellenic tribes conquered and largely destroyed the Ægean civilization that had preceded their arrival; upon its ashes they built up a civilization of their own. They took to the sea and crossed by way of the islands to Asia Minor; and, sailing through the Dardanelles and Bosphorus,

plicity, we represent the shifting of nomadic peoples by a straight line; but really they moved in annual swings, as the broom of a servant who is sweeping out a passage swishes from side to side as she advances. Spreading round the north of the Black Sea, and probably to the north of the Caspian, from the range of the original Teutonic tribes of Central and North-central Europe to the Iranian peoples who became the Medes and Persians and (Aryan) Hindus, were the grazing lands of a confusion of tribes, about whom it is truer to be vague than precise, such as the Cimmerians, the Sarmatians, and those Scythians who, together with the Medes and Persians came into effective contact with the Assyrian Empire by 1,000 B.C. or earlier.

East and south of the Black Sea, between the Danube and the Medes and Persians, and to the north of the Semitic and Mediterranean peoples of the sea coasts and peninsulas, ranged another series of equally ill-defined Aryan tribes, moving easily from place to place and spread their settlements along the south, and presently along the north borders of the Black Sea. They spread also over the south of Italy, which was called at last Magna Græcia, and round the northern coast of the Mediterranean. They founded the town of Marseilles on the site of an earlier Phœnician colony. They began settlements in Sicily in rivalry with the Carthaginians as early as 735 B.C.

In the rear of the Greeks proper came the kindred Macedonians and Thracians; on their left wing, the Phrygians crossed by the Bosphorus into Asia Minor.

We find all this distribution of the Greeks effected before the beginnings of written history. By the seventh century B.C.—that is to say, by the time of the Babylonian captivity of the Jews—the landmarks of the ancient world of the pre-Hellenic civilization in Europe have been obliterated. Tiryns and Cnossos are unimportant sites; Mycenæ and Troy survive in legend; the great cities of this new Greek world are Athens, Sparta (the capital of Lacedemon), Corinth, Thebes, Samos, Miletus. The world our grandfathers called "Ancient Greece" had arisen on the forgotten ruins of a still more Ancient Greece, in many ways as civilized and artistic, of which to-day we are only beginning to learn through the labours of the excavator. But the newer Ancient Greece, of which we are now telling, still lives vividly in the imaginations and institutions of men because it spoke a beautiful and most expressive Aryan tongue akin to our own, and because it had taken over the Mediterranean alphabet and perfected it by the addition of vowels, so that reading and writing were now easy arts to learn and practise, and great numbers of people

could master them and make a record for later ages.[1]

§ 2

Now this Greek civilization that we find growing up in South Italy and Greece and Asia **Distinctive Features of Hellenic Civilization.** Minor in the seventh century B.C., is a civilization differing in many important respects from the two great civilized systems whose growths we have already traced, that of the Nile and that of the Two Rivers of Mesopotamia. These civilizations grew through long ages where they are found; they grew slowly about a temple life out of a primitive agriculture; priest kings and god kings consolidated such early city states into empires. But the barbaric Greek herdsmen raiders came southward into a world whose civilization was already an old story. Shipping and agriculture, walled cities and writing, were already there. The Greeks did not grow a civilization of their own; they wrecked one and put another together upon and out of the ruins.

To this we must ascribe the fact that there is no temple-state stage, no stage of priest kings, in the Greek record. The Greeks got at once to the city organization that in the east had grown round the temple. They took over the association of temple and city; the idea was ready-made for them. What impressed them most about the city was probably its wall. It is doubtful if they took to city

[1] Vowels were less necessary for the expression of a Semitic language. In the early Semitic alphabets only A, I, and U were provided with symbols, but for such a language as Greek in which many of the inflectional endings are vowels, a variety of vowel signs was indispensable.

An early Greek sea-fight.

From a painted vase, about 550 B.C.

life and citizenship straight away. At first they lived in open villages outside the ruins of the cities they had destroyed, but there stood the model for them, a continual suggestion. They thought first of a city as a safe place in a time of strife, and of the temple uncritically as a proper feature of the city. They came into this inheritance of a previous civilization with the ideas and traditions of the woodlands still strong in their minds. The heroic social system of the *Iliad* took possession of the land, and adapted itself to the new conditions. As history goes on the Greeks became more religious and superstitious as the faiths of the conquered welled up from below.[1]

We have already said that the social structure of the primitive Aryans was a two-class system of nobles and commoners, the classes not very sharply marked off from each other, and led in warfare by a king who was simply the head of one of the noble families, *primus inter pares*, a leader among his equals. With the conquest of the aboriginal population and with the building of towns there was added to this simple social

[1] See Zimmern's *Greek Commonwealth,* Bury's *History of Greece,* and Barker's *Greek Political Theory.*

Photo: Alinari.

THE GOLD AND IVORY STATUE OF ATHENE PARTHENOS WHICH STOOD INSIDE THE PARTHENON.

From a marble copy (first century B.C.). This is a patriot goddess like Britannia or Germania, and not a priestly theological divinity like Anubis or Bel-Marduk.

arrangement of two classes a lower stratum of farm-workers and skilled and unskilled workers, who were for the most part slaves. But all the Greek communities were not of this "conquest" type. Some were "refugee" cities representing smashed communities, and in these the aboriginal substratum would be missing.

In many of the former cases the survivors of the earlier population formed a subject class, slaves of the state as a whole, as, for instance, the Helots in Sparta. The nobles and commoners became landlords and gentlemen farmers; it was they who directed the shipbuilding and engaged in trade. But some of the poorer free citizens followed mechanic arts, and, as we have already noted, would even pull an oar in a galley for pay. Such priests as there were in this Greek world were either the guardians of shrines and temples or sacrificial functionaries; Aristotle, in his *Politics*, makes them a mere subdivision of his official class. The citizen served as warrior in youth, ruler in his maturity, priest in his old age. The priestly *class*, in comparison with the equivalent class in Egypt and Babylonia, was small and insignificant. The gods of the Greeks proper, the gods of the heroic

Photo : Mansell.

ARCHAIC (FIFTH OR SIXTH CENTURY B.C.) BRONZE STATUETTE OF GREEK WARRIOR ON HORSEBACK.

Greeks, were, as we have already noted, glorified human beings, and they were treated without very much fear or awe ; but beneath these gods of the conquering freemen lurked other gods of the subjugated peoples, who found their furtive followers among slaves and women. The original Aryan gods were not expected to work miracles or control men's lives. But Greece, like most of the Eastern world in the thousand years B.C., was much addicted to consulting *oracles* or soothsayers. Delphi was particularly famous for its oracle. "When the Oldest Men in the tribe could not tell you the right thing to do," says Gilbert Murray, "you went to the blessed dead. All oracles were at the tombs of Heroes. They told you what was 'Themis,' what was the right thing to do, or, as religious people would put it now, what was the Will of the God."

The priests and priestesses of these temples were not united into one class, nor did they exercise any power as a class. It was the nobles and free commoners, two classes which, in some cases, merged into one common body of citizens, who constituted the Greek state. In many cases, especially in great city states, the population of slaves and unenfranchised strangers greatly outnumbered the citizens. But for them the State did not exist ; it existed for the select body of citizens alone. It might or might not tolerate the outsider and the slave, but they had no legal voice in their treatment—any more than if it had been a despotism.[1]

This is a social structure differing widely from that of the Eastern monarchies. The exclusive importance of the Greek citizen reminds one a little of the exclusive importance of the children of Israel in the later Jewish state, but there is no equivalent on the Greek

[1] "For them the state did not exist." This needs qualification. Cephalus, at whose house the conversation of Plato's *Republic* is placed, was a resident alien. He was a wealthy man in the best society, and taken as a type of the "happy man." His son, Lysias, was a leading orator. Even in the matter of the slaves : the Old Oligarch, in the "Constitution of Athens," complains that the Athenian slaves had no distinctive dress or manners, and so a gentleman could not even push one of them ! In the *Republic* itself there is a description of the Democratic State, in which the slaves push you off the pavement. Moreover, even during the Peloponnesian War, there was no persecution of aliens and no expulsion of aliens from Athens. They were evidently a loyal and contented class. True, in time of food-shortage, the claims of everybody to true citizenship were scrutinized more and more closely ; but that was unavoidable.—G. M.

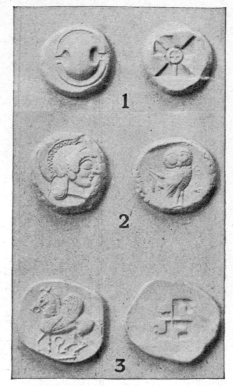

Photo : Mansell.

EARLY GREEK COINS (SIXTH AND FIFTH CENTURIES B.C.).

1. Thebes. 2. Athens (bearing head of Goddess Athena and owl with olive branch). 3. Corinth.

side to the prophets and priests, nor to the idea of an overruling Jehovah.

Another contrast between the Greek states and any of the human communities to which we have hitherto given attention is their continuous and incurable division. The civilizations of Egypt, Sumeria, China, and no doubt North India, all began in a number of independent city states, each one a city with a few miles largest city states of Greece remained smaller than many English counties; and some had an area of only a few square miles. Athens, the largest of the Greek cities, at the climax of its power had a population of perhaps a third of a million. Hardly any other Greek cities ever exceeded 50,000. Of this, half or more were slaves and strangers, and two-thirds of the free body women and children.

Photo: Alinari.
THE TEMPLE OF NEPTUNE AT PAESTUM IN ITALY (MAGNA GRÆCIA) NEAR NAPLES (SIXTH CENTURY B.C.).

of dependent agricultural villages and cultivation around it, but out of this phase they passed by a process of coalescence into kingdoms and empires. But to the very end of their independent history the Greeks did not coalesce. Commonly, this is ascribed to the geographical conditions under which they lived. Greece is a country cut up into a multitude of valleys by mountain masses and arms of the sea that render intercommunication difficult; so difficult that few cities were able to hold many of the others in subjection for any length of time. Moreover, many Greek cities were on islands and scattered along remote coasts. To the end the

§ 3

The government of these city states varied very widely in its nature. As they settled down after their conquests the Greeks retained for a time the rule of their kings, but these kingdoms drifted back more and more to the rule of the aristocratic class. In Sparta (Lacedemon) kings were still distinguished in the sixth century B.C. The Lacedemonians had a curious system of a double kingship; two kings, drawn from different royal families, ruled together. But most of the Greek city states had become aristocratic republics long before the sixth

Monarchy Aristocracy and Democracy in Greece.

century. There is, however, a tendency towards slackness and inefficiency in most families that rule by hereditary right; sooner or later they decline; and as the Greeks got out upon the seas and set up colonies and commerce extended, new rich families arose to jostle the old and bring new personalities into power. These *nouveaux riches* became members of an expanded ruling class, a mode of government known as oligarchy—in opposition to aristocracy —though, strictly, the term oligarchy (= government by the few) should of course include hereditary aristocracy as a special case.

In many cities there arose persons of exceptional energy, who, taking advantage of some social conflict or class grievance, secured a more or less irregular power in the state. This combination of personality and opportunity has occurred in the United States of America, for example, where men exercising various kinds of informal power are called *bosses*. In Greece they were called *tyrants*. But the tyrant was rather more than a boss; he was recognized as a monarch, and claimed the authority of a monarch. The modern boss, on the other hand, shelters behind legal forms which he has "got hold of" and uses for his own ends. Tyrants were distinguished from kings, who claimed some sort of right, some family priority, for example, to rule. They were supported, perhaps, by some poor class with a grievance; Peisistratus, for example, who was tyrant of Athens, with two intervals of exile, between 560 and 527 B.C., was supported by the poverty-struck Athenian hillmen. Sometimes, as in Greek Sicily, the tyrant stood for the rich against the poor. When, later on, the Persians began to subjugate the Greek cities of Asia Minor, they set up pro-Persian tyrants.

Aristotle, the great philosophical teacher, who was born under

Photo: Alinari.

VASE SHOWING THE CROWNING OF A GREEK BRIDE.

(Greek *paintings* being all lost, the vases reproduced here and on the next page are interesting as pictorial representations of social life, apart from their artistic value.)

the hereditary Macedonian monarchy, and who was for some years tutor to the king's son, distinguishes in his *Politics* between kings who ruled by an admitted and inherent right, such as the King of Macedonia, whom he served, and tyrants who ruled without the consent of the government. As a matter of fact, it is hard to conceive of a tyrant ruling without the consent of many, and the active participation of a substantial number of his subjects; and the devotion and unselfishness of your "true kings" has been known to rouse resentment and questioning. Aristotle was also able to say that while the king ruled for the good of the state, the tyrant ruled for his own good. Upon this point, as in his ability to regard slavery as a natural thing and to consider women unfit for freedom and political rights, Aristotle was in harmony with the trend of events about him.

A third form of government that prevailed increasingly in Greece in the sixth, fifth, and fourth centuries B.C., was known as *democracy*. As the modern world nowadays is constantly talking of democracy, and as the modern idea of democracy is something widely different from the democracy of the Greek city states, it will be well to be very explicit upon the meaning of democracy in Greece. Democracy then was government by the commonalty, the Demos; it was government by the whole body of the citizens, by the many as distinguished from the few. But let the modern reader mark that word "citizen." The slave was excluded, the freedman was excluded, the stranger; even the Greek born in the city, whose father had come eight or ten miles from the city beyond the headland, was excluded. The earlier democracies (but not all) demanded a property qualification from the citizen, and property in those days was land; this was subsequently relaxed, but the modern reader will grasp that here was something very different from modern democracy. At the end of the fifth century B.C. this property qualification had been abolished in Athens, for example ; but Pericles, a great Athenian statesman of whom we shall have more to tell later, had established a law (451 B.C.) restricting citizenship to those who could establish Athenian descent on both sides. Thus, in the Greek democracies quite as much as in the oligarchies, the citizens formed *a close corporation*, ruling sometimes, as in the case of Athens in its great days, a big population of serfs, slaves, and " outlanders." A modern politician used to the idea, the entirely new and different idea, that democracy in its perfected form means that every adult man and woman shall have a voice in the government, would, if suddenly spirited back to the extremist Greek democracy, regard it as a kind of oligarchy. The only real difference between a Greek " oligarchy " and a Greek democracy was that in the former, the poorer and less important citizens had no voice in the government, and in the latter every citizen had. Aristotle, in his *Politics*, betrays very clearly the practical outcome of this difference. Taxation sat lightly on the rich in the oligarchies ; the democracies, on the other hand, taxed the rich, and gener-

Photo : Manseli.
GREEK VASE SHOWING FEMININE COSTUME.

ally paid the impecunious citizen a maintenance allowance and special fees. In Athens fees were paid to citizens even for attending the general assembly. But the generality of people outside the happy order of citizens worked and did what they were told, and if one desired the protection of the law, one sought a citizen to plead for one. For only the citizen had any standing in the law courts. Greek democracy was, in fact, a sort of government by a swarm of hereditary barristers. Our modern idea, that any one in the state is a citizen, would have shocked the privileged democrats of Athens profoundly.[1]

One obvious result of this monopolization of the state by the class of citizens was that the patriotism of these privileged people took an intense and narrow form. They would form alliances, but never coalesce with other city states. That would have obliterated every advan-

[1] I do not agree with " hereditary barristers " or " fee-hunting." The Athenian dicasts were not barristers, but judges : they sat in panels (sometimes a panel of some hundreds) and judged. They had to be paid for attendances as judges (don't we pay jurymen ?) because it took them away from their work as potters, dyers, and stone-masons. Pay was a genuine and good democratic institution ; it was just what made possible the ordinary citizen's co-operation in the life of the state, and stopped its business from being the perquisite of the rich. I feel strongly that the text is unjust to Athens.—E. B.

See Zimmern, *Greek Commonwealth*, and Barker's *Greek Political Theory*, pp. 29-30.

tage by which they lived. There would have been no more fees, no more privileges. The narrow geographical limits of these Greek states added to the intensity of their feeling. A man's love for his country was reinforced by his love for his native town, his religion, and his home; for these were all one. Of course the slaves did not share in these feelings, and in the oligarchic states very often the excluded class got over its dislike of foreigners in its greater dislike of the class at home which oppressed it. But, in the main, patriotism in the Greek was a personal passion of an inspiring and dangerous intensity. Like rejected love, it was apt to turn into something very like hatred. The Greek exile resembled the French or Russian *emigré* in being ready to treat his beloved country pretty roughly in order to save her from the devils in human form who had taken possession of her and turned *him* out.

In the fifth century B.C. Athens formed a system of relationships with a number of other Greek city states which is often spoken of by historians as the Athenian Empire. But all the other city states retained their own governments. One "new fact" added by the Athenian Empire was the complete and effective suppression of piracy; another was the institution of a sort of international law. The law, indeed, was Athenian law; but actions could now be brought and justice administered between citizens of the different states of the League, which of course had not been possible before. The Athenian Empire had really developed out of a league of mutual defence against Persia; its seat had originally been in the island of Delos, and the allies had contributed to a common treasure at Delos; the treasure of Delos was carried off to Athens because it was exposed to a possible Persian raid. Then one city after another offered a monetary contribution instead of military service, with the result that in the end Athens was doing almost all the work and receiving almost all the money. She was supported by one or two of the larger islands. The "League" in this way became gradually an "Empire," but the citizens of the allied states remained, except where there were special treaties of intermarriage and the like, practically foreigners to one another. And it was chiefly the poorer citizens of Athens who sustained this empire by their most vigorous and incessant personal service. Every citizen was liable to military service at home or abroad between the ages of eighteen and sixty, sometimes on purely

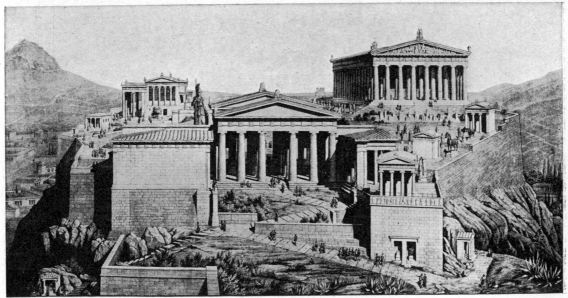

Photo: Mansell.

RESTORATION OF THE ACROPOLIS OF ATHENS, SHOWING THE CENTRAL BUILDINGS OF THE GREATEST GREEK CITY STATE.

The dominating temple to the right is the Parthenon, in which was the great statue of Athene; the smaller but very beautiful temple to the left is the Erechtheum (Erechtheus was a legendary snake-king of Athens). The entrance building is the Propylæa. This is the Athens rebuilt after the destruction by Xerxes.

Photo: Alinari.

RUINS OF THE ERECHTHEUM, ATHENS.

Athenian affairs and sometimes in defence of the cities of the Empire whose citizens had bought themselves off. There was probably no single man over twenty-five in the Athenian Assembly who had not served in several campaigns in different parts of the Mediterranean or Black Sea, and who did not expect to serve again. Modern imperialism is denounced by its opponents as the exploitation of the world by the rich ; Athenian imperialism was the exploitation of the world by the poorer citizens of Athens.

Another difference from modern conditions, due to the small size of the Greek city states, was that in a democracy every citizen had the right to attend and speak and vote in the popular assembly. For most cities this meant a gathering of only a few hundred people ; the greatest had no more than some thousands of citizens. Nothing of this sort is possible in a modern " democracy " with, perhaps, several million voters. The modern " citizen's " voice in public affairs is limited to the right to vote for one or other of the party candidates put before him. He, or she, is then supposed to have "assented" to the resultant government. Aristotle, who would have enjoyed the electoral methods of our modern democracies keenly, points out very subtly how the outlying farmer class of citizens in a democracy can be virtually disenfranchised by calling the popular assembly too frequently for their regular attendance. In the later Greek democracies (fifth century) the appointment of public officials, except in the case of officers requiring very special knowledge, was by casting lots. This was supposed to protect the general corporation of privileged citizens from the continued predominance of rich, influential, and conspicuously able men.

Some democracies (Athens and Miletus, *e.g.*) had an institution called the ostracism,[1] by which in times of crisis and conflict the decision was made whether some citizen should go into exile for ten years. This may strike a modern reader as an envious institution, but that was not its essential quality. It was, says Gilbert Murray, a way of arriving at a decision in a case when political feeling was so divided

[1] From ostrakon, a tile; the voter wrote the name on a tile or shell.

as to threaten a deadlock. There were in the Greek democracies parties and party leaders, but no regular government in office and no regular opposition. There was no way, therefore, of carrying out a policy, although it might be the popular policy, if a strong leader or a strong group stood out against it. But by the ostracism, the least popular or the least trusted of the chief leaders in the divided community was made to retire for a period without loss of honour or property. Professor Murray suggests that a Greek democracy, if it had found itself in such a position of deadlock as the British Empire did upon the question of Home Rule for Ireland in 1914, would have probably first ostracized Sir Edward Carson, and then proceeded to carry out the provisions of the Home Rule Bill.

This institution of the ostracism has immortalized one obscure and rather illiterate member of the democracy of Athens. A certain Aristides had gained a great reputation in the law court for his righteous dealing. He fell into a dispute with Themistocles upon a question of naval policy; Aristides was for the army, Themistocles was a "strong navy" man, and a deadlock was threatened. There

Photo : Bonfils.

RUINS OF THE ERECHTHEUM, ATHENS.

was resort to an ostracism to decide between them. Plutarch relates that as Aristides walked through the streets while the voting was in progress, he was accosted by a strange citizen from the agricultural environs unaccustomed to the art of writing, and requested to write his own name on the proffered potsherd.

"But why?" he asked. "Has Aristides ever injured you?"

"No," said the citizen. "No. Never have

Rowers in an Athenian warship, about 400 B.C. (Fragment of relief found on the Acropolis)

I set eyes on him. But, oh! I am so *bored* by hearing him called Aristides the Just."

Whereupon, says Plutarch, without further parley, Aristides wrote as the man desired. . . .

When one understands the true meaning of these Greek constitutions, and, in particular, the limitation of all power, whether in the democracies or the oligarchies, to a locally privileged class, one realizes how impossible was any effective union of the hundreds of Greek cities scattered about the Mediterranean region, or even of any effective co-operation between them for a common end. Each city was in the hands of a few or a few hundred men, to whom its separateness meant everything that was worth having in life. Only conquest from the outside could unite the Greeks, and until Greece was conquered they had no political unity. When at last they were conquered, they were conquered so completely that their unity ceased to be of any importance even to themselves; it was a unity of subjugation.

Yet there was always a certain tradition of unity between all the Greeks, based on a common language and script, on the common possession of the heroic epics, and on the continuous

intercourse that the maritime position of the states made possible. And, in addition, there were certain religious bonds of a unifying kind. Certain shrines, the shrines of the god Apollo in the island of Delos and at Delphi, for example, were sustained, not by single states, but by leagues of states or Amphictyonies (= League of neighbours), which in the case of the Delphic amphictyony, for example, became very wide-reaching unions. The league protected the shrine and the safety of pilgrims, saw to the roads leading thereunto, secured peace at the time of special festivals, upheld certain rules to mitigate the usages of war among its members, and—the Delian league especially—suppressed piracy. A still more important link of Hellenic union was the Olympian games that were held every four years at Olympia. Foot races, boxing, wrestling, javelin throwing, quoit throwing, jumping, and chariot and horse racing were the chief sports, and a record of victors and distinguished visitors was kept. From the year 776 B.C. onward[1] these games were held regularly for over a thousand years, and they did much to maintain that sense of a common Greek life (pan-Hellenic) transcending the narrow politics of the city states.

Such links of sentiment and association were of little avail against the intense "separatism" of the Greek political institutions. From the History of Herodotus the student will be able to gather a sense of the intensity and persistence of the feuds that kept the Greek world in a state of chronic warfare. In the old days (say, to the sixth century B.C.) fairly large families prevailed in Greece, and something of the old Aryan great household system (see Chap. XV), with its strong clan feeling and its capacity for maintaining an enduring feud, still endured. The history of Athens circles for many years about the feud of two great families, the Alcmæonidæ and the Peisistratidæ; the latter equally an aristocratic family, but founding

[1] 776 B.C. is the year of the First Olympiad, a valuable starting-point in Greek chronology.

its power on the support of the poorer class of the populace and the exploitation of their grievances. Later on, in the sixth and fifth centuries, a limitation of births and a shrinkage of families to two or three members—a process Aristotle notes without perceiving its cause—led to the disappearance of the old aristocratic clans, and the later wars were due rather to trade disputes and grievances caused and stirred up by individual adventurers than to family vendettas.

It is easy to understand, in view of this intense separatism of the Greeks, how readily the Ionians of Asia and of the islands fell first under the domination of the kingdom of Lydia, and then under that of the Persians when Cyrus overthrew Crœsus, the king of Lydia. They rebelled only to be reconquered. Then came the turn of European Greece. It is a matter of astonishment, the Greeks themselves were astonished, to find that Greece itself did not fall under the dominion of the Persians, these barbaric Aryan masters of the ancient civilizations of Western Asia. But before we tell of this struggle we must give some attention to these Asiatics against whom they were pitted; and particularly to these Medes and Persians who, by 538 B.C., were already in possession of the ancient civilizations of Assyria, Babylonia, and about to subjugate Egypt.

§ 4

We have had occasion to mention the kingdom of Lydia, and it may be well to give a short note here upon the Lydians before proceeding with our story. The original population of the larger part of Asia Minor may perhaps have been akin to the original population of Greece and Crete. If so, it was of "Mediterranean" race. Or it may have been another branch of those still more generalized and fundamental darkish peoples from whom arose the Mediterranean race to the west and the Dravidians to the east. Remains of the same sort of art that distinguishes Cnossos and Mycenæ are to be found scattered over Asia Minor. But just as the Nordic Greeks poured southward into Greece to conquer and mix with the aborigines, so did other and kindred Nordic tribes pour over the Bosphorus into Asia Minor. Over some areas these Aryan peoples prevailed altogether, and became the bulk of the inhabitants and retained their Aryan speech. Such were the Phrygians, a people whose language was almost as close to that of the Greeks as the Macedonian. But over other areas the Aryans did not so prevail.

The kingdom of Lydia.

Photo: Mansell.

GENERAL VIEW OF THE TEMPLE OF ZEUS AT OLYMPIA.

Photo: Mansell.

FIGURES FROM THE PARTHENON FRIEZE (ELGIN MARBLES).

In Lydia the original race and their language held their own. The Lydians were a non-Aryan people speaking a non-Aryan speech, of which at the present time only a few words are known. Their capital city was Sardis.

Their religion was also non-Aryan. They worshipped a Great Mother goddess. The Phrygians also, though retaining their Greek-like language, became infected with mysterious religion, and much of the mystical religion and secret ceremonial that pervaded Athens at a later date was Phrygian (when not Thracian) in origin.

At first the Lydians held the western sea-coast of Asia Minor, but they were driven back from it by the establishment of Ionian Greeks coming by the sea and founding cities. Later on, however, these Ionian Greek cities were brought into subjection by the Lydian kings.

The history of this country is not clearly known, and were it known it would scarcely be of sufficient importance to be related in this historical outline, but in the eighth century B.C. one monarch, named Gyges, becomes note-worthy. The country under his rule was subjected to another Aryan invasion, certain nomadic tribes called the Cimmerians came pouring across Asia Minor, and they were driven back with difficulty by Gyges and his son and grandson. Sardis was twice taken and burnt by these barbarians. And it is on record that Gyges paid tribute to Sardanapalus, which serves to link him up with our general ideas of the history of Assyria, Israel, and Egypt. Later, Gyges rebelled against Assyria, and sent troops to help Psammetichus I to liberate Egypt from its brief servitude to the Assyrian.

It was Alyattes, the grandson of Gyges, who made Lydia into a considerable power. He reigned for seven years, and he reduced most of the Ionian cities of Asia Minor to subjection. The country became the centre of a great trade between Asia and Europe ; it had always been productive and rich in gold, and now the Lydian monarch was reputed the richest in Asia. There was a great coming and going between the Black and Mediterranean Seas, and between the East and West. We have already noted that Lydia was reputed to be the first country in the world to produce coined money, and to provide the convenience of inns for travellers and traders. The Lydian dynasty seems to have been a trading dynasty of the type of Minos in Crete, with a banking and financial development. . . . So much we may note of Lydia by way of preface to the next section.

§ 5

The Rise of the Persians in the East Now, while one series of Aryan-speaking invaders had developed along the lines we have described in Greece, Magna Græcia, and around the shores of the Black Sea, another series of Aryan-speaking peoples, whose originally Nordic blood was perhaps already mixed with a Mongolian element, were settling and spreading to the north and east of the Assyrian and Babylonian empires. We have already spoken of the arc-like dispersion of the Nordic Aryan peoples to the north of the Black and Caspian Seas; it was probably by this route that the Aryan-speaking races gradually came down into what is now the Persian country, and spread, on the one hand, eastward to India (? 2,000 to 1,000 B.C.), and on the other, increased and multiplied in the Persian uplands until they were strong enough to assail first Assyria (650 B.C.) and then Babylon (538 B.C.).

There is much that is not yet clear about the changes of climate that have been going on in Europe and Asia during the last 10,000 years. The ice of the last glacial age receded gradually, and gave way to a long period of steppe or prairie-like conditions over the great plain of Europe. About 12,000 or 10,000 years ago, as it is reckoned now, this state of affairs was giving place to forest conditions. We have already noted how, as a consequence of these changes, the Solutrian horse hunters gave place to Magdalenian fishers and forest deer hunters; and these, again, to the Neolithic herdsmen and agriculturists. For some thousands of years the European climate seems to have been warmer than it is to-day. A great sea spread from the coast of the Balkan peninsula far into Central Asia, and extended northward into Central Russia, and the shrinkage of that sea and the consequent hardening of the climate of South Russia and Central Asia was going on contemporaneously with the development of the first civilizations in the river valleys. Many facts seem to point to a more genial climate in Europe and Western Asia, and still more strongly to a greater luxuriance of plant and vegetable life, 4,000 to 3,000 years ago, than we find to-day. There were forests then in South Russia and in the country which is now Western Turkestan, where now steppes and deserts prevail. On the other hand, between 1,500 and 2,000 years ago, the Aral Caspian region was probably drier and those seas smaller than they are at the present time.

We may note in this connection that Thotmes III (say, the fifteenth century B.C.), in his expedition beyond the Euphrates, hunted a herd of 120 elephants in that region. Again, an Ægean dagger from Mycenæ, dating about 2,000 B.C., shows a lion-hunt in progress. The hunters carry big shields and spears, and stand in rows one behind the other. The first man spears the lion, and when the wounded beast leaps at him, drops flat under the protection

Scythians ... *as portrayed by a Greek artist* ......

ONE OF THE FEW REPRESENTATIONS OF THE ANCIENT SCYTHIANS IN EXISTENCE, FROM A GREEK ELECTRUM VASE.

of his big shield, leaving the next man to repeat his stroke, and so on, until the lion is speared to death. This method of hunting is practised by the Masai to-day, and could only have been worked out by a people in a land where lions were abundant. But abundant lions imply abundant game, and that again means abundant vegetation. About 2,000 B.C. the hardening of the climate in the central parts of the Old World, to which we have already referred, which put an end to elephants and lions in Asia Minor and Greece,[1] was turning the faces of the nomadic

Map showing the relation of the MEDIAN and Second BABYLONIAN (Chaldæan) EMPIRES in the reign of Nebuchadnezzar the Great [MOUNTAINS shaded vertically.]

Aryan peoples southward towards the fields and forests of the more settled and civilized nations.

These Aryan peoples come down from the East Caspian regions into history about the time that Mycenæ and Troy and Cnossos are falling to the Greeks. It is difficult to dis-

entangle the different tribes and races that appear under a multitude of names in the records and inscriptions that record their first appearance, but, fortunately, these distinctions are not needed in an elementary outline such as this present history. A people called the Cimmerians appear in the districts of Lake Urumiya and Van, and shortly after Aryans have spread from Armenia to Elam. In the ninth century B.C., a people called the Medes, very closely related to the Persians to the east of them, appear in the Assyrian inscriptions.

Tiglath Pileser III and Sargon II, names already familiar in this story, profess to have made them pay tribute. They are spoken of in the inscriptions as the "dangerous Medes." They are as yet a tribal people, not united under one king.

About the ninth century B.C. Elam and the Elamites, whose capital was Susa, a people which possessed a tradition and civilization at least as old as the Sumerian, suddenly vanish from history. We do not know what happened. They seem to have been overrun and the population absorbed by the conquerors. Susa is in the hands of the Persians.

A fourth people, related to these Aryan tribes, who appear at this time in the narrative of Herodotus, are the "Scythians." For a while the monarchs of Assyria play off these various kindred peoples, the Cimmerians, the Medes, the Persians, and the Scythians, against each other. Assyrian princesses (a daughter of Esarhaddon, e.g.) are married to Scythian chiefs. Nebuchadnezzar the Great, on the other hand, marries a daughter of Cyaxares, who has become king of all the Medes. The Aryan Scythians are for the Semitic Assyrians; the Aryan Medes for the Semitic Babylonians. It was this Cyaxares who took Nineveh, the Assyrian capital, in 606 B.C., and so released Babylon from the Assyrian yoke to establish,

[1] It is, at least, doubtful whether any change of climate expelled either lion or elephant from South-East Europe and Asia Minor: the cause of their gradual disappearance was—I think—nothing but Man, increasingly well armed for the chase. Lions lingered in the Balkan peninsula till about the fourth century B.C., if not later. Elephants had, perhaps, disappeared from Western Asia by the eighth century B.C. The lion (much bigger than the existing form) stayed on in Southern Germany till the Neolithic period. The panther inhabited Greece, Southern Italy, and Southern Spain likewise till the beginning of the historical period (say 1,000 B.C.).—H. H. J.

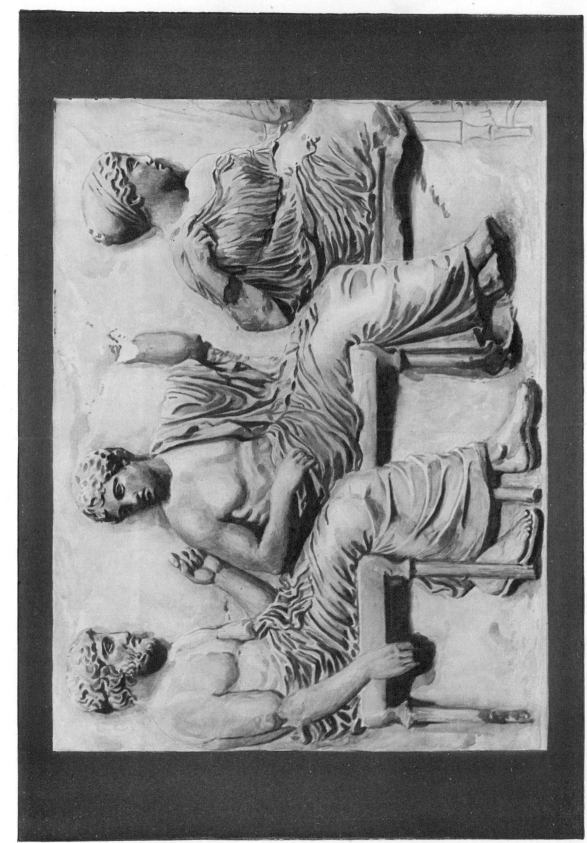

GREEK DIVINITIES (POSEIDON, DIONYSUS, AND DEMETER) ON THE PARTHENON FRIEZE.

under Chaldean rule, the Second Babylonian Empire. The Scythian allies of Assyria drop out of the story after this. They go on living their own life away to the north without much interference with the peoples to the south. A glance at the map of this period shows how, for two-thirds of a century, the Second Babylonian Empire lay like a lamb within the embrace of the Median lion.

Into the internal struggles of the Medes and Persians, that ended at last in the accession of Cyrus "the Persian" to the throne of Cyaxares in 550 B.C., we will not enter. In that year Cyrus was ruling over an empire that

short the power of the Persians, if by any means he might, while yet it was in growth and before they should have become great."

He then made trial of the various oracles. His method of trial we will not relate here, but it led him to the belief that the Delphi Oracle was alone trustworthy. What follows is rather a lengthy passage, but it is so characteristic of the garrulousness and wonder-loving mind of the Father of History, and with such a pleasant touch of spite against the Lacedemonians, that it is impossible to resist the quotation.

"After this, with great sacrifices, he endeavoured to win the favour of the god at

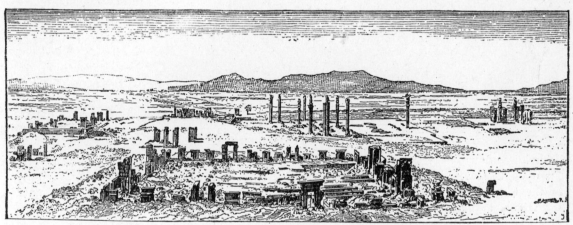

RUINS OF PERSEPOLIS. (After M. Dieulafoy, *L'art antique de la Perse*.)

reached from the boundaries of Lydia to Persia and perhaps to India. Nabonidus, the last of the Babylonian rulers, was, as we have already told, digging up old records and building temples in Babylonia.

§ 6

But one monarch in the world was alive to the threat of the new power that lay in the hands of Cyrus. This was Crœsus,

The Story of Crœsus. the Lydian king. His son had been killed in a very tragic manner, which Herodotus relates, but which we will not describe here. Says Herodotus:

"For two years then, Crœsus remained quiet in great mourning, because he was deprived of his son; but after this period of time, the overthrowing of the rule of the son of Cyaxares by Cyrus, and the growing greatness of the Persians, caused Crœsus to cease from his mourning, and led him to a care of cutting

Delphi: for of all the animals that are fit for sacrifice he offered three thousand of each kind, and he heaped up couches overlaid with gold and overlaid with silver, and cups of gold, and robes of purple, and tunics, making of them a great pyre, and this he burnt up, hoping by these means the more to win over the god to the side of the Lydians; and he proclaimed to all the Lydians that every one of them should make sacrifice with that which each man had. And when he had finished the sacrifice, he melted down a vast quantity of gold, and of it he wrought half-plinths, making them six palms in length and three in breadth, and in height one palm; and their number was one hundred and seventeen. Of these four were of pure gold weighing two talents and a half each, and the others of gold alloyed with silver weighing two talents. And he caused to be made also an image of a lion of pure gold weighing ten talents; which lion, when the temple at Delphi was

13

Photo : Mansell.

500 B.C. MEN BRINGING CHARIOTS, RINGS AND WREATHS. RELIEF FROM PERSEPOLIS.

being burnt down, fell from off the half-plinths, for upon these it was set, and is placed now in the treasury of the Corinthians, weighing six talents and a half, for three talents and a half were melted away from it. So Crœsus, having finished all these things, sent them to Delphi, and with them these besides : two mixing-bowls of great size, one of gold and the other of silver, of which the golden bowl was placed on the right hand as one enters the temple, and the silver on the left, but the places of these also were changed after the temple was burnt down. . . . Moreover, Crœsus sent four silver wine-jars, which stand in the treasury of the Corinthians, and two vessels for lustral water, one of gold and the other of silver, of which the gold one is inscribed ' from the Lacedemonians,' who say that it is their offering ; therein, however, they do not speak rightly, for this also is from Crœsus, but one of the Delphians wrote the inscription upon it, desiring to gratify the Lacedemonians ; and his name I know, but I will not make mention of it. . . . And many other votive offerings Crœsus sent with these, not specially distinguished, among which are certain castings of silver of a round shape, and also a golden figure of a woman three cubits high, which the Delphians say is a statue of the baker of Crœsus. Moreover, Crœsus dedicated the ornaments from his wife's neck and her girdles. . . .

" To the Lydians who were to carry these gifts to the temples Crœsus gave charge that they should ask the Oracles this question also : whether Crœsus should march against the Persians, and, if so, whether he should join with himself any army of men as his friends. And when the Lydians had arrived at the places to which they had been sent and had dedicated the votive offerings, they inquired of the Oracles, and said : ' Crœsus, king of the Lydians and of other nations, considering that these are the only true Oracles among men, presents to you gifts such as your revelations deserve, and asks you again now whether he shall march against the Persians, and, if so, whether he shall join with himself any army of men as allies.' They inquired thus, and the answers of both the Oracles agreed in one, declaring to Crœsus that if he should march against the Persians he should destroy a great empire. . . . So when the answers were brought back and Crœsus heard them, he was delighted with the oracles, and expecting that he would certainly destroy the kingdom of Cyrus, he sent again to Pytho, and presented to the men of Delphi, having ascertained the number of them, two staters of gold for each man : and in return for this the Delphians gave to Crœsus and to the Lydians precedence in consulting the Oracle and freedom from all payments, and the right to front seats at the games, with this privilege also for all time, that any one of them who wished should be allowed to become a citizen of Delphi."

But here we may not run on as Herodotus loved to do. Suffice it to say that Crœsus made a defensive alliance both with the Lacedemonians and the Egyptians. We will not quote the story of how a great bronze mixing-bowl that the Lacedemonians sent to Crœsus went astray, but we will note a light on the life of the Medes and Persians of that time.

" Thus, then it happened about the mixing-bowl; but meanwhile Crœsus, mistaking the meaning of the Oracle, was making a march into Cappadocia, expecting to overthrow Cyrus and the power of the Persians ; and while Crœsus was preparing to march against the Persians, one of the Lydians, who even before this time was thought to be a wise man, but in consequence of this opinion got a very great name for wisdom among the Lydians, had advised Crœsus as follows : ' O king, thou art preparing to march against men who wear breeches of leather, and the rest of their clothing is of leather also ; and they eat food not such as they desire, but such as they can obtain, dwelling in a land which is rugged ; and, more-over, they make no use of wine but drink water ; and no figs have they for dessert, nor any other good thing. On the one hand, if thou shalt overcome them, what wilt thou take away from them, seeing they have nothing ? and, on the other

Photo: Major W. J. P. Rodd, D.S.O.

A CORNER IN SUSA TO-DAY.

hand, if thou shalt be overcome, consider how many good things thou wilt lose ; for once having tasted our good things, they will cling to them fast, and it will not be possible to drive them away. I, for my own part, feel gratitude to the gods that they do not put it into the minds of the Persians to march against the Lydians.' Thus he spoke not persuading Crœsus ; for it is true indeed that the Persians before they subdued the Lydians had no luxury nor any good thing."

Crœsus and Cyrus fought an indecisive battle at Pteria, from which Crœsus retreated. Cyrus followed him up, and he gave battle outside his capital town of Sardis. The chief strength of the Lydians lay in their cavalry ; they were excellent, if undisciplined, horsemen, and fought with long spears.

" Cyrus, when he saw the Lydians being arrayed for battle, fearing their horsemen, did on the suggestion of Harpagos, a Mede, as follows : All the camels which were in the train of his army carrying provisions and baggage he gathered together, and he took off their burdens and set men upon them provided with the equipment of cavalry ; and, having thus furnished them, forth he appointed them to go in front of the rest of the army towards the horsemen of Crœsus ; and after the camel-troop he ordered the infantry to follow ; and behind the infantry he placed his whole force of cavalry. Then, when all his men had been placed in their several positions, he charged them to spare none of the other Lydians, slaying all who might come in their way, but Crœsus himself they were not to slay, not even if he should make resistance when he was being captured. Such was his charge : and he set the camels opposite the horsemen for this reason,—because the horse has a fear of the camel and cannot endure either to see his form or to scent his smell : for this reason then the trick had been devised, in order that the cavalry of Crœsus might be useless, that very force wherewith the Lydian king was expecting most to shine. And as they were coming together to the battle, so soon as the horses scented the camels and saw them, they turned away back, and the hopes of Crœsus were at once brought to nought. The Lydians, however, for their part did not upon that act as cowards, but when they perceived what was coming to pass, they leapt from their horses and fought with the Persians on foot. At length, however, when many had fallen on either side, the Lydians turned to flight ; and

to Crœsus as he stood upon the pyre there came, although he was in such evil case, a memory of the saying of Solon, how he had said with divine inspiration that no one of the living might be called happy. And when this thought came into his mind, they say that he sighed deeply and groaned aloud, having been for long silent, and three times he uttered the name of Solon. Hearing this, Cyrus bade the interpreters ask Crœsus who was this person on whom he called ; and they came near and asked. And Crœsus for a time, it is said, kept silence when he was asked this, but afterwards, being pressed, he said : ' One whom more than much wealth I should have desired to have speech with all monarchs.' Then, since his

Photo : Major W. J. P. Rodd.

SUSA TO-DAY.

having been driven within the wall of their fortress, they were besieged by the Persians."

In fourteen days Sardis was stormed and Crœsus taken prisoner. . . .

"So the Persians having taken him brought him into the presence of Cyrus ; and he piled up a great pyre and caused Crœsus to go up upon it bound in fetters, and along with him twice seven sons of Lydians, whether it was that he meant to dedicate this offering as first-fruits of his victory to some god, or whether he desired to fulfil a vow, or else had heard that Crœsus was a god-fearing man, and so caused him to go up on the pyre because he wished to know if any one of the divine powers would save him, so that he should not be burnt alive. He, they say, did this ; but

words were of doubtful import, they asked again of that which he said ; and as they were urgent with him and gave him no peace, he told how once Solon, an Athenian, had come and having inspected all his wealth had made light of it, with such and such words ; and how all had turned out for him according as Solon had said, not speaking at all especially with a view to Crœsus himself, but with a view to the whole human race, and especially those who seem to themselves to be happy men. And while Crœsus related these things, already the pyre was lighted and the edges of it round about were burning. Then they say that Cyrus, hearing from the interpreters what Crœsus had said, changed his purpose and considered that he himself also was but a man, and that he was delivering another man, who had been not inferior to himself in felicity, alive to the fire; and, moreover, he feared the requital, and reflected that there was nothing of that which men possessed which was secure; therefore, they say, he ordered them to extinguish as quickly as possible the fire that was burning, and to bring down Crœsus and those who were with him from the pyre; and they, using endeavours, were not able now to get the mastery of the flames. Then it is related by the Lydians that Crœsus, having learned how Cyrus had changed his mind, and seeing that every one was trying to put out the fire, but that they were no longer able to check it, cried aloud, entreating Apollo that if any gift had ever been given by him which was acceptable to the god, he would come to his aid and rescue him from the evil which was now upon him. So he with tears entreated the god, and suddenly, they say, after clear sky and calm weather clouds gathered and a storm burst, and it rained with a very violent shower, and the pyre was extinguished. Then Cyrus, having

perceived that Crœsus was a lover of the gods and a good man, caused him to be brought down from the pyre and asked him as follows: ' Crœsus, tell me who of all men was it who persuaded thee to march upon my land and so to become an enemy to me instead of a friend?' And he said: ' O king, I did this to thy felicity and to my own misfortune, and the causer of this was the god of the Hellenes, who incited me to march with my army. For no one is so senseless as to choose of his own will war rather than peace, since in peace the sons bury their fathers, but in war the fathers bury their sons. But it was pleasing, I suppose, to the divine powers that these things should come to pass thus.' "

But Herodotus is too alluring a companion for one who would write an Outline of History; and the rest of the life of Crœsus, and how he gave wise counsels to Cyrus, must be read in his ampler page.

When Lydia was subdued, Cyrus turned his attention to Nabonidus in Babylon. He defeated the Babylonian army, under Belshazzar, outside Babylon, and then laid siege

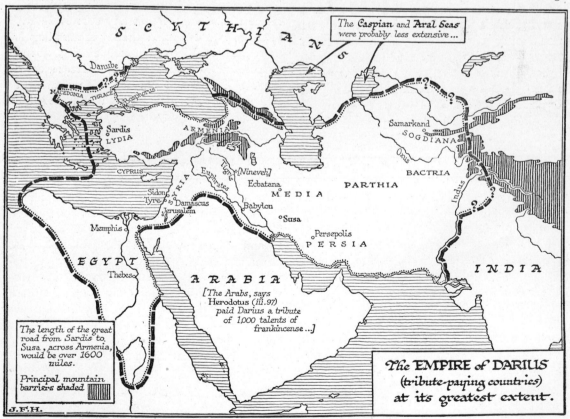

The Caspian and Aral Seas were probably less extensive ...

[The Arabs, says Herodotus (iii.97) paid Darius a tribute of 1,000 talents of frankincense ...]

The length of the great road from Sardis to Susa, across Armenia, would be over 1600 miles.

Principal mountain barriers shaded

The EMPIRE of DARIUS (tribute-paying countries) at its greatest extent.

to the town. He entered the town (538 B.C.), probably as we have already suggested, with the connivance of the priests of Bel.

§ 7

Cyrus was succeeded by his son Cambyses, who took an army into Egypt (525 B.C.). **Darius invades Russia.** There was a battle in the delta, in which Greek mercenaries fought on both sides. Herodotus declares that he saw the bones of the slain still lying on the field fifty or sixty years later, and comments on the comparative thinness of the Persian skulls. After this battle Cambyses took Memphis and most of Egypt.

Photo: Major W. J. P. Rodd.
AN OLD UNFINISHED LION FROM THE TIME OF DARIUS.
This lion lies neglected beside an old side-road close to Hamadan, Persia.

In Egypt, we are told, Cambyses went mad. He took great liberties with the Egyptian temples, and remained at Memphis "opening ancient tombs and examining the dead bodies." He had already murdered both Crœsus, ex-king of Lydia, and his own brother Smerdis before coming to Egypt, and he died in Syria on the way back to Susa of an accidental wound, leaving no heirs to succeed him. He was presently succeeded by Darius the Mede (521 B.C.), the son of Hystaspes, one of the chief councillors of Cyrus.

The empire of Darius I was larger than any one of the preceding empires whose growth we have traced. It included all Asia Minor and Syria, that is to say, the ancient Lydian and Hittite empires, all the old Assyrian and Babylonian empires, Egypt, the Caucasus and Caspian regions, Media, Persia, and it extended, perhaps, into India to the Indus. The nomadic Arabians alone of all the peoples of what is nowadays called the Near East, did not pay tribute to the satraps (provincial governors) of Darius. The organization of this great empire seems to have been on a much higher level of efficiency than any of its precursors. Great arterial roads joined province to province, and there was a system of royal posts;[1] at stated intervals post horses stood always ready to carry the government messenger, or the traveller if he had a government permit, on to the next stage of his journey. Apart from this imperial right-of-way and the payment of tribute, the local governments possessed a very considerable amount of local freedom. They were restrained from internecine conflict, which was all to their own good. And at first the Greek cities of the mainland of Asia paid the tribute and shared in this Persian Peace.

Darius was first incited to attack the Greeks in Europe by a homesick Greek physician at his court, who wanted at any cost to be back in Greece. Darius had already made plans for an expedition into Europe, aiming not at Greece, but to the northward of Greece, across the Bosphorus and Danube. He wanted to strike at South Russia, which he believed to be the home country of the Scythian nomads who threatened him on his northern and northeastern frontiers. But he lent an attentive ear to the tempter, and sent agents into Greece.[2]

This great expedition of Darius opens out our view in this history. It lifts a curtain upon the Balkan country behind Greece about which we have said nothing hitherto; it carries us to and over the Danube. The nucleus of his army marched from Susa, gathering up contingents as they made their way to the Bosphorus. Here Greek allies (Ionian Greeks from Asia) had made a bridge of boats, and the army crossed over while the Greek allies sailed on in their ships to the Danube, and, two days' sail up from its mouth, landed to make another

---

[1] But a thousand years earlier the Hittites seem to have had paved high roads running across their country.

[2] But cp. Bury's *History of Greece*, ch. vi., § 5.

Photo: Major W. J. P. Rodd.

TABLETS CUT IN THE ROCKS BESIDE AN ANCIENT ROAD USED BY DARIUS THROUGH THE HILLS WITHIN FIVE MILES OF HAMADAN.

floating bridge. Meanwhile, Darius and his host advanced along the coast of what is now Bulgaria, but which was then called Thrace. They crossed the Danube, and prepared to give battle to the Scythian army and take the cities of the Scythians.

But the Scythians had no cities, and they evaded a battle, and the war degenerated into a tedious and hopeless pursuit of more mobile enemies. Wells were stopped up and pastures destroyed by the nomads. The Scythian horsemen hung upon the skirts of the great army, which consisted mostly of foot soldiers, picking off stragglers and preventing foraging; and they did their best to persuade the Ionian Greeks, who had made and were guarding the bridge across the Danube, to break up the bridge, and so ensure the destruction of Darius. So long as Darius continued to advance, however, the loyalty of his Greek allies remained unshaken.

But privation, fatigue, and sickness hindered and crippled the Persian army; Darius lost many stragglers and consumed his supplies, and at last the melancholy conviction dawned upon

him that a retreat across the Danube was necessary to save him from complete exhaustion and defeat.

In order to get a start in his retreat he sacrificed his sick and wounded. He had these men informed that he was about to attack the Scythians at nightfall, and under this pretence stole out of the camp with the pick of his troops and made off southward, leaving the camp fires burning and the usual noises and movements of the camp behind him. Next day the men left in the camp realized the trick their monarch had played upon them, and surrendered themselves to the mercy of the Scythians; but Darius had got his start, and was able to reach the bridge of boats before his pursuers came upon him. They were more mobile than his troops, but they missed their quarry in the darkness. At the river the retreating Persians "were brought to an extremity of fear," for they found the bridge partially broken down and its northern end destroyed.

At this point a voice echoes down the centuries to us. We see a group of dismayed Persians standing about the Great King upon the bank of the streaming river; we see the masses of halted troops, hungry and war-worn; a trail of battered transport stretches away towards the horizon, upon which at any time the advance guards of the pursuers may appear. There is not much noise in spite of the multitude, but rather an inquiring silence. Standing out like a pier from the further side of the great stream are the remains of the bridge of boats, an enigma. . . . We cannot discern whether there are men over there or not. The shipping of the Ionian Greeks seems still to be drawn up on the further shore, but it is all very far away.

"Now there was with Darius an Egyptian who had a voice louder than that of any other man on earth, and this man Darius ordered to take his stand upon the bank of the Ister (Danube) and to call Histiæus of Miletus."

This worthy—a day is to come, as we have already noted, when his decapitated head will be sent to Darius at Susa—appears approaching slowly across the waters in a boat.

There is a parley, and we gather that it is "all right."

The explanation Histiæus has to make is a complicated one. Some Scythians have been and have gone again. Scouts, perhaps, these were. It would seem there had been a discussion between the Scythians and the Greeks. The Scythians wanted the bridge broken down; they would then, they said, undertake to finish up the Persian army and make an end to Darius and his empire, and the Ionian Greeks of Asia could then free their cities again. Miltiades, the Athenian, was for accepting this proposal. But Histiæus had been more subtle. He would prefer, he said, to see the Persians completely destroyed before definitely abandoning their cause. Would the Scythians go back and destroy the Persians to make sure of them while the Greeks on their part destroyed the bridge? Anyhow, whichever side the Greeks took finally, it was clear to him that it would be wise to destroy the northern end of the bridge, because otherwise the Scythians might

THE CARVINGS AT BISITUN, NEAR KERMANSHAH, PERSIA, SHOWING DARIUS, NINE KINGS HE CONQUERED BEFORE HIM, ONE OTHER BENEATH HIS FEET, AND TWO OF HIS MINISTERS OR COUNCILLORS BEHIND HIM. TO ONE SIDE AND BENEATH ARE TABLETS IN THREE LANGUAGES DESCRIBING HIS EXPLOITS.

rush it. Indeed, even as they parleyed the Greeks set to work to demolish the end that linked them to the Scythians as quickly as possible. In accordance with the suggestions of Histiæus the Scythians rode off in search of the Persians, and so left the Greeks safe in either event. If Darius escaped, they could be on his side ; if he was destroyed, there was nothing of which the Scythians could complain.

Histiæus did not put it quite in that fashion to Darius. He had at least kept the shipping and most of the bridge. He represented himself as the loyal friend of Persia, and Darius was not disposed to be too critical. The Ionian ships came over. With a sense of immense relief the remnant of the wasted Persians were presently looking back at the steely flood of the Danube streaming wide between themselves and their pursuers. . . .

The pleasure and interest had gone out of the European expedition for Darius. He returned to Susa, leaving an army in Thrace, under a trusted general Megabazus. This Megabazus set himself to the subjugation of Thrace, and among other states which submitted reluctantly to Darius was a kingdom, which thus comes into our history for the first time, the kingdom of Macedonia, a country inhabited by a people so closely allied to the Greeks that one of its princes had already been allowed to compete and take a prize in the Olympian games.

Darius was disposed to reward Histiæus by allowing him to build a city for himself in Thrace, but Megabazus had a different opinion of the trustworthiness of Histiæus, and prevailed upon the king to take him to Susa, and, under the title of councillor, to keep him a prisoner there. Histiæus was at first flattered by this

Photo : Major W. J. P. Rodd.
ANOTHER VIEW OF THE CARVINGS AT BISITUN, NEAR KERMANSHAH, PERSIA.

court position, and then realized its true meaning. The Persian court bored him, and he grew homesick for Miletus. He set himself to make mischief, and was able to stir up a revolt against the Persians among the Ionian Greeks on the mainland. The twistings and turnings of the story, which included the burning of Sardis by the Ionians and the defeat of a Greek fleet at the battle of Ladé (495 B.C.), are too complicated to follow here. It is a dark and intricate story of treacheries, cruelties, and hate, in which the death of the wily Histiæus shines almost cheerfully. The Persian governor of Sardis, through which town he was being taken on his way back to Susa as a prisoner, having much the same opinion of him as Megabazus had, and knowing his ability to humbug Darius, killed him there and then, and sent on the head only to his master.

Cyprus and the Greek islands were dragged into this contest that Histiæus had stirred up, and at last Athens. Darius realized the error he had made in turning to the right and not to the left when he had crossed the Bosphorus, and he now set himself to the conquest of all Greece. He began with the islands. Tyre and Sidon were subject to Persia, and ships of the

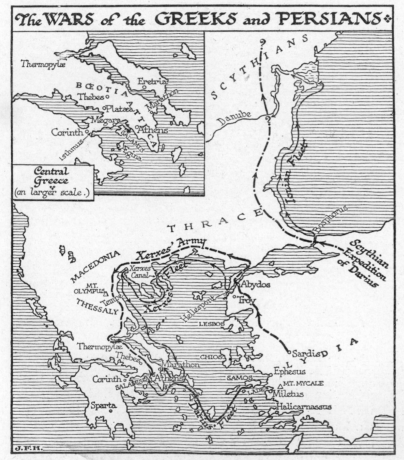

The WARS of the GREEKS and PERSIANS

Central Greece (on larger scale.)

Phœnician and of the Ionian Greeks provided the Persians with a fleet by means of which one Greek island after another was subjugated.

§ 8

The first attack upon Greece proper was made in 490 B.C. It was a sea attack upon Athens, with a force long and carefully prepared for the task, the fleet being provided with specially built transports for the conveyance of horses. This

The Battle of Marathon.

expedition made a landing near Marathon in Attica. The Persians were guided into Marathon by a renegade Greek, Hippias, the son of Peisistratus, who had been tyrant of Athens. If Athens fell, then Hippias was to be its tyrant, under the protection of the Persians. Meanwhile, so urgent was the sense of a crisis in the affairs of Hellas, that a man, a herald and runner, went from Athens to Sparta, forgetful of all feuds, to say : " Lacedemonians, the Athenians make request of you to come to their help, and not to allow a city most anciently established among the Hellenes to fall into slavery by the means of Barbarians; for even now Eretria has been enslaved and Hellas has become the weaker by a city of renown." This man, Pheidippides, did the distance from Athens to Sparta, nearly a hundred miles as the crow flies, and much more if we allow for the contours and the windings of the way, in something under eight and forty hours.

But before the Spartans could arrive on the scene the battle was joined. The Athenians charged the enemy. They fought— " in a memorable fashion: for they were the first of all the Hellenes about whom we know who went to attack the enemy at a run, and they were the first also who endured to face the Median garments and the men who wore them, whereas up to this time the very name of the Medes was to the Hellenes a terror to hear."

The Persian wings gave before this impetuous attack, but the centre held. The Athenians, however, were cool as well as vigorous ; they let the wings run and closed in on the flanks of the centre, whereupon the main body of the Persians fled to their ships. Seven vessels fell into the hands of the Athenians ; the rest got away, and, after a futile attempt to sail round to Athens and seize the city before the army returned thither, the fleet made a retreat to Asia. Let Herodotus close the story with a paragraph that still further enlightens us upon the tremendous prestige of the Medes at this time :

" Of the Lacedemonians there came to Athens two thousand after the full moon, making great haste to be in time, so that they arrived in Attica on the third day after leaving Sparta : and though they had come too late for the battle, yet they desired to behold the Medes ; and accordingly they went on to Marathon and looked at the bodies of the slain : then afterwards they departed home, commending the Athenians and the work which they had done."

§ 9

So Greece, unified for a while by fear, gained her first victory over Persia. The news came **Thermopylæ and Salamis.** to Darius simultaneously with the news of a rebellion in Egypt, and he died while still undecided in which direction to turn. His son and successor, Xerxes, turned first to Egypt and set up a Persian satrap there ; then for four years he prepared a second attack upon Greece. Says Herodotus, who was, one must remember, a patriotic Greek, approaching now to the climax of his History :

" For what nation did Xerxes not lead out of Asia against Hellas ? and what water was not exhausted, being drunk by his host, except only the great rivers ? For some supplied ships, and others were appointed to serve in the land-army ; to some it was appointed to furnish cavalry, and to others vessels to carry horses, while they served in the expedition themselves also ; others were ordered to furnish ships of war for the bridges, and others again ships with provisions."

Xerxes passed into Europe, not as Darius did at the half-mile crossing of the Bosphorus, but at the Hellespont (= the Dardanelles). In his account of the assembling of the great army, and its march from Sardis to the Hellespont, the poet in Herodotus takes possession of the historian. The great host passes in splendour by Troy, and Xerxes, who although a Persian and a Barbarian, seems to have had the advantages of a classical education, turns aside, says our historian, to visit the citadel of Priam. The Hellespont was bridged at Abydos, and upon a hill was set a marble throne from which Xerxes surveyed the whole array of his forces.

" And seeing all the Hellespont covered over with the ships and all the shores and the plains

Photo : Alinari.

REMAINS OF THE SUPPOSED TOMB OF MILTIADES AT MARATHON.

of Abydos full of men, then Xerxes pronounced himself a happy man, and after that he fell to weeping. Artabanus, his uncle, therefore perceiving him—the same who at first boldly declared his opinion advising Xerxes not to march against Hellas—this man, I say, having observed that Xerxes wept, asked as follows : ' O king, how far different from one another are the things which thou hast done now and a short while before now ! for having pronounced thyself a happy man, thou art now shedding tears.' He said : ' Yea, for after I had reckoned up, it came into my mind to feel pity at the thought how brief was the whole life

where, at that time—2,300 years have altered these things greatly—there was a great cliff on the landward side and the sea to the east, with a track scarcely wide enough for a chariot between. The great advantage to the Greeks of this position at Thermopylæ was that it prevented the use of either cavalry or chariots, and narrowed the battle front so as to minimize their numerical inequality. And there the Persians joined battle with them one summer day in the year 480 B.C.

For three days the Greeks held this great army, and did them much damage with small loss to themselves, and then on the third day

Photo : Alinari.

FRIEZE FROM THE TREASURY OF THE CNIDIANS (DATING FROM 530 B.C.) AT DELPHI, SHOWING GREEK WARRIORS.

of man, seeing that of these multitudes not one will be alive when a hundred years have gone by.'

This may not be exact history, but it is great poetry. It is as splendid as anything in *The Dynasts*.

The Persian fleet, coasting from headland to headland, accompanied this land multitude during its march southward ; but a violent storm did the fleet great damage and 400 ships were lost, including much corn transport. At first the united Hellenes marched out to meet the invaders at the Vale of Tempe near Mount Olympus, but afterwards retreated through Thessaly, and chose at last to await the advancing Persians at a place called Thermopylæ,

a detachment of Persians appeared upon the rear of the Greeks, having learnt of a way over the mountains from a peasant. There were hasty discussions among the Greeks ; some were for withdrawing, some for holding out. The leader of the whole force, Leonidas, was for staying ; and with him he would keep, he said, 300 Spartans. The rest of the Greek army could, meanwhile, make good its retreat to the next defensible pass. The Thespian contingent of 700, however, refused to fall back. They preferred to stay and die with the Spartans. Also a contingent of 400 Thebans remained. As Thebes afterwards joined the Persians, there is a story that these Thebans were detained by force against their will, which seems on military as well as historical grounds improbable. These 1,400 stayed, and were, after a conflict of heroic quality, slain to a man. Two Spartans happened to be away, sick with ophthalmia. When they heard the news, one was too ill to move ; the other made his helot guide him to the battle, and there struck blindly until he was killed. The other, Aristodemus, was taken away with the retreating troops, and returned to Sparta, where he was not actually punished for his conduct, but was known as Tresas, " the man who retreated." It was enough to distinguish him from all other Spartans, and he got himself killed at the Battle of Platæa a year later, performing prodigies of reckless courage. . . . For a whole day this little band had held the pass, assailed in front and rear by the whole force of the Persians. They had covered the retreat of the main Greek army, they had inflicted great losses on the invaders, and they had raised the prestige of the Greek warrior over that of the Mede higher even than the victory of Marathon had done.

The Persian cavalry and transport filtered slowly through the narrow passage of Thermopylæ, and marched on towards Athens, while a series of naval encounters went on at sea. The Hellenic fleet retreated before the advance of the Persian shipping, which suffered seriously through its comparative ignorance of the intricate coasts and of the tricks of the local weather. Weight of numbers carried the Persian army forward to Athens; now that Thermopylæ was lost, there was no line of defence nearer than the Isthmus of Corinth, and this meant the abandonment of all the intervening territory, including Athens. The population had either to fly or submit to the Persians. Thebes with all Bœotia submitted, and was pressed into the Persian army, except one town, Platæa, whose inhabitants fled to Athens. The turn of Athens came next, and great efforts were made to persuade her to make terms ; but, instead, the whole population determined to abandon everything and take to the shipping. The women and non-combatants were carried to Salamis and various adjacent islands. Only a few people too old to move and a few dissentients remained in the town, which was occupied by the Persians and burnt. The

sacred objects, statues, etc., which were burnt at this time, were afterwards buried in the Acropolis by the returning Athenians, and have been dug up in our own day with the marks of burning visible upon them. Xerxes sent off a mounted messenger to Susa with the news, and he invited the sons of Peisistratus, whom he had brought back with him, to enter upon their inheritance and sacrifice after the Athenian manner upon the Acropolis.

Meanwhile, the Hellenic confederate fleet had come round to Salamis, and in the council of war there were bitter differences of opinion. Corinth and the states behind the Isthmus wanted the fleet to fall back to that position, abandoning the cities of Megara and Ægina. Themistocles insisted with all his force on fighting in the narrows of Salamis. The majority was steadily in favour of retreat, when there suddenly arrived the news that retreat was cut off. The Persians had sailed round Salamis and held the sea on the other side. This news was brought by that Aristides the Just, of whose ostracism we have already told ; his sanity and eloquence did much to help Themistocles to hearten the hesitating commanders. These two men had formerly been bitter antagonists ; but, with a generosity rare in those days, they forgot their differences before the common danger. At dawn the Greek ships pulled out to battle.

The fleet before them was a fleet more composite and less united than their own. But it was about three times as great. On one wing were the Phœnicians, on the other Ionian Greeks from Asia and the Islands. Some of the latter fought stoutly ; others remembered that they too were Greeks. The Greek ships, on the other hand, were mostly manned by freemen fighting for their homes. Throughout the early hours the battle raged confusedly. Then it became evident to Xerxes, watching the combat, that his fleet was attempting flight. The flight became disaster.

Xerxes had taken his seat to watch the battle. He saw his galleys rammed by the sharp prows of other galleys ; his fighting-men shot down ; his ships boarded. Much of the sea-fighting in those days was done by ramming ; the big galleys bore down their opponents by superior weight of impact, or sheared off their oars and so destroyed their manœuvring power and left them helpless. Presently, Xerxes saw that some of his broken ships were surrendering. In the water he could see the heads of Greeks swimming to land; but " of the Barbarians the greater number perished in the sea, not knowing how to swim." The clumsy attempt of the hard-pressed first line of the Persian fleet to put about led to indescribable confusion. Some were rammed by the rear ships of their own side. This ancient shipping was poor, unseaworthy stuff by any modern standards. The west wind was blowing, and many of the broken ships of Xerxes were now drifting away out of his sight to be wrecked on the coast

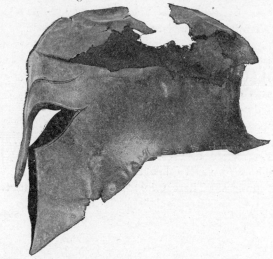

Photo: Mansell.
HELMET OF "CORINTHIAN" TYPE, INSCRIBED WITH DEDICATION TO ZEUS, FROM NEAR OLYMPIA.

beyond. Others were being towed towards Salamis by the Greeks. Others, less injured and still in fighting trim, were making for the beaches close beneath him that would bring them under the protection of his army. Scattered over the further sea, beyond the headlands, remote and vague, were ships in flight and Greek ships in pursuit. Slowly, incident by incident, the disaster had unfolded under his eyes. We can imagine something of the coming and going of messengers, the issuing of futile orders, the changes of plan, throughout the day. In the morning Xerxes had come out provided with tables to mark the most successful of his commanders for reward. In the gold of the sunset he beheld the sea power of Persia utterly scattered, sunken, and destroyed, and

the Greek fleet over against Salamis unbroken and triumphant, ordering its ranks, as if still incredulous of victory.

The Persian army remained as if in indecision for some days close to the scene of this sea fight, and then began to retreat to Thessaly, where it was proposed to winter and resume the campaign. But Xerxes, like Darius I before him, had conceived a disgust for European campaigns. He was afraid of the destruction of the bridge of boats. With part of the army he went on to the Hellespont, leaving the main force in Thessaly under a general, Mardonius. Of his own retreat the historian relates :

" Whithersoever they came on the march and to whatever nation they seized the crops of that people and used them for provisions ; and if they found no crops, then they took the grass which was growing up from the earth, and stripped off the bark from the trees and plucked down the leaves and devoured them ; alike of the cultivated trees and of those growing wild ; and they left nothing behind them : thus they did by reason of famine. Then plague too seized upon the army and dysentery, which destroyed them by the way, and some of them also who were sick the king left behind, laying charge upon the cities where at the time he chanced to be in his march, to take care of them and support them ; of these he left some in Thessaly, and some at Siris in Paionia, and some in Macedonia. . . . When, passing on from Thrace they came to the passage, they crossed over the Hellespont in haste to Abydos by means of the ships, for they did not find the floating bridges still stretched across, but broken up by a storm. While staying there for a time they had distributed to them an allowance of food more abundant than they had had by the way, and from satisfying their hunger without restraint and also from the changes of water there died many of those in the army who had remained safe till then. The rest arrived with Xerxes at Sardis."

§ 10

Platæa and Mycale. The rest of the Persian army remained in Thessaly under the command of Mardonius, and for a year he maintained an aggressive campaign against the Greeks. Finally, he was defeated and killed in a pitched battle at Platæa (479 B.C.), and on the same day the Persian fleet and a land army met with joint disaster under the shadow of Mount Mycale on the Asiatic mainland, between Ephesus and Miletus. The Persian ships, being in fear of the Greeks, had been drawn up on shore and a wall built about them; but the Greeks disembarked and stormed this enclosure. They then sailed to the Hellespont to destroy what was left of the bridge of boats, so that later the Persian fugitives, retreating from Platæa, had to cross by shipping at the Bosphorus, and did so with difficulty.

Encouraged by these disasters of the imperial power, the Ionian cities in Asia began for a second time to revolt against the Persians.

With this the ninth book of the *History of Herodotus* comes to an end. He was born about 484 B.C., so that at the time of the battle of Platæa he was a child of five years old. Much of the substance of his story was gathered by him from actors in, and eye-witnesses of, the great events he relates. The war still dragged on for a long time; the Greeks supported a rebellion against Persian rule in Egypt, and tried unsuccessfully to take Cyprus; it did not end until about 449 B.C. Then the Greek coasts of Asia Minor and the Greek cities in the Black Sea remained generally free, but Cyprus and Egypt continued under Persian rule. Herodotus, who had been born a Persian subject in the Ionian city of Halicarnassus, was five and thirty years old by that time, and he must have taken an early opportunity after this peace of visiting Babylon and Persia. He probably went to Athens, with his History ready to recite, about 438 B.C.

The idea of a great union of Greece for aggression against Persia was not altogether strange to Herodotus. Some of his readers suspect him of writing to enforce it. It was certainly in the air at that time. He describes Aristagoras, the son-in-law of Histiæus, as showing the Spartans " a tablet of bronze on which was engraved a map of the whole earth with all the seas and rivers." He makes Aristagoras say: " These Barbarians are not valiant in fight. You, on the other hand, have now attained to the utmost skill in war. They fight with bows and arrows and a short spear; they go into battle wearing trousers and having caps on their heads. You have perfected your weapons and discipline. They are easily to be conquered. Not all the other nations of the world have what they possess: gold, silver, bronze, embroidered garments, beasts and slaves; *all this you might have for yourselves, if you so desired.*"

It was a hundred years before these suggestions bore fruit.

Xerxes was murdered in his palace about 465 B.C., and thereafter Persia made no further attempts at conquest in Europe. We have no such knowledge of the things that were happening in the empire of the Great King as we have of the occurrences in the little states of Central Greece. Greece had suddenly begun to produce literature, and put itself upon record as no other nation had ever done hitherto. After 479 B.C. (Platæa) the spirit seems to have gone out of the government of the Medes and Persians. The empire of the Great King enters upon a period of decay. An Artaxerxes, a second Xerxes, a second Darius, pass across the stage; there are rebellions in Egypt and Syria; the Medes rebel; a second Artaxerxes and a second Cyrus, his brother, fight for the throne. This history is even as the history of Babylonia, Assyria, and Egypt in the older times. It is autocracy reverting to its normal state of palace crime, blood-stained magnificence, and moral squalor. But the last-named struggle produced a Greek masterpiece, for this second Cyrus collected an army of Greek mercenaries and marched into Babylonia, and was there killed at the moment of victory over Arta-xerxes II. Thereupon, the Ten Thousand Greeks, left with no one to employ them, made a retreat to the coast again (401 B.C.), and this retreat was immortalized in a book, one of the first of personal war books, the *Anabasis*, by their leader Xenophon.

Murders, revolts, chastisements, disasters, cunning alliances, and base betrayals, and no Herodotus to record them. Such is the texture of Persian history. An Artaxerxes III, covered with blood, flourishes dimly for a time. "Arta-xerxes III is said to have been murdered by Bagoas, who places Arses, the youngest of the king's sons, on the throne only to slay him in turn when he seemed to be contemplating independent action." [1] So it goes on. Beneath the crimes and disorders of the palaces, the life of the city and country ran a similar course.

Justice was fitful and law venal. Wars that were unmeaning catastrophies swept down upon any little gleam of prosperity or decency to which this or that community clambered: Athens, prospering for a time after the Persian repulse, was smitten by the plague, in which Pericles, its greatest ruler, died (428 B.C.). But, as a noteworthy fact amidst these con-fusions, the Ten Thousand of Xenophon were scattering now among the Greek cities, repeating from their own experience the declaration of Aristagoras that the Persian empire was a rich confusion which it would be very easy to conquer.

[1] Winckler, in Helmolt's *Universal History*.

XXIII

GREEK THOUGHT AND LITERATURE [1]

§ 1

GREEK history for the next forty years after Platæa and Mycale is a story of comparative peace and tranquillity. There were wars, but they were not intense wars. For a little while in Athens, for a section of the better sort, there was leisure **The Athens of Pericles.** and opportunity. And by a com-bination of accidents, and through the character of a small group of people, this leisure and opportunity produced the most remarkable and memorable results. A beauti-ful literature was produced ; the plastic arts flourished, and the foundations of modern science were laid. Then, after an interlude of fifty odd years, the long-smouldering hostility between Athens and Sparta broke out into a fierce and exhausting war, which sapped at last the vitality of this creative movement.

This war is known in history as the Pelopon-nesian War ; it went on for nearly thirty years, and wasted all the power of Greece. At first Athens was in the ascendant, then Sparta.

Then arose Thebes, a city not fifty miles from Athens, to overshadow Sparta. Once more Athens flared into importance as the head of a confederation. The story must be told at considerable length or not told at all. It is a story of narrow rivalries and inexplicable hatreds, that would have vanished long ago out of the memories of men, were it not that it is recorded and reflected in a great literature.

Through all this time Persia appears and reappears as the ally first of this league and then of that. About the middle of the fourth century B.C., Greece becomes aware of a new influence in its affairs, that of Philip, King of Macedonia. Macedonia does, indeed, arise in the background of this incurably divided Greece, as the Medes and Persians arose behind the Chaldean Empire. A time comes when the Greek mind turns round, so to speak, from

[1] See in relation to this chapter, Zimmern's *Greek Commonwealth*. A very handy book for the student in this section is Abbott's *Skeleton Outline of Greek History*.

The time chart, page 209, represents seven centuries. Throughout the rest of this History we shall give a series of time charts on the same scale, ending with 1920 A.D. This chart is on a scale of roughly $8\frac{1}{2}$ times that of the time chart on page 111. By this scale that chart would have to be about 4 feet long ; the time diagram on page 58, 377 inches ; that on page 38, 377 feet ; and the diagram of geological time between $8\frac{1}{2}$ and 85 miles !

THE PARTHENON OF ATHENS SEEN FROM THE PROPYLÆA.

Column headings: MEDITERRANEAN (WESTERN / EASTERN) — EGYPT — JUDEA — MESOPOTAMIA & PERSIA — INDIA — CHINA

CHINA

HUNS

551 Confucius born

The Period assigned by Chinese historians to the Chow Dynasty

INDIA

ARYANS

Aryans in India

Dravidians

Buddha

EASTERN ARYANS

Scythians

Medes & Persians

MESOPOTAMIA & PERSIA

The Middle Assyrian Empire and Babylonia independent of one another until

745 Tiglath Pileser III founds (the New Assyrian Empire
Ten Tribes deported by Sargon II. 722
704 Sennacherib
680 Esarhaddon
667 Sardanapalus
ASSYRIAN EMPIRE
606 Nineveh falls.
Nebuchadnezzar the Great
Babylonian captivity of the Jews
CHALDEAN EMPIRE
539 Cyrus takes Babylon
521 Darius I
485 Xerxes
465 Xerxes murdered
PERSIA — PERSIAN EMPIRE
401 Retreat of the Ten Thousand
330 Darius III killed
326 Defeat of Porus
321 Chandragupta

JUDEA

Saul king of Israel
David
Solomon
930 Israel splits from Judah
Syrian Kingdom
Israel
Judah
590 Babylonian captivity of the Jews
530 Ezra rebuilds Jerusalem.

EGYPT

XXI Dynasty in decay
Shishak I (XXII Dyn.) loots Temple
790 Ethiopian conquest of Egypt
takes Thebes in Egypt
608 Necho II — Battle of Megiddo
Settlement of Jews in Egypt
525 Cambyses in E
521 in Egypt.
EGYPT in decay
331 Alexander visits Ammon

MEDITERRANEAN

Cnossus destroyed
GREEKS
Phoenician colonists
WESTERN ARYANS
Carthage built
753 Rome built
776 First Olympiad
Ionian Greeks
Greeks in Sicily & Magna Graecia
Rome expels her Etruscan kings
527 Peisistratus died
490 Battle of Marathon
480 " Salamis
474 Etruscan fleet destroyed
470 Hanno's voyage
466 Pericles
431 Peloponnesian War
428 Herodotus died
404
Plato
338 Battle of Chaeronea
Aristotle
323 Death of Alexander the Great
331 Alexander the Great
Hellenism spreads eastward
390 Brennus sacks Rome
366 Camillus builds Temple of Concord
Rise of ROME

Time scale: 1000 B.C. — 900 B.C. — 800 B.C. — 700 B.C. — 600 B.C. — 500 B.C. — 400 B.C. — 300 B.C.

(See footnote on page 208.)

its disputes, and stares in one united dismay at the Macedonian.

Planless and murderous squabbles are still planless and murderous squabbles even though Thucydides tells the story, even though the great beginnings of a new civilization are wrecked by their disorders, and in this general outline we can give no space at all to the particulars of these internecine feuds, to the fights and flights that sent first this Greek city and then that up to the sky in flames. Upon a one-foot globe Greece becomes a speck almost too small to recognize, and in a short history of mankind, all this century and more of dissension between the days of Salamis and Platæa and the rise of King Philip, shrinks to a little, almost inaudible clash of disputation, to a mere note upon the swift passing of opportunity for nations as for men.

But what does not shrink into insignificance, because it has entered into the intellectual process of all subsequent nations, because it is inseparably a part of our mental foundation, is the literature that Athens produced during such patches and gleams of tranquillity and security as these times afforded her.

Says Professor Gilbert Murray : [1]

" Their outer political history, indeed, like that of all other nations, is filled with war and diplomacy, with cruelty and deceit. It is the inner history, the history of thought and feeling and character, that is so grand. They

[1] *Ancient Greek Literature*, by Gilbert Murray (Heinemann, 1911).

Photo: Mansell.

PERICLES. (BUST FOUND NEAR TIVOLI.)

had some difficulties to contend with which are now almost out of our path. They had practically no experience, but were doing everything for the first time ; they were utterly weak in material resources, and their emotions, their ' *desires and fears and rages,*' were probably wilder and fiercer than ours. Yet they produced the Athens of Pericles and of Plato."

This remarkable outbreak of creative power, which for three and twenty centuries has been to men of intelligence a guiding and inspiring beacon out of the past, flared up after the battles of Marathon and Salamis had made Athens free and fearless, and, without any great excesses of power, predominate in her world. It was the work of a quite small group of men. A number of her citizens lived for the better part of a generation under conditions which, in all ages, have disposed men to produce good and beautiful work ; they were secure, they were free, and they had pride ; and they were without that temptation of apparent and unchallenged power which disposes all of us to inflict wrongs upon our fellow men. When political life narrowed down again to the waste and crimes of a fratricidal war with Sparta, there was so broad and well-fed a flame of intellectual activity burning that it lasted through all the windy distresses of this war and beyond the brief lifetime of Alexander the Great, for a period altogether of more than a hundred years after the wars began.

Athens, it must be understood, was by far the largest of all the Greek city democracies.

Flushed with victory and the sense of freedom fairly won, her people did for a time rise towards nobility. Under the guidance of a great demagogue, Pericles, the chief official of the Athenian general assembly, and a politician statesman rather of the calibre of Gladstone or Lincoln in modern history, they were set to the task of rebuilding their city and expanding their commerce. For a time they were capable of following a generous leader generously, and Fate gave them a generous leader. In Pericles there was mingled in the strangest fashion political ability with a real living passion for deep and high and beautiful things. He kept in power for over thirty years. He was a man of extraordinary vigour and liberality of mind. He stamped these qualities upon his time. As Winckler has remarked, the Athenian democracy had for a time " the face of Pericles." He was sustained by what was probably a very great and noble friendship. There was a woman of unusual education, Aspasia, from Miletus, whom he could not marry because of the law that restricted the citizenship of Athens to the home-born, but who was in effect his wife. She played a large part in gathering about him men of unusual gifts. All the great writers of the time knew her, and several have praised her wisdom. Plutarch, it is true, accuses her of instigating a troublesome and dangerous but

ARCHAIC STATUE OF APOLLO (SIXTH CENTURY B.C.) BEFORE THE GREAT PERIOD OF ATHENIAN ART.

finally successful war against Samos, but, as he himself shows later, this was necessitated by the naval hostility of the Samians, which threatened the overseas trade of Athens, upon which all the prosperity of the republic depended.

Men's ambitions are apt to reflect the standards of their intimates. Pericles was content, at any rate, to serve as a leader in Athens rather than to dominate as a tyrant. Alliances were formed under his guidance, new colonies and trading stations were established from Italy to the Black Sea; and the treasures of the league at Delos were brought to Athens. Convinced of his security from Persia, Pericles spent the war hoard of the allies upon the beautification of his city. This was an unrighteous thing to do by our modern standards, but it was not a base or greedy thing to do. Athens had accomplished the work of the Delian League, and is not the labourer worthy of his hire? This sequestration made a time of exceptional opportunity for architects and artists. The Parthenon of Athens, whose ruins are still a thing of beauty, was but the crown set upon the clustering beauty of the Athens Pericles rebuilt. Such sculptures as those of Phidias, Myron, and Polyclitus that still survive, witness to the artistic quality of the time.

The reader must bear in mind that illuminating remark of Winckler's, which says that this renascent Athens bore for a time the face of Pericles. It was the peculiar genius of this man and of his atmosphere that let loose the genius of men about him, and attracted men of great intellectual vigour to Athens. Athens wore his face for a time as one wears a mask, and then became restless and desired to put him aside. There was very little that was great and generous about the common Athenian. We have told of the spirit of one sample voter for the ostracism of Aristides, and Lloyd (in his *Age of Pericles*) declares that the Athenians would not suffer the name of Miltiades to be mentioned in connection with the battle of Marathon. The sturdy self-respect of the common voters revolted presently against the beautiful buildings rising about them; against the favours shown to such sculptors as Phidias over popular worthies in the same line of business; against the donations made to a mere foreigner like Herodotus of Halicarnassus; against the insulting preference of Pericles for the company and conversation of a Milesian woman. The public life of Pericles was conspicuously orderly, and that presently set the man in the street thinking that his private life must be very corrupt. One gathers that Pericles was " superior " in his demeanour; he betrayed at times a contempt for the citizens he served.

" Pericles acquired not only an elevation of sentiment, and a loftiness and purity of style far removed from the low expression of the vulgar, but likewise a gravity of countenance which relaxed not into laughter, a firm and even tone of voice, an easy deportment, and a decency of dress which no vehemence of speaking ever put into disorder. These things, and others of a like nature, excited admiration in all that saw him. Such was his conduct, when a vile and abandoned fellow loaded him a whole day with reproaches and abuse; he bore it with patience and silence, and continued in public for the despatch of some urgent affairs. In the evening he walked softly home, this impudent wretch following, and insulting him all the way with the most scurrilous language. And as it was dark when he came to his own door, he ordered one of his servants to take a torch and light the man home. The poet Ion, however, says he was proud and supercilious in conversation, and that there was a great deal of vanity and contempt of others mixed with his dignity of manner. . . . He appeared not in the streets except when he went to the forum or the senate house. He declined the invitations of his friends, and all social entertainments and recreations; insomuch that in the whole time of his administration, which was a considerable length, he never went to sup with any of his friends but

Photo : Anderson.
THE DORYPHORUS—SPEAR-BEARER—OF POLYCLITUS.

once, which was at the marriage of his nephew Euryptolemus, and he staid there only until the ceremony of libation was ended. He considered that the freedom of entertainments takes away all distinction of office, and that dignity is but little consistent with familiarity. . . ." [1]

There was as yet no gutter journalism to tell the world of the vileness of the conspicuous and successful; but the common man, a little out of conceit with himself, found much consolation in the art of comedy, which flourished exceedingly. The writers of comedy satisfied that almost universal craving for the depreciation of those whose apparent excellence offends our self-love. They threw dirt steadily and industriously at Pericles and his friends. Pericles was portrayed in a helmet; a helmet became him, and it is to be feared he knew as much. This led to much joy and mirth over the pleasant suggestion of a frightfully distorted head, an onion head. The " goings on " of Aspasia were of course a fruitful vineyard for the inventions of the street. . . .

Dreaming souls, weary of the vulgarities of our time, have desired to be transferred to the sublime Age of Pericles. But, plumped down into that Athens, they would have found themselves in very much the atmosphere of the lower sort of contemporary music-hall, very much in the vein of our popular newspapers; the same hot blast of braying libel, foul imputation, greedy " patriotism," and general baseness would have blown upon them, the " modern note " would have pursued them. As the memories of Platæa and Salamis faded and the new buildings grew familiar, Pericles and the pride of Athens became more and more offensive to the homely humour of the crowd. He was never ostracized—his prestige with the quieter citizens saved him from that; but he was attacked with increasing boldness and steadfastness. He lived and died a poor man; he was perhaps the most honest of demagogues; but this did not save him from an abortive prosecution for peculation. Defeated in that, his enemies resorted to a more devious method; they began to lop away his friends.

Religious intolerance and moral accusations are the natural weapons of the envious against the leaders of men. His friend Damon was

[1] *Plutarch.*

ostracized. Phidias was attacked for impiety. On the shield of the great statue of the goddess Athenè, Phidias had dared to put, among the combatants in a fight between Greeks and Amazons, portraits of Pericles and himself. Phidias died in prison. Anaxagoras, a stranger welcomed to Athens by Pericles—when there were plenty of honest fellows already there

COPY OF MYRON'S DISCOBOLUS.

quite willing to satisfy any reasonable curiosities—was saying the strangest things about the sun and stars, and hinting not obscurely that there were no gods, but only one animating spirit (*nous*) in the world.[2] The comedy writers suddenly found they had deep religious feelings that could be profoundly and even dangerously shocked, and Anaxagoras fled the threat of a prosecution. Then came the turn of Aspasia. Athens seemed bent upon deporting her, and Pericles was torn between the woman who was

[2] For an account of his views, see Burnet's *Greek Philosophy.*

the soul of his life and the ungracious city he had saved, defended, and made more beautiful and unforgettable than any other city in history. He stood up to defend Aspasia, he was seized by a storm of very human emotion, and as he spoke he wept—a gleeful thing for the rabble. His tears saved Aspasia for a time.

The Athenians were content to humiliate Pericles, but he had served them so long that they were indisposed to do without him. He had been their leader now for a third of a century.

In 431 B.C. came the war with Sparta. Plutarch accuses Pericles of bringing it on, because he felt his popularity waned so fast that a war was needed to make him indispensable.

" And as he himself was become obnoxious to the people upon Phidias's account, and was afraid of being called in question for it, he urged on the war, which as yet was uncertain, and blew up that flame, which till then was stifled and suppressed. By this means he hoped to obviate the accusations that threatened him, and to mitigate the rage of envy, because such was his dignity and power, that in all important affairs, and in every great danger, the republic could place its confidence in him alone."

But the war was a slow and dangerous war, and the Athenian people were impatient. A

Photo: Anderson.

VENUS OF PRAXITELES.

certain Cleon arose, ambitious to oust Pericles from his leadership. There was a great clamour for a swift ending of the war. Cleon set out to be " the man who won the war." The popular poets got to work in this fashion:

" Thou king of satyrs . . .
    why boast thy prowess,
Yet shudder at the sound of sharpened swords,
Spite of the flaming Cleon ? "

An expedition under the leadership of Pericles was unsuccessful, and Cleon seized the opportunity for a prosecution. Pericles was suspended from his command and fined. The story goes that his eldest son—this was not the son of Aspasia, but of a former wife —turned against him, and pursued him with vile and incredible accusations. This young man was carried off by the plague. Then the sister of Pericles died, and then his last legitimate son. When, after the fashion of the time, he put the funeral garlands on the boy he wept aloud. Presently he himself took the contagion and died (428 B.C.).

The salient facts of this brief summary will serve to show how discordant Pericles was with the normal life of his time and city. This intellectual and artistic outbreak in Athens was no doubt favoured by the conditions of the time, but it was also due in part to the appearance of some very unusual men. It was not a general movement; it was the movement of a small group of people exceptionally placed and gifted.

§ 2

Another leading figure in this Athenian movement,·a figure still more out of harmony with

Socrates.

the life around him, and quite as much an original source and stimulant of the enduring greatness of his age, was a man called Socrates, the son of a stone-mason. He was born about sixteen years later than Herodotus, and he was beginning to be heard of about the time when Pericles died. He himself wrote nothing, but it was his custom to talk in public places. There was in those days a great searching for wisdom going on; there was a various multitude of teachers called sophists who reasoned upon truth, beauty, and right living, and instructed the developing curiosities and imaginations of youth. This was so because there were no great priestly schools in Greece. And into these discussions this man came, a clumsy and slovenly figure, barefooted, gathering about him a band of admirers and disciples.

His method was profoundly sceptical; he believed that the only possible virtue was true knowledge; he would tolerate no belief, no hope that could not pass the ultimate acid test. For himself this meant virtue, but for many of his weaker followers it meant the loss of beliefs and moral habits that would have restrained their impulses. These weaklings became self-excusing, self-indulging scoundrels. Among his young associates were Plato, who afterwards immortalized his method in a series of philosophical dialogues, and founded the philosophical school of the Academy, which lasted nine hundred years, Xenophon, of the Ten Thousand, who described his death, and Isocrates, one of the wisest of Greek political thinkers; but there were also Critias, who, when Athens was utterly defeated by Sparta, was leader among the Thirty Tyrants appointed by the Spartans to keep the crushed city under; [1]

Charmides, who was killed beside Critias when the Thirty were overthrown; and Alcibiades, a brilliant and complex traitor, who did much to lead Athens into the disastrous expedition against Syracuse which destroyed her strength, who betrayed her to the Spartans, and who was at last assassinated while on his way to the Persian court to contrive mischief against Greece. These latter pupils were not the only young men of promise whose vulgar faith and

Photo : Mansell.

ANCIENT COPY FROM SHIELD OF THE ATHENE OF THE PARTHENON BY PHIDIAS. BATTLE OF GREEKS AND AMAZONS.

Among the Greeks is Phidias as a bald-headed old man and Pericles with his arm across his face.

patriotism Socrates destroyed to leave nothing in its place. His most inveterate enemy was a certain Anytus, whose son, a devoted disciple of Socrates, had become a hopeless drunkard.

[1] "But it was not only against the lives, properties, and liberties of Athenian citizens that the Thirty made war. They were not less solicitous to extinguish the intellectual force and education of the city, a project so perfectly in harmony both with the sentiment and practice of Sparta, that they counted on the support of their foreign allies. Among the ordinances which they promulgated was one, expressly forbidding any one ' to teach the art of words.' The edict of the Thirty was, in fact, a general suppression of the higher class of teachers or professors, above the rank of the elementary (teacher of letters or) grammatist. If such an edict could have been maintained in force for a generation, combined with the other mandates of the Thirty—the city out of which Sophocles and Euripides had just died, and in which Plato and Isocrates were in vigorous age, would have been degraded to the intellectual level of the meanest community in Greece. It was not uncommon for a Grecian despot to suppress all those assemblies wherein youths came together for the purpose of common training, either intellectual or gymnastic, as well as the public banquets and clubs or associations, as being dangerous to his authority, tending to elevation of courage, and to a consciousness of political rights among the citizens."—Grote's *History of Greece.*

Through Anytus it was that Socrates was at last prosecuted for " corrupting " the youth of Athens, and condemned to death by drinking a poisonous draught made from hemlock (399 B.C.).

His death is described with great beauty in the dialogue of Plato called by the name of *Phædo*.

§ 3

The preceding section raised an interesting discussion between Professor Gilbert Murray

What was the Quality of the Common Athenians?

and the writer upon the character and quality of the common Athenian citizen. Professor Murray thought several phrases used by the writer harsh and unjust. But what he had to say was so interesting and informing, and the writer was so entirely in agreement with his spirit, that it seemed better, instead of modifying what has been written in § 1, to leave that as it stood and to supplement it by quoting Professor Murray. He objected to the parallelism with a twentieth-century crowd. " What I want you to do," he wrote, " is to take them at the level of the people round them and before them and see how they differ. For example, the first thing that strikes one is that they use all their powers for a different purpose than most peoples:

for intellectual and artistic things. No more enormous works here to glorify divine kings ; no private splendour, no luxury, but a wonderful output of art, poetry, philosophy, and—within limits—science. Compare them with Rome.

" In the matter of slavery : all nations had slaves ; some treated them very cruelly, some with moderate cruelty. The Greeks alone argued whether it was right to have them—and ' cranks ' occasionally proposed emancipation. You get strong testimony, sometimes indignant testimony, that the Athenians were too soft altogether in their treatment of slaves. As soon as you get to Carthaginian or Roman history you get appalling cruelty (the 6,000 crucified by Crassus, the gladiatorial games, the habitual leg-breaking of slaves, etc.) ; such things seem never to have occurred in Greece. As soon as you get to Alexander you get, of course, the Oriental despotic touch—fantastic vanity and cruelty ; and at length the recurrence of human sacrifice.

" The greatness of Greece comes out only in the art and literature and thought ; not in the political and social history—except in dim flashes. By all means emphasize clearly to start with that the Greeks of, say, the ninth century, were practically savages, and those of

THE PLATFORM ON THE ATHENIAN PLACE OF ASSEMBLY, FROM WHICH PERICLES MUST HAVE SPOKEN.

even the sixth and in places right on to the fifth and fourth were in many things on the 'Lower Cultures' level. Clothes like Polynesians; tools very poor; religion ... fragments of the Polynesian all about, when you got outside the educated Attic world. But the *characteristic* is that, on this very low level, you have extraordinary flashes of very high inspiration, as the poetry and art and philosophy witness. Also, an actual achievement in social life—what one calls 'Hellenism,' *i.e.*, republicanism, simplicity of life, sobriety of thought, almost complete abolition of torture, mutilation, etc., and an amazing emancipation of the individual and of the human intellect. It is impossible to speak, really, of the 'Greek view' of anything. Because all the different views are put forward and represented. polytheism, monotheism, atheism; pro-slavery, anti-slavery; duty to animals, no duty to animals; democracy, monarchy, aristocracy. The characteristic is that *human thought got free.* (Not absolutely, of course; only to an amazing extent.) This emancipation was paid for by all sorts of instability; awful political instability, because stability in such things is produced exactly by the opposite —by long firm tradition and cohesiveness.

" It is not fair to say I idealize the Athenian mob; see, for example, my *Euripides and his Age.* But I don't think it was like our music-hall mob. It was much more artistic, much more intellectual and yet more primitive, more indecent but less lascivious; more capable of atrocious misconduct; also probably more capable of idealism. But we don't really know much about the crowd. It is only a hostile average-sensual-man background against which

Photo: Alinari.

SOCRATES. (BUST IN THE VATICAN.)

the philosophers and poets stand out. There was no ' city mob,' as in Rome. They were nearly all small farmers or craftsmen. I can't help thinking that their badness was more like the faults of a superior South Sea Islander than like the viler side of the ' crowd ' to-day."

§ 4

The most characteristic feature of the opening years of this brilliant century and a half (475 to 325 B.C.) of Greek intellectual life was the appearance of the great tragedies.

Greek Tragedy and Comedy.

Before the age of Pericles the main literature of the Greek peoples had been their epic poetry, of which we have already said something in our account of the earlier nomadic Aryan life. It was made up of songs of free adventure, aristocratic and valiant in spirit. The main Greek epics were reduced to writing, and the text of the chief ones put in its present order in the time of the tyrant Peisistratus (*i.e.*, immediately before the first Persian wars). Chanted originally to the chiefs and leading men in hall, they were now recited at the public festivals. In addition, there were also poems of more homely character, love songs, war lyrics, and the like.

A third stream of poetry also ran into the Greek tradition, perhaps not of Aryan origin at all, but preserving the religious ideas of the dark whites whom the Greeks had conquered. These were religious chants and hymns associated with the secret religious practices of the worship of Demeter, the earth goddess, and of Orpheus and Dionysus. They are mixed up with ideas of self-abasement, self-mutilation, and the like, that were altogether foreign to the healthy directness of the hardy barbarians from the north. These ideas were creeping out from their hiding-places, and expressing themselves in Greek in Athens during this period in the Orphic religious poetry. It seems probable that in the Athenian population among all the Greek cities the pre-Aryan strain was unusually strong. This dark strain was subtle, artistic, creative—Cnossos witnesses to that; but it had no great courage of the mind; it was afraid of the stars and of life. Whenever that strain is

through the rural life of Greece was the tradition of a dressing-up and a dancing and chanting associated with the worship of another God, who is killed and lives again as a part of the ceremonies, the God Dionysus. After the coming of the Aryans into Greece, the vocal element became stronger in these proceedings, and thrust into the dance came a recitation. There was first one reciter, then two, and then three, and the rest of the company became the chorus to the declamations of these principal actors. Out of the public performance at festivals and anniversaries of these choir songs or dithyrambs with one actor grew the great art of tragedy with three and more. Side by side with tragedy, comedy developed from another and merrier series of dressings-up and singing. Here we can but name those who were supreme in these arts who flourished in the days of Pericles, Æschylus, Sophocles, and Euripides, the masters of tragedy, and Aristophanes, the writer of comedies. We can say nothing of the splendour and beauty of the former, nor of the fantastic invention and wit of the latter. Æschylus won his first prize for tragedy in the year that Herodotus was born (484 B.C.); Sophocles came some eighteen years later; Euripides was four years old when Æschylus was beginning his career. The mockery of Aristophanes broke out (427 B.C.) only when the days of great tragedy and sculpture and building were drawing to a close.

Photo: Alinari.

HEAD OF THE HERMES OF PRAXITELES
(Fine example of Greek ideal type.)

found in any race, there is to be found also thoughts and legends of sacrificial murders.

And perhaps also indigenous to the Greek soil, rooted deeply there in the time of the world-wide ancient heliolithic culture, were religious dances. Such dances we can trace from the Atlantic to Peru. There is a drawing in a Spanish cave at Cogul, near the Ebro, which is supposed to represent a later palæolithic ritual dance. There is little evidence of the primitive Aryans engaging in religious dances. But running

§ 5

The influence of Socrates also began to bear fruit after the days of Pericles and Aspasia.

Plato and the Academy.
This old questioner, at whose touch faith, speculation, and illusion shrivelled together, was the centre of a group of young men who lived through and after the years of the Peloponnesian War. Of all the young men, one stands out as the greatest of them all, Plato. He was born 427 B.C., the year of the first performance of

the work of Aristophanes, and he lived for eighty years.

In mental temperament Plato was of an altogether different type from the older man. He was a most artistic and delicate writer, and Socrates could write nothing consecutive. He cared for beautiful things and Socrates despised them. He was supremely concerned with the ordering of public affairs and the scheming of happier human relationships, while Socrates, heedless of heat and cold and the opinion of his fellow creatures, concentrated his mind upon a serene disillusionment. Life, said Socrates, was deception; only the Soul lived. Plato had a very great affection for this rugged old teacher, he found his method of the utmost value in disentangling and cleaning up opinions, and he made him the central figure of his immortal dialogues; but his own thoughts and disposition turned him altogether away from the sceptical attitude. In many of the dialogues the voice is the voice of Socrates, but the thought is the thought of Plato. Plato was living in a time of doubt and questioning about all human relationships. In the great days of Pericles, before 450 B.C., there seems to have been a complete satisfaction in Athens with social and political institutions. Then there seemed no reason for questioning. Men felt free; the community prospered; one suffered chiefly from jealousy. The History of Herodotus displays little or no dissatisfaction with Athenian political institutions.

But Plato, who was born about the time Herodotus died, and who grew up in the atmosphere of a disastrous war and great social distress and confusion, was from the first face to face with human discord and the misfit of human institutions. To that challenge his mind responded. One of his earlier works and his latest are bold and penetrating discussions of the possible betterment of social relations. Socrates had taught him to take nothing for granted, not even the common relations of husband and wife or parent and child. His *Republic*, the first of all Utopian books, is a young man's dream of a city in which human life is arranged according to a novel and a better plan; his last unfinished work, the *Laws*, is a discussion of the regulation of another such Utopia. There is much in Plato at which we cannot even glance here, but it is a landmark in this history, it is a new thing in the development of mankind, this appearance of the idea of wilfully and com-

Photo: Bonfils. SEATS IN THE THEATRE OF DIONYSUS, ATHENS.

pletely recasting human conditions. So far mankind has been living by tradition under the fear of the gods. Here is a man who says boldly to our race, and as if it were a quite reasonable and natural thing to say, " Take hold of your lives. Most of these things that distress you, you can avoid ; most of these

Photo : Anderson.
PLATO. (BUST FROM NAPLES MUSEUM). IT IS POSSIBLE THAT THIS IS WRONGLY ASCRIBED TO PLATO, AND THAT IT REPRESENTS THE INDIAN BACCHUS.

things that dominate you, you can overthrow. You can do as you will with them."

One other thing besides the conflicts of the time perhaps stimulated the mind of Plato in this direction. In the days of Pericles Athens had founded many settlements overseas, and the setting up of these settlements had familiarized men with the idea that a community need not grow, it could also be made.

Closely associated with Plato was a younger man, who later also maintained a school in Athens and lived to an even greater age. This was Isocrates. He was what we should call a publicist, a writer rather than an orator, and his peculiar work was to develop the idea of Herodotus, the idea of a unification of Greece against the Persian Empire, as a remedy for the baseness and confusion of her politics and the waste and destruction of her internecine wars. His political horizon was in some respects broader than Plato's, and in his later years he

looked towards monarchy, and particularly towards the Macedonian monarchy of Philip, as a more unifying and broadening method of government than city democracy. The same drift to monarchist ideas had occurred in the case of that Xenophon whose *Anabasis* we have already mentioned. In his old age this retired mercenary wrote the *Cyropædia*, a "vindication both theoretically and practically of absolute monarchy as shown in the organization of the 'Persian Empire." [1]

§ 6

Plato taught in the Academy. To him in his old age came a certain good-looking youngster from Stagira in Macedonia, Aristotle, who was the son of the Macedonian king's physician, and a man with a very different type of mind from that of the great Athenian. He was naturally sceptical of the imaginative will, and with a great respect for and comprehension of established fact. Later on, after Plato was dead, he set up a school at the Lyceum in Athens and taught, criticizing Plato and Socrates with a certain hardness. When he taught, the shadow of Alexander the Great lay across the freedom of Greece, and he favoured slavery and constitutional kings. He had previously been the tutor of Alexander for several years at the court of Philip of Macedon.[2] Intelligent men were losing heart in those days, their faith in the power of men to make their own conditions of life was fading. There were no more Utopias. The rush of events was manifestly too powerful for such organized effort as was then practicable between men of fine intelligence. It was possible to think of recasting human society when human society was a little city of a few thousand citizens, but what was happening about them was something cataclysmal ; it was the political recasting of the whole known world, of the affairs of what even then must have amounted to something between fifty and a hundred million people. It was recasting upon a scale no human mind was yet equipped to grasp. It drove thought back upon the idea of a vast and

Aristotle and the Lyceum.

[1] Mahaffy.
[2] There is not a single sentence in praise of Alexander, no dedication, no compliments, in all Aristotle. On the other hand, he never mentions Demosthenes nor quotes him in the Rhetoric.—G. M.

implacable Fate. It made men snatch at whatever looked stable and unifying. Monarchy, for instance, for all its manifest vices, was a conceivable government for millions; it had, to a certain extent, *worked*; it imposed a ruling will where it would seem that a collective will was impossible. This change of the general intellectual mood harmonized with Aristotle's natural respect for existing fact. If, on the one hand, it made him approve of monarchy and slavery and the subjection of women as reasonable institutions, on the other hand it made him eager to understand fact and to get some orderly knowledge of these realities of nature and human nature that were now so manifestly triumphant over the creative dreams of the preceding generation. He is terribly sane and luminous, and terribly wanting in self-sacrificial enthusiasm. He questions Plato when Plato would exile poets from his Utopia, for poetry is a power; he directs his energy along a line diametrically opposed to Socrates' depreciation of Anaxagoras. He anticipates Bacon and the modern scientific movement in his realization of the importance of ordered knowledge. He set himself to the task of gathering together and setting down knowledge. He was the first natural historian. Other men before him had speculated about the nature of things, but he, with every young man he could win over to the task, set himself to classify and compare things. Plato says in effect: " Let us take hold of life and remodel it "; this soberer successor: " Let us first know more of life and meanwhile serve the king." It was not so much a contradiction as an immense qualification of the master.

The peculiar relation of Aristotle to Alexander the Great enabled him to procure means for his work such as were not available again for scientific inquiry for long ages. He could command hundreds of talents (a talent = about £240) for his expenses. At one time he had at his disposal a thousand men scattered throughout Asia and Greece, collecting matter for his natural history.[1][2] They were, of course, very

---

[1] Wheeler.

[2] Bauer, in *Vom Griechentum zum Christentum*, says that Alexander sent a mission of exploration to Abyssinia to enable Aristotle to settle the question of the cause of the Nile inundations (melting of mountain snows), and that he also had tropical flora and other material collected for him.—E. B.

untrained observers, collectors of stories rather than observers; but nothing of the kind had ever been attempted, had even been thought of, so far as we know, before his time. Political and natural science were both attempted. The students of the Lyceum under his direction made an analysis of 158 political constitutions. . . .

This was the first gleam of organized science in the world. The early death of Alexander, and the breaking up of his empire almost before it had begun, put an end to endowments on this scale for 2,000 years. Only in Egypt at the Alexandria Museum did any scientific research continue, and that only for a few generations. Fifty years after Aristotle's death the Lyceum had already dwindled to insignificance.

§ 7

The general drift of thought in the concluding years of the fourth century B.C. was not with Aristotle, nor towards the laborious and necessary accumulation of ordered knowledge. It is possible that without his endowments from the king he would have made but a small figure in intellectual history. Through them he was able to give his splendid intelligence substance and effect. The ordinary man prefers easy ways so long as they may be followed, and is almost wilfully heedless whether they end at last in a cul-de-sac. Finding the stream of events too powerful to control at once, the generality of philosophical teachers drifted in those days from the scheming of model cities and the planning of new ways of living into the elaboration of beautiful and consoling systems of evasion.

Philosophy becomes Unworldly.

Perhaps that is putting things coarsely and unjustly. But let Professor Gilbert Murray speak upon this matter.[3]

" The Cynics cared only for virtue and the relation of the soul to God; the world and its learning and its honours were as dross to them. The Stoics and Epicureans, so far apart at first sight, were very similar in their ultimate aim. What they really cared about was ethics—the practical question how a man should order his life. Both, indeed, gave themselves to some science—the Epicureans to physics, the Stoics

[3] *Ancient Greek Literature.*

to logic and rhetoric—but only as a means to an end. The Stoic tried to win men's hearts and convictions by sheer subtlety of abstract argument and dazzling sublimity of thought and expression. The Epicurean was determined to make Humanity go its way without cringing to capricious gods and without sacrificing Free-Will. He condensed his gospel into four maxims: "God is not to be feared; Death cannot be felt; the Good can be won; all that we dread can be borne and conquered."

And meanwhile the stream of events flowed on, with a reciprocal indifference to philosophy.

§ 8

If the Greek classics are to be read with any benefit by modern men, they must be read as the work of men like ourselves. Regard must be had to their traditions, their opportunities, and their limitations. There is a disposition to exaggeration in all human admiration; men will treat the rough notes of Thucydides or Plato for work they never put in order as miracles of style, and the errors of their transcribers as hints of unfathomable mysteries; most of our classical texts are very much mangled, and all were originally the work of human beings in difficulties, living in a time of such darkness and narrowness of outlook as makes our own time by comparison a time of dazzling illumination. What we shall lose in reverence by this familiar treatment, we shall gain in sympathy for that group of troubled, uncertain, and very modern minds. The Athenian writers were, indeed, the first of modern men. They were discussing questions that we still discuss; they began to struggle with the great problems that confront us to-day. Their writings are our dawn.

They began an inquiry, and they arrived at no solutions. We cannot pretend to-day that we have arrived at solutions to most of the questions they asked. The mind of the Hebrews, as we have already shown, awoke suddenly to the endless miseries and disorders of life, saw that these miseries and disorders were largely due to the lawless acts of men, and concluded that salvation could come only through subduing ourselves to the service of the one God who rules heaven and earth. The Greek, rising to the same perception, was not prepared with

The Quality and Limitations of Greek Thought.

the same idea of a patriarchal deity; he lived in a world in which there was not God but the gods; if perhaps he felt that the gods themselves were limited, then he thought of Fate behind them, cold and impersonal. So he put his problem in the form of an enquiry as to what was right living, without any definite correlation of the right-living man with the will of God. . . . To us, looking at the matter from a standpoint purely historical, the common problem can now be presented in a form that, for the purposes of history, covers both the Hebrew and Greek way of putting it. We have seen mankind rising out of the unconsciousness of animals to a continuing racial self-consciousness, realizing the unhappiness of its wild diversity of aims, realizing the inevitable tragedy of individual self-seeking, and feeling their way blindly towards some linking and subordinating idea to save them from the pains and accidents of mere individuality. The gods, the god-king, the idea of the tribe, the idea of the city; here are ideas that have claimed and held for a time the devotion of men, ideas in which they have a little lost their individual selves and escaped to the realization of a life larger and more enduring. Yet, as their wars and disasters prove, none of these greater ideas were yet great enough. The gods failed to protect, the tribe proved itself vile and cruel, the city ostracized one's best and truest friends, the god-king made a beast of himself. . . .

As we read over the speculative literature of this great period of the Greeks, we realize three barriers set about the Greek mind, from which it rarely escapes, but from which we now perhaps are escaping.

The first of these limitations is the obsession of the Greek mind by the idea of the city as the ultimate state. In a world in which empire had followed empire, each greater than its predecessor, in a world through which men and ideas drive ever more loosely and freely, in a world visibly unifying even then, the Greeks, because of their peculiar physical and political circumstances, were still dreaming impossibly of a compact little city state, impervious to outer influences, valiantly secure against the whole world. Plato's estimate of the number of citizens in a perfect state varied between 1,000 (the *Republic*) and 5,040 (the *Laws*) citizens.[1] This state was to go to war and hold its own against other cities of the same size. And this was not a couple of generations after the hosts of Xerxes had crossed the Hellespont!

Perhaps these Greeks thought the day of world empires had passed for ever, whereas it was only beginning. At the utmost their minds reached out to alliances and leagues. There must have been men at the court of Artaxerxes thinking far away beyond these little ideas of the rocky creek, the island, and the mountain-encircled valley. But the need for unification against the greater powers that moved outside the Greek-speaking world, the Greek mind disregarded wilfully. These outsiders were barbarians, not to be needlessly thought about; they were barred out now from Greece for ever. One took Persian money; everybody took Persian money; what did it matter? Or one enlisted for a time in their armies (as Xenophon did) and hoped for his luck with a rich prisoner. Athens took sides in Egyptian affairs, and carried on minor wars with Persia, but there was no conception of a common policy or a common future for Greece. . . . Until at last a voice in Athens began to shout "Macedonia!" to clamour like

Photo: Anderson.

ZENO, FOUNDER OF STOIC PHILOSOPHY.

"The Hellenistic type—that is, the Oriental who combined the religious instinct of Asia with the philosophic spirit of Greece—such an Oriental as (to take two very great names) the Stoic apostle Zeno, a Phœnician of Cyprus, or the Christian apostle Saul, the Jew of Tarsus."—HOGARTH (*Ancient East*).

a watch-dog, "Macedonia!" This was the voice of the orator and demagogue, Demosthenes; hurling warnings and threats and denunciations at King Philip of Macedon, who had learnt his politics not only from Plato and Aristotle, but also from Isocrates and Xenophon, and from Babylon and Susa, and who was preparing quietly, ably, and steadfastly to dominate all Greece, and through Greece to conquer the known world. . . .

There was a second thing that cramped the Greek mind, the institution of domestic slavery. Slavery was implicit in Greek life; men could conceive of neither comfort nor dignity without it. But slavery shuts off one's sympathy not only from a class of one's fellow subjects; it puts the slave-owner into a class and organization against all stranger men. One is of an elect tribe. Plato, carried by his clear reason and the noble sanity of his spirit beyond the things of the present, would have abolished slavery; much popular feeling and the New Comedy were against it; the Stoics and Epicureans, many of whom were slaves, condemned it as unnatural, but finding it too strong to upset, decided that it did not affect the soul and might be ignored. With the wise there was no bound or free. To the matter-of-fact Aristotle, and probably to most practical men, its abolition was inconceivable. So they declared that there were in the world men "naturally slaves." . . .

Finally, the thought of the Greeks was hampered by a want of knowledge that is almost inconceivable to us to-day. They had no knowledge of the past of mankind at all; at best they had a few shrewd guesses. They had no knowledge of geography beyond the range of the Mediterranean basin and the frontiers of Persia.

[1] "For the proper administration of justice, and for the distribution of authority, it is necessary that the citizens be acquainted with each other's characters, so that, where this cannot be, much mischief ensues, both in the use of authority and in the administration of justice; for it is not just to decide arbitrarily, as must be the case with excessive population." Aristotle's *Politics*, quoted by Wheeler, who adds, "Aristotle comes to the conclusion that the natural 'limit to the size of the state must be found in the capability of being easily taken in at a glance.'" But Murray notes that the word Eusunopton means also "capable of being comprehended as a unity"—a very different and wider idea.

We know far more to-day of what was going on in Susa, Persepolis, Babylon, and Memphis in the time of Pericles than he did. Their astronomical ideas were still in the state of rudimentary speculations. Anaxagoras, greatly daring, thought the sun and moon were vast globes, so vast that the sun was probably " as big as all the Peloponnesus." The forty-seventh proposition of the first book of Euclid was regarded as one of the supreme triumphs of the human mind. Their ideas in physics and chemistry were the results of profound cogitation; it is wonderful that they did guess at atomic structure. One has to remember their extraordinary poverty in the matter of experimental apparatus. They had coloured glass for ornament, but no white glass; no accurate means of measuring the minor intervals of time, no really efficient numerical notation, no very accurate scales, no rudiments of telescope or microscope. A modern scientific man dumped down in the Athens of Pericles would have found the utmost difficulty in demonstrating the elements of his knowledge, however crudely, to the men he would have found there. He would have had to rig up the simplest apparatus under every disadvantage, while Socrates pointed out the absurdity of seeking Truth with pieces of wood and string and metal such as small boys use for fishing. And he would have been in constant danger of a prosecution for impiety.

Our world to-day draws upon relatively immense accumulations of knowledge of fact. In the age of Pericles scarcely the first stone of our comparatively tremendous cairn of things recorded and proved had been put in place. When we reflect upon this difference, then it ceases to be remarkable that the Greeks, with all their aptitude for political speculation, were blind to the insecurities of their civilization from without and from within, to the necessity for effective unification, to the swift rush of events that was to end for long ages these first brief freedoms of the human mind.

It is not in the results it achieved, but in the attempts it made that the true value for us of this group of Greek talkers and writers lies. It is not that they answered questions, but that they dared to ask them. Never before had man challenged his world and the way of life to which he found his birth had brought him.

Never had he said before that he could alter his conditions. Tradition and a seeming necessity had held him to life as he had found it grown up about his tribe since time immemorial. Hitherto he had taken the world as children still take the homes and habits in which they have been reared.

So in the fifth and fourth centuries B.C. we perceive, most plainly in Judea and in Athens, but by no means confined to those centres, the beginnings of a moral and an intellectual process in mankind, an appeal to righteousness and an appeal to the truth from the passions and confusions and immediate appearances of existence. It is like the dawn of the sense of responsibility in a youth, who suddenly discovers that life is neither easy nor aimless. Mankind is growing up. The rest of history for three and twenty centuries is threaded with the spreading out and development and interaction and the clearer and more effective statement of these main leading ideas. Slowly more and more men apprehend the reality of human brotherhood, the needlessness of wars and cruelties and oppression, the possibilities of a common purpose for the whole of our kind. In every generation thereafter there is the evidence of men seeking for that better order to which they feel our world must come. But everywhere and wherever in any man the great constructive ideas have taken hold, the hot greeds, the jealousies, the suspicions and impatience that are in the nature of every one of us, war against the struggle towards greater and broader purposes. The last twenty-three centuries of history are like the efforts of some impulsive, hasty immortal to think clearly and live rightly. Blunder follows blunder; promising beginnings end in grotesque disappointments; streams of living water are poisoned by the cup that conveys them to the thirsty lips of mankind. But the hope of men rises again at last after every disaster. . . .

We pass on now to the story of one futile commencement, one glorious shattered beginning of human unity. There was in Alexander the Great knowledge and imagination, power and opportunity, folly, egotism, detestable vulgarity, and an immense promise, broken by the accident of his early death while men were still dazzled by its immensity.

ALEXANDER AT THE BATTLE OF ISSUS

This vigorous and unaffected battle piece is from a mosaic found at Pompeii. Alexander is to the left on horseback, Darius to the right in his chariot. Probably very like the real thing.

XXIV
THE CAREER OF ALEXANDER THE GREAT[1]

§ 1

THE true hero of the story of Alexander is not so much Alexander as his father Philip. The author of a piece does not shine in the limelight as the actor does, and it was Philip who planned much of the greatness that his son achieved, who laid the foundations and forged the tools, who had indeed already begun the Persian expedition at the time of his death. Philip, beyond doubting, was one of the greatest monarchs the world has ever seen; he was a man of the utmost intelligence and ability, and his range of ideas was vastly beyond the scope of his time. He made Aristotle his friend; he must have discussed with him those schemes for the organization of real knowledge which the philosopher was to realize later through Alexander's endowments. Philip, so far as we can judge, seems to have been Aristotle's "Prince"; to him Aristotle turned as men turn only to those whom they admire and trust. To Philip also Isocrates appealed as the great leader who should unify and ennoble the chaotic public life of Greece.

Philip of Macedonia.

In many books it is stated that Philip was a man of incredible cynicism and of uncontrolled lusts. It is true that at feasts, like all the Macedonians of his time, he was a hard drinker and sometimes drunken —it was probably considered unamiable not to drink excessively at feasts; but of the other accusations there is no real proof, and for evidence we have only the railings of such antagonists as Demosthenes, the Athenian demagogue and

orator, a man of reckless rhetoric. The quotation of a phrase or so will serve to show to what the patriotic anger of Demosthenes could bring him. In one of the *Philippics*, as his denunciations of Philip are called, he gives vent in this style :

"Philip—a man who not only is no Greek, and no way akin to the Greeks, but is not even a barbarian from a respectable country—no, a pestilent fellow of Macedon, a country from which we never get even a decent slave." And so on and so on. We know, as a matter of fact, that the Macedonians were an Aryan people very closely akin to the Greeks, and that Philip was probably the best educated man of his time. This was the spirit in which the adverse accounts of Philip were written.

When Philip became king of Macedonia in 359 B.C., his country was a little country without a seaport or industries or any considerable city. It had a peasant population, Greek almost in language and ready to be Greek in sympathies, but more purely Nordic in blood than any people to the south of it. Philip made this little barbaric state into a great one ; he created the most efficient military organization the world had so far seen, and he had brought most of Greece into one confederacy under his leadership at the time of his death. And his extraordinary quality, his power of thinking out beyond the current ideas of his time, is shown not so much in those matters as in the care with which he had his son trained to carry on the policy he had created. He is one of the few monarchs in history who cared for his successor. Alexander was, as few other monarchs have ever been, a specially educated king ; he was educated for em-

[1] Benjamin Ide Wheeler's *Alexander the Great* and G. D. Hogarth's *Philip and Alexander* have been very useful here.

PHILIP OF MACEDON.
One of the Gold Medallions of Tarsus.

pire. Aristotle was but one of the several able tutors his father chose for him. Philip confided his policy to him, and entrusted him with commands and authority by the time he was sixteen. He commanded the cavalry at Chæronea under his father's eye. He was nursed into power—generously and unsuspiciously.

To any one who reads his life with care it is evident that Alexander started with an equipment of training and ideas of unprecedented value. As he got beyond the wisdom of his upbringing he began to blunder and misbehave —sometimes with a dreadful folly. The defects of his character had triumphed over his upbringing long before he died.

Philip was a king after the old pattern, a leader-king, first among his peers, of the ancient Nordic Aryan type. The army he found in Macedonia consisted of a general foot levy and a noble equestrian order called the "companions." The people were farmers and hunters and somewhat drunken in their habits, but ready for discipline and good fighting stuff. And if the people were homely, the government was intelligent and alert. For some generations the court language had been Attic (=Athenian) Greek, and the court had been sufficiently civilized to shelter and entertain such great figures as Euripides, who died there in 406 B.C., and Zeuxis the artist. Moreover, Philip, before his accession, had spent some years as a hostage in Greece. He had had as good an education as Greece could give at that time. He was, therefore, quite familiar with what we may call the idea of Isocrates—the idea of a great union of the

Photo: Alinari.

DEMOSTHENES.

Greek states in Europe to dominate the Eastern world; and he knew, too, how incapable was the Athenian democracy, because of its constitution and tradition, of taking the opportunity that lay before it. For it was an opportunity that would have to be shared. To the Athenians or the Spartans it would mean letting in a "lot of foreigners" to the advantages of citizenship. It would mean lowering themselves to the level of equality and fellowship with Macedonians —a people from whom "*we*" do not get "even a decent slave."[1]

There was no way to secure unanimity among the Greeks for the contemplated enterprise except by some revolutionary political action. It was no love of peace that kept the Greeks from such an adventure; it was their political divisions. The resources of the several states were exhausted in a series of internecine wars— wars arising out of the merest excuses and fanned by oratorical wind. The ploughing of certain sacred lands near Delphi by the Phocians was, for example, the pretext for a sanguinary Sacred War.

Philip's first years of kingship were devoted to the discipline of his army. Hitherto most of the main battle fighting in the world had been done by footmen in formation. In the very ancient Sumerian battle-pieces we see spearmen in close order forming the main battle, just as

[1] To the common Athenians, that is. But to many thoughtful Greeks the rôle of Macedonia in their future was a matter of earnest speculation. Herodotus (viii. 137) tells a long story of a prophecy by which the inheritance of Perdiccas, the ancestor of the Macedonian kings, was to embrace at last the whole round world. This was written a hundred years before Philip and Alexander.

they did in the Zulu armies of the nineteenth century; the Greek troops of Philip's time were still fighting in that same style; the Theban "phalanx" was a mass of infantry holding spears, the hinder ranks thrusting their longer spears between the front-line men. Such a formation went through anything less disciplined that opposed it. Mounted archers could, of course, inflict considerable losses on such a mass of men, and accordingly, as the horse came into warfare, horsemen appeared on either side as an accessory to this main battle. The reader must remember that the horse did not come into very effective use in western war until the rise of the Assyrians, and then at first only as a chariot horse. The chariots drove full tilt at the infantry mass and tried to break it. Unless its discipline was very solid they succeeded. The Homeric fighting is chariot fighting. It is not until the last thousand years B.C. that we begin to find mounted soldiers, as distinct from charioteers, playing a part in warfare. At

first they appear to have fought in a scattered fashion, each man doing his personal feats. So the Lydians fought against Cyrus. It was Philip who seems to have created charging cavalry. He caused his "companions" to drill for a massed charge. And also he strengthened his phalanx by giving the rear men longer spears than had been used hitherto, and so deepening its mass. The Macedonian phalanx was merely a more solid version of the Theban phalanx. None of these massed infantry formations was flexible enough to stand a flank or rear attack. They had very slight manœuvring power. Both Philip's and his son's victories followed, therefore, with variations, one general scheme of co-operation between these two arms. The phalanx advanced in the centre and held the enemy's main body; on one wing or the other the cavalry charges swept away the enemy cavalry, and then swooped round upon the flank and rear of the enemy phalanx, the front of which the Macedonian phalanx was already smiting. The

The growth of
MACEDONIA
under Philip

Kingdom of Macedonia at Philip's accession....
At his death

Macedonian warrior.

Bas-relief from Pella...

enemy main battle then broke and was massacred. As Alexander's military experience grew, he also added a use of catapults in the field, big stone-throwing affairs, to break up the enemy infantry. Before his time catapults had been used in sieges, but never in battles. He invented " artillery preparation."

With the weapon of his new army in his hand, Philip first turned his attention to the north of Macedonia. He carried expeditions into Illyria and as far as the Danube ; he also spread his power along the coast as far as the Hellespont. He secured possession of a port, Amphipolis, and certain gold mines adjacent. After several Thracian expeditions he turned southward in good earnest. He took up the cause of the Delphic amphictyony against those sacrilegious Phocians, and so appeared as the champion of Hellenic religion.

There was a strong party of Greeks, it must be understood, a Pan-Hellenic party, in favour of the Greek headship of Philip. The chief writer of this Pan-Hellenic movement was Isocrates. Athens, on the other hand, was the head and front of the opposition to Philip, and Athens was in open sympathy with Persia, even sending emissaries to the Great King to warn him of the danger to him of a united Greece. The comings and goings of twelve years cannot be related here. In 338 B.C. the long struggle between division and pan-Hellenism came to a decisive issue, and at the battle of Chæronea Philip inflicted a crushing defeat upon Athens and her allies. He gave Athens peace upon astonishingly generous terms ; he displayed himself steadfastly resolved to propitiate and favour that implacable city ; and in 338 B.C. a congress of Greek states recognized him as captain-general for the war against Persia.

He was now a man of forty-seven. It seemed as though the world lay at his feet. He had made his little country into the leading state in a great Græco-Macedonian confederacy. That unification was to be the prelude to a still greater one, the unification of the Western world with the Persian empire into one world state of all known peoples. Who can doubt he had that dream ? The writings of Isocrates convince us that he had it. Who can deny that he might have realized it ? He had a reasonable hope of living for perhaps another quarter century of activity. In 336 B.C. his advanced guard crossed into Asia. . . .

But he never followed with his main force. He was assassinated.

§ 2

It is necessary now to tell something of the domestic life of King Philip. The lives of both

ARISTOTLE.
Bust in the Hall of Philosophers, Museum of the Capitol, Rome.

Philip and his son were pervaded by **The Murder of King Philip.** the personality of a restless and evil woman, Olympias, the mother of Alexander.

She was the daughter of the king of Epirus, a country to the west of Macedonia, and, like Macedonia, a semi-Greek land. She met Philip, or was thrown in his way, at some religious gathering in Samothrace. Plutarch declares the marriage was a love-match, and there seems to be at least this much in the charges against Philip that, like many energetic and imaginative men, he was prone to impatient love impulses. He married her when he was already a king, and Alexander was born to him three years later.

It was not long before Olympias and Philip were bitterly estranged. She was jealous of him, but there was another and graver source of trouble in her passion for religious mysteries. We have already noted that beneath the fine and restrained Nordic religion of the Greeks the land abounded with religious cults of a darker and more ancient kind, aboriginal cults with secret initiations, orgiastic celebrations, and often with cruel and obscene rites. These religions of the shadows, these practices of the women and peasants and slaves, gave Greece her Orphic, Dionysic, and Demeter cults; they have lurked in the tradition of Europe down almost to our own times. The witchcraft of the Middle Ages, with its resort to the blood

Photo: Mansell.   ALEXANDER THE GREAT.

of babes, scraps of executed criminals, incantations and magic circles, seems to have been little else than the lingering vestiges of these solemnities of the dark whites. In these matters Olympias was an expert and an enthusiast, and Plutarch mentions that she achieved considerable celebrity by a use of tame serpents in these pious exercises. The snakes invaded her domestic apartments, and history is not clear whether Philip found in them matter for exasperation or religious awe. These occupations of his wife must have been a serious inconvenience to Philip, for the Macedonian people were still in that sturdy stage of social development in which neither enthusiastic religiosity nor uncontrollable wives are admired.

The evidence of a bitter hostility between mother and father peeps out in many little things in the histories. She was evidently jealous of Philip's conquests; she hated his fame. There are many signs that Olympias did her best to set her son against his father and attach him wholly to herself. A story survives (in Plutarch's *Life*) that " whenever news was brought of Philip's victories, the capture of a city or the winning of some great battle, he never seemed greatly rejoiced to hear it; on the contrary he used to say to his play-fellows: ' Father will get everything in advance, boys; he won't leave any great task for me to share with you.' " . . .

It is not a natural thing for a boy to envy his

father in this fashion without some inspiration. That sentence sounds like an echo.

We have already pointed out how manifest it is that Philip planned the succession of Alexander, and how eager he was to thrust fame and power into the boy's hands. He was thinking of the political structure he was building—but the mother was thinking of the glory and pride of that wonderful lady Olympias. She masked her hatred of her husband under the cloak of a mother's solicitude for her son's future. When in 337 B.C. Philip, after the fashion of kings in those days, married a second wife who was a native Macedonian, Cleopatra, "of whom he was passionately enamoured," Olympias made much trouble.

Plutarch tells of a pitiful scene that occurred at Philip's marriage to Cleopatra. There was much drinking of wine at the banquet, and Attalus, the father of the bride, being "intoxicated with liquor," betrayed the general hostility to Olympias and Epirus by saying he hoped there would be a child by the marriage to give them a truly Macedonian heir. Whereupon Alexander, taut for such an insult, cried out, "What then am I?" and hurled his cup at Attalus. Philip, enraged, stood up

and, says Plutarch, drew his sword, only to stumble and fall. Alexander, blind with rage and jealousy, taunted and insulted his father.

"Macedonians," he said. "See there the general who would go from Europe to Asia! Why! he cannot get from one table to another!"

How that scene lives still, the sprawl, the flushed faces, the angry voice of the boy! Next day Alexander departed with his mother—and Philip did nothing to restrain them. Olympias went home to Epirus; Alexander departed to Illyria. Thence Philip persuaded him to return.

Fresh trouble arose. Alexander had a brother of weak intellect, Aridæus, whom the Persian governor of Caria sought as a son-in-law. "Alexander's friends and his mother now infused notions into him again, though perfectly groundless, that by so noble a match, and the support consequent upon it, Philip designed the crown for Aridæus. Alexander, in the uneasiness these suspicions gave him, sent one Thessalus, a player, into Caria, to desire the grandee to pass by Aridæus, who was of spurious birth, and deficient in point of understanding, and to take the lawful heir to the crown into his al-

Photo: Mansell.

THE MAUSOLEUM AT HALICARNASSUS.

Built about 350 B.C. by Queen Artemisia of Caria to the memory of her husband Mausolus. Restoration by C. R. Cockerell, R.A., British Museum.

liance. Pixodarus was infinitely more pleased with this proposal. But Philip no sooner had intelligence of it, than he went to Alexander's apartment, taking along with him Philotas, the son of Parmenio, one of his most intimate friends and companions, and, in his presence, reproached him with his degeneracy and meanness of spirit, in thinking of being son-in-law to a man of Caria, one of the slaves of a barbarian king. At the same time he wrote to the Corinthians, insisting that they should send Thessalus to him in chains. Harpalus and Niarchus, Phrygius and Ptolemy, some of the other companions of the prince, he banished. But Alexander afterwards recalled them, and treated them with great distinction."

There is something very touching in this story of the father pleading with the son he manifestly loved, and baffled by the web of mean suggestion which had been spun about the boy's imagination.

It was at the marriage of his daughter to her uncle, the king of Epirus and the brother of Olympias, that Philip was stabbed. He was walking in a procession into the theatre unarmed, in a white robe, and he was cut down by one of his bodyguard. The murderer had a horse waiting, and would have got away, but the foot of his horse caught in a wild

Photo: Mansell.

MAUSOLUS, PRINCE OF CARIA.
One of the two marble statues believed to have stood in the chariot which surmounted the Mausoleum at Halicarnassus.

vine and he was thrown from the saddle by the stumble and slain by his pursuers. . . .

So at the age of twenty Alexander was at the end of his anxiety about the succession, and established king in Macedonia.

Olympias then reappeared in Macedonia, a woman proudly vindicated. It is said that she insisted upon paying the same funeral honours to the memory of the murderer as to Philip, and that she consecrated the fatal weapon to Apollo, inscribed with the name Myrtalis, by which Philip had been wont to address her when their loves first began.[1] In Greece there were great rejoicings over this auspicious event, and Demosthenes, when he had the news, although it was but seven days after the death of his own daughter, went into the public assembly at Athens in gay attire wearing a chaplet.

Whatever Olympias may have done about her husband's assassin, history does not doubt about her treatment of her supplanter, Cleopatra. So soon as Alexander was out of the way—and a revolt of the hillmen in the north called at once for his attention — Cleopatra's newly born child was killed in its mother's

[1] Goldsmith's *History of Greece*. The picturesque disposition of the novelist, rather than the austere method of the historian, is apparent here.

arms, and Cleopatra—no doubt after a little taunting—was then strangled. These excesses of womanly feeling are said to have shocked Alexander, but they did not prevent him from leaving his mother in a position of considerable authority in Macedonia. She wrote letters to him upon religious and political questions, and he showed a dutiful disposition in sending her always a large share of the plunder he made.

Photo: Brogi.

BRONZE FIGURE FROM THE NAPLES MUSEUM. COPY OF AN OLDER GREEK ORIGINAL PROBABLY REPRESENTING ALEXANDER.

§ 3

Alexander's First Conquests. These stories have to be told because history cannot be understood without them. Here was the great world of men between India and the Adriatic ready for union, ready, as it had never been before, for a unifying control. Here was the wide order of the Persian empire with its roads, its posts, its general peace and prosperity, ripe for the fertilizing influence of the Greek mind. And these stories display the quality of the human beings to whom those great opportunities came. Here was this Philip who was a very great and noble man, and yet he was drunken, he could keep no order in his household. Here was Alexander in many ways gifted above any man of his time,

and he was vain, suspicious, and passionate, with a mind set awry by his mother.

We are beginning to understand something of what the world might be, something of what our race might become, were it not for our still raw humanity. It is barely a matter of seventy generations between ourselves and Alexander; and between ourselves and the savage hunters our ancestors, who charred their food in the embers or ate it raw, intervene some four or five hundred generations. There is not much scope for the modification of a species in four or five hundred generations. Make men and women only sufficiently jealous or fearful or drunken or angry, and the hot red eyes of the cave-man will glare out at us to-day. We have writing and teaching, science and power; we have tamed the beasts and schooled the lightning; but we are still only shambling towards the light. We have tamed and bred the beasts, but we have still to tame and breed ourselves.

From the very beginning of his reign the deeds of Alexander showed how well he had assimilated his father's plans, and how great were his own abilities. A map of the known world is needed to show the course of his life. At first, after receiving assurances from Greece that he was to be captain-general of the Grecian forces, he marched through Thrace to the Danube; he crossed the river and burnt a village, the second great monarch to raid the Scythian country beyond the Danube; then recrossed it and marched westward and so came down by Illyria. By that time the city of Thebes was in rebellion, and his next blow was at Greece. Thebes—unsupported of course by Athens—was taken and looted; it was treated with extravagant violence; all its buildings, except the temple and the house of the poet Pindar, were razed, and thirty thousand people sold into slavery. Greece was stunned, and Alexander was free to go on with the Persian campaign.

This destruction of Thebes betrayed a streak of crazy violence in the new master of human destinies. It was too heavy a blow to have dealt. It was a barbaric thing to do. No Greeks would have gone so far with conquered Greeks. If the spirit of rebellion was killed, so also was the spirit of help. The Greek states remained inert thereafter, neither troublesome

SARCOPHAGUS OF ALEXANDER (NOW AT CONSTANTINOPLE). GREEKS AND PERSIANS HUNTING LIONS WITH ALEXANDER THE GREAT, ABOUT 300 B.C.

nor helpful. They would not support Alexander with their shipping, a thing which was to prove a very grave embarrassment to him.[1]

There is a story told by Plutarch about this Theban massacre, as if it redounded to the credit of Alexander, but indeed it shows only how his saner and his crazy sides were in conflict. It tells of a Macedonian officer and a Theban lady. This officer was among the looters, and he entered this woman's house, inflicted unspeakable insults and injuries upon her, and at last demanded whether she had gold or silver hidden. She told him all her treasures had been put into the well, conducted him thither, and, as he stooped to peer down, pushed him suddenly in and killed him by throwing great stones upon him. Some allied soldiers came upon this scene and took her forthwith to Alexander for judgment.

She defied him. Already the extravagant impulse that had ordered the massacre was upon the wane, and he not only spared her, but had her family and property and freedom restored to her. This Plutarch makes out to be a generosity, but the issue is more complicated than that. It was Alexander who was outraging and plundering and enslaving all Thebes. That poor crumpled Macedonian brute in the well had been doing only what he had been told he had full liberty to do. Is a commander first to give cruel orders, and then to forgive and reward those who slay his instruments? This gleam of remorse at the instance of one woman who was not perhaps wanting in tragic dignity and beauty, is a poor set-off to the murder of a great city.

Mixed with the craziness of Olympias in Alexander was the sanity of Philip and sane teaching from Aristotle. This Theban business certainly troubled the mind of Alexander. Whenever afterwards he encountered Thebans, he tried to show them special favour. Thebes, to his credit, haunted him.

[1] But Phocis was treated in the same way by Philip and his friends in 346, and Mantinea by Sparta in 385. It was a regular Greek punishment of a city to break it up into villages; and as for selling into slavery, Callicratidas the Spartan, in the Peloponnesian War, was held to be very noble when he said he would not sell Greeks into slavery. Anyhow, the destruction of Thebes was due to the *Greek* enemies of Thebes, who pressed it on Alexander.—E. B.

Yet the memory of Thebes did not save three other great cities from similar brain storms; Tyre he destroyed, and Gaza, and a city in India, in the storming of which he was knocked down in fair fight and wounded; and of the latter place not a soul, not a child, was spared. He must have been badly frightened to have taken so evil a revenge.

At the outset of the war the Persians had this supreme advantage, they were practically masters of the sea. The ships of the Athenians and their allies sulked unhelpfully. Alexander, to get at Asia, had to go round by the Hellespont; and if he pushed far into the Persian empire, he ran the risk of being cut off completely from his base. His first task, therefore, was to cripple the enemy at sea, and this he could only do by marching along the coast of Asia Minor and capturing port after port until the Persian sea bases were destroyed. If the Persians had avoided battle and hung upon his lengthening line of communications they could probably have destroyed him, but this they did not do. A Persian army not very much greater than his own gave battle on the banks of the Granicus (334 B.C.) and was destroyed. This left him free to take Sardis, Ephesus, Miletus, and, after a fierce struggle, Halicarnassus. Meanwhile the Persian fleet was on his right flank and between him and Greece, threatening much but accomplishing nothing.

In 333 B.C., pursuing this attack upon the sea bases, he marched along the coast as far as the head of the gulf now called the Gulf of Alexandretta. A huge Persian army, under the great king Darius III, was inland of his line of march, separated from the coast by mountains, and Alexander went right beyond this enemy force before he or the Persians realized their proximity. Scouting was evidently very badly done by Greek and Persian alike. The Persian army was a vast, ill-organized assembly of soldiers, transport, camp followers, and so forth. Darius, for instance, was accompanied by his harem, and there was a great multitude of harem slaves, musicians, dancers, and cooks. Many of the leading officers had brought their families to witness the hunting down of the Macedonian invaders. The troops had been levied from every province in the empire; they had no tradition or principle of combined action.

Seized by the idea of cutting off Alexander from Greece, Darius moved this multitude over the mountains to the sea; he had the luck to get through the passes without opposition, and he encamped on the plain of Issus between the mountains and the shore. And there Alexander, who had turned back to fight, struck him. The cavalry charge and the phalanx smashed this great brittle host as a stone smashes a bottle. It was routed. Darius escaped from his war chariot—that out-of-date instrument—and fled on horseback, leaving even his harem in the hands of Alexander.

All the accounts of Alexander after this battle show him at his best. He was restrained and

face with an inviolate city which had stood siege after siege, which had resisted Nebuchadnezzar the Great for fourteen years. For the standing of sieges Semitic peoples hold the palm. Tyre was then an island half a mile from the shore, and her fleet was unbeaten. On the other hand, Alexander had already learnt much by the siege of the citadel of Halicarnassus; he had gathered to himself a corps of engineers from Cyprus and Phœnicia, the Sidonian fleet was with him, and presently the king of Cyprus came over to him with a hundred and twenty ships, which gave him the command of the sea. Moreover, great Carthage, either relying on the strength of the mother city or being disloyal to

Rischgitz Collection.

THE DEFEAT OF DARIUS AT ARBELA (PIETRO DE CORTONA, CAPITOL GALLERY, ROME).
To contrast the sentimentalized sham-heroic Alexander of the classical Italian painters with the vigorous reality of the Pompeïan artist who painted the picture of the battle of the Issus which is reproduced in our colour plate.

magnanimous. He treated the Persian princesses with the utmost civility. And he kept his head; he held steadfastly to his plan. He let Darius escape, unpursued, into Syria, and he continued his march upon the naval bases of the Persians—that is to say, upon the Phœnician ports of Tyre and Sidon.

Sidon surrendered to him; Tyre resisted.

Here, if anywhere, we have the evidence of great military ability on the part of Alexander. His army was his father's creation, but Philip had never shone in the siege of cities. When Alexander was a boy of sixteen, he had seen his father repulsed by the fortified city of Byzantium upon the Bosphorus. Now he was face to

her, and being furthermore entangled in a war in Sicily, sent no help.

The first measure of Alexander was to build a pier from the mainland to the island, a dam which remains to this day; and on this, as it came close to the walls of Tyre, he set up his towers and battering-rams. Against the walls he also moored ships in which towers and rams were erected. The Tyrians used fire-ships against this flotilla, and made sorties from their two harbours. In a big surprise raid that they made on the Cyprian ships they were caught and badly mauled; many of their ships were rammed, and one big galley of five banks of oars and one of four were captured outright.

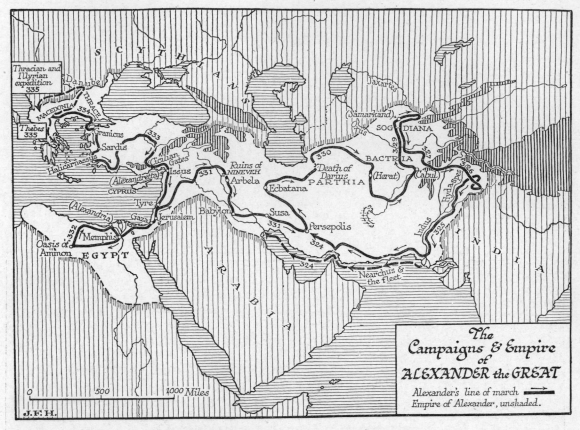

The Campaigns & Empire of ALEXANDER the GREAT

Alexander's line of march ➝
Empire of Alexander, unshaded.

J.F.H.

Finally a breach in the walls was made, and the Macedonians, clambering up the debris from their ships, stormed the city.

The siege had lasted seven months. Gaza held out for two. In each case there was a massacre, the plundering of the city, and the selling of the survivors into slavery. Then towards the end of 332 B.C. Alexander entered Egypt, and the command of the sea was assured. Greece, which all this while had been wavering in its policy, decided now at last that it was on the side of Alexander, and the council of the Greek states at Corinth voted its "captain-general" a golden crown of victory. From this time onward the Greeks were with the Macedonians.

The Egyptians also were with the Macedonians. But they had been for Alexander from the beginning. They had lived under Persian rule for nearly two hundred years, and the coming of Alexander meant for them only a change of masters; on the whole, a change for the better. The country surrendered without a blow. Alexander treated its religious feelings with extreme respect. He unwrapped no mummies as Cambyses had done; he took no liberties with Apis, the sacred bull of Memphis. Here, in great temples and upon a vast scale, Alexander found the evidences of a religiosity, mysterious and irrational, to remind him of the secrets and mysteries that had entertained his mother and impressed his childhood. During his four months in Egypt he flirted with religious emotions.

He was still a very young man, we must remember, divided against himself. The strong sanity he inherited from his father had made him a great soldier; the teaching of Aristotle had given him something of the scientific outlook upon the world. He had destroyed Tyre; in Egypt, at one of the mouths of the Nile, he now founded a new city, Alexandria, to replace that ancient centre of trade. To the north of Tyre, near Issus, he founded a second port, Alexandretta. Both of these cities flourish to this day, and for a time Alexandria was perhaps the greatest city in the world. The sites, therefore, must have been wisely chosen. But also

Alexander had the unstable emotional imaginativeness of his mother, and side by side with such creative work he indulged in religious adventures. The gods of Egypt took possession of his mind. He travelled four hundred miles to the remote oasis of the oracle of Ammon. He wanted to settle certain doubts about his true parentage. His mother had filled his mind by hints and vague speeches of some deep mystery about his parentage. Was so ordinary a human being as Philip of Macedon really his father?

For nearly four hundred years Egypt had been a country politically contemptible, overrun now by Ethiopians, now by Assyrians, now by Babylonians, now by Persians. As the indignities of the present became more and more disagreeable to contemplate, the past and the other world became more splendid to Egyptian eyes. It is from the festering humiliations of peoples that arrogant religious propagandas spring. To the triumphant the downtrodden can say, "It is naught in the sight of the true gods." So the son of Philip of Macedon, the master-general of Greece, was made to feel a small person amidst the gigantic temples. And he had an abnormal share of youth's normal ambition to impress everybody. How gratifying then for him to discover presently that he was no mere successful mortal, not one of these modern vulgar Greekish folk, but ancient and divine, the son of a god, the Pharaoh god, son of Ammon Ra!

Already in a previous chapter we have given a description of that encounter in the desert temple.

Not altogether was the young man convinced. He had his moments of conviction; he had his saner phases when the thing

Photo: Mansell.

HEAD OF APOLLO. A FINE EXAMPLE OF HELLENISTIC ART.

was almost a jest. In the presence of Macedonians and Greeks he doubted if he was divine. When it thundered loudly, the ribald Aristarchus could ask him: "Won't *you* do something of the sort, oh Son of Zeus?" But the crazy notion was, nevertheless, present henceforth in his brain, ready to be inflamed by wine or flattery.

Next spring (331 B.C.) he returned to Tyre, and marched thence round towards Assyria, leaving the Syrian desert on his right. Near the ruins of forgotten Nineveh he found a great Persian army, that had been gathering since the battle of Issus, awaiting him. It was another huge medley of contingents, and it relied for its chief force upon that now antiquated weapon, the war chariot. Of these Darius had a force of two hundred, and each chariot had scythes attached to its wheels and to the pole and body of the chariot. There seem to have been four horses to each chariot, and it will be obvious that if one of those horses was wounded by javelin or arrow, that chariot was incapacitated. Against broken footmen or a crowd of individualist fighters such vehicles might be formidable; but Darius began the battle by flinging these instruments against the cavalry and light infantry. Few reached their objective, and those that did were readily disposed of. There was some manœuvring for position. The well-drilled Macedonians moved obliquely across the Persian front, keeping good order; the Persians, following this movement to the flank, opened gaps in their array. Then suddenly the disciplined Macedonian cavalry charged at one of these torn places and smote the centre of the Persian host. The infantry followed close upon their charge. The centre and left of the Persians crumpled up. For a while the light cavalry on the Persian right gained ground against Alexander's left, only to be cut to pieces by the cavalry from Thessaly, which by this time had become almost as good as its Macedonian model. The Persian forces ceased to resemble an army. They dissolved into a vast multitude of fugitives streaming under

Photo: Alinari.

THE WINGED NIKÉ (VICTORY) OF SAMOTHRACE.
Carved to commemorate a naval victory gained by Demetrius Poliorcetes over the Egyptian General Ptolemy, 306 B.C., off the Island of Cyprus.
Inset—coin of Demetrius, showing the entire statue—the figure on the prow of a galley.

reigned seventeen hundred years before) and of Nebuchadnezzar the Great and of Nabonidus, unlike Nineveh, was still a prosperous and important centre. Like the Egyptians, the Babylonians were not greatly concerned at a change of rule to Macedonian from Persian. The temple of Bel-Marduk was in ruins, a quarry for building material, but the tradition of the Chaldean priests still lingered, and Alexander promised to restore

great dust clouds and without a single rally across the hot plain towards Arbela. Through the dust and the flying crowd rode the victors, slaying and slaying until darkness stayed the slaughter. Darius led the retreat.

Such was the battle of Arbela. It was fought on October the 1st, 331 B.C. We know its date so exactly, because it is recorded that, eleven days before it began, the sooth-sayers on both sides had been greatly exercised by an eclipse of the moon.

Darius fled to the north into the country of the Medes. Alexander marched on to Babylon. The ancient city of Hammurabi (who had

the building. Thence he marched on to Susa, once the chief city of the vanished and forgotten Elamites, and now the Persian capital. He went on to Persepolis, where, as the climax of a drunken carouse, he burnt down the great palace of the king of kings. This he afterwards declared was the revenge of Greece for the burning of Athens by Xerxes.

§ 4

And now begins a new phase in the story of Alexander. For the next seven years he wandered with an army chiefly of Macedonians in the north and east of what was then the known world. At first it was a pursuit of Darius. Afterwards it became——? Was it **The Wanderings of Alexander.** a systematic survey of a world he meant to consolidate into one great order, or was it a wild-goose chase? His own soldiers, his own intimates, thought the latter, and at last stayed his career beyond the Indus. On the map it looks very like a wild-goose chase; it seems to aim at nothing in particular and to get nowhere.

The pursuit of Darius III soon came to a pitiful end. After the battle of Arbela his own generals seem to have revolted against his weakness and incompetence; they made him a prisoner, and took him with them in spite of his desire to throw himself upon the generosity of his conqueror. Bessus, the satrap of Bactria, they made their leader. There was at last a hot and exciting chase of the flying caravan which conveyed the captive king of kings. At dawn, after an all-night pursuit, it was sighted far ahead. The flight became a headlong bolt. Baggage, women, everything was abandoned by Bessus and his captains; and one other impediment also they left behind. By the side of a pool of water far away from the road a Macedonian trooper presently found a deserted mule-cart with its mules still in the traces. In this cart lay Darius, stabbed in a score of places and bleeding to death. He had

refused to go on with Bessus, refused to mount the horse that was brought to him. So his captains had run him through with their spears and left him. . . . He asked his captors for water. What else he may have said we do not know. The historians have seen fit to fabricate a quite impossible last dying speech for him. Probably he said very little. . . .

When, a little after sunrise, Alexander came up, Darius was already dead. . . .

To the historian of the world the wanderings of Alexander have an interest of their own quite apart from the light they throw upon his character. Just as the campaign of Darius I lifted the curtain behind Greece and Macedonia, and showed us something of the silent background to the north of the audible and recorded history of the early civilizations, so now Alexander's campaigns take us into regions about which there had hitherto been no trustworthy record made.

We discover they were not desert regions, but full of a gathering life of their own.

He marched to the shores of the Caspian, thence he travelled eastward across what is now called Western Turkestan. He founded a city that is now known as Herat; whence he went northward by Cabul and by what is now Samarkand, right up into the mountains of Central Turkestan. He returned southward, and came down into

Photo: Anderson.
LATER HELLENISTIC SCULPTURE—LAOCOON AND HIS SONS— THE WORK OF RHODIAN SCULPTORS.

THE ACROPOLIS OF PERGAMUM.
From the proposed design for restoration by Richard Bohn.

India by the Khyber Pass. He fought a great battle on the Upper Indus against a very tall and chivalrous king, Porus, in which the Macedonian infantry encountered an array of elephants and defeated them. Possibly he would have pushed eastward across the deserts to the Ganges valley, but his troops refused to go further. Possibly, had they not done so, then or later he would have gone on until he vanished eastward out of history. But he was forced to turn about. He built a fleet and descended to the mouth of the Indus. There he divided his forces. The main army he took along the desolate coast back to the Persian Gulf, and on the way it suffered dreadfully and lost many men through thirst. The fleet followed him by sea, and rejoined him at the entrance to the Persian Gulf. In the course of this six-year tour he fought battles, received the submission of many strange peoples, and founded cities. He saw the dead body of Darius in June 330 B.C.; he returned to Susa in 324 B.C. He found the empire in disorder: the provincial satraps raising armies of their own, Bactria and Media in insurrection, and Olympias making government impossible in Macedonia. Harpalus, the royal treasurer, had bolted with all that was portable of the royal treasure, and was making his way, bribing as he went, towards Greece. Some of the Harpalus money is said to have reached Demosthenes.

But before we deal with the closing chapter of the story of Alexander, let us say a word or so about these northern regions into which he wandered. It is evident that from the Danube region right across South Russia, right across the country to the north of the Caspian, right across the country to the east of the Caspian, as far as the mountain masses of the Pamir Plateau and eastward into the Tarim basin of Eastern Turkestan, there spread then a series of similar barbaric tribes and peoples all at about the same stage of culture, and for the most part Aryan in their language and possibly Nordic in their race. They had few cities, mostly they were nomadic; at times they settled temporarily to cultivate the land. They were certainly already mingling in Central Asia with Mongolian tribes, but the Mongolian tribes were not then prevalent there.

An immense process of drying up and elevation has been going on in these parts of the world during the last ten thousand years. Ten thousand years ago there was probably a continuous water barrier between the basin of the Obi and the Aral-Caspian sea. As this had

HEAD OF ALEXANDER FROM A SILVER COIN OF LYSIMACHUS (321–281 B.C.)

Alexander wears the ram's horns of Jupiter Ammon, his divine father

dried up and the marshy land had become steppe-like country, Nordic nomads from the west and Mongolian nomads from the east had met and mixed, and the riding horse had come back into the western world. It is evident this great stretch of country was becoming a region of accumulation for these barbaric peoples. They were very loosely attached to the lands they occupied. They lived in tents and wagons rather than houses. A brief cycle of plentiful and healthy years, or a cessation of tribal warfare under some strong ruler, would lead to considerable increases of population ; then two

across Asia Minor, the southward coming of the Scythians and Medes and Persians, and the Aryan descent into India. About a century before Alexander there had been a fresh Aryan invasion of Italy by a Keltic people, the Gauls, who had settled in the valley of the Po. Those various races came down out of their northern obscurity into the light of history ; and meanwhile beyond that light the reservoir accumulated for fresh discharges. Alexander's march in Central Asia brings now into our history names that are fresh to us; the Parthians, a race of mounted bowmen who were destined to

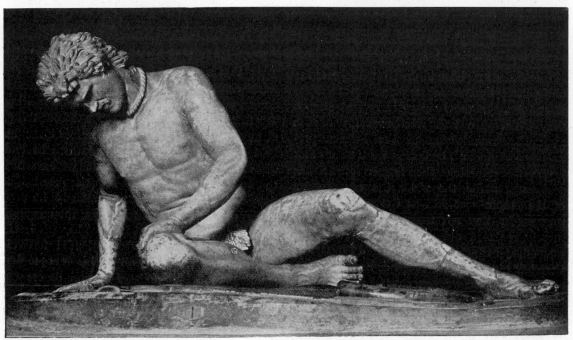

Photo: Anderson.

THE DYING GAUL (OF PERGAMUM).

or three hard years would suffice to send the tribes wandering again in search of food.

From before the dawn of recorded history this region of human accumulation between the Danube and China had been, as it were, intermittently *raining* out tribes southward and westward. It was like a cloud bank behind the settled landscape that accumulated and then precipitated invaders. We have noted how the Keltic peoples drizzled westward, how the Italians, the Greeks, and their Epirote, Macedonian, and Phrygian kindred came south. We have noted too the Cimmerian drive from the east, like a sudden driving shower of barbarians

play an important rôle in history a century or so later, and the Bactrians who lived in the sandy native land of the camel. Everywhere he seems to have met Aryan-speaking peoples. The Mongolian barbarians to the north-eastward were still unsuspected, no one imagined there was yet another great cloud bank of population, beyond the Scythians and their kind, in the north of China that was presently also to begin a drift westward and southward, mixing as it came with the Nordic Scythians and every other people of kindred habits that it encountered. As yet only China knew of the Huns ; there were no Turks in Western Tur-

16

kestan or anywhere else then, no Tartars in the world.

This glimpse of the state of affairs in Turkestan in the fourth century B.C. is one of the most interesting aspects of the wanderings of Alexander ; another is his raid through the Punjab. From the point of view of the teller of the human story it is provocative that he did not go on into the Ganges country, and that consequently we have no independent accounts by Greek writers of the life in ancient Bengal. But there is a considerable literature in various Indian languages dealing with Indian history and social life that still needs to be made accessible to European readers.

§ 5

Alexander had been in undisputed possession of the Persian empire for six years. He was now thirty-one. In those six years he had created very little. He had retained most of the organization of the Persian provinces, appointing fresh satraps or retaining the former ones ; the roads, the ports, the organization of the empire was still as Cyrus, his greater predecessor, had left them ; in Egypt he had merely replaced old provincial governors by new ones; in India he had defeated Porus, and then left him in power much as he found him, except that Porus was now called a satrap by the Greeks. Alexander had, it is true, planned out a number of towns, and some of them were to grow into great towns ; seventeen Alexandrias he founded altogether ; [1] but he had destroyed Tyre, and with Tyre the security of the sea routes which had hitherto been the chief westward outlet for Mesopotamia. Historians say that he Hellenized the east. But Babylonia and Egypt swarmed with Greeks before his time ; he was not the cause, he was a part of the Hellenization. For a time the whole world, from the Adriatic to the Indus, was under one ruler ; so far he had realized the dreams of Isocrates and Philip his father. But how far was he making this a permanent and enduring union ? How far as yet was it anything more than a dazzling but transitory flourish of his own magnificent self ?

Was Alexander indeed Great ?

[1] Mahaffy. Their names have undergone various changes—e.g. Candahar (Iskender) and Secunderabad.

He was making no great roads, setting up no sure sea communications. It is idle to accuse him of leaving education alone, because the idea that empires must be cemented by education was still foreign to human thought. But he was forming no group of statesmen about him ; he was thinking of no successor ; he was creating no tradition—nothing more than a personal legend. The idea that the world would have to go on after Alexander, engaged in any other employment than the discussion of his magnificence, seems to have been outside his mental range. He was still young, it is true, but well before Philip was one and thirty he had been thinking of the education of Alexander.

Was Alexander a statesman at all ?

Some students of his career assure us that he was ; that now from Susa he planned a mighty world empire, seeing it not simply as a Macedonian conquest of the world, but as a melting together of racial traditions. He did one thing, at any rate, that gives colour to this idea ; he held a great marriage feast, in which he and ninety of his generals and friends were married to Persian brides. He himself married a daughter of Darius, though already he possessed an Asiatic wife in Roxana, the daughter of the king of Samarkand. This wholesale wedding was made a very splendid festival, and at the same time all of his Macedonian soldiers, to the number of several thousands, who had married Asiatic brides, were given wedding gifts. This has been called the Marriage of Europe and Asia ; the two continents were to be joined, wrote Plutarch, " in lawful wedlock and by community of offspring." And next he began to train recruits from Persia and the north, Parthians, Bactrians, and the like, in the distinctive disciplines of the phalanx and the cavalry. Was that also to assimilate Europe and Asia, or was it to make himself independent of his Macedonians ? They thought the latter, at any rate, and mutinied, and it was with some difficulty that he brought them to a penitent mood and induced them to take part in a common feast with the Persians. The historians have made a long and eloquent speech for him on this occasion, but the gist of it was that he bade his Macedonians begone, and gave no sign of how he proposed they should get home out of

Greek statuette of a Gaul ..

(From Myrina)

Persia. After three days of dismay they submitted to him and begged his forgiveness.

Here is the matter for a very pretty discussion. Was Alexander really planning a racial fusion or had he just fallen in love with the pomp and divinity of an Oriental monarch, and wished to get rid of these Europeans to whom he was only a king-leader? The writers of his own time, and those who lived near to his time, lean very much to the latter alternative. They insist upon his immense vanity. They relate how he began to wear the robes and tiara of a Persian monarch. "At first only before the barbarians and privately, but afterwards he came to wear it in public when he sat for the dispatch of business." And presently he demanded Oriental prostrations from his friends.

One thing seems to support the suggestion of great personal vanity in Alexander. His portrait was painted and sculptured frequently, and always he is represented as a beautiful youth, with wonderful locks flowing backward from a broad forehead. Previously most men had worn beards. But Alexander, enamoured of his own youthful loveliness, would not part with it; he remained a sham boy at thirty-two; he shaved his face, and so set a fashion in Greece and Italy for many centuries.

The stories of violence and vanity in his closing years cluster thick upon his memory.

He listened to tittle-tattle about Philotas, the son of Parmenio, one of his most trusted and faithful generals. Philotas, it was said, had boasted to some woman he was making love to that Alexander was a mere boy; that, but for such men as his father and himself, there would have been no conquest of Persia, and the like. Such assertions had a certain element of truth in them. The woman was brought to Alexander, who listened to her treacheries. Presently Philotas was accused of conspiracy, and, upon very insufficient evidence, tortured and executed. Then Alexander thought of Parmenio, whose other two sons had died for him in battle. He sent swift messengers to assassinate the old man before he could hear of his son's death! Now Parmenio had been one of the most trusted of Philip's generals; it was Parmenio who had led the Macedonian armies into Asia before the murder of Philip. There can be little doubt of the substantial truth of this story, nor about the execution of Callisthenes, the nephew of Aristotle, who refused

Photo: Mansell.

COINS OF THE HELLENISTIC PERIOD.

1. Alexander the Great. 2. Lysimachus. 3. Rhodian coin.

Alexander divine honours, and "went about with as much pride as if he had demolished a tyranny, while the young men followed him as the only freeman among thousands." Mixed with such incidents we have the very illuminating story of the drunken quarrel in which he killed Clitus. The monarch and his company had been drinking hard, and the drink had made the talk loud and free. There was much flattery of the "young god," much detraction of Philip, at which Alexander had smiled with satisfaction.[1] Was he not the son of a god? This drunken self-complacency was more than the honest Macedonians could stand; it roused Clitus, his foster-brother, to a frenzy. Clitus reproached Alexander with his Median costume and praised Philip, there was a loud quarrel, and, to end it, Clitus was hustled out of the room by his friends. He was, however, in the obstinate phase of drunkenness, and he returned by another entrance. He was heard outside quoting Euripides "in a bold and disrespectful tone":

"Are these your customs? Is it thus that Greece
   Rewards her combatants? Shall one man claim
   The trophies won by thousands?"

[1] D. G. Hogarth.

Whereupon Alexander snatched a spear from one of his guards and ran Clitus through the body as he lifted the curtain to come in. . . .

One is forced to believe that this was the real atmosphere of the young conqueror's life. Then the story of his frantic and cruel display of grief for Hephæstion can scarcely be all invention. If it is true, or in any part true, it displays a mind ill-balanced and altogether wrapped up in personal things, to whom empire was no more than opportunity for egoistic display, and all the resources of the world, stuff for freaks of that sort of "generosity" which robs a thousand people to extort the admiration of one astounded recipient.

Hephæstion, being ill, was put upon a strict diet, but in the absence of his physician at the theatre he ate a roasted fowl and drank a flagon of iced wine, in consequence of which he died. Thereupon Alexander decided upon a display of grief. It was the grief of a lunatic. He had the physician crucified! He ordered every horse and mule in Persia to be shorn, and pulled down the battlements of the neighbouring cities. He prohibited all music in his camp for a long time, and, having taken certain villages of the

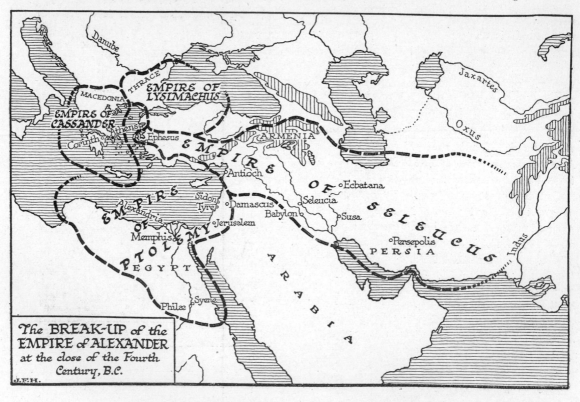

The BREAK-UP of the EMPIRE of ALEXANDER at the close of the Fourth Century, B.C.

Cusæans, he caused all the adults to be massacred, as a sacrifice to the manes of Hephæstion. Finally he set aside ten thousand talents (a talent = £240) for a tomb. For those days this was an enormous sum. None of which things did any real honour to Hephæstion, but they served to demonstrate to an awe-stricken world what a tremendous thing the sorrow of Alexander could be.

This last story and many such stories may be lies or distortions or exaggerations. But they have a vein in common. After a bout of hard drinking in Babylon a sudden fever came upon Alexander (323 B.C.), and he sickened and died. He was still only thirty-three years of age. Forthwith the world empire he had snatched at and held in his hands, as a child might snatch at and hold a precious vase, fell to the ground and was shattered to pieces.

Whatever appearance of a worldwide order may have gleamed upon men's imaginations, vanished at his death. The story becomes the story of a barbaric autocracy in confusion. Everywhere the provincial rulers set up for themselves. In the course of a few years the entire family of Alexander had been destroyed.

Roxana, his barbarian wife, was prompt to murder, as a rival, the daughter of Darius. She herself presently bore Alexander a post-humous son, who was also called Alexander. He was murdered, with her, a few years later (311 B.C.). Hercules, the only other son of Alexander, was murdered also. So too was Aridæus, the weak-minded half-brother (see § 2). Plutarch gives a last glimpse of Olympias during a brief interval of power in Macedonia, accusing first this person and then that of poisoning her wonderful son. Many she killed in her fury. The bodies of some of his circle who had died after his death she caused to be dug up, but we do not know if any fresh light was shed upon his death by these disinterments. Finally Olympias was killed in Macedonia by the friends of those she had slain.

§ 6

From this welter of crime there presently emerged three leading figures. Much of the old Persian empire, as far as the Indus eastward and almost to Lydia in the west, was held by one general Seleucus, who founded a dynasty, the Seleucid

The Successors of Alexander.

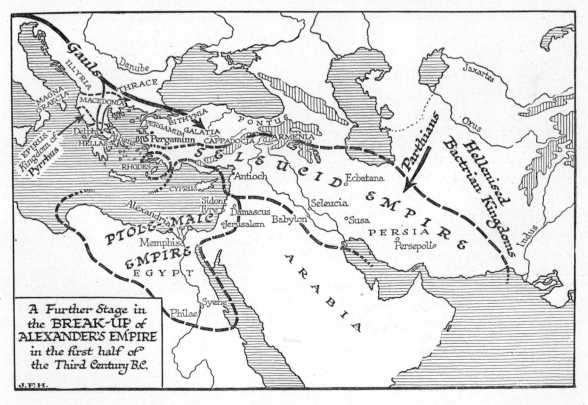

A Further Stage in the BREAK-UP of ALEXANDER'S EMPIRE in the first half of the Third Century B.C.

J.F.H.

Dynasty; Macedonia fell to another Macedonian general, Antigonus; a third Macedonian, Ptolemy, secured Egypt, and, making Alexandria his chief city, established a sufficient naval ascendancy to keep also Cyprus and most of the coast of Phœnicia and Asia Minor. The Ptolemaic and Seleucid empires lasted for a considerable time; the forms of government in Asia Minor and the Balkans were more unstable. Two maps will help the reader to a sense of the kaleidoscopic nature of the political boundaries of the third century B.C. Antigonus was defeated and killed at the battle of Ipsus (301), leaving Lysimachus, the governor of Thrace, and Cassander, of Macedonia and Greece, as equally transitory successors (see Map). Minor governors carved out smaller states. Meanwhile the barbarians swung down into the broken-up and enfeebled world of civilization from the west and from the east. From the west came the Gauls, a people closely related to the Kelts. They raided down through Macedonia and Greece to Delphi, and (277 B.C.) two sections of them crossed the Bosphorus into Asia Minor, being first employed as mercenaries and then setting up for themselves as independent plunderers; and after raiding almost to the Taurus, they settled in the old Phrygian land, holding the people about them to tribute. (These Gauls of Phrygia became the Galatians of St. Paul's Epistle.) Armenia and the southern shores of the Black Sea became a confusion of changing rulers. Kings with Hellenistic ideas appeared in Cappadocia, in Pontus (the south shore of the Black Sea), in Bithynia, and in Pergamum (see Map). From the east the Scythians and the Parthians and Bactrians also drove southward. . . . For a time there were Greek-ruled Bactrian states becoming more and more Orientalized; in the second century B.C. Greek adventurers from Bactria raided down into North India and founded short-lived kingdoms there, the last eastward fling of the Greek; then gradually barbarism fell again like a curtain between the Western civilizations and India.[1]

[1] The stages by which Bactria degenerated into Afghanistan may be studied neatly in the progressive deterioration of its coinage from a decent standard of Hellenic accomplishment into the vague flourishes of Orientalism; it began by displaying a Heracles of pure Greek blood and a pair of horsemen who would hardly

§ 7

Amidst all these shattered fragments of the burst bubble of Hellenic empire one small state *Pergamum a Refuge of Culture.* stands out and demands at least a brief section to itself, the kingdom of Pergamum. We hear first of this town as an independent centre during the struggle that ended in the battle of Ipsus. While the tide of the Gaulish invasion swirled and foamed to and fro about Asia Minor between the years 277 and 241, Pergamum for a time paid them tribute, but she retained her general independence, and at last, under Attalus I, refused her tribute and defeated them in two decisive battles. For more than a century thereafter (until 133 B.C.) Pergamum remained free, and was perhaps during that period the most highly civilized state in the world. On the hill of the acropolis was reared a rich group of buildings, palaces, temples, a museum, and a library, rivals of those of Alexandria, of which we shall presently tell, and almost the first in the world. Under the princes of Pergamum, Greek art blossomed afresh, and the reliefs of the altar of the temple of Zeus and the statues of the fighting and dying Gauls which were made there, are among the great artistic treasures of mankind.

In a little while, as we shall tell later, the influence of a new power began to be felt in the Eastern Mediterranean, the power of the Roman republic, friendly to Greece and to Greek civilization; and in this power the Hellenic communities of Pergamum and Rhodes found a natural and useful ally and supporter against the Galatians and against the Orientalized Seleucid empire. But we shall tell later of how at last the Roman power came into Asia, how it defeated the Seleucid empire at the battle of Magnesia (190 B.C.), and drove it out of Asia Minor and beyond the Taurus mountains, and how at last in 133 B.C. Attalus III, the last king of Pergamum, bowing to his sense of an inevitable destiny, made the Roman republic the heir to his kingdom, which became then the Roman province of "Asia."

have seemed out of place on the frieze of the Parthenon, and it fell steadily to a level of incompetence only equalled by the crude imitations of Roman currency that were being made in pre-Roman Britain about the same time.—P. G.

§ 8

Nearly all historians are disposed to regard the career of Alexander the Great as marking an epoch in human affairs. It drew together all the known world, excepting only the Western Mediterranean, into one drama.

Alexander as a Portent of World Unity. But the opinions men have formed of Alexander himself vary enormously. They fall, most of them, into two main schools. One type of scholar is fascinated by the youth and splendour of this young man. These Alexander-worshippers seem disposed to take him at his own valuation, to condone every crime and folly either as the mere ebullience of a rich nature or as the bitter necessity to some gigantic scheme, and to regard his life as framed upon a design, a scheme of statesmanship, such as all the wider knowledge and wider ideas of these later times barely suffice to bring into the scope of our understanding. On the other hand, there are those who see him only as a wrecker of the slowly maturing possibilities of a free and tranquil Hellenized world.

Before we ascribe to Alexander or to his father Philip schemes of world policy such as a twentieth-century historian-philosopher might approve, we shall do well to consider very carefully the utmost range of knowledge and thought that was possible in those days. The world of Plato, Isocrates, and Aristotle had practically no historical perspective at all ; there had not been such a thing as history in the world, history, that is, as distinguished from mere priestly chronicles, until the last couple of centuries. Even highly educated men had the most circumscribed ideas of geography and foreign countries. For most men the world was still flat and limitless. The only systematic political philosophy was based on the experiences of minute city states, and took no thought of empires. Nobody knew anything of the origins of civilization. No one had speculated upon economics.[1] No one had worked out the reaction of one social class upon another. We are too apt to consider

[1] Before that time. But such speculation was going on then. There is some interesting economic theory in Plato's *Republic*, and Aristotle was writing the *Œconomica*. Xenophon wrote on Athenian revenues and other economic matters. Thucycides wrote an excellent passage on the Greek past, and Aristotle dealt with barbaric customs.—E. B.

the career of Alexander as the crown of some process that had long been afoot ; as the climax of a crescendo. In a sense, no doubt, it was that ; but much more true is it that it was not so much an end as a beginning ; it was the first revelation to the human imagination of the oneness of human affairs. The utmost reach of the thought of Greece before his time was of a Persian empire Hellenized, a predominance in the world of Macedonians and Greeks. But before Alexander was dead, and much more after he was dead and there had been time to think him over, the conception of a world law and organization was a practicable and assimilable idea for the minds of men.

For some generations Alexander the Great was for mankind the symbol and embodiment of world order and world dominion. He became a fabulous being. His head, adorned with the divine symbols of the demi-god Hercules or the god Ammon Ra, appears on the coins of such among his successors as could claim to be his heirs. Then the idea of world dominion was taken up by another great people, a people who for some centuries exhibited considerable political genius, the Romans ; and the figure of another conspicuous adventurer, Cæsar, eclipsed for the western half of the old world the figure of Alexander.

So by the beginning of the third century B.C. we find already arisen in the Western civilization of the old world three of the great structural ideas that rule the mind of contemporary mankind. We have already traced the escape of writing and knowledge from the secrets and mysteries and initiations of the old-world priesthoods, and the development of the idea of a universal knowledge, of a universally understandable and communicable history and philosophy. We have taken the figures of Herodotus and Aristotle as typical exponents of this first great idea, the idea of *science*—using the word science in its widest and properest sense, to include history and signify a clear vision of man in relation to the things about him. We have traced also the generalization of religion among the Babylonians, Jews, and other Semitic peoples, from the dark worship in temples and consecrated places of some local or tribal god to the open service of *one universal God of Righteousness*, whose temple is the whole world. And now we have traced also the first germination of the idea of *a world polity*. The rest of the history of mankind is very largely the history of those three ideas of science, of a universal righteousness, and of a human commonweal, spreading out from the minds of the rare and exceptional persons and peoples in which they first originated, into the general consciousness of the race, and giving first a new colour, then a new spirit, and then a new direction to human affairs.

XXV

SCIENCE AND RELIGION AT ALEXANDRIA[1]

§ 1

ONE of the most prosperous fragments of the brief world empire of Alexander the Great was Egypt, which fell to the share of the Ptolemy whose name we have already noted as one of the associates of Alexander whom King Philip had banished. The country was at a secure distance from plundering Gaul or Parthian, and the destruction of Tyre and the Phœnician navy and the creation of Alexandria gave Egypt a temporary naval ascendancy in the Eastern Mediterranean. Alexandria grew to proportions that rivalled Carthage; eastward she had an overseas' trade through the Red Sea with Arabia and India; and westward her traffic competed with the Carthaginian. In the Macedonian and Greek governors of the Ptolemies, the Egyptians found a government more sympathetic and tolerable than any they had ever known since they ceased to be a self-governing empire. Indeed it is rather that Egypt conquered and annexed the Ptolemies politically, than that the Macedonians ruled Egypt.

The Science of Alexandria.

There was a return to Egyptian political ideas, rather than any attempt to Hellenize the government of the country. Ptolemy became Pharaoh, the god king, and his administration continued the ancient tradition of Pepi, Thotmes, Rameses, and Necho. Alexandria, however, for her town affairs, and subject to the divine overlordship of Pharaoh, had a constitution of the Greek city type. And the language of the court and administration was Attic Greek. Greek became so much the general language of educated people in Egypt, that the Jewish community there found it necessary to translate their Bible into the Greek language, many men of their own people being no longer able to understand Hebrew. Attic Greek for some centuries before and after Christ was the language of all educated men from the Adriatic to the Persian Gulf.

Of all Alexander's group of young men, Ptolemy seems to have done most to carry out those ideas of a systematic organization of knowledge with which Aristotle had no doubt familiarized the court of Philip of Macedon. Ptolemy was a man of very extraordinary intellectual gifts, at once creative and modest, with a certain understandable cynicism towards the strain of Olympias in the mind of Alexander. His contemporary history of Alexander's cam-

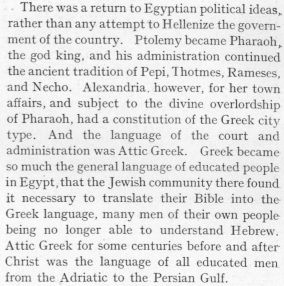

Tetradrachm with head of Seleucus I.

---

[1] *Vide* Mahaffy's *Greek Life and Thought* and his *Progress of Hellenism in Alexander's Empire*, Marvin's *Living Past*, Legge's *Forerunners and Rivals of Christianity*, and Reinach's *Orpheus*.

paigns has perished; but it was a source to which all the surviving accounts are deeply indebted.

The Museum he set up in Alexandria was in effect the first university in the world. As its name implies, it was dedicated to the service of the Muses, which was also the case with the Peripatetic school at Athens. It was, however, a religious body only in form, in order to meet the legal difficulties of endowment in a world that had never foreseen such a thing as a secular intellectual process. It was essentially a college of learned men engaged chiefly in research and record, but also to a certain extent

Photo: Brogi.

PTOLEMY SOTER, FIRST KING OF EGYPT,
323–285 B.C.

in teaching. At the outset, and for two or three generations, the Museum at Alexandria presented such a scientific constellation as even Athens at its best could not rival. Particularly sound and good was the mathematical and geographical work. The names of Euclid, familiar to every schoolboy, Eratosthenes, who measured the size of the earth and came within fifty miles of the true diameter, Apollonius, who wrote on conic sections, stand out. Hipparchus made the first attempt to catalogue and map the stars with a view to checking any changes that might be occurring in the heavens. Hero devised the first steam engine. Archimedes came to Alexandria to study, and remained a frequent correspondent of the Museum. The medical school of Alexandria was equally famous. For the first time in the world's history a standard of professional knowledge was set up. Herophilus, the greatest of the Alexandrian anatomists, is said to have conducted vivisections upon con-

demned criminals.[1] Other teachers, in opposition to Herophilus, condemned the study of anatomy and developed the science of drugs. But this scientific blaze at Alexandria did not endure altogether for more than a century. The organization of the Museum was not planned to ensure its mental continuity. It was a "royal" college; its professors and fellows (as we may call them) were appointed and paid by Pharaoh. "The republican character of the private corporations called the schools or academies at Athens was far more stable and inde-

[1] The question whether the vivisection of human beings, or, indeed, whether any vivisection at all occurred at Alexandria, is one of considerable importance because of the light it throws upon the moral and intellectual quality of the time. One of the editors of this book was inclined to throw doubt upon it, as a thing antipathetic to the Greek spirit. The writer has taken some pains to find out the facts of the case, and he has been so fortunate as to have the help of Dr. Singer, one of the greatest living authorities upon the history of medicine. There are statements made by Tertullian (De Anima, chap. xxv.), but he was a biased and untrustworthy witness. The conclusive passage is taken from Celsus, who wrote during the reign of Tiberius, three centuries after the great days of Alexandria. "If you are to have one witness," writes Dr. Singer, "you could hardly have a better. In my own mind I am satisfied with the evidence of Celsus, and I have asked Dr. E. T. Wittrington, our best authority on Greek medicine, and he also is satisfied."

The following is a translation of the passage in Celsus, De Re Medica. One school says that "it is necessary to dissect the bodies of the dead, and to examine their viscera and intestines. Herophilus and Erasistratus adopted by far the best method, for they obtained criminals from prison by royal permission, and dissected them alive, and they examined, while they still

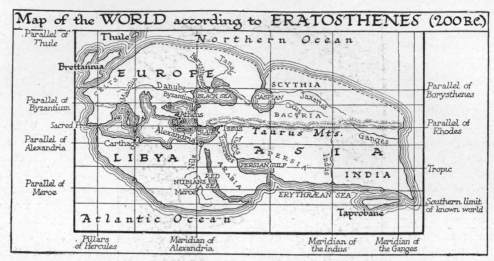

Map of the WORLD according to ERATOSTHENES (200 B.C.)

pendent."[1] Royal patronage was all very well so long as Pharaoh was Ptolemy I, or Ptolemy II, but the strain degenerated, and the long tradition of Egyptian priestcraft presently swallowed up the Ptolemies—and destroyed the Aristotelian mentality of the Museum altogether. The Museum had not existed for a hundred years before its scientific energy was extinct.

Side by side with the Museum, Ptolemy I created a more enduring monument to himself in the great library. This was a combination of state library and state publishing upon a scale hitherto unheard of. It was to be altogether encyclopædic. If any stranger brought an unknown book to Egypt, he had to have it copied for the collection, and a considerable staff of copyists was engaged continually in making duplicates of all the more popular and necessary works. The library, like a university press, had

breathed, the parts which Nature had concealed, noting their position, warmth (or possibly ' colour '—*colorem* instead of *calorem*), shape, size, relation, hardness, softness, smoothness, and feel; also the projections and depressions of each and how they fit into one another. For if there happen any inward pain, he who has not learned where the viscera and intestines are placed, cannot know where the pain is; nor can the diseased part be cured by one who does not know what part it is. Again, if the viscera of any one are exposed by a wound, he who is ignorant of the natural colour of that part in the healthy state cannot know whether it be sound or corrupted, and therefore cannot cure the corrupted part. Moreover, remedies can be applied more appropriately externally when the position, shape, and size of the internal parts is known, and the same argument holds for all the other matters that we have mentioned. Nor is it a cruel act, as many would have it, to seek remedies for innocent mankind throughout the ages by torture of a few criminals."

Against this view, says Celsus, the other school argues that " to cut open the abdomen and thorax of living men, and thus to turn that art which concerns itself with the health of mankind not only into an instrument of death (*pestem*—lit. ' a plague '), but (death) in its most horrible form, and this although some of the things that we seek thus barbarously can by no means be known, while others may be learned without cruelty. For the colour, smoothness, softness, hardness, and all

their like are not the same when the body is cut open as when it is whole; and, moreover, even in bodies that have not been thus ravaged, these properties are often changed by fear, grief, want of food, or of digestion, fatigue, and a thousand other lesser causes. It is thus more likely that the inner organs, which are more tender, and to which the light is a new experience, are changed by serious wounds and by mangling.

" Further, nothing can be more foolish than to think that any things are the same in a live man as in a moribund one, or, rather, in one practically dead. It is indeed true that the abdomen, with which our argument is less concerned, can be opened while a man yet lives, but as soon as the knife reaches the thorax (præcordium), and cuts the transverse septum, which is a membrane dividing the superior parts from the inferior and called diaphragma by the Greeks, the man at once gives up the ghost, and thus it is the breast and its viscera of a dead and not a living man which the murderous physician examines. He has thus but performed a cruel murder, and has not learned what the viscera of a living man are like."

Celsus' own judgment is given a little later : " To dissect a living body is both cruel and unnecessary ; to dissect dead bodies is necessary."

It is to be noted, says Professor Murray, that Herophilus and Erasistratus were not living in a Greek city state, but under an *oriental despot*.

[1] Mahaffy.

an outward trade. It was a book-selling affair. Under Callimachus, the head of the library during the time of Ptolemy II and III, the arrangement and cataloguing of the accumulations was systematically undertaken. In those days, it must be remembered, books were not in pages, but rolled like the music-rolls of the modern piano-player, and in order to refer to any particular passage, a reader had to roll back or roll forward very tediously, a process which wore out books and readers together. One thinks at once of a simple and obvious little machine by which such a roll could have been quickly wound to and fro for reference, but nothing of the sort seems to have been used. Every time a roll was read it was handled by two perspiring hands. It was to minimize the waste of time and trouble that Callimachus broke up long works, such as the History of Herodotus, into " books " or volumes, as we should call them, each upon a separate roll. The library of Alexandria drew a far vaster crowd of students than the teachers of the Museum. The lodging and catering for these visitors from all parts of the world became a considerable business interest for the Alexandrian population.

It is curious to note how slowly the mechanism of the intellectual life improves. Contrast the ordinary library facilities of a middle-class English home, such as the present writer is now working in, with the inconveniences and deficiencies of the equipment of an Alexandrian writer, and one realizes the enormous waste of time, physical exertion, and attention that went on through all the centuries during which that library flourished. Before the present writer lie half a dozen books, and there are good indices to three of them. He can pick up any one of these six books, refer quickly to a statement, verify a quotation, and go on writing. Contrast with that the tedious unfolding of a rolled manuscript. Close at hand are two encyclopædias, a dictionary, an atlas of the

before it could reach any considerable circle of readers, and every copyist introduced some new error.[1] Whenever a need for maps or diagrams arose, there were fresh difficulties. Such a science as anatomy, for example, depending as it does upon accurate drawing, must have been enormously hampered by the natural limitations of the copyist. The transmission of geographical fact again must have been almost incredibly tedious. No doubt a day will come when a private library and writing-desk of the year A.D. 1919 will seem quaintly clumsy and difficult; but, measured by the standards of Alexan-

GREEN SCHIST:— SEAL OF KHASHKHAMER, VICEROY OF ISHKUN-SIN; REIGN OF UR-GUR, KING OF UR, B.C. 2500 SCENE: WORSHIP OF THE MOON-GOD.

Photo: Mansell.

A SUMERIAN SEAL USED FOR PRINTING BEFORE THE DAWN OF HISTORY; THE SEAL TO THE LEFT, THE IMPRESSION TO THE RIGHT.

world, a biographical dictionary, and other books of reference. They have no marginal indices, it is true; but that perhaps is asking for too much at present. There were no such resources in the world in 300 B.C. Alexandria had still to produce the first grammar and the first dictionary. This present book is being written in manuscript; it is then taken by a typist and typewritten very accurately. It can then, with the utmost convenience, be read over, corrected amply, rearranged freely, retyped, and recorrected. The Alexandrian author had to dictate or recopy every word he wrote. Before he could turn back to what he had written previously, he had to dry his last words by waving them in the air or pouring sand over them; he had not even blotting-paper. Whatever an author wrote had to be recopied again and again

dria, they are astonishingly quick, efficient, and economical of nervous and mental energy.

No attempt seems to have been made at Alexandria to print anything at all. That strikes one at first as a very remarkable fact. The world was crying out for books, and not simply for books. There was an urgent public need for notices, proclamations, and the like. Yet there is nothing in the history of the Western civilizations that one can call printing until the fifteenth century A.D. It is not as though printing was a recondite art or dependent upon any precedent and preliminary discoveries.

[1] It has been suggested that new books were perhaps dictated to a roomful of copyists, and so issued in a first edition of some hundreds at least. In Rome, Horace and Virgil seem to have been issued in quite considerable editions.

Printing is the most obvious of dodges. In principle it has always been known. As we have already stated, there is ground for supposing that the Palæolithic men of the Magdalenian period may have printed designs on their leather garments. The " seals " of ancient Sumeria again were printing devices. Coins are print. Illiterate persons in all ages have used wooden or metal stamps for their signatures ; William I, the Norman Conqueror of England, for example, used such a stamp with ink to sign documents. In China the classics were being printed by the second century A.D. Yet either because of a complex of small difficulties about ink or papyrus or the form of books, or because of some protective resistance on the part of the owners of the slave copyists, or because the script was too swift and easy to set men thinking how to write it still more easily, as the Chinese character or the Gothic letters did, or because of a gap in the social system between men of thought and knowledge and men of technical skill, printing was not used—not even used for the exact reproduction of illustrations.

The chief reason for this failure to develop printing systematically lies, no doubt, in the fact that there was no abundant supply of printable material of a uniform texture and convenient form. The supply of papyrus was strictly limited, strip had to be fastened to strip, and there was no standard size of sheet. Paper had yet to come from China to release the mind of Europe. Had there been presses, they would have had to stand idle while the papyrus rolls were slowly made. But this explanation does not account for the failure to use block printing in the case of illustrations and diagrams.

These limitations enable us to understand why it was that Alexandria could at once achieve the most extraordinary intellectual triumphs—for such a feat as that of Eratosthenes, for instance, having regard to his poverty of apparatus, is sufficient to put him on a level with Newton or Pasteur—and yet have little or no effect upon the course of politics or the lives and thoughts of people round about her. Her Museum and library were a centre of light, but it was light in a dark lantern hidden from the general world. There were no means of carrying its results even to sympathetic men abroad except by tedious letter-writing. There was no possibility of communicating what was known there to the general body of men. Students had to come at great cost to themselves to this crowded centre because there was no other way of gathering even scraps of knowledge. At Athens and Alexandria there were bookstalls where manuscript note-books of variable quality could be bought at reasonable prices, but any extension of education to larger classes and other centres would have produced at once a restrictive shortage of papyrus. Education did not reach into the masses at all ; to become more than superficially educated one had to abandon the ordinary life of the times and come for long years to live a hovering existence in the neighbourhood of ill-equipped and overworked sages. Learning was not indeed so complete a withdrawal from ordinary life as initiation into a priesthood, but it was still something in that nature.

And very speedily that feeling of freedom, that openness and directness of statement, which is the vital air of the true intellectual life, faded out of Alexandria. From the first the patronage even of Ptolemy I set a limit to political discussion. Presently the dissensions of the schools let in the superstitions and prejudices of the city mob to scholastic affairs.

Wisdom passed away from Alexandria and left pedantry behind. For the use of books was substituted the worship of books. Very speedily the learned became a specialized queer class with unpleasant characteristics of its own. The Museum had not existed for half a dozen generations before Alexandria was familiar with a new type of human being ; shy, eccentric, unpractical, incapable of essentials, strangely fierce upon trivialities of literary detail, as bitterly jealous of the colleague within as of the unlearned without, the bent Scholarly Man. He was as intolerant as a priest, though he had no altar ; as obscurantist as a magician, though he had no cave. For him no method of copying was sufficiently tedious and no rare book sufficiently inaccessible. He was a sort of by-product of the intellectual process of mankind. For many precious generations the new-lit fires of the human intelligence were to be seriously banked down by this by-product.

Right thinking is necessarily an open process, and the only science and history of full value to men consist of what is generally and clearly known; this is surely a platitude, but we have still to discover how to preserve our centres of philosophy and research from the caking and darkening accumulations of narrow and dingy-spirited specialists. We have still to ensure that a man of learning shall be none the less a man of affairs, and that all that can be thought and known is kept plainly, honestly, and easily available to the ordinary men and women who are the substance of mankind.

§ 2

At first the mental activities of Alexandria centred upon the Museum, and

Philosophy at Alexandria. were mainly scientific. Philosophy, which in a more vigorous age had been a doctrine of power over self and the material world, without abandoning these pretensions, became in reality a doctrine of secret consolation. The stimulant changed into an opiate. The philosopher let the world, as the vulgar say, *rip*, the world of which he was a part, and consoled himself by saying in very beautiful and elaborate forms that the world was illusion and that there was in him something quintessential and sublime, outside and above the world. Athens,[1] politically insignificant, but still a great and crowded mart throughout the fourth century, decaying almost imperceptibly so far as outer seeming went, and treated with a strange respect that was half contempt by all the warring powers and adventurers of the world, was the fitting centre of such philosophical teaching. It was quite a couple of centuries before the schools of Alexandria became as important in philosophical discussion.

But of Philo the Jew in the first century A.D.,

[1] See Ferguson's *Hellenistic Athens*.

Photo: Mansell.
SERAPIS.

and of Plotinus in the third, interesting as the thought and influence of these men were, the scale of this outline will not permit us to treat.

§ 3

If Alexandria was late to develop a distinctive philoso-

Alexandria as a Factory of Religions. phy, she was early prominent as a great factory and exchange of religious ideas.

The Museum and Library represented only one of the three sides of the triple city of Alexandria. They represented the Aristotelian, the Hellenic, and Macedonian element. But Ptolemy I had brought together two other factors to this strange centre. First there were a great number of Jews, brought partly from Palestine, but largely also from those settlements in Egypt which had never returned to Jerusalem; these latter were the Jews of the Diaspora or Dispersion, a race of Jews who, as we have already noted in Chapter XXI, had not shared the Babylonian Captivity, but who were nevertheless in possession of the Bible and in close correspondence with their co-religionists throughout the world. These Jews populated so great a quarter of Alexandria that the town became the largest Jewish city in the world, with far more Jews in it than there were in Jerusalem. We have already noted that they had found it necessary to translate their scriptures into Greek. And, finally, there was a great population of native Egyptians, also for the most part speaking Greek, but with the superstitious temperament of the dark whites and with the vast tradition of forty centuries of temple religion and temple sacrifices at the back of their minds. In Alexandria three types of mind and spirit met, the three main types of the white race, the clear-headed criticism of the Aryan Greek, the moral fervour and monotheism of the Semitic Jew, and the deep Mediterranean tradition of mysteries and sacrifices that we have already seen at work in the secret cults and occult practices of Greece, ideas which in Hamitic Egypt ruled proudly in great temples in the open light of day.

These three were the permanent elements of the Alexandrian blend. But in the seaport and markets mingled men of every known race, comparing their religious ideas and customs. It is even related that in the third century B.C. Buddhist missionaries came from the court of King Asoka in India. Aristotle remarks in his *Politics* that the religious beliefs of men are apt to borrow their form from political institutions, " men assimilate the lives no less than the bodily forms of the gods to their own," and this age of Greek-speaking great empires under autocratic monarchs was bearing hardly upon those merely local celebrities, the old tribal and city deities. Men were requiring deities with an outlook at least as wide as the empires, and except where the interests of powerful priesthoods stood in the way, a curious process of assimilation of gods was going on. Men found that though there were many gods, they were all very much alike. Where there had been many gods, men came to think there must be really only one god under a diversity of names. He had been everywhere— under an alias. The Roman Jupiter, the Greek Zeus, the Egyptian Ammon, the putative father of Alexander and the old antagonist of Amenophis IV, the Babylonian Bel Marduk, were all sufficiently similar to be identified.

" Father of all in every age, in every clime adored
By saint, by savage and by sage, Jehovah, Jove or Lord."

Where there were distinct differences, the difficulty was met by saying that these were different *aspects* of the same god. Bel Marduk,

Photo: Mansell.
ISIS AND HORUS (XIXTH DYNASTY).

however, was now a very decadent god indeed, who hardly survived as a pseudonym ; Assur, Dagon, and the like, poor old gods of fallen nations, had long since passed out of memory, and did not come into the amalgamation. Osiris, a god popular with the Egyptian commonality, was already identified with Apis, the sacred bull in the temple of Memphis, and somewhat confused with Ammon. Under the name of Serapis he became the great god of Hellenic Alexandria. He was Jupiter-Serapis. The Egyptian cow goddess, Hathor or Isis, was also represented now in human guise as the wife of Osiris, to whom she bore the infant Horus, who grew up to be Osiris again. These bald statements sound strange, no doubt, to a modern mind, but these identifications and mixing up of one god with another are very illustrative of the struggle the quickening human intelligence was making to cling still to religion and its emotional bonds and fellowship, while making its gods more reasonable and universal.

This fusing of one god with another is called *theocrasia*, and nowhere was it more vigorously going on than in Alexandria. Only two peoples resisted it in this period: the Jews, who already had their faith in the One God of Heaven and Earth, Jehovah, and the Persians, who had a monotheistic sun worship.

It was Ptolemy I who set up not only the Museum in Alexandria, but the Serapeum, which was devoted to the worship of a trinity of gods, which represented the result of a process of theocrasia applied more particularly to the gods of Greece and Egypt.

This trinity consisted of the god Serapis (= Osiris + Apis), the goddess Isis (= Hathor, the cow-moon goddess), and the child-god Horus. In one way or another almost every other god was identified with one or other of these three aspects of the one God, even the sun god Mithras of the Persians. And they were each other; they were three, but they were also one. They were worshipped with great fervour, and the jangling of a peculiar instrument, the *sistrum*, a frame set with bells and used rather after the fashion of the tambourine in the proceedings of the modern Salvation Army, was a distinctive accessory to the ceremonies. And now for the first time we find the idea of immortality becoming the central idea of a religion that extended beyond Egypt. Neither the early Aryans nor the early Semites seem to have troubled very much about immortality, it has affected the Mongolian mind very little, but the continuation of the individual life after death had been from the earliest times an intense preoccupation of the Egyptians. It played now a large part in the worship of Serapis. In the devotional literature of his cult he is spoken of as " the saviour and leader of souls, leading souls to the light and receiving them again." It is stated that " he raises the dead, he shows forth the longed-for light of the sun to those who see, whose holy tombs contain multitudes of sacred books "; and again, " we never can escape him, he will save us, after death we shall still be the care of his providence." [1]

[1] Legge, *Forerunners and Rivals of Christianity.*

The ceremonial burning of candles and the offering of ex-votos, that is to say of small models of parts of the human body in need of succour, was a part of the worship of the Serapeum. Isis attracted many devotees, who vowed their lives to her. Her images stood in the temple, crowned as the Queen of Heaven and bearing the infant Horus in her arms. The candles flared and guttered before her, and the wax ex-votos hung about the shrine. The novice was put through a long and careful preparation, he took vows of celibacy, and when he was initiated his head was shaved and he was clad in a linen garment. . . .

In this worship of Serapis, which spread very widely throughout the civilized world in the third and second centuries B.C., we see the most remarkable anticipations of usages and forms of expression that were destined to dominate the European world throughout the Christian era. The essential idea, the living spirit, of Christianity was, as we shall presently show, a new thing in the history of the mind and will of man; but the garments of ritual and symbol and formula that Christianity has worn, and still in many countries wears to this day, were certainly woven in the cult and temples of Jupiter, Serapis, and Isis, that spread now from Alexandria throughout the civilized world in the age of theocrasia in the second and first centuries before Christ.

KING ASOKA.

From a Tibetan painted banner.

XXVI

THE RISE AND SPREAD OF BUDDHISM [1]

§ 1

IT is interesting to turn from the mental and moral activities of Athens and Alexandria, and the growth of human ideas in the Mediterranean world, to the almost entirely separate intellectual life of India. Here was a civilization which from the first seems to have grown up upon its own roots and with a character of its own. It was cut off from the civilizations to the west and the east by vast mountain barriers and desert regions. The Aryan tribes who had come down into the peninsula soon lost touch with their kindred to the west and north, and developed upon lines of their own. This was more particularly the case with those who had passed on into the Ganges country and beyond. They found a civilization already scattered over India, the Dravidian civilization. This had arisen independently, just as the Sumerian, Cretan, and Egyptian civilizations seem to have arisen, out of that widespread development of the neolithic culture, the heliolithic culture, whose characteristics we have already described. They revived and changed this Dravidian civilization much as the Greeks did the Ægean or the Semites the Sumerian.

The Story of Gautama.

These Indian Aryans were living under different conditions from those that prevailed to the north-west. They were living in a warmer climate, in which a diet of beef and fermented liquor was destructive; they were forced, therefore, to a generally vegetarian dietary, and the prolific soil, almost unasked, gave them all the food they needed. There was no further reason for them to wander; the crops and seasons were trustworthy. They wanted little clothing or housing. They wanted so little that trade was undeveloped. There was still land for every one who desired to cultivate a patch— and a little patch sufficed. Their political life was simple and comparatively secure; no great

conquering powers had arisen as yet in India, and her natural barriers sufficed to stop the early imperialisms of west and east. Thousands of comparatively pacific little village republics and chieftainships were spread over the land. There was no sea life, there were no pirate raiders, no strange traders. One might write a history of India coming down to four hundred years ago and hardly mention the sea.

The history of India for many centuries had been happier, less fierce, and more dreamlike than any other history. The noblemen, the rajahs, hunted; life was largely made up of love stories. Here and there a maharajah arose amidst the rajahs and built a city, caught and tamed many elephants, slew many tigers, and left a tradition of his splendour and his wonderful processions.

It was somewhen between 500 and 600 B.C., when Crœsus was flourishing in Lydia and Cyrus was preparing to snatch Babylon from Nabonidus, that the founder of Buddhism was born in India. He was born in a little republican tribal community in the north of Bengal under the Himalayas, in what is now overgrown jungle country on the borders of Nepal. The little state was ruled by a family, the Sakya clan, of which this man, Siddhattha Gautama, was a member. Siddhattha was his personal name, like Caius or John; Gautama, or Gôtama, his family name, like Cæsar or Smith; Sakya his clan name, like Julius. The institution of caste was not yet fully established in India, and the Brahmins, though they were privileged and influential, had not yet struggled to the head of the system; but there were already strongly marked class distinctions and a practically impermeable partition between the noble Aryans and the darker common people. Gautama belonged to the former race. His teaching, we may note, was called the Aryan Path, the Aryan Truth.

It is only within the last half-century that the increasing study of the Pali language, in which most of the original sources were written, has

---

[1] Rhys Davids' *Buddhism* and other writings by him have been our chief guide here.

17

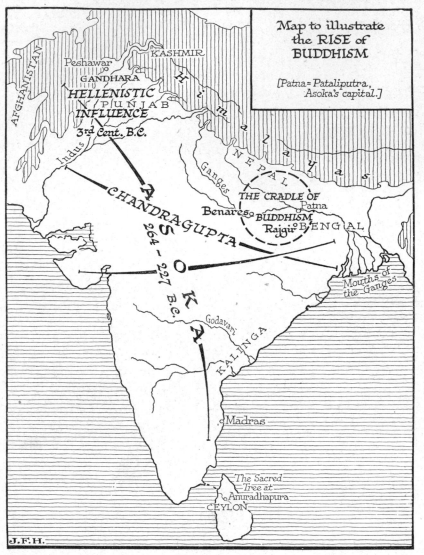

Map to illustrate the RISE of BUDDHISM

[Patna = Pataliputra, Asoka's capital.]

about a hundred miles away. The chief amusements were hunting and love-making. All the good that life seemed to offer, Gautama enjoyed. He was married at nineteen to a beautiful cousin. For some years they remained childless. He hunted and played and went about in his sunny world of gardens and groves and irrigated rice-fields. And it was amidst this life that a great discontent fell upon him. It was the unhappiness of a fine brain that seeks employment. He lived amidst plenty and beauty, he passed from gratification to gratification, and his soul was not satisfied. It is as if he heard the destinies of the race calling to him. He felt that the existence he was leading was not the reality of life, but a holiday—a holiday that had gone on too long.

While he was in this mood he saw four things that served to point his thoughts. He was driving on some excursion of pleasure, when he came upon a man dreadfully broken down by age. The poor bent, enfeebled creature struck his imagination. "Such is the way of life," said Channa, his charioteer, and "to that we must all come." While this was yet in his mind he chanced upon a man suffering horribly from some loathsome disease. "Such is the way of life," said Channa. The third vision was of an unburied body, swollen, eyeless, mauled by passing birds and beasts and altogether terrible. "That is the way of life," said Channa.

The sense of disease and mortality, the insecurity and the unsatisfactoriness of all

given the world a real knowledge of the life and actual thought of Gautama. Previously his story was overlaid by monstrous accumulations of legend, and his teaching violently misconceived. But now we have a very human and understandable account of him.

He was a goodlooking, capable young man of fortune, and until he was twenty-nine he lived the ordinary aristocratic life of his time. It was not a very satisfying life intellectually. There was no literature except the oral tradition of the Vedas, and that was chiefly monopolized by the Brahmins; there was even less knowledge. The world was bound by the snowy Himalayas to the north and spread indefinitely to the south. The city of Benares, which had a king, was

happiness, descended upon the mind of Gautama. And then he and Channa saw one of those wandering ascetics who already existed in great numbers in India. These men lived under severe rules, spending much time in meditation and in religious discussion. For many men before Gautama in that land of un-eventful sunshine had found life distressing and mysterious. These ascetics were all supposed to be seeking some deeper reality in life; and a passionate desire to do likewise took possession of Gautama.

He was meditating upon this project, says the sweetly, surrounded by flowers, with his infant son in her arm. He felt a great craving to take up the child in one first and last embrace before he departed, but the fear of waking his wife prevented him, and at last he turned away and went out into the bright Indian moonshine to Channa waiting with the horses, and mounted and stole away.

As he rode through the night with Channa, it seemed to him that Mara, the Tempter of Mankind, filled the sky and disputed with him. "Return," said Mara, "and be a king, and I will make you the greatest of kings. Go on,

Krishna   Kali, *as an impersonation of Vengeance*   Ganesa

HINDU DEITIES.

story, when the news was brought to him that his wife had been delivered of his first-born son. "This is another tie to break," said Gautama.

He returned to the village amidst the rejoicings of his fellow clansmen. There was a great feast and a Nautch dance to celebrate the birth of this new tie, and in the night Gautama awoke in a great agony of spirit, "like a man who is told that his house is on fire." In the ante-room the dancing girls were lying in strips of darkness and moonlight. He called Channa, and told him to prepare his horse. Then he went softly to the threshold of his wife's chamber, and saw her by the light of a little oil lamp, sleeping and you will fail. Never will I cease to dog your footsteps. Lust or malice or anger will betray you at last in some unwary moment; sooner or later you will be mine."

Very far they rode that night, and in the morning he stopped outside the lands of his clan, and dismounted beside a sandy river. There he cut off his flowing locks with his sword, removed all his ornaments, and sent them and his horse and sword back to his house by Channa. Then going on he presently met a ragged man and exchanged clothes with him, and so having divested himself of all worldly entanglements, he was free to pursue his search after wisdom. He made his way southward to a resort of hermits and teachers in a hilly spur running into Bengal northward from the Vindhya Mountains, close to the town of Rajgir. There a number of wise men lived in a warren of caves, going into the town for their simple supplies and imparting their knowledge by word of mouth to such as cared to come to them.

This instruction must have been very much in the style of the Socratic discussions that were going on in Athens a couple of centuries later. Gautama became versed in all the metaphysics of his age. But his acute intelligence was dissatisfied with the solutions offered him.

recovered, the preposterousness of these semi-magic ways of attempting wisdom was plain to him.

He amazed and horrified his five companions by demanding ordinary food and refusing to continue his self-mortifications. He had realized that whatever truth a man may reach is reached best by a nourished brain in a healthy body. Such a conception was absolutely foreign to the ideas of the land and age. His disciples deserted him, and went off in a melancholy state to Benares. The boom of the great bell ceased. Gautama the wonderful had fallen.

Vishnu   Brahma   Siva

HINDU DEITIES.

The Indian mind has always been disposed to believe that power and knowledge may be obtained by extreme asceticism, by fasting, sleeplessness, and self-torment, and these ideas Gautama now put to the test. He betook himself with five disciple companions to the jungle in a gorge in the Vindhya Mountains, and there he gave himself up to fasting and terrible penances. His fame spread, "like the sound of a great bell hung in the canopy of the skies." [1] But it brought him no sense of truth achieved. One day he was walking up and down, trying to think in spite of his enfeebled state. Suddenly he staggered and fell unconscious. When he

[1] The *Burmese Chronicle*, quoted by Rhys Davids.

For a time Gautama wandered alone, the loneliest figure in history, battling for light.

When the mind grapples with a great and intricate problem, it makes its advances, it secures its positions step by step, with but little realization of the gains it has made, until suddenly, with an effect of abrupt illumination, it realizes its victory. So it would seem it happened to Gautama. He had seated himself under a great tree by the side of a river to eat, when this sense of clear vision came to him. It seemed to him that he saw life plain. He is said to have sat all day and all night in profound thought, and then he rose up to impart his vision to the world.

§ 2

Such is the plain story of Gautama as we gather it from a comparison of early writings. But common men must have their cheap marvels and wonders. It is nothing to them that this little planet should at last produce upon its surface a man thinking of the past and the future and the essential nature of existence. And so we must have this sort of thing by some worthy Pali scribe, making the most of it :

Teaching and Legend in Conflict.

"When the conflict began between the Saviour of the World and the Prince of Evil a thousand appalling meteors fell. . . . Rivers flowed back towards their sources ; peaks of lofty mountains where countless trees had grown for ages rolled crumbling to the earth, . . . the sun enveloped itself in awful darkness, and a host of headless spirits filled the air." [1]

Of which phenomena history has preserved no authentication. Instead we have only the figure of a lonely man walking towards Benares.

Extraordinary attention has been given to the tree under which Gautama had this sense of mental clarity. It was a tree of the fig genus, and from the first it was treated with peculiar veneration. It was called the Bo Tree. It has long since perished, but close at hand lives another great tree which may be its descendant, and in Ceylon there grows to this day a tree, the oldest historical tree in the world, which we know certainly to have been planted as a cutting from the Bo Tree in the year 245 B.C. From that time to this it has been carefully tended and watered ; its great branches are supported by pillars, and the earth has been terraced up about it so that it has been able to put out fresh roots continually. It helps us to realize the shortness of all human history to see so many generations spanned by the endurance of one single tree. Gautama's disciples unhappily have cared more for the preservation of his tree than of his thought, which from the first they misconceived and distorted.

At Benares Gautama sought out his five pupils, who were still leading the ascetic life. There is an account of their hesitation to receive him when they saw him approaching. He was a backslider. But there was some power of personality in him that prevailed over their coldness, and he made them listen to his new convictions. For five days the discussion was carried on. When he had at last convinced them that he was now enlightened, they hailed him as the Buddha. There was already in those days a belief in India that at long intervals Wisdom returned to the earth and was revealed to mankind through a chosen person known as the Buddha. According to Indian belief there have been many such Buddhas ; Gautama Buddha is only the latest one of a series. But it is doubtful if he himself accepted that title or

Photo by courtesy of the Victoria and Albert Museum.

BUDDHA PREACHING HIS FIRST SERMON IN THE DEER-PARK AT SARNATH NEAR BENARES.

From a relief of (*circa*) the second century A.D.

[1] The *Madhurattha Vilasini*, quoted by Rhys Davids.

recognized that theory. In his discourses he never called himself the Buddha.

He and his recovered disciples then formed a sort of Academy in the Deer Park at Benares. They made themselves huts, and accumulated other followers to the number of threescore or more. In the rainy season they remained in discourse at this settlement, and during the dry weather they dispersed about the country, each giving his version of the new teachings. All their teaching was done, it would seem, by word

Photo: W. C. Fox.
THE DHAMER STUPA AT SARNATH (THE DEER-PARK) NEAR BENARES, A FAMOUS OBJECT OF PILGRIMAGE.

of mouth. There was probably no writing yet in India at all. We must remember that in the time of Buddha it is doubtful if even the Iliad had yet been committed to writing. Probably the Mediterranean alphabet, which is the basis of most Indian scripts, had not yet reached India. The master, therefore, worked out and composed pithy and brief verses, aphorisms, and lists of "points," and these were expanded in the discourse of his disciples. It greatly helped them to have these points and aphorisms numbered. The modern mind is apt to be impatient of the tendency of Indian thought to a numerical statement of things, the Eightfold Path, the Four Truths, and so on, but this enumeration was a mnemonic necessity in an undocumented world.

§ 3

The fundamental teaching of Gautama, as it is now being made plain to us by the study of original sources, is clear and simple and in the closest harmony with modern ideas. It is beyond all dispute the achievement of one of the most penetrating intelligences the world has ever known.

The Gospel of Gautama Buddha.

We have what are almost certainly the authentic heads of his discourse to the five disciples which embodies his essential doctrine. All the miseries and discontents of life he traces to insatiable selfishness. Suffering, he teaches, is due to the craving individuality, to the torment of greedy desire. Until a man has overcome every sort of personal craving his life is trouble and his end sorrow. There are three principal forms the craving of life takes, and all are evil. The first is the desire to gratify the senses, sensuousness. The second is the desire for personal immortality. The third is the desire for prosperity, worldliness. All these must be overcome—that is to say, a man must no longer be living for himself—before life can become serene. But when they are indeed overcome and no longer rule a man's life, when the first personal pronoun has vanished from his private thoughts, then he has reached the higher wisdom, Nirvana, serenity of soul. For Nirvana does not mean, as many people wrongly believe, extinction, but the extinction of the futile personal aims that necessarily make life base or pitiful or dreadful.

Now here, surely, we have the completest analysis of the problem of the soul's peace. Every religion that is worth the name, every philosophy, warns us to lose ourselves in something greater than ourselves. "Whosoever would save his life, shall lose it;" there is exactly the same lesson.

The teaching of history, as we are unfolding it in this book, is strictly in accordance with this teaching of Buddha. There is, as we are seeing, no social order, no security, no peace or happiness, no righteous leadership or kingship, unless men lose themselves in something greater than themselves. The study of biological progress again reveals exactly the same process—the merger of the narrow globe of the individual experience in a wider being (compare what has been said in Chaps. XII and XVIII). To forget oneself in greater interests is to escape from a prison.

The self-abnegation must be complete. From the point of view of Gautama, that dread of death, that greed for an endless continuation of his mean little individual life which drove the Egyptian and those who learnt from him with propitiations and charms into the temples, was of mankind as a great Brotherhood pursuing an endless destiny under the God of Righteousness, the idea that was already dawning upon the Semitic consciousness in Babylon at this time, did not exist in his world. Yet his account of the Eightfold Path is, nevertheless, wi hin these limitations, profoundly wise.

Let us briefly recapitulate the eight elements of the Aryan Path. First, Right Views ; Gautama placed the stern examination of views and

Photo: W. C. Fox.

TWO PILLARS OF THE EARLY BUDDHIST MONASTERY NOW BEING EXCAVATED AT SARNATH.

as mortal and ugly and evil a thing as lust or avarice or hate. The religion of Gautama is flatly opposite to the "immortality" religions. And his teaching is set like flint against asceticism, as a mere attempt to win personal power by personal pains.

But when we come to the rule of life, the Aryan Path, by which we are to escape from the three-fold base cravings that dishonour human life, then the teaching is not so clear. It is not so clear for one very manifest reason, Gautama had no knowledge nor vision of history ; he had no clear sense of the vast and many-sided adventure of life opening out in space and time. His mind was confined within the ideas of his age and people, and their minds were shaped into notions of perpetual recurrence, of world following world and of Buddha following Buddha, a stagnant circling of the universe. The idea ideas, the insistence upon *truth* as the first research of his followers. There was to be no clinging to tawdry superstitions. He condemned, for instance, the prevalent belief in the trans-migration of souls. In a well-known early Buddhist dialogue there is a destructive analysis of the idea of an enduring individual soul. Next to Right Views came Right Aspirations ; because nature abhors a vacuum, and since base cravings are to be expelled, other desires must be encouraged—love for the service of others, desire to do and secure justice and the like. Primitive and uncorrupted Buddhism aimed not at the destruction of desire, but at the change of desire. Devotion to science and art, or to the betterment of things manifestly falls into harmony with the Buddhistic Right Aspirations, provided such aims are free from jealousy or the craving for fame. Right Speech, Right

Conduct, and Right Livelihood, need no expansion here. Sixthly in this list came Right Effort, for Gautama had no toleration for good intentions and slovenly application ; the disciple had to keep a keenly critical eye upon his activities. The seventh element of the path, Right Mindfulness, is the constant guard against a lapse into personal feeling or glory for whatever is done or not done. And, finally, comes Right Rapture, which seems to be aimed against the pointless ecstacies of the devout, those witless gloryings, for instance, that went to the jingle of the Alexandrian sistrum.

We will not discuss here the Buddhistic doctrine of *Karma*, because it belongs to a world of thought that is passing away. The good or evil of every life was supposed to determine the happiness or misery of some subsequent life, that was in some inexplicable way identified with its predecessor. Nowadays we realize that a life goes on in its consequences for ever, but we find no necessity to suppose that any particular life resumes again. The Indian mind was full of the idea of cyclic recurrence ; everything was supposed to come round again. This is a very natural supposition for men to make ; so things seem to be until we analyse them. Modern science has made clear to us that there is no such exact recurrence as we are apt to suppose ; every day is by an infinitesimal quantity a little longer than the day before ; no generation repeats the previous generation precisely ; history never repeats itself ; change, we realize now, is inexhaustible ; all things are eternally new. But these differences between our general ideas and those Buddha must have possessed need not in any way prevent us from appreciating the unprecedented wisdom, the goodness, and the greatness of this plan of an emancipated life as Gautama laid it down somewhen in the sixth century before Christ.

And if he failed in theory to gather together all the wills of the converted into the one multifarious activity of our race battling against death and deadness in time and space, he did in practice direct his own life and that of all his immediate disciples into one progressive adventure, which was to preach and spread the doctrine and methods of Nirvana or soul-serenity throughout our fevered world. For them at least his teaching was complete and full. But all

men cannot preach or teach ; doctrine is but one of many of the functions of life that are fundamentally righteous. To the modern mind it seems at least equally acceptable that a man may, though perhaps against greater difficulties, cultivate the soil, rule a city, make roads, build houses, construct engines, or seek and spread knowledge, in perfect self-forgetfulness and serenity. As much was inherent in Gautama's teaching, but the stress was certainly laid upon the teaching itself, and upon withdrawal from rather than upon the ennoblement of the ordinary affairs of men.

In certain other respects this primitive Buddhism differed from any of the religions we have hitherto considered. It was primarily a religion of conduct, not a religion of observances and sacrifices. It had no temples, and since it had no sacrifices, it had no sacred order of priests. Nor had it any theology. It neither asserted nor denied the reality of the innumerable and often grotesque gods who were worshipped in India at that time. It passed them by.

§ 4

From the very first this new teaching was misconceived. One corruption was perhaps inherent in its teaching. Because the **Buddhism and Asoka.** world of men had as yet no sense of the continuous progressive effort of life, it was very easy to slip from the idea of renouncing self to the idea of renouncing active life. As Gautama's own experiences had shown, it is easier to flee from this world than from self. His early disciples were strenuous thinkers and teachers, but the lapse into mere monastic seclusion was a very easy one, particularly easy in the climate of India, where an extreme simplicity of living is convenient and attractive, and exertion more laborious than anywhere else in the world.

And it was early the fate of Gautama, as it has been the fate of most religious founders since his days, to be made into a wonder by his less intelligent disciples in their efforts to impress the outer world. We have already noted how one devout follower could not but believe that the moment of the master's mental irradiation must necessarily have been marked by an epileptic fit of the elements. This is but a sample of the vast accumulation of vulgar marvels

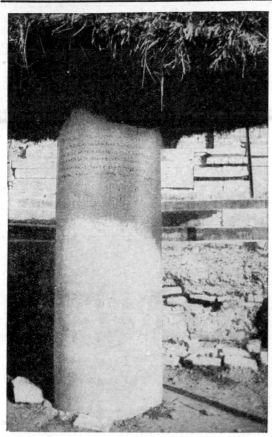

BASE OF THE ASOKA PILLAR, OF RED SANDSTONE, AT SARNATH, NEAR BENARES (NOTE THE INSCRIPTION).

ment with which the Brahminical teachers had already familiarized their minds. They represented Buddha as the saviour from almost unlimited torment.

There seems to be no limit to the lies that honest but stupid disciples will tell for the glory of their master and for what they regard as the success of their propaganda. Men who would scorn to tell a lie in everyday life will become unscrupulous cheats and liars when they have given themselves up to propagandist work ; it is one of the perplexing absurdities of our human nature. Such honest souls, for most of them were indubitably honest, were presently telling their hearers of the miracles that attended the Buddha's birth—they no longer called him Gautama, because that was too familiar a name —of his youthful feats of strength, of the marvels of his everyday life, winding up with a sort of illumination of his body at the moment of death.

ASOKA'S PILLAR, DELHI, THE OLDEST CAST-IRON PILLAR IN THE WORLD.

Asoka caused the Fourteen Edicts, or moral rules, to be engraved on certain pillars and rocks and set up for the instruction of his people.

that presently sprang up about the memory of Gautama.

There can be no doubt that for the great multitude of human beings then as now the mere idea of an emancipation from self is a very difficult one to grasp. It is probable that even among the teachers Buddha was sending out from Benares there were many who did not grasp it and still less were able to convey it to their hearers. Their teaching very naturally took on the aspect of salvation not from oneself—that idea was beyond them—but from misfortunes and sufferings here and hereafter. In the existing superstitions of the people, and especially in the idea of the transmigration of the soul after death, though this idea was contrary to the Master's own teaching, they found stuff of fear they could work upon. They urged virtue upon the people lest they should live again in degraded or miserable forms, or fall into some one of the innumerable hells of tor-

Of course it was impossible to believe that Buddha was the son of a mortal father. He was miraculously conceived through his mother dreaming of a beautiful white elephant! Previously he had himself been a marvellous elephant with six tusks; he had generously given them all to a needy hunter—and even helped him to saw them off. And so on.

Moreover, a theology grew up about Buddha. He was discovered to be a god. He was one of a series of divine beings, the Buddhas. There was an undying "Spirit of all the Buddhas"; there was a great series of Buddhas past and Buddhas (or Buddisatvas) yet to come. But we cannot go further into these complications of Asiatic theology. "Under the overpowering influence of these sickly imaginations the moral teachings of Gautama have been almost hid from view. The theories grew and flourished; each new step, each new hypothesis, demanded another; until the whole sky was filled with forgeries of the brain, and the nobler and simpler lessons of the founder of the religion were smothered beneath the glittering mass of metaphysical subtleties." [1]

In the third century B.C. Buddhism was gaining wealth and power, and the little groups of simple huts in which the teachers of the Order gathered in the rainy season were giving place to substantial monastic buildings. To this period belong the beginnings of Buddhistic art. Now if we remember how recent was the adventure of Alexander, that all the Punjab was still under Seleucid rule, that all India abounded with Greek adventurers, and that there was still quite open communication by sea and land with Alexandria, it is no great wonder to find that this early Buddhist art was strongly Greek in character, and that the new Alexandrian cult of Serapis and Isis was extraordinarily influential in its development.

The kingdom of Gandhara on the north-west frontier near Peshawar, which flourished in the third century B.C., was a typical meeting-place of the Hellenic and Indian worlds. Here are to be found the earliest Buddhist sculptures, and interwoven with them are figures which are recognizably the figures of Serapis and Isis and Horus already worked into the legendary net that gathered about Buddha. No doubt the

[1] Rhys Davids, *Buddhism*.

Greek artists who came to Gandhara were loth to relinquish a familiar theme. But Isis, we are told, is no longer Isis but Hariti, a pestilence goddess whom Buddha converted and made benevolent. So adapted, she seems to have travelled with Buddhist art, as Buddhism extended its range. In China there is a popular goddess Kwannon, that nice little madonna on a lotus whose image is familiar to every one who has ever looked into a shop window of imported Chinese goods.[2] She has been identi-

Reproduced by permission of M. Paul Geuthner from "The Beginnings of Buddhist Art," by A. Foucher.
INDO-GREEK IMAGE OF HARITI (IN GANDHARA).

fied with Isis, but that identification is questioned by several authorities. The Isis quality about her is very remarkable.

The precise route by which Buddhism acquired the same outward garments of worship as Christianity is difficult to determine. They may have been derived directly from the Isis cult or they may have reached eastern Asia centuries later by means of the Nestorian Christians. We read in Huc's Travels how perplexing he and his fellow missionary found this possession of a

[2] See Foucher, *Beginnings of Buddhist Art*, translated by L. A. and F. W. Thomas.

common tradition of worship. "The cross," he says, "the mitre, the dalmatica, the cope, which the Grand Lamas wear on their journeys, or when they are performing some ceremony out of the temple ; the service with double choirs, the psalmody, the exorcisms, the censer, suspended from five chains, which you can open or close at pleasure ; the benedictions given by the Lamas by extending the

Reproduced by permission of M. Paul Geuthner from " The Beginnings of Buddhist Art," by A. Foucher.
CHINESE IMAGE OF KWANNON.

right hand over the heads of the faithful ; the chaplet, ecclesiastical celibacy, spiritual retirement, the worship of the saints, the fasts, the processions, the litanies, the holy water, all these are analogies between the Buddhists and ourselves." [1]

The cult and doctrine of Gautama, gathering corruptions and variations from Brahminism

[1] Huc's *Travels in Tartary, Tibet, and China.*

and Hellenism alike, was spread throughout India by an increasing multitude of teachers in the fourth and third centuries B.C. For some generations at least it retained much of the moral beauty and something of the simplicity of the opening phase. Many people who have no intellectual grasp upon the meaning of self-abnegation and disinterestedness have nevertheless the ability to appreciate a splendour in the reality of these qualities. Early Buddhism was certainly producing noble lives, and it is not only through reason that the latent response to nobility is aroused in our minds. It spread rather in spite of than because of the concessions that it made to vulgar imaginations. It spread because many of the early Buddhists were sweet and gentle, helpful and noble and admirable people, who compelled belief in their sustaining faith.

Quite early in its career Buddhism came into conflict with the growing pretensions of the Brahmins. As we have already noted, this priestly caste was still only struggling to dominate Indian life in the days of Gautama. They had already great advantages. They had the monopoly of tradition and religious sacrifices. But their power was being challenged by the development of kingship, for the men who became clan-leaders and kings were usually not of the Brahminical caste.

Kingship received an impetus from the Persian and Greek invasions of the Punjab. We have already noted the name of King Porus whom, in spite of his elephants, Alexander defeated and turned into a satrap. There came also to the Greek camp upon the Indus a certain low-caste [2] adventurer named Chandragupta Maurya, whom the Greeks called Sandracottus, with a scheme for conquering the Ganges country. The scheme was not welcome to the Macedonians, who were in revolt against marching any further into India, and he had to fly the camp. He wandered among the tribes upon the north-west frontier, secured their support, and after Alexander had departed, overran the Punjab, ousting the Macedonian representatives. He then conquered the Ganges country (321 B.C.), waged a successful war (303 B.C.) against Seleucus (Seleucus I) when the latter attempted to re-

[2] Rhys Davids. He was the son of a king by a low-caste mother.

cover the Punjab, and consolidated a great empire reaching across all the plain of northern India from the western to the eastern sea. And this King Chandragupta came into much the same conflict with the growing power of the Brahmins, into the conflict between crown and priesthood, that we have already noted as happening in Babylonia and Egypt and China. He saw in the spreading doctrine of Buddhism an ally against the growth of priestcraft and caste. He supported and endowed the Buddhistic Order, and encouraged its teachings.

ANURADHAPURA, THE SACRED BO TREE. FIRST FLIGHT OF STEPS ON THE NORTH FACE, LEADING TO THE FIRST TERRACE.

peace and with great ability. He was no mere religious fanatic. But in the year of his one and only war he joined the Buddhist community as a layman, and some years later he became a full member of the Order, and devoted himself to the attainment of Nirvana by the Eightfold Path. How entirely compatible that way of living then was with the most useful and beneficent activities his life shows. Right Aspiration, Right Effort, and Right Livelihood distinguished his

He was succeeded by his son, who conquered Madras and was in turn succeeded by Asoka (264 to 227 B.C.), one of the great monarchs of history, whose dominions extended from Afghanistan to Madras. He is the only military monarch on record who abandoned warfare after victory. He had invaded Kalinga (255 B.C.), a country along the east coast of Madras, perhaps with some intention of completing the conquest of the tip of the Indian peninsula. The expedition was successful, but he was disgusted by what he saw of the cruelties and horrors of war. He declared, in certain inscriptions that still exist, that he would no longer seek conquest by war, but by religion, and the rest of his life was devoted to the spreading of Buddhism throughout the world.

He seems to have ruled his vast empire in career. He organized a great digging of wells in India, and the planting of trees for shade. He appointed officers for the supervision of charitable works. He founded hospitals and public gardens. He had gardens made for the growing of medicinal herbs. Had he had an Aristotle to inspire him, he would no doubt have endowed scientific research upon a great scale. He created a ministry for the care of the aborigines and subject races. He made provision for the education of women. He made, he was the first monarch to make, an attempt to educate his people into a common view of the ends and way of life. He made vast benefactions to the Buddhist teaching orders, and tried to stimulate them to a better study of their own literature. All over the land he set up long inscriptions rehearsing the teaching of Gautama, and it is the simple and human teaching and not the preposterous accretions.

Thirty-five of his inscriptions survive to this day. Moreover, he sent missionaries to spread the noble and reasonable teaching of his master throughout the world, to Kashmir, to Ceylon, to the Seleucids, and the Ptolemies. It was one of these missions which carried that cutting of the Bo Tree, of which we have already told, to Ceylon.

For eight and twenty years Asoka worked sanely for the real needs of men. Amidst the tens of thousands of names of monarchs that crowd the columns of history, their majesties and graciousnesses and serenities and royal highnesses and the like, the name of Asoka shines, and shines almost alone, a star. From the Volga to Japan his name is still honoured. China, Tibet, and even India, though it has left his doctrine, preserve the tradition of his greatness. More living men cherish his memory to-day than have ever heard the names of Constantine or Charlemagne.

§ 5

Two Great Chinese Teachers. It is thought that the vast benefactions of Asoka finally corrupted Buddhism by attracting to its Order great numbers of mercenary and insincere adherents, but there can be no doubt that its rapid extension throughout Asia was very largely due to his stimulus.

It made its way into Central Asia through Afghanistan and Turkestan, and so reached China. "Buddhist writings were circulated far and wide"[1] before 200 B.C. Buddhism found in China another very similar religion of conduct, Taoism, founded by a certain Lao Tse, who had been a contemporary of Gautama's. Tao means the Way, which corresponds closely with the idea of the Aryan Path. The two religions spread side by side and underwent similar changes, so that nowadays their outward practice is very similar. It also encountered Confucianism, which was even less theological and even more a code of personal conduct.

Confucius, the founder of Confucianism, like Lao Tse (whom he met and admired) and Gautama, lived also in the sixth century B.C. His life has some interesting parallelisms with that of some of the more political of the Greek philosophers of the fifth and fourth. The sixth century B.C. falls into the period assigned by Chinese historians to the Chow Dynasty, but in those days the rule of that dynasty had become little more than nominal; the emperor conducted the traditional sacrifices of the Son of Heaven, and received a certain formal respect. Even his nominal empire was not a sixth part

Photo by courtesy of the Victoria and Albert Museum.

GAUTAMA BUDDHA, AS A BODHISATTVA, ATTENDED BY HIS DISCIPLES MAUDGALYAYANA AND SARIPUTRA.

Panel of grey stone (granulite) found amongst the debris round the Mahabodhi Temple at Bodh-Gaya, Bengal. Period, sixth century A.D.

[1] A Chinese writer quoted in the *Encyclopædia Britannica.*

of the China of to-day. In Chapter XVI we have already glanced at the state of affairs in China at this time; practically China was a multitude of warring states open to the northern barbarians. Confucius was a subject in one of those states, Lu; he was of aristocratic birth, but poor; and, after occupying various official positions, he set up a sort of Academy in Lu for the discovery and imparting of Wisdom. And we also find Confucius travelling from state to state in China, seeking a prince who would make him his counsellor and become the centre of a reformed world. Plato, two centuries later, in exactly the same spirit, went as advisor to the tyrant Dionysius of Syracuse, and we have already noted the attitudes of Aristotle and Isocrates towards Philip of Macedonia.

The teaching of Confucius centred upon the idea of a noble life which he embodied in a standard or ideal, the Aristocratic Man. This phrase is often translated into English as the Superior Person, but as "superior" and "person," like "respectable" and "genteel," have long become semi-humorous terms of abuse, this rendering is not fair to Confucianism. He did present to his time the ideal of a very fine and devoted public man. The public side was very important to him. He was far more of a political thinker than Gautama or Lao Tse. His mind was full of the condition of China, and he sought to call the Aristocratic Man into existence very largely in order to produce the noble state. One of his sayings may be quoted here: "It is impossible to withdraw from the world, and associate with birds and beasts that have no affinity with us. With whom should I associate but with suffering men? The disorder that prevails is what requires my efforts. If right principles ruled through the kingdom, there would be no necessity for me to change its state."

The political basis of his teaching seems to be characteristic of Chinese moral ideas; there is a much directer reference to the State than is the case with most Indian and European moral and religious doctrine. For a time he was appointed magistrate in Chung-tu, a city of the dukedom of Lu, and here he sought to regulate life to an extraordinary extent, to subdue every relationship and action indeed to the rule of an elaborate etiquette. "Cere-

monial in every detail, such as we are wont to see only in the courts of rulers and the households of high dignitaries, became obligatory on the people at large, and all matters of daily life were subject to rigid rule. Even the food which the different classes of people might eat was regulated; males and females were kept apart in the streets; even the thickness of coffins and the shape and situation of graves were made the subject of regulations.[1]

This is all, as people say, very Chinese. No other people have ever approached moral order and social stability through the channel of manners. Yet in China, at any rate, the methods of Confucius have had an enormous effect, and no nation in the world to-day has such a universal tradition of decorum and self-restraint.

Later on the influence of Confucius over his duke was undermined, and he withdrew again into private life. His last days were saddened by the deaths of some of his most promising disciples. "No intelligent ruler," he said, "arises to take me as his master, and my time has come to die." . . .

But he died to live. Says Hirth, "There can be no doubt that Confucius has had a greater influence on the development of the Chinese national character than many emperors taken together. He is, therefore, one of the essential figures to be considered in connection with any history of China. That he could influence his nation to such a degree was, it appears to me, due more to the peculiarity of the nation than to that of his own personality. Had he lived in any other part of the world, his name would perhaps be forgotten. As we have seen, he had formed his character and his personal views on man's life from a careful study of documents closely connected with the moral philosophy cultivated by former generations. What he preached to his contemporaries was, therefore, not all new to them; but, having himself, in the study of old records, heard the dim voice of the sages of the past, he became, as it were, the megaphone phonograph through which were expressed to the nation those views which he had derived from the early development of the nation itself. . . . The great influence of Confucius's personality on national life in China was due not only to his writings and his teachings as

[1] Hirth's *The Ancient History of China.*

recorded by others, but also to his doings. His personal character, as described by his disciples and in the accounts of later writers, some of which may be entirely legendary, has become the pattern for millions of those who are bent on imitating the outward manners of a great man. . . . Whatever he did in public was regulated to the minutest detail by ceremony. This was no invention of his own, since ceremonial life had been cultivated many centuries before Confucius; but his authority and example did much to perpetuate what he considered desirable social practices."

The Chinese speak of Buddhism and the doctrines of Lao Tse and Confucius as the Three Teachings. Together they constitute the basis and point of departure of all later Chinese thought. Their thorough study is a necessary preliminary to the establishment of any real intellectual and moral community between the great people of the East and the Western world.

There are certain things to be remarked in common of all these three teachers, of whom Gautama was indisputably the greatest and profoundest, whose doctrines to this day dominate the thought of the great majority of human beings; there are certain features in which their teaching contrasts with the thoughts and feelings that were soon to take possession of the western world. Primarily they are personal and tolerant doctrines; they are doctrines of a Way, of a Path, of a Nobility, and not doctrines of a church or a general rule. And they offer nothing either for or against the existence and worship of the current gods. The Athenian philosophers, it is to be noted, had just the same theological detachment; Socrates was quite willing to bow politely or sacrifice formally to almost any divinity,—reserving his private thoughts. This attitude is flatly antagonistic to the state of mind that was growing up in the Jewish communities of Judea, Egypt, and Babylonia, in which the thought of the one God was first and foremost. Neither Gautama nor Lao Tse nor Confucius had any inkling of this idea of a *jealous* God, a God who would have " none other gods," a God of terrible Truth, who would not tolerate any lurking belief in magic, witchcraft, or old customs, or any sacrificing to the god-king or any trifling with the stern unity of things.

§ 6

The intolerance of the Jewish mind did keep its essential faith clear and clean. The theological disregard of the great Eastern teachers, neither assenting nor denying, did on the other hand permit elaborations of explanation and accumulations of ritual from the very beginning. Except for Gautama's insistence upon Right Views, which was easily disregarded, there was no *self-cleansing* element in either Buddhism, Taoism, or Confucianism. There was no effective prohibition of superstitious practices, spirit raising,

The Corruptions of Buddhism.

Photo by courtesy of the Victoria and Albert Museum.
SCENES FROM THE LEGENDARY LIFE OF BUDDHA.
From a carving of the third century A.D.

incantations, prostrations, and supplementary worships. At an early stage a process of encrustation began, and continued. The new faiths caught almost every disease of the corrupt religions they sought to replace; they took over the idols and the temples, the altars and the censers.

Tibet to-day is a Buddhistic country, yet Gautama, could he return to earth, might go from end to end of Tibet seeking his own teaching in vain. He would find that most ancient type of human ruler, a god king, enthroned, the Dalai Lama, the " living Buddha." At Lhassa he would find a huge temple filled with priests, abbots, and lamas—he whose only buildings were huts and who made no priests —and above a high altar he would behold a huge golden idol, which he would learn was called "Gautama Buddha!" He would hear services intoned before this divinity, and certain precepts, which would be dimly familiar to him, murmured as responses. Bells, incense, prostrations, would play their part in these amazing proceedings. At one point in the service a bell would be rung and a mirror lifted up, while the whole congregation, in an access of reverence, bowed lower. . . .

About this Buddhist countryside he would discover a number of curious little mechanisms, little wind-wheels and water-wheels spinning, on which brief prayers were inscribed. Every time these things spin, he would learn, it counts as a prayer. "To whom?" he would ask. Moreover, there would be a number of flagstaffs in the land carrying beautiful silk flags, silk flags which bore the perplexing inscription, "Om Mani padme hum," "the jewel is in the lotus." Whenever the flag flaps, he would learn, it was a prayer also, very beneficial to the gentleman who paid for the flag and to the land generally. Gangs of workmen, employed by pious persons, would be going about the country cutting this precious formula on cliff and stone. And this, he would realize at last, was what the world had made of his religion! Beneath this gaudy glitter was buried the Aryan Way to serenity of soul.[1]

[1] See Huc's *Travels in Tartary, Thibet, and China.*

We have already noted the want of any progressive idea in primitive Buddhism. In that again it contrasted with Judaism. The idea of a Promise gave to Judaism a quality no previous or contemporary religion displayed; it made Judaism historical and dramatic. It justified its fierce intolerance because it pointed to an aim. In spite of the truth and profundity of the psychological side of Gautama's teaching, Buddhism stagnated and corrupted for the lack of that directive idea. Judaism, it must be confessed, in its earlier phases, entered but little into the souls of men; it let them remain lustful, avaricious, worldly or superstitious; but because of its persuasion of a promise and of a divine leadership to serve divine ends, it remained in comparison with Buddhism bright and expectant, like a cared-for sword.

§ 7

For some time Buddhism flourished in India. But Brahminism, with its many gods and its **The Present Range of Buddhism.** endless variety of cults, always flourished by its side, and the organization of the Brahmins grew more powerful, until at last they were able to turn upon this caste-denying cult and oust it from India altogether. The story of that struggle is not to be told here; there were persecutions and reactions, but by the eleventh century, except for Orissa, Buddhist teaching was extinct in India. Much of its gentleness and charity had, however, become incorporated with Brahminism.

Over great areas of the world, as our map has shown, it still survives; and it is quite possible that in contact with western science, and inspired by the spirit of history, the original teaching of Gautama, revived and purified, may yet play a large part in the direction of human destiny.

But with the loss of

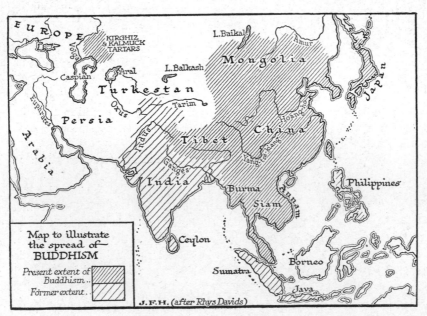

Map to illustrate the spread of BUDDHISM

Present extent of Buddhism..

Former extent..

J.F.H. (after Rhys Davids)

EIGHTEENTH-CENTURY TIBETAN TEMPLE PICTURE OF BUDDHA ENTHRONED.

(Note that the picture has been injured and the face of Buddha distorted.)

India the Aryan Way ceased to rule the lives of any Aryan peoples. It is curious to note that while the one great Aryan religion is now almost exclusively confined to Mongolian peoples, the Aryans themselves are under the sway of two religions, Christianity and Islam, which are, as we shall see, essentially Semitic. And both Buddhism and Christianity wear garments of ritual and formula that seem to be derived through Hellenistic channels from that land of temples and priestcraft, Egypt, and from the mentality of the brown Hamitic peoples.

Book V

THE RISE AND COLLAPSE OF THE ROMAN EMPIRE

XXVII

THE TWO WESTERN REPUBLICS[1]

§ 1

The Beginnings of the Latins. IT is now necessary to take up the history of the two great republics of the Western Mediterranean, Rome and Carthage, and to tell how Rome succeeded in maintaining for some centuries an empire even greater than that achieved by the conquests of Alexander. But this new empire was, as we shall try to make clear, a political structure differing very profoundly in its nature from any of the great Oriental empires that had preceded it. Great changes in the texture of human society and in the conditions of social interrelations had been going on for some centuries. The flexibility and transferability of money was becoming a power and, like all powers in inexpert hands, a danger in human affairs. It was altering the relations of rich men to the state and to their poorer fellow citizens. This new

empire, the Roman empire, unlike all the preceding empires, was not the creation of a great conqueror. No Sargon, no Thotmes, no Nebuchadnezzar, no Cyrus nor Alexander nor Chandragupta, was its fountain head. It was made by a republic. It grew by a kind of necessity through new concentrating and unifying forces that were steadily gathering power in human affairs.

But first it is necessary to give some idea of the state of affairs in Italy in the centuries im-

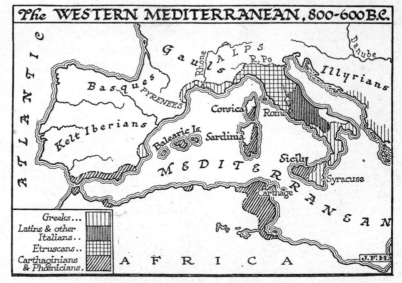

[1] A very convenient handbook for this and the next two chapters is Matheson's *Skeleton Outline of Roman History*.

mediately preceding the appearance of Rome in the world's story.

Before 1,200 B.C., that is to say before the rise of the Assyrian empire, the siege of Troy, and the final destruction of Cnossos, but after the time of Amenophis IV, Italy, like Spain, was probably still inhabited mainly by dark white people of the more fundamental Iberian or Mediterranean race.[1] This aboriginal population was probably a thin and backward one. But already in Italy, as in Greece, the Aryans were coming southward. By 1,000 B.C. immigrants from the north had settled over most of the north and centre of Italy, and, as in Greece, they had intermarried with their darker predecessors and established a group of Aryan languages, the Italian group, more akin to the Keltic (Gaelic)[2] than to any other, of which the most interesting from the historical point of view was that spoken by the Latin tribes in the plains south and east of the river Tiber. Meanwhile the Greeks had been settling down in Greece, and now they were taking to the sea and crossing over to South Italy and Sicily and establishing themselves there. Subsequently they established colonies along the French Riviera and founded Marseilles upon the site of an older Phœnician colony. Meanwhile another people also had come into Italy by sea. These were a brownish sturdy people, to judge from the pictures they have left of themselves; very probably they were a tribe of those Ægean "dark whites" who were being driven out of Greece and Asia Minor and the islands in between by the Greeks. We have already told the tale of Cnossos (Chapter XVII) and of the settlement of the kindred Philistines in Palestine (Chapter XXI, §1). These Etruscans, as they were called in Italy, were known even in ancient times to be of Asiatic origin, and it is tempting, but probably unjustifiable, to connect this tradition with the Æneid, the sham epic of the Latin poet Virgil, in which the Latin civilization is ascribed to Trojan immigrants from Asia Minor. (But the Trojans themselves were probably an Aryan people allied to the Phrygians.) These Etruscan people conquered most of Italy north

of the Tiber from the Aryan tribes who were scattered over that country. Probably the Etruscans ruled over a subjugated Italian population, so reversing the state of affairs in Greece, in which the Aryans were uppermost.

Our map, which may be taken to represent roughly the state of affairs about 750 B.C., also shows the establishments of the Phœnician traders, of which Carthage was the chief, along the shores of Africa and Spain.

Of all the peoples actually in Italy, the Etruscans were by far the most civilized. They built sturdy fortresses of the Mycænean type of architecture; they had a metal industry; they used imported Greek pottery of a very fine type. The Latin tribes on the other side of the Tiber were by comparison barbaric.

The Latins were still a rude farming people. The centre of their worship was a temple to the tribal god Jupiter, upon the Alban Mount. There they gathered for their chief festivals very much after the fashion of the early tribal gathering we have already imagined at Avebury (Chapter XII). This gathering-place was not a town. It was a high place of assembly. There was no population permanently there. There were, however, twelve townships in the Latin league. At one point upon the Tiber there was a ford, and here there was a trade between Latins and Etruscans. At this ford Rome had its beginnings. Traders assembled there, and refugees from the twelve towns found an asylum and occupation at this trading centre. Upon the seven hills near the ford a number of settlements sprang up, which finally amalgamated into one city.

Most people have heard the story of the two brothers Romulus and Remus, who founded Rome, and the legend of how they were exposed as infants and sheltered and suckled by a wolf. Little value is now attached to this tale by modern historians, but the wolf serves to remind us that Italy was not then the smiling land of vine and olive it has since become. It was still a rough country of marsh and forest, in which the farmers grazed their cattle and made their clearings. Rome, on the very boundary of Latin and Etruscan, was not in a very strong position for defence. At first there were perhaps Latin kings in Rome, then it would seem the city fell into the hands of

[1] For Italian pre-history see Modestov's *Introduction à l'histoire Romaine*, and Peet's *Stone and Bronze Age in Italy and Sicily*.

[2] See Lloyd's *Making of the Roman People*.

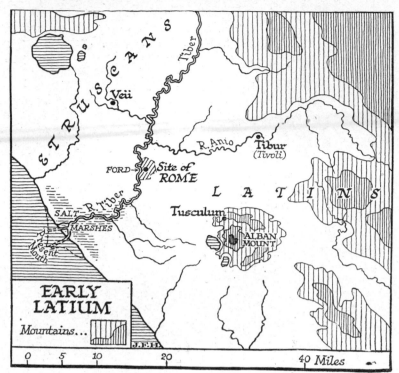

EARLY
LATIUM

Mountains...

0   5   10   20   40 Miles

disasters happened to the Etruscans which so weakened them that the Romans were able at last to master them altogether. The first of these was a war with the Greeks of Syracuse in Sicily which destroyed the Etruscan fleet (474 B.C.), and the second was a great raid of the Gauls from the north into Italy. These latter people swarmed into North Italy and occupied the valley of the Po towards the end of the fifth century B.C., as a couple of centuries later their kindred were to swarm down into Greece and Asia Minor and settle in Galatia. The Etruscans were thus caught between hammer and anvil, and after a long and intermittent war the Romans

Etruscan rulers whose tyrannous conduct led at last to their expulsion, and Rome became a Latin-speaking republic. The Etruscan kings were expelled from Rome in the sixth century B.C., while the successors of Nebuchadnezzar were ruling by the suffrance of the Medes in Babylon, while Confucius was seeking a king to reform the disorders of China, and while Gautama was teaching the Aryan Way to his disciples at Benares.

Of the struggle between the Romans and the Etruscans we cannot tell in any detail here. The Etruscans were the better armed, the more civilized, and the more numerous, and it would probably have gone hard with the Romans if they had had to fight them alone. But two

were able to capture Veii, an Etruscan fortress, a few miles from Rome, which had hitherto been a great threat and annoyance to them.

It is to this period of struggle against the Etruscan monarchs, the Tarquins, that Macaulay's *Lays of Ancient Rome*, familiar to every schoolboy, refer.

Photo: Anderson.

THE CAPITOLINE WOLF.

Photo: Mansell.

ETRUSCAN HELMET, WITH INSCRIBED DEDICATION BY
HIERO OF SYRACUSE, AFTER HIS NAVAL VICTORY,
474 B.C.

But the invasion of the Gauls was one of those
convulsions of the nations that leave nothing
as it has been before. They carried their raiding right down the Italian peninsula, devasting
all Etruria. They took and sacked Rome
(390 B.C.). According to Roman legends—
on which doubt is thrown—the citadel on the
Capitol held out, and this also the Gauls would
have taken by surprise at night, if certain geese
had not been awakened by their stealthy movements and set up such a cackling as to arouse
the garrison. After that the Gauls, who were
ill-equipped for siege operations, and perhaps
suffering from disease in their camp, were
bought off, and departed to the northward
again, and, though they made subsequent raids,
they never again reached Rome.

The leader of the Gauls who sacked Rome was
named Brennus. It is related of him that as the
gold of the ransom was being weighed, there was
some dispute about the justice of the counter-
poise, whereupon he flung his sword into the
scale, saying, *" Væ victis !"* (" Woe to the
vanquished !")—a phrase that has haunted the
discussions of all subsequent ransoms and
indemnities down to the present time.

For half a century after this experience Rome
was engaged in a series of wars to establish
herself at the head of the Latin tribes. For the
burning of the chief city seems to have stimulated rather than crippled her energies. How-

ever much she had suffered, most of her neighbours seem to have suffered more. By 290 B.C.
Rome was the mistress city of all Central Italy
from the Arno to south of Naples. She had
conquered the Etruscans altogether, and her
boundaries marched with those of the Gauls
to the north and with the regions of Italy under
Greek dominion (Magna Græcia) to the south.
Along the Gaulish boundary she had planted
garrisons and colonial cities, and no doubt it
was because of that line of defence that the raiding enterprises of the Gauls were deflected
eastward into the Balkans.

After what we have already told of the history
of Greece and the constitutions of her cities,
it will not surprise the reader to learn that the
Greeks of Sicily and Italy were divided up into
a number of separate city governments, of which
Syracuse and Tarentum (the modern Taranto)
were the chief, and that they had no common
rule of direction or policy. But now, alarmed
at the spread of the Roman power, they looked
across the Adriatic for help, and found it in the
ambitions of Pyrrhus, the king of Epirus. Between the Romans and Pyrrhus these Greeks
of Magna Græcia were very much in the same
position that Greece proper had been in, between the Macedonians and the Persians half a
century before.

Photo: Mansell.

PRIMITIVE ETRUSCAN STATUETTE (PROBABLY FROM
SARDINIA).

ETRUSCAN SARCOPHAGUS IN TERRA-COTTA.
From the British Museum.

Photo: Mansell.

The reader will remember that Epirus, the part of Greece that is closest to the heel of Italy, was the native land of Olympias, the mother of Alexander. In the kaleidoscopic changes of the map that followed the death of Alexander, Epirus was sometimes swamped by Macedonia, sometimes independent. This Pyrrhus was a kinsman of Alexander the Great, and a monarch of ability and enterprise, and he seems to have planned a career of conquest in Italy and Sicily. He commanded an admirable army, against which the comparatively inexpert Roman levies could at first do little. His army included all the established military devices of the time, an infantry phalanx, Thessalian cavalry, and twenty fighting elephants from the east. He routed the Romans at Heraclea (280 B.C.), and, pressing after them, defeated them again at Ausculum (279 B.C.) in their own territory. Then, instead of pursuing the Romans further, he made a truce with them, turned his attention to the subjugation of Sicily, and so brought the sea power of Carthage into alliance against him. For Carthage could not afford to have a strong power established so close to her as Sicily. Rome in those days seemed to the Carthaginians a far less serious threat than the possibility of another Alexander the Great ruling Sicily. A Carthaginian fleet appeared off the mouth of the Tiber, therefore, to encourage or induce the Romans to renew the struggle, and Rome and Carthage were definitely allied against the invader.

This interposition of Carthage was fatal to Pyrrhus. Without any decisive battle his power wilted, and, after a disastrous repulse in an attack upon the Roman camp of Beneventum, he had to retire to Epirus (275 B.C.).

It is recorded that when Pyrrhus left Sicily, he said he left it to be the battleground of Rome and Carthage. He was killed three years later in a battle in the streets of Argos. The war against Pyrrhus was won by the Carthaginian fleet, and Rome reaped a full half of the harvest of victory. Sicily fell completely to Carthage, and Rome came down to the toe and heel of Italy, and looked across the Straits of Messina at her new rival. In eleven years' time (264

Samnite warriors .... (from painted vases.)

B.C.) the prophecy of Pyrrhus was fulfilled, and the first war with Carthage, the first of the three Punic[1] Wars, had begun.

§ 2[2]

But we write " Rome " and the " Romans," and we have still to explain what manner of

A New Sort of State.

people these were who were playing a rôle of conquest that had hitherto been played only by able and aggressive monarchs.

Their state was, in the fifth century B.C., a republic of the Aryan type very similar to a Greek aristocratic republic. The earliest accounts of the social life of Rome give us a picture of a very primitive Aryan community. " In the second half of the fifth century before Christ, Rome was still an aristocratic community of free peasants, occupying an area of nearly 400 square miles, with a population certainly not exceeding 150,000, almost entirely

[1] Latin *Pœni* = Carthaginians. *Punicus (adj.)* = Carthaginian, *i.e.* Phœnician.

[2] See Pelham, *Outlines of Roman History*; Mommsen, *History of Rome*; and the histories of the Roman Empire by Bury, H. Stuart Jones, and W. E. Heitland.

dispersed over the country-side and divided into seventeen districts or rural tribes. Most of the families had a small holding and a cottage of their own, where father and sons lived and worked together, growing corn for the most part, with here and there a strip of vine or olive. Their few head of cattle were kept at pasture on the neighbouring common land ; their clothes and simple implements of husbandry they made for themselves at home. Only at rare intervals and on special occasions would they make their way into the fortified town, which was the centre at once of their religion and their government. Here were the temples of the gods, the houses of the wealthy, and the shops of the artizans and traders, where corn, oil, or wine could be bartered in small quantities for salt or rough tools and weapons of iron. "[3]

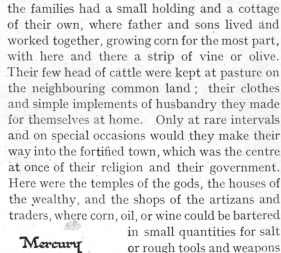

Mercury
The plebeian god of commerce.

[From a Roman bronze.]

This community followed the usual tradition of a division into aristocratic and common citizens, who were called in Rome patricians and plebeians. These were the citizens; the slave or outlander had no more part in the state than he had in Greece. But the constitution differed from any

[3] Ferrero, *The Greatness and Decline of Rome.*

Greek constitution in the fact that a great part of the ruling power was gathered into the hands of a body called the Senate, which was neither purely a body of hereditary members nor directly an elected and representative one. It was a nominated one, and in the earlier period it was nominated solely from among the patricians. It existed before the expulsion of the kings, and in the time of the kings it was the king who nominated the senators. But after the expulsion of the kings (510 B.C.), the supreme government was vested in the hands of two elected rulers, the *consuls*; and it was the consuls who took over the business of appointing senators. In the early days of the Republic only patricians were eligible as consuls or senators, and the share of the plebeians in the government consisted merely in a right to vote for the consuls and other public officials. Even for that purpose their votes did not have the same value as those of their patrician fellow citizens. But their votes had at any rate sufficient weight to induce many of the patrician candidates to profess a more or less sincere concern for plebeian grievances. In the early phases of the Roman state, moreover, the plebeians were not only excluded from public office, but from intermarriage with the patrician class. The administration was evidently primarily a patrician affair.

The early phase of Roman affairs was therefore an aristocracy of a very pronounced type, and the internal history of Rome for the two centuries and a half between the expulsion of the last Etruscan king, Tarquin the Proud, and the beginning of the first Punic War (264 B.C.), was very largely a struggle for mastery between those two orders, the patricians and the plebeians. It was, in fact, closely parallel with the struggle of aristocracy and democracy in the city states of Greece, and, as in the case of Greece, there were whole classes in the community, slaves, freed slaves, unpropertied free men, outlanders, and the like, who were entirely outside and beneath the struggle. We have

already noted the esential difference of Greek democracy and what is called democracy in the world to-day. Another misused word is the Roman term *proletariat*, which in modern jargon means all the unpropertied people in a modern state. In Rome the *proletarii* were a voting division of fully qualified citizens whose property was less than 10,000 copper asses (= £275). They were an enrolled class; their value to the state consisted in their raising families of citizens (proles = offspring), and from their ranks were

Photo: Anderson.
REMAINS OF THE SERVIAN WALL, ROME.

drawn the colonists who went to form new Latin cities or to garrison important points. But the proletarii were quite distinct in origin from slaves or freedmen or the miscellaneous driftage of a town slum, and it is a great pity that modern political discussion should be confused by an inaccurate use of a term which has no exact modern equivalent and which expresses nothing real in modern social classification.

The mass of the details of this struggle between patricians and plebeians we can afford to ignore in this outline. It was a struggle which showed the Romans to be a people of a curiously shrewd character, never forcing things to a destructive crisis, but being within the limits of their discretion grasping hard dealers. The patricians made a mean use of their political advantages to grow rich through the national conquests at the expense not only of the defeated enemy, but of the poorer plebeian, whose farm had been neglected and who had fallen into debt during his military service. The plebeians were ousted from any share in the conquered lands, which the patricians divided up among themselves. The introduction of money[1] probably increased the facilities of the usurer and the difficulties of the borrowing debtor.

Photo : Anderson.

THE TARPEIAN ROCK.

Three sorts of pressure won the plebeians a greater share in the government of the country and the good things that were coming to Rome as she grew powerful. The first of these (1) was the general strike of plebeians; the plebeians seem to have invented the strike, which now makes its first appearance in history. Twice they actually marched right out of Rome, threatening to make a new city higher up the Tiber, and twice this threat proved conclusive. The second method of pressure (2) was the threat of a tyranny. Just as in Attica (the little state of which Athens was the capital), Peisistratus raised himself to power on the support of the poorer districts, so there was to be found in most periods of plebeian discontent some ambitious man ready to figure as a leader and wrest power from the senate. For a long time the Roman

[1] J. Wells, *Short History of Rome to the Death of Augustus.*

patricians were clever enough to beat every such potential tyrant by giving in to a certain extent to the plebeians. And finally (3) there were patricians big-minded and far-seeing enough to insist upon the need of reconciliation with the plebians.

Thus in 509 B.C., Valerius Poplicola (3), the consul, enacted that whenever the life or rights of any citizen were at stake, there should be an appeal from the magistrates to the general assembly. This Lex Valeria was " the Habeas Corpus of Rome," and it freed the Roman plebeians from the worst dangers of class vindictiveness in the law courts.

In 494 B.C. occurred the first strike (1). " After the Latin war the pressure of debt had become excessive, and the plebeians saw with indignation their friends, who had often served the state bravely in the legions, thrown into chains and reduced to slavery at the demand of patrician creditors. War was raging against the Volscians, but the legionaries, on their victorious return, refused any longer to obey the consuls, and marched, though without any disorder, to the Sacred Mount beyond the Anio (up the Tiber). There they prepared to found a new city, since the rights of citizens were denied to them in the old one. The patricians were compelled to give way, and the plebeians, returning to Rome from the " First Secession," received the privilege of having officers of their own, tribunes and ædiles." [1]

[1] J. Wells.

In 486 B.C. arose Spurius Cassius (2), a consul who carried an Agrarian Law securing public land for the plebeians. But the next year he was accused of aiming at royal power, and condemned to death. His law never came into operation.

There followed a long struggle on the part of the plebeians to have the laws of Rome written down, so that they would no longer have to trust to patrician memories. In 451–450 B.C. the law of the Twelve Tables was published, the basis of all Roman law.

But in order that the Twelve Tables should be formulated, a committee of ten (the *decemvirate*) was appointed in the place of the ordinary magistrates. A second decemvirate, appointed in succession to the first, attempted a sort of aristocratic counter-revolution under Appius Claudius. The plebeians withdrew again a second time to the Sacred Mount, and Appius Claudius committed suicide in prison.

In 440 came a famine, and a second attempt to found a popular tyranny upon the popular wrongs, by Spurius Mælius, a wealthy plebeian, which ended in his assassination.

After the sack of Rome by the Gauls (390 B.C.), Marcus Manlius, who had been in command of the Capitol when the geese had saved it, came forward as a popular leader. The plebeians were suffering severely from the after-war usury and profiteering of the patricians, and were incurring heavy debts in rebuilding and restocking their farms. Manlius spent his fortune in releasing debtors. He was accused by the patricians of tyrannous intentions, condemned, and suffered the fate of condemned traitors in Rome, being flung from the Tarpeian Rock,

Photo: Mansell.
ROMAN PORTRAIT BUST. TIME OF THE REPUBLIC.

the precipitous edge of that same Capitoline Hill he had defended.

In 376 B.C., Licinius, who was one of the ten tribunes for the people, began a long struggle with the patricians by making certain proposals called the Licinian Rogations, that there should be a limit to the amount of public land taken by any single citizen, so leaving some for everybody, that outstanding debts should be forgiven without interest upon the repayment of the principal, and that henceforth one at least of the two consuls should be a plebeian. This precipitated a ten-year struggle. The plebeian power to stop business by the veto of their representatives, the tribunes, was fully exercised. In cases of national extremity it was the custom to set all other magistrates aside and appoint one leader, the Dictator. Rome had done such a thing during times of military necessity before, but now the patricians set up a Dictator in a time of profound peace, with the idea of crushing Licinius altogether. They appointed Camillus, who had besieged and taken Veii from the Etruscans. But Camillus was a wiser man than his supporters; he brought about a compromise between the two orders in which most of the demands of the plebeians were conceded (366 B.C.), dedicated a temple to Concord, and resigned his power.

Thereafter the struggle between the orders abated. It abated because, among other influences, the social differences between patricians and plebeians were diminishing. Trade was coming to Rome with increasing political power, and many plebeians were growing rich and many patricians becoming relatively poor. Intermarriage had been rendered possible by a change in the law, and social intermixture was going on. While the rich plebeians were becoming, if not aristocratic, at least oligarchic in habits and sympathy, new classes were springing up in Rome with fresh interests and no political standing. Particularly abundant were the freedmen, slaves set free, for the most part artizans, but some of them traders, who were growing wealthy. And the Senate, no longer a purely patrician body—since various official positions were now open to plebeians, and such plebeian officials became senators—was becom-

combination of sagacity and aggressive selfishness that had distinguished the war of her orders at home and enabled her population to worry out a balance of power without any catastrophe, marks her policy abroad. She understood the value of allies ; she could assimilate ; abroad as at home she could in those days at least " give and take " with a certain fairness and sanity. There lay the peculiar power of Rome. By that it was she succeeded where Athens, for example, had conspicuously failed.

Photo : Alinari.

THE APPIAN WAY.

ing now an assembly of all the wealthy, able, energetic, and influential men in the state. The Roman power was expanding, and as it expanded these old class oppositions of the early Latin community were becoming unmeaning. They were being replaced by new associations and new antagonisms. Rich men of all origins were being drawn together into a common interest against the communistic ideas of the poor.

In 390 B.C. Rome was a miserable little city on the borders of Etruria, being sacked by the Gauls ; in 275 B.C. she was ruling and unifying all Italy, from the Arno to the Straits of Messina. The compromise of Camillus (367 B.C.) had put an end to internal dissensions, and left her energies free for expansion. And the same queer

The Athenian democracy suffered much from that narrowness of " patriotism " which is the ruin of all nations. " Athens for the Athenians " was the guiding principle of her rule, and " tax the foreigner " her substitute for political wisdom.[1] Even Pericles used the funds of the

[1] But note that Athens had (1) no taxes on foreigners, and inflicted no disabilities on them except absence of citizenship. No "expulsions of aliens" such as were regular at Sparta, and common in most places. This is a frequent Athenian boast. Cp. Thucydides ii. 39, " Our city is thrown open to the world. We never expel a foreigner or prevent him from seeing and learning anything of which the secret, if revealed, might be useful to an enemy." (2) Practically Free Trade ; only a general 5 per cent. import duty. (3) Great interest in foreign places, constitutions, customs, etc. Athens was very oppressive—by modern stan-

allies to beautify the capital city. So Athens was disliked and envied by her own empire ; her disasters were not felt and shared as disasters by her subject-cities. The shrewder, nobler Roman senators of the great years of Rome, before the first Punic War overstrained her moral strength and began her degeneration, were not only willing in the last resort to share their privileges with the mass of their own people, but eager to incorporate their sturdiest antagonists upon terms of equality with themselves. They extended their citizenship cautiously but steadily. Some cities became Roman, with even a voting share in the government. Others had self-government and the right to trade or marry in Rome, without full Roman citizenship. Garrisons of full citizens were set up at strategic points, and colonies with variable privileges established amidst the purely conquered peoples. The need to keep communications open in this great and growing mass of citizenship was evident from the first. Printing and paper were not yet available for intercourse, but a system of high roads followed the Latin speech and the Roman rule. The first of these, the Appian Way, ran from Rome ultimately into the heel of Italy. It was begun by the censor Appius Claudius (who must not be confused with the decemvir Appius Claudius of a century earlier) in 312 B.C.

According to a census made in 265 B.C., there were already in the Roman dominions, that is to say in Italy south of the Arno, 300,000 citizens. They all had a common interest in the welfare of the state ; they were all touched a little with the diffused kingship of the republic. This was, we have to note, an absolutely new thing in the history of mankind. All considerable states and kingdoms and empires hitherto had been communities by mere obedience to some head, some monarch, upon whose moods and character the public welfare was helplessly dependent. No republic had hitherto succeeded in being anything more than a city state. The so-called Athenian " empire " was simply a city state directing its allies and its subjugated cities. In a few decades the Roman republic was

dards—to its subject-allies ; chiefly because there was no representation, and because she was so much at war. But even here, after her defeat in 404, they voluntarily gathered to her again. The second Athenian Empire was not in any way forced upon them.—G. M.

destined to extend its citizenship into the valley of the Po, to assimilate the kindred Gauls, replacing their language by Latin, and to set up a Latin city, Aquileia, at the very head of the Adriatic Sea. In 89 B.C. all free inhabitants of Italy became Roman citizens ; in 212 A.D. the citizenship was extended to all free men in the empire.[1]

This extraordinary political growth was

Photo : Alinari.
EARLY ROMAN BRONZE STATUE.

manifestly the precursor of all modern states of the western type. It is as interesting to the political student, therefore, as a carboniferous amphibian or an *archæopteryx* to the student of zoological development. It is the primitive type

[1] Haverfield says—and I think he is right—that Rome had a great advantage in her imperial development—viz., that she was a city and not a nation. A nation implies some unity of race, and race prejudice. A city is based on the mere fact of citizenship. We should have said to St. Paul : " Citizen or no citizen, you are only a Levantine Jew." But a Roman, apparently, did not think of saying so. Hence the great freedom with which emperors and senators are taken from other races.—G. M.

of the now dominant order. Its experiences throw light upon all subsequent political history.

One natural result of this growth of a democracy of hundreds of thousands of citizens scattered over the greater part of Italy was the growth in power of the Senate. There had been in the development of the Roman constitution a variety of forms of the popular assembly, the plebeian assembly, the assembly by tribes, the assembly by centuries, and the like, into which variety we cannot enter here with any fullness; but the idea was established that with the popular assembly lay the power of initiating laws. It is to be noted that there was a sort of parallel government in this system. The assembly by tribes or by centuries was an assembly of the *whole citizen body*, patrician and plebeian together; the assembly of the plebeians was of course an assembly only of the plebeian class. Each assembly had its own officials: the former, the consuls, etc.; the latter, the tribunes. While Rome was a little state, twenty miles square, it was possible to assemble something like a representative gathering of the people, but it will be manifest that with the means of communication existing in Italy at that time, it was now impossible for the great bulk of the citizens even to keep themselves informed of what was going

Photo: Mansell.
A ROMAN IN CIVIL COSTUME (ABOUT FIRST CENTURY B.C.)

on at Rome, much less to take any effective part in political life there. Aristotle in his *Politics* had already pointed out the virtual disenfranchisement of voters who lived out of the city and were preoccupied with agricultural pursuits, and this sort of disenfranchisement by mechanical difficulties applied to the vast majority of Roman citizens. With the growth of Rome an unanticipated weakness crept into political life through these causes, and the popular assembly became more and more a gathering of political hacks and the city riff-raff, and less and less a representation of the ordinary worthy citizens. The popular assembly came nearest to power and dignity in the fourth century B.C. From that period it steadily declined in influence, and the new Senate, which was no longer a patrician body, with a homogeneous and on the whole a noble tradition, but a body of rich men, ex-magistrates, powerful officials, bold adventurers and the like, pervaded by a strong disposition to return to the idea of hereditary qualification, became for three centuries the ruling power in the Roman world.

There are two devices since known to the world which might have enabled the popular government of Rome to go on developing beyond its climax in the days of Appius Claudius the Censor, at the close of the fourth century B.C., but neither of them occurred to the Roman mind. The first of these devices was a proper use of print. In our account of early Alexandria we have already remarked upon the strange fact that printed books did not come into the world in the fourth or third century B.C. This account of Roman affairs forces us to repeat that remark.

ment. For the old Popular Assembly (in its threefold form) it would have been possible to have substituted a gathering of delegates. Later on in history, the English did, as the state grew, realize this necessity. Certain men, the Knights of the Shire, were called up to Westminster to speak and vote for local feeling, and

THE TEMPLE OF MATER MATUTA, ROME.
" Probably a temple of ' Mother Dawn ' . . . most complete example of the round temple still existing."—*Stobart.*
(The tiled roof is, of course, modern.)

To the modern mind it is clear that a widespread popular government demands, as a necessary condition for health, a steady supply of correct information upon public affairs to all the citizens and a maintenance of interest. The popular governments in the modern states that have sprung up on either side of the Atlantic during the last two centuries have been possible only through the more or less honest and thorough ventilation of public affairs through the press. But in Italy the only way in which the government at Rome could communicate with any body of its citizens elsewhere was by the antiquated device of sending a herald, and with the individual citizen it could hold no communication by any means at all.

The second device, for which the English are chiefly responsible in the history of mankind, which the Romans never used, was the almost equally obvious one of representative govern-

were more or less formally elected for that end. The Roman situation seems to a modern mind to have called aloud for such a modification. It was never made.[1]

[1] The point raised here that Rome never developed representation is a very interesting one. There was a golden chance in the Social War (90 B.C.). The allies of Rome (socii) revolted, and set up a counter Rome in Corfinium. Now, to our minds, the obvious thing for them to do was (1) to make Corfinium just a capital ; (2) to set up a parliament there, consisting of representatives drawn from the allies, who lived, of course, all over Italy. Not a bit of it. They made Corfinium a city state (not a capital), and feigned themselves all to be citizens of it, meeting in a primary assembly there. They also set up, it is true, a senate of 500 ; but this was just a copy of the Roman senate, and not a representative body (see Mommsen, vol. iii. pp. 237–8, Eng. trans.). Under the Roman Empire there were germs of representation in provincial assemblies : see Bury, *Student's Roman Empire,* on the *concilium Lugdunense* in Gaul and τὰ κοινὰ in Asia Minor.—E. B.

The method of assembling the *comitia tributa* [1] (one of the three main forms of the Popular Assembly) was by the proclamation of a herald, who was necessarily inaudible to most of Italy, seventeen days before the date of the gathering. The augurs, the priests of divination whom Rome had inherited from the Etruscans, examined the entrails of sacrificial beasts on the night before the actual assembly, and if they thought fit to say that these gory portents were unfavourable, the *comitia tributa* dispersed. But if the augurs reported that the livers were propitious, there was a great blowing of horns from the Capitol and from the walls of the city, and the assembly went on. It was held in the open air, either in the little Forum beneath the Capitol or in a still smaller recess opening out of the Forum, or in the military exercising ground, the Campus Martius, now the most crowded part of modern Rome, but then an open space. Business began at dawn with prayer. There were no seats, and this probably helped to reconcile the citizen to the rule that everything ended at sunset.

After the opening prayer came a discussion of the measures to be considered by the assembly, and the proposals before the meeting were read out. Is it not astonishing that there were no printed copies distributed? If any copies were handed about, they must have been in manuscript, and each copy must have been liable to errors and deliberate falsification. No questions seem to have been allowed, but private individuals might address the gathering with the permission of the presiding magistrate.

The multitude then proceeded to go into enclosures like cattle-pens according to their tribes, and each tribe voted upon the measure under consideration. The decision was then taken not by the majority of the citizens, but by the majority of tribes, and it was announced by the heralds.

The Popular Assembly by centuries, *comitia centuriata*, was very similar in its character, except that instead of thirty-five tribes there were, in the third century B.C., 373 centuries, and there was a sacrifice as well as prayer to begin with. The centuries, originally military (like the "hundreds" of primitive English local

[1] Seyffert's *Dictionary of Classical Antiquities*. (Nettleship Sandys.)

government), had long since lost any connection with the number one hundred. Some contained only a few people; some very many. There were eighteen centuries of knights (equites), who were originally men in a position to maintain a horse and serve in the cavalry, though later the Roman knighthood, like knighthood in England, became a vulgar distinction of no military, mental, or moral significance. (These equites became a very important class as Rome traded and grew rich; for a time they were the real moving class in the community. There was as little chivalry left among them at last as there is in the "honours list" knights of England of to-day. The senators from about 200 B.C. were excluded from trade. The equites became, therefore, the great business men, *negotiatores*, and as *publicani* they farmed the taxes.) There were, in addition, eighty (!) centuries of wealthy men (worth over 100,000 asses), twenty-two of men worth over 75,000 asses, and so on. There were two centuries each of mechanics and musicians, and the *proletarii* made up one century. The decision in the *comitia centuriata* was by the majority of centuries.

Is it any wonder that with the growth of the Roman state and the complication of its business, power shifted back from such a Popular Assembly to the Senate, which was a comparatively compact body varying between three hundred as a minimum, and, at the utmost, nine hundred members (to which it was raised by Cæsar), men who had to do with affairs and big business, who knew each other more or less, and had a tradition of government and policy? The power of nominating and calling up the senators vested in the Republic first with the consuls, and when, some time after, "censors" were created, and many of the powers of the consuls had been transferred to them, it was shifted to them. Appius Claudius, one of the first of the censors to whom this power was given, enrolled freedmen in the tribes and called sons of freedmen to the Senate. But this was a shocking arrangement to the conservative instincts of the time; the consuls would not recognize his Senate, and the next censors (304 B.C.) set aside his invitations. His attempt, however, serves to show how far the Senate had progressed from its original condition as a purely patrician body. Like the contemporary

Photo : Anderson.

THE TEMPLE OF VESTA, TIVOLI (SEEN THROUGH THE ARCH).

British House of Lords, it had become a gathering of big business men, energetic politicians, successful adventurers, great landowners, and the like ; its patrician dignity was a picturesque sham ; but, unlike the British House of Lords, it was unchecked legally by anything but the inefficient Popular Assembly we have already described, and by the tribunes elected by the plebeian assembly. Its legal control over the consuls and proconsuls was not great ; it had little executive power ; but in its prestige and experience lay its strength and influence. The interests of its members were naturally antagonistic to the interests of the general body of citizens, but for some generations that great mass of ordinary men was impotent to express its dissent from the proceedings of this oligarchy. Direct popular government of a state larger than a city state had already failed therefore in Italy, because as yet there was no public education, no press, and no representative system ; it had failed through these mere mechanical difficulties, before the first Punic War. But its appearance is of enormous interest, as the first appearance

of a set of problems with which the whole political intelligence of the world wrestles at the present time.

The Senate met usually in a Senate House in the Forum, but on special occasions it would be called to meet in this or that temple ; and when it had to deal with foreign ambassadors or its own generals (who were not allowed to enter the city while in command of troops), it assembled in the Campus Martius outside the walls.

§ 3

It has been necessary to deal rather fully with the political structure of the Roman republic because of its immense importance to this day. The constitution of Carthage [1] need not detain us long. Italy under Rome was a republican country ; Carthage was that much older thing, a republican city. She had an '' empire,'' as

The Carthaginian Republic of Rich Men.

---

[1] Aristotle, *Politics*, Bk. ii. ch. xi. ; and J. Wells, *Rome to the Death of Augustus.*

The ROMAN POWER after the SAMNITE WARS

[Beginning of the 3rd Century..Compare with contemporary map of the Break-up of Alexander's Empire]

Roman power ▓▓▓

§ 4

The First Punic War. It would be interesting, and not altogether idle, to speculate what might have happened to mankind if Rome and Carthage could have settled their differences and made a permanent alliance in the Western world. If Alexander the Great had lived, he might have come westward and driven these two powers into such a fusion of interests. But that would not have suited the private schemes and splendours of the Carthaginian oligarchy, and the new Senate of greater Rome was now growing fond of the taste of plunder and casting covetous eyes across the Straits of Messina upon the Carthaginian possessions in Sicily. They were covetous, but they were afraid of the Carthaginian sea-power. Roman popular "patriotism," however, was also jealous and fearful of these Carthaginians, and less inclined to count the cost of a conflict. The alliance Pyrrhus had forced upon Rome and Carthage held good for eleven years, but Rome was ripe for what is called in modern political jargon an "offensive defensive" war. The occasion arose in 264 B.C.

At that time Sicily was not completely in

Athens had an "empire," of tributary states which did not love her, and she had a great and naturally disloyal industrial slave population.

In the city there were two elected "kings," as Aristotle calls them, the *suffetes*, who were really equivalent to the Roman censors; their Semitic name was the same as that used for the Jewish *judges*. There was an impotent public assembly and a senate of leading personages; but two committees of this senate, nominally elected, but elected by easily controlled methods, the Hundred and Four and the Thirty, really constituted a close oligarchy of the richest and most influential men. They told as little as they could to their allies and fellow citizens, and consulted them as little as possible. They pursued schemes in which the welfare of Carthage was no doubt subordinated to the advantage of their own group. They were hostile to new men or novel measures, and confident that a sea ascendancy that had lasted two centuries must be in the very nature of things.

COIN STRUCK TO COMMEMORATE THE VICTORY OVER PYRRHUS (AND HIS ELEPHANTS).

Carthaginian hands. The eastward end was still under the power of the Greek king of

THE APPIAN WAY TO-DAY.

Map of
ITALY
after 275 B.C.
Roman power

the history of mankind. But this is how one historian, soaked with the fantastic political ideas of our times, is pleased to write of this evil expedition. "The Romans knew they were entering on war with Carthage; but the political instincts of the people were right, for a Carthaginian garrison on the Sicilian Straits would have been a dangerous menace to the peace of Italy." So they protected the peace of Italy from this "menace" by a war that lasted nearly a quarter of a century. They wrecked their own slowly acquired political *morale* in the process.

The Romans captured Messina, and Hiero deserted from the Carthaginians to the Romans. Then for some time the struggle centred upon the town Agrigentum. This the Romans besieged, and a period of trench warfare ensued. Both sides suffered greatly from plague and irregular supplies; the Romans lost 30,000 men; but in the end (261 B.C.) the Carthaginians evacuated the place and retired to their fortified towns on the western coast of the island of which Lilybæum was the chief. These they could supply easily from the African mainland, and, as long as their sea ascendancy held, they could exhaust any Roman effort against them.

And now a new and very extraordinary phase of the war began. The Romans came out upon the sea, and to the astonishment of the Carthaginians and themselves defeated the Carthaginian fleet. Since the days of Salamis there had been a considerable development of naval architecture. Then the ruling type of battleship was a trireme, a galley with three banks (rows) of oars; now the leading Carthaginian battleship was a quinquereme, a much bigger galley with five banks of oars, which could ram or shear the oars of any feebler vessel. The Romans had

Syracuse, Hiero, a successor of that Dionysius to whom Plato had gone as resident court philosopher. A band of mercenaries who had been in the service of Syracuse seized upon Messina (289 B.C.), and raided the trade of Syracuse, so that at last Hiero was forced to take measures to suppress them (270 B.C.). Thereupon Carthage, which was also vitally concerned in the suppression of piracy, came to his aid, and put in a Carthaginian garrison at Messina. This was an altogether justifiable proceeding. Now that Tyre had been destroyed, the only capable guardian of sea law in the Mediterranean was Carthage, and the suppression of piracy was her task by habit and tradition.

The pirates of Messina appealed to Rome, and the accumulating jealousy and fear of Carthage decided the Roman people to help them. An expedition was dispatched to Messina under the consul Appius Claudius (the third Appius Claudius we have had to mention in this history).

So began the first of the most wasteful and disastrous series of wars that has ever darkened

SYRACUSE.

come into the war with no such shipping. Now they set to work to build quinqueremes, being helped, it is said, in their designing by one of these Carthaginian vessels coming ashore. In two months they built a hundred quinqueremes and thirty triremes. But they had no skilled navigators, no experienced oarsmen, and these deficiencies they remedied partly with the assistance of their Greek allies and partly by the invention of new tactics. Instead of relying upon ramming or breaking the oars of the adversary, which demanded more seamanship than they possessed, they decided to board the enemy, and they constructed a sort of long drawbridge on their ships, held up to a mast by a pulley and with grappling-hooks and spikes at the end. They also loaded their galleys with soldiers. Then as the Carthaginian rammed or swept alongside, this *corvus*, as it was called, could be let down and the boarders could swarm aboard him.

Simple as this device was, it proved a complete success. It changed the course of the war and the fate of the world. The small amount of invention needed to counteract the *corvus* was not apparently within the compass of the Carthaginian rulers. At the battle of Mylæ (260 B.C.) the Romans gained their first naval victory and captured or destroyed fifty vessels. At the great battle of Ecnomus (256 B.C.), "probably the greatest naval engagement of antiquity," [1] in which seven or eight hundred big ships were engaged, the Carthaginians showed that they had learnt nothing from their former disaster. According to rule they outmanœuvred and defeated the Romans, but the *corvus* again

[1] J. Wells *op. cit.*

defeated them. The Romans sank thirty vessels and captured sixty-four.

Thereafter the war continued with violent fluctuations of fortune, but with a continuous demonstration of the greater energy, solidarity, and initiative of the Romans. After Ecnomus the Romans invaded Africa by sea, and sent an insufficiently supported army, which after many successes and the capture of Tunis (within ten miles of Carthage) was completely defeated. They lost their sea ascendancy through a storm, and regained it by building a second fleet of two hundred and twenty ships within three months. They captured Palermo, and defeated a great Carthaginian army there (251 B.C.), capturing one hundred and four elephants, and making such a triumphal procession into Rome as that city had never seen before. They made an unsuccessful siege of Lilybæum, the chief surviving Carthaginian stronghold in Sicily. They lost their second fleet in a great naval battle at Drepanum (249 B.C.), losing one hundred and eighty out of two hundred and ten vessels ; and a third fleet of one hundred and twenty battleships and eight hundred transports was lost in the same year partly in battle and partly in a storm.

For seven years a sort of war went on between the nearly exhausted combatants, a war of raids and feeble sieges, during which the Carthaginians had the best of it at sea. Then by a last supreme effort Rome launched a fourth fleet of two hundred keels, and defeated the last strength of the Carthaginians at the battle of the Ægatian Isles (241 B.C.), after which Carthage (240 B.C.) sued for peace.

By the terms of this peace, all Sicily, except for

Roman As (bronze, 4ᵗʰ Cent. B.C. Half size.)

A COPPER COIN SUCH AS THE ABOVE WEIGHED 290 g.
HEAD OF JANUS ON ONE SIDE ; ON REVERSE, PROW OF
A GALLEY (A COMMON DESIGN ON GREEK COINS).

the dominions of Hiero of Syracuse, became an "estate" of the Roman people. There was no such process of assimilation as had been practised in Italy ; Sicily became a conquered province, paying tribute and yielding profit like the provinces of the older empires. And, in addition, Carthage paid a war indemnity of 3,200 talents (= £788,000).

§ 5

For twenty-two years there was peace between Rome and Carthage. It was peace without prosperity. Both combatants were

Cato the Elder and the Spirit of Cato. suffering from the want and disorganization that follow naturally and necessarily upon all great wars. The territories of Carthage seethed with violent disorder ; the returning soldiers could not get their pay, and mutinied and looted ; the land went uncultivated. We read of horrible cruelties in the suppression of these troubles by Hamilcar, the Carthaginian general ; of men being crucified by the thousand. Sardinia and Corsica revolted. The "peace of Italy" was scarcely happier. The Gauls rose and marched south ; they were defeated, and 40,000 of them killed at Telamon. It is manifest that Italy was incomplete until it reached the Alps. Roman colonies were planted in the valley of the Po, and the great northward artery, the Via Flaminia, was begun. But it shows the moral and intellectual degradation of this post-war period that when the Gauls were threatening Rome, human sacrifices were proposed and carried out. The old Carthaginian sea law was broken up—it may have been selfish and monopolistic, but it was at least orderly—the Adriatic swarmed with

Illyrian pirates, and as the result of a quarrel arising out of this state of affairs, Illyria, after two wars, had to be annexed as a second "province." By sending expeditions to annex Sardinia and Corsica, which were Carthaginian provinces in revolt, the Romans prepared the way for the Second Punic War.

The First Punic War had tested and demonstrated the relative strength of Rome and Carthage. With a little more wisdom on either side, with a little more magnanimity on the part of Rome, there need never have been a renewal of the struggle. But Rome was an ungracious conqueror. She seized Corsica and Sardinia on no just grounds, she increased the indemnity by 1,200 talents, she set a limit, the Ebro, to Carthaginian developments in Spain. There was a strong party in Carthage, led by Hanno, for the propitiation of Rome ; but it was natural that many Carthaginians should come

Carthaginian coins.

The lower coin was struck for the pay of the Carthaginian mercenaries during the Second Punic War. Note, in both, the palm-tree, an essentially Carthaginian symbol.

to regard their national adversary with a despairing hostility.

So began that age-long hostility between the lands north and south of the Mediterranean which lasts down to our own day, the conflict of the Semiticized Berber and the Aryanized south European, in spite of the fact that these two divisions of Mediterranean man have so much physically in common. Henceforth they

Photo : Brogi.

TAORMINA, MAGNA GRÆCIA.

"The theatre (Greek) at Taormina, reconstructed during the Roman period, was wonderfully situated, opening on the sea and on Mount Etna."—Durny (Histoire des Grecs),

took different sides in religion, in language, in costume and culture.

Hatred is one of the passions that can master a life, and there is a type of temperament very prone to it, ready to see life in terms of vindictive melodrama, ready to find stimulus and satisfaction in frightful demonstrations of "justice" and revenge. The fears and jealousies of the squatting-place and the cave still bear their dark blossoms in our lives; we are not four hundred generations yet from the old Stone Age. Great wars, as all Europe knows, give this "hating" temperament the utmost scope, and the greed and pride and cruelty that the First Punic War had released were now producing a rich crop of anti-foreign monomania. The outstanding figure upon the side of Carthage was a great general and administrator, Hamilcar Barca, who now set himself to circumvent and shatter Rome. He was the father-in-law of Hasdrubal and the father of a boy Hannibal, destined to be the most dreaded enemy that ever scared the Roman Senate. The most obvious course before Carthage was the reconstruction of its fleet and naval administration, and the recovery of sea power, but this, it would seem, Hamilcar could not effect. As an alternative he resolved to organize Spain as the base of a land attack upon Italy. He went to Spain as governor in 236 B.C., and Hannibal related afterwards that his father then—he was a boy of eleven—made him vow deathless hostility to the Roman power.

This quasi-insane concentration of the gifts and lives of the Barca family upon revenge is but one instance of the narrowing and embitterment of life that the stresses and universal sense of insecurity of this great struggle produced in the minds of men. A quarter of a century of war had left the whole western world miserable and harsh. While the eleven-year-old Hannibal was taking his vow of undying hatred, there was running about a farmhouse of Tusculum a small but probably very disagreeable child of two named Marcus Porcius Cato. This boy lived to be eighty-five years old, and his ruling passion seems to have been hatred for any human happiness but his own. He was a good soldier, and had a successful political career. He held a command in Spain, and distinguished himself by his cruelties. He posed

as a champion of religion and public morality, and under this convenient cloak carried on a lifelong war against everything that was young, gracious, or pleasant. Whoever roused his jealousy, incurred his moral disapproval. He was energetic in the support and administration of all laws against dress, against the personal adornment of women, against entertainments and free discussion. He was so fortunate as to be made censor, which gave him great power over the private lives of public people. He was thus able to ruin public opponents through private scandals. He expelled Manlius from the Senate for giving his wife a kiss in the daytime in the sight of their daughter. He persecuted Greek literature, about which, until late in life, he was totally ignorant. Then he read and admired Demosthenes. He wrote in Latin upon agriculture and the ancient and lost virtues of Rome. From these writings much light is thrown upon his qualities. One of his maxims was that when a slave was not sleeping he should be working. Another was that old oxen and slaves should be sold off. He left the war horse that had carried him through his Spanish campaigns behind him when he returned to Italy in order to save freight. He hated other people's gardens, and cut off the supply of water for garden use in Rome. After entertaining company, when dinner was over he would go out to correct any negligence in the service with a leather thong. He admired his own virtues very greatly, and insisted upon them in his writings. There was a battle at Thermopylæ against Antiochus the Great, of which he wrote, "those who saw him charging the enemy, routing and pursuing them, declared that Cato owed less to the people of Rome than the people of Rome owed to Cato."[1] In his old age Cato became lascivious, and misconducted himself with a woman slave. Finally, when his son protested against this disorder of their joint household, he married a young wife, the daughter of his secretary, who was not in a position to refuse his offer. (What became of the woman slave is not told. Probably he sold her.) This compendium of all the old Roman virtues died at an advanced age, respected and feared. Almost his last public act was to urge on the Third Punic War and the final destruc-

[1] Plutarch, *Life of Cato.*

tion of Carthage. He had gone to Carthage as a commissioner to settle certain differences between Carthage and Numidia, and he had been shocked and horrified to find some evidences of prosperity and even of happiness in that country.

From the time of that visit onward Cato concluded every speech he made in the Senate by croaking out "*Delenda est Carthago*" ("Carthage must be destroyed").

Such was the type of man that rose to prominence in Rome during the Punic struggle, such was the protagonist of Hannibal and the Carthaginian *revanche*, and by him and by Hannibal we may judge the tone and quality of the age.

The two great western powers, and Rome perhaps more than Carthage, were strained mentally and morally by the stresses of the First War. The evil side of life was uppermost. The history of the Second and Third Punic Wars (219 to 201 and 149 to 146 B.C.), it is plain, is not the history of perfectly sane peoples. It is nonsense for historians to write of the "political instincts" of the Romans or Carthaginians. Quite other instincts were loose. The red eyes of the ancestral ape had come back into the world. It was a time when reasonable men were howled down or murdered ; the true spirit of the age is shown in the eager examination for signs and portents of the still quivering livers of those human victims who were sacrificed in Rome during the panic before the battle of Telamon. The western world was indeed black with homicidal monomania. Two great peoples, both very necessary to the world's development, fell foul of one another,

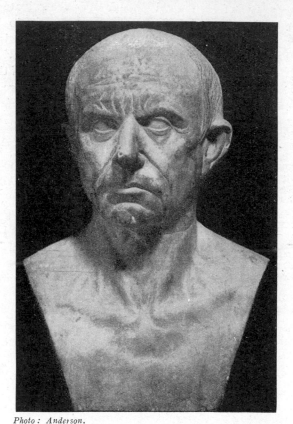

Photo: Anderson.

CATO.
Bust in the Capitoline Museum, Rome.)

and at last Rome succeeded in murdering Carthage.

§ 6

We can only tell very briefly here of the particulars of the Second and Third Punic Wars. We have told how Hamilcar began to organize Spain, and how the Romans forbade him to cross the Ebro. He died in 228 B.C., and was followed by his son-in-law Hasdrubal, who was assassinated in 221 B.C., and succeeded by Hannibal, who was now twenty-six. The actual war was precipitated by the Romans making a breach of their own regulations, and interfering with affairs south of the Ebro. Whereupon Hannibal marched straight through the south of Gaul, and crossed the Alps (218 B.C.) into Italy.

The Second Punic War.

The history of the next fifteen years is the story of the most brilliant and futile raid in history. For fifteen years Hannibal held out in Italy, victorious and unconquered. The Roman generals were no match for the Carthaginian, and whenever they met him they were beaten. But one Roman general, P. Cornelius Scipio, had the strategic sense to take a course that robbed all Hannibal's victories of fruit. At the outbreak of the war he had been sent by sea to Marseilles to intercept Hannibal ; he arrived three days late, and, instead of pursuing him, he sent on his army into Spain to cut up Hannibal's supplies and reinforcements. Throughout all the subsequent war there remained this Roman army of Spain between Hannibal and his base. He was left "in the air," in-

Photo: Anderson.

SPOLETO—A TYPICAL ITALIAN HILL-TOWN. FAMOUS IN EARLY ROMAN HISTORY FOR ITS
REPULSE OF HANNIBAL.

capable of conducting sieges or establishing conquests.

Whenever he met the Romans in open fight he beat them. He gained two great victories in North Italy, and won over the Gauls to his side. He pressed south into Etruria, and ambushed, surrounded, and completely destroyed a Roman army at Lake Trasimene. In 216 B.C. he was assailed by a vastly superior Roman force under Varro at Cannæ, and destroyed it utterly. Fifty thousand men are said to have been killed and ten thousand prisoners taken. He was, however, unable to push on and capture Rome because he had no siege equipment.

But Cannæ produced other fruits. A large part of Southern Italy came over to Hannibal, including Capua, the city next in size to Rome, and the Macedonians allied themselves with him. Moreover, Hiero of Syracuse, the faithful ally of Rome, was now dead, and his successor Hieronymus turned over to the Carthaginians. The Romans carried on the war, however, with great toughness and resolution; they refused to treat with Hannibal after Cannæ, they pressed a slow but finally successful blockade and siege of Capua, and a Roman army set itself to reduce Syracuse. The siege of Syracuse is chiefly memorable for the brilliant inventions of the philosopher Archimedes, which long held the Romans at bay. We have already named this Archimedes as one of the pupils and corre-

spondents of the school of the Alexandrian Museum. He was killed in the final storm of the town. Tarentum (209 B.C.), Hannibal's chief port and means of supply from Carthage, at last followed Syracuse (212 B.C.) and Capua (211 B.C.), and his communications became irregular.

Spain also was wrested bit by bit from the Carthaginian grip. When at last reinforcements for Hannibal under his brother Hasdrubal (not to be confused with his brother-in-law of the same name who was assassinated) struggled through into Italy, they were destroyed at the battle of the Metaurus (207 B.C.), and the first news that came to Hannibal of the disaster was the hacked-off head of his brother thrown into his camp.

Thereafter Hannibal was blockaded into Calabria, the toe of Italy. He had no forces for further operations of any magnitude, and he returned at last to Carthage in time to command the Carthaginians in the last battle of the war.

This last battle, the battle of Zama (202 B.C.), was fought close to Carthage.

It was the first defeat Hannibal experienced, and so it is well to give a little attention to the personality of his conqueror, Scipio Africanus the Elder, who stands out in history as a very fine gentleman indeed, a great soldier and a generous man. We have already mentioned a certain P. Cornelius Scipio who struck at Hannibal's base in Spain; this was his son; until after Zama this son bore the same name of P. Cornelius Scipio, and then the surname of Africanus was given him. (The younger Scipio Africanus, Scipio Africanus Minor, who was later to end the Third Punic War, was the adopted son of this first Scipio Africanus, Scipio Africanus the Elder.) Scipio Africanus was

Photo: Brogi.

SCIPIO AFRICANUS:
(From the Naples Museum.)

everything that aroused the distrust, hatred, and opposition of old-fashioned Romans of the school of Cato. He was young, he was happy and able, he spent money freely, he was well versed in Greek literature, and inclined rather to Phrygian novelties in religion than to the sterner divinities of Rome. And he did not believe in the extreme discretion that then ruled Roman strategy.

After the early defeats of the Second Punic War, Roman military operations were domi-nated by the personality of a general, Fabius, who raised the necessity of avoiding battle with Hannibal into a kind of sacred principle. For ten years "Fabian tactics" prevailed in Italy. The Romans blockaded, cut up convoys, attacked stragglers, and ran away whenever Hannibal appeared. No doubt it was wise for a time after their first defeats to do this sort of thing, but the business of the stronger power, and Rome was the stronger power throughout the Second Punic War, is not to tolerate an interminable war, but to repair losses, discover able generals, train better armies, and destroy the enemy power. Decision is one of the duties of strength.

To such men as young Scipio, the sly, ineffective artfulness of Fabianism, which was causing both Italy and Carthage to bleed slowly to death, was detestable. He clamoured for an attack upon Carthage itself.

"But Fabius, on this occasion, filled the city with alarms, as if the commonwealth was going to be brought into the most extreme danger by a rash and indiscreet young man; in short, he scrupled not to do or say anything he thought likely to dissuade his countrymen from embracing the proposal. With the Senate he carried his point. But the people believed that his opposition to Scipio proceeded either from envy of his success, or from a secret fear that if this young hero should perform some signal exploit, put an end to the war, or even remove it out of Italy, his own slow proceedings through the course of so many years might be imputed to indolence or timidity. . . . He applied to Crassus, the colleague of Scipio, and endeavoured to persuade him not to yield that province to Scipio, but, if he thought it proper to conduct the war in that manner, to go himself against Carthage. Nay, he even hindered the raising of money for that expedition, so that Scipio was obliged to find the supplies as he could. . . . He endeavoured to prevent the young men who offered to go as volunteers from giving in their names, and loudly declared, both in the Senate and Forum, 'That Scipio did not only himself avoid Hannibal, but intended to carry away with him the remaining strength of Italy, persuading the young men to abandon their parents, their wives, and native city, while an unsubdued and potent enemy was still at their doors.' With these assertions he so terrified the people, that they allowed Scipio to take with him only the legions that were in Sicily, and three hundred of those men who had served him with so much fidelity in Spain. . . . After Scipio was gone over into Africa, an account was soon brought to Rome of his glorious and wonderful achievements. This account was followed by rich spoils, which confirmed it. A Numidian king was taken prisoner; two camps were burned and destroyed; and in them a vast number of men, arms, and horses; and the Carthaginians sent orders to Hannibal to quit his fruitless hopes in Italy, and return home to defend his own country. Whilst every tongue was applauding these exploits of Scipio, Fabius proposed that his successor should be appointed, without any shadow or reason for it, except what this well-known maxim implies: viz., 'That it is dangerous to trust affairs of such importance to the fortune of one man, because it is not likely that he will be always successful.' . . . Nay, even when Hannibal embarked his army and quitted Italy, Fabius ceased not to disturb the general joy and to damp the spirits of Rome, for he took the liberty to affirm, 'That the commonwealth was now come to her last and worst trial; that she had the most reason to dread the efforts of Hannibal when he should arrive in Africa, and attack her sons under the walls of Carthage; that Scipio would have to do with an army yet warm with the blood of so many Roman generals, dictators, and consuls.' The city was alarmed with these declamations, and though the war was removed into Africa, the danger seemed to approach nearer Rome than ever."

Before the battle of Zama there were a brief truce and negotiations, which broke down through the fault of the Carthaginians. As with the battle of Arbela, so the exact day of the battle of Zama can be fixed by an eclipse, which in this case occurred during the fighting. The Romans had been joined by the Numidians, the hinterland people of Carthage, under their king Massinissa, and this gave them—for the first time in any battle against Hannibal—a great superiority of cavalry. Hannibal's cavalry wings were driven off, while at the same time the sounder discipline of Scipio's infantry enabled them to open lanes for the charge of the Carthaginian war elephants without being

thrown into confusion. Hannibal attempted to extend his infantry line to envelop the Roman infantry mass, but while at Cannæ all the advantage of training and therefore of manœuvring power had been on his side, and he had been able to surround and massacre a crowd of infantry, he now found against him an infantry line better than his own. His own line broke as it extended, the Roman legion charged home, and the day was lost. The Roman cavalry came back from the pursuit of Hannibal's horse to turn what was already a defeat into a disastrous rout.

Carthage submitted without any further struggle. The terms were severe, but they left it possible for her to hope for an honourable future. She had to abandon Spain to Rome, to give up all her war fleet except ten vessels, to pay 10,000 talents (£2,400,000), and, what was the most difficult condition of all, to agree not to wage war without the permission of Rome. Finally a condition was added that Hannibal, as the great enemy of Rome, should be surrendered. But he saved his countrymen from this humiliation by flying to Asia.

These were exorbitant conditions, with which Rome should have been content. But there are nations so cowardly that they dare not merely conquer their enemies; they must *mak siccar* and destroy them. The generation of Romans that saw greatness and virtue in a man like Cato the Censor, necessarily made their country a mean ally and a cowardly victor.

§ 7

The history of Rome for the fifty-six years that elapsed between the battle of Zama and the last act of the tragedy, the Third Punic War, tells of a hard ungracious expansion of power abroad and of a slow destruction, by the usury and greed of the rich, of the free agricultural population at home.

The Third Punic War.

The spirit of the nation had become harsh and base; there was no further extension of citizenship, no more generous attempts at the assimilation of congenial foreign populations. Spain was administered badly, and settled slowly and with great difficulty. Complicated interventions led to the reduction of Illyria and Macedonia to the position of tribute-paying provinces;

Rome, it was evident, was going to " tax the foreigner " now and release her home population from taxation. After 168 the old land tax was no longer levied in Italy, and the only revenue derived from Italy was from the state domains and through a tax on imports from overseas. The revenues from the province of " Asia " defrayed the expenses of the Roman state.[1] At home men of the Cato type were acquiring farms by loans and foreclosure, often the farms of men impoverished by war service;

Photo: Anderson.
A ROMAN PUGILIST (GLADIATOR).

they were driving the free citizens off their land, and running their farms with the pitilessly driven slave labour that was made cheap and abundant. Such men regarded alien populations abroad merely as unimported slaves. Sicily was handed over to the greedy enterprise of tax-farmers. Corn could be grown there by rich men using slaves, and imported very profitably into Rome, and so the home land could be turned over to cattle and sheep feeding. Consequently a drift of the uprooted Italian population to the towns, and particularly to Rome, began.

[1] Mommsen says the other provinces cost as much as they paid.

Of the first conflicts of the spreading power of Rome with the Seleucids, and how she formed an alliance with Egypt, we can tell little here, nor of the tortuous fluctuations of the Greek cities under the shadow of her advance until they fell into actual subjugation. A map must suffice to show the extension of her empire at this time.

The general grim baseness of the age was not without its protesting voices. We have already told how the wasting disease of the Second Punic War, a disease of the state which was producing avaricious rich men exactly as diseases of the body will sometimes produce great pustules, was ended by the vigour of Scipio Africanus. When it had seemed doubtful whether the Senate would let him go as the Roman general, he had threatened an appeal to the people. Thereafter he was a marked man for the senatorial gang, who were steadily changing Italy from a land of free cultivators to a land of slave-worked cattle ranches; they attempted to ruin him before ever he reached Africa; they gave him forces insufficient, as they hoped, for victory; and after the war they barred him strictly from office. Interest and his natural malice alike prompted Cato to attack him.

Scipio Africanus the Elder seems to have been of a generous and impatient temperament, and indisposed to exploit the popular discontent with current tendencies and his own very great popularity to his own advantage. He went as subordinate to his brother Lucius Scipio, when the latter commanded the first Roman army to pass into Asia. At Magnesia in Lydia a great composite army under Antiochus III, the Seleucid monarch, suffered the fate (190 B.C.) of the very similar Persian armies of a hundred and forty years before. This victory drew down upon Lucius Scipio the hostility of the Senate, and he was accused of misappropriating moneys received from Antiochus. This filled Africanus with honest rage. As Lucius stood up in the Senate with his accounts in his hands ready for the badgering of his accusers, Africanus snatched the documents from him, tore them up, and flung the fragments down. His brother, he said, had paid into the treasury 200,000 sestertii (=£2,000,000). Was he now to be pestered and tripped up upon this or that item ?

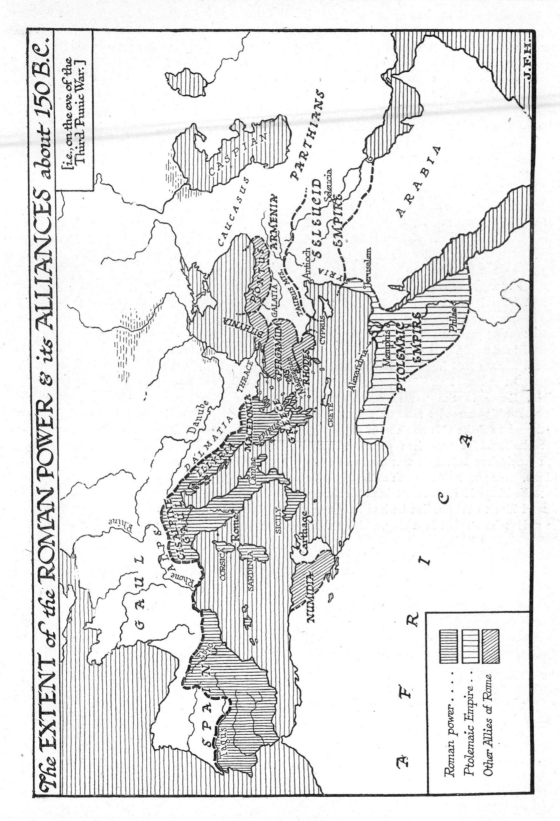

The EXTENT of the ROMAN POWER & its ALLIANCES about 150 B.C.

[i.e., on the eve of the Third Punic War.]

J.F.H.

Roman power....
Ptolemaic Empire...
Other Allies of Rome

SPAIN

GAUL

Rhine

Rhone

ALPS

CISALPINE

CORSICA

SARDINIA

Rome

Carthage

SICILY

NUMIDIA

AFRICA

ARABIA

Danube

DALMATIA

ILLYRIA

MACEDONIA

EPIRUS

THRACE

GREECE

CRETE

CYPRUS

RHODES

CAUCASUS

CASPIAN

ARMENIA

PONTUS

BITHYNIA

GALATIA

PERGAMUM

TAURUS MTS.

PARTHIANS

SELEUCID EMPIRE

SYRIA

Antioch

Seleucia

Jerusalem

PTOLEMAIC EMPIRE

Alexandria

Memphis

Philae

When, later on, Lucius was prosecuted and condemned, Africanus rescued him by force. Being impeached, he reminded the people that the day was the anniversary of the battle of Zama, and defied the authorities amidst the plaudits of the crowd.

The Roman people seem to have liked and supported Scipio Africanus, and, after an interval of two thousand years, men must like him still. He was able to throw torn paper in the face of the Senate, and when Lucius was attacked again, one of the tribunes of the people interposed his veto and quashed the proceedings. But Scipio Africanus lacked that harder alloy which makes men great democratic leaders. He was no Cæsar. He had none of the qualities that subdue a man to the base necessities of political life. After these events he retired in disgust from Rome to his estates, and there he died in the year 183 B.C.

In the same year died Hannibal. He poisoned himself in despair. The steadfast fear of the Roman Senate had hunted him from court to court. In spite of the indignant protests of Scipio, Rome in the peace negotiations had demanded his surrender from Carthage, and she continued to make this demand of every power that sheltered him. When peace was made with Antiochus III, this was one of the conditions. He was run to earth at last in Bithynia; the king of Bithynia detained him in order to send him to Rome, but he had long carried the poison he needed in a ring, and by this he died.

It adds to the honour of the name of Scipio that it was another Scipio, Scipio Nasica, who parodied Cato's *Delenda est Carthago* by ending all his speeches in the Senate with " Carthage must stand." He had the wisdom to see that the existence and stimulus of Carthage contributed to the general prosperity of Rome.[1]

Yet it was the second Scipio Africanus, the adopted son of Scipio Africanus the Elder, who took and destroyed Carthage. The sole offence of the Carthaginians, which brought about the third and last Punic War, was that they continued to trade and prosper. Their trade was not a trade that competed with that of Rome; when Carthage was destroyed, much of her trade died with her, and North Africa entered upon a phase of economic retrogression; but her prosperity aroused that passion of envy which was evidently more powerful even than avarice in the " old Roman" type. The rich Equestrian order resented any wealth in the world but its own. Rome provoked the war by encouraging the Numidians to encroach upon Carthage until the Carthaginians were goaded to fight in despair. Rome then pounced upon Carthage, and declared she had broken the treaty! She had made war without permission.

The Carthaginians sent the hostages Rome demanded, they surrendered their arms, they prepared to surrender territory. But submission only increased the arrogance of Rome and the pitiless greed of the rich Equestrian order which swayed her counsels. She now demanded

[1] But it was this Scipio Nasica who was responsible for the killing of Tiberius Gracchus. On the whole, he seems to have been a statesman of very distinguished abilities. He was the means of bringing the Asiatic Great Mother Goddess to Rome. " People at Rome generally were beginning to see that they would have to take over Asia. Had they any right? Nasica was sent on a mission to invite the Magna Mater at Pessinus to come to Rome. Her image nodded ' yes.' She was brought and installed in Rome. Now this is a policy of peaceful assimilation. Just as in Babylon you get gods of other cities brought to Babylon, just as Nabonidus (see Chap. xix. § 6) was trying to get an amicable pantheon as a way of peaceful assimilation, and failing to do so because he did not bring the priesthoods as well as the gods, so Rome was at this time thinking on the same lines. Camillus had shown the way when he suggested the invitation of Juno of Veii to Rome. Now Nasica, it may be suggested, wanted to treat Carthage in the same fashion. He opposed the destruction of Carthage in 146 (Mommsen iii. p. 23, p. 39). If he had had his way, one may guess, he would have invited the Carthaginian gods to Rome, and the corollary would have been the enfranchisement of the Carthaginian population—the treatment of the Carthaginians as equals, whose gods had been received in Rome, and stood in Rome. Mummius did the same in carrying off the statues of Greek gods to Rome, only, being stupid he did not understand why (146 B.C.)."

Nasica's visit to Pessinus was as important as the testament of Attalus. His policy is not the policy of Rome the conqueror, but Rome the assimilator. He is trying to get a nexus by a common pantheon. If this had been done, the Republic might have survived. As it was, the deification of the ruler had to provide the nexus, as in Alexander's empire. The " Synœcism of gods " or the " deification of rulers," those are the only ways of amalgamating peoples. It is a pity Alexander and Rome did not attempt the former.—J. L. M. and E. B.

that Carthage should be abandoned, and the population remove to a spot at least ten miles from the sea. This demand they made to a population that subsisted almost entirely by overseas trade !

This preposterous order roused the Carthaginians to despair. They recalled their exiles and prepared for resistance. The military efficiency of the Romans had been steadily declining through a half-century of narrowminded and base-spirited government, and the first attacks upon the town in 149 B.C. almost ended in disaster. Young Scipio, during these

lated, there were fifty thousand Carthaginians left alive out of an estimated population of half a million. These survivors went into slavery, the whole city was burnt, the ruins were ploughed to express final destruction, and a curse was invoked with great solemnities upon anyone who might attempt to rebuild it.

In the same year (146 B.C.) the Roman Senate and Equestrians also *murdered* another great city that seemed to limit their trade monopolies, Corinth. They had a justification, for Corinth had been in arms against them, but it was inadequate justification.

Photo: Bonfils.

ALL THAT REMAINS OF CORINTH.

operations, distinguished himself in a minor capacity. The next year was also a year of failure for the incompetents of the Senate. That august body then passed from a bullying mood to one of extreme panic. The Roman populace was even more seriously scared. Young Scipio, chiefly on account of his name, although he was under the proper age, and in other respects not qualified for the office, was made consul, and bundled off to Africa to save his precious country.

There followed the most obstinate and dreadful of sieges. Scipio built a mole across the harbour, and cut off all supplies by land or sea. The Carthaginians suffered horribly from famine ; but they held out until the town was stormed. The street fighting lasted for six days, and when at last the citadel capitu-

§ 8

We must note here, in a brief section, a change in the military system of Rome, after the Second Punic War, that was of How the enormous importance in her later Punic War development. Up to that period undermined the Roman armies had been levies Roman of free citizens. Fighting power Liberty. and voting power were closely connected ; the public assembly by centuries followed the paraphernalia of a military mobilization, and marched, headed by the Equestrian centuries, to the Campus Martius. The system was very like that of the Boers before the last war in South Africa. The ordinary Roman citizen, like the ordinary Boer, was a farmer ; at the summons of his country he went " on commando." The Boers were, indeed, in many respects, the last survivors of Aryanism. They fought extraordinarily well, but at the back of their minds was an anxious desire to go back to their farms. For prolonged operations, such as the siege of Veii, the Romans reinforced and relieved their troops in relays; the Boers did much the same at the siege of Ladysmith.

The necessity for subjugating Spain after the Second Punic War involved a need for armies of a different type. Spain was too far off for periodic reliefs, and the war demanded a more thorough training than was possible with these on and off soldiers. Accordingly men were enlisted for longer terms and *paid*. So the paid soldier first appeared in Roman affairs. And to pay was added booty. Cato distributed silver treasure among his command in Spain; and it is also on record that he attacked Scipio Africanus for distributing booty among his troops in Sicily. The introduction of military pay led on to a professional army, and this, a century later, to the disarmament of the ordinary Roman citizen, who was now drifting in an impoverished state into Rome and the larger towns. The great wars had been won, the foundations of the empire had been well and truly laid by the embattled farmers of Rome before 200 B.C. In the process the embattled farmers of Rome had already largely disappeared. The change that began after the Second Punic War was completed towards the close of the century in the reorganization of the army by Marius, as we will tell in its place. After his time we shall begin to write of " the army," and then of " the legions," and we shall find we are dealing with a new kind of army altogether, no longer held together in the solidarity of a common citizenship. As that tie fails, the legions discover another in *esprit de corps*, in their common difference from and their common interest against the general community. They begin to develop a warmer interest in their personal leaders, who secure them pay and plunder. Before the Punic Wars it was the tendency of ambitious men in Rome to court the plebeians; after that time they began to court the legions.

§ 9

The history of the Roman Republic thus far, is in many respects much more modern in

flavour, especially to the American or Western European reader, than anything that has preceded it. For the first time we have something like a self-govern-ing " nation," something larger than a mere city state, seeking to control its own destinies. For the first time we have a wide countryside under one conception of law. We get in the Senate and the popular assembly a conflict of groups and personalities, an argumentative process of control, far more stable and enduring than any autocracy can be, and far more flexible and adaptable than any priesthood. For the first time also we encounter social conflicts comparable to our own. Money has superseded barter, and financial capital has become fluid and free; not perhaps so fluid and free as it is to-day, but much more so than it had ever been before. The Punic Wars were wars of peoples, such as were no other wars we have yet recorded. Indubitably the broad lines of our present world, the main ideas, the chief oppositions, were already appearing in those days.

Comparison of the Roman Republic with a Modern State.

But, as we have already pointed out, certain of the elementary facilities and some of the current political ideas of our time were still wanting in the Rome of the Punic Wars. There were no newspapers,[1] and there was practically no use of elected representatives in the popular assemblies. And another deficiency, very understandable to us nowadays, but quite beyond the scope of anyone then, was the absence of any general elementary political education at all. The plebeians of Rome had shown some glimmering of the idea that without knowledge votes cannot make men free, when they had insisted upon the publication of the

[1] Julius Cæsar (60 B.C.) caused the proceedings of the Senate to be published by having them written up upon bulletin boards, *in albo* (upon the white). It had been the custom to publish the annual edict of the prætor in this fashion. There were professional letter-writers who sent news by special courier to rich country correspondents, and these would copy down the stuff upon the Album (white board). Cicero, while he was governor in Cicilia, got the current news from such a professional correspondent. He complains in one letter that it was not what he wanted; the expert was too full of the chariot races and other sporting intelligence, and failed to give any view of the political situation. Obviously this news-letter system was available only for public men in prosperous circumstances.

law of the Twelve Tables ; but they had never been able, it was beyond the possibilities of the time, to imagine any further extension of knowledge to the bulk of the people. It is only nowadays that men are beginning to understand fully the political significance of the maxim that "knowledge is power." Two British Trade Unions, for example, have recently set up a Labour College to meet the special needs of able working-men in history, political and social science, and the like. But education in republican Rome was the freak of the individual parent, and the privilege of wealth and leisure. It was mainly in the hands of Greeks, who were in many cases slaves. There was a thin small stream of very fine learning and very fine thinking up to the first century of the monarchy, let Lucretius and Cicero witness, but it did not spread into the mass of the people. The ordinary Roman was not only blankly ignorant of the history of mankind, but also of the conditions of foreign peoples ; he had no knowledge of economic laws nor of social possibilities. Even his own interests he did not clearly understand.

Of course, in the little city states of Greece and in that early Roman state of four hundred square miles, men acquired by talk and observation a sufficient knowledge for the ordinary duties of citizenship, but by the beginning of the Punic Wars the business was already too big and complicated for illiterate men. Yet nobody seems to have observed the gap that was opening between the citizen and his state,

Photo: Mansell.
HEAD OF A BARBARIAN PRISONER.
(Græco-Roman bust.)

and so there is no record at all of any attempt to enlarge the citizen by instruction to meet his enlarged duties. From the second century B.C. and onward everyone is remarking upon the ignorance of the common citizen and his lack of political wisdom, everything is suffering from the lack of political solidarity due to this ignorance, but no one goes on to what we should now consider the inevitable corollary, no one proposes to destroy the ignorance complained of. There existed no means whatever for the instruction of the masses of the people in a common political and social ideal. It was only with the development of the great propagandist religions in the Roman world, of which Christianity was the chief and the survivor, that the possibility of such a systematic instruction of great masses of people became apparent in the world. That very great political genius, the Emperor Constantine the Great, six centuries later, was the first to apprehend and to attempt to use this possibility for the preservation and the mental and moral knitting-together of the world community over which he ruled.

But it is not only in these deficiencies of news and of education and of the expedient of representative government that this political system of Rome differed from our own. True, it was far more like a modern civilized state than any other state we have considered hitherto, but in some matters it was strangely primordial and "sub-civilized." Every now and then the reader of Roman history, reading it in terms of debates and measures, policies and campaigns, capital and labour, comes upon something that gives him much the same shock he would feel if he went down to some unknown caller in his house and extended his hand to meet the misshapen hairy paw of *Homo Neanderthalensis* and looked up to see a chinless, bestial face. We have noted the occurrence of human sacrifice in the third century B.C., and much that we learn of the religion of republican Rome carries us far back beyond the days of decent gods, to the age of shamanism and magic. We talk of a legislative gathering, and the mind flies to Westminster; but how should we feel if we went to see the beginning of a session of the House of Lords, and discovered the Lord Chancellor, with bloody fingers, portentously fiddling about among the entrails of a newly killed sheep? The mind would recoil from Westminster to the customs of Benin. And the slavery of Rome was a savage slavery, altogether viler than the slavery of Babylon. We have had a glimpse of the virtuous Cato among his slaves in the second century B.C.

Photo: *Mansell.*
A CAPTIVE BARBARIAN CHIEF.
(From the Louvre.)

Moreover, in the third century B.C., when King Asoka was ruling India in light and gentleness, the Romans were reviving an Etruscan sport, the setting on of slaves to fight for their lives. One is reminded of West Africa again in the origin of this amusement; it grew out of the prehistoric custom of a massacre of captives at the burial of a chief. There was a religious touch about this sport, the slaves with hooks, who dragged the dead bodies out of the arena, wore masks to represent the infernal ferryman-god, Charon. In 264 B.C., the very year in which Asoka began to reign and the First Punic War began, the first recorded gladiatorial combat took place

in the forum at Rome, to celebrate the funeral of a member of the old Roman family of Brutus. This was a modest display of three couples, but soon gladiators were fighting by the hundred. The taste for these combats grew rapidly, and the wars supplied an abundance of captives.

The old Roman moralists, who were so severe upon kissing and women's ornaments and Greek philosophy, had nothing but good to say for this new development. So long as pain was inflicted, Roman morality, it would seem, was satisfied.

If republican Rome was the first of modern self-governing national communities, she was certainly the 'Neanderthal' form of them.

In the course of the next two or three centuries the gladiatorial shows of Rome grew to immense proportions. To begin with, while wars were frequent, the gladiators were prisoners of war. They came with their characteristic national weapons, tattooed Britons, Moors, Scythians, negroes, and the like, and there was perhaps some military value in these exhibitions. Then criminals of the lower classes [1] condemned to death were also used. The ancient world did not understand that a criminal condemned to death still has rights, and at any rate the use of a criminal as a gladiator was not so bad as his use as "material" for the vivisectors of the Museum at Alexandria. But as the profits of this sort of show business grew and the demand for victims increased, ordinary slaves were sold to the trainers of gladiators, and any slave who had aroused his owner's spite might find himself in an establishment for letting out gladiators. And dissipated young men who had squandered their property, and lads of spirit, would go voluntarily into the trade for a

[1] Seyffert, *op. cit.*

AN ETRUSCAN REPRESENTATION OF A CEREMONIAL BURNING OF THE DEAD PAINTED ON TERRA-COTTA SLABS.

(From the Louvre.)

304]

stated time, trusting to their prowess to survive. As the business developed, a new use was found for gladiators as armed retainers ; rich men would buy a band, and employ it as a body-guard or hire it out for profit at the shows. The festivities of a show began with a cere-monial procession (*pompa*) and a sham fight (*prælusio*). The real fighting was heralded by trumpets. Gladiators who objected to fight for any reason were driven on by whips and hot irons. A wounded man would sometimes call for pity by holding up his forefinger. The spec-tators would then either wave their handker-chiefs in token of mercy, or condemn him to death by holding out their clenched fists with the thumbs up. The slain and nearly dead were dragged out to a particular place, the *spoliarium*, where they were stripped of their arms and possessions, and those who had not already expired were killed.

This organization of murder as a sport and show serves to measure the great gap in moral standards between the Roman community and our own. No doubt cruelties and outrages upon human dignity as monstrous as this still go on in the world, but they do not go on in the name of the law and without a single dissentient voice. For it is true that until the time of Seneca (first century A.D.) there is no record of any plain protest against this business. The conscience of mankind was weaker and less intelligent then than now. Presently a new power was to come into the human conscience through the spread of Christianity. The spirit of Jesus in Christianity became the great antagonist in the later Roman state of these cruel shows and of slavery, and, as Christianity spread, these two evil things dwindled and disappeared.[1]

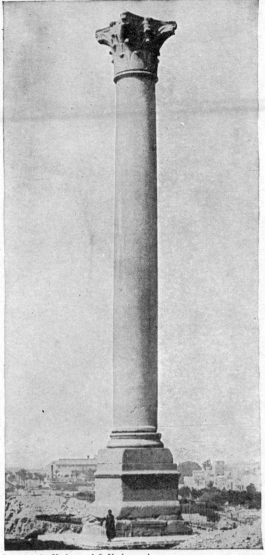

POMPEY'S PILLAR, THE SAILOR'S LANDMARK, AT ALEXANDRIA.

"The shaft was erected as a landmark for sailors by one of the Roman governors of Egypt. In the Middle Ages it was mistakenly connected with the tomb of Pompey, who was murdered on this coast, and it has therefore been called Pompey's Pillar. This column is the only surviving monument of any size from the days of Alexandria's splendour."

---

[1] "A little more needs to be said on this matter. The Greeks cited gladiatorial shows as a reason for re-garding the Romans as *Barbaroi*, and there were riots when some Roman proconsul tried to introduce them in Corinth. Among Romans, the better people evidently disliked them, but a sort of shyness prevented them from frankly denouncing them as cruel. For instance, Cicero, when he had to attend the Circus, took his tablets and his secretary with him, and didn't look. He expresses particular disgust at the killing of an elephant ; and somebody in Tacitus (Drusus, Ann. I. 76), was unpopular because he was too fond of gladiatorial bloodshed—"*quamquam vili sanguine nimis gaudens*" ("rejoicing too much in blood, worthless blood though it was"). The games were unhesitatingly condemned by Greek philosophy, and at different times two Cynics and one Christian gave their lives in the arena, protesting against them, before they were abolished.

"I do not think Christianity had any such relation to slavery as is here stated. St. Paul's action in sending back a slave to his master, and his injunction, 'Slaves, obey your masters,' were regularly quoted on the pro-slavery side, down to the nineteenth century ; on the other hand, both the popular philosophies and the Mystery religions were against slavery in their

20

whole tendency, and Christianity of course in time became the chief representative of these movements. Probably the best test is the number of slaves who occupied posts of honour in the religious and philosophic systems, like Epictetus, for instance, or the many slaves who hold offices in the Mithraic Inscriptions. I do not happen to know if any slaves were made Christian bishops, but by analogy I should think it likely that some were. In all the Mystery religions, as soon as you entered the community, and had communion with God, earthly distinctions shrivelled away."—G. M.

The Spirit of Jesus is something different from formal Christianity, which I regard as the vehicle, the largely unsympathetic vehicle, by which that spirit was carried about the world.—H. G. W.

XXVIII

FROM TIBERIUS GRACCHUS TO THE GOD EMPEROR IN ROME

§ 1

WE have already twice likened the self-governing community of Rome to a "Neanderthal" variety of the modern "democratic" civilized state, and we shall recur again to this comparison. In form the two things, the first great primitive essay and its later relations, are extraordinarily similar; in spirit they differ very profoundly.

The Science of Thwarting the Common Man.

Roman political and social life, and particularly Roman political and social life in the century between the fall of Carthage and the rise of Cæsar and Cæsarism, has a very marked general resemblance to the political and social life in such countries as the United States of America or the British Empire to-day. The resemblance is intensified by the common use, with a certain inaccuracy in every case, of such terms as "senate," "democracy," "proletariat," and the like. But everything in the Roman state was earlier, cruder, and clumsier; the injustices were more glaring, the conflicts harsher. There was comparatively little knowledge and few general ideas. Aristotle's scientific works were only beginning to be read in Rome in the first century B.C.; Ferrero,[1] it is true, makes Cæsar familiar with the Politics of Aristotle, and ascribes to him the dream of making a "Periclean Rome," but in doing so, Ferrero seems to be indulging in one of those lapses into picturesque romancing which are at once the joy and the snare of all historical writers.

Attention has already been drawn to the profound difference between Roman and modern conditions due to the absence of a press, of any popular education or of the representative idea in the popular assembly. Our world to-day is still far from solving the problem of representation and from producing a public assembly which will really summarize, crystallize, and express the thought and will of the community; our elections are still largely an ingenious mockery of the common voter who finds himself helpless in the face of party organizations which reduce his free choice of a representative to the less unpalatable of two political hacks, but, even so, his vote, in comparison with the vote of an ordinary honest Roman citizen, is an effective instrument. Too many of our histories dealing with this period of Roman history write of "the popular party," and of the votes of the people and so forth, as though such things were as much working realities as they are to-day. But the senators and politicians of Rome saw to it that such things never did exist as clean and wholesome realities. These modern phrases are very misleading unless they are carefully qualified.

We have already described the gatherings of the popular comitia; but that clumsy assembly in sheep pens does not convey the full extent to which the gerrymandering of popular representation could be carried in Rome. Whenever there was a new enfranchisement of citizens

[1] *Greatness and Decline of Rome*, bk. i. ch. xi.

in Italy, there would be the most elaborate trickery and counter-trickery to enrol the new voters into as few or as many of the thirty old "tribes" as possible, or to put them into as few as possible new tribes. Since the vote was taken by tribes, it is obvious that however great the number of new additions made, if they were all got together into one tribe, their opinion would only count for one tribal vote, and similarly if they were crowded into just a few tribes, old or new. On the other hand, if they were put into too many tribes, their effect in any particular tribe might be inconsiderable. Here was the sort of work to fascinate every smart knave in politics. The *comitia trib ta* could be *worked* at times so as to vote right counter to the general feeling of the people. And as we have already noted, the great mass of voters in Italy were also disenfranchised by distance. About the middle period of the Carthaginian wars there were upwards of 300,000 Roman citizens; about 100 B.C. there were more than 900,000, but in effect the voting of the popular assembly was confined to a few score thousand resident in and near Rome, and mostly men of a base type. And the Roman voters were "organized" to an extent that makes the Tammany machine of New York seem artless and honest. They belonged to clubs, *collegia sodalicia*, the latter having some elegant religious pretensions; and the rising politician working his way to office went first to the usurers and then with the borrowed money to these clubs. If the outside voters were moved enough by any question to swarm into the city, it was always possible to put off the voting by declaring the omens unfavourable. If they came in unarmed, they could be intimidated; if they brought in arms, then the cry was raised that there was a plot to overthrow the republic, and a massacre would be organized.

There can be no doubt that all Italy, all the empire was festering with discomfort, anxiety, and discontent in the century after the destruction of Carthage; a few men were growing very rich, and the majority of people found themselves entangled in an inexplicable net of uncertain prices, jumpy markets, and debts; but yet there was no way at all of stating and clearing up the general dissatisfaction. There is no record of a single attempt to make the popular assembly a straightforward and workable public organ. Beneath the superficial appearances of public affairs struggled a mute giant of public opinion and public will, who sometimes made some great political effort, a rush to vote or such like, and sometimes broke into actual violence. So long as there was no actual violence, the Senate and the financiers kept on in their own disastrous way. Only when they were badly frightened would governing cliques or parties desist from some nefarious policy and heed the common good. The real method of popular expression in Italy in those days was not the *comitia tributa*, but the strike and insurrection, the righteous and necessary methods of all cheated or suppressed peoples. We have seen in our own days in Great Britain a decline in the prestige of parliamentary government and a drift towards unconstitutional methods on the part of the masses through exactly the same cause, through the incurable disposition of politicians to gerrymander the electoral machine until the community is driven to explosion.

For insurrectionary purposes a discontented population needs a leader, and the political history of the concluding century of Roman republicanism is a history of insurrectionary leaders and counter-revolutionary leaders. Most of the former are manifestly unscrupulous adventurers who try to utilize the public necessity and unhappiness for their own advancement. Many of the historians of this period betray a disposition to take sides, and are either aristocratic in tone or fiercely democratic; but, indeed, neither side in these complex and intricate disputes has a record of high aims or clean hands. The Senate and the rich equestrians were vulgar and greedy spirits, hostile and contemptuous towards the poor mob; and the populace was ignorant, unstable, and at least equally greedy. The Scipios in all this record shine by comparison, a group of gentlemen. To the motives of one or the other figures of the time, to Tiberius Gracchus, for example, we may perhaps extend the benefit of the doubt. But for the rest, they do but demonstrate how clever and cunning men may be, how subtle in contention, how brilliant in pretence, and how utterly wanting in wisdom or grace of spirit. " A shambling, hairy, brutish, but probably very cunning creature with a big brain *behind* ; " so someone, I think it was Sir Harry Johnston, has described *Homo neanderthalensis*.

To this day we must still use similar terms to describe the soul of the politician. The statesman has still to oust the politician from his lairs and weapon heaps. History has still to become a record of human dignity.

§ 2

Another respect in which the Roman system was a crude anticipation of our own, and different **Finance in** from any preceding political system **the Roman** we have considered, was that it was **State.** a cash and credit-using system. Money had been in the world as yet for only a few centuries. But its use had been growing ; it was providing a fluid medium for trade and enterprise and changing economic conditions profoundly. In republican Rome, the financier and the " money " interest begin to play a part recognizably similar to their rôles to-day.

We have already noted—in our account of Herodotus—that a first effect of money was to give freedom of movement and leisure to a number of people who could not otherwise have enjoyed these privileges. And that is the peculiar value of money to mankind. Instead of a worker or helper being paid in kind and in such a way that he is tied as much in his enjoyment as in his labour, money leaves him free to do as he pleases amidst a wide choice of purchasable aids, eases, and indulgences. He may eat his money or drink it or give it to a temple or spend it in learning something or save it against some foreseen occasion. That is the good of money, the freedom of its universal convertibility. But the freedom money gives the poor man is nothing to the freedom money has given the rich man. With money rich men ceased to be tied to lands, houses, stores, flocks and herds. They could change the nature and locality of their possessions with an unheard-of freedom. In the third and second century B.C., this release, this untethering of wealth, began to tell upon the general economic life of the Roman and Hellenized world. People began to buy land and the like not for use, but to sell again at a profit ; people borrowed to buy, speculation developed. No doubt there were bankers in the Babylon of 1,000 B.C., but they lent in a far more limited and solid way, bars of metal and stocks of goods. That earlier world was a world of barter and payment in kind, and it went slowly—and much more staidly and stably—for that reason. In that state the vast realm of China has remained almost down to the present time.

The big cities before Rome were trading and manufacturing cities. Such were Corinth and Carthage and Syracuse. But Rome never produced a very considerable industrial population, and her warehouses never rivalled those of Alexandria. The little port of Ostia was always big enough for her needs. Rome was a political and financial capital, and in the latter respect, at least, she was a new sort of city. She imported profits and tribute, and very little went out from her in return. The wharves of Ostia were chiefly busy unloading corn from Sicily and Africa and loot from all the world.

After the fall of Carthage the Roman imagination went wild with the hitherto unknown possibilities of finance. Money, like most other inventions, had " happened " to mankind, and men had still to develop—to-day they have still to perfect—the science and morality of money. One sees the thing " catching on " in the recorded life and the writings of Cato the Censor. In his early days he was bitterly virtuous against usury ; in his later he was devising ingenious schemes for safe usury.

In this curiously interesting century of Roman history we find man after man asking, " What has happened to Rome ? " Various answers are made—a decline in religion, a decline from the virtues of the Roman forefathers, Greek " intellectual poison," and the like. We who can look at the problem with a large perspective, can see that what had happened to Rome was " money "—the new freedoms and chances and opportunities that money opened out. Money floated the Romans off the firm ground, everyone was getting hold of money, the majority by the simple expedient of running into debt ; the eastward expansion of the empire was very largely a hunt for treasure in strong rooms and temples to keep pace with the hunger of the new need. The Equestrian order, in particular, became the money power.

Photo: Giraudon.

"FATHER TIBER" (LATE ROMAN).

Everyone was developing property. Farmers were giving up corn and cattle, borrowing money, buying slaves, and starting the more intensive cultivation of oil and wine. Money was young in human experience and wild, nobody had it under control. It fluctuated wildly. It was now abundant and now scarce. Men made sly and crude schemes to corner it, to hoard it, to send up prices by releasing hoarded metals. A small body of very shrewd men was growing immensely rich. Many patricians were growing poor and irritated and unscrupulous. Among the middle sort of peoples there was much hope, much adventure, and much more disappointment. The growing mass of the expropriated was permeated by that vague, baffled, and hopeless sense of being explicably bested, which is the preparatory condition for all great revolutionary movements.

§ 3

The first conspicuous leader to appeal to the gathering revolutionary feeling in Italy was Tiberius Gracchus. He looks more like an honest man than any other figure in this period of history, unless it be Scipio Africanus the Elder. At first Tiberius Gracchus was a moderate reformer of a rather reactionary type. He wished to restore the yeoman class to property, very

The Last Years of Republican Politics.

largely because he believed that class to be the backbone of the army, and his military experience in Spain before and after the destruction of Carthage had impressed upon him the declining efficiency of the legions. He was what we should call nowadays a "Back-to-the-land" man. He did not understand, and few people understand to-day, how much easier it is to shift population from the land into the towns, than to return it to the laborious and simple routines of agricultural life. He wanted to revive the Licinian laws, which had been established when Camillus built his temple of Concord nearly two centuries and a half before (see Chap. xxvii, § 2), so far as they broke up great estates and restrained slave labour.

These Licinian laws had repeatedly been revived and repeatedly lapsed to a dead letter again. It was only when the big proprietors in the Senate opposed this proposal that Tiberius Gracchus turned to the people and began a furious agitation for popular government. He created a commission to inquire into the title of all landowners. In the midst of his activities occurred one of the most extraordinary incidents in history. Attalus, the king of the rich country of Pergamus in Asia Minor, died (133 B.C.), and left his kingdom to the Roman people.

It is difficult for us to understand the motives of this bequest. Pergamus was a country allied to Rome, and so moderately secure from aggression ; and the natural consequence of such a will was to provoke a violent scramble among the senatorial gangs and a dispute between them and the people for the spoils of the new acquisition. Practically Attalus handed over his country to be looted. The act is so amazing that one is driven towards the hypothesis of forgery.[1] There were of course many Italian business people established in the country and a strong party of native rich men in close relations with Rome. To them, no doubt, a coalescence with the Roman system would have been acceptable. Josephus bears witness to such a desire for annexation among the rich men of Syria, a desire running counter to the wishes of both king and people. This Pergamus bequest, astonishing in itself, had the still more astonishing result of producing imitations in other quarters. In 96 B.C. Ptolemy Apion bequeathed Cyrenaica, in North Africa, to the Roman people ; in 81 B.C. Alexander II, King of Egypt, followed suit with Egypt, a legacy too big for the courage if not for the appetite of the Senators, and they declined it ; in 74 B.C. Nicomedes, King of Bithynia, demised Bithynia. Of these latter testamentary freaks we will say no more here. But it will be manifest how great an opportunity was given Tiberius Gracchus by the bequest of Attalus, of accusing the rich of greed and of proposing to decree the treasures of Attalus to the commonalty. He proposed to use this new wealth to provide seed, stock, and agricultural implements for the resettlement of the land.

His movement was speedily entangled in the complexities of the Roman electoral system— without a simple and straightforward electoral method, all popular movements in all ages necessarily become entangled and maddened in constitutional intricacies, and almost as necessarily lead to bloodshed. It was needed,

if his work was to go on, that Tiberius Gracchus should continue to be tribune, and it was illegal for him to be tribune twice in succession. He overstepped the bounds of legality, and stood for the tribuneship a second time ; the peasants who came in from the countryside to vote for him came in armed ; the cry that he was aiming at a tyranny, the cry that had long ago destroyed Mælius and Manlius, was raised in the Senate, the friends of "law and order" went to the Capitol in state, accompanied by a rabble of dependents armed with staves and bludgeons; there was a conflict, or rather a massacre of the revolutionaries, in which nearly three hundred people were killed, and Tiberius Gracchus was beaten to death with the fragments of a broken bench by two Senators.

Thereupon the Senators attempted a sort of counter-revolution, and proscribed many of the followers of Tiberius Gracchus ; but the state of public opinion was so sullen and threatening that this movement was dropped and Scipio Nasica, who was implicated in the death of Tiberius, though he occupied the position of pontifex maximus, and should have remained in Rome for the public sacrifices which were the duties of that official, went abroad to avoid trouble.

The uneasiness of Italy next roused Scipio Africanus the Younger to propose the enfranchisement of all Italy. But he died suddenly before he could carry the proposal into effect.

Then followed the ambiguous career of Caius Gracchus, the brother of Tiberius, who followed some tortuous "policy" that still exercises the mind of historians. He increased the burthens of taxation laid upon the provinces, it is supposed with the idea of setting the modern financiers (the Equites) against the senatorial landowners. He gave the former the newly bequeathed taxes of Asia to farm, and, what is worse, he gave them control of the special courts set up to prevent extortion. He started enormous public works and particularly the construction of new roads, and he is accused of making a political use of the contracts. He revived the proposal to enfranchise Italy. He increased the distribution of subsidized cheap corn to the Roman citizens. . . . Here we cannot attempt to disentangle his schemes, much less to judge him. But that his policy was offensive to the groups

---

[1] There is no evidence of forgery and no contemporary suggestion of the sort. The bequest of Attalus, even if it was a forgery (Mommsen accepts it, iii. p. 55), is of importance, as showing that a great many people did think that Rome was the best administrator. Otherwise, the story (if it is only a story) could not have caught on. *A priori* there seems good reason for the testament. The Attalid dynasty was "petering out" ; there were troublesome Gauls about (Mommsen, iii. p. 53).—J. L. M., and E. B.

THE FORUM, ROME.
The Column of Phocas, the Tabularium, and the Arch of Septimius Severus.

that controlled the Senate there can be no doubt whatever. He was massacred by the champions of "law and order," with about three thousand of his followers, in the streets of Rome in 121 B.C. His decapitated head was carried to the Senate on the point of a pike.

(A reward of its weight in gold, says Plutarch, had been offered for this trophy ; and its captor, acting in the true spirit of a champion of "big business," filled the brain-case with lead on its way to the scales.)

In spite of these prompt firm measures the Senate was not to enjoy the benefits of peace and the advantages of a control of the imperial resources for long. Within ten years the people were in revolt again.

In 118 B.C. the throne of Numidia, the semi-barbaric kingdom that had arisen in North Africa upon the ruins of the civilized Carthaginian power, was seized by a certain able Jugurtha, who had served with the Roman armies in Spain, and had a knowledge of the Roman character. He provoked the military intervention of Rome. But the Romans found that their military power, under a Senate of financiers and landlords, was very different from what it had been even in the days of the younger Scipio Africanus. " Jugurtha bought over the Commissioners sent out to watch him, the Senators charged with their prosecution, and the generals in command against him."[1] There is a mistaken Roman proverb : ' *pecunia non olet* ' (money does not stink), for the money of Jugurtha stank even in Rome. There was a great popular outcry, and a capable soldier of lowly origin, Marius, was carried to the consulship (107 B.C.) on the wave of popular indignation. Marius made no attempt on the model of the Gracchi to restore the backbone of the army by rehabilitating the yeoman class. He was a professional soldier with a high standard of efficiency and a disposition to take short cuts. He simply raised troops from among the poor, whether countrymen or townsmen, paid them well, disciplined them thoroughly, and

[1] Ferrero.

(106 B.C.) ended the seven years' war with Jugurtha by bringing that chieftain in chains to Rome. It did not occur to anybody that incidentally Marius had also created a professional army with no interest to hold it together but its pay. He then held on to the consulship more or less illegally for several years, and in 102 and 101 B.C. repelled a threatening move of the Germans (who thus appear in our history for the first time), who were raiding through Gaul towards Italy. He gained two victories; one on Italian soil. He was hailed as the saviour of his country, a second Camillus (100 B.C.).

The social tensions of the time mocked that comparison with Camillus. The Senate benefited by the greater energy in foreign affairs and the increased military efficiency that Marius had introduced, but the sullen, shapeless discontent of the mass of the people was still seeking some effective outlet. The rich grew richer and the poor poorer. It was impossible to stifle the consequences of that process for ever by political trickery. The Italian people were still unenfranchised. Two extreme democratic leaders, Saturninus and Glaucia, were assassinated, but that familiar senatorial remedy failed to assuage the populace on this occasion. In 92 B.C. an aristocratic official, Rutilius Rufus, who had tried to restrain the exactions of the financiers in Asia Minor, was condemned on a charge of corruption so manifestly trumped up that it deceived no one; and in 91 B.C., Livius Drusus, a newly elected tribune of the people, who was making capital out of the trial of Rutilius Rufus, was assassinated. He had proposed a general enfranchisement of the Italians, and he had foreshadowed not only another land law, but a general abolition of debts. Yet for all this vigour on the part of the senatorial usurers, landgrabbers, and forestallers, the hungry and the anxious were still insurgent. The murder of Drusus was the last drop in the popular cup; Italy blazed into a desperate insurrection.

There followed two years of bitter civil war, the Social War. It was a war between the idea of a united Italy and the idea of the rule of the Roman Senate. It was not a " social " war in the modern sense, but a war between Rome and her Italian allies (allies = Socii). " Roman generals, trained in the traditions of colonial warfare, marched ruthlessly up and down Italy, burning farms, sacking towns, and carrying off men, women, and children, to sell them in the open market or work them in gangs upon their estates." [1] Marius and an aristocratic general, Sulla, who had been with him in Africa and who was his bitter rival, both commanded on the side of Rome. But though the insurgents experienced defeats and looting, neither of these generals brought the war to an end. It was ended in a manner (89 B.C.) by the practical surrender of the Roman Senate to the idea of reform. The spirit was taken out of the insurrection by the concession of their demands " in principle " ; and then as soon as the rebels had dispersed, the usual cheating of the new voters, by such methods as we have explained in § 1 of this chapter, was resumed.

By the next year (88 B.C.) the old round had begun again. It was mixed up with the personal intrigues of Marius and Sulla against each other; but the struggle had taken on another complexion through the army reforms of Marius, which had created a new type of legionary, a landless professional soldier with no interest in life but pay and plunder, and with no feeling of loyalty except to a successful general. A popular tribune, Sulpicius, was bringing forward some new laws affecting debt, and the consuls were dodging the storm by declaring a suspension of public business. Then came the usual resort to violence, and the followers of Sulpicius drove the consuls from the forum. But here it is that the new forces which the new army had made possible came into play. King Mithridates of Pontus, the Hellenized king of the southern shores of the Black Sea east of Bithynia, was pressing Rome into war. One of the proposed laws of Sulpicius was that Marius should command the armies sent against this Mithridates. Whereupon Sulla marched the army he had commanded throughout the Social War to Rome, Marius and Sulpicius fled, and a new age, an age of military pronunciamentos, began.

Of how Sulla had himself made commander against Mithridates and departed, and of how legions friendly to Marius then seized power, how Marius returned to Italy and enjoyed a thorough massacre of his political opponents

[1] Ferrero.

and died, sated, of fever, we cannot tell in any detail. But one measure during the Marian reign of terror did much to relieve the social tension, and that was the abolition of three-quarters of all outstanding debts. Nor can we tell here how Sulla made a discreditable peace with Mithridates (who had massacred a hundred thousand Italians in Asia Minor) in order to bring his legions back to Rome, defeat the Marians at the battle of the Colline Gate of Rome, and reverse the arrangements of Marius. Sulla restored law and order by the proscription and execution of over five thousand people. He desolated large parts of Italy, restored the Senate to power, repealed many of the recent laws, though he was unable to restore the cancelled burden of debt, and then, feeling bored by politics and having amassed great riches, he retired with an air of dignity into private life, gave himself up to abominable vices, and so presently died, eaten up with some disgusting disease produced by debauchery.[1]

Photo: Brogi.

POMPEY THE GREAT.

relying more and more on the support of the legions, presently began to scheme and intrigue again for dictatorial power in Rome. In 73 B.C. all Italy was terrified by a rising of the slaves, and particularly of the gladiators, led by a gladiator from Thessaly, Spartacus. He and seventy others had fled out from a gladiatorial " farm" at Capua. Similar risings had already occurred in Sicily. The forces under Spartacus necessarily became a miscellaneous band drawn from east and west, without any common idea except the idea of dispersing and getting home; nevertheless, he held out in Southern Italy for two years, using the then apparently extinct crater of Vesuvius for a time as a natural fortress. The Italians, for all their love of gladiatorial display, failed to appreciate this conversion of the whole country into an arena, this bringing of the gladiatorial sword to the door, and when at last Spartacus was overthrown, their terror changed to frantic cruelty, six thousand of his captured followers were crucified—long miles of nailed and drooping victims—along the Appian Way.

§ 4

The Era of the Adventurer Generals.

Political life in Italy was not so much tranquillized as stunned by the massacres and confiscations of Marius and Sulla. The scale upon which this history is planned will not permit us to tell here of the great adventurers who,

Here we cannot deal at any length with Lucullus, who invaded Pontus and fought Mithridates, and brought the cultivated cherry-tree to Europe; nor can we tell how ingeniously Pompey the Great stole the triumph and most of the prestige Lucullus had won in Armenia beyond Pontus. Lucullus, like Sulla, retired into an opulent private life, but with more elegance and with a more gracious end. We cannot relate in any detail how Julius Cæsar accumulated reputation in the west, by conquering Gaul, defeating the German tribes upon

[1] Plutarch. To which, however, G. M. adds the following note. " It is generally believed that Sulla died through bursting a blood-vessel in a fit of temper. The story of abominable vices seems to be only the regular slander of the Roman mob against anyone who did not live in public."

the Rhine, and pushing a punitive raid across the Straits of Dover into Britain. More and more important grow the legions ; less and less significant are the Senate and the assemblies of Rome. But there is a certain grim humour about the story of Crassus that we cannot altogether neglect.

This Crassus was a great money-lender and forestaller. He was a typical man of the new Equestrian type, the social equivalent of a modern munition profiteer. He first grew rich by buying up the property of those proscribed by Sulla. His earliest exploits in the field were against Spartacus, whom finally he crushed by great payments and exertions after a prolonged and expensive campaign. He then, as the outcome of complicated bargains, secured the command in the east and prepared to emulate the glories of Lucullus, who had pushed east from Pergamus and Bithynia into Pontus, and of Pompey, who had completed the looting of Armenia.

His experiences serve to demonstrate the gross ignorance with which the Romans were conducting their affairs at that time. He crossed the Euphrates, expecting to find in Persia another Hellenized kingdom like Pontus. But, as we have already intimated, the great reservoirs of nomadic peoples that stretched round from the Danube across Russia into Central Asia, had been raining back into the lands between the Caspian Sea and the Indus that Alexander had conquered for Hellenism. Crassus found himself against the "Scythian" again ; against mobile tribes of horsemen led by a monarch in Median costume.[1] The particular variety of "Scythian" he encountered was called the Parthian. It is possible that in the Parthians a Mongolian (Turanian) element was now mingled with the Aryan strain ; but the campaign of Crassus beyond the Euphrates is curiously like the campaign of Darius beyond the Danube ; there is the same heavy thrusting of an infantry force against elusive light horsemen. But Crassus was less quick than Darius to realize the need of withdrawal, and the Parthians were better bowmen than the Scythians Darius met. They seem to have had some sort of noisy projectile of unusual strength and force, something different from

[1] Plutarch.

an ordinary arrow.[2] The campaign culminated in that two days' massacre of the hot, thirsty, hungry, and weary Roman legions, which is known as the battle of Carrhæ (53 B.C.) They toiled through the sand, charging an enemy who always evaded their charge and rode round them and shot them to pieces. Twenty thousand of them were killed, and ten thousand marched on eastward as prisoners into slavery in Iran.

What became of Crassus is not clearly known. There is a story, probably invented for our moral benefit and suggested by his usuries, that he fell alive into the hands of the Parthians and was killed by having molten gold poured down his throat.

But this disaster has a very great significance indeed to our general history of mankind. It serves to remind us that from the Rhine to the Euphrates, all along to the north of the Alps and Danube and Black Sea, stretched one continuous cloud of nomadic and semi-nomadic peoples, whom the statescraft of imperial Rome was never able to pacify and civilize, nor her military science subdue. We have already called attention to a map showing how the Second Babylonian Empire, the Chaldean Empire, lay like a lamb in the embrace of the Median power. In exactly the same way the Roman Empire lay like a lamb in the embrace of this great crescent of outer barbarians. Not only was Rome never able to thrust back or assimilate that superincumbent crescent, but she was never able to organize the Mediterranean Sea into a secure and orderly system of communication between one part of her empire and another. Quite unknown as yet to Rome, the Mongolian tribes from North-eastern Asia, the Huns and their kin, walled back and driven out from China by the Tsi and Han dynasties,

[2] The bow was probably the composite bow, so-called because it is made of several plates (five or so) of horn, like the springs of a carriage : it discharges a high-speed arrow with a twang. This was the bow the Mongols used. This short composite bow (it was not a long bow) was quite old in human experience. It was the bow of Odysseus ; the Assyrians had it in a modified form. It went out in Greece, but it survived as the Mongol bow. It was quite short, very stiff to pull, with a flat trajectory, a remarkable range, and a great noise (cp. Homer's reference to the twang of the bow). It went out in the Mediterranean because the climate was not good for it, and because there were insufficient animals to supply the horn.—J. L. M.

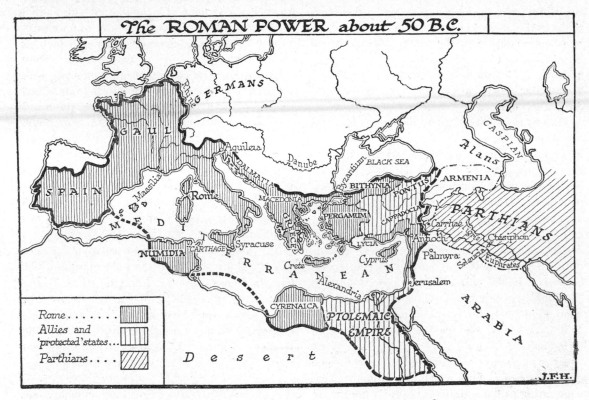

The ROMAN POWER about 50 B.C.

Rome ....
Allies and 'protected' states...
Parthians....

were drifting and pressing westward, mixing with the Parthians, the Scythians, the Teutons and the like, or driving them before them.

Never at any time did the Romans succeed in pushing their empire beyond Mesopotamia, and upon Mesopotamia their hold was never very secure. Before the close of the republic that power of assimilation which had been the secret of their success was giving way to "patriotic" exclusiveness and "patriotic" greed. Rome plundered and destroyed Asia Minor and Babylonia, which were the necessary basis for an eastward extension to India, just as she had destroyed and looted Carthage and so had no foothold for extension into Africa, and just as she had destroyed Corinth and so cut herself off from an easy way into the heart of Greece. Western European writers, impressed by the fact that later on Rome Romanized and civilized Gaul and South Britain and restored the scene of her earlier devastations in Spain to prosperity, are apt to ignore that over far greater areas to the south and east her influence was to weaken and so restore to barbarism the far wider conquests of Hellenic civilization.

§ 5

But among the politicians of Italy in the first century B.C. there were no maps of Germany and Russia, Africa and Central Asia, and no sufficient intelligence to study them had they existed. Rome never developed the fine curiosities that sent Hanno and the sailors of Pharaoh Necho down the coasts of Africa. When, in the first century B.C., the emissaries of the Han dynasty reached the eastern shores of the Caspian Sea, they found only stories of a civilization that had receded. The memory of Alexander still lived in these lands, but of Rome men only knew that Pompey had come to the western shores of the Caspian and gone away again, and that Crassus had been destroyed. Rome was preoccupied at home. What mental energy remained over in the Roman citizen from the attempt to grow personally rich and keep personally safe was intent upon the stratagems and strokes and counter-strokes of the various adventurers who were now manifestly grappling for the supreme power.

It is the custom of historians to treat these struggles with extreme respect. In particular

Caius Julius Cæsar and his Death.

the figure of Julius Cæsar is set up as if it were a star of supreme brightness and importance in the history of mankind.[1] Yet a dispassionate consideration of the known facts fails altogether to justify this demi-god theory of Cæsar. Not even that precipitate wrecker of splendid possibilities, Alexander the Great, has been so magnified and dressed up for the admiration of careless and uncritical readers. There is a type of scholar who, to be plain, sits and *in-*

Photo: *Alinari.*

JULIUS CÆSAR.
(In the Uffizi Gallery, Florence.)

vents marvellous world policies for the more conspicuous figures in history with the merest scraps of justification or with no justification at all. We are told that Alexander planned the conquest of Carthage and Rome and the complete subjugation of India, and that only his death shattered these schemes. What we know for certain is that he conquered the Persian Empire, and never went far beyond its boundaries; and that when he was supposed to be making these vast and noble plans, he was in fact indulging in such monstrous antics as his mourning for his favourite Hephæstion, and as his main occupation he was drinking himself to

death. So too Julius Cæsar is credited with the intention of doing just that one not impossible thing which would have secured the Roman Empire from its ultimate collapse—namely, the systematic conquest and civilization of Europe as far as the Baltic and the Dnieper. He was to have marched upon Germany, says Plutarch, through Parthia and Scythia, round the north of the Caspian and Black Seas. Yet the fact we have to reconcile with this wise and magnificent project is that at the crest of his power, Cæsar, already a bald, middle-aged man, past the graces and hot impulses of youthful love, spent the better part of a year in Egypt, feasting and entertaining himself in amorous pleasantries with the Egyptian queen Cleopatra. And afterwards he brought her with him to Rome, where her influence over him was bitterly resented. Such complications with a woman mark the elderly sensualist or sentimentalist—he was fifty-four at the commencement of the *affaire*—rather than the master-ruler of men.

On the side of the superman idea of Cæsar, we have to count a bust in the Naples Museum. It represents a fine and intellectual face, very noble in its expression, and we can couple with that the story that his head, even at birth, was unusually large and finely formed. But there is really no satisfying evidence that this well-known bust does represent Cæsar, and it is hard to reconcile its austere serenity with the reputation for violent impulse and disorderliness that clung to him. Other busts of a quite different man are also, with more probability, ascribed to him.

There can be little doubt that he was a dissolute and extravagant young man—the scandals cluster thick about his sojourn in Bithynia, whither he fled from Sulla; he was the associate of the reprobate Clodius and the conspirator Catiline, and there is nothing in his political career to suggest any aim higher or remoter than his own advancement to power, and all the personal glory and indulgence that power makes possible. We will not attempt to tell here of the turns and devices of his career. Although he was of an old patrician family, he came into politics as the brilliant darling of the people. He spent great sums and incurred heavy debts to provide public festivals on the most lavish scale. He opposed the

---

[1] For a good compact account of Cæsar, much more appreciative of him than our text, see Warde Fowler's *Julius Cæsar.*

tradition of Sulla, and cherished the memory of Marius, who was his uncle by marriage. For a time he worked in conjunction with Crassus and Pompey, but after the death of Crassus he and Pompey came into conflict. By 49 B.C. he and Pompey, with their legions, he from the west and Pompey from the east, were fighting openly for predominance in the Roman state. He had broken the law by bringing his legions across the Rubicon, which was the boundary between his command and Italy proper. At the battle of Pharsalus in Thessaly (48 B.C.), Pompey was routed, and, fleeing to Egypt, was

Photo: Mansell.
ANOTHER BUST ASCRIBED TO JULIUS CÆSAR
(British Museum).
"Undoubtedly a close copy of an authentic original."—*Stobart.*

murdered, leaving Cæsar more master of the Roman world than ever Sulla had been.

He was then created dictator for ten years in 46 B.C., and early in 45 B.C. he was made dictator for life. This was monarchy; if not hereditary monarchy, it was at least electoral life monarchy. It was unlimited opportunity to do his best for the world. And by the spirit and quality of his use of this dictatorial power during these four years we are bound to judge him. A certain reorganization of local administration he effected, and he seems to have taken up what was a fairly obvious necessity of the times, a project for the restoration of the two murdered seaports of Corinth and Carthage, whose destruction had wrecked the sea-life of the Mediterranean. But much more evident was the influence of Cleopatra and Egypt upon his mind. Like Alexander before him, his head seems to have been turned by the king-god tradition, assisted no doubt in his case by the adulation of that charming hereditary-goddess,

Cleopatra. We find evidence of exactly that same conflict upon the score of divine pretensions, between him and his personal friends, that we have already recorded in the case of Alexander. So far as the Hellenized east was concerned, the paying of divine honours to rulers was a familiar idea; but it was still repulsive to the lingering Aryanism of Rome.

Antony, who had been his second in command at Pharsalus, was one of the chief of his flatterers. Plutarch describes a scene at the public games in which Antony tried to force a crown upon Cæsar, which Cæsar, after a little coyness and in face of the manifested displeasure of the crowd, refused. But he had adopted the ivory sceptre and throne, which were the traditional insignia of the ancient kings of Rome. His image was carried amidst that of the gods in the opening *pompa* of the arena, and his statue was set up in a temple with an inscription, "To the Unconquerable God!" Priests even were appointed for his godhead. These things are not the symptoms of greatmindedness, but of a common man's megalomania. Cæsar's record of vulgar scheming for the tawdriest mockeries of personal worship is a silly and shameful record; it is incompatible with the idea that he was a wise and wonderful superman setting the world to rights.

Finally (44 B.C.) he was assassinated by a group of his own friends and supporters, to whom these divine aspirations had become intolerable. He was beset in the Senate, and stabbed in three and twenty places, dying at the foot of the statue of his fallen rival Pompey the

Great. The scene marks the complete demoralization of the old Roman governing body. Brutus, the ringleader of the murderers, would have addressed the senators, but, confronted by this crisis, they were scuttling off in every direction. For the best part of a day Rome did not know what to make of this event ; the murderers marched about with their bloody weapons through an undecided city, with no one gainsaying them and only a few joining them ; then public opinion turned against them, some of their houses were attacked, and they had to hide and fly for their lives.

§ 6

But the trend of things was overwhelmingly towards monarchy. For thirteen years more **The End of the Republic.** the struggle of personalities went on. One single man is to be noted as inspired by broad ideas and an ambition not entirely egoistic, Cicero. He was a man of modest origin, whose eloquence and literary power had won him a prominent place in the Senate. He was a little tainted by the abusive tradition of Demosthenes, nevertheless he stands out, a noble and pathetically ineffective figure, pleading with the now utterly degenerate, base, and cowardly Senate for the high ideals of the Republic. He was a writer of great care and distinction, and the orations and private letters he has left us make him one of the most real and living figures of this period to the modern reader.[1] He was prosecuted and killed in 43 B.C., the year after the murder of Julius Cæsar, and his head and hands were nailed up in the Roman forum. Octavian, who became at last the monarch of Rome, seems to have made an effort to save Cicero; that murder was certainly not his crime.

Here we cannot trace out the tangle of alliances and betrayals that ended in the ascendancy of this Octavian, the adopted heir of Julius Cæsar. The fate of the chief figures is interwoven with that of Cleopatra.

After the death of Cæsar, she set herself to capture the emotions and vanity of Antony, a much younger man than Cæsar, with whom she was probably already acquainted. For a time Octavian and Antony and a third figure,

[1] See Strachan Davidson's *Cicero*, or, better, his own letters to Atticus.

Lepidus, divided the Roman world just as Cæsar and Pompey had divided it before their final conflict. Octavian took the hardier west, and consolidated his power ; Antony had the more gorgeous east—and Cleopatra. To Lepidus fell that picked bone, Carthaginian Africa. He seems to have been a good man of good traditions, set upon the restoration of

Photo: Bonfils.

CLEOPATRA.
From an Egyptian relief.

Carthage rather than upon wealth or personal vanities. The mind of Antony succumbed to those same ancient ideas of divine kingship that had already proved too much for the mental equilibrium of Julius Cæsar. In the company of Cleopatra he gave himself up to love, amusements, and a dream of sensuous glory, until Octavian felt that the time was ripe to end these two Egyptian divinities.

In 32 B.C. Octavian induced the Senate to depose Antony from the command of the east, and proceeded to attack him. A great naval battle at Actium (31 B.C.) was decided by the sudden desertion of Cleopatra with sixty ships in the midst of the fight. It is quite impossible for us to decide now whether this was due to premeditated treachery or to the sudden whim of a charming woman. The departure of these ships threw the fleet of Antony into hopeless confusion, which was increased by the headlong flight of this model lover in pursuit. He

Photo: Mansell.

CLEOPATRA.

From a Roman bust in the British Museum ; obviously the same woman as the Egyptian portrait, but by a less appreciative artist.

went off in a swift galley after her without informing his commanders. He left his followers to fight and die as they thought fit, and for a time they were incredulous that he had gone. The subsequent encounter of the two lovers and their reconciliation is a matter for ironical speculation on the part of Plutarch.

Octavian's net closed slowly round his rival. It is not improbable that there was some sort of understanding between Octavian and Cleopatra, as perhaps in the time of Julius Cæsar there may have been between the queen and Antony. Antony gave way to much mournful posturing, varied by love scenes, during this last stage of his little drama. For a time he posed as an imitator of the cynic Timon, as one who had lost all faith in mankind, though one may think that his deserted sailors at Actium had better reason for such an attitude. Finally he found himself and Cleopatra besieged by Octavian in Alexandria. There were some sallies and minor successes, and Antony was loud with challenges to Octavian to decide the matter by personal combat. Being led to believe that Cleopatra had committed suicide, this star of romance stabbed himself, but so ineffectually as to die lingeringly, and he was carried off to expire in her presence (30 B.C.).

Plutarch's account of Antony, which was derived very largely from witnesses who had seen and known him, describes him as of heroic mould. He is compared to the demi-god Hercules, from whom indeed he claimed descent, and also to the Indian Bacchus. There is a disgusting but illuminating description of a scene in the Senate when he attempted to speak while drunk, and was overtaken by one of the least dignified concomitants of intoxication.

For a little while Cleopatra still clung to life, and perhaps to the hope that she might reduce Octavian to the same divine rôle that had already been played by Julius Cæsar and Antony. She had an interview with Octavian, in which she presented herself as beauty in distress and very lightly clad. But when it became manifest that Octavian lacked the godlike spark, and that his care for her comfort and welfare was dictated chiefly by his desire to exhibit her in a triumphal procession through the streets of Rome, she also committed suicide. An asp was smuggled to her past the Roman sentries, concealed in a basket of figs, and by its fangs she died.

Octavian seems to have been almost entirely free from the divine aspirations of Julius Cæsar and Antony. He was neither God nor romantic hero ; he was a man. He was a man of far greater breadth and capacity than any other player in this last act of the Republican drama in Rome. All things considered, he was perhaps the best thing that could have happened to Rome at that time. He " voluntarily resigned the extraordinary powers which he had held since 43, and, to quote his own words, ' handed over the republic to the control of the senate and the people of Rome.' The old constitutional machinery was once more set in motion; the senate, assembly, and magistrates resumed their functions, and Octavian himself was hailed as the 'restorer of the commonwealth and the champion of freedom.' It was not so easy to determine what relation he himself, the actual master of the Roman world, should occupy towards this revived republic. His abdication, in any real sense of the word, would have simply thrown everything back into confusion. The interests of peace and order required that he should retain at least the substantial part of his authority; and this object was in fact accomplished, and the rule of the emperors founded, in a manner which has no parallel in history. Any revival of the kingly title was out of the question, and Octavian himself expressly refused the dictatorship. Nor was any new office created or any new official title invented for his benefit. But by senate and people he was invested according to the old constitutional forms with certain powers, as many citizens had been before him, and so took his place by the side of the lawfully appointed magistrates of the republic; only, to mark his pre-eminent dignity, as the first of them all, the senate decreed that he should take as an additional cognomen that of 'Augustus,' while in common parlance he was henceforth styled Princeps, a simple title of courtesy, familiar to republican usage and conveying no other idea than that of a recognized primacy and precedence over his fellow-citizens. The ideal

Photo : Mansell.
AUGUSTUS, WHEN A BOY (British Museum).

sketched by Cicero in his *De Republica*, of a constitutional president of a free republic, was apparently realized; but it was only in appearance. For in fact the special prerogatives conferred upon Octavian gave him back in substance the autocratic authority he had resigned, and as between the restored republic and its new *princeps* the balance of power was overwhelmingly on the side of the latter." [1]

§ 7

In this manner it was that Roman republicanism ended in a *princeps* or ruling prince, and the first great experiment in a self-governing community on a scale larger than that of tribe or city, collapsed and failed.

Why the Roman Republic Failed.

The essence of its failure was that it could not sustain unity. In its early stages its citizens, both patrician and plebeian, had a certain tradition of justice and good faith, and of the loyalty of all citizens to the law, and of the goodness of the law for all citizens; it clung to this idea of the importance of the law and of law-abidingness nearly into the first century B.C. But the unforeseen invention and development of money, the temptations and disruptions of imperial expansion, the entanglement of electoral methods, weakened and swamped this tradition by presenting old issues in new disguises under which the judgment did not recognize them, and by enabling men to be

[1] H. S. Jones in *The Encyclopædia Britannica*, article "Rome." His contribution is admirably verified and exact, and we are greatly indebted to it.

A STREET IN POMPEII, THE BRIGHTON OF ROME, TO-DAY.

321]

loyal to the professions of citizenship and disloyal to its spirit. The bond of the Roman people had always been a moral rather than a religious bond; their religion was sacrificial and superstitious; it embodied no such great ideas of a divine leader and of a sacred mission as Judaism was developing. As the idea of citizenship failed and faded before the new occasions, there remained no inner, that is to say no real, unity in the system at all. Every man tended more and more to do what was right in his own eyes.

Under such conditions there was no choice between chaos and a return to monarchy, to the acceptance of some chosen individual as the one unifying will in the state. Of course in that return there is always hidden the expectation that the monarch will become as it were magic, will cease to be merely a petty human being, and will think and feel as something greater and more noble, as indeed a state personage; and of course monarchy invariably fails to satisfy that expectation. We shall glance at the extent of this failure in the brief review we shall presently make of the emperors of Rome. We shall find at last one of the more constructive of these emperors, Constantine the Great, conscious of his own inadequacy as a unifying power, turning to the faith, the organization, and teaching network of one of the new religious movements in the empire, to supply just that permeating and correlating factor in men's minds that was so manifestly wanting.

With Cæsar, the civilization of Europe and Western Asia went back to monarchy, and, through monarchy, assisted presently by organized Christianity, it sought to achieve peace, righteousness, happiness, and world order for close upon eighteen centuries. Then almost suddenly it began reverting to republicanism, first in one country and then in another, and, assisted by the new powers of printing and the press and of organized general education, and by the universalist religious ideas in which the world had been soaked for generations, it has now resumed again the effort to create a republican world-state and a world-wide scheme of economic righteousness which the Romans had made so prematurely and in which they had so utterly and disastrously failed.

Certain conditions, we are now beginning to perceive, are absolutely necessary to such a

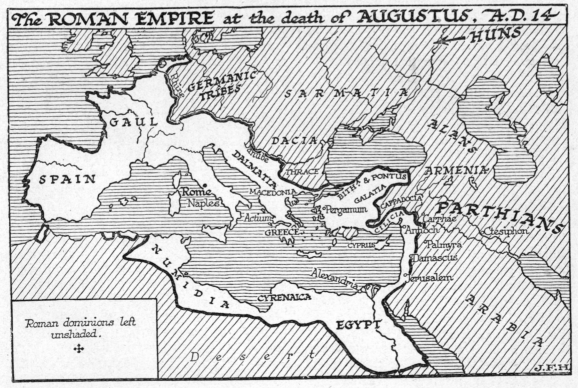

The ROMAN EMPIRE at the death of AUGUSTUS, A.D. 14

Roman dominions left unshaded.

creation; conditions which it is inconceivable that any pre-Christian Roman could have regarded as possible. We may still think the attainment of these conditions a vastly laborious and difficult and uncertain undertaking, but we understand that the attempt must be made because no other prospect before us gives even a promise of happiness or self-respect or preservation of our kind. The first of these conditions is that there should be a common political idea in the minds of all men, an idea of the state thought of as the personal possession of each individual and as the backbone fact of his scheme of duties. In the early days of Rome, when it was a little visible state, twenty miles square, such notions could be and were developed in children in their homes, and by what they saw and heard of the political lives of their fathers; but in a larger country such as Rome had already become before the war with Pyrrhus, there was a need of an organized teaching of the history, of the main laws, and of the general intentions of the state towards everyone if this moral unity was to be maintained. But the need was never realized, and no attempt at any such teaching was ever made. At the time it could not have been made. It is inconceivable that it could have been made. The knowledge was not there, and there existed no class from which the needed teachers could be drawn and no conception of an organization for any such systematic moral and intellectual training as the teaching organization of Christianity, with its creeds and catechisms and sermons and confirmations, presently supplied.

Moreover, we know nowadays that even a universal education of this sort supplies only the basis for a healthy republican state. Next to education there must come abundant, prompt, and truthful information of what is going on in the state, and frank and free discussion of the issues of the time. Even nowadays these functions are performed only very imperfectly and badly by the press we have and by our publicists and politicians; but badly though it is done, the thing is done, and the fact that it is done at all argues that it may ultimately be done well. In the Roman state it was not even attempted. The Roman citizen got his political facts from rumour and the occasional orator. He stood wedged in the forum, imperfectly hearing a distant speaker. He probably misconceived every issue upon which he voted.

And of the monstrous ineffectiveness of the Roman voting system we have already written.

Unable to surmount or remove these obstacles to a sane and effective popular government, the political instincts of the Roman mind turned towards monarchy. But it was not monarchy of the later European type, not hereditary monarchy, which was now installed in Rome. The *princeps* was really like an American war-time president elected not for three years, but for life, able to appoint senators instead of being restrained by an elected senate, and with a rabble popular meeting in the place of the house of representatives. He was also *pontifex maximus*, chief of the sacrificial priests, a function unknown at Washington; and in practice it became usual for him to designate and train his successor and to select for that honour a son or an adopted son or a near relation whom he could trust. The power of the *princeps* was in itself enormous to entrust to the hands of a single man, without any adequate checks, but it was further enhanced by the tradition of monarch-worship which had now spread out from Egypt over the entire Hellenized east, and which was coming to Rome in the head of every Oriental slave and immigrant. By natural and imperceptible degrees the idea of the god-emperor came to dominate the whole Romanized world.

Only one thing presently remained to remind the god-emperor that he was mortal, and that was the army. The god-emperor was never safe upon the Olympus of the Palatine Hill at Rome. He was only secure while he was the beloved captain of his legions. And as a consequence only the hardworking emperors who kept their legions active and in close touch with themselves had long reigns. The sword overhung the emperor and spurred him to incessant activity. If he left things to his generals, one of those generals presently replaced him. This spur was perhaps the redeeming feature of the Roman Imperial system. In the greater, compacter, and securer empire of China there was not the same need of legions, and so there was not the same swift end for lazy or dissipated or

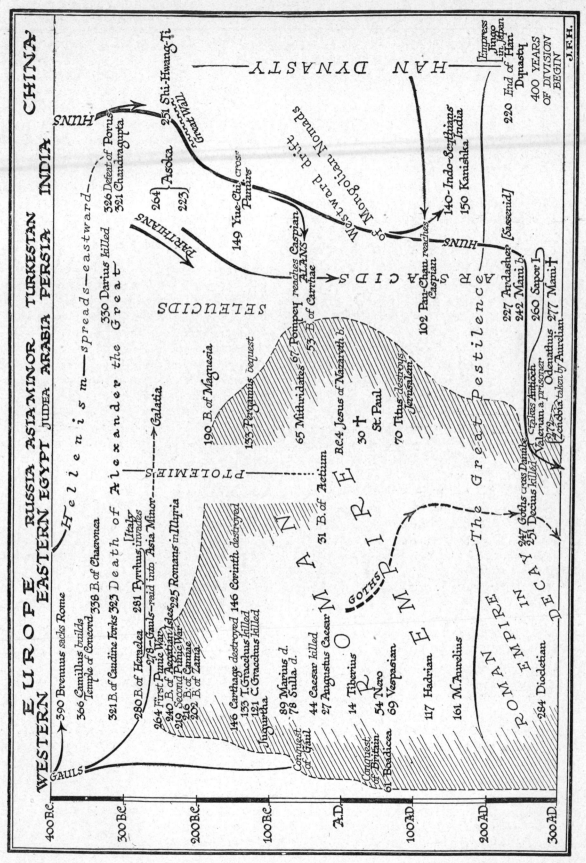

CHINA

WESTERN EUROPE RUSSIA ASIA MINOR TURKESTAN
EASTERN EGYPT JUDEA ARABIA PERSIA INDIA

Hellenism — spreads — eastward

HUNS

251 Shi-Hwang-Ti
Great Wall

HAN DYNASTY

330 Darius killed
326 Defeat of Porus
321 Chandragupta

Death of Alexander the Great

264
Asoka
223

Galatia

149 Yue-Chi cross
Parthus

Westward drift
of Mongolian Nomads

140-Indo-Scythians
150 Kanishka India

220 End of
Han Dynasty

400 YEARS
OF DIVISION
BEGIN

Empress
Jingo
in Japan

PARTHIANS

SELEUCIDS

67 Pompey reaches Caspian
ALANS
53 B. of Carrhae

HUNS

102 Pau-Chau reaches
Caspian

SASSACIDS
ARSACIDS

227 Ardashir [Sassenid]
242 Mani b.
260 Sapor I
277 Mani †

PTOLEMIES

190 B. of Magnesia

155 Pergamus bequest

65 Mithridates

B.C.4 Jesus of Nazareth b.
30 †
St. Paul

70 Titus destroys
Jerusalem

The Great Pestilence

takes Antioch
Valerian a prisoner
272 Odenathus
Zenobia taken by Aurelian

321 B. of Caudine Forks

280 B. of Heraclea
281 Pyrrhus invades Italy
278 Gauls raid into Asia Minor

264 First Punic War
240 B. of Aegatian Isles
225 Romans in Illyria
219 Second Punic War
216 B. of Cannae
202 B. of Zama

146 Carthage destroyed 146 Corinth destroyed
135 T. Gracchus killed
121 C. Gracchus killed
Jugurtha

89 Marius d.
78 Sulla d.

44 Caesar killed
27 Augustus Caesar

MAN

51 B. of Actium

EMPIRE

247 Goths cross Danube
251 Decius killed

390 Brennus sacks Rome
366 Camillus builds
Temple of Concord 338 B. of Chaeronea

GAULS

14 Tiberius
ROME
54 Nero
69 Vespasian

Conquest
of Gaul

Conquest
of Britain
61 Boadicea

117 Hadrian

161 M.Aurelius

GOTHS

ROMAN EMPIRE IN DECAY

284 Diocletian

J.F.H.

400 B.C.   300 B.C.   200 B.C.   100 B.C.   A.D.   100 A.D.   200 A.D.   300 A.D.

juvenile monarchs that overtook such types in Rome.

§ 8

It may be convenient to the reader to have here a few chronological landmarks for these last three hundred and twenty years B.C.

In 325, Rome, having consolidated her power over the Latin states, is fighting the Samnites in South Italy.

323. *Death of Alexander the Great.*

321. *Rise of Chandragupta in the Punjab.* Serious Roman reverse against the Samnites at the battle of the Caudine Forks.

281. Pyrrhus invades Italy.
280. Battle of Heraclea.
279. Battle of Ausculum.
278. *Gauls raid into Asia Minor and settle down in Galatia.*
275. Pyrrhus leaves Italy.

264. First Punic War. (*Asoka begins to reign in Behar.*) First gladiatorial games in Rome.
260. Battle of Mylæ.
256. Battle of Ecnomus.
250. *Shi Hwang Ti in China.*
242. Battle of Ægatian Isles.
241. End of First Punic war.

225. Battle of Telamon. Roman armies in Illyria.

219. Second Punic War.
216. Battle of Cannæ.
214. *Great Wall of China begun.*

202. Battle of Zama.
201. End of Second Punic War.

200–197. Rome at war with Macedonia.
192. War with the Seleucids.
190. Battle of Magnesia.

149. Third Punic War. *The Yueh-Chi come into Western Turkestan.*
146. Carthage destroyed. Corinth destroyed.

133. Attalus bequeaths Pergamum to Rome. Tiberius Gracchus killed.

121. Caius Gracchus killed.
118. War with Jugurtha.

106. War with Jugurtha ends.
102. Marius drives back Germans.
100. Triumph of Marius. *Wu-ti conquering the Tarim valley.*

91. Social war.
89. All Italians become Roman citizens.
86. Death of Marius.
78. Death of Sulla.
73. The revolt of the slaves under Spartacus.
71. Defeat and end of Spartacus.
66. Pompey leads Roman troops to the Caspian and Euphrates. He encounters the Alani.
64. Mithridates of Pontus dies.
53. Crassus killed at Carrhæ. *Mongolian elements with Parthians.*
48. Julius Cæsar defeats Pompey at Pharsalus.
44. Julius Cæsar assassinated.

31. Battle of Actium.
27.—Augustus Cæsar *princeps* (until 14 A.D.).
Hunnish peoples drifting westward, gathering between the Volga and Central Asia, and (Alans) raiding through the Caucasus into Armenia.

XXIX

THE CÆSARS BETWEEN THE SEA AND THE GREAT PLAINS OF THE OLD WORLD[1]

§ 1

WESTERN writers are apt, through their patriotic predispositions, to overestimate the organization, civilizing work, and security of the absolute monarchy that established itself in Rome after the accession of Augustus Cæsar. From **A Short Catalogue of Emperors.** it we derive the political traditions of Britain, France, Spain, Germany, and Italy, and these countries loom big in the perspectives of European writers. By the scale of a world history the Roman Empire ceases to seem so overwhelmingly important. It lasted about four centuries in all before it was completely shattered. The Byzantine Empire was no genuine continuation of it; it was a resumption of the Hellenic Empire of Alexander; it spoke Greek; its monarch had a Roman title no doubt, but so for that matter had the late Tzar of Bulgaria. During its four centuries of life the empire of Rome had phases of division and complete chaos; its prosperous years, if they are gathered together and added up, do not amount in all to a couple of centuries. Compared with the quiet steady expansion, the secu-

Photo: Anderson.

AUGUSTUS CÆSAR.
From the Vatican Museum.

rity, and the civilizing task of the contemporary Chinese Empire, or with Egypt between 4,000 and 1,000 B.C., or with Sumeria before the Semitic conquest, this amounts to a mere incident in history. The Persian Empire of Cyrus again, which reached from the Hellespont to the Indus, had as high a standard of civilization; and its homelands remained unconquered and fairly prosperous for over two hundred years. Its predecessor, the Median Empire, had endured for half a century. After a brief submergence by Alexander the Great, it rose again as the Seleucid Empire, which endured for some centuries. The Seleucid dominion shrank at last to the west of the Euphrates, and became a part of the Roman Empire; but Persia, revived by the Parthians as a new Persian Empire, first under the Arsacids and then under the Sassanids, outlived the empire of Rome. The Sassanids repeatedly carried war into the Byzantine Empire, and held the line of the Euphrates steadfastly. In 616 A.D., under Chosroes II, they were holding Damascus, Jerusalem, and Egypt, and threatening the Hellespont. But there has been no tradition to keep alive the glories of the Sassanids. The reputation of Rome has

[1] The best book in a compact compass for expanding this chapter is H. Stuart Jones's *The Roman Empire.*

flourished through the prosperity of her heirs. The tradition of Rome is greater than its reality.

History distinguishes two chief groups of Roman emperors who were great administrators. The first of these groups began with :—

Augustus Cæsar (27 B.C. to 14 A.D.), the Octavian of the previous section, who worked hard at the reorganization of the provincial governments and at financial reform. He established a certain tradition of lawfulness and honesty in the bureaucracy, and he restrained the more monstrous corruptions and tyrannies by giving the provincial citizen the right to appeal to Cæsar. But he fixed the European boundaries of the empire along the Rhine and Danube, so leaving Germany, which is the necessary backbone of a safe and prosperous Europe, to barbarism; and he made a similar limitation in the east at the Euphrates, leaving Armenia independent, to be a constant bone of contention with the Arsacids and Sassanids. It is doubtful whether he considered that he was fixing the final boundaries of the empire along these lines, or whether he thought it desirable to consolidate for some years before any further attempts at expansion.

Tiberius (14 to 37 A.D.) is also described as a capable ruler, but he became intensely unpopular in Rome, and it would seem that he was addicted to gross and abominable vices. But his indulgence in these and his personal tyrannies and cruelties did not interfere with the general prosperity of the empire. It is difficult to judge him; all our sources of information are hostile to him.

Caligula (37 to 41 A.D.) was insane, but the empire carried on during four years of eccentricity at its head. Finally he was murdered in his palace by his servants, and there seems to have been an attempt to restore the senatorial government, an attempt which was promptly suppressed by the household legions.

Claudius (41 to 54 A.D.), the uncle of Caligula, upon whom the choice of the soldiers fell, was personally uncouth, but he seems to have been a hardworking and fairly capable administrator. He advanced the westward boundary of the empire by annexing the southern half of Britain. He was poisoned by Agrippina, the mother of his adopted son, Nero, and a woman of great charm and force of character.

Nero (54 to 68 A.D.), like Tiberius, is credited with monstrous vices and cruelties, but the empire had acquired sufficient momentum to carry on through his fourteen years of power. He certainly murdered his devoted but troublesome mother and his wife, the latter as a mark of devotion to a lady, Poppæa, who then married him; but the domestic infelicities of the Cæsars are no part of our present story. The reader greedy for criminal particulars must go to the classical source, Suetonius. These various Cæsars and their successors and their womenkind were probably no worse essentially than most weak and passionate human beings, but they had no real religion, being themselves gods; they had no wide knowledge on which to build high ambitions, their women were fierce and often illiterate, and they were under no restraints of law or custom. They were surrounded by creatures ready to stimulate their slightest wishes and to translate their vaguest impulses into action. What are mere passing black thoughts and angry impulses with most of us became therefore deeds with them. Before a man condemns Nero as a different species of being from himself, he should examine his own secret thoughts very carefully. Nero became intensely unpopular in Rome, and it is interesting to note that he became unpopular not because he murdered and poisoned his intimate relations, but because there was an insurrection in Britain under a certain Queen Boadicea, and the Roman forces suffered a great

Photo: Mansell.

TRAJAN

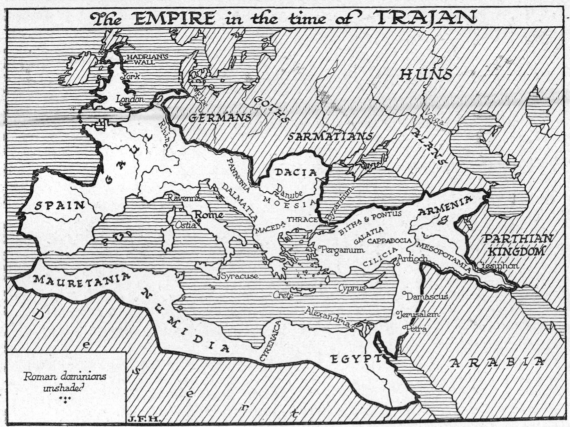

The EMPIRE in the time of TRAJAN

Roman dominions unshaded

disaster (61 A.D.), and because there was a destructive earthquake in Southern Italy. The Roman population, true to its Etruscan streak, never religious and always superstitious, did not mind a wicked Cæsar, but it did object strongly to an unpropitious one. The Spanish legions rose in insurrection under an elderly general of seventy-three, Galba, whom they acclaimed emperor. He advanced upon Rome carried in a litter. Nero, hopeless of support, committed suicide (68 A.D.).

Galba, however, was only one of a group of would-be emperors. The generals in command of the Rhine legions, the Palatine troops, and the eastern armies, each attempted to seize power. Rome saw four emperors in a year, Galba, Otho, Vitellus, and Vespasian ; the fourth, Vespasian (69—79 A.D.), from the eastern command, had the firmest grip, and held and kept the prize. But with Nero the line of Cæsars born or adopted ended. Cæsar ceased to be the family name of the Roman emperors, and became a title, Divus Cæsar, the Cæsar god. The monarchy took a step forward towards orientalism by an increased insistence upon the worship of the ruler.

Vespasian (69 to 79 A.D.) and his sons Titus (79 A.D.) and Domitian (81 A.D.) constitute, as it were, a second dynasty, the Flavian ; then after the assassination of Domitian came a group of emperors related to one another not by blood, but by adoption, the adoptive emperors. Nerva (96 A.D.) was the first of this line, and Trajan (98 A.D.) the second. They were followed by the indefatigable Hadrian (117 A.D.), Antoninus Pius (138 A.D.), and Marcus Aurelius (161 to 180 A.D.). Under both the Flavians and the Antonines the boundaries of the empire crept forward again. North Britain was annexed in 84 A.D., the angle of the Rhine and Danube was filled in, and what is now Transylvania was made into a new province, Dacia. Trajan also invaded Parthia and annexed Armenia, Assyria, and Mesopotamia. Under his rule the empire reached its maximum extent. Hadrian, his successor, was of a cautious and retractile disposition. He abandoned these new eastern conquests of Trajan's, and he also abandoned North Britain. He adopted the Chinese idea of the limiting wall against barbarism, an excellent idea so long as the pressure of population on the

THE ROMAN WALL (HADRIAN'S WALL), NORTHUMBERLAND.

imperial side of the wall is greater than the pressure from without, but worthless otherwise. He built Hadrian's wall across Britain, and a palisade between the Rhine and the Danube. The full tide of Roman expansion was past, and in the reign of his successor the North European frontier was already actively on the defensive against the aggression of Teutonic and Slavic tribes.

Marcus Aurelius Antoninus is one of those figures in history about which men differ widely and intensely. To some critics he seems to have been a priggish person; he dabbled in religions, and took a pleasure in conducting priestly ceremonies in priestly garments—a disposition offensive to common men—and they resent his alleged failure to restrain the wickedness of his wife Faustina. The stories of his domestic infelicity, however, rest on no very good foundations, though certainly his son Commodus was a startling person for a good home to produce. On the other hand, he was unquestionably a devoted and industrious emperor, holding social order together through a series of disastrous years of vile weather, great floods, failing harvests and famine, barbaric raids and revolts, and at last a terrible universal pestilence.

Says F. W. Farrar, quoted in the *Encyclopædia Britannica*, "He regarded himself as being, in fact, the servant of all. The registry of the citizens, the suppression of litigation, the elevation of public morals, the care of minors, the retrenchment of public expenses, the limitation of gladiatorial games and shows, the care of roads, the restoration of senatorial privileges, the appointment of none but worthy magistrates, even the regulation of street traffic, these and numberless other duties so completely absorbed his attention that, in spite of indifferent health, they often kept him at severe labour from early morning till long after midnight. His position, indeed, often necessitated his presence at games and shows; but on these occasions he occupied himself either in reading, or being read to, or in writing notes. He was one of those who held that nothing should be done hastily, and that few crimes were worse than waste of time."

But it is not by these industries that he is now remembered. He was one of the greatest exponents of the Stoical philosophy, and in his *Meditations*, jotted down in camp and court, he has put so much of a human soul on record as to raise up for himself in each generation a fresh series of friends and admirers.

With the death of Marcus Aurelius this long phase of unity and comparative good government came to an end, and his son Commodus inaugurated an age of disorder. Practically the empire had been at peace within itself for two hundred years. Now for a hundred years the student of Roman history must master the various criminology of a number of inadequate emperors, while the frontier crumbled and receded under barbarian pressure. One or two names only seem to be the names of able men : such were Septimius Severus, Aurelian, and Probus. Septimius Severus was a Carthaginian, and his sister was never able to master Latin. She conducted her Roman household in the Punic language, which must have made Cato the elder turn in his grave. The rest of the emperors of this period were chiefly adventurers too unimportant to the general scheme of things for us to note. At times there were separate emperors ruling in different parts of the distracted empire. From our present point of view the Emperor Decius, who was defeated and killed during a great raid of the Goths into Thrace in 251 A.D., and the Emperor Valerian, who, together with the great city of Antioch, was captured by the Sassanid Shah of Persia in 260 A.D., are worthy of notice because they mark the insecurity of the whole Roman system, and the character of the outer pressure upon it. So too is Claudius, " the Conqueror of the Goths," because he gained a great victory over these people at Nish in Serbia (270 A.D.), and because he died, like Pericles, of the plague.

Through all these centuries intermittent pestilences were playing a part in weakening races and altering social conditions, a part that has still to be properly worked out by historians. There was, for instance, a great plague throughout the empire between the years 164 and 180 A.D. in the reign of the Emperor Marcus Aurelius. It probably did much to disorganize social life and prepare the way for the troubles that followed the accession of Commodus. This same pestilence devastated China, as we shall note in § 4 of this chapter. Considerable fluctuations of climate had also been going on in the first and second centuries, producing stresses and shiftings of population, whose force historians have still to appraise. But before we go on to tell of the irruptions of the barbarians

and the attempts of such later emperors as Diocletian (284 A.D.) and Constantine the Great (312 A.D.) to hold together the heaving and splitting vessel of the state, we must describe something of the conditions of human life in the Roman Empire during its two centuries of prosperity.

§ 2

The impatient reader of history may be disposed to count the two centuries of order between 27 B.C. and 180 A.D. as among the **Roman Civilization at its Zenith.** wasted opportunities of mankind. It was an age of spending rather than of creation, an age of architecture and trade in which the rich grew richer and the poor poorer and the soul and spirit of man decayed. Looked at superficially, as a man might have looked at it from an aeroplane a couple of thousand feet in the air, there was a considerable flourish of prosperity. Everywhere, from York to Cyrene and from Lisbon to Antioch, he would have noted large and well-built cities, with temples, theatres, amphitheatres, markets, and the like ; thousands of such cities, supplied by great aqueducts and served by splendid high roads, whose stately remains astonish us to this day. He would have noted an abundant cultivation, and have soared too high to discover that this cultivation was the grudging work of slaves. Upon the

Photo: Mansell.

MARCUS AURELIUS
Head from Cyrene.

Mediterranean and the Red Sea a considerable traffic would be visible ; and the sight of two ships alongside each other would not at that altitude reveal the fact that one was a pirate and plundering the other.

And even if the observer came down to a closer scrutiny, there would still be much accumulated improvement to note. There had been a softening of manners and a general refinement since the days of Julius Cæsar. With this there had been a real increase of humane feeling. During the period of the Antonines, laws for the protection of slaves from extreme

was used abundantly, and there was a steady flow of the precious metals eastward in exchange. There had been very considerable advances in gastronomy and the arts of entertainment. Petronius describes a feast given by a wealthy man under the early Cæsars, a remarkable succession of courses, some delicious, some amazing, exceeding anything that even the splendours and imagination of modern New York could produce ; and the festival was varied by music and by displays of tight-rope dancing, juggling, Homeric recitations, and the like. There was a considerable amount of

Photo : Moscioni.

DETAIL FROM TRAJAN'S COLUMN. ROMAN CAVALRY CHARGING MAIL-CLAD SARMATIANS.

cruelty came into existence, and it was no longer permissible to sell them to the gladiatorial schools. Not only were the cities outwardly more splendidly built, but within the homes of the wealthy there had been great advances in the art of decoration. The gross feasting, animal indulgence, and vulgar display of the earlier days of Roman prosperity were now tempered by a certain refinement. Dress had become richer, finer, and more beautiful. There was a great trade in silk with remote China, for the mulberry tree and the silkworm had not yet begun to move west. By the time silk had ended its long and varied journey to Rome it was worth its weight in gold. Yet it

what we may describe as "rich men's culture" throughout the empire. Books were far more plentiful than they had been before the time of the Cæsars. Men prided themselves upon their libraries, even when the cares and responsibilities of property made them too busy to give their literary treasures much more than a passing examination. The knowledge of Greek spread eastward and of Latin westward, and if the prominent men of this or that British or Gallic city lacked any profound Greek culture themselves, they could always turn to some slave or other, whose learning had been guaranteed of the highest quality by the slave-dealer, to supply the deficiency.

ROMAN AMPHITHEATRE AT NÎMES.

The generation of Cato had despised Greeks and the Greek language, but now all that was changed. The prestige of Greek learning of an approved and settled type was as high in the Rome of Antoninus Pius as it was in the Oxford and Cambridge of Victorian England. The Greek scholar received the same mixture of unintelligent deference and practical contempt. There was a very considerable amount of Greek scholarship, and of written criticism and commentary. Indeed there was so great an admiration for Greek letters as almost completely to destroy the Greek spirit; and the recorded observations of Aristotle were valued so highly as to preclude any attempt to imitate his organization of further inquiry. It is noteworthy that while Aristotle in the original Greek fell like seed upon stony soil in the Roman world, he was, in Syrian and Arabic translations, immensely stimulating to the Arabic civilization of a thousand years later. Nor were the æsthetic claims of Latin neglected in this heyday of Greek erudition. As Greece had her epics and so forth, the Romans felt that they too must have their epics. The age of Augustus was an age of imitative literature. Virgil in the Æneid set himself modestly but resolutely, and with an elegant sort of successfulness, to parallel Homer, just as Lord Tennyson, the poet laureate of Queen Victoria, using the mediæval literature about King Arthur as his material, did a similar service for Great Britain in his *Idylls of the King*.

All this wide-spread culture of the wealthy householder is to the credit of the early Roman Empire, and Gibbon makes the most of it in the sunny review of the age of the Antonines with which he opens his *Decline and Fall of the Roman Empire*. His design for that great work demanded a prelude of splendour and

PONT DU GARD, NÎMES. AQUEDUCT BUILT TO CARRY WATER ACROSS THE VALLEY OF THE GARD. SPAN OF 880 FEET.

Photo: Frith.

FORTIFIED GATEWAY AT TREVES. TYPICAL ROMAN MILITARY ARCHITECTURE.

tranquillity. But he was far too shrewd and subtle not to qualify his apparent approval of the conditions he describes. "Under the Roman Empire," he writes, "the labour of an industrious and ingenious people was variously but incessantly employed in the service of the rich. In their dress, their table, their houses, and their furniture, the favourites of fortune united every refinement of convenience, of elegance, and of splendour, whatever could soothe their pride, or gratify their sensuality. Such refinements, under the odious name of luxury, have been severely arraigned by the moralists of every age ; and it might perhaps be more conducive to the virtue, as well as happiness, of mankind, if all possessed the necessaries, and none the superfluities of life. But in the present imperfect condition of society, luxury, though it may proceed from vice or folly, seems to be the only means that can correct the unequal distribution of property. The diligent mechanic and the skilful artist, who have obtained no share in the division of the earth, receive a voluntary tax from the possessors of land ; and the latter are prompted, by a sense of interest, to improve those estates, with whose produce they may purchase additional pleasure. This operation, the particular effects of which are

felt in every society, acted with much more diffuse energy in the Roman world. The provinces would soon have been exhausted of their wealth, if the manufactures and commerce of luxury had not insensibly restored to the industrious subjects the sums which were exacted from them by the arms and authority of Rome." And so on, with a sting of satire in every fold of the florid description.

If we look a little more widely than a hovering aeroplane can do at the movement of races upon the earth, or a little more closely than an inspection of streets, amphitheatres, and banquets goes, into the souls and thoughts of men, we shall find that this impressive display of material prosperity is merely the shining garment of a polity blind to things without and things within, and blind to the future. If, for instance, we compare the two centuries of Roman ascendancy and opportunity, the first and second centuries A.D., with the two centuries of Greek and Hellenic life beginning about 466 B.C. with the supremacy of Pericles in Athens, we are amazed by—we cannot call it an inferiority, it is a complete absence of science. The incuriousness of the Roman rich and the Roman rulers was more massive and monumental even than their architecture.

In one field of knowledge particularly we might have expected the Romans to have been alert and enterprising, and that was geography. Their political interests demanded a steadfast inquiry into the state of affairs beyond their frontiers, and yet that inquiry was never made. There is practically no literature of Roman travel beyond the imperial limits, no such keen and curious accounts as Herodotus gives of the Scythians, the Africans, and the like. There is nothing in Latin to compare with the early descriptions of India and Siberia that are to be found in Chinese. The Roman legions went at one time into Scotland, yet there remains no really intelligent account of Picts or Scots, much less any glance at the seas beyond. Such explorations as those of Hanno or Pharaoh Necho seem to have been altogether beyond the scope of the Roman imagination. It is probable that after the destruction of Carthage the amount of shipping that went out into the Atlantic through the Straits of Gibraltar fell to inconsiderable proportions. Still more impossible in this world of vulgar wealth, enslaved intelligence, and

bureaucratic rule was any further development of the astronomy and physiography of Alexandria. The Romans do not seem even to have inquired what manner of men wove the silk and prepared the spices or collected the amber and the pearls that came into their markets. Yet the channels of inquiry were open and easy; pathways led in every direction to the most convenient "jumping-off places" for explorers it is possible to imagine.

"The most remote countries of the ancient world were ransacked to supply the pomp and delicacy of Rome. The forests of Scythia afforded some valuable furs. Amber was brought overland from the shores of the Baltic to the Danube, and the barbarians were astonished at the price which they received in exchange for so useless a commodity. There was a considerable demand for Babylonian carpets and other manufactures of the East; but the most important branch of foreign trade was carried on with Arabia and India. Every year, about the time of the summer solstice, a fleet of a hundred and twenty vessels sailed

Photo: American Colony, Jerusalem.   THE TEMPLE OF BACCHUS, BAALBEK.

from Myos-hormos, a port of Egypt on the Red Sea. By the periodical assistance of the monsoons, they traversed the ocean in about forty days. The coast of Malabar, or the island of Ceylon, was the usual term of their navigation, and it was in those markets that the merchants from the more remote countries of Asia expected their arrival. The return of the fleet to Egypt was fixed to the months of December or January, and as soon as their rich cargo had been transported, on the backs of camels, from the Red Sea to the Nile, and had descended that river as far as Alexandria, it was poured, without delay, into the capital of the empire."[1]

Yet Rome was content to feast, exact, grow rich, and watch its gladiatorial shows without the slightest attempt to learn anything of India, China, Persia or Scythia, Buddha or Zoroaster, or about the Huns, the Negroes, the people of Scandinavia, or the secrets of the western sea.

When we realize the uninspiring quality of the social atmosphere which made this indifference possible, we are able to account for the failure of Rome during its age of opportunity to develop any physical or chemical science, and as a consequence to gain any increased control over matter. Most of the physicians in Rome were Greeks and many of them slaves—for the Roman wealthy did not even understand that a bought mind is a spoilt mind. Yet this was not due to any want of natural genius among the Roman people; it was due entirely to their social and economic conditions. From the Middle Ages to the present day Italy has produced a great number of brilliant scientific men. And one of the most shrewd and inspired of scientific writers was an Italian, Lucretius, who lived between the time of Marius and Julius Cæsar (about 100 B.C. to about 55 B.C.). This amazing man was of the quality of Leonardo da Vinci (also an Italian) or Newton. He wrote a long Latin poem about the processes of Nature, *De Rerum Natura*, in which he guessed with astonishing insight about the constitution of matter and about the early history of mankind. Osborn in his *Old Stone Age* quotes with admiration long passages from Lucretius about primitive man, so good and true are they to-day. But this was an individual display, a seed that

bore no fruit. Roman science was still-born, into a suffocating atmosphere of vile wealth and military oppression. The true figure to represent the classical Roman attitude to science is not Lucretius, but that Roman soldier who hacked Archimedes to death at the storming of Syracuse.

And if physical and biological science wilted and died on the stony soil of Roman prosperity, political and social science never had a chance to germinate. Political discussion would have been treason to the emperor, social or economic inquiry would have threatened the rich. So Rome, until disaster fell upon her, never examined into her own social health, never questioned the ultimate value of her hard officialism. Consequently, there was no one who realized the gravity of her failure to develop any intellectual imagination to hold her empire together, any general education in common ideas that would make men fight and work for the empire as men will fight and work for a dear possession. But the rulers of the Roman Empire did not want their citizens to fight for anything in any spirit at all. The rich had eaten the heart out of their general population, and they were content with the meal they had made. The legions were filled with Germans, Britons, Numidians, and the like; and until the very end the wealthy Romans thought they could go on buying barbarians to defend them against the enemy without and the rebel poor within. How little was done in education by the Romans is shown by an account of what was done. Says Mr. H. Stuart Jones,[2] " Julius Cæsar bestowed Roman citizenship on ' teachers of the liberal arts'; Vespasian endowed professorships of Greek and Latin oratory at Rome; and later emperors, especially Antoninus Pius, extended the same benefits to the provinces. Local enterprise and munificence were also devoted to the cause of education; we learn from the correspondence of the younger Pliny that public schools were founded in the towns of Northern Italy. But though there was a wide diffusion of knowledge under the empire, there was no true intellectual progress. Augustus, it is true, gathered about him the most brilliant writers of his time, and the debut of the new monarchy coincided with the Golden Age of Roman litera-

[1] Gibbon.

[2] *Encyclopædia Britannica*, article "Rome."

Photos: *W. C. Fox.*
BOTTOM FLOOR AND DRAIN OF TEMPERATE ROOM AT ROMAN BATHS UNEARTHED AT GAER FACH, PENGAM, S. WALES.
These baths were probably built about A.D. 100.

ture; but this was of brief duration, and the beginnings of the Christian era saw the triumph of classicism and the first steps in the decline which awaits all literary movements which look to the past rather than the future.''

There is a diagnosis of the intellectual decadence of the age in a treatise upon the sublime by a Greek writer who wrote somewhen in the second, third, or fourth century A.D., and who may possibly have been Longinus Philologus,[1] which states very distinctly one manifest factor in the mental sickness of the Roman world. He is cited by Gibbon: "The sublime Longinus, who, in somewhat a later period, and in the court of a Syrian queen, preserved the spirit of ancient Athens, observes and laments the degeneracy of his contemporaries, which debased their sentiments, enervated their courage, and de-

[1] See *Encyclopædia Britannica*, article "Longinus." The Syrian queen referred to by Gibbon is Zenobia. Longinus was put to death by Aurelian. See ch. xxxii., § 2.

pressed their talents. 'In the same manner,' says he, 'as some children always remain pigmies, whose infant limbs have been too closely confined, thus our tender minds, fettered by the prejudices and habits of a just servitude, are unable to expand themselves or to attain that well-proportioned greatness which we admire in the ancients; who, living under a popular government, wrote with all the same freedom as they acted.'"

But this critic grasped only one aspect of the restraints upon mental activity. The leading-strings that kept the Roman mind in a permanent state of infantilism constituted a double servitude; they were economic as well as political. The account Gibbon gives of the life and activities of a certain Herodes Atticus, who lived in the time of Hadrian, shows just how little was the share of the ordinary citizen in the outward magnificence of the time. This Atticus had an immense fortune, and he amused himself by huge architectural benefactions to various cities. Athens was given a racecourse, and a theatre of cedar, curiously carved, was set up there to the memory of his wife; a theatre was built at Corinth, a racecourse was given to Delphi, baths to Thermopylæ, an aqueduct to Canusium, and so on and so on. One is struck by the spectacle of a world of slaves and common people who were not consulted and over whose heads, without any participation on their part, this rich man indulged in his displays of "taste." Numerous inscriptions in Greece and Asia still preserve the name of Herodes Atticus, "patron and benefactor," who ranged about the empire as though it was his private garden, commemorating himself by these embellishments. He did not confine himself to splendid buildings. He was also a philosopher, though none of his wisdom has survived. He had a large villa near Athens, and there philosophers were welcome guests so long as they convinced their patron of the soundness of their pretensions, received his discourses with respect, and did not offend him by insolent controversy.

The world, it is evident, was not progressing during these two centuries of Roman prosperity. But was it happy in its stagnation? There are signs of a very unmistakable sort that the great mass of human beings in the empire, a mass numbering something between a hundred and a hundred and fifty millions, was not happy, was probably very acutely miserable, beneath its outward magnificence. True there were no great wars and conquests within the empire, little of famine or fire or sword to afflict mankind; but, on the other hand, there was a terrible restraint by government, and still more by the property of the rich, upon the free activities of nearly everyone. Life for the great majority who were neither rich nor official, nor the womankind and the parasites of the rich and official, must have been laborious, tedious, and lacking in interest and freedom to a degree that a modern mind can scarcely imagine.

Three things in particular may be cited to sustain the opinion that this period was a period of widespread unhappiness. The first of these is the extraordinary apathy of the population to political events. They saw one upstart pretender to empire succeed another with complete indifference. Such things did not seem to matter to them; hope had gone. When presently the barbarians poured into the empire, there was nothing but the legions to face them. There was no popular uprising against them at all. Everywhere the barbarians must have been outnumbered if only the people had resisted. But the people did not resist. It is manifest that to the bulk of its inhabitants the Roman Empire did not seem to be a thing worth fighting for. To the slaves and common people the barbarian probably seemed to promise more freedom and less indignity than the pompous rule of the imperial official and grinding employment by the rich. The looting and burning of palaces and an occasional massacre did not shock the folk of the Roman underworld as it shocked the wealthy and cultured people to whom we owe such accounts as we have of the breaking down of the imperial system. Great numbers of slaves and common people probably joined the barbarians, who knew little of racial or patriotic prejudices, and were openhanded to any promising recruit. No doubt in many cases the population found that the barbarian was a worse infliction even than the tax-gatherer and the slave-driver. But that discovery came too late for resistance or the restoration of the old order.

And as a second symptom that points to the same conclusion that life was hardly worth living for the poor and the slaves and the majority of people during the age of the Antonines, we must reckon the steady depopulation of the empire. People refused to have children. They did so, we suggest, because their homes were not safe from oppression, because in the case of slaves there was no security that the husband and wife would not be separated, because there was no pride nor reasonable hope in children any more. In modern states the great breeding-ground has always been the agricultural countryside where there is a more or less secure peasantry; but under the Roman Empire the peasant and the small cultivator was either a worried debtor, or he was held in a network of restraints that made him a spiritless serf, or he had been ousted altogether by the gang production of slaves.

A third indication that this outwardly flourishing period was one of deep unhappiness and mental distress for vast multitudes, is to be

THE ARCH OF SEPTIMIUS SEVERUS IN THE FORUM AT ROME.

found in the spread of new religious movements throughout the population. We have seen how in the case of the little country of Judea a whole nation may be infected by the persuasion that life is unsatisfactory and *wrong*, and that something is needed to set it right. The mind of the Jews, as we know, had crystallized about the idea of the Promise of the One True God and the coming of a Saviour or Messiah. Rather different ideas from these were spreading through the Roman Empire. They were but varying answers to one universal question: "What must we do for salvation?" One frequent and natural consequence of disgust with life as it is, is to throw the imagination forward to an after-life, which is to redeem all the miseries and injustices of this one. The belief in such compensation is a great opiate for present miseries. Egyptian religion had long been saturated with anticipations of immortality, and we have seen how central was that idea to the cult of Serapis and Isis at Alexandria. The ancient mysteries of Demeter and Orpheus, the mysteries of the Mediterranean race, revived and made a sort of *theocrasia* with these new cults.

A second great religious movement was Mithraism, a development of Zoroastrianism, a religion of very ancient Aryan origin, traceable back to the Indo-Iranian people before they split into Persians and Hindus. We cannot here examine its mysteries in any detail.[1] Mithras was a god of light, a Sun of Righteousness, and in the shrines of the cult he was always represented as slaying a sacred bull whose blood was the seed of life. Suffice it that, complicated with many added ingredients, this worship of Mithras came into the Roman Empire about the time of Pompey the Great, and began to spread very widely under the Cæsars and Antonines. Like the Isis religion, it promised immortality. Its followers were mainly slaves, soldiers, and distressed people. In its methods of worship, in the burning of candles before the altar and so forth, it had a certain superficial resemblance to the later developments of the ritual of the third great religious movement in the Roman world, Christianity.

Christianity also was a doctrine of immortality and salvation, and it too spread at first chiefly among the lowly and unhappy. Christianity has been denounced by modern writers as a "slave religion." It was. It took the slaves and the downtrodden, and it gave them hope and restored their self-respect, so that they stood up for righteousness like men and faced persecution and torment. But of the origins and quality of Christianity we will tell more fully in a later chapter.

§ 3

We have already shown reason for our statement that the Roman imperial system was a very unsound political growth indeed. It is **Limitations of the Roman Mind.** absurd to write of its statecraft; it had none. At its best it had a bureaucratic administration which kept the peace of the world for a time and failed altogether to secure it.

Let us note here the main factors in its failure.

The clue to all its failure lies in the absence of any free mental activity and any organization for the increase, development, and application of knowledge. It respected wealth and it despised science. It gave government to the rich, and imagined that wise men could be bought and bargained for in the slave markets when they were needed. It was, therefore, a colossally ignorant and unimaginative empire. It foresaw nothing.

It had no strategic foresight, because it was blankly ignorant of geography and ethnology. It knew nothing of the conditions of Russia, Central Asia, and the East. It was content to keep the Rhine and Danube as its boundaries, and to make no effort to Romanize Germany. But we need only look at the map of Europe and Asia showing the Roman Empire to see that a willing and incorporated Germany was absolutely essential to the life and security of Western Europe. Excluded, Germany became a wedge that needed only the impact of the Hunnish hammer to split up the whole system.

Moreover, this neglect to push the boundaries northward to the Baltic left that sea and the North Sea as a region of experiment and training and instruction in seamanship for the Northmen of Scandinavia, Denmark, and the Frisian coast. But Rome went on its way quite stupidly, oblivious to the growth of a newer and more powerful piracy in the North.

[1] See Legge, *Forerunners and Rivals of Christianity.*

22

Photo : *Underwood & Underwood.*

THE COLOSSEUM, ROME.

The same unimaginative quality made the Romans leave the seaways of the Mediterranean undeveloped. When presently the barbarians pressed down to the warm water, we read of no swift transport of armies from Spain or Africa or Asia to the rescue of Italy and the Adriatic coasts. Instead, we see the Vandals becoming masters of the Western Mediterranean without so much as a naval battle.

The Romans had been held at the Euphrates by an array of mounted archers. It was clear that as the legion was organized it was useless in wide open country, and it should have been equally clear that sooner or later the mounted nomads of East Germany, South Russia or Parthia were bound to try conclusions with the empire. But the Romans, two hundred years after Cæsar's time, were still marching about, the same drilled and clanking cohorts they had always been, easily ridden round and shot to pieces. The empire had learnt nothing even from Carrhæ.

The incapacity of the Roman imperialism for novelty in methods of transport again is amazing. It was patent that their power and unity depended upon the swift movement of troops and supplies from one part of the empire to another. The republic made magnificent roads ; the empire never improved upon them. Four hundred years before the Antonines, Hero of Alexandria had made the first steam-engine. Beautiful records of such beginnings of science were among the neglected treasures of the rich men's libraries throughout the imperial domains. They were seed lying on stony soil. The armies and couriers of Marcus Aurelius drudged along the roads exactly as the armies of Scipio Africanus had done three centuries before them.

The Roman writers were always lamenting the effeminacy of the age. It was their favourite cant. They recognized that the free men of the forest and steppes and desert were harder and more desperate fighters than their citizens, but the natural corollary of developing the industrial power of their accumulations of population to make a countervailing equipment never entered their heads. Instead they took the barbarians into their legions, taught them the arts of war, marched them about the empire, and returned them, with their lesson well learnt, to their own people.

In view of these obvious negligences, it is no wonder that the Romans disregarded that more subtle thing, the soul of the empire, altogether, and made no effort to teach or train or win its common people into any conscious participation with its life. Such teaching or training would indeed have run counter to all the ideas of the rich men and the imperial officials. They had made a tool of religion; science, literature, and education they had entrusted to the care of slaves, who were bred and trained and sold like dogs or horses; ignorant, pompous, and base, the Roman adventurers of finance and property who created the empire, lorded it with a sense of the utmost security while their destruction gathered without the empire and within.

By the second and third centuries A.D. the overtaxed and overstrained imperial machine was already staggering towards its downfall.

§ 4[1]

And now it is necessary, if we are to understand clearly the true situation of the Roman Empire, to turn our eyes to the world beyond its northern and eastern borders, the world of the plains, that stretches, with scarcely a break, from Holland across Germany and Russia to the mountains of Central Asia and Mongolia, and to give a little attention to the parallel empire in China that was now consolidating and developing a far tougher and more enduring moral and intellectual unity than the Romans ever achieved.

The Stir of the Great Plains.

"It is the practice," says Mr. E. H. Parker, "even amongst our most highly educated men in Europe, to deliver sonorous sentences about being 'masters of the world,' 'bringing all nations of the earth under her sway,' and so on, when in reality only some corner of the Mediterranean is involved, or some ephemeral sally into Persia and Gaul. Cyrus and Alexander, Darius and Xerxes, Cæsar and Pompey, all made very interesting excursions, but they were certainly not on a larger scale or charged with greater human interest than the campaigns which were going on at the other end of Asia. Western civilization possessed much in art and science for which China never cared, but, on the other hand, the Chinese developed a historical and critical literature, a courtesy of demeanour, a luxury of clothing, and an administrative system of which Europe might have been proud. In one word, the history of the Far East is quite as interesting as that of the Far West. It only requires to be able to read it. When we brush away contemptuously from our notice the tremendous events which took place on the plains of Tartary, we must not blame the Chinese too much for declining to interest themselves in the doings of what to them appear insignificant states dotted round the Mediterranean and Caspian, which, at this time, was practically all the world of which we knew in Europe." [2]

We have already mentioned (in chap. xvi. and elsewhere) the name of Shi-Hwang-Ti, who consolidated an empire much smaller, indeed, than the present limits of China, but still very great and populous, spreading from the valleys of the Hwang-ho and the Yang Tse. His name is a convenient historical datum point. He began to reign in 250 B.C., and he reigned until 210 B.C., and during those forty years he effected much the same work of consolidation that Augustus Cæsar carried out in Rome two centuries later. At his death there was dynastic trouble for four years, and then (206 B.C.) a fresh dynasty, the Han, established itself and ruled for two hundred and twenty-nine years. The opening quarter century of the Christian era was troubled by a usurper; then what is called the Later Han Dynasty recovered power and ruled for another century and a half, until China, in the time of the Antonines, was so devastated by an eleven-year pestilence as to fall into disorder. This same pestilence, we may note, also helped to produce a century of confusion in the Western world (see § 1). But altogether until this happened, for more than four hundred years Central China was generally at peace, and on the whole well governed, a cycle of strength,

[1] No really good, full, and popular descriptive history, with maps and illustrations, of early and medieval China, nor of the Mongol (Hun) and Turkish peoples, seems to exist in the English language. The writer has consulted Skrine and Ross's *Heart of Asia*, Hirth's *Ancient History of China*, S. Wells Williams' *History of China, A Thousand Years of the Tartars*, by E. H. Parker, H. H. Howorth's *History of the Mongols*, and has found much useful material scattered through Ratzel and Helmolt. He has later on made a useful section from Watters' translation and commentary upon the *Travels of Yuan Chwang*, supplemented by the *Life of Yuan Chwang*, edited by L. Cranmer Byng. Yule's edition of Marco Polo has also been a very inspiring source of material.

[2] E. H. Parker, *A Thousand Years of the Tartars.*

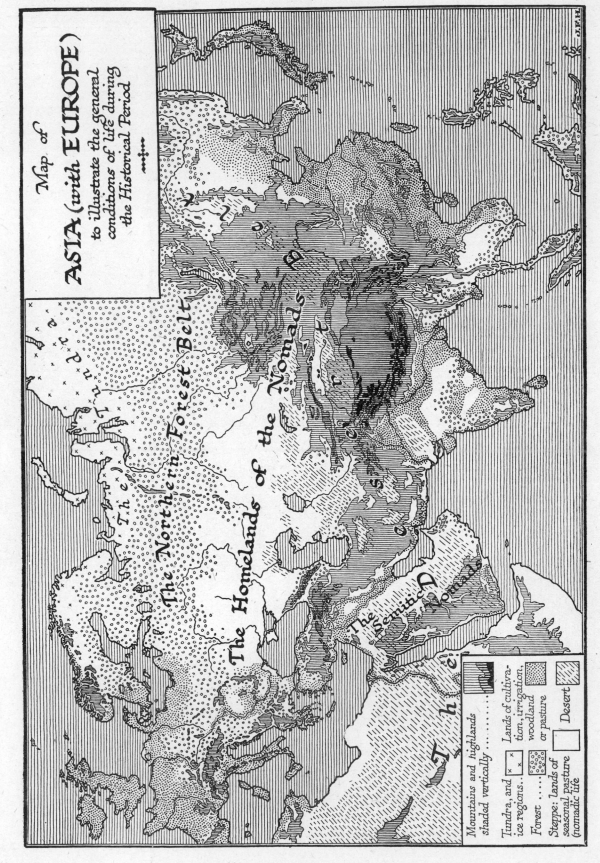

Map of
ASIA (with EUROPE)
to illustrate the general
conditions of life during
the Historical Period

J.F.H.

The Northern Forest Belt

The Homelands of the Nomads

The Tundra

The Semi-D Nomads

The

Mountains and highlands
shaded vertically . . . .

Tundra, and
ice regions . . . . .

Forest . . . .

Steppe: lands of
seasonal pasture
(nomadic life

Lands of cultiva-
tion, irrigation,
woodland
or pasture

Desert

and prosperity unparalleled by anything in the experience of the Western world.

Only the first of the Han monarchs continued the policy of Shi-Hwang-Ti against the *literati*. His successor restored the classics, for the old separatist tradition was broken, and in the uniformity of learning throughout the empire lay, he saw, the cement of Chinese unity. While the Roman world was still blind to the need of any universal mental organization, the Han emperors were setting up a uniform system of education and of literary degrees throughout China that has maintained the intellectual solidarity of that great and always expanding country into modern times. The bureaucrats of Rome were of the most miscellaneous origins and traditions; the bureaucrats of China were, and are still, made in the same mould, all members of one tradition. Since the Han days China has experienced great vicissitudes of political fortune, but they have never changed her fundamental character; she has been divided, but she has always recovered her unity; she has been conquered, and she has always absorbed and assimilated her conquerors.

But from our present point of view, the most important consequences of this consolidation of China under Shi-Hwang-Ti and the Hans was in its reaction upon the unsettled tribes of the northern and western border of China. Throughout the disordered centuries before the time of Shi-Hwang-Ti, the Hi-ung-nu or Huns had occupied Mongolia and large portions of Northern China, and had raided freely into China and interfered freely in Chinese politics. The new power and organization of the Chinese civilization began to change this state of affairs for good and all.

We have already, in our first account of Chinese beginnings, noted the existence of these Huns. It is necessary now to explain briefly who and what they were. Even in using this word Hun as a general equivalent for the Hi-ung-nu, we step on to controversial ground. In our accounts of the development of the Western world we have had occasion to name the Scythians, and to explain the difficulty of distinguishing clearly between Cimmerians, Sarmatians, Medes, Persians, Parthians, Goths, and other more or less nomadic, more or less Aryan peoples who drifted to and fro in a great

arc between the Danube and Central Asia. While sections of the Aryans were moving south and acquiring and developing civilization, these other Aryan peoples were developing mobility and nomadism; they were learning the life of the tent, the wagon, and the herd. They were learning also to use milk as a food basis, and were probably becoming less agricultural, less disposed to take even snatch crops, than they had been. Their development was being aided by a slow change in climate that was replacing the swamps and forests and parklands of South Russia and Central Asia by steppes, by wide grazing lands that is, which favoured a healthy, unsettled life, and necessitated an annual movement between summer and winter pasture. These peoples had only the lowest political forms; they split up, they mingled together; the various races had identical social habits; and so it is that the difficulty, the impossibility of sharp distinctions between them arises. Now the case of the Mongolian races to the north and northwest of the Chinese civilization is very parallel. There can be little doubt that the Hi-ung-nu, the Huns, and the later people called the Mongols, were all very much the same people, and that the Turks and Tartars presently branched off from this same drifting Mongolian population. Kalmucks and Buriats are later developments of the same strain. Here we shall favour the use of the word "Hun" as a sort of general term for these tribes, just as we have been free and wide in our use of "Scythian" in the West.

The consolidation of China was a very serious matter for these Hunnish peoples. Hitherto their overflow of population had gone adventuring southward into the disorders of divided China as water goes into a sponge. Now they found a wall built against them, a firm government, and disciplined armies cutting them off from winter pasture. And though the wall held them back, it did not hold back the Chinese. They were increasing and multiplying through these centuries of peace, and as they increased and multiplied, they spread steadily with house and plough wherever the soil permitted. They spread westward into Tibet and northward and north-westwardly up to the very edge of the Gobi desert. They spread into the best winter pasturing and hunting-grounds of the Hunnish nomads, exactly as the white people of the United States spread westward into the hunting-grounds of the Red Indians. And in spite of raid and massacre, they were just as invincible because they had the pressure of numbers and a strong avenging government behind them. Even without the latter support the cultivating civilization of China has enormous powers of permeation and extension. It has spread slowly and continuously for three thousand years. It is spreading in Manchuria

THE GREAT WALL OF CHINA AT KOU PEI KO PASS.

and Siberia to-day. It roots deeply where it spreads.

Partly the Huns were civilized and assimilated by the Chinese. The more northerly Huns were checked and their superabundant energies were turned westward. The southern Huns were merged into the imperial population.

If the reader will examine a map of Central Asia, he will see that very great mountain barriers separate the Southern, Western, and Eastern peoples of Asia. (But he should be wary of forming his ideas from a map upon Mercator's projection, which enormously exaggerates the

areas and distances of Northern Asia and Siberia.) He will find that from the central mountain masses three great mountain systems radiate eastward; the Himalayas going south-eastward, south of Tibet, the Kuen Lun eastward, north of Tibet, and the Thian Shan north-eastward to join the Altai mountains. Further to the north is the great plain, still steadily thawing and drying. Between the Thian Shan and the Kuen Lun is an area, the Tarim Basin (= roughly Eastern Turkestan), of rivers that never reach the sea, but end in swamps and intermittent lakes. This basin was much more fertile in the past than it is now. The mountain barrier to the west of this Tarim Basin is high, but not forbidding; there are many practicable routes downward into Western Turkestan, and it is possible to travel either along the northern foothills of the Kuen Lun or by the Tarim valley westward from China to Kashgar (where the roads converge), and so over the mountains to Kokand, Samarkand, and Bokhara. Here then is the natural meeting-place in history of Aryan and Mongolian. Here or round by the sea.

We have already noted how Alexander the Great came to one side of the barrier in 329 B.C. High among the mountains of Turkestan a lake preserves his name. Indeed, so living is the tradition of his great raid, that almost any stone ruin in Central Asia is still ascribed to " Iskander." After this brief glimpse, the light of history upon this region fades again, and when it becomes bright once more it is on the eastern and not upon the western side. Far away to the east Shi Hwang Ti had routed the Huns and walled them out of China proper. A portion of these people remained in the north of China, a remnant which was destined to amalgamate with Chinese life under the Hans, but a considerable section had turned westward and (second and first centuries B.C.) driven before them a kindred people called the Yueh-Chi, driving them from the eastern to the western extremity of the Kuen Lun, and at

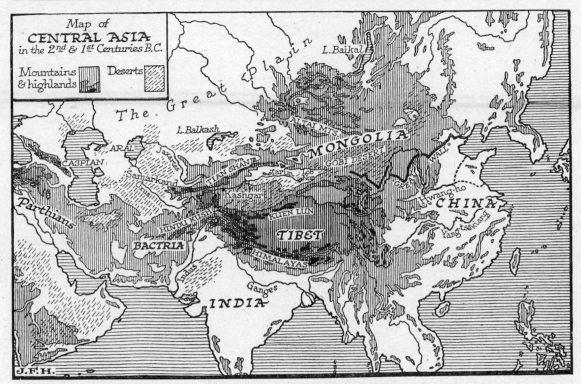

Map of
CENTRAL ASIA
in the 2nd & 1st Centuries B.C.

Mountains & highlands   Deserts

The Great Plain

L. Baikal

L. Balkash

ALTAI MTS.

MONGOLIA

GOBI DESERT

GREAT WALL

ARAL

CASPIAN

Jaxartes

Samarkand

Oxus

TIAN SHAN

Tarim R.

Lob Nor

Hwang-ho

CHINA

Kashgar

Parthians

HINDU KUSH

KUEN LUN

Yang-tse-kiang

BACTRIA

TIBET

Indus

HIMALAYAS

Ganges

INDIA

J.F.H.

last right over the barrier into the once Aryan region of Western Turkestan. These Yueh-Chi conquered the slightly Hellenized kingdom of Bactria, and mixed with Aryan people there. Later on these Yueh-Chi became, or were merged with Aryan elements into, a people called the Indo-Scythians, who went on down the Khyber Pass and conquered northern portions of India as far as Benares (100–150 A.D.), wiping out the last vestiges of Hellenic rule in India. This big splash over of the Mongolian races westward was probably not the first of such splashes, but it is the first recorded splash. In the rear of the Yueh-Chi were the Huns, and in the rear of the Huns and turning them now northward was the vigorous Han Dynasty of China. In the reign of the greatest of the Han monarchs, Wu-Ti (140–86 B.C.), the Huns had been driven northward out of the whole of Eastern Turkestan or subjugated, the Tarim Basin swarmed with Chinese settlers, and caravans were going over westward with silk and lacquer and jade to trade for the gold and silver of Armenia and Rome.

The splash over of the Yueh-Chi is recorded, but it is fairly evident that much westward movement of sections of the Hunnish peoples is not recorded. From 200 B.C. to 200 A.D. the Chinese Empire maintained a hard, resolute, advancing front towards nomadism, and the surplus of the nomads drifted steadily west. There was no such settling down behind a final frontier on the part of the Chinese as we see in the case of the Romans at the Rhine and Danube. The drift of the nomads before this Chinese thrust, century by century, turned southward at first towards Bactria. The Parthians of the first century B.C. probably mingled Scythian and Mongolian elements. The "singing arrows" that destroyed the army of Crassus came, it would seem, originally from the Altai and the Tian Shan. After the first century B.C. the line of greater attraction and least resistance lay for a time towards the north of the Caspian. In a century or so all the country known as Western Turkestan was "Mongolized," and so it remains to this day. A second great thrust by China began about 75 A.D., and accelerated the westward drift of the nomads. In 102, Pan Chau, a great Chinese general, was sending explorers from his advanced camp upon the Caspian to learn particulars of the Roman power. But their reports upon the task he contemplated decided him not to proceed.

By the first century A.D. nomadic Mongolian peoples are in evidence upon the eastern boundaries of Europe, already greatly mixed with Aryan nomads and with uprooted Aryan elements from the Caspian-Pamir region. There are Hunnish peoples established between the Caspian Sea and the Urals. West of them were the Alans, probably also a Mongolian people with Aryan elements ; they had fought against Pompey the Great when he was in Armenia in 65 B.C. These are as yet the furthest westward peoples of the new Mongolian advance, and they made no further westward push until the fourth century A.D. To the north-west the Finns, a Mongolian people, had long been established as far west as the Baltic.

West of the Huns, beyond the Don, there were Aryan tribes, the Goths. These Goths had spread south-eastward from their region of origin in Scandinavia. They were a Teutonic people, and we have already marked them crossing the Baltic in the map on page 177. They continued to move south-eastward across Russia, using the rivers and never forgetting their Baltic watercraft. No doubt they assimilated much Scythian population as they spread down to the Black Sea. In the first century A.D. they were in two main divisions, the Ostrogoths, the east Goths, who were between the Don and the Dnieper, and the Visigoths, or West Goths, west of the Dnieper. During the first century there was an air of quiescence over the great plains, but population was accumulating and the tribes were fermenting. The second and third centuries seem to have been a phase of comparatively moist seasons and abundant grass. Presently in the fourth and fifth centuries the weather grew drier and the grass became scanty, and the nomads stirred afresh.

But it is interesting to note that in the opening century of the Christian era, the Chinese Empire was strong enough to expel and push off from itself the surplus of this Mongolian nomadism to the north of it which presently conquered North India and gathered force and mingled with Aryan nomadism, and fell at last like an avalanche upon the weak-backed Roman Empire.

Before we go on to tell of the blows that now began to fall upon the Roman Empire and of the efforts of one or two great men to arrest the collapse, we may say a few words about the habits and quality of these westward-drifting barbaric Mongolian peoples who were now spreading from the limits of China towards the Black and Baltic Seas. It is still the European custom to follow the lead of the Roman writers and write of these Huns and their associates as of something incredibly destructive and cruel. But such accounts as we have from the Romans were written in periods of panic, and the Roman could lie about his enemies with a freedom and vigour that must arouse the envy even of the modern propagandist. He could talk of " Punic faith " as a byword for perfidy while committing the most abominable treacheries against Carthage, and his railing accusations of systematic cruelty against this people or that were usually the prelude and excuse for some frightful massacre or enslavement or robbery on his own part. He had quite a modern passion for self-justification. We must remember that these accounts of the savagery and frightfulness of the Huns came from a people whose chief amusement was gladiatorial shows, and whose chief method of dealing with insurrection and sedition was nailing the offender to a cross to die. From first to last the Roman Empire must have killed hundreds of thousands of men in that way. A large portion of the population of this empire that could complain of the barbarism of its assailants consisted of slaves subject practically to almost any lust or caprice at the hands of their owners. It is well to bear these facts in mind before we mourn the swamping of the Roman Empire by the barbarians as though it was an extinction of all that is fine in life by all that is black and ugly.

The facts seem to be that the Hunnish peoples were the eastern equivalent of the primitive Aryans of whom we have given an account in Chapter XV, and that, in spite of their profound racial and linguistic differences, they mixed with the nomadic and semi-nomadic residuum of the Aryan races north of the Danube and Persia very easily and successfully. Instead of killing, they enlisted and intermarried with the peoples they invaded. They had that necessary gift for all peoples destined to political predominance, tolerant assimilation. They came rather later in time, and their nomadic life was more highly developed than that of the primitive Aryans. The primitive Aryans were a forest and ox-wagon people who took to the horse later. The Hunnish peoples had grown up with the horse. Somewhen about 1,200 or 1,000 years B.C. they began to ride the horse. The bit, the saddle, the stirrup, these are not primitive things, but they are necessary if man and horse are to keep going for long stretches. It is well to bear in mind how modern a thing is riding. Altogether man has not been in the saddle for much more than three thousand years.[1] We have already noted the gradual appearance of the war chariot, the mounted man, and finally of disciplined cavalry in this history. It was from the Mongolian regions of Asia that these things came. To this day men in Central Asia go rather in the saddle than on their proper feet. Says Ratzel,[2] "Strong, long-necked horses are found in enormous numbers on the steppes. For Mongols and Turcomans riding is not a luxury; even the Mongol shepherds tend their flocks on horseback. Children are taught to ride in early youth; and the boy of three years old often takes his first riding-lesson on a safe child's saddle and makes quick progress."

It is impossible to suppose that the Huns and the Alans could have differed very widely in character from the present nomads of the steppe regions, and nearly all observers are agreed in describing these latter as open and pleasant people. They are thoroughly honest and free-spirited. "The character of the herdsmen of Central Asia," says Ratzel,[3] "when unadulterated, is ponderous eloquence, frankness, rough good-nature, pride, but also indolence, irritability, and a tendency to vindictiveness. Their faces show a considerable share of frankness combined with amusing naïvete. . . . Their courage is rather a sudden blaze of pugnacity than cold boldness. Religious fanaticism they have none. Hospitality is universal." This is not an entirely disagreeable picture. Their personal bearing, he says further, is quieter and more dignified than that of the townsmen of Turkestan and Persia. Add to this that the nomadic life prevents any great class inequalities or any extensive development of slavery.

[1] See Roger Pocock, *Horses*, a very interesting and picturesque little book.
[2] *The History of Mankind*, book v., C.
[3] *Ibid*.

Of course these peoples out of Asia were totally illiterate and artistically undeveloped. But we must not suppose, on that account, that they were primitive barbarians, and that their state of life was at the level from which the agricultural civilization had long ago arisen. It was not. They too had developed, but they had developed along a different line, a line with less intellectual complication, more personal dignity perhaps, and certainly with a more intimate contact with wind and sky.

§ 5

The first serious irruptions of the German tribes into the Roman Empire began in the third century with the decay of the central power.[4] We will not entangle the reader here with the vexed and intricate question of the names, identity, and inter-relationships of the various Germanic tribes. Historians find great difficulties in keeping them distinct, and these difficulties are enhanced by the fact that they themselves took little care to keep themselves distinct. We find in 236 A.D. a people called the Franks breaking bounds upon the Lower Rhine, and another, the Alamanni, pouring into Alsace. A much more serious push southward was that of the Goths. We have already noted the presence of these people in South Russia, and their division by the Dnieper into Western and Eastern Goths. They had become a maritime people again upon the Black Sea— probably their traditional migration from Sweden was along the waterways, for it is still possible to row a boat, with only a few quite practicable portages, from the Baltic right across Russia to either the Black or Caspian Sea—and they had wrested the command of the eastern seas from the control of Rome. They were presently raiding the shores of Greece. They also crossed the Danube in a great land raid in 247, and defeated and killed the Emperor Decius in what is now Serbia. The province of Dacia vanished from the Roman history. In 270 they were defeated at Nish in Serbia by Claudius, and in 276 they were raiding Pontus. It is characteristic of the invertebrate nature of the empire that the legions of Gaul found that

The Western (true Roman) Empire crumbles up.

[4] See *Migrations*, by Flinders Petrie, the 1906 Huxley Lecture of the Royal Anthrop. Institute.

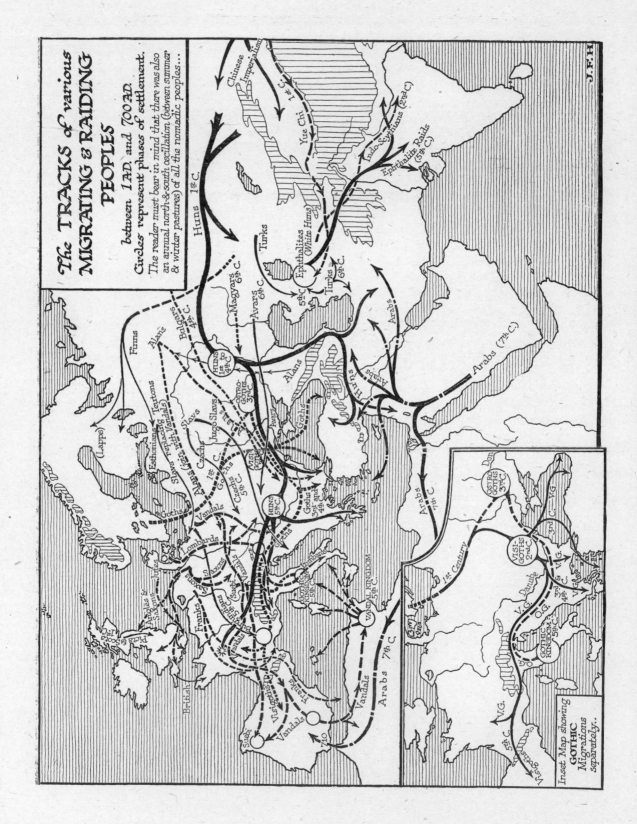

The TRACKS of various MIGRATING & RAIDING PEOPLES

between 1 A.D. and 700 A.D.
Circles represent phases of settlement.
The reader must bear in mind that there was also an annual north-&-south oscillation (between summer & winter pastures) of all the nomadic peoples...

Chinese Imperialism

Yue Chi 1st C.

Indo-Scythians (2nd C.)

Ephthalite Raids (5th C.)

Huns 1st C.

Turks

Ephthalites (White Huns)

5th C.

Turks 6th C.

Turks 6th C.

Arabs

Magyars 6th C.

Avars 6th C.

Alans

Finns

Budgers 4th C.

HUNS 1st to 4th C.

OSTRO-GOTHS 3rd C.

Alans

Goths

Huns

Arabs

Arabs (7th C.)

(Lapps)

Teutons

Esthonians

Slavs (1st with Vandals)

Slavs replacing Vandals

Alans (1st with Vandals)

Slavs

Czechs 1st C.

Jugo-Slavs

Goths 1st C.

Czechs 5th C.

VISI-GOTHS

Avars

Goths 3rd and 4th C.

HUNS 5th C.

Goths

Goths

Arabs 7th C.

Goths

Lombards

Vandals

Lombards

Saxons

Suebi

Vandals

GOTHIC KINGDOM 5th C.

VANDAL KINGDOM 5th C.

Angles & Saxons

Jutes

Franks

Frisians

Suebi

Vandals

Picts & Scots 1st C.

British

Visigoths 5th C.

Vandals

710

Vandals

Arabs 7th C.

Suebi

Visigoths 5th C.

Don

OSTRO-GOTHS 3rd C.

V.G.

VISI-GOTHS 2nd C.

V.G. 3rd C.

V.G. 4th C.

1st Century

(3rd C.) 300 A.D.

V.G.

Danube

O.G.

GOTHIC KINGDOM 5th C.

V.G.

V.G.

5th C.

Visigoths 5th-6th C.

Inset Map showing GOTHIC Migrations separately...

J.F.H.

346

the most effective method of dealing with the Franks and the Alamanni at this time was by setting up a separate emperor in Gaul and doing the job by themselves.

Then for a while the barbarians were held, and the Emperor Probus in 276 forced the Franks and the Alamanni back over the Rhine. But it is significant of the general atmosphere of insecurity created by these raids that Aurelian (270–275) fortified Rome, which had been an open and secure city for all the earlier years of the empire.

In 321 A.D. the Goths were again over the Danube, plundering what is now Serbia and Bulgaria. They were driven back by Constantine the Great, of whom we shall have more to tell in the next chapter. About the end of his reign (337 A.D.) the Vandals, a people closely kindred to the Goths, being pressed by them, obtained permission to cross the Danube into Pannonia, which is now that part of Hungary west of the river.

But by the middle of the fourth century the Hunnish people to the east were becoming aggressive again. They had long subjugated the Alani, and now they made the Ostrogoths, the east Goths, tributary. The Visigoths (or west Goths) followed the example of the Vandals, and made arrangements to cross the Danube into Roman territory. There was some dispute upon the terms of this settlement, and the Visigoths, growing fierce, assumed the offensive, and at Adrianople defeated the Emperor Valens, who was killed in this battle. They were then allowed to settle in what is now Bulgaria, and their army became nominally a Roman army, though they retained their own chiefs, the foremost of whom was Alaric. It exhibits the complete " barbarization " of the Roman empire that had already occurred, that the chief opponent of Alaric the Goth, Stilicho, was a Pannonian Vandal. The legions in Gaul were under the command of a Frank, and the Emperor Theodosius I (emp. 379–395) was a Spaniard chiefly supported by Gothic auxiliaries.

The empire was now splitting finally into an eastern (Greek-speaking) and a western (Latin-speaking) half. Theodosius the Great was succeeded by his sons Arcadius at Constantinople and Honorius at Ravenna. Alaric made a puppet of the eastern monarch and Stilicho

of the western. Huns now first appear within the empire as auxiliary troops enlisted under Stilicho. In this struggle of East and West, the frontier—if we can still speak of a frontier between the unauthorized barbarian without and the barbarian in possession within—gave way. Fresh Vandals, more Goths, Alans, Suevi, marched freely westward, living upon the country. Amidst this confusion occurred a crowning event. Alaric the Goth marched down Italy, and after a short siege captured Rome (410).

By 425 or so, the Vandals (whom originally we noted in East Germany) and a portion of the Alani (whom we first mentioned in South-east Russia) had traversed Gaul and the Pyrenees, and had amalgamated and settled in the south of Spain. There were Huns in possession of Pannonia and Goths in Dalmatia. Into Bohemia and Moravia came and settled a Slavic people, the Czechs (451). In Portugal and north of the Vandals in Spain were Visigoths and Suevi. Gaul was divided among Visigoths, Franks, and Burgundians. Britain was being invaded by Low German tribes, the Jutes, Angles and Saxons, before whom the Keltic British of the south-west were flying across the sea to what is now " Brittany " in France. The usual date given for this invasion is 449, but it was probably earlier.[1] And as the result of intrigues between two imperial politicians, the Vandals of the south of Spain, under their king Genseric, embarked *en masse* for North Africa (429), became masters of Carthage (439), secured the mastery of the sea, raided, captured, and pillaged Rome (455), crossed into Sicily, and set up a kingdom in West Sicily, which endured there for a hundred years (up to 534). At the time of its greatest extent (477) this Vandal kingdom included also Corsica, Sardinia, and the Balearic Isles, as well as much of North Africa.

About this Vandal kingdom facts and figures are given that show very clearly the true nature of these barbarian irruptions. They were not really the conquest and replacement of one people or race by another ; what happened was something very different ; it was a social revolution started and masked by a superficial foreign conquest. The whole Vandal nation,

[1] E. B.

men, women, and children, that came from Spain to Africa, for example, did not number more than eighty thousand souls. We know this because we have particulars of the transport problem. In their struggle for North Africa, Dr. Schurtz tells us,[1] " there is no trace of any serious resistance offered by the inhabitants ; Boniface (the Roman governor of North Africa) had defended Hippo with Gothic mercenaries, while the native population lent no appreciable assistance, and the nomad tribes of the country either adopted a dubious attitude or availed themselves of the difficulties of the Roman governor to make attacks and engage in predatory expeditions. This demoralization resulted from social conditions, which had perhaps developed more unfavourably in Africa than in other parts of the Roman Empire. The free peasants had long ago become the serfs of the great landed proprietors, and were little superior in position to the masses of slaves who were everywhere to be found. And the great landowners had become in their turn easy victims of the policy of extortion followed by unscrupulous governors to an increasingly unprecedented extent in proportion as the dignity of the imperial power sank lower. No man who had anything to lose would now take a place in the senate of the large towns, which had once been the goal of the ambitious, for the senators were required to make up all deficiencies in the revenue, and such deficiencies were now frequent and considerable. . . . Bloody insurrections repeatedly broke out, always traceable ultimately to the pressure of taxation. . . ."

Manifestly the Vandals came in as a positive relief to such a system.[2] They exterminated the great landowners, wiped out all debts to Roman money-lenders, and abolished the last vestiges of military service. The cultivators found themselves better off ; the minor officials kept their places ; it was not so much a conquest as a liberation from an intolerable deadlock.

It was while the Vandals were still in Africa that a great leader, Attila, arose among the Huns. The seat of his government was in the plains east of the Danube. For a time he swayed a considerable empire of Hunnish and Germanic tribes, and his rule stretched from the Rhine into Central Asia. He negotiated on equal terms with the Chinese emperor. He bullied Ravenna and Constantinople for ten years. Honoria, the grand-daughter of Theodosius II, Emperor of the Eastern empire, one of those passionate young ladies who cause so much trouble in the world, having been put under restraint because of a love affair with a court chamberlain, sent her ring to Attila and called upon him to be her husband and deliverer. He was also urged to attack the Eastern empire by Genseric the Vandal, who was faced by an alliance of the Western and Eastern emperors. He raided southward to the very walls of Constantinople, completely destroying, says Gibbon, seventy cities in his progress, and forcing upon the emperor an onerous peace, which apparently did not involve the liberation of Honoria to her hero. At this distance of time we are unable to guess at the motives for this omission. Attila continued to speak of her as his affianced bride, and to use the relationship as a pretext for aggressions. In the subsequent negotiations a certain Priscus accompanied an embassy to the camp of the Hunnish monarch, and the fragments that still survive of the narrative he wrote give us a glimpse of the camp and way of living of the great conqueror.

The embassy was itself a curiously constituted body. Its head was Maximin, an honest diplomatist who went in good faith. Quite unknown to him and, at the time, to Priscus, Vigilius, the interpreter of the expedition, had also a secret mission from the court of Theodosius which was to secure by bribery the assassination of Attila. The little expedition went by way of Nish ; it crossed the Danube in canoes, dug out of a single tree, and it was fed by contributions from the villages on the route. Differences in dietary soon attracted the attention of the envoys. Priscus mentions mead in the place of wine, millet for corn, and a drink either distilled [3] or brewed from barley. The journey through Hungary will remind the reader in many of its incidents of the journeys of travellers in Central Africa during the Victorian period. The travellers were politely offered temporary wives.

---

[1] In Helmolt's *History of the World*.

[2] E. B. disagrees with this view. He regards it as the pro-Teutonic view of the German historians.

[3] Gibbon.

Attila's capital was rather a vast camp and village than a town. There was only one building of stone, a bath constructed on the Roman model. The mass of the people were in huts and tents; Attila and his leading men lived in timber palaces in great stockaded enclosures with their numerous wives and ministers about them. There was a vast display of loot, but Attila himself affected a nomadic simplicity; he was served in wooden cups and platters, and never touched bread. He worked hard, kept open court before the gate of his palace, and was commonly in the saddle. The primitive custom of both Aryans and Mongols of holding great feasts in hall still held good, and there was much hard drinking. Priscus describes how bards chanted before Attila. They "recited the verses which they had composed, to celebrate his valour and his victories. A profound silence prevailed in the hall, and the attention of the guests was captivated by the vocal harmony, which revived and perpetuated the memory of their own exploits; a martial ardour flashed from the eyes of the warriors, who were impatient for battle; and the tears of the old men expressed their generous despair, that they could no longer partake the danger and glory of the field. This entertainment, which might be considered as a school of military virtue, was succeeded by a farce that debased the dignity of human nature. A Moorish and Scythian buffoon successively excited the mirth of the rude spectators by their deformed figures, ridiculous dress, antic gestures, absurd speeches, and the strange, unintelligible confusion of the Latin, the Gothic, and the Hunnish languages, and the hall resounded with loud and licentious peals of laughter. In the midst of this intemperate riot, Attila alone, without change of countenance, maintained his steadfast and inflexible gravity." [1]

Although Attila was aware, through the confession of the proposed assassin, of the secret work of Vigilius, he allowed this embassy to return in safety, with presents of numerous horses and the like, to Constantinople. Then he despatched an ambassador to Theodosius II to give that monarch, as people say, a piece of his mind. "Theodosius," said the envoy, "is the son of an illustrious and respectable parent;

[1] Gibbon.

Attila, likewise, is descended from a noble race; and *he* has supported, by his actions, the dignity which he inherited from his father Munzuk. But Theodosius has forfeited his parental honours, and, by consenting to pay tribute, has degraded himself to the condition of a slave. It is therefore just that he should reverence the man whom fortune and merit have placed above him; instead of attempting, like a wicked slave, clandestinely to conspire against his master."

This straightforward bullying was met by abject submission. The emperor sued for pardon, and paid a great ransom.

In 451 Attila declared war on the western empire. He invaded Gaul. So far as the imperial forces were concerned, he had things all his own way, and he sacked most of the towns of France as far south as Orleans. Then the Franks and Visigoths and the imperial forces united against him, and a great and obstinate battle at Troyes (451), in which over 150,000 men were killed on both sides, ended in his repulse and saved Europe from a Mongolian overlord. This disaster by no means exhausted Attila's resources. He turned his attention southward, and overran North Italy. He burnt Aquileia and Padua, and looted Milan, but he made peace at the entreaty of Pope Leo I. He died in 453. . . .

Hereafter the Huns, so far as that name goes in Europe, the Huns of Attila, disappeared out of history. They dissolve into the surrounding populations. They were probably already much mixed, and rather Aryan than Mongolian. They did not become, as one might suppose, the inhabitants of Hungary, though they have probably left many descendants there. About a hundred years after came another Hunnish or mixed people, the Avars, out of the east into Hungary, but these were driven out eastward again by Charlemagne in 791–5. The Magyars, the modern Hungarians, came westward later. They were a Turko-Finnish people. The Magyar is a language belonging to the Finno-Ugrian division of the Ural-Altaic tongues. The Magyars were on the Volga about 550. They settled in Hungary about 900. . . . But we are getting too far on in our story, and we must return to Rome.

In 493 Theodoric, a Goth, became King of

Rome, but already for seventeen years there had been no Roman emperor. So it was in utter social decay and collapse that the great slave-holding "world-ascendancy" of the God-Cæsars and the rich men of Rome came to an end.

§ 6

But though throughout the whole of Western Europe and North Africa the Roman imperial system had collapsed, though credit had vanished, luxury production had ceased and money was hidden, though creditors were going unpaid and slaves masterless, the tradition of the Cæsars was still being carried on in Constantinople. We have already had occasion to mention as two outstanding figures among the late Cæsars, Diocletian (284) and Constantine the Great (312), and it was to the latter of these that the world owes the setting up of a fresh imperial centre at Constantinople. Very early during the imperial period the unsuitability of the position of Rome as a world capital, due to the Roman failure to use the sea, was felt. The destruction of Carthage and Corinth had killed the shipping of the main Mediterranean sea-routes. For a people who did not use the sea properly, having the administrative centre at Rome meant that every legion, every draft of officials, every order, had to travel northward for half the length of Italy before it could turn east or west. Consequently nearly all the more capable emperors set up their headquarters at some subordinate centre in a more convenient position. Sirmium (on the River Save), Milan, Lyons, and Nicomedia (in Bithynia) were among such supplementary capitals. For a time under Diocletian, Durazzo was the imperial capital. Ravenna, near the head of the Adriatic, was the capital of the last Roman emperors in the time of Alaric and Stilicho.

It was Constantine the Great who determined upon the permanent transfer of the centre of imperial power to the Bosphorus. We have already noted the existence of the city of Byzantium, which Constantine chose to develop into his new capital. It played a part in the story of the intricate Histiæus (chap. xxii, § 4); it repulsed Philip of Macedon

The Eastern (revived Hellenic) Empire.

(chap. xxiv, § 3). If the reader will examine its position, he will see that, in the hands of a line of capable emperors, and as the centre of a people with some solidarity and spirit and seacraft (neither of which things were vouchsafed to it), it was extraordinarily well-placed. Its galleys could have penetrated up the rivers to the heart of Russia and outflanked every barbarian advance. It commanded practicable trade routes to the east, and it was within a reasonable striking distance of Mesopotamia, Egypt, Greece, and all the more prosperous and civilized regions of the world at that period. And even under the rule of a series of inept monarchs and under demoralized social conditions, the remains of the Roman Empire centring at Constantinople held out for nearly a thousand years.

It was the manifest intention of Constantine the Great that Constantinople should be the centre of an undivided empire. But having regard to the methods of travel and transport available at the time, the geographical conditions of Europe and Western Asia do not point to any one necessary centre of government. If Rome faced westward instead of eastward, and so failed to reach out beyond the Euphrates, Constantinople on the other hand was hopelessly remote from Gaul. The enfeebled Mediterranean civilization, after a certain struggle for Italy, did in fact let go of the west altogether and concentrated upon what were practically the central vestiges, the stump, of the empire of Alexander. The Greek language resumed its sway, which had never been very seriously undermined by the official use of Latin. This "Eastern" or Byzantine empire is generally spoken of as if it were a continuation of the Roman tradition. It is really far more like a resumption of Alexander's.

The Latin language had not the intellectual vigour behind it, it had not the literature and the science, to make it a necessity to intelligent men and so to maintain an ascendancy over the Greek. For no language, whatever officialdom may do, can impose itself in competition with another that can offer the advantages of a great literature or encyclopædic information. Aggressive languages must bring gifts, and the gifts of Greek were incomparably greater than the gifts of Latin. The Eastern empire

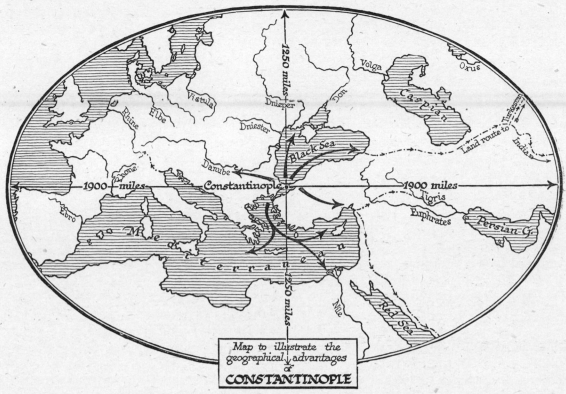

Map to illustrate the
geographical advantages
of
CONSTANTINOPLE

was from the beginnings of its separation Greek-speaking, and a continuation, though a degenerate continuation, of the Hellenic tradition. Its intellectual centre was no longer in Greece, but Alexandria. Its mentality was no longer the mentality of free-minded plain-speaking citizens, of the Stagirite Aristotle and the Greek Plato ; its mentality was the mentality of the pedants and of men politically impotent ; its philosophy was a pompous evasion of real things, and its scientific impulse was dead. Nevertheless, it was Hellenic. The Roman had come, and he had gone again. Indeed he had gone very extensively from the west also. By the sixth century A.D. the populations of Europe and North Africa had been stirred up like sediment. When presently in the seventh and eighth centuries the sediment begins to settle down again and populations begin to take on a definite localized character, the Roman is only to be found by name in the region about Rome. Over large parts of his Western empire we find changed and changing modifications of his Latin speech : in Gaul, where the Frank is learning a Gallic form of Latin and evolving French in the process ; in Italy, where, under the influence of Teutonic invaders, the Lombards and Goths, Latin is being modified into various Italian dialects ; in Spain and Portugal, where it is becoming Spanish and Portuguese. The fundamental Latinity of the languages in these regions serves to remind us of the numerical unimportance of the various Frankish, Vandal, Avar, Gothic, and the like German-speaking invaders, and serves to justify our statement that what happened to the Western empire was not so much conquest and the replacement of one population by another as a political and social revolution. The district of Valais in South Switzerland also retained a fundamentally Latin speech ; and, what is more curious and interesting, is that in Dacia and Mœsia Inferior, large parts of which to the north of the Danube became the modern Roumania (=Romania), although these regions were added late to the empire and lost soon, the Latin speech also remained.

In Britain Latin was practically wiped out by the conquering Anglo-Saxons, from among whose various dialects the root-stock of English presently grew.

But while the smashing of the Roman social

and political structure was thus complete, while in the east it was thrown off by the older and stronger Hellenic tradition, and while in the west it was broken up into fragments that began to take on a new and separate life of their own, there was one thing that did not perish, but grew, and that was the tradition of the world empire of Rome and of the supremacy of the Cæsars.

and leaders and kings of the barbarians, who raided through the prostrate but vast disorder of the decayed empire, were capable of conceiving of some mighty king of kings greater than themselves and giving a real law for all men, and they were ready to believe that elsewhere in space and time, and capable of returning presently to resume his supremacy, Cæsar had been such a king of kings. Far above their own titles, therefore, they esteemed and envied the title of Cæsar. The international history of Europe from this time henceforth is largely the story of kings and adventurers setting up to be Cæsar and Imperator (Emperor). We shall tell of some of them in their places. So universal did this "Cæsaring" become, that the Great War of 1914–18 mowed down no less than four Cæsars, the German Kaiser (= Cæsar), the Austrian Kaiser, the Tsar (= Cæsar) of Russia, and that fantastic figure, the Tsar of Bulgaria. The French "Imperator" (Napoleon III) had already fallen in 1871. There is now (1919) no one left in the world to carry on the Imperial title or the tradition of Divus Cæsar except the Turkish Sultan and British monarch. The former commemorates his lordship over Constantinople as Kaisar-i-Roum; the latter is called the Cæsar of India (a country no real Cæsar ever looked upon), Kaisar-i-Hind.

The EASTERN ROMAN EMPIRE circa 500 A.D.

when Theodoric was king of Italy & Sicily, & nominally subject to the Emperor at Constantinople

Kingdom of Theodoric.......

When the reality was destroyed, the legend had freedom to expand. Removed from the possibility of verification, the idea of a serene and splendid Roman world-supremacy grew up in the imagination of mankind, and still holds it to this day.

Ever since the time of Alexander, human thought has been haunted by the possible political unity of the race. All the sturdy chiefs

SECOND CENTURY PORTRAIT OF CHRIST FROM THE ROMAN CATACOMBS.
Drawing by T. Heaphy, in the British Museum.

[353

BOOK VI[1]

CHRISTIANITY AND ISLAM

XXX

THE BEGINNINGS, THE RISE, AND THE DIVISIONS OF CHRISTIANITY

§ 1

BEFORE we can understand the qualities of Christianity, which must now play a large part in our history, and which opened men's eyes to fresh aspects of the possibility of a unified world, we must go back some centuries and tell of the condition of affairs in Palestine and Syria, in which countries Christianity arose. We have already told in Chapter XXI the main facts about the origin of the Jewish nation and tradition, about the Diaspora, about the fundamentally scattered nature of Jewry even from the beginning, and the gradual development of the idea of one just God ruling the earth and bound by a special promise to preserve and bring to honour

Judea at the Christian Era.

GALILEE and surrounding provinces.

Principal routes -----

J.F.H.

0   50   100   200 Miles

the Jewish people. The Jewish idea was and is a curious combination of theological breadth and an intense racial patriotism. The Jews looked for a special saviour, a Messiah, who was to redeem mankind by the agreeable process of restoring the fabulous glories of David and Solomon, and bringing the whole world at last under the benevolent but firm Jewish heel. As the political power of the Semitic peoples declined, as Carthage followed Tyre into the darkness and Spain became a Roman province, this dream grew and spread. There can be little doubt that the scattered Phœnicians in Spain and Africa and throughout the Mediterranean, speaking as they did a language closely akin to Hebrew and being deprived of their authentic political rights, became proselytes to Judaism. For phases of vigorous proselytism alternated with phases of exclusive jealousy in Jewish

[1] The student desirous of developing this and the following book cannot do better than proceed to the *Cambridge Medieval History*.

23

JERUSALEM.

history. On one occasion the Idumeans, being conquered, were all forcibly made Jews.[1] There were Arab tribes who were Jews in the time of Mohammed, and a Turkish people who were mainly Jews in South Russia in the ninth century. Judaism is indeed the reconstructed political ideal of many shattered peoples— mainly Semitic. It is to the Phœnician contingent and to Aramean accessions in Babylon that the financial and commercial tradition of the Jews is to be ascribed. But as a result of these coalescences and assimilations, almost everywhere in the towns throughout the Roman Empire, and far beyond it in the east, Jewish communities traded and flourished, and were kept in touch through the Bible and through a religious and educational organization. The main part of Jewry never was in Judea and had never come out of Judea.

Manifestly this intercommunicating series of Judaized communities had very great financial and political facilities. They could assemble resources, they could stir up, they could allay. They were neither so abundant nor so civilized as the still more widely diffused Greeks, but they had a tradition of greater solidarity. Greek was hostile to Greek ; Jew stood by Jew. Wherever a Jew went, he found men of like mind and like tradition with himself. He could get shelter, food, loans, and legal help. And by reason of this solidarity rulers had everywhere to take account of this people as a help, as a

[1] Josephus.

source of loans or as a source of trouble. So it is that the Jews have persisted as a people while Hellenism has become a universal light for mankind.

We cannot tell here in any detail the history of that smaller part of Jewry that lived in Judea. These Jews had returned to their old position of danger ; again they were seeking peace in, so to speak, the middle of a highway. In the old time they had been between Syria and Assyria to the north and Egypt to the south ; now they had the Seleucids to the north and the Ptolemys to the south, and when the Seleucids went, then down came the Roman power upon them. The independence of Judea was always a qualified and precarious thing. The reader must go to the *Antiquities* and the *Wars of the Jews* of Flavius Josephus, a copious, tedious, and maddeningly patriotic writer, to learn of the succession of their rulers, of their high-priest monarchs, and of the Maccabæans, the Herods and the like. These rulers were for the most part of the ordinary eastern type, cunning, treacherous, and blood-stained. Thrice Jerusalem was taken and twice the temple was destroyed. It was the support of the far more powerful Diaspora that prevented the little country from being wiped out altogether, until 70 A.D., when Titus, the adopted son and successor of the Emperor Vespasian, after a siege that ranks in bitterness and horror with that of Tyre and Carthage, took Jerusalem and destroyed city and temple altogether. He did

Photo: American Colony, Jerusalem.

JERUSALEM.

this in an attempt to destroy Jewry, but indeed he made Jewry stronger by destroying its one sensitive and vulnerable point.

Throughout a history of five centuries of war and civil commotion between the return from captivity and the destruction of Jerusalem, certain constant features of the Jew persisted. He remained obstinately monotheistic; he would have none other gods but the one true God. In Rome, as in Jerusalem, he stood out manfully against the worship of any god-Cæsar. And to the best of his ability he held to his covenants with his God. No graven images could enter Jerusalem; even the Roman standards with their eagles had to stay outside.

Two divergent lines of thought are traceable in Jewish affairs during these five hundred years. On the right, so to speak, are the high and narrow Jews, the Pharisees, very orthodox, very punctilious upon even the minutest details of the law, intensely patriotic and exclusive. Jerusalem on one occasion fell to the Seleucid monarch Antiochus IV. because the Jews would not defend it on the Sabbath day, when it is forbidden to work; and it was because the Jews made no effort to destroy his siege train on the Sabbath that Pompey the Great was able to take Jerusalem. But against these narrow Jews were pitted the broad Jews, the Jews of the left, who were Hellenizers, among whom are to be ranked the Sadducees, who did

not believe in immortality. These latter Jews, the broad Jews, were all more or less disposed to mingle with and assimilate themselves to the Greeks and Hellenized peoples about them. They were ready to accept proselytes, and so to share God and his promise with all mankind. But what they gained in generosity they lost in rectitude. They were the worldlings of Judea. We have already noted how the Hellenized Jews of Egypt lost their Hebrew, and had to have their Bible translated into Greek.

In the reign of Tiberius Cæsar a great teacher arose out of Judea who was to liberate the intense realization of the righteousness and unchallengeable oneness of God and of man's moral obligation to God, which was the strength of orthodox Judaism, from that greedy and exclusive narrowness with which it was so extraordinarily intermingled in the Jewish mind. This was Jesus of Nazareth, the seed rather than the founder of Christianity.

§ 2

The audience to which this book will first be presented will be largely an audience of Christians, with perhaps a sprinkling of Jewish readers, and the former at least will regard Jesus of Nazareth as being much more than a human teacher, and

The Teaching of Jesus of Nazareth.

Photo: H. J. Shepstone.

JERUSALEM, SHOWING SILOAM AND MOUNT OF OLIVES.

his appearance in the world not as a natural event in history, but as something of a supernatural sort interrupting and changing that steady development of life towards a common consciousness and a common will, which we have hitherto been tracing in this book. But these persuasions, dominant as they are in Europe and America, are nevertheless not the persuasions of all men or of the great majority of mankind, and we are writing this outline of the story of life with as complete an avoidance of controversial matter as may be. We are trying to write as if this book was to be read as much by Hindus or Moslems or Buddhists as by Americans and Western Europeans. We shall therefore hold closely to the apparent facts, and avoid, without any disputation or denial, the theological interpretations that have been imposed upon them. We shall tell what men have believed about Jesus of Nazareth, but him we shall treat as being what he appeared to be, a man, just as a painter must needs paint him as a man. The documents that testify to his acts and teachings we shall treat as ordinary human documents. If the light of divinity shine through our recital, we will neither help nor hinder it. This is what we have already done in the case of Buddha, and what we shall do later with Mohammed. About Jesus we have to write not theology but history, and our concern is not with the spiritual and theological significance of his life, but with its effects upon the political and everyday life of men.

Almost our only sources of information about the personality of Jesus are derived from the four gospels, all of which were certainly in existence a few decades after his death. The first three, the gospels of Matthew, Mark, and Luke, many suppose to be derived from some earlier documents; the gospel of St. John has more idiosyncrasy and is coloured by theology of a strongly Hellenic type. Critics are disposed to regard the gospel of St. Mark as being the most trustworthy account of the personality and actual words of Jesus.[1] But all four agree in giving us a picture of a very definite personality; they carry the same conviction of reality that the early accounts of Buddha do. In spite of miraculous and incredible additions, one is obliged to say, "Here was a man. This part of the tale could not have been invented."

But just as the personality of Gautama Buddha has been distorted and obscured by the stiff squatting figure, the gilded idol of later Buddhism, so one feels that the lean and strenuous personality of Jesus is much wronged by the unreality and conventionality that a mistaken reverence had imposed upon his figure in modern Christian art. Jesus was a penniless teacher, who wandered about the dusty, sun-bit country of Judea, living upon casual gifts of food; yet he is always represented clean, combed, and sleek, in spotless raiment, erect, and with something motionless about him as

[1] See *Encyclopædia Biblica*; article "Jesus."

though he was gliding through the air. This alone has made him unreal and incredible to many people who cannot distinguish the core of the story from the ornamental and unwise additions of the unintelligently devout.

And it may be that the early parts of the gospels are accretions of the same nature. The miraculous circumstances of the birth of Jesus, the great star that brought wise men from the east to worship at his manger cradle, the massacre of all the infant children in Judea by Herod—a massacre of which there is no single scrap of evidence in any contemporary history —and the flight into Egypt, are all supposed to be such accretionary matter by many authorities. At the best they are events unnecessary to the teaching, and they rob it of much of the strength and power it possesses when we strip it of such accompaniment. So, too, do the discrepant genealogies given by Matthew and Luke, in which there is an endeavour to trace the direct descent of Joseph, his father, from King David, as though it was any honour to Jesus or to anyone to have such a man as an ancestor. The insertion of these genealogies is the more peculiar and unreasonable, because, according to the legend, Jesus was not the son of Joseph at all, but miraculously conceived.

We are left, if we do strip this record of these difficult accessories, with the figure of a being, very human, very earnest and passionate, capable of swift anger, and teaching a new and simple and profound doctrine—namely, the universal loving Fatherhood of God and the coming of the Kingdom of Heaven. He was clearly a person—to use a common phrase—of intense personal magnetism. He attracted followers and filled them with love and courage. Weak and ailing people were heartened and healed by his presence. Yet he was probably of a delicate physique, because of the swiftness with which he died under the pains of crucifixion. There is a tradition that he fainted when, according to the custom, he was made to bear his cross to the place of execution.[1] When

[1] John says he carried his cross, but the three other gospels say that it was carried for him.

A VIEW FROM THE MOUNT OF OLIVES, LOOKING ACROSS THE WILDERNESS OF JUDEA AND THE DEAD SEA AND JORDAN VALLEY. MOUNTAINS OF MOAB IN THE DISTANCE.

he first appeared as a teacher he was a man of about thirty. He went about the country for three years spreading his doctrine, and then he came to Jerusalem and was accused of trying to set up a strange kingdom in Judea; he was tried upon this charge, and crucified together with two thieves. Long before they were dead, his sufferings were over.

Now it is a matter of fact that in the gospels all that body of theological assertion which constitutes Christianity finds little support. There is, as the reader may see for himself, no clear and emphatic assertion in these books of the doctrines which Christian teachers of all denominations find generally necessary to salvation. It is difficult to get any words that actually came from Jesus in which he claimed to be the Jewish Messiah (rendered in Greek by " the Christ ") or to be a part of the godhead, or in which he explained the doctrine of the Atonement or urged any sacrifices or sacraments (that is to say, priestly offices) upon his followers. We shall see presently how later on all Christendom was torn by disputes about the Trinity. There is no evidence that the apostles of Jesus ever heard of the Trinity— at any rate from him. The observance of the Jewish Sabbath, again, transferred to the Mithraic Sun-day, is an important feature of many Christian cults; but Jesus deliberately broke the Sabbath, and said that it was made for man and not man for the Sabbath. Nor did he say a word about the worship of his mother Mary, in the guise of Isis, the Queen of

THE " SUN-BIT COUNTRY OF JUDEA."

Heaven. All that is most characteristically Christian in worship and usage, he ignored. Sceptical writers have had the temerity to deny that Jesus can be called a Christian at all. For light upon these extraordinary gaps in his teaching, each reader must go to his own religious guides. Here we are bound to mention these gaps on account of the difficulties and controversies that arose out of them, and we are equally bound not to enlarge upon them.

As remarkable is the enormous prominence given by Jesus to the teaching of what he called the Kingdom of Heaven, and its comparative insignificance in the procedure and teaching of most of the Christian churches.

This doctrine of the Kingdom of Heaven, which was the main teaching of Jesus, and which plays so small a part in the Christian creeds, is certainly one of the most revolutionary doctrines that ever stirred and changed human thought. It is small wonder if the world of that time failed to grasp its full significance, and recoiled in dismay from even a half apprehension of its tremendous challenges to the established habits and institutions of mankind. It is small wonder if the hesitating convert and disciple presently went back to the old familiar ideas of temple and altar, of fierce deity and propitiatory observance, of consecrated priest and magic blessing, and—these things being attended to—reverted then to the dear old habitual life of hates and profits and competition and pride. For the doctrine of the Kingdom of Heaven, as Jesus seems to have preached it, was no less than a bold and uncompromising demand for a complete change and cleansing of the life of our struggling race, an utter cleansing, without and within. To the gospels the reader must go for all that is preserved of this tremendous teaching; here we are only concerned with the jar of its impact upon established ideas.

The Jews were persuaded that God, the one God of the whole world, was a righteous god, but they also thought of him as a trading god who had made a bargain with their Father

creeds and other races. In the parable of the labourers he thrust aside the obstinate claim of the Jews to have a sort of first mortgage upon God. All whom God takes into the kingdom, he taught, God serves alike; there is no distinction in his treatment, because there is no measure to his bounty. From all, moreover, as the parable of the buried talent witnesses, and as the incident of the widow's mite enforces, he demands the utmost. There are no privileges, no rebates, and no excuses in the Kingdom of Heaven.

Photo : American Colony, Jerusalem.

THE LOWER POOL OF GIHON, JERUSALEM.

Abraham about them, a very good bargain indeed for them, to bring them at last to predominance in the earth. With dismay and anger they heard Jesus sweeping away their dear securities. God, he taught, was no bargainer; there were no chosen people and no favourites in the Kingdom of Heaven. God was the loving father of all life, as incapable of showing favour as the universal sun. And all men were brothers —sinners alike and beloved sons alike—of this divine father. In the parable of the Good Samaritan Jesus cast scorn upon that natural tendency we all obey, to glorify our own people and to minimise the righteousness of other

But it was not only the intense tribal patriotism of the Jews that Jesus outraged. They were a people of intense family loyalty, and he would have swept away all the narrow and restrictive family affections in the great flood of the love of God. The whole Kingdom of Heaven was to be the family of his followers. We are told that, " While he yet talked to the people, behold, his mother and his brethren stood without, desiring to speak with him. Then one said unto him, Behold, thy mother and thy brethren stand without, desiring to speak with thee. But he answered and said unto him that told him, Who is my mother ? and who are my brethren? And he stretched forth his hand toward his disciples, and said, Behold my mother and my brethren! For whosoever shall do the will of my Father which is in heaven, the same is my brother, and sister, and mother."[1]

And not only did Jesus strike at patriotism and the bonds of family loyalty in the name of God's universal fatherhood and the brotherhood of all mankind, but it is clear that his teaching condemned all the gradations of the economic system, all private wealth, and personal advantages. All men belonged to the kingdom; all their possessions belonged to the kingdom;

him loved him, and said unto him, One thing thou lackest: go thy way, sell whatsoever thou hast, and give to the poor, and thou shalt have treasure in heaven: and come, take up the cross, and follow me. And he was sad at that saying, and went away grieved: for he had great possessions.

"And Jesus looked round about, and saith unto his disciples, How hardly shall they that have riches enter into the kingdom of God! And the disciples were astonished at his words. But Jesus answered again, and saith unto them, Children, how hard is it for them that trust in

TIBERIAS AND THE LAKE OF GALILEE.

the righteous life for all men, the only righteous life, was the service of God's will with all that we had, with all that we were. Again and again he denounced private riches and the reservation of any private life.

"And when he was gone forth into the way, there came one running, and kneeled to him, and asked him, Good Master, what shall I do that I may inherit eternal life? And Jesus said unto him, Why callest thou me good? there is none good but one, that is, God. Thou knowest the commandments, Do not commit adultery, Do not kill, Do not steal, Do not bear false witness, Defraud not, Honour thy father and mother. And he answered and said unto him, Master, all these things have I observed from my youth. Then Jesus beholding

[1] Matt. xii. 46–50.

riches to enter into the kingdom of God! It is easier for a camel to go through the eye of a needle, than for a rich man to enter into the kingdom of God."[2]

Moreover, in his tremendous prophecy of this kingdom which was to make all men one together in God, Jesus had small patience for the bargaining righteousness of formal religion. Another large part of his recorded utterances is aimed against the meticulous observance of the rules of the pious career. "Then came together unto him the Pharisees, and certain of the scribes, which came from Jerusalem. And when they saw some of his disciples eat bread with defiled, that is to say, with unwashen, hands, they found fault. For the Pharisees, and all the Jews, except they wash their hands

[2] Mark x. 17–25.

oft, eat not, holding the tradition of the elders. And when they come from the market, except they wash, they eat not. And many other things there be, which they have received to hold, as the washing of cups, and pots, brazen vessels, and of tables. Then the Pharisees and scribes asked him, Why walk not thy disciples according to the tradition of the elders, but eat bread with unwashen hands? He answered and said unto them, Well hath Isaiah prophesied of you hypocrites, as it is written,

" This people honoureth me with their lips,

" But their heart is far from me.

" Howbeit in vain do they worship me,

" Teaching for doctrines the commandments of men.

" For laying aside the commandment of God, ye hold the tradition of men, as the washing of pots and cups: and many other such things ye do. And he said unto them, Full well ye reject the commandment of God, that ye may keep your own tradition." [1]

So, too, we may note a score of places in which he flouted that darling virtue of the formalist, the observance of the Sabbath.

It was not merely a moral and a social revolution that Jesus proclaimed; it is clear from a score of indications that his teaching had a political bent of the plainest sort. It is true that he said his kingdom was not of this world, that it was in the hearts of men and not upon a throne; but it is equally clear that wherever and in what measure his kingdom was set up in the hearts of men, the outer world would be in that measure revolutionized and made new.

Whatever else the deafness and blindness of his hearers may have missed in his utterances, it is plain that they did not miss his resolve to revolutionize the world. Some of the questions that were brought to Jesus and the answers he gave enable us to guess at the drift of much of his unrecorded teaching. The directness of his political attack is manifest by such an incident as that of the coin—

" And they send unto him certain of the Pharisees and of the Herodians, to catch him in his words. And when they were come, they say unto him, Master, we know that thou art true, and carest for no man: for thou regardest not the person of men, but teachest the way of God in truth: Is it lawful to give tribute to Cæsar, or not? Shall we give, or shall we not give? But he, knowing their hypocrisy, said unto them, Why tempt ye me? bring me a penny, that I may see it. And they brought it. And he saith unto them, Whose is this image and superscription? And they said unto him, Cæsar's. And Jesus answering said unto them, Render to Cæsar the things that are Cæsar's, and to God the things that are God's " [2]—which, in view of all else that he had taught, left very little of a man or his possessions for Cæsar.

The whole tenor of the opposition to him and the circumstances of his trial and execution show clearly that to his contemporaries he seemed to propose plainly, and did propose plainly to change and fuse and enlarge all human life. But even his disciples did not grasp the profound and comprehensive significance of that proposal. They were ridden by the old Jewish dream of a king, a Messiah to overthrow the Hellenized Herods and the Roman overlord, and restore the fabled glories of David. They disregarded the substance of his teaching, plain and direct though it was; evidently they thought it was merely his mysterious and singular way of setting about the adventure that would at last put him on the throne of Jerusalem. They thought he was just another king among the endless succession of kings, but of a quasi-magic kind, and making quasi-magic professions of an impossible virtue.

" And James and John, the sons of Zebedee, come unto him, saying, Master, we would that thou shouldest do for us whatsoever we shall desire. And he said unto them, What would ye that I should do for you? They said unto him, Grant unto us that we may sit, one on thy right hand, and the other on thy left hand, in thy glory. But Jesus said unto them, Ye know not what ye ask: can ye drink of the cup that I drink of? and be baptized with the baptism that I am baptized with? And they said unto him, We can. And Jesus said unto them, Ye shall indeed drink of the cup that I drink of; and with the baptism that I am baptized withal shall ye be baptized: but to sit on my right hand and on my left hand is not mine to give;

[1] Mark vii. 1–9.

[2] Mark xii. 13–17.

but it shall be given to them for whom it is prepared. And when the ten heard it, they began to be much displeased with James and John. But Jesus called them to him, and saith unto them, Ye know that they which are accounted to rule over the Gentiles exercise lordship over them ; and their great ones exercise authority upon them. But so shall it not be among you : but whosoever will be great among you, shall be your minister : and whosoever of you will be the chiefest, shall be servant of all. For even the Son of man came not to be ministered unto, but to minister, and to give his life a ransom for many." [1]

This was cold comfort for those who looked for a due reward for their services and hardships in his train. They could not believe this hard doctrine of a kingdom of service which was its own exceeding great reward. Even when he was dead upon the cross, they could not believe that he was not still in the vein of the ancient world of pomps and privileges, that presently by some amazing miracle he would become undead again and return, and set up his throne with much splendour and graciousness in Jerusalem. They thought his life was a stratagem and his death a trick.

He was too great for his disciples. And in view of what he plainly said, is it any wonder that all who were rich and prosperous felt a horror of strange things, a swimming of their world at his teaching ? Perhaps the priests and the rulers and the rich men understood him better than his followers. He was dragging out all the little private reservations they had made from social service into the light of a universal religious life. He was like some terrible moral huntsman digging mankind out of the snug burrows in which they had lived hitherto. In the white blaze of this kingdom of his there was to be no property, no privilege, no pride and precedence ; no motive indeed and no reward but love. Is it any wonder that men were dazzled and blinded and cried out against him ? Even his disciples cried out when he would not spare them the light. Is it any wonder that the priests realized that between this man and themselves there was no choice but that he or priestcraft should perish ? Is it any wonder that the Roman soldiers, con-

[1] Mark x. 35–45.

fronted and amazed by something soaring over their comprehension and threatening all their disciplines, should take refuge in wild laughter, and crown him with thorns and robe him in purple and make a mock Cæsar of him ? For to take him seriously was to enter upon a strange and alarming life, to abandon habits, to control instincts and impulses, to essay an incredible happiness. . . .

Is it any wonder that to this day this Galilean is too much for our small hearts ?

§ 3

Yet be it noted that while there was much in the real teachings of Jesus that a rich man or a priest or a trader or an imperial official or any ordinary respectable citizen could not accept without the most revolutionary changes in his way of living, yet there was nothing that a follower of the actual teaching of Gautama Sakya might not receive very readily, nothing to prevent a primitive Buddhist from being also a Nazarene, and nothing to prevent a personal disciple of Jesus from accepting all the recorded teachings of Gautama Buddha.

The New Universal Religions.

Again consider the tone of this extract from the writings of a Chinaman, Mo Ti, who lived somewhen in the fourth century B.C., when the doctrines of Confucius and Lao Tse prevailed in China, before the advent of Buddhism to that country, and note how " Nazarene " it is.

" The mutual attacks of state on state ; the mutual usurpations of family on family ; the mutual robberies of man on man ; the want of kindness on the part of the sovereign and of loyalty on the part of the minister ; the want of tenderness and filial duty between father and son—these, and such as these, are the things injurious to the empire. All this has arisen from want of mutual love. If but that one virtue could be made universal, the princes loving one another would have no battle-fields ; the chiefs of families would attempt no usurpations ; men would commit no robberies ; rulers and ministers would be gracious and loyal ; fathers and sons would be kind and filial ; brothers would be harmonious and easily reconciled. Men in general loving one another, the strong would not make prey of the weak ; the many would not plunder the few, the rich

Photo : H. J. Shepstone.
RUINS OF A LARGE JEWISH SYNAGOGUE AT CAPERNAUM ON THE SHORES OF THE LAKE OF GALILEE

would not insult the poor, the noble would not be insolent to the mean ; and the deceitful would not impose upon the simple." [1]

This is extraordinarily like the teaching of Jesus of Nazareth cast into political terms. The thoughts of Mo Ti came close to the Kingdom of Heaven.

This essential identity is the most important historical aspect of these great world religions. They were in their beginnings quite unlike the priest, altar and temple cults, those cults for the worship of definite finite gods that played so great and so essential a part in the earlier stages of man's development between 15,000 B.C. and 600 B.C. These new world religions, from 600 B.C. onward, were essentially religions of the heart and of the universal sky. They swept away all those various and limited gods that had served the turn of human needs since the first communities were welded together by fear and hope. And presently when we come to Islam we shall find that for a third time the same fundamental new doctrine of the need of a universal devotion of all men to one Will reappears. Islam indeed is marred, as Judaism

[1] Hirth, *The Ancient History of China.* Chap. viii.

is marred, by a streak of primitive exclusiveness ; its founder was manifestly of a commoner clay than either Jesus or Gautama, and he had to tack on to his assertion of the supremacy of God an assertion that Mohammed was in especial his prophet, a queer little lapse into proprietorship, a touchingly baseless claim for the copyright of an idea which, as a matter of fact, he had picked up from the Jews and Christians about him. Yet, warned by the experiences of Christianity, Mohammed was very emphatic in insisting that he himself was merely a man. And the broad idea of human brotherhood under God that he preached, and the spirit in which his followers have carried it among black and fallen races, puts his essential teaching little lower than that of its two greater but far more abundantly corrupted and misrepresented rivals.

We speak of these great religions of mankind which arose between the Persian conquest of Babylon and the break-up of the Roman empires as rivals ; but it is their defects, their accumulations and excrescences, their differences of language and phrase, that cause the rivalry ; and it is not to one overcoming the other or to any new variant replacing them that we must look, but to the white truth in each being burnt free from its dross, and becoming manifestly the same truth—namely, that the hearts of men, and therewith all the lives and institutions of men, must be subdued to one common Will, ruling them all.[1]

And though much has been written foolishly about the antagonism of science and religion, there is indeed no such antagonism. What all these world religions declare by inspiration and insight, history as it grows clearer and science as its range extends display, as a reasonable and demonstrable fact, that men form one universal brotherhood, that they spring from one common origin, that their individual lives, their nations and races, interbreed and blend and go on to merge again at last in one common human destiny upon this little planet amidst the stars. And the psychologist can now stand beside the preacher and assure us that there is no reasoned peace of heart, no balance and no safety in the soul, until a man in losing his life has found it, and has schooled and disciplined his interests and will beyond greeds, rivalries, fears, instincts, and narrow affections. The history of our race and personal religious experience run so closely parallel as to seem to a modern observer almost the same thing; both tell of a being at first scattered and blind and utterly confused, feeling its way slowly to the serenity and salvation of an ordered and coherent purpose. That, in the simplest, is the outline of history; whether one have a religious purpose or disavow a religious purpose altogether, the lines of the outline remain the same.

§ 4

The Crucifixion of Jesus of Nazareth.

In the year 30 A.D.,[2] while Tiberius, the second Emperor, was Emperor of Rome and Pontius Pilate was procurator of Judea, a little while before the Feast of the Passover, Jesus of Nazareth came into Jerusalem. Probably he

[1] "St. Paul understood what most Christians never realize, namely, that the Gospel of Christ is not *a* religion, but religion itself in its most universal and deepest significance."—Dean Inge in *Outspoken Essays*.

[2] Authorities vary considerably upon this date, and upon most of the dates of the life of Jesus. See *Encyclopædia Biblica*, art. "Chronology."

came then for the first time. Hitherto he had been preaching chiefly in Galilee, and for the most part round and about the town of Capernaum. In Capernaum he had preached in the synagogue.

His entry into Jerusalem was a pacific triumph. He had gathered a great following in Galilee—he had sometimes to preach from a boat upon the Lake of Galilee, because of the pressure of the crowd upon the shore—and his fame had spread before him to the capital. Great crowds came out to greet him. It is clear they did not understand the drift of his teaching, and that they shared the general persuasion that by some magic of righteousness he was going to overthrow the established order. He rode into the city upon the foal of an ass that had been borrowed by his disciples. The crowd accompanied him with cries of triumph and shouts of "Hosanna," a word of rejoicing.

He went to the temple. Its outer courts were cumbered with the tables of money-changers and with the stalls of those who sold doves to be liberated by pious visitors to the temple. These traders upon religion he and his followers cast out, overturning the tables. It was almost his only act of positive rule.

Then for a week he taught in Jerusalem, surrounded by a crowd of followers who made his arrest by the authorities difficult. Then officialdom gathered itself together against this astonishing intruder. One of his disciples, Judas, dismayed and disappointed at the apparent ineffectiveness of this capture of Jerusalem, went to the Jewish priests to give them his advice and help in the arrest of Jesus. For this service he was rewarded with thirty pieces of silver. The high priest and the Jews generally had many reasons for dismay at this gentle insurrection that was filling the streets with excited crowds; for example, the Romans might misunderstand it or use it as an occasion to do some mischief to the whole Jewish people. Accordingly the high priest Caiaphas, in his anxiety to show his loyalty to the Roman overlord, was the leader in the proceedings against this unarmed Messiah, and the priests and the orthodox mob of Jerusalem the chief accusers of Jesus.

How he was arrested in the garden of Gethsemane, how he was tried and sentenced by

Pontius Pilate, the Roman procurator, how he was scourged and mocked by the Roman soldiers and crucified upon the hill called Golgotha, is told with unsurpassable simplicity and dignity in the gospels.

The revolution collapsed utterly. The disciples of Jesus with one accord deserted him, and Peter, being taxed as one of them, said, "I know not the man." This was not the end they had anticipated in their great coming to Jerusalem. His last hours of aching pain and thirst upon the cross were watched only by a few women and near friends.

of nature indulged in any such meaningless comments. Far more tremendous is it to suppose a world apparently indifferent to those three crosses in the red evening twilight, and to the little group of perplexed and desolated watchers. The darkness closed upon the hill; the distant city set about its preparations for the Passover; scarcely anyone but that knot of mourners on the way to their homes troubled whether Jesus of Nazareth was still dying or already dead. . . .

The souls of the disciples were plunged for a time into utter darkness. Then presently came

ANTIOCH, NORTHERN SYRIA.

Towards the end of the long day of suffering this abandoned leader roused himself to one supreme effort, cried out with a loud voice, "My God! my God! why hast thou forsaken me?" and, leaving these words to echo down the ages, a perpetual riddle to the faithful, died.

It was inevitable that simple believers should have tried to enhance the stark terrors of this tragedy by foolish stories of physical disturbances similar to those which had been invented to emphasize the conversion of Gautama. We are told that a great darkness fell upon the earth, and that the veil of the temple was rent in twain; but if indeed these things occurred, they produced not the slightest effect upon the minds of people in Jerusalem at that time. It is difficult to believe nowadays that the order

a whisper among them and stories, rather discrepant stories, that the body of Jesus was not in the tomb in which it had been placed, and that first one and then another had seen him alive. Soon they were consoling themselves with the conviction that he had risen from the dead, that he had shown himself to many, and had ascended visibly into heaven. Witnesses were found to declare that they had positively seen him go up, visibly in his body. He had gone through the blue—to God. Soon they had convinced themselves that he would presently come again, in power and glory, to judge all mankind. In a little while, they said, he would come back to them; and in these bright revivals of their old-time dream of an assertive and temporal splendour they forgot the greater measure, the giant measure he had given them of the Kingdom of God.

§ 5 [1]

The story of the early beginnings of Christianity is the story of the struggle between the real teachings and spirit of Jesus **Doctrines added to the Teachings of Jesus.** of Nazareth and the limitations, amplifications, and misunderstandings of the very inferior men who had loved and followed him from Galilee, and who were now the bearers and custodians of his message to mankind. The gospels and the Acts of the Apostles present a patched and uneven record, but there can be little question that on the whole it is a quite honest record of those early days.

The early Nazarenes, as the followers of Jesus were called, present from the first a spectacle of a great confusion between these two strands, his teaching on the one hand, and the glosses and interpretations of the disciples on the other. They continued for a time his disciplines of the complete subjugation of self; they had their goods in common, they had no bond but love. Nevertheless, they built their faith upon the stories that were told of his resurrection and magical ascension, and the promised return. Few of them understood that the renunciation of self is its own reward, that it is itself the Kingdom of Heaven; they regarded it as a sacrifice that entitled them to the compensation of power and dominion when presently the second coming occurred. They had now all identified Jesus with the promised Christ, the Messiah so long expected by the Jewish people. They found out prophecies of the crucifixion in the prophets—the Gospel of Matthew is particularly insistent upon these prophecies. Revived by these hopes, enforced by the sweet and pure lives of many of the believers, the Nazarene doctrine began to spread very rapidly in Judea and Syria.

And presently there arose a second great teacher, whom many modern authorities regard as the real founder of Christianity, Saul of Tarsus, or Paul. Saul apparently was his Jewish and Paul his Roman name; he was a Roman citizen, and a man of much wider education and a much narrower intellectuality than Jesus seems to have been. By birth he was probably a Jew, though some Jewish writers deny this; he had certainly studied under Jewish teachers. But he was well versed in the Hellenic theologies of Alexandria, and his language was Greek. Some classical scholars profess to find his Greek unsatisfactory; he did not use the Greek of Athens, but the Greek of Alexandria; but he used it with power and freedom.[2] He was a religious theorist and teacher long before he heard of Jesus of Nazareth, and he appears in the New Testament narrative at first as the bitter critic and antagonist of the Nazarenes.

The present writer has been unable to find any discussion of the religious ideas of Paul before he became a follower of Jesus. They must have been a basis, if only a basis of departure, for his new views, and their phraseology certainly supplied the colour of his new doctrines. We are almost equally in the dark as to the teachings of Gamaliel, who is named as the Jewish teacher at whose feet he sat. Nor do we know what Gentile teachings had reached him. It is highly probable that he had been influenced by Mithraism. He uses phrases curiously like Mithraistic phrases. What will be clear to anyone who reads his various Epistles, side by side with the Gospels, is that his mind was saturated by an idea which does not appear at all prominently in the reported sayings and teaching of Jesus, the idea of a sacrificial person, who is offered up to God as an atonement for sin. What Jesus preached was a new birth of the human soul; what Paul preached was the ancient religion of priest and altar and propitiatory bloodshed. Jesus was to him the Easter lamb, that traditional human victim without spot or blemish who haunts all the religions of the dark white peoples. Paul came to the Nazarenes with overwhelming force because he came to them with this completely satisfactory explanation

---

[1] See *Judaism and St. Paul*, by C. G. Montefiore for some interesting speculations on the religion of Paul before his conversion. See also the very interesting paper on St. Paul in Dean Inge's *Outspoken Essays* already quoted in a footnote.

[2] Paul's Greek is very good. He is affected by the philosophical jargon of the Hellenistic schools and by that of Stoicism. But his mastery of sublime language is amazing.—G. M.

of the disaster of the crucifixion. It was a brilliant elucidation of what had been utterly perplexing.

Paul had never seen Jesus. His knowledge of Jesus and his teaching must have been derived from the hearsay of the original disciples. It is clear that he apprehended much of the spirit of Jesus and his doctrine of a new birth, but he built this into a theological system, a very subtle and ingenious system, whose appeal to this day is chiefly intellectual. And it is clear that the faith of the Nazarenes, which he found as a doctrine of motive and a way of living, he made into a doctrine of *belief*. He found the Nazarenes with a spirit and hope, and he left them Christians with the beginning of a creed.

But we must refer the reader to the Acts of the Apostles and the Pauline Epistles for an account of Paul's mission and teaching. He was a man of enormous energy, and he taught at Jerusalem, Antioch, Athens, Corinth, Ephesus, and Rome.

Possibly he went into Spain. The manner of his death is not certainly known, but it is said that he was killed in Rome during the reign of Nero. A great fire had burnt a large part of Rome, and the new sect was accused of causing this. The rapid spread of Christian teaching certainly owes more to Paul than to any other single man. Within two decades of the crucifixion this new religion was already attracting the attention of the Roman rulers in several provinces. If it had acquired a theology in the hands of Saint Paul, it still retained much of the revolutionary and ele-

Photo: Mansel..

ISIS AND HORUS.

mentary quality of the teachings of Jesus. It had become somewhat more tolerant of private property; it would accept wealthy adherents without insisting upon the communization of their riches, and Saint Paul has condoned the institution of slavery ("Slaves, be obedient to your masters"),[1] but it still set its face like flint against certain fundamental institutions of the Roman world. It would not tolerate the godhead of Cæsar; not even by a mute gesture at the altar would the Christians consent to worship the Emperor, though their lives were at stake in the matter. It denounced the gladiatorial shows. Unarmed, but possessing enormous powers of passive resistance, Christianity thus appeared at the outset plainly as rebellion, striking at the political if not at the economic essentials of the imperial system. The first evidences of Christianity in non-Christian literature we find when perplexed Roman officials began to write to one another and exchange views upon the strange problem presented by this infectious rebellion of otherwise harmless people.

Much of the history of the Christians in the first two centuries of the Christian era is very obscure. They spread far and wide throughout the world, but we know very little of their ideas

[1] The spirit of Jesus, the animating spirit of Christianity, which breathes through the gospels, was flatly opposed both to private property and slavery, but the attitude of the Christians was never so definite. Generally they ameliorate1 rather than abolished.—H. G. W.

Patristic theory justified slavery as a result of the Fall. See Carlyle, *Medieval Political Theory in the West.*—E. B.

or their ceremonies and methods during that time. As yet they had no settled creeds, and there can be little doubt that there were wide local variations in their beliefs and disciplines during this formless period. But whatever their local differences, everywhere they seem to have carried much of the spirit of Jesus; and though everywhere they aroused bitter enmity and active counter-propaganda, the very charges made against them witness to the general goodness of their lives.

During this indefinite time a considerable amount of a sort of theocrasia seems to have gone on between the Christian cult and the almost equally popular and widely diffused Mithraic cult, and the cult of Serapis[1]-Isis-Horus.

to speak of Jesus shedding his blood for mankind is really a most inaccurate expression. But Mithraism centred upon some now forgotten mysteries about Mithras sacrificing a sacred and benevolent bull; all the Mithraic shrines seem to have contained a figure of Mithras killing this bull, which bleeds copiously, and from this blood a new life sprang. The Mithraist votary actually bathed in the blood of the sacrificial bull, and was "born again" thereby. At his initiation he went beneath a scaffolding on which the bull was killed, and the blood ran down on him.[2]

The contributions of the Alexandrine cult to Christian thought and practices were even more considerable. In the personality of

Photo : Mansell.

MITHRAS AND THE BULL.

From the former it would seem the Christians adopted Sun-day as their chief day of worship instead of the Jewish Sabbath, the abundant use of candles in religious ceremonies, the legend of the adoration by the shepherds, and probably also those ideas and phrases, so distinctive of certain sects to this day, about being "washed in the blood" of Christ, and of Christ being a blood sacrifice. For we have to remember that a death by crucifixion is hardly a more bloody death than hanging;

[1] Serapis was a synthesis of Osiris and Apis.

Horus, who was at once the son of Serapis and identical with Serapis, it was natural for the Christians to find an illuminating analogue in their struggles with the Pauline mysteries. From that to the identification of Mary with Isis, and her elevation to a rank quasi-divine —in spite of the saying of Jesus about his

[2] See Legge, *Forerunners and Rivals of Christianity*, chap. xii. See also Cumont's *Oriental Religions in Roman Paganism* for a very clear account of the gradual development of Roman Paganism into a religion very similar to Christianity *pari passu* with the development of Christianity.

"THE DARKNESS CLOSED UPON THE HILL; THE DISTANT CITY SET ABOUT ITS PREPARATIONS FOR THE PASSOVER; SCARCELY ANYONE BUT THAT KNOT OF MOURNERS ON THE WAY TO THEIR HOMES TROUBLED WHETHER JESUS OF NAZARETH WAS STILL DYING OR ALREADY DEAD. . . ."

mother and his brothers that we have already quoted—was also a very natural step. Natural, too, was it for Christianity to adopt, almost insensibly, the practical methods of the popular religions of the time. Its priests took on the head-shaving and the characteristic garments of the Egyptian priests, because that sort of thing seemed to be the right way of distinguishing a priest. One accretion followed another. Almost insensibly the originally revolutionary teaching was buried under these customary acquisitions. We have already tried to imagine Gautama Buddha returning to Tibet, and his amazement at the worship of his own image in Lhassa. We will but suggest the parallel amazement of some earnest Nazarene who had known and followed his dusty and travel-worn Master through the dry sunlight of Galilee, restored suddenly to this world and visiting, let us say, a mass in St. Peter's at Rome, at learning that the consecrated wafer upon the altar was none other than his crucified teacher.[1]

Religion in a world community is not many things but one thing, and it was inevitable that all the living religious faiths in the world at the time, and all the philosophy and religious thought that came into contact with Christianity, should come to an account with Christianity and exchange phrases and ideas. The hopes of the early Nazarenes had identified Jesus with the Christ; the brilliant mind of Paul had surrounded his career with mystical significance. Jesus had called men and women to a giant undertaking, to the renunciation of self, to the new birth into the kingdom of love. The line of least resistance for the flagging convert was to intellectualize himself away from this plain doctrine, this stark proposition, into complicated

Photo : Mansell.

MITHRAS.

theories and ceremonies—that would leave his essential self alone. How much easier is it to sprinkle oneself with blood than to purge oneself from malice and competition ; to eat bread and drink wine and pretend one had absorbed divinity, to give candles rather than the heart, to shave the head and retain the scheming privacy of the brain inside it ! The world was full of such evasive philosophy and theological stuff in the opening centuries of the Christian Era. It is not for us here to enlarge upon the distinctive features of Neo-platonism, Gnosticism, Philonism, and the like teachings which abounded in the Alexandrian world. But it was all one world with that in which the early Christians were living. The writings of such men as Origen, Plotinus, and Augustine witness to the inevitable give and take of the time.

Jesus called himself the Son of God and also the Son of Man ; but he laid little stress on who he was or what he was, and much upon the teachings of the Kingdom. In declaring that he was more than a man and divine, Paul and his other followers, whether they were right or wrong, opened up a vast field of argument. Was Jesus God ? Or had God created him ? Was he identical with God or separable from God ? It is not the function of the historian to answer such questions, but he is bound to note them, and to note how unavoidable they were, because of the immense influence they have had upon the whole subsequent life of western mankind. By the fourth century of the Christian Era we find all the Christian communities so agitated and exasperated by tortuous and elusive arguments about the nature of God as to be largely negligent of the simpler teachings of charity, service, and brotherhood that Jesus had inculcated.

[1] Cp. Father Hugh Benson's account of the procession of the Host in his book *Lourdes*.

The chief views that the historian notices are those of the Arians, the Sabellians, and the Trinitarians. The Arians followed Arius, who taught that Christ was less than God; the Sabellians taught practically that there were three equal Gods, God the Father, God the Son (with whom Jesus was identified), and God the Holy Ghost; the Trinitarians, of whom Athanasius was the great leader, taught that the Father, the Son, and the Holy Ghost were not three gods, but one God. The reader is referred to the Athanasian Creed [1] for the exact expression of the latter doctrine, and for the alarming consequences to him of any failure to grasp and believe it. To Gibbon he must go for a derisive statement of these controversies. The present writer can deal with them neither with awe nor derision; they seem to him, he must confess, a disastrous ebullition of the human mind entirely inconsistent with the plain account of Jesus preserved for us in the gospels. Orthodoxy became a test not only for Christian office, but for Christian trade and help. A small point of doctrine might mean affluence or beggary to a man. It is difficult to read the surviving literature of the

Photo: Mansell.
TITUS, WHO BESIEGED AND DESTROYED JERUSALEM.

time without a strong sense of the dogmatism, the spites, rivalries, and pedantries of the men who tore Christianity to pieces for the sake of these theological refinements. Most of the Trinitarian disputants—for it is chiefly Trinitarian documents that survive—accuse their antagonists, probably with truth, of mean and secondary motives, but they do so in a manner that betrays their own base spirit very clearly. Arius, for example, is accused of heretical opposition because he was not appointed Bishop of Alexandria. Riots and excommunications

[1] In any prayer book of the Episcopalian Church.

and banishments punctuated these controversies, and finally came official persecutions. These fine differences about the constitution of the Deity interwove with politics and international disputes. Men who quarrelled over business affairs, wives who wished to annoy their husbands, developed antagonistic views upon this exalted theme. Most of the barbarian invaders of the empire were Arians; probably because their simple minds found the Trinitarian position incomprehensible.

It is easy for the sceptic to mock at these disputes. But even if we think that these attempts to say exactly how God was related to himself were presumptuous and intellectually monstrous, nevertheless we are bound to recognize that beneath these preposterous refinements of impossible dogmas there lay often a real passion for truth —even if it was truth ill conceived. Both sides produced genuine martyrs. And the zeal of these controversies, though it is a base and often malicious zeal, did at any rate make the Christian sects very energetically propagandist and educational. Moreover, because the history of the Christian body in the fourth and fifth centuries is largely a record of these unhappy disputes, that must not blind us to the fact that the spirit of Jesus did live and ennoble many lives among the Christians. The text of the gospels, though it was probably tampered with during this period, was not destroyed, and Jesus of Nazareth, in his own manifest inimitable greatness, still taught through that text. Nor did these unhappy quarrels prevent Christianity from maintaining a united front against gladiatorial shows and against slavery, and against the degrading worship of idols and of the god-Cæsar.

§ 6

So far as it challenged the divinity of Cæsar and the characteristic institutions of the empire, Christianity is to be regarded as a rebellious and disintegrating movement, and so it was regarded by most of the emperors before Constantine the Great. It encountered considerable hostility, and at last systematic attempts to suppress it. Decius was the first emperor to organize an official persecution, and the great era of the martyrs was in the time of Diocletian (303 and following years). The persecution of Diocletian was indeed the crowning struggle of the old idea of the god-emperor against the already great and powerful organization that denied his divinity. Diocletian had reorganized the monarchy upon lines of extreme absolutism; he had abolished the last vestiges of republican institutions; he was the first emperor to surround himself completely with the awe-inspiring etiquette of an eastern monarch. He was forced by the logic of his assumptions to attempt the complete eradication of a system that flatly denied them. The test in the persecution was that the Christian was required to offer sacrifice to the emperor.

The Struggles and Persecutions of Christianity.

"Though Diocletian, still averse to the effusion of blood, had moderated the fury of Galerius, who proposed that everyone refusing to offer sacrifice should immediately be burnt alive, the penalties inflicted on the obstinacy of the Christians might be deemed sufficiently rigorous and effectual. It was enacted that their churches, in all the provinces of the empire, should be demolished to their foundations; and the punishment of death was denounced against all who should presume to hold any secret assemblies for the purpose of religious worship. The philosophers, who now assumed the unworthy office of directing the blind zeal of persecution, had diligently studied the nature and genius of the Christian religion; and as they were not ignorant that the speculative doctrines of the faith were supposed to be contained in the writings of the prophets, of the evangelists, and of the apostles, they most probably suggested the order, that the bishops and presbyters should deliver all their sacred books into the hands of the magistrates, who were commanded under the severest penalties, to burn them in a public and solemn manner. By the same edict, the property of the church was at once confiscated; and the several parts of which it might consist were either sold to the highest bidder, united to the imperial domain, bestowed on the cities or corporations, or granted to the solicitations of rapacious courtiers. After taking such effectual measures to abolish the worship, and to dissolve the government of the Christians, it was thought necessary to subject to the most intolerable hardships the condition of those perverse individuals who should still reject the religion of nature, of Rome, and of their ancestors. Persons of a liberal birth were declared incapable of holding any honours or employments; slaves were for ever deprived of the hopes of freedom; and the whole body of the Christians were put out of the protection of the law. The judges were authorized to hear and to determine every action that was brought against a Christian; but the Christians were not permitted to complain of any injury which they themselves had suffered; and those unfortunate sectaries were exposed to the severity, while they were excluded from the benefits, of public justice. . . . This edict was scarcely exhibited to the public view, in the most conspicuous place in Nicomedia, before it was torn down by the hands of a Christian, who expressed at the same time, by the bitterest of invectives, his contempt as well as abhorrence for such impious and tyrannical governors. His offence, according to the mildest laws, amounted to treason, and deserved death, and if it be true that he was a person of rank and education, those circumstances could serve only to aggravate his guilt. He was burnt, or rather roasted, by a slow fire; and his executioners, zealous to revenge the personal insult which had been offered to the emperors, exhausted every refinement of cruelty without being able to subdue his patience, or to alter the steady and insulting smile which in his dying agonies he still preserved in his countenance." [1]

So with the death of this unnamed martyr the great persecution opened. But, as Gibbon points out, our information as to its severity is of very doubtful value. He estimates the

[1] Gibbon, *The Decline and Fall of the Roman Empire*, chap. xvi.

total of victims as about two thousand, and contrasts this with the known multitudes of Christians martyred by their fellow Christians during the period of the Reformation. Gibbon was strongly prejudiced against Christianity, and here he seems disposed to minimize the fortitude and sufferings of the Christians. In many provinces, no doubt, there must have been a great reluctance to enforce the edict. But there was a systematic hunt for the copies of Holy Writ, and in many places a systematic destruction of Christian churches. There were tortures and executions, as well as a great crowding of the gaols with Christian presbyters and bishops. We have to remember that the Christian community was now a very considerable element of the population, and that an influential proportion of the officials charged with the execution of the edict were themselves of the proscribed faith. Galerius, who was in charge of the eastern provinces, was among the most vigorous of the persecutors, but in the end, on his death bed (311), he realized the futility of his attacks upon this huge community, and granted toleration in an edict, the gist of which Gibbon translates as follows :—

"Among the important cares which have occupied our mind for the utility and preservation of the empire, it was our intention to correct and re-establish all things according to the ancient laws and public discipline of the Romans. We were particularly desirous of reclaiming into the way of reason and nature the deluded Christians who had renounced the religion and ceremonies instituted by their fathers; and presumptuously despising the practice of antiquity, had invented extravagant laws and opinions according to the dictates of their fancy, and had collected a various

society from the different provinces of our empire. The edicts which we have published to enforce the worship of the gods having exposed many of the Christians to danger and distress, many having suffered death, and many more who still persist in their impious folly, being left destitute of any public exercise of religion, we are disposed to extend to those unhappy men the effects of our wonted clemency. We permit them, therefore, freely to profess their private opinions and to assemble in their conventicles without fear or molestation, provided always that they preserve a due respect to the established laws and government. By another rescript we shall signify our intentions to the judges and magistrates ; and we hope that our indulgence will engage the Christians to offer up their prayers to the deity whom they adore, for our safety and prosperity, for their own, and for that of the republic."

In a few years Constantine the Great was reigning, first as associated emperor (312) and then as the sole ruler (324), and the severer trials of Christianity were over. If Christianity was a rebellious and destructive force towards a pagan Rome, it was a unifying and organizing force within its own communion. This fact the genius of Constantine grasped. The spirit of Jesus, for all the doctrinal dissentions that prevailed, made a great freemasonry throughout and even beyond the limits of the empire. The faith was spreading among the barbarians beyond the border ; it had extended into Persia and Central Asia. It provided the only hope of moral solidarity he could discern in the great welter of narrow views and selfseeking over which he had to rule. It, and it alone, had the facilities for organizing *will*, for the need of which the empire was

Photo: *A. Giraudon.*
CONSTANTINE (FROM THE LOUVRE).

falling to pieces like a piece of rotten cloth. In 312 Constantine had to fight for Rome and his position against Maxentius. He put the Christian monogram upon the shields and banners of his troops, and claimed that the God of the Christians had fought for him in his complete victory at the battle of the Milvian Bridge just outside Rome. By this act he renounced all those pretensions to divinity that the vanity of Alexander the Great had first brought into the western world, and with the applause and enthusiastic support of the Christians he established himself as a monarch more absolute even than Diocletian.

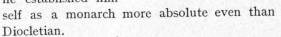

Photo : Anderson.   CONSTANTINE.

§ 7

Constantine the Great.

The figure of Constantine the Great is at least as cardinal in history as that of Alexander the Great or Augustus Cæsar. We know very little of his personality or

In a few years' time Christianity had become the official religion of the empire, and in A.D. 337 Constantine upon his death bed was baptized as a Christian.[1]

[1] Here, from another point of view, are some remarks upon the acceptance of Christianity by the empire. Evidently the Church—*i.e.* the Secret Friendly Society, based on the proletariat of the eastern manufacturing towns—was becoming stronger and stronger. (The evidence of this is plentiful.) Diocletian summoned his two associated Cæsars to a conference on the subject, and they decided to persecute, to try to crush the "camorra." They persecuted and failed, and Diocletian resigned. Constantine the Great, the next claimant to the empire, made terms with the camorra and succeeded. He established it as official, and overcame its hatred of Rome by showering wealth and power on it. Eventually, when in fear of death, he got baptized. If one imagines a blend of Lenin and some Indian sect, drawing its strength from the "hunkey" populations of big American towns, and secret in its organization . . . you will perhaps get something like the Christianity of this time. The conception of the blameless and saintly Early Christian is, I think, romance. No

doubt there were many saintly people ; but consider the appalling accusations made by all the Christian sects against each other, and the furious denunciation of the turbulent Christian monastics by Augustine. Also consider what a spirit lies behind the Book of Revelation ! We should certainly hang and shoot if we found such a book circulating in India : a series of elaborate and horrific curses on the Roman Empire, until at last the Christians march in Roman blood "up to the bridles of the horses," rejoicing and praising the name of the Lamb. I do not blame the Revelationist ; such hatred is the natural answer to persecution. But do not let us call it lamb-like innocence."—G. M.

I do not understand the reference to the Book of the Revelation of St. John. (1) That book came long prior to Constantine ; (2) it says nothing about Christians marching in Roman blood " up to the bridles of the horses." The whole note hurts me, and I should be glad to see it deleted.—E. B.

I have too much respect for G. M. to delete his note, and too much for E. B. to suppress his protest. And indeed these two notes do tell, as nothing in the text could do, the unsettled and controversial nature of all judgments upon popular quality and popular movements in history. The shrewd reader of the early chapters of this *Outline* will already have detected evidences of a dispute between G. M. and the writer about the quality of the Athenian crowd. Upon such questions, even when the case is a contemporary one, judgments seem to be inseparable from temperamental and social bias. Witness the conflicting estimates reasonable men will make of the Bolsheviki and of the American labour extremities to-day. Whatever one's private opinion may be, the proper course when one is writing a history seems to be to state it simply as a personal opinion—and to quote contrasting representative views.—H. G. W.

of his private life; no Plutarch, no Suetonius, has preserved any intimate and living details about him. Abuse we have of him from his enemies, and much obviously fulsome panegyric to set against it; but none of these writers give us a living character of him; he is a party symbol for them, a partisan flag. It is stated by the hostile Zosimus that, like Sargon I, he was of illegitimate birth; his father was a distinguished general and his mother, Helena; an innkeeper's daughter of Nish in Serbia. Gibbon,[1] however, is of opinion that there was a valid marriage. In any case it was a lowly marriage, and the personal genius of Constantine prevailed against serious disadvantages. He was comparatively illiterate, he knew little or no Greek. It appears to be true that he banished his eldest son Crispus, and caused him to be executed at the instigation of the young man's stepmother, Fausta; and it is also recorded that he was afterwards convinced of the innocence of Crispus, and caused Fausta to be executed—according to one account by being boiled to death in her bath, and according to another by being exposed naked to wild beasts on a desolate mountain—while there is also very satisfactory documentary evidence that she survived him. If she was executed, the fact remains that her three sons, together with two nephews, became the appointed heirs of Constantine. Clearly there is nothing solid to be got from this libellous tangle, and such soufflé as is possible with these scanty materials is to be found admirably done by Gibbon (chap. xviii.). Gibbon, because of his anti-Christian animus, is hostile to Constantine; but he admits that he was temperate and chaste. He accuses him of prodigality because of his great public buildings, and of being vain and dissolute (!) because in his old age he wore a wig—Gibbon wore his own hair tied with a becoming black bow—and a diadem and magnificent robes. But all the later emperors after Diocletian wore diadems and magnificent robes.

But if the personality of Constantine the Great remains phantom-like, if the particulars of his domestic life reveal nothing but a vague tragedy, we can still guess at much that was in

[1] q.v., *The Decline and Fall of the Roman Empire,* chap. xiv.

his mind. It must, in the closing years of his life, have been a very lonely mind. He was more of an autocrat than any previous emperor had been—that is to say, he had less counsel and help. No class of public-spirited and trustworthy men remained; no senate nor council shared and developed his schemes. How much he apprehended the geographical weakness of the empire, how far he saw the complete disaster that was now so near, we can only guess. He made his real capital at Nicomedia in Bithynia; Constantinople across the Bosphorus was still being built when he died. Like Diocletian, he seems to have realized the broken-backed outline of his dominions, and to have concentrated his attention in foreign affairs and more particularly on the affairs of Hungary, South Russia, and the Black Sea. He reorganized all the official machinery of the empire; he gave it a new constitution and sought to establish a dynasty. He was a restless remaker of things; the social confusion he tried to fix by assisting in the development of a caste system. This was following up the work of his great predecessor Diocletian. He tried to make a caste of the peasants and small cultivators, and to restrict them from moving from their holdings. In fact he sought to make them serfs. The supply of slave labour had fallen off because the empire was no longer an invading but an invaded power; he turned to serfdom as the remedy. His creative efforts necessitated unprecedently heavy taxation. All these things point to a lonely and forcible mind. It is in his manifest understanding of the need of some unifying moral force if the empire was to hold together that his claim to originality lies.

It was only after he had turned to Christianity that he seems to have realized the fierce dissensions of the theologians. He made a great effort to reconcile these differences in order to have one uniform and harmonious teaching in the community, and at his initiative a general council of the Church was held at Nicæa, a town near Nicomedia and over against Constantinople, in 325. Eusebius gives a curious account of this strange gathering, over which the Emperor, although he was not yet a baptized Christian, presided. It was not his first council of the Church, for he had already (in 313) presided over a council at Arles. He sat in the midst of the council of Nicæa upon a golden throne, and as he had little Greek, we must suppose he was reduced to watching the countenances and gestures of the debaters, and listening to their intonations. The council was a stormy one. When old Arius rose to speak, one Nicholas of Myra struck him in the face, and afterwards many ran out, thrusting their fingers into their ears in affected horror at the old man's heresies. One is tempted to imagine the great emperor, deeply anxious for the soul of his empire, firmly resolved to end these divisions, bending towards his interpreters to ask them the meaning of the uproar.

This council produced the Nicene Creed, a strictly Trinitarian statement, and the Emperor sustained it. But afterwards, when Athanasius bore too hardly upon the Arians, he had him banished from Alexandria ; and when the church at Alexandria would have excommunicated Arius, he obliged it to readmit him to communion.

§ 8

This date 325 A.D. is a very convenient date in our history. It is the date of the first complete general ("œcumenical") council of the entire Christian world. (That at Arles we have mentioned had been a gathering of only the western half.) It marks the definite entry upon the stage of human affairs of the Christian church and of Christianity as it is generally understood in the world to-day. It marks the exact definition of Christian teaching by the Nicene Creed.

The Establishment of Official Christianity.

It is necessary that we should recall the reader's attention to the profound differences between this fully developed Christianity of Nicæa and the teachings of Jesus of Nazareth. All Christians hold that the latter is completely contained in the former, but that is a question outside our province. What is clearly apparent is that the teaching of Jesus of Nazareth was a *prophetic teaching* of the new type that began with the Hebrew prophets. It was not priestly, it had no consecrated temple and no altar. It had no rites and ceremonies. Its sacrifice was " a broken and a contrite heart." Its only organization was an organization of preachers, and its chief function was the sermon.

But the fully fledged Christianity of the fourth century, though it preserved as its nucleus the teachings of Jesus in the gospels, was mainly a *priestly religion* of a type already familiar to the world for thousands of years. The centre of its elaborate ritual was an altar, and the essential act of worship the sacrifice, by a consecrated priest, of the mass. And it had a rapidly developing organization of deacons, priests, and bishops.

But if Christianity had taken on an extraordinary outward resemblance to the cults of Serapis, Ammon, or Bel-Marduk, we must remember that even its priestcraft had certain novel features. Nowhere did it possess any quasi-divine image of God. There was no head temple containing the god, because God was everywhere. There was no holy of holies. Its widespread altars were all addressed to the unseen universal Trinity. Even in its most archaic aspects there was in Christianity something new.

A very important thing for us to note is the rôle played by the Emperor in the fixation of Christianity. Not only was the council of Nicæa assembled by Constantine the Great, but all the great councils, the two at Constantinople (381 and 553), Ephesus (431), and Chalcedon (451) were called together by the imperial power. And it is very manifest that in much of the history of Christianity at this time the spirit of Constantine the Great is as evident or more evident than the spirit of Jesus. He was, we have said, a pure autocrat. The last vestiges of Roman republicanism had vanished in the days of Aurelian and Diocletian. To the best of his lights he was trying to remake the crazy empire while there was yet time, and he worked without any councillors, any public opinion, or any sense of the need of such aids and checks. The idea of stamping out all controversy and division, stamping out all thought, by imposing one dogmatic creed upon all believers, is an altogether autocratic idea, it is the idea of the single-handed man who feels that to work at all he must be free from opposition and criticism. The history of the Church under his influence becomes now therefore a history of the violent struggles that were bound to follow upon his sudden and rough summons to unanimity. From him the Church acquired the disposition to be authoritative and unquestioned, to develop a centralized organization and run parallel to the empire.

A second great autocrat who presently contributed to the stamping upon Catholic Christianity of a distinctly authoritative character was Theodosius I, Theodosius the Great (379-395). He forbade the unorthodox to hold meetings, handed over all churches to the Trinitarians, and overthrew the heathen temples throughout the empire, and in 390 he caused the great statue of Serapis at Alexandria to be destroyed. There was to be no rivalry, no qualification to the rigid unity of the Church.

Here we cannot tell of the vast internal troubles of the Church,[1] its indigestions of heresy ; of Arians and Paulicians, of Gnostics and Manicheans. Had it been less authoritative and more tolerant of intellectual variety, it might perhaps have been a still more powerful body than it became. But in spite of all these disorders, it did for some time maintain a

[1] On the rise of dogma or tradition in the Church, especially at Rome, see Davis, *Mediæval Europe* (Home University Library).—E. B.

conception of human unity more intimate and far wider than was ever achieved before. By the fifth century Christendom was already becoming greater, sturdier, and more enduring than any empire had ever been because it was something not merely imposed upon men, but interwoven with the texture of their minds. It reached out far beyond the utmost limits of the empire, into Armenia, Persia, Abyssinia, Ireland, Germany, India, and Turkestan. "Though made up of widely scattered congregations, it was thought of as one body of Christ, one people of God. This ideal unity found expression in many ways. Intercommunication between the various Christian communities was very active. Christians upon a journey were always sure of a warm welcome and hospitable entertainment from their fellow-disciples. Messengers and letters were sent freely from one church to another. Missionaries and evangelists went continually from place to place. Documents of various kinds, including gospels and apostolic epistles, circulated widely. Thus in various ways the feeling of unity found expression, and

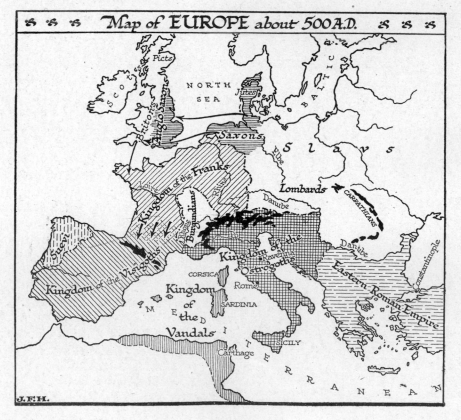

Photo: Alinari.
REMAINS OF THE PALACE OF THEODORIC, RAVENNA.

the development of widely separated parts of Christendom conformed more or less closely to a common type." [1]

Christendom retained at least the formal tradition of this general unity of spirit until 1054, when the Latin-speaking Western church and the main and original Greek-speaking church, the "Orthodox" church, severed themselves from one another, ostensibly upon the question of adding two words to the creed. The older creed had declared that the "Holy Ghost proceeded from the Father." The Latins wanted to add, and did add "*Filioque*" (= and from the son), and placed the Greeks out of their communion because they would not follow this lead. But already as early as the fifth century the Christians in Eastern Syria, Persia, Central Asia—there were churches at Merv, Herat, and Samarkand—and India had detached themselves on a similar score. These

[1] *Encyclopædia Britannica*, art. "Church History," p. 336.

extremely interesting Asiatic Christians are known in history as the Nestorian Church, and their influence extended into China. The Egyptian and Abyssinian churches also detached themselves very early upon similarly inexplicable points. Long before this formal separation of the Latin and Greek-speaking halves of the main church, however, there was a practical separation following upon the breaking up of the empire. Their conditions diverged from the first. While the Greek-speaking Eastern Empire held together and the emperor at Constantinople remained dominant in the Church, the Latin half of the empire, as we have already told, collapsed, and left the Church free of any such imperial control. Moreover, while ecclesiastical authority in the empire of Constantinople was divided between the high-bishops, or patriarchs, of Constantinople, Antioch, Alexandria, and Jerusalem, authority in the West was concentrated in the patriarch, or Pope, of Rome. The Bishop of

Rome had always been recognized as first among the patriarchs, and all these things conspired to justify exceptional pretensions upon his part to a quasi-imperial authority. With the final fall of the Western Empire, he took over the ancient title of *pontifex maximus* which the emperors had held, and so became the supreme sacrificial priest of the Roman tradition. Over the Christians of the West his supremacy was fully recognized, but from the beginning it had to be urged with discretion within the dominions of the Eastern emperor and the jurisdictions of the other four patriarchs.

Ideas of worldly rule by the Church were already prevalent in the fourth century. Saint Augustine, a citizen of Hippo in North Africa, who wrote between 354 and 430, gave expression to the developing political ideas of the Church in his book *The City of God*. *The City of God* represents the possibility of making the world into a theological and organized Kingdom of Heaven. The city, as Augustine puts it, is "a spiritual society of the predestined faithful,"[1] but the step from that to a political application was not a very wide one. The Church was to be the ruler of the world over all nations, the divinely led ruling power over a great league of terrestrial states. In later years these ideas developed into a definite political theory and policy. As the barbarian races settled and became Chris-

[1] E. B. (quoted from Tröltsch).

Photo : Alinari.

TOMB OF THEODORIC, RAVENNA.

tian, the Pope began to claim an overlordship of their kings. In a few centuries the Pope had become in theory, and to a certain extent in practice, the high priest, censor, judge, and divine monarch of Christendom ; his influence extended in the west far beyond the utmost range of the old empire, to Ireland, Norway and Sweden, and over all Germany. For more than a thousand years this idea of the unity of Christendom, of Christendom as a sort of vast Amphictyony, whose members even in war time were restrained from many extremities by the idea of a common brotherhood and a common loyalty to the Church, dominated Europe. The history of Europe from the fifth century onward to the fifteenth is very largely the history of the failure of this great idea of a divine world government to realize itself in practice.

§ 9

We have already given an account in the previous chapter of the chief irruptions of the barbarian races. We may now, with the help of a map, make a brief review of the political divisions of Europe at the close of the fifth century. No vestige of the Western Empire, the original Roman Empire, remained as such. Over many parts of Europe a sort of legendary overlordship of the Hellenic Eastern Empire held its place in men's minds. The emperor at Constantinople was, in theory at

The Map of Europe, A.D. 500.

Photo: Alinari.

INTERIOR OF THE CHURCH OF S. APOLLINARE IN CLASSE, RAVENNA.

least, still emperor. In Britain, the quite barbaric Teutonic Angles, Saxons and Jutes had conquered the eastern half of England; in the west of the island the Britons still held out, but were gradually being forced back into Wales and Cornwall. The Anglo-Saxons seem to have been among the most ruthless and effective of barbarian conquerors, for wherever they prevailed, their language completely replaced the Keltic or Latin speech—it is not certain which[1]—used by the British. These Anglo-Saxons were as yet not Christianized. Most of Gaul, Holland, and the Rhineland was under the fairly vigorous, Christianized, and much more civilized kingdom of the Franks. But the Rhone valley was under the separate kingdom of the Burgundians. Spain and some of the south of France were under the rule of the Visigoths, but the Suevi were in possession of the north-west corner of the peninsula. Of the Vandal kingdom in Africa we have already written; and Italy, still in its population and habits Roman, came under the

[1] See Haverfield, *The Romanization of Roman Britain.* —E. B.

rule of the Ostrogoths. There was no emperor in Rome, but Theodoric I ruled there as the first of a line of Gothic kings, and his rule extended across the Alps into Pannonia and down the Adriatic to Dalmatia and Serbia. To the east of the Gothic kingdom the emperors of Constantinople ruled definitely. The Bulgars were still at this time a Mongolian tribe of horse-riding nomads in the region of the Volga; the Aryan Serbs had recently come southward to the shores of the Black Sea into the original home of the Visigoths; the Turko-Finnish Magyars were not yet in Europe. The Lombards were as yet north of the Danube.

The sixth century was marked by a phase of vigour on the part of the Eastern Empire under the Emperor Justinian (527-565). The Vandal kingdom was recovered in 534; the Goths were expelled from Italy in 553. So soon as Justinian was dead (565), the Lombards descended into Italy and settled in Lombardy, but they left Ravenna, Rome, Southern Italy, and North Africa under the rule of the Eastern Empire.

Such was the political condition of the world

Photo : Anderson.

HADRIAN'S TOMB, ROME (CASTLE OF THE HOLY ANGEL).

in which the idea of Christendom developed. The daily life of that time was going on at a very low level indeed physically, intellectually, and morally.   It is frequently said that Europe in the sixth and seventh centuries relapsed into barbarism, but that does not express the reality of the case very well. Barbarism is a social order of an elementary type, orderly within its limits ; the state of Europe beneath its political fragmentation was a social disorder. Its *morale* was not that of a kraal, but that of a slum.   In a savage kraal a savage knows that he belongs to a community, and lives and acts accordingly ; in a slum, the individual neither knows of nor acts in relation to any greater being.

Only very slowly and weakly did Christianity restore that lost sense of community and teach men to rally about the idea of Christendom. The social and economic structure of the Roman Empire was in ruins. That civilization had been a civilization of wealth and political power sustained by the limitation and slavery of the great mass of mankind. It had presented a

spectacle of outward splendour and luxurious refinement, but beneath that brave outward show were cruelty, stupidity, and stagnation. It had to break down, it had to be removed before anything better could replace it.

We have already called attention to its intellectual deadness. For three centuries it had produced neither science nor literature.[1] It is only where men are to be found neither too rich and powerful to be tempted into extravagant indulgences nor too poor and limited to care for anything beyond the daily need that those disinterested curiosities and serene impulses can have play that give sane philosophy and

[1] No literature ! I demur entirely.   Apuleius, Ammianus, St. Augustine, the Vulgate, Claudian, Sidonius Apollinaris, Ausonius—I mention but a few names—are not these literature ?—E. B.

I forgot the *Golden Ass* and St. Augustine as coming into the Imperial period, but do these two names save the situation ? E. B. ekes out with one second-rate historian, a translation, three court poets. Yet we are dealing here with the literature of a " world " empire. —H. G. W.

science and great art to the world, and the plutocracy of Rome had made such a class impossible. When men and women are unlimited and unrestrained, the evidence of history shows clearly that they are all liable to become monsters of self-indulgence; when, on the other hand, they are driven and unhappy, then their impulse is towards immoderate tragical resorts, towards wild revolts or towards the austerities and intensities of religion.

It is not perhaps true to say that the world became miserable in these " dark ages " to which we have now come; much nearer the truth is it to say that the violent and vulgar fraud of Roman imperialism, that world of politicians, adventurers, landowners and financiers, collapsed into a sea of misery that was already there. Our histories of these times are very imperfect: there were few places where men could write, and little encouragement to write at all; no one was sure even of the safety of his manuscript or the possibility of its being read. But we know enough to tell that this age was an age not merely of war and robbery, but of famine and pestilence. No effective sanitary organization had yet come into the world, and the migrations of the time must have destroyed whatever hygienic balance had been established. Attila's ravages in North Italy were checked by an outbreak of fever in 452. There was a great epidemic of bubonic plague towards the end of the reign of Justinian (565) which did much to weaken the defence of Italy against the Lombards. In 543 ten thousand people had died in one day in Constantinople. (Gibbon says " each day.") Plague was raging in Rome in 590. The seventh century was also a plague-stricken century. The Englishman Bede, one of the few writers of the time, records pestilences in England in 664, 672, 678, and 683, no less than four in twenty years! Gibbon couples the Justinian epidemic with the great comet of 531, and with the very frequent and serious earthquakes of that reign. " Many cities of the east were left vacant, and in several districts of Italy the harvest and the vintage withered on the ground." He alleges " a visible decrease of the human species which has never been made good in some of the fairest countries of the globe." To many in those dark days it

seemed that all learning and all that made life seemly and desirable was perishing.[1]

How far the common lot was unhappier under these conditions of squalor and insecurity than it had been under the grinding order of the imperial system it is impossible to say. There was possibly much local variation, the rule of violent bullies here and a good-tempered freedom there, famine this year and plenty the next. If robbers abounded, tax-gatherers and creditors had disappeared. Such kings as those of the Frankish and Gothic kingdoms were really phantom rulers to most of their so-called subjects; the life of each district went on at a low level, with little trade or travel. Greater or lesser areas of country-side would be dominated by some able person, claiming with more or less justice the title of lord or count or duke from the tradition of the later empire or from the king. Such local nobles would assemble bands of retainers and build themselves strongholds. Often they adapted pre-existing buildings. The Colosseum at Rome, for example, the arena of many great gladiatorial shows, was converted into a fortress, and so was the amphitheatre at Arles. So also was the great tomb of Hadrian at Rome. In the decaying and now insanitary towns and cities shrunken bodies of artisans would hold together and serve the needs of the cultivating villages about them by their industry, placing themselves under the protection of some adjacent noble.

§ 10

A very important share in the social recrystallization that went on in the sixth and seventh centuries after the breakdown and fusion of the fourth and fifth was taken by the Christian monastic orders that were now arising in the Western world.

The Salvation of Learning by Christianity.

Monasteries had existed in the world before Christianity. During the period of social unhappiness among the Jews before the time of Jesus of Nazareth, there was a sect of Essenes who lived apart in communities vowed to austere lives of solitude, purity, and self-denial.

[1] A very interesting and suggestive book bearing on this question of disease in relation to political history is *Malaria : a Neglected Factor in the History of Greece and Rome*, by W. H. S. Jones.

Photo : Alinari.
THE PRESENT-DAY MONASTERY OF MONTE CASSINO, ON THE SITE OF ST. BENEDICT'S ORIGINAL FOUNDATION

Buddhism, too, had developed its communities of men who withdrew from the general effort and commerce of the world to lead lives of austerity and contemplation. Indeed, the story of Buddha, as we have told it, shows that such ideas must have prevailed in India long before his time, and that at last he repudiated them. Quite early in the history of Christianity there arose a similar movement away from the competition and heat and stress of the daily life of men. In Egypt, particularly, great numbers of men and women went out into the desert and there lived solitary lives of prayer and contemplation, living in absolute poverty in caves or under rocks, and subsisting on the chance alms of those whom their holiness impressed. Such lives would signify little to the historian, they are indeed of their very nature lives withdrawn from history, were it not for the turn this monastic tendency presently took among the more energetic and practical Europeans.

One of the central figures in the story of the development of monasticism in Europe is Saint Benedict, who lived between 480 and 544. He was born at Spoleto in Italy, and he was a young man of good family and ability. The shadow of the times fell upon him, and, like Buddha, he took to the religious life and at first set no limit to his austerities. Fifty miles from Rome is Subiaco, and there at the end of a gorge of the Anio, beneath a jungle growth of weeds and bushes, rose a deserted palace built by the Emperor Nero, overlooking an artificial lake that had been made in those days of departed prosperity by damming back the waters of the river. Here, with a hair shirt as his chief possession, Benedict took up his quarters in a cave in the high southward-looking cliff that overhangs the stream, in so inaccessible a position that his food had to be lowered to him on a cord by a faithful admirer.[1] Three years he lived here, and his fame spread as Buddha's did nearly a thousand years before under similar circumstances.

As in the case of Buddha, the story of Benedict has been overlaid by foolish and credulous disciples with a mass of silly stories of miracles and manifestations. But presently we find him, no longer engaged in self-torment, but controlling a group of twelve monasteries, and the resort of a great number of people. Youths are brought to him to be educated, and the whole character of his life has changed.

From Subiaco he removed further southward to Monte Cassino, half-way between Rome and Naples, a lonely and beautiful mountain, in the midst of a great circle of majestic heights. Here, it is interesting to note that in the sixth century A.D. he found a temple of Apollo and a sacred grove and the country-side still worshipping at this shrine. His first labours had to be missionary labours, and it was with difficulty that he persuaded the simple pagans to demolish their temple and cut down their grove. The establishment upon Monte Cassino became a famous and powerful centre within the lifetime of its founder. Mixed up with the imbecile inventions of marvel-loving monks about

[1] Baring Gould's *Lives of the Saints*.

demons exorcised, disciples walking on the water, and dead children restored to life, we can still detect something of the real spirit of Benedict. Particularly significant are the stories that represent him as discouraging extreme mortification. He sent a damping message to a solitary who had invented a new degree in saintliness by chaining himself to a rock in a narrow cave. "Break thy chain," said Benedict, " for the true servant of God is chained not to rocks by iron, but to righteousness by Christ."

And next to the discouragement of solitary self-torture it is Benedict's distinction that he insisted upon hard work. Through the legends shines the clear indication of the trouble made by his patrician students and disciples who found themselves obliged to toil instead of leading lives of leisurely austerity under the ministrations of the lower-class brethren. A third remarkable thing about Benedict was his political influence. He set himself to reconcile Goths and Italians, and it is clear that Totila, his Gothic king, came to him for counsel and was greatly influenced by him. When Totila retook Naples from the Greeks, the Goths pro-tected the women from insult and treated even the captured soldiers with humanity. When Belisarius, Justinian's general, had taken the same place ten years previously, he had cele-brated his triumph by a general massacre.

Now the monastic organization of Benedict was a very great beginning in the western world.[1] One of his prominent followers was Pope Gregory the Great (540-604), the first monk to become Pope (590) ; he was one of the most capable and energetic of the popes, sending successful missions to the unconverted, and particularly to the Anglo-Saxons. He ruled in Rome like an independent king, organiz-ing armies, making treaties. It is clear that Augustine's *City of God* was a very real thing to him. To his influence is due the imposition of the Benedictine rule upon nearly the whole of Latin monasticism.

Closely associated with these two names in the development of a civilizing monasticism out of the merely egotistic mortifications of the early recluses is that of Cassiodorus (490-585). He was evidently much senior to Pope Gregory,

[1] On Benedictinism, see Dom. Berlière's *L'Ordre Monastique.*—E. B.

Photo: Anderson.

LATERAN PALACE, ROME—THE ORIGINAL PALACE OF THE POPES.

and younger by ten years than Benedict, and, like these two, he belonged to a patrician family, a Syrian family settled in Italy. He had a considerable official career under the Gothic kings; and when, between 545 and 553, the overthrow of those kings and the great pestilence paved the way for the new barbaric rule of the Lombards, he took refuge in a monastic career. He founded a monastery upon his private estates, and set the monks he gathered to work in quite the Benedictine fashion, though whether his monks actually followed the Benedictine rule that was being formulated about the same time from Monte Cassino we do not know. But there can be no question of his influence upon the development of this great working, teaching, and studying order. It is evident that he was profoundly impressed by the universal decay of education and the possible loss of all learning and of the ancient literature by the world; and from the first he directed his brethren to the task of preserving and restoring these things. He collected ancient MSS. and caused them to be copied. He made sundials, water clocks, and similar apparatus, a little last gleam of experimental science in the gathering ignorance. He wrote a history of the Gothic kings, and, what is more significant of his sense of the needs of the time, he produced a series of school books on the liberal arts and a grammar. Probably his influence was even greater than that of Saint Benedict in making monasticism into a powerful instrument for the restoration of social order in the Western world.

The spread of monasteries of the Benedictine order or type in the seventh and eighth centuries was very considerable. Everywhere we find them as centres of light, restoring, maintaining, and raising the standard of cultivation, preserving some sort of elementary education, spreading useful arts, multiplying and storing books, and keeping before the eyes of the world the spectacle and example of a social backbone. For eight centuries thenceforth the European monastic system remained a system of patches and fibres of enlightenment in what might otherwise have been a wholly chaotic world. Closely associated with the Benedictine monasteries were the schools that grew presently into the medieval universities. The schools of the Roman world had been altogether swept away in the general social breakdown. There was a time when very few priests in Britain or Gaul could read the gospel or their service books. Only gradually was teaching restored to the world. But when it was restored, it came back not as the duty work of a learned slave, but as the religious service of a special class of devoted men.

In the east also there was a breach of educational continuity, but there the cause was not so much social disorder as religious intolerance, and the break was by no means so complete. Justinian closed and dispersed the schools of Athens (529), whose origins we have described in chap. xxiii, §§ 1 and 2; but he did this very largely in order to destroy a rival to the new school he was setting up in Constantinople, which was more directly under imperial control. Since the new Latin learning of the developing western universities had no text-books and literature of its own, it had, in spite of its strong theological bias to the contrary, to depend very largely upon the Latin classics and the Latin translations of the Greek literature. It was obliged to preserve far more of that splendid literature than it had a mind to do.

Enlightenment

Enlightenment

SARAH PERRY

JONATHAN CAPE
LONDON

1 3 5 7 9 10 8 6 4 2

Jonathan Cape, an imprint of Vintage, is part of the Penguin Random House group of companies
whose addresses can be found at global.penguinrandomhouse.com

First published by Jonathan Cape in 2024

Illustrations by Neil Gower

penguin.co.uk/vintage

Typeset in 13.5/16pt Garamond MT Std by Jouve (UK), Milton Keynes

Printed and bound in Great Britain by Clays Ltd, Elcograf S.p.A.

The authorised representative in the EEA is Penguin Random House Ireland,
Morrison Chambers, 32 Nassau Street, Dublin D02 YH68

A CIP catalogue record for this book is available from the British Library

HB ISBN 9781787334991
TPB ISBN 9781787335004

Penguin Random House is committed to a sustainable future
for our business, our readers and our planet. This book is made
from Forest Stewardship Council® certified paper.

In memory of
David George Perry
A good Baptist
And a very good friend

There are two hungers, hunger for bread
And hunger of the uncouth soul
For the light's grace. I have seen both . . .

R. S. Thomas, 'The Dark Well'

PART ONE

1997

The Law of Ellipses

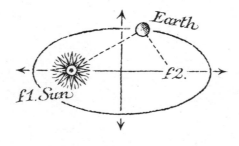

Fig. 1

Monday: late winter, bad weather. The River Alder, fattened by continuous rain, went in spate through Aldleigh and beyond it, taking carp and pike and pages torn from pornographic magazines past war memorials and pubs and new industrial estates, down to the mouth of the Blackwater and on in due course to the sea. Toppled shopping trolleys glistened on the riverbank; so also did unwanted wedding rings, and beer cans, and coins struck by empires in the years of their decline. Herons paced like white-coated orderlies in the muddy reeds; and at half past four a fisherman caught a cup untouched since the ink was wet on *The Battle of Maldon*, spat twice, and threw it back.

Late winter, bad weather: the town oppressed by cloud as low as a coffin lid. A place spoken of in passing, if at all: neither Boudicca nor Wat Tyler had given it a second glance when they took their vengeances to London; and war had reached it only as an afterthought, when a solitary Junkers discharged the last of its ordnance and extinguished four souls without notice.

Thomas Hart was at his desk in the offices of the *Essex Chronicle*, surveying the town through a dissolving window. At that hour and from that vantage, lights appeared as fires set by travellers that crossed a soaking fen: strip-lights in the shoe shops and newsagent's not yet shuttered for the night, and in the cinema and bowling alley opening for business two miles out of town; lamplight in the bar of the Jackdaw and Crow, and streetlights coming on down London Road.

A man of fifty, Thomas Hart, and a man of Essex, for his sins: tall, and retaining as much hair as he had at forty, which is to say more above the collar than the brow. Dressed, as has always been his habit, in clothes chosen to be admired by the observant – a jacket, single-breasted, in Harris tweed; a white shirt cuffed with silver links; a tie of oatmeal knitted silk. A face he does not deceive himself is handsome, but understands to be memorable: the nose not symmetrical, but of a pleasing emphatic size; the eyes large, direct, and approaching green. An air altogether of occupying a time not his own – might he be more at ease in an Edwardian dining room, say, or on a pitching clipper's deck? Very likely.

Thomas was surveying an object on his desk. Two leather discs about the diameter of his own hand were fastened with a tarnished pin; the lower disc was painted blue, and mottled with markings he couldn't have made out even if he'd been inclined to try. The blue showed through a large hole cut in the upper part, and gilded letters at the rim showed the months of the year, and the days of the month, and the hours of the day. Thomas touched it as if it carried a contagious disease. 'What,' he said, 'do you imagine I should do with this?'

A younger man was sitting at the edge of the desk, swinging his foot. With the downcast gaze of the guilty he turned the upper disc with his finger. The hole moved. The blue persisted. 'It belonged to my father,' he said. 'I thought you might make something of it.' Nick Carleton, editor of the *Chronicle* and grieving son, looked with unconcealed amusement about the small office, which – despite the plastic venetian blinds, and the computer's hard drive humming as it laboured at its work; despite the twentieth century wearing

4

itself out on the pavements three floors down – gave the impression that at any moment a gramophone might strike up a Schubert *lieder*.

'I was sorry,' said Thomas gravely, 'to hear of your loss. The death of a father,' he said, frowning at the window, 'is at the same time both quite proper in the order of things, and incomprehensibly stupid.'

'I never saw him use it,' said Carleton, containing tears, 'and I don't know how it works. It is a planisphere. A map of the stars.'

'I see. And what do you imagine I should do with it?'

The evening was coming doggedly in. Wind seeped over the concrete windowsill, and a bewildered pigeon struck the glass and slipped from view.

'You're our longest-serving contributor,' said Carleton, flinching at the bang. 'Our most admired. Indeed I should say our most popular.' I'm beginning to speak like him, he thought: Thomas Hart is catching, that's the trouble. 'I've often heard it said that it's a consolation – that's the general feeling, as I said to the board – to wake on Thursday morning, and find your thoughts on Essex ghosts and literature and so on, before turning to the matters of the day.'

'Literature,' said Thomas mildly to the planisphere, 'is the matter of the day.'

'Your work has an old-fashioned feel,' Carleton pressed on. 'You'll allow me that. I argue that's your charm. Other papers might seek out some young person to be the voice of their generation, but here at the *Essex Chronicle* we pride ourselves on our loyalty.'

'I could hardly have asked to be the voice of a generation,' said Thomas, 'since there is only one of me.'

Briefly Carleton considered the other man, of whom he'd made such a study he might have been appointed professor of

Thomas Studies at the University of Essex. He knew, for example, that Thomas was a confirmed bachelor, as they say, never seen in the company of a beautiful young person or a stately older one; that he had about him the melancholy religious air of a defrocked priest, and was known to attend a peculiar little chapel on the outskirts of town. He had a courtly manner considered an affectation by those who didn't like him, and irresistible by those who did; and if it couldn't be fairly said that he was strange, there was certainly the impression of his being the lone representative of his species. Of Thomas Hart's family, companions, politics, tastes in music and weekend pursuits, Carleton knew nothing, wondered often, and would never ask. That Thomas had worked for the *Chronicle* since 1976 was easily established, as was the fact that he'd published three brief novels since that date. Out of a sense of delicacy Carleton never mentioned that he owned all three of these, and found them elegant and elliptical, couched in prose that had the cadence of the King James Bible, and concerned with deep feeling suppressed until the final pages (when some confusing event ensued, generally in bad weather). Were Carleton his literary agent, he might have pleaded with the other man to allow himself, in fiction at any rate, to say what he really felt, and not veil it all in atmosphere and metaphor; but he confined himself to glancing sometimes at the cheap green notebooks that attended Thomas like spoor, and were now stacked three deep on his desk (*Monday*, he read surreptitiously; *late winter. Bad weather* –). It hadn't occurred to him that Thomas wouldn't know a planisphere when he had his hands on it, or that a tentative suggestion he looked to the stars would be so unwelcome. Blinking, he recalibrated his idea of Thomas Hart, and became persuasive: 'Loyalty,' he said, 'is a key concern of ours. But it is increasingly felt that you might benefit from new material, and it struck me you might like to write about astronomy. You see' – he reached for the planisphere, and moved it – 'this is today's date, and so you'll find Orion in the south.'

'Astronomy,' said Thomas, with the look of a man tasting a bitter substance. He turned the disc. He extinguished the stars.

'In fact,' said the editor, 'it struck me that you could write about this new comet.' He made a withdrawal from the store of knowledge inherited from his father: 'It's a Great Comet, you know, with naked-eye visibility. People really go in for that sort of thing. Bird's Custard once put a comet on their adverts. Perhaps it's a bad omen, and there'll be a disaster, then we'll have something for our front page' (he brightened here at visions of catastrophic fires).

'What comet?'

'Thomas! Do you never look up? They call it Hale–Bopp. It's been on the news.'

'Hale–Bopp,' said Thomas. 'I see. I never watch the news.' He raised the planisphere towards the editor. 'I have no interest in astronomy. This comet could crash through the window and land on the carpet and I'd have nothing to say about it.'

Carleton refused the planisphere with a gesture. 'Keep it. Give it a try. We have to think of something, Thomas: circulation is down. Do you want to write about this sheep they've cloned in Scotland, or about the general election? Celebrity gossip, perhaps, or the sexual intrigues of the Tory cabinet?' He received a look of admonition, as if he'd stained one of those pristine white cuffs.

'I am too old,' said Thomas, 'for new tricks.'

'These days,' said Carleton, hardening his heart, and further depleting the store of his inheritance, 'a good pair of

7

binoculars offers more or less the same magnitude as Galileo's telescope. Five hundred words, please. Why don't you start with the moon?'

'Is there a moon tonight?'

'How should I know?' – Carleton was at the door; Carleton was almost free – 'I've always found it unreliable. Five hundred words, please, and six if the night is clear.'

'These days,' said Thomas, 'the nights are never clear.' With bad grace he lifted the planisphere to the weak light seeping in, and turned the upper part. The perforation slid over the painted leather, and half-familiar names appeared on the ground of blue: Aldebaran. Bellatrix. Hyades. Well, then. Five hundred words, and six if the night was clear; and meanwhile he was behind on his correspondence. A solitary letter in the steel tray, the flap lifting and the stamp not straight; the letter signed boldly in blue ink:

James Bower
Essex Museum Services
17 February 1997

Dear Mr Hart

I think I have some information that might interest you.

As I'm sure you know, we're doing renovation work at Lowlands House, and it has turned up some interesting documents. We think they may relate to a woman who lived at Lowlands in the nineteenth century, who disappeared and was never discovered. I've always enjoyed your column, and remember especially your account of going in search of the Lowlands ghost – and it occurred to me the legend might even be connected with this disappearance! Could

8

you be persuaded to come and visit me at the museum?
We are open daily from 10 a.m. to 4 p.m. I'm always at
my desk.

Yours sincerely

James Bower

Thomas put down the letter. Was it possible the strip-light briefly dimmed, and summoned out of shadow the figure of a vanished woman, now returned? It was not. Thomas smiled, and turned again towards the window. The stunned pigeon had left its greasy imprint on the glass, and it rose like the Holy Ghost behind the venetian blinds.

Late winter, thought Thomas, bad weather – he buttoned himself into his coat; he left the offices of the *Chronicle* – that was as good a beginning as any. The planisphere was in his pocket, and pricked him with its bent brass pin. The adamant cloud was burnished by streetlight; and somewhere behind it, he thought, Carleton's comet was concealed like a letter in an envelope, and no doubt bringing bad news.

Gone five in the evening, and traffic pursuing itself out of town; Aldleigh coming into view, and Thomas passing women labouring with plastic shopping bags, and schoolboys that bickered and swore. The rain eased into particles of mist that swarmed about the streetlights like flies, and Thomas conversed with himself. What could account for his indifference to the stars? The troubling thought occurred that perhaps he was afraid the annihilating vastness of a comet's orbit would end his tentative faith. Then again (Thomas was consoling himself) Virginia Woolf had written about a solar eclipse, and there was Gerard Manley Hopkins's slip of comet to

9

consider: there were precedents. 'Bellatrix,' he said, feeling the discomfort of the planisphere, but grudgingly delighted by the syllables: 'Hyades.' He stood now at a crossroads, where traffic went in haste to London or down to Aldleigh's shops and office blocks. Slipping between cars, Thomas crossed to the opposing pavement and stood there for a time. At his left, there was the broad road to town; at his right, the road that narrowed to a shallow bridge over the River Alder. Thomas looked neither left nor right, but rather surveyed a chapel behind iron railings on London Road. It was flanked by a mossy wall, and by a derelict patch of ground known to him as Potter's Field; its iron gate was fastened with a chain. Mutely the chapel looked back at him across a car park glossed by rain. Its door was closed, and newly painted green; beside the door a green bay tree flourished like the wicked in the thirty-seventh psalm. An east wind blowing up the Alder moved the cold illuminated air, and the bay tree danced in its small black bed. The chapel did not dance. Its bricks were pale, its proportions austere: it was a sealed container for God. No passer-by would ever take it for a place of worship, and Aldleigh's children believed it to be a crematorium where old men were converted into ashes and smoke. No sacred carvings flanked the door, and no bells rang; its pitched slate roof shone blue when wet. Its seven tapered windows had the look of eyes half-closed against the sun, and on brighter days, light picked out a single disc of coloured glass set in each window's apex. This was Bethesda Chapel, as fixed in time's flow as a boulder in a river: Aldleigh ran past it, and round it, and could never change it. Above the door a narrow plaque read 1888, and beyond the bristled threshold mat, 1888 persisted. All the dreadful business of the modern world – its exchange rates, tournaments, profanities, publications, elections, music and changes of administration – washed up against the green door and fell back, dammed.

'Bethesda,' said Thomas, leaning on the gate, speaking to himself and inclined to smile; then the iron chain, which ought to have been locked, unlatched and fell on his foot. Thomas, stifling surprise, peered in confusion through the haze. 'What was that?' he said. 'Did you see that?' Nobody heard, or could answer. He leaned further in and doubted himself: it was shadows shifted by the passing traffic, nothing more. Still – 'I wonder,' he said. The chain moved over his shoe. Thomas felt the animal of his body respond: stiffened hairs at the nape of his neck, and on his forearms; the chambers of his heart compressed – it's the Lowlands ghost, he said to himself, amused by his own fear, she's come vaulting over the wall!

The wet air parted, and briefly there was the impression of a shadow thickening and persisting against the green door, and slipping out of sight. Then, under brief headlight illumination, Thomas saw a mark painted by the chapel's iron knocker: something like a cross, if badly done, and blotted with a circle. The headlights went out. The mark returned to the shadows. Thomas, in whom disbelief equalled curiosity, went through the gate. Sound of bad-tempered traffic, of girls on the high street calling to each other from the pavements; sound also of some furtive motion by the green bay tree. Then abruptly a shadow there detached itself, became substantial, and crossed the car park towards Thomas. It came with such spiteful speed he called out, 'Mind how you go!' with useless good manners, and stumbled as a creature with a white hood knocked him in passing. Briefly, three things: thin face; pale eyes; thin hand clutching a can of paint. Possibly also something said, but this consumed by the traffic and the muffling air – then Thomas, slowly turning, saw the intruder seep into the small crowd going up to town.

'Dear me,' said Thomas. He approached the door. Paint ran between the boards; the circle surmounting the cross dribbled like an open mouth. Youths, he understood, were given to tagging railway arches in cheerful acts of defiance; but there was nothing cheerful in this inscrutable symbol already blurred by rain, which instead conveyed a kind of incompetent malice that left Thomas obscurely depressed. He took his notebook from his pocket, and one by one tore out pages that softened quickly in the wet air; and using these he cleaned the door as best he could. Then he turned his back and headed for the town, leaving the rest to the weather.

Bethesda receded. It kept the peace. Up ahead the news-agent's and grocer's were drawing down their shutters for the night, and a train leaving for Liverpool Street rattled the glasses in the Jackdaw and Crow. A man in a red velvet coat spread cardboard boxes at the foot of the war memorial, and made himself a pillow with the *News of the World*: 'Evening,' said Thomas, and received an imperious nod. He headed down a sloping alley and on to Upper Bridge Road, which passed in Essex for a hill, so that the red-brick terraces going over the hump had the look of a sleeping dragon's long articulated spine. So uphill, then down, and on into Lower Bridge Road, which ran under the dripping railway arch, and led neither into Aldleigh nor out of it – led nowhere, in fact. Here thirty-four Victorian terraces built for the engin-eers that had laboured on the London line faced each other, withdrawn behind their cars, and gardens, and signs urging passers-by to vote Labour, or Conservative, or to beware the dog. One house alone resisted the modern age. Here there was never any modern music heard, or exclamations from soap operas or films; and certainly no evidence of allegiance to any political party or social tribe. There was instead an insistent quiet, and the impression of a house set back behind a faint but impenetrable mist. Thomas Hart was home.

Nick Carleton, wondering how the other man lived, pictured with affectionate pity a solitary life in a fastidious apartment, and a narrow bed made each morning without fail. He was mistaken. Thomas lived where he'd been born, and where (so he often thought without rancour) he'd very likely die; and if he lived alone he was not lonely, that being a condition not of solitude but of longing, and Thomas was not a discontented man. The habits and tastes of his parents, which had been those of austere children of Bethesda's particular God, had been stripped with the wallpaper and carpets, and nothing remained of them now but Thomas himself. It was all exactly as he wanted it to be. The oak table by the window was burnished with decades of meals and work, and shone on fat turned legs. The sofa was deep, and blue, and partly concealed by a quilt his mother hadn't had time to finish. Edwardian and Victorian and art deco lamps which ought not to have agreed with each other nonetheless got on for the sake of Thomas, and shone from the sideboard and the floor. A broad bay window facing east allowed a single hour of rising sun before the room dimmed in the shadow of the railway bridge; and when a fire was lit in the grate, yellow marigolds bloomed on the surrounding tiles. The walls were obscured by books in arrangements that might have pleased a librarian, save that those by Thomas Hart were interposed here and there, since it pleased his vanity to imagine the phantoms of his imagination conversing all night with Emma Bovary in her vulgar gown, or Mrs Dalloway fretting over shopping lists. Pictures were hung in curated disorder: a lithograph signed by Picasso in the plate, a skilled oil of a turbulent sea. Occupying a large space it did not deserve, a small photograph showed Bethesda Chapel on the day of its opening: 1888, and a godless sun scorching the lawn, while bearded men stood sombrely with women in their summer hats, and beyond the chapel wall on Lowlands Park's unconsecrated land, a bare-headed woman stood in the shade of an elm, only ever looking up. Thomas, turning on the lamps, regarded her a while. He'd feared her in childhood, since her face in shadow had been featureless; but these days considered her a lodger, her dress and her bent neck increasingly distinct behind the glass.

He prepared himself a meal: radishes in a saucer with Maldon salt and grassy olive oil; good rye bread, and red wine poured with the pleasure of a man who's elected to sin. He brought these to the table with the letter and the planisphere, and surveyed these as he ate and drank. Perhaps there'll be a disaster, Carleton had said; and Thomas felt again the blow of the hooded creature fleeing Bethesda with paint on its hands. But that had been no disaster, only something strange and soon forgotten in the order and quiet of his home – so Thomas, who had a gift for self-persuasion, placidly ate a radish.

Late, now: the man in the red coat sleeping on the *News of the World*, last orders at the Jackdaw and Crow; a baffled robin singing on the streetlight, James Bower's letter stained with wine. The table was heaped with cheap green notebooks banked against a laptop computer that looked insolently modern against the polished oak, and the empty gold-rimmed glass. Sighing, Thomas raised the lid, and looked with the writer's longing and reluctance at the blank document paining his eyes with its glare. He wanted nothing more than to write, he would rather do anything but; it was the purpose of his life, it was the bane of it. 'All hopeless anyway,' he said to the woman in the photograph, 'nothing wrecks a thing like trying to describe it. Besides, I've got nothing to say.' Sound of the robin singing – sound, perhaps, of the woman in the photograph speaking from behind the glass, from behind Bethesda's wall: *Get on with it, won't you? You're in your fifty-first year, and time is getting on.*

Well, then. Late winter, bad weather. As good a beginning as any. Get on with it, Thomas Hart.

THE LOWLANDS GHOST

THOMAS HART *ESSEX CHRONICLE,*
31 OCTOBER 1996

Since it's Halloween, and the wall between the worlds of the living and the dead has got a hole in it, this night is as good as any to confess: I don't believe in ghosts, but I am afraid of them.

Humour me, my old friends! The fear arrived like this: when I was eleven, a friend of mine was absent from school for days, and it was said he'd gone mad because he'd seen the Lowlands ghost. I'd never heard of this ghost, and so listened with disbelief to stories of a gaunt and terrible lady who looked up at the sky with a neck that looked half-broken, and cursed those who saw her to be lonely and unloved, so that the workmen who'd seen her hanged themselves, and nobody cut them down; and children who saw her were thrown out by their parents to starve in the streets.

But there was a plan. My friends were going to break into Lowlands House on Halloween, and wait for the ghost. Did I want to come, too, and meet on the steps at midnight? Here I was in a difficulty. My father was the pastor at Bethesda Chapel, and our theology had no room for haunting. But since I believed in God I also believed in his adversary, and it struck me there was no ghost at Lowlands, but perhaps a demon. Here was a test of faith for which an early Christian martyr would give his right arm! All right, I said: I'll go.

So on the night of Halloween I crept out of the house and set off for Lowlands Park. There was no colour in the world that night, only a kind of shining grey; and when I came to Lowlands House it seemed to me it was sinking in the grass, and that the boards on the windows were like the coins they put on the eyes of the dead. Then I waited and waited for the other boys, but nobody ever came.

I'd never been lonely before and have rarely been lonely since, but felt that night I was the only living thing in the world. When I called for my friends, nobody answered; when I tried to pray, I couldn't remember how. Then my heart turned and slammed, because I saw a light drifting back and forth in the upper rooms, as if someone was gliding on a kind of trolley past one window and then another, and passing through walls. Stupidly I began to walk towards the moving light without knowing why I did it, until my foot caught in a tree root, and I fell. The house disappeared from view as if it had finally sunk. Everything was quiet. The owls were gone. It occurred to me that every living thing in Essex, even the worms, was leaving me in disgust. An enormous tiredness came over me, and I turned my face into the mud, and waited for the demon, or the ghost, or God – but there was only nothing after nothing.

At dawn a woman out walking her dog found me, and took me home with a cough that kept me from school for days, and prevented my parents from punishing me as they might have done. During my illness, I found that whenever I looked up I could see an old photo hanging at the head of the stairs. The photo showed a woman standing by the wall of Lowlands Park, and in certain lights it seemed that she turned and looked at me out of a featureless face in which there were no eyes.

As I say: I didn't believe in ghosts then, and I don't believe in them now; but I'd always call for my mother, and ask her to close the door.

The following Sunday, James Bower waited at the lights on London Road. The dissatisfaction that had dogged him all his life was amplified by the monotony of the day, and he was struck by the sensation that he'd always been waiting for events that never came. Then guilt arrived: he had a house mortgaged at a competitive rate of interest; a wife whose company he still enjoyed, and children of whom he was fond: what more could a man of fifty ask? But his watch ticked, and each tick portioned off an hour, and everything in view represented his failure to have lived the life he'd expected of himself. And would the lights never change – would he never be on his way? Sighing, he wound the window down, and music came over the lip of the glass: voices, an instrument of some kind – a melody he knew and couldn't place, departing the open doors of an austere grey building set behind iron railings, and flanked by the wall to Lowlands Park. James Bower regarded this building with surprise, as if it had been struck up at that moment with the instrument and singers. Its pale bricks had a pearly look, its narrow windows glistered; the music paused, and James saw a man come quickly through the gate. He was tall, and wore a tweed coat with a collar raised against anticipated winds; he carried a leather satchel, and seemed an object set down in a place where it didn't belong. When he arrived at the chapel threshold, he paused and twice turned irresolute towards the gate and back again. Then he stooped for a moment to examine the painted green door, patted it twice as if satisfied with it and with himself, and went in.

Then James Bower, startled by the changing lights and by impatient drivers at the rear, shook off the brief enchantment, departed Bethesda, and thought no more of it for days.

Thomas Hart, who'd come home that afternoon from London on the train, latched Bethesda's gate. The planisphere was in his pocket, and there were binoculars in his bag: five hundred words, he thought, resigned to the task, and six if the night is clear. He heard the congregation singing, '*It is well, it is well with my soul,*' and the sound caused him to turn back twice to the gate, as if he'd left his own soul on the pavement. Then he went resolutely to the door, and inspected it: a little stain between the painted boards perhaps, but no remnant of the meaningless symbol, no shadow unlatching from behind the green bay tree. He tapped the door twice. He went in.

Bethesda on the evening of the Lord's Day, and clouds receding over the roof: forty-seven members of the congregation on their feet with their souls in their mouths. The pews were hard and narrow, enclosed by high sides against which it was possible to lean when the sermon was long. Strips of brown carpet had been nailed down the aisles between the pews; the floorboards were pine. The walls were of a green so pale it couldn't be detected in certain lights, and in all seasons were cold to the touch: by the close of the service the worshippers' breath would run down like alcohol made in a still. Gas lamps fixed high on the wall could no longer be lit, since their pipes had been severed; their green glass shades had the look of tulips past their best. Light came instead from narrow tapered windows, and opaque globes of milky glass hanging overhead like ten halted moons. The pulpit, raised against the chapel's furthest wall, also had the look of a tulip blooming on a broad oak stem, and directly beneath it, always under the eye of the preacher, the communion table rested on the carpeted stage and issued its instruction: THIS DO IN REMEMBRANCE OF ME. The preacher in the pulpit, gazing ahead, would see Bethesda's gallery, held up on the opposing wall by painted iron pillars; this gallery was painted white, and a clock like the clock in a railway station hung there. A woman with a feather nodding in her hat was playing the old harmonium, which had once been found floating in the chapel in 1952 at the time of the North Sea flood, when women on Canvey Island had draped their children over cottage doors to preserve them from the water (and so, said Thomas, the hymns puffed out on briny air).

Thomas, coming through the door, felt he'd walked into a dense illuminated cloud, through which the rest of the world was faint and distant as a town across a valley. The congregation sat. Thomas sat with them, and looked not at the preacher, but at a black-haired girl seated beside a narrow window. She wore a drooping velvet hat, from which only a round chin protruded, and a shawl with tangled fringes falling over the raised back of her pew. Having heard the door admit the latecomer, she turned and acknowledged him, then looked scowling up at the railway clock and down again: You are late, Thomas Hart!

I am late, Grace Macaulay, it is true, he conveyed in a smiling nod, but I'm not sorry.

Grace Macaulay, then: seventeen, small and plump, with skin that went brown by the end of May. Her hair was black and oily, and had the hot consoling scent of an animal in summer. She disliked books, and was by nature a thief if she found a thing to be beautiful, but not hers. She didn't know she couldn't sing. She was inclined to be cross. She had the sudden wordless affection of a farmyard animal, and a habit of butting her small body like a lamb against Thomas, who loved and resented her as he imagined a father might love and resent a daughter. As the diligent congregation opened their Bibles and began the reading of the psalm, Thomas recalled first seeing her when she was six days old, with the petals of her skull not yet closed. That had been a cold fine day in 1980, and Thomas a man of thirty-three, unhappily seated in the pew where he was sometimes told his nature was an affront to God. That Sunday, he'd resolved, would be his last, and with gratitude he'd lock Bethesda's gates behind him and seal up what remained of his faith, and go to flourish in London, godless and at liberty. But a man had come in, carrying a baby in a wicker basket: Ronald Macaulay, of all men in Bethesda the most pious and most stern, whose wife Rachel had died in giving birth. He wore a stunned expression, as if shown something he'd puzzle over for the rest of his life, and there was milky vomit on his lapel. Instinctively, and with the faith he never could shake off, Thomas had commended the grieving man to God, and at the end of the service gone to say with truth and good manners how sorry he was for such a loss. Then – without pleasure; without interest – he'd looked into the basket. There she was, Grace Macaulay, black-haired and ugly with fur at the tips of her ears. Her eyes with their newborn lustre of oil on water had roved about the strangers' faces without interest, then lighted on Thomas and looked with sudden focus on him: 'Oh!' he'd said – a man of thirty-three, he was, who liked children no more and no less than any other human being, which is to say according to their merits – 'Oh!' he'd said, and 'There you are!' She existed. She had not existed, and then she had, summoned out of whatever matter her consciousness had been made, and had stuck her small bare foot in his door. It was disastrous. There was a pain in his heart, as if it had acquired a new chamber to contain her, and so all his life he'd be carting her about. Then the infant had begun to howl with the indignant rage of a creature that had never asked to be born, and Thomas was fixed in place by duty towards a love he'd never sought, and could not explain.

Now the congregation turned to their Bibles with the sound of wind passing over the pages, and there was the reading of a psalm. The planisphere pricked Thomas, and he took it out and put it with his Bible: *Andromeda*, it said. *Perseus*. The blue was remarkable against the Bible's thin black type. '*I will lift up mine eyes to the hills*,' the pastor said, and Thomas lifted his own eyes to the vaulted ceiling, from which white flakes of paint sometimes drifted canting down. 'Almighty God,' the pastor said, 'our heavenly Father' – Thomas turned and turned the planisphere, and the brass pin shone like the Pole Star.

Then the preacher said 'amen', and at that moment Bethesda's holy air was moved by the sound of broken glass. Something had come in from the world, and struck the window where Grace Macaulay sat. Fragments of glass winked on the carpet. A golf ball rolled among them and butted up against a pew. Half the congregation, signalling devotion to their prayers, would not open their eyes; half looked at the girl in the velvet hat who now stood with her Bible in her left hand, exploring a cut on her neck with her right. Through the breach came noises: wind disturbing the bay tree, traffic going on to Aldleigh and all its worldly pursuits. Into this a single syllable arrived, and the effect was of a drop of ink spilled on a laundered tablecloth: 'Shit!' The pastor grasped his lectern and repeated his amen. 'Shit,' came the voice again, with a despairing cadence; and Grace, standing with her thumb to a thin stream of blood, looked expectantly at the door, as if reminded of an appointment she'd failed to keep.

'*I was glad when they said unto me*,' said the pastor with his rare dry wit, '*let us go to the house of the Lord*.' Then the inner door was thrown back and Thomas saw a boy come in. He wore a green coat, and his hair was cut to glinting stubble. Astounded by the faces of the congregation, he said, 'Oh God'; and since that name had never been said aloud under Bethesda's roof with anything but reverence the atmosphere broke as the window had broken. Attending to the change of air, the boy spoke quietly: 'Sorry,' he said, 'lost my ball,' and mimed the twisting, upward motion of a golfer's swing. Grace, inducing blood from her cut, said, 'It's over there.' Abruptly it struck her that despite her lesser sex she'd spoken aloud during a chapel service. Scowling, she sat.

The boy came up the aisle. He looked about with the peering, intent gaze of the short-sighted; his eyes were thickly fringed with remarkable dark lashes. Water ran down the sleeves of his coat and dripped on the carpet, and his trainers had green laces. The pastor looked helplessly down at his congregation. The boy quickly reached for the ball in the broken glass, and met Grace's eye as he stood. The brim of her hat made the upper part of her face dim; the weak chapel light struck her plump white chin and the bloody thumb at her neck. The trespasser gave her a kindly nod that struck off the pews, and the harmonium, and the wet green walls; then he tossed the ball from hand to hand, and left the chapel.

The door went quietly into the wall, and 'Shall we sing?'

23

the pastor said. The grateful congregation rose, and lifted Thomas with it. He sang; he saw Grace look back to the chapel doors with a watchful, hopeful frown, and was uneasy. It seemed to him that the earth had halted its ordinary turning, and began again tilted a little further on its axis.

With the service ended, and the rain gone east to Aldwinter and Walton-on-the-Naze, the pastor and Ronald Macaulay surveyed the breached window. What a pity it was, they said, and what a sad thing to hear the name of God abused so casually; and would a square of cardboard make do for a mend, until a glazier could do his work? Grace Macaulay, hoping for a scar, showed Thomas the little cut. 'Who was that boy,' she said, 'and why did he come in?'

'It was only an accident. He won't come back.'

'But if God makes everything happen, then everything happens on purpose, and it wasn't an accident. So why did he come in?'

'If I knew the mind of God, I'd have better things to do than talk to children.' He pulled at the fringe of her shawl: no harm meant, none done.

'What is that, Thomas?' she said, noting the planisphere as he put it in his pocket. 'Is it a clock?'

'It's a way of finding the stars.'

'The stars don't need finding. You go out and look up and there they always are.'

'I suppose so,' said Thomas. 'But do you ever look up? I don't. Besides: there rivers always are, but you might still need a map to find them.' He showed her the planisphere, and turned the leather disc. 'Aldebaran,' she said. 'Pollux. Am I saying it right?'

'I don't know, but I doubt it. Now give it back: I'm off to Lowlands Park to find my way through stars,' said Thomas, 'and if the moon comes up, I suppose I'd better take a look.'

He clasped her shoulder and shook her a little roughly, as if she were a pet: 'Sleep well,' he said, 'you wretched child. Now look. Your father's calling, and they're turning out the lights.'

Behind the chapel was a steeply sloping lawn, where Grace as a child had played alone. This lawn was boundaried by a line of silver birches that screened the chapel from the world as a curtain screens a patient dying on a ward, and beyond the silver birches lay the five hundred acres of Lowlands Park. It was by that time gone halfway to ruin, and the careful planting of its oaks and limes gave the impression of an exhausted battalion marching on the house. The lawns were left largely untended, and stems of mullein and cow parsley dead since the end of summer rattled when the wind got up. Immense formal beds had sunk and spread, and become indistinguishable from the lawn, though occasionally a valiant plant seeding itself down through the generations bloomed in high summer. There was a lake left to silt up and become shallow; it was hedged by reeds, and plagued all summer by midges dancing with terminal glee. Sometimes in good weather the lawns died back and the earth cracked, and it was possible to make out the remnants of a brick path going aimlessly down to the lake, the bricks marked here and there with stars.

Lowlands House, which listed on a shallow promontory at the end of the vanished path, was – at certain times, on certain days – a lovely place. The white facade responded to the Essex light, seeming sometimes pink as flesh, and in stormy weather grey as Bethesda's brick. Once it had been one of the great houses of Essex: not remarkable (sniffed Pevsner), but designed and constructed with all the terraces and Doric columns the fashion of the day could ask. When the family money had been dwindled down by venality and bad advice, and the sinking Essex clay had caused subsidence that cracked the plaster audibly at night, the last of the family line had staked the house he despised on a horse, and lost it to a man who never once crossed the threshold and soon forgot he owned it. So Lowlands quickly became disconsolate and damp, and was bought in due course by a wool merchant named John Bell. With his care and bright new money it had briefly flourished: it was Bell who'd laid the starry path and dug out the lake, and commissioned a statue of a woman to stand forever looking over the water (though some tragedy to which Thomas had never paid attention had put an end to all that, and quickly the rose garden choked on its own thorns, and the statue hurled herself into the lake).

A childish bad temper settled on Thomas. This was the effect of the chapel, and the broken window, and of Nick Carleton's impertinence: what business was a comet of his? What was the moon to do with him? It waxed and waned, and that was all he knew, and all he needed to know. His head ached. He walked on. It was getting dark. The dense stands of oak thinned into solitary sentinels as the lawn rose faintly to the house. Overhead, streaks of high cloud split, and showed clear inky reaches not yet marked by stars. Somewhere, no doubt: the unreliable moon. He walked on, fetching the planisphere and notebook out of his pocket, and diligently recording the date and time. From this vantage, he could make out the pale house drifting down its shallow promontory, and steps descending to a wire fence that kept nobody out. Doric columns flanked oak doors surmounted by a shield of heraldry, and secured by steel plates. The windows were blinded by boards that split and buckled in bad weather, so that trespassers beyond the boundary fence could sometimes make out the fireplace in the hall, and pale frescoes half-obscured by obscene and amatory graffiti.

Meanwhile the ornamental lake was ceding to the Essex clay, and drowned the stone woman in silt.

Thomas walked on. The cloud thinned over a rising moon. Mist pooled in the hollows between the oaks. There was no wind. 'Where are you,' said Thomas, 'where did you go?', seeking out his old companion in the windows, inclined to persuade himself a light moved behind the splitting boards. Naturally: nothing. He shrugged; he turned to the sky. From east to west it was a featureless dark canopy, save for a pale place where the low cloud, startled by the rising moon, was dispersing into shining fragments. It seemed to Thomas he was looking up into a sea in which a silver shoal of herring swam; and after a time, when the cloud was gone, he raised his binoculars, and looked again.

FIRST LIGHT

THOMAS HART *ESSEX CHRONICLE*,
24 FEBRUARY 1997

Dear reader, you have on your hands an altered man. This is the editor's fault, because he sent me to look at the moon.

But Thomas, you're thinking: have you never seen the moon before? Well, of course – I know its habit of pitching up at two in the afternoon, or tilting back like a rocking chair, but never found it any more interesting than any other thing. So I set off for Lowlands Park last Sunday without hope, and in a temper. There'd been rain that day, and there were no birds, no stars, and no moon: it was obviously all a waste of time, and my shoes were being ruined by the mud.

I was busily employed in cursing my editor when I realised that in fact the night had begun to clear, and that my temper was clearing with it. Stars had come out without my noticing, and there was an immense radiant place just above Lowlands where the moon was concealed by the last of the cloud. Then the wind took the cloud, and the moon came out; so for the first time in my life I gave the moon my full attention. First, I saw a melancholy face looking down at me, and was half-inclined to wave. But I was not after all a child, and really it looked to me like a greasy white plate, and I was tempted to shrug, and get back to my books. Then I remembered I had binoculars with me, and for a while fumbled with the focus wheel, at first seeing nothing but a shining blot. I swore. My feet were wet. I tried again; the blot dwindled down, and the moon came fully into view. The flat melancholy face had gone, and in its place was an astonishing and terrible thing bellying out of the sky. The more I looked, the larger it became. You mustn't think it came down to meet me – it was a question of flight! I saw nearby the lip of craters lit by the sun, and shadows falling behind them; I saw vast dark plains, and places so bright you'd think they'd turned the lights on for my benefit. Towards the rim, where the hour hand on a clock stands at half past four, I saw a shining centre out of which radiated lines too straight to have been made by chance – it is a city, I thought, and all roads lead to it!

A man in a red velvet coat was walking nearby, and laughed at me, because I was saying, 'Who are you? Who are you, up there?' I wanted to know who travelled on those roads, and in what vehicles – what was the name of the celestial city, and what were the laws and regulations of their principalities and powers? Were our sins their virtues, and their virtues our sins? What were the intervals of their music, and what did they eat in bad weather?

I put the binoculars down. I was bewildered and amazed: there was mud in the tread of my shoes, and lunar dust in the pockets of my coat. I saw the man in the red coat shaking his head, and heading for town; I heard a woman calling in her dog, and music thudding from a car on London Road. But all that seemed as remote as foreign customs in foreign lands. What on earth did it have to do with me? I had become a citizen of the empire of the moon.

Nick Carleton, reading this despatch from the shore of the Sea of Tranquillity, looked up at Thomas Hart.

'Do you like it? Will it do?'

'I do,' said the editor, truthfully, 'but it's very strange.'

'Ah, well,' said Thomas, and left it at that.

'My father told me,' said Carleton, 'that when a telescope is used for the first time, whatever the astronomer sees that night is called the "first light". You're like a telescope yourself, Thomas: we took the lens cap off, and this is your first light. Well, then! We have a title.' He was pleased with this; but when he looked for the other man's responding pleasure saw he was looking out between the slatted blinds. Half past three in the afternoon, but all the same: the moon.

Several cold days went. Thomas roamed at night with the litter and drinkers and foxes, consulting the planisphere by streetlight. Overcast nights were a personal affront; his neck ached with all the looking. The scattered stars assembled themselves. He had the wonderlust. The moon waned: lights out in the great city, calm on the dry black seas. He consulted books on physics and astronomy, and when he understood Kepler's laws was brought almost to tears by such exacting beauty. I am superterrestrial, he thought, and passed untouched through crowds on Aldleigh High Street with the waters of his body drawn up by the moon with the tides.

From the last night of February, Comet Hale–Bopp could not be ignored. It came as a chalk smudge of light, and bright as a star of the second magnitude, so that men and women generally indifferent to the stars were compelled beyond the limit of their interest, and wondered what it was, and why it didn't move. In the Colchester barracks, bragging squaddies drunk on valour saw it, and argued over the cause; a girl coming out of the Jackdaw and Crow in tears over a broken shoe saw it, and tried to describe it, and couldn't. (The vagrant in the red coat saw it from the steps of the war memorial, but all day he'd been diligently drinking, so all the stars had tails.)

Ronald Macaulay saw it, and said to himself that the heavens declared the glory of God, but admitted that of that glory he felt nothing. Anne Macaulay saw it, standing at the kitchen sink. Grace Macaulay saw it, and shrugged. She was taking off her clothes. It was her habit to examine herself every evening by lamplight, as if her body were a bit of clay being worked on against her will. The hair between her legs was reddish: she thought this odd and beautiful. There was a spot on her shoulder she couldn't reach, and a splay of violet lines fading over hips that had broadened shockingly the year before. Her breasts and stomach were round, and she set her feet on the ground like an animal refusing to budge; muscles were visible in her arms and thighs. She hadn't grown an inch since she was twelve. There was a steep inward curve to the small of her back; there was a birthmark on her upper arm, and a quickly healing cut on her neck. She touched it, and wished it were worse. Her hands were small, and her nails bitten short. In this light she found herself erotic, and wondered if this was a form of desire that constituted a sin. Then she wondered if the boy who'd broken the chapel window would also find her erotic, and winced as her conscience pricked. She got into bed. In the front garden a silver birch stood between her window and the streetlight, and its shadow flinched against the wall. She prayed sincerely, and slept.

Thomas Hart, seeing the comet as he came home from work, felt he'd been waiting for it all his life: 'Look,' he said, grasping the sleeve of a stranger, 'look at that! It is circumpolar,' he said, 'it will never set' (the stranger shook him off and went home with his hangover). Later that evening it struck Thomas there was something he ought to have been doing, and remembered what it was, and did it:

Dear Mr Bower

I hope you're well. I'm sorry it has taken me this long to reply to your kind letter, which did indeed interest me. I am not so old that I'm unmoved by the prospect of solving the problem of the Lowlands ghost! If you can forgive my bad manners, and would still like to speak to the *Chronicle* about your research into Lowlands, I would be pleased to visit and see what you've found. I will come this Friday, if I may, at about eleven.

Yours sincerely

THOMAS HART

SIGNS AND WONDERS

THOMAS HART *ESSEX CHRONICLE*,
21 MARCH 1997

Well: have you seen it yet? We have a visitor. Look north-west after dusk in good weather, and you'll find it: Comet Hale–Bopp, tearing out of space and headed for the sun.

I imagine it brings trouble. In 1910, for example, people in the United States bought gas masks and sealed up their keyholes with lumps of soap and wax, believing Halley's Comet would release clouds of deadly cyanogen gas. In Haiti and Texas it was possible to buy anti-comet pills, and in Washington State a shepherd nailed himself hand and foot to a wooden cross and begged the authorities to leave him there. That same year in Essex, two wealthy sisters locked themselves in the attic and set themselves on fire, and were buried the following week in the same grave; and in London a pastor preached for twenty hours without pausing before collapsing in the street (his last words were said to have been 'flee from the wrath to come'). In the end, Halley reached its perihelion without causing any greater harm than terror (though

some said it had been possible to smell something like burning vege-tables, and marsh gas).

Comets have always caused a bit of a stir – in 1456, Pope Callixtus III excommunicated Halley as an 'instrument of the devil', and in 1835 it was said to have caused a devastating fire in New York. Natu-rally ours is an age of reason, and that's a fine thing – but the arrival of Comet Hale–Bopp has shown our pleasure in fear isn't as dimin-ished as we'd like to think. I've heard of a group in California who see in the comet's wake a 'dark compan-ion' they believe to be a spaceship; and this week alone the *Chronicle* has received three letters from people believing Hale–Bopp is the Star of Bethlehem, signalling the arrival of a new Messiah, or possibly the return of the old one.

And though it seems to me little more than a blurred star, I some-times look up and remember a Bible phrase that frightened me when I was young: that in the last days there would be wars, and rumours of

33

wars. You see how easily we're fooled by a new light! And in fact Hale–Bopp will reach its perihelion on April Fool's Day, which I suppose is fitting – but I think on the whole I'd rather be prone to being fooled, than be too wise a man for wonder.

Friday, about eleven, and March going out like a lamb: Aldleigh lively under drifts of cherry blossom that blotted the steps of the old town hall and caused women in high heels to slip. Here Aldleigh Museum kept its stores of coins and mosaics retrieved from new roads and housing estates in the nick of time, together with its dancing bear stuffed and chained at the foot of the stairs, and its single mummified Egyptian cat which (so children claimed) could be smelt through panes of glass. Students from Colchester and Cambridge came now and then to examine its library, and its manuscripts pertaining to witch trials, saffron, Blackwater serpents, and the growth and manufacture of thatch; and meanwhile a model of Boudicca, her hard breasts bare, drove her chariot forever across a carpet stained with gum.

James Bower's office was cold, and could never be lit beyond permanent dusk. The windows rattled when an east wind blew, and if on certain days he was charmed by the panelled walls, and by the Essex coat of arms above the door, now he sighed over the tedium of his work. I've been bored all my life, he thought, and now I am fifty: everything is behind me, and nothing is ahead. The clock ticked. He watched it. It was about eleven, and there were voices in the hall. This, he supposed, was Thomas Hart, whose letter and columns suggested a man who shed dust as he walked. James stood. He straightened the papers on his desk. Now there was a deep voice, accentless and precise. 'Thank you,' it said. 'Should I wait here?'

'No need,' said James, coming through the door. 'Thomas Hart, I presume? In here, and we'll have tea, or coffee if you prefer.' Dust drifted in the narrow hall, and briefly it seemed the morning guest, indistinct and featureless, was at that moment being formed out of a swirling mass of particles. Then he came into the clarifying light, and James was brought up hard against a memory. 'Oh!' he said, fumbling his good manners, and frowning at the visitor with startled recognition. What was he, or what had he been? An old schoolfriend perhaps, but for the life of him – 'Come in,' he said, 'and sit down.'

With graceful deliberation Thomas Hart took off his coat, and James Bower understood it was not the features that were familiar, but the atmosphere attending the man. He wore a tie, and the line of a folded handkerchief showed above the breast pocket of his jacket: the effect was to give James the impression that his own shirt and jeans were in some way offensive. It would have been unkind and untrue to say he was a strange man; but all the same he conveyed the impression he belonged elsewhere.

'I hope you'll forgive my delay in replying, Mr Bower,' said Thomas Hart. 'I've had the moon on my hands, you see.'

'Please,' said the other man, bewildered by the formality, 'call me James.'

'Ah yes: force of habit. James, then.' He took out a notebook; he opened it on his knee. James began to hear a thin melody, as plainly as if coming through the broken window frame. 'Oh!' he said again. That was it, he thought, that was it: the pearly grey brick, the solitary man – *It is well, it is well with my soul!*

'So then, James: you've found some documents relating to Lowlands House? I love the old place,' he said with charming sorrow, 'and hate to see it sink so low.' (James wouldn't have been surprised if he had said: I was there when it was built, and saw the last tile set on the roof.)

A silent woman brought tea in green cups on a green tin tray, and left.

'I could let you in,' said James, 'I have the keys.' He was startled by a desire to interest this man. 'I visit often of course, and never did believe in the ghost; but these days find myself listening for footsteps — you're making notes?'

'I write everything down,' said Thomas, with the suggestion of an apology. 'It is how I make sense of things.' Then he became professional, brisk: if there were footsteps at Lowlands he was evidently resolved not to hear them. 'Now,' he said, leaning faintly forwards, 'about these documents?'

James willingly followed Thomas from the supernatural to the ordinary, and opened a file. 'What do you know,' he said, 'about Maria Văduva?'

'Nothing,' said Thomas. 'In fact, I've never heard the name.'

'She was the wife of John Bell, who owned Lowlands until his death in 1889, and we've never known anything more about her: it's as if she's been cut out of time. We have records of their marriage, but not of her death; we have no portraits of her anywhere, and when the house and contents were sold none of her possessions were listed in the inventory. We only know that in 1887 John Bell commissioned a statue of her to stand by the lake — look: we have a photo — but soon after this she disappeared, and now the statue has gone, too.'

'I see.' Thomas examined the image of a stone woman stuck on the verges of the lake. Black moss stained her skirts, and something was falling from her right hand. 'I suppose she's in the water now,' he said. 'What is she holding?'

'I have always thought,' said James, 'it looked like a shotgun – don't you want your tea? I don't blame you.'

Thomas looked at the cup he'd put down, and moved it further away. 'You've told me what you don't know,' he said, 'but I understood you wanted to show me something you do know?'

James, puzzled by his desire to impress and excite this visitor beyond the ordinary professional interest, reached again for his file. 'We've been taking up the carpets,' he said, 'in the east wing. The floorboards are lifting up with damp, there's all kinds down there – a silver fork, a lens from a pair of glasses, bits of old clothing – and also, shoved down between the boards as if deliberately, we found these.' He handed the other man a square of foxed and buckled paper, together with a larger document.

Thomas took the document and raised it to the window. Daylight seeped through seams where it was unfolded. It was a long letter, in a looping exuberant scrawl: '. . . *beloved inhabitant*,' he read aloud. '. . . *Foolish Street* . . .' Briefly defeated by the ink, he frowned more deeply still: '*though truly it seems to me that I am a static object, changeless as the noble gases, condemned only to observe and never to move* . . . She goes on at length,' said Thomas. 'I see it was never sent.'

'Not finished, and never sent. But dated, as you see, and the name is clear: Maria Văduva, writing at Lowlands on the twenty-second of May 1887.'

Thomas put the letter down and considered it. 'So then,' he said, 'certain facts can be deduced. Firstly, that her name was Maria Văduva, which is certainly not English. Secondly, that she was remarkable enough to have justified a statue, in which she may possibly have been holding a weapon. Thirdly, that she was alive and resident in Lowlands at this date. Fourthly, that she had at least one friend, to whom she sometimes wrote. It is very strange,' he said, with a direct assessing look at James, 'that so little is left of her. This letter is long. I suppose there's more information here?'

'I've made copies,' said James. 'You can take one home, and read it.'

'Thank you.'

'Anything,' said James, becoming magnanimous, 'for the *Essex Chronicle*. And then, you see, we have this.' This: a smaller sheet of paper, folded once, and showing an inked circle drawn with a schoolboy's exactitude. Within this circle, there was a kind of scribbled blot. Thomas surveyed it. It was without form, and void: no sense could be made of it. 'You almost feel,' he said, 'that if you touch it your finger would sink through the paper and be lost in it. But this is signed, too: "Maria Văduva, M42, 1887". M42.' He shook his head. 'As if she means to indicate March, or May; only no month has forty-two days.'

'Perhaps,' said James. 'But really it might mean nothing at all.' Currents of air in the dim roof shifted and brought down dust.

'Well: perhaps she was mad, and was shut away for it.'

'Any of us might go mad at any time,' said James.

'We might,' said Thomas, 'I suppose'; and there was the suggestion that he at any rate was a man beyond the reach of insanity.

'One last thing,' said James. 'This had fallen behind a window seat. So now we have an image of her, and we are all in love. She is not young, and no beauty' – here, gentle disappointment – 'but striking, you might say.'

Thomas took the photo he was given, and saw a woman in a black silk dress, the constricting high neck trimmed with lace. Her face in profile showed straight black brows and a Roman nose; her black hair was kept back from her temples with a diamond pin. 'How cross she looks,' said Thomas, 'but not, I think, insane.' He frowned then, as if mocking the woman's concentrated severity. 'Mr Bower – James, I should say – I wonder if I've seen her before?'

'This image, you mean? This photo?'

'No.' He put the woman down. 'I have a photograph at home,' he said, 'from the day Bethesda opened.' He hesitated then, and James was astonished to see colour rise from beneath the other man's collar, and stain his neck. 'That is: the old chapel on London Road, that backs on to Lowlands Park. Perhaps you know it. At any rate, a photo was taken on the day it opened. It shows the chapel of course, and the first congregation; but what interests me most is that towards the edge of the picture, caught by mistake and almost out of sight, a black-haired woman stands the other side of the chapel wall, on Lowlands land. It is dated August 1888; so if it is her, it keeps her alive and in Lowlands for a further year. Perhaps I'll bring it and show you,' he said; and it seemed to James that he leaned with shyness against the high back of his chair, and inspected his fingernails, as if to indicate that a refusal wouldn't trouble him at all.

'Yes,' said James, 'bring it, by all means.' It would be quite natural then to say: And of course I know the chapel, Thomas, everybody does, and I saw you there – but this felt impossibly intimate. 'I wonder,' he said, smiling to demonstrate that he was aware of his own foolishness, 'I wonder if we have named the Lowlands ghost? A strange woman, suddenly vanished – a statue drowned in the lake – what more could we ask. Is it worth writing about, do you think? Can you make something of it?'

'Certainly I can,' said Thomas. He was returning his

notebook to his pocket. 'My readers are fond of Lowlands, and they're very fond of the ghost. They tell me she's come back, you know – that lights have been seen, where there should be no lights. But a real woman who has vanished interests me more than an imagined one who persists in showing up. We'll keep in touch' – he was standing; he was putting on his coat – 'and you can tell me what more you find, and I'll tell you what I find. Like a mystery,' he said (a smile then, passing quickly), 'like schoolboys.' He held out his hand.

There was a brief dry touch of palm on palm. The windows of the room turned with the earth and admitted the sun. A beam of light divided the room in two, and also divided the men.

'Well then,' said James. 'You have my number, and I have yours.'

'Yes,' said Thomas, 'I think so'; and with a peculiarly intimate smile headed for the door. Quite a strange man, thought James, watching him go – but what a relief to discover he still contained the capacity to be taken by surprise. He returned to his work, and with his old sense of tedium and futility put his name to a pink requisition slip, which concerned graves disinterred in the village of Aldwinter in 1954.

Maria Văduva Bell
Lowlands House
22 MAY 1887

To the only beloved inhabitant of Foolish Street!

Very well: since you ask, I will make a record of what is
happening – though truly it seems to me I am as
changeless as the noble gases – and by the time you reach
my signature, you'll cast poor dull Maria to the dogs –

So you see – I have left my homeland – I exchange both
warmth and cold for the nothingness of English
weather! John Bell conveyed me first by train and in due
course by means of a bone-rattling carriage to Lowlands,
not a mile distant from the village of Aldleigh, which I
do not like and cannot pronounce. I daresay I must call
this my home – though truly there never was so dank and
drear a place – though Essex being flat and featureless at
least has in its favour the kind of skies which all my life I
have sought –

I confess to having been surprised by affection for my
husband – this dreadful emotion roused by discovering
that he has commissioned a rose garden, and an orchard,
and a lake, and beside this lake a statue of a woman
holding certain instruments of her trade – and this
woman is intended to be me. You would laugh to see it –
she is as fragile as women are intended to be, and as you
and I are not – and lifts her skirt above the water, but
never above her toes – but it caused me to soften against
any man who could conceive of me in this way! Then I
regretted this softness – and made a quick summation of

42

his faults: that he is without humour, without intelligence, and without style; and furthermore – you will not deny this material fact – that he possesses a face like a boiled potato. (You must deploy this method for your own husband, since it is wise never to think too well of any man – or you will find, as I have found, they may become the rocks on which your ship is wrecked!)

24 MAY

How lax I have been in my task! I offer in mitigation that I have taken up my old nocturnal habits – since the weather has been good for hunting –

John Bell of course dislikes these habits and speaks to his land agent as if I were a madwoman. But I sharpen my wits to keener points, and speak to the land agent, and to the various house-keepers, ground-keepers, accountants, scullery maids &c. &c. (knowing you consort with socialists and radicals, I blush to confess that my husband is rich beyond virtue), with such precision and prolixity in their own language they appear first astonished – and in due course, when I apologise for the paucity of my vocabulary and the stupidity of my grammar, quite ashamed. So my sanity is not in question, and the instruments of my trade are preserved –

These are my days – I wake early, and rise late. My room adjoins that of my husband – the wallpaper is patterned with ducks that swim forever to the floor – my bed would require a ladder were I not the height of a man. Then I assemble myself in such grand array it is said of me that positively I clank as I walk (indeed I have in mind a gown to dazzle the admirer with whole galaxies of pearl and

43

silver – one day you shall admire it on me). If there has
been a good night hunting, I pass an hour anatomising
what I have caught, and the place I caught it, and labelling
its parts – then it is lunch with John Bell, and I attend to
his remarks on the stock exchange, and the growth or
diminution in the value of merino, Shetland, lambswool,
angora, and so on, until I feel I must sink under a soft hot
heap of his words –

I have entered sadness as one might enter a room – this
after weeks of my heart having for its habitation a place
as unyielding and flat as an Essex field in winter! John Bell
says: What ails you, wife? He produces gardenias, hair-
combs, lenses, bracelets in amber and jet, celestial
almanacs, a white hen – reminds me that the whole
exchequer of his affection and his accounts is at my
disposal – as if I were a capricious king, and he a
chancellor fearing for his neck – let me pluck and eat the
hen, I said – but relented for the sake of her fine eyes and
set her free to peck about on the terrace. What ails you,
he says! – as if he did not know, for I told him, that I love
a man who does not love me!

I lack the heart for hunting.

I walked this afternoon with John Bell in the gardens –
and my heart lifted (I gave it no permission) at the first
flush of roses – but I ought not to be happy! Isn't the
value of my love for M. set by the heap of my sorrow?
This is my calculation: to diminish my sorrow is to
diminish my love to an equal degree!

Three women were walking the grounds – as the people of Aldleigh are inclined to do, having no respect for the law – this being the Essex disposition. They were young, and of the type M. loved – for he confided in me often that he was no proof against beauty and youth – so I despised them, for the cheap coin of their good looks! And John Bell bowed deeply as M. would have done – only more deeply, and with more grace – so my lifting heart fell, and resumed its proper position: at my feet, having been trampled.

Oh C. – if he had only liked my looks – if his tastes had not been so devoutly fixed on Veronica, who in her dreadful prettiness might have been his sister! Still I recall the words of the English queen: that she might well blush to show her face, but of her mind she would never be ashamed –

What have I told you of the man I love? You have seen his beauty in photographs – and it is remarkable – but you must not think that is the cause! It is that he stands on a high ledge, and I could not reach him – and you know what a weakness I have for what I cannot reach!

I learn that John Bell has sold a piece of land at the boundary of Lowlands, beside the new London Road. Astonishment and consternation above stairs and below it! Does my husband's exchequer falter? It does not: it grows fat on wool and the women that wear it. He confides in me that he was petitioned particularly by gentlemen of a dissident sect, which is called the Strict and Particular Baptists (I trust I shall never meet any man living under so pinched a faith), who have no place of worship, and should like to build one. My husband has a fondness for any religion not overseen by the state – indeed at any mealtime he would speak at length on Wycliffe, the morning star of the Reformation, if I were to let him – so he has sold a half-acre at last year's prices, and the foundations are soon to be laid.

Now, my beloved: no cloud, no moon. I believe I see Lucifer at my window. Your friend must dress herself, and go out . . .

———

I am on the floor – there is torn paper all about me – John Bell possesses a capacity for anger which I could not have imagined – indeed I like him for it! Why did I marry him, he asks – forgetting that I accepted him with these bare facts: that I love a man who does not love me – that I delivered my heart wholesale to M., who had no use for it – so that nothing remains now but to marry without feeling, only sense – and after all, John Bell is rich!

Then John in his envy commanded me to remain indoors, though the night was clear and fine – he is jealous of M., and of whatever else I love – though it would be better to instruct a priest not to pursue his God! So he tore my papers, and I liked him in his anger – and was faithful neither to M. nor to my sorrow –

How little you'll think of me now!

Thomas Hart, pleasantly if only slightly drunk, read this letter for the third time, and spoke to the woman who wrote it. He'd taken down the photo of Bethesda on the day of its opening, and propped it against the bottle of wine now empty on the table. 'So was it you,' he said, 'that haunts Lowlands, and haunted me?' (Maria Vāduva, leaning on Bethesda's wall, refused to meet his eye.)

'It's no use,' said Thomas. 'I'm already coming to know you, whether you like it or not. A little mad, I think; handsome and rich; bad-tempered and clever and miserably in love. And I'm mad too, I suppose, talking to a dead woman – what's got into me?' He was laughing at himself and all the world, and what had got into him was this – that superimposed on all the world was James Bower's startled look of recognition: oh, but it is you, Thomas, here you are at last! *He knew me*, he'd said to himself, stumbling home past the war memorial and the market square: *he knew me!* How to explain such surprised and impossible knowledge – the unearned intimacy that had made his mouth dry up, so that he couldn't even drink his tea? Providence, thought Thomas, that was it: providence – God had directed Thomas Hart, and had directed James Bower – he'd set them in motion, and their orbits were fixed! Then again (Thomas was an honest man) there was the fact of James Bower's beauty, which in that dim closed room had made everything intimate and strange, which in the course of an hour he had memorised, as he'd once memorised passages of scripture in Bethesda's Sunday School. 'Everything about him,' he told Maria, indifferent behind the glass, 'was gold – he radiated light – I could read in the dark by standing in his shadow!' Now Thomas numbered off James Bower's virtues one by one: his fair hair kept too long, out of vanity or neglect; his narrow copper eyes, the whites of which had been remarkably clear; a burnished look to forearms bared by a T-shirt he was really too old to have worn, but which Thomas was prepared to forgive. The bones of his wrists had been too prominent, and the glass on his watch had been cracked. His hands were large and expressive, and he had moved easily in his chair, as if he felt it a pleasure to inhabit a body of which he'd never been ashamed – he'd smelt not of soap or fragrance but of clean skin. His lips had looked as if they had ashes on them: 'He needs to drink more water,' said Thomas tenderly, 'or he'll get headaches.'

Never think too well of any man, said cautious Maria, leaning over Bethesda's wall and speaking urgently, *or you will find, as I have found –*

'Yes, yes: they become the rocks on which your ship is wrecked. So you said. But how can you understand? How can you know?' He fetched more wine; he cut a pork pie and smeared it with mustard. When he returned to the table Maria vaulted the wall to join the congregation on Bethesda's lawn; with her arm around the pastor's waist she looked unsmilingly at Thomas and shook her head. 'Let me explain,' he said (if he was going mad, he was inclined to let it happen). 'I've read your private letters: isn't it fair I tell you my secrets in return? I have only ever wanted men. I have wanted them all my life. I knew I wanted them before I knew all the words they have for it, and long before I had heard them say from the pulpit that men like me lived beyond God's grace – I knew when I was thirteen, and went camping in the summer and watched boys shave out of enamel bowls on the trestle table, and felt the pain it caused me to see their throats move when they swallowed – their bodies were so miraculous and strange to me you'd think they were nothing like mine!' Maria, frowning and solemn, looked once over her shoulder towards Bethesda, and its narrow bricks. 'Yes,' said Thomas, spilling his wine, 'yes, and every week I sat in my pew between my parents, and after they died I sat in my pew without them, and I tried to make sense of it. Do you think you lose your faith, because your faith does not want you? That would be easy! My life would have been a happier one! But all these years there have been two fires in me and neither puts the other out! So this is how I make sense of it: in London I live that part of my life, and I never feel it to be a sin, and on the train between Liverpool Street and Aldleigh I set it aside, and come to Bethesda and I am another man. I've never had love,' he said, frowning now, and looking at the letter on the table, 'I've never expected it. It seemed to me that God would withhold it from me, for my sins. That has been the bargain, you understand? But if it was God's providence that sent me to James Bower – if this man has been looking for me, and found me – was it ever a sin, after all? Was I never a sinner, and never a saint, but only Thomas Hart?' There was pain in the sockets of his eyes, and at the base of his skull: I'm drunk and foolish, he thought, and I ask too much of life. The table was inviting and cool to the touch, and the robin was singing on the streetlight. I just need to sleep it off, thought Thomas, I just need forty winks – so he rested his head on his folded arms, and there was the scent of polish and mustard and paper. Easily, he slept; and as he slept, the woman in the photograph took her arm from the pastor's waist, and crossed the parched lawn towards the camera. Her black skirts, thickly beaded at the hem, obscured the view of Bethesda; then her fine and muddied boots came over the frame, and were first set squarely on the table, then one by one on the floor: Maria Văduva Bell, assembled out of ink and speculation, and taking up residence on Lower Bridge Road.

ON THE MOTION OF BODIES IN ORBIT

THOMAS HART *ESSEX CHRONICLE*,
28 MARCH 1997

Since I now divide my time between Essex and the moon, I go out whenever nights are clear to explore my second home, and give myself a constant headache what with all that looking up.

Keeping note of the moon's transit over Aldleigh, I've pictured it moving down the thread of its orbit like a bead on a length of string. Did you think an orbit formed a circle? So did I, but we are both mistaken. In 1609 Johannes Kepler published his laws regarding the motion of bodies in orbit, and in the first of these ruled that the shape of an orbit is not a circle, but rather the form of an ellipse (I'm as much a baffled student as any child, and have found it helpful to picture a drawing of a rugby ball).

As every child knows, a body must orbit something – so the earth orbits the sun, and the moon orbits the earth. The sun is the earth's focal point, and the earth is the moon's focal point.

This is quite straightforward – but I have discovered that the more I learn, the more I'm apt to be confused. In fact, there are two focal points inside the orbital ellipse: two dots drawn on the side of our rugby ball. The first is the primary focal point – the sun, for example, or the earth – and then there is another focus. There is no star or planet there: there is only space. You cannot see it, because there is nothing to see but maths. It is there, because it must be there.

Sometimes I think of my own body in motion. What moves me on? What moves you? I suppose I could tell you what kind of sun draws me down my orbit, but there must be other forces at work that I can't make out. It comforts me to think of us all in motion, helpless against the forces of time and fate. We are just like the earth, I think: 'insignificantly small', as Kepler said once, 'but borne through stars'.

The following Sunday, Thomas Hart went out through Bethesda's gates when the evening service was done. Grace Macaulay was in his wake and the comet was overhead: 'Look up,' he said, 'you wretched child – see it hanging over the roof?' Grace looked obediently at the pearly blur skimming the slates. Her soul was not moved. 'Is that it?' she said. 'Is that all?' She wore her Sunday best: a skirt sewn from a faded bedcover bought for a pound, and printed with a child's idea of birds; a silk blouse stolen from her aunt (it was too small, and its torn seams were concealed by a schoolboy's blazer). Her black curls, released from the loathed velvet hat, needed washing: they gleamed with oil from her scalp, and the rosemary and lavender oils she'd used as a perfume mixed unpleasantly on her skin. She carried her Bible. She walked with quick small steps as if always on the verge of tumbling over. 'I think it's probably a sign,' she said, 'don't you? I think things are changing' (she looked at Potter's Field, and found nothing in it). 'And you're different, too. Something's going on. Why don't you tell me what it is? I bet it's all to do with that bloody comet,' she said, and with this little profanity she smiled.

'It is not the comet exactly,' said Thomas, declining either to applaud or chastise. 'It's all of it. Look here, I've found a mystery.'

'Thomas! Are you having an adventure?'

'I am,' said Thomas. 'They've found some papers at Low-lands House. Drawings nobody can make out, a letter from a woman called Maria, who was certainly a lunatic, and is pos-sibly a ghost.'

'The one you saw when you were a boy?'

'I imagine so, don't you? And sometimes I even see her these days, when I think to look – it seems her name was Maria Văduva. In 1888 she disappeared, and nobody knows what became of her. James Bower says –'

'Who's that?'

'A man at the museum. It's not important.' Thomas was afraid he blushed, and that she'd see it.

'No: who's that?' said Grace. She stood rigid as a sight-hound in the slips, scowling into darkness punctuated at intervals by the streetlights on London Road. Look at her, thought Thomas. More animal than human, sniffing the air – he looked where she looked, and saw a figure moving ahead of them away from town. It leaped and weaved with happy devilry across the path, pausing whenever it found light, and basking briefly before dashing on.

'It's him,' said Grace, with the wonder of astronomers. 'It's him, it's that boy.' She dashed forward, then turned to Thomas. 'What should I do?' she said, with a curious sort of helplessness that was in no way childish. 'I don't know what to do. Let's go back to Bethesda. They might not have locked the doors.'

'But he's seen you.'

'He has? Thomas, what should I do?' Hale–Bopp came out again. Nobody saw it. The boy, leaping into light, stood distantly surveying Grace. Cropped fair hair glinted on his scalp. He wore a denim jacket that was stuck all over with patches, which would certainly have been as inscrutable to the girl as they were to Thomas: a yellow circle marked with an idiot grin, a blue skull through which a serpent moved. The laces of his trainers were undone. He wore a splint on his wrist, and had grazed his cheek; he peered myopically out of his extraordinarily deep-fringed eyes. He carried something. 'Hello?' he said.

'He can't actually see who I am,' said Grace, affronted. 'Why doesn't he wear his glasses?' She went forward. 'It's me,' she said. 'Can't you see it's me?'

'Oh.' The boy blinked, waved, came nearer. 'That's funny,' he said. 'I was coming to see you.'

'You hurt me,' said Grace. 'You cut my neck. I'll have a scar. What do you mean, you were coming to see me – were you coming to tell me you were sorry?'

'It was an accident!' said the boy, in the way of a child to whom an injustice has been done. 'How can I say I'm sorry, when I didn't mean to do it?'

Grace, seeming to examine this from a theological perspective, visibly relented. 'All right,' she said, 'I'm Grace. But how could you come to see me, when you don't even know who I am?'

'Everyone knows' – he looked apologetic – 'because, well: you know.' A gesture with his splinted wrist took in her long skirt, under which filthy lace petticoats showed, and her boy's boots, and the Bible half-concealed under her hat. 'But I like it,' he said, with hasty kindness. 'I'm Nathan.'

'In the Book of Samuel,' said Grace, 'Nathan was a prophet who tricked a king.'

'All right,' said Nathan.

'What's that? Is it for me?' Grace Macaulay, inveterate thief, put her small hand on what he carried.

'I bought you chocolates. Not because I'm sorry, I just thought you'd like them. I ate some, to be honest. But there's lots left.' He opened the box. Together they examined the contents, and placidly began to eat. Thomas watched, bewildered: here again was the sense that some significant thing was taking place, and perhaps had always been taking place – the comet had come out. 'Hello,' he said, intending a reproof.

'Hello,' said the boy. He had the ease of a creature never told it was a sinner from the womb.

'This is Thomas,' said Grace, without explanation. She stood close by the boy with the ease of long acquaintance, and seemed to Thomas they were in some way ranged against him – that it was possible to make out some connective tissue dissolving between himself and Grace, and re-forming between the other two.

'You busy?' said the boy to Grace. 'Do you want to do something? What do you want to do?'

She looked astonished. What did she want to do? 'I don't know,' she said. The thought had rarely occurred to her. She knew what she ought to do, and what she ought not to do; the idea that she was allowed to want anything at all was appalling.

'Want to go in there?' said the boy, gesturing towards Potter's Field, a place of absolute darkness between Bethesda and the lights on London Road. 'Someone's been lighting fires. Want to go and see?'

Grace looked at Thomas, who saw, superimposed on the child he loved, a woman arrived from further down her orbit, and exhausted by all her daily calculations of how to be good. She is seventeen, he thought, and eighteen soon – there's been so little liberty, and there may never be any more than this. The lights were out in Bethesda. The boy, despite the broadening shoulders and the scent of cigarettes sewn into his jacket with the coloured patches, did not seem unsafe. 'Go on, then,' said Thomas, 'just for a while. I'll go slowly, and you can catch me up.' Grace made a wordless sound of delight, and squeezed his arm with bruising gratitude – then the children (surely, thought Thomas, that was what they were) had gone, talking of fires. Thomas waited. The comet ticked on.

Meanwhile: Anne Macaulay in the kitchen of the house on Beechwood Avenue stood frowning over her copy of the *Essex Chronicle*: *insignificantly small,* Thomas had written, *and borne through stars.* This troubled her. The people of Bethesda gave the stars very little thought: God had riveted them in place on the fourth day, and that was that. To think any further entailed reaches of time and distance at odds with Genesis, and so at odds with God – she put the paper down.

Thomas Hart, she felt, was becoming untethered from the pulpit. She'd pray for him, but this was no bother: she'd prayed for him nightly since they first met on the day they buried Rachel Macaulay. After the funeral Anne had sat against Bethesda's chilly wall with the infant Grace in her arms, feeling not an ounce of affection for the squalling child. That had been ten days since she was summoned by her brother out of a life she supposed nobody would have envied or admired, but which she'd remembered then with the baffled wonder of a dreamer: a flat overlooking a wind-scoured hill; a small cold classroom she kept in good order and pupils, likewise; psalms sung in the chapel where she'd been born and baptised and where she'd still thought she might marry; an unreliable yellow car she'd loved. Then her brother had phoned, and said with dumb unemphatic syllables that Rachel had died, and was dead, and now there was a baby, and would she come down. So she did go down, on a single ticket to a county she despised, with its miserable fields of oil-seed rape and its new flatland towns. Her little life had ended for the sake of a scowling black-haired infant she didn't love, and at the funeral she'd mourned less for Rachel than for herself. This lack of goodness had compounded her grief with guilt, and she'd wept tearlessly as they brought out the silver tea urn and unhappy sandwiches, until Thomas Hart had quietly come to where she sat by the wall. 'I'm sorry for your loss,' he'd said, and the form of words was renewed when he said it, as if he grasped that Anne's loss was not that of the woman who'd laboured into her own grave, but of the gorse and the hill and the classroom and the fifteen children in it. 'I'm very sorry,' he'd said, and reached for the baby's fist, and shaken it twice as if they were business associates who had a prior understanding. 'We meet again,' he'd said; and Grace Macaulay, ten days old, had vomited on his sleeve.

Then seventeen years passed without notice, and now came Grace's familiar impatient rap at the door. 'It's late,' said Anne to Thomas, 'and the tea's gone cold in the pot. And whatever's happened?' she said, looking now at Grace, who it seemed had become disproportionately tired in the brief time she'd been gone. 'Is someone hurt?'

'Nobody is hurt,' said Thomas, 'and nothing has happened. The comet came out, that's all.'

'Auntie Anne,' said Grace, seeming smaller even than her small stature, 'can I go to bed?' Then without any apparent cause she began to cry in resigned quiet sobs; and Thomas, watching her wipe her nose on her sleeve as she went into the house, created fact by stating it: 'You see,' he said, 'she is really just a child.'

Midnight in Essex, and Hale–Bopp heading west in the company of Cassiopeia. Earlier that same day, in China and Mongolia and Siberia, a total eclipse of the sun had caused the comet to be visible shortly before noon. It turned anticlockwise every eleven and a quarter hours, and by the views and calculations of astronomers its tail gave the effect of ripples spreading from a stone thrown in a pond. Since perihelion wouldn't be attained until April Fool's Day, the comet had not yet reached its fullest magnitude; but it was bright enough, and it was new. So rats on the banks of the River Alder, conversing in a sunken shopping trolley, saw it, and paused, and took up their conversation; and pigeons on the roof of the Jackdaw and Crow saw it, and bloated themselves against the chill. In Lowlands House someone saw it, and in haste and terror spilled black paint on the steps. (Bethesda saw it and was untroubled, having its mind on higher matters.)

A fox in Potter's Field saw it, and began to caper and dash in the ruins, having no idea why. And what a reek there was hereabouts, the fox thought, kicking up cigarette butts and nosing at paper greased with scraps of food – what a reek, what a stench! It searched as it capered, and discovered a man sitting under a hazel, and leaning against the wall that divided Potter's Field from Bethesda's sanctified ground. He was occupied in unknotting rope. This was difficult, since all the knuckles of his hands were swollen, and his left thumb, seeming to have moved an inch or so down the wrist towards the elbow, was of no use. The watchful fox could not make out the size of the body inside the clothing, which consisted of several layers surmounted by a red velvet coat that must once have been a woman's. He wore torn jeans; he wore unmatched boots. The sun had stained his scalp through its thin pelt of white hair, and his eyes were blue. After a time he finished his business with the rope, raised himself with difficulty, and surveyed the hazel tree. It was young and pliant: it would do. He took a sheet of tarpaulin from a leather holdall, and with that same difficulty tied the tarpaulin to the hazel and made himself a shelter, then withdrew a piece of carpet, put it in the shade of the tarpaulin, and lay down to sleep. The fox, who was not by nature unkind, moved quietly on: there would be other larks elsewhere.

Thomas Hart on Lower Bridge Road, hearing the bark of foxes and the pain of rutting cats, sat by a dying fire. He averted his eyes from the corner of the room, since he was certain he'd see, if only he looked long enough, a black-browed woman cross-legged against the skirting board, scribbling on a square of paper: Maria Văduva Bell, going at her drawings like mad. Thomas thought of Grace with love and worry. She'd emerged from Potter's Field talking intently with the boy, who with exaggerated bows had left them by the lights on London Road, and gone capering home on his own. 'All right?' Thomas had said, understanding that she was both untouched, and altered absolutely.

'There'd been a fire,' she'd said, 'but it was out.' She smelt of cigarettes; her cheeks were flushed. Furtively, and feeling despondently like a spy, Thomas had assessed her hair, and her clothing, and found nothing more untidy than it had ever been.

'All right?' he'd said again, and with more meaning; and crossly she said that of course she was. Did he think she'd never spoken to a boy before – did he think she couldn't look after herself? Thomas certainly did think these things, but pointed instead at Orion loping over the roof of the Jack-daw and Crow. 'Be gone soon,' he'd said, 'and we won't see him again until it gets cold. Let's get you home.'

Now Thomas turned his mind from Grace, and permitted himself to think of James Bower, and to imagine that Maria Văduva, crouching in the corner in her yards of black bro-cade, looked up from her lunatic scribbles and solemnly tipped him a wink. I've been moving towards this all my life, thought Thomas: a stranger who knew me, and a scowling ghost taking up residence in the sitting room. Then he resumed his new habit of reciting to himself everything

James Bower had said, and all the looks and gestures that had signalled understanding, until he became ashamed of himself, and set aside his recollections, and began to write –

Thomas Hart
Lower Bridge Road
Aldleigh
30 March 1997

Dear James

I was so pleased to meet you the other day. I hope you remember my saying I have a photograph that might interest you? I'm going away for a few days, so I enclose it for you here: you'll see it's dated August 1888. Surely this woman standing just out of sight is our lost Maria? I've always kept it near to hand, and was scared of it when I was a child, thinking it was the Lowlands ghost and she was so lonely she'd followed me home. But perhaps she is both?

I also enclose a newspaper clipping you might find interesting. It's from the *Essex Chronicle* the week following the opening of Bethesda Chapel. I'm not a member there myself – I have one foot in sea and one in shore, so to speak – but go often out of habit, and out of the kind of love one might have for a family member. It's a strange place, I suppose, and the people keep themselves separate from the world – though I'm quite often in the world, and never feel quite at home either in the pew or out of it!

Yours sincerely

THOMAS HART

ALDLEIGH, ESSEX: CHAPEL OPENS FOR WORSHIP

ESSEX CHRONICLE,
25 AUGUST 1888

Religious affairs correspondent writes: The first service has taken place at the new Strict and Particular Baptist Chapel on London Road, Aldleigh. Members have until now met in the home of Pastor John Brandon, late of Wattisham, Suffolk. It is hoped the Chapel will attract those of the Non-conformist tradition in the town who currently lack a place of worship.

What's in a name?

Anglican readers puzzled by the term *Strict Baptist* should be advised the members are not themselves of a strict disposition; the point is a doctrinal and not a behavioural one, and refers to the question of *Particular Redemption*, and to the *Restriction of Communion* to those baptised by immersion. To this end, the Chapel is fitted with a baptistery capable of accommodating a fully grown adult.

'All welcome'

Services will take place at 11 a.m. and 6.30 p.m. on the Lord's Day, with Sunday School at 3 p.m., and Weekly Prayer Meetings on Wednesdays at 7 p.m. *All welcome.*

Lowlands House at dawn was unmoored on a pale sea. Mist drifting from the Alder had crossed the lawns, and now reached the steps and terrace as a soft tide coming in. A man in a yellow hat was on his knees, scrubbing at black paint spilled on the steps; as he worked the hat appeared repeatedly above the pale bank, and the effect was that of a signal transmitted and never received.

'I feel,' said James Bower, who was unbuttoning his coat, 'as if I were a boy again.' He held a bunch of keys in his right hand, and these rattled in the stultifying silence of the queer wet light. 'A boy,' said James, 'solving a mystery. What's this, and what does it mean? What does it have to do with Maria Văduva? Perhaps she stood here once. But where did she go, and what was she doing with her bits of paper? You probably think I'm being childish.'

'Not at all,' said Thomas Hart.

The men had entered through a vacant doorway from which brass hinges had been broken. Rags of mist entered at ankle height and dissipated quickly. A further door was set in the opposing wall, and this was padlocked shut. Boarded windows let in narrow shafts of light, revealing wallpaper that recoiled from the rotting plaster, and obscenities painted without much conviction. A long table on turned legs was pushed between the open door and the locked one; a pot of black paint was on it. At the table's furthest end, James Bower had made himself a place of work. A file marked VĂDUVA was propped against the wall beside the Bethesda photograph, and Maria looked hopelessly out towards the blinded windows. A grey marble mantelpiece with a deep shelf enclosed a vacant fireplace, and dead moths were ranged there like ornaments in the dust; a chandelier hung listing from its hook, and stripped of its glass drops made a grasping iron claw. Absent paintings had left their vacancies on wallpaper peeling like the bark of silver birch, and on the wall beside the window a black symbol, recently painted, dripped on floorboards that warped and gaped. The men regarded it.

'I've seen this before,' said Thomas, with the note of an apology. He was conscious of the proximity of the other man, who still had about him the scent of his morning shower, and the coffee he'd drunk after it. He'd nicked himself shaving, and Thomas looked with disproportionate solicitude at the bit of tissue sticking to the cut. 'Someone was painting it on Bethesda's door. They seemed quite thin and frightened, and did a bad job. This one is better.'

'There's another painted on the steps,' said James. 'We're having trouble getting rid of it. But of course it's only students, it's just pranks.'

'I'm not sure,' said Thomas, returning to the symbol on the wall: crossed lines surmounted with a teardrop, signifying nothing. 'But I'm glad I came.'

James took his phone out of a leather case clipped to his belt, and looked at it, and sighed. 'The men are late, as always – they'll leave early, as always.' Dismally he began to speak of regulations concerning the preservation of listed buildings, and all this was incomprehensible to Thomas: 'I'm sure it will be all right,' he said, with optimism he knew to be both unhelpful and unfounded. Then the man on the terrace came in, removing his hat as if he stood on sanctified ground. He was young and tired. 'The paint won't come off,' he said, 'you would think it had been there decades, not an hour or two.'

'What about a pressure washer?' said James, drifting from Thomas in body and spirit, and peering between boards at the marred stone steps. 'What about some kind of solvent?'

'Perhaps it has been there for decades,' said Thomas, 'only nobody noticed'; but James was too preoccupied for this whimsy. So Thomas left him to his business, and paced about the room conscious of a kind of pricking unease that seemed to have no cause. It was possible to think the dead moths were rousing in the dust and that the silence beyond the pad-locked door was that of a creature holding its breath – are you there, Maria, thought Thomas, have you followed me all the way from Lower Bridge Road? He turned to the window, where slips of light entered between the boards, and a pan-elled window seat retained rags of its upholstery. Where the floorboards bucked with the sinking of the house, the window seat had split. Thomas gazed at the fissure. Behind him James Bower receded on his private orbit, speaking dully of what ought to be done, and when it ought to be done by. The splitting seat split wider as Thomas pressed the floor-boards down.

Then a rat with a severed tail passed between his feet: with swivelling black eyes it made a study of the intruder, shrugged him off, and went about its business. Abruptly it slipped between two panels of the window seat, showing its little stump. There was silence. It was gone absolutely. A peculiar loneliness settled on Thomas. The other men had drifted from the room, and were examining the steps; the pitch and rhythm of their voices travelled clearly through the mist, but their words were obscured. 'Where did you go?' asked Thomas of the rat. No answer. He went down on his knees. 'Where did you go?' Dust on the floorboards, thickly felting in the corners; moss where the wood was damp. The press of his knee caused the split to open further. Thomas listened with longing to the rat's diligent clever feet, and detected also the impression of paper rustling, as if a reader had grown impatient with a book. He put his hand into the seat and patted blindly about in the chilly cavity, anticipating the rump of the rat, or possibly an iron nail. He held his nerve. He reached paper. He grasped it. Distantly the rat made noises. Thomas pulled his clenched fist quickly back, and the split wood rasped his wrist. The little pain was welcome. He looked at the paper he held. 'Oh, James,' he said. 'James?' Carefully he stood, and went to the table. The mist was clearing from the lawns – the light was less diffuse, and noises arrived from traffic on London Road.

James came in. He'd taken off his coat, and the scent of soap was fading from his body. 'What have you been doing?' he said. 'What's that?'

'There was a rat,' said Thomas, concealing blood on his wrist with his cuff. He put the paper down.

'What is it?' said James with pleasant authority. 'What have you found?' There were three sheets. Two of these were written in a familiar hand on fine blue notepaper, and in the poor light certain words asserted themselves – *Lucifer*, for example, and *goose-down pillows*. 'Oh, Maria!' said James, as if exasperated with a friend. The third fragment was a smaller sheet of card, folded with precision; when Thomas opened it, the paper split on the fold and severed the square. 'Oh,' he said. Together they attended to it in silence. Here again was a circle drawn in black ink, enclosing a dark blot, and now divided into hemispheres; here again something inked at the rim, not possible to make out. The natural thing would be to bring the halves together, but Thomas was disinclined to touch the paper, and participate in Maria Văduva's madness.

A rotting board, dislodged by ivy and time, fell from a window and broke on the terrace outside. The men flinched. 'Maria!' said Thomas, feigning terror to conceal genuine fright. Wind entered, bringing voices. 'There's somebody in there,' a woman said. 'Somebody's in there. Didn't I tell you? Didn't I say?'

It was certainly a woman's voice, and not a child's; but Thomas knew it. He said, as if the sin were his, 'I know who this is.' He put his face to the breach, and looked. The mist was clearing into shining particles that revealed wet lawns and solitary oaks, and revealed also the scarlet fabric of a red skirt held out from the body by stiff petticoats, and a pair of jeans torn over the knee. The skirt drifted over the jeans.

'A friend of mine,' said Thomas to James, 'and a friend of hers.' He went out. James went with him.

Now: mild March weather, and nothing strange in it. Yellow aconites arriving at the foot of the oaks; the drooping wire fence plainly visible, and broken in new places. Grace Macaulay in a flowered shawl stood on the steps, and Nathan stood with her. The smell of Silk Cut adhered to their clothes. 'Oh,' said Grace, seeing Thomas approaching, and it struck him with resentment that she'd never before greeted him with disappointment. Well, he thought: you've wrecked my morning and I've wrecked yours. Fair's fair. She looked at James. 'Who's this, then?'

'James Bower,' said Thomas. 'Grace Macaulay. And this is Nathan.' The boy hopped from foot to foot, animated by cold or by feeling, and grown broader in the days since Thomas had seen him last, so that the sleeves of his denim jacket were too short on his wrists.

'Yes,' said Grace, examining James. 'Yes, but who is he? What are you doing?'

'We are solving a mystery,' said James, examining Grace with pleasure, and becoming extraordinarily handsome. 'Would you like to see?'

'Is somebody dead?' This was Nathan, wandering to the window, looking in. 'Did somebody die in there?'

Grace tugged with a possessive gesture at Nathan's sleeve. 'Thomas thinks a woman went off her head,' she said, 'and vanished. He wants to find out all about it, so he can put it in his newspaper, which is the only reason he ever does anything.'

'That is true,' said Thomas mildly.

'Why don't you come on in,' said James. 'See what Thomas found.' But no, thought Thomas, don't come in, leave us alone. The mist was gone. He could no longer smell the soap on James Bower's body.

'Come on,' said James, 'come in'; and Thomas watched Grace run ahead, tripping on her skirt. She stood under the lightless chandelier. 'I knew it would be like this,' she said. 'All my life I've wanted to be in here, and they wouldn't let me. Well I'm here now, aren't I?' She delighted in the ceiling, the shattered windows, the obscene graffiti on the plaster; she delighted in Nathan, who leaped backwards on to the window seat, swaying as the wood cracked.

'Come and see what Thomas found,' said James. He took them to the table where Maria looked over his files: 'See here,' he said, then silenced himself with an exclamation. Quickly Thomas came forward. 'What is it?' he said.

'It was here,' said James. 'It was right here a moment ago – what have you done with it,' he said, turning to Thomas, 'what have you done with it?' The photograph of Maria Văduva had fallen face down on the table beside the file, but the severed square and the illegible letter were gone.

66

'What's happened?' said Grace. 'What have you lost?'

'I found something under the window,' said Thomas, showing her the wound on his wrist, 'but now it isn't there.'

'Did you take it?' said James, looking at the children one after the other. Abruptly he seemed remote and stern, and desirable because of this; so Thomas turned away in shame.

'I didn't take anything!' said Nathan. He leaped down from the window seat; he raised his arms: 'I didn't see anything to take.'

'He didn't,' said Grace, 'he isn't a thief!'

'Was it the wind?' said Thomas, stooping to look under the table. No paper down there, but a cracked glass disc. He left it.

'Listen,' said James, 'there isn't any wind.' They listened. Sound only of traffic, of scrubbing on the steps.

'This house,' said James Bower, 'has taken against me. And what have you done to your hand – you're bleeding – why didn't you say?' His attention affected Thomas like tenderness. Briefly the whole morning struck him again as miraculous, and he was unable to speak.

Grace shook out her skirts and said, 'What's through there, then?' She was looking at the second door. It had been unlocked, and stood open. Through the aperture it was possible to see a pale wall diminishing into darkness, and dust moving in eddies. The padlock still hung on its chain.

'Christ!' said James Bower, and received from Grace and Thomas a double reproof. 'What the hell is going on in here?' he said, laughing, and shaking his head. 'Did you hear that? Was that footsteps?'

Together the children and the men listened, and persuaded themselves there were footsteps in the adjoining room, and that every quarter of the house rang with the footsteps of all its residents and visitors.

'Wasn't it always open?' said Grace. 'Wasn't it always like that?'

Nathan crossed to the door, and examined the padlock. 'Didn't actually lock it, you see, didn't turn the wheels. You have to actually turn it,' he said, looking at James with kindly pity for the frailties of old men. 'It doesn't work unless you lock it, shall I show you?'

Solemnly James said, 'Thank you. But I think I understand.'

'Then somebody is in here,' said Grace. Her hands were on her hips. 'Somebody is painting on the walls and stealing things.' She stood beside Nathan in the shadow of the open door; and it seemed to Thomas that he saw them as children and adults simultaneously, their bodies flickering between time past, and time to come. It suits me to think them children, he thought with pain, but they are not: here is a man with cigarettes in his pocket and God knows what else, here is a woman defying me to defy her – 'It won't be safe,' said Thomas, 'nothing will be safe through there.'

'Things fall,' said James, 'and are lost. Men have been going in and out.'

'Certainly,' said Thomas, 'things do fall'; but the atmosphere in the room had altered, as if each were guilty, and conscious of being watched.

Then men came tramping adamantly into the hall, and a general consensus arose among them: bracing was required, certain reinforcements in certain places, it was a sodding wonder the chimney hadn't dropped into the hearth.

'Come on, then,' said James, 'let's go'; and with a gesture impossible to refuse removed them all from the room.

Out on the Lowlands terrace Thomas fell into despondency. Something had been gained in that room, and quickly lost – 'Besides,' he said, turning to Grace, 'shouldn't you be at school?'

'Yes,' said Grace. 'But I have sinned.'

'Thomas,' said James Bower, swinging a hard hat on a strap, 'I'd better get on. I'm glad you could come.' He put on the hat, and this made him ridiculous. 'Off you go,' he said, taking them all in with his kindly dismissal. 'Maria's bound to turn up soon. She always does.' Thomas received a quick touch on the shoulder, and felt this was longer than it ought to have been, and concealed something in it; so his despondency lifted.

Now there was neither mist nor sunlight. All the world was uniformly dull, the brassy aconites tarnished, the palsied limbs of the oaks leafless and dry. A solitary point of colour was coming across the park towards them, seeming at that distance to bob aimlessly like a plastic ball on the surface of a pond – a pink thing, unnaturally bright, resolving itself in due course into a long full-skirted coat fastened with buttons, everything that same flat, lifeless pink. It was a woman, speaking volubly in long unemphatic sentences, everything about her insistently artificial, her hair set like curls of butter back from a white forehead; and walking beside her, seeming to be formed as she walked out of the drab colours of the Essex soil, turning again and again to her companion as if enraptured by all that unbroken silly speech, was Anne Macaulay.

Dear child – now it is June, and you will think I have forgotten you in your fine rooms at Foolish Street – and indeed you think correctly! I forget what I ought to remember, and remember most clearly what I most wish to forget – so I have perhaps been mad, though I should like to know what committees of men in their good wool coats set about their taxonomies of sanity, and say this man is sane, and this woman, but not this man, or that one! Indeed I believe my body has lost its reason, and not my mind – my intellect I assure you is entirely undiminished, yet there is at all times a harsh note in my ears, like that of a musician sounding a broken instrument, and the palms of my hands become numb, or pricked all over with invisible pins – I sleep and wake a dozen times and on waking my heart is lodged throbbing in my throat – meanwhile Lucifer at the window attends my mornings and beckons me out and is fastened by the Belt of Venus and beneath him the shadow we cast upon the universe is so dreadful and so immense there is a dark place extending far beyond the reach of my vision –

[All that was yesterday, and is done. I was induced to sleep, and woke to find Lucifer departed. This has been a great relief to me – I never could resist that light, for all that it disturbs my rest – for that is the consensus: that there is no ill in me that cannot be solved with three goose-down pillows and what John Bell's doctor dispenses from his bag – I am ashamed of my distress, and ashamed of the cause, and ashamed of these pages – so I remove them and hide them, and will not send them, that I may keep the good opinion of my friend – nonetheless I do confess myself to myself: MV]

'Do you think so,' said Anne Macaulay, 'do you really think so?' It is an ordinary Tuesday, she thought, and I'm going to have lunch with my friend. She flushed with childish pride: her own friend, acquired not in Bethesda but in the world. This was Lorna Greene, dazzlingly alive in pink satin, whose kitten-heeled shoes audibly struck the wet pavements with the noise of clacking teeth; who'd just then been saying how much she admired Anne's winter coat, with its black felt collar folded over rubbed grey wool, and how well it suited her.

Had Anne believed in chance, she might have said that chance was how they met: by virtue of having waited so often at the same bus stop that in the end not speaking would have been stranger than speaking. That Anne should notice Lorna against the granite of the nearby war memorial, the municipal bins, was not surprising. All winter she'd dressed in rustling layers of mauve and pink, and set her yellow hair in curls that resisted the weather; she wore a powdery scent that never faded from the folds of her clothes, and at all times looked about her with the bright assessing gaze of a blackbird. That Anne should herself be noticed she felt to be astounding, and she'd received Lorna's first attention with a confused shyness that looked aloof. But Lorna had pecked smilingly away, seeking her out in well-modulated tones from which the Essex accent had been excised: she was Scottish? How lovely. She lived on Beechwood Avenue? Such a lovely road, with its silver birches. How lovely to have a niece, to be grey-haired, to have a brother named Ronald, to have once been a teacher, to attend chapel – quickly Anne became 'dear Anne', and it had been impossible not to soften against the endearments, the praise, the unsought gift of a dragonfly pin with a crystal thorax and wing. They'd exchanged phone numbers; they'd taken walks. Now they were going to lunch at the Jackdaw and Crow ('my treat, dear Anne!'), because it had not been possible for Anne to explain that she'd never set foot inside a pub and had never intended to do so. Besides (she exculpated herself), nothing was ever chance, but only providence, and she might win a soul for Christ – 'Do you really think it suits me?' she said, looking down at her sleeve, and thinking that perhaps after all neither her coat nor herself were as drab as she had feared.

Meanwhile Thomas Hart, in carriage D of the 10.42 from Liverpool Street, submitted dumbly to the affection of a red-haired young man with whom he'd spent the past three days. 'You live in Aldleigh too?' the boy had said that morning in New Cross, delighted by coincidence and the prospect of further proximity to Thomas Hart, whose age and diffident expert affection he liked. 'Awful little place,' he'd said, shuddering as he dressed, 'we should move'; and Thomas had quickly concealed his disquiet. He survived, as he put it to himself, by dividing his nature from his soul; so he left his nature in London on the station platform, and picked up his soul in Aldleigh as if it were left luggage. How he could explain to this ardent boy that no, he didn't want to get coffee, and sit together on the train; that yes, he was aware of the various places in Essex they could visit and he disliked them all? So arm in arm they caught the train, and 'Nobody cares, do they,' the young man had said, 'I got a black eye a few years back, but all a bit different from your day, I'm sure.' Then with thoughtless touches, never having believed himself a sinner, he'd told Thomas of his ambitions and sorrows and revenges, all of which struck Thomas as petty, and only became pettier as the train passed Stratford, Shenfield, Chelmsford; as Aldleigh cast its shadow on the line. Now it was no longer possible to conceal his distaste for the boy's company – for his youth, his thin ideas, his clothing and speech, all of which marked him out in a way Thomas himself had never been marked out – and imperceptibly the red head had moved away from the tweed shoulder, and leaned now against the smeared window (and on the platform at Colchester a black-browed woman rapped fiercely on the glass: *You coward, Thomas Hart!*).

Then they were at Aldleigh, and there was Upper Bridge Road in view, there was the Jackdaw and Crow – there, if passengers cared to look, a further view of a white house sinking into the lawns. Already the boy, resilient in youth, had recovered his brief petulance at a rare rejection, and was preoccupied with his prospects that night, and all the nights after – 'Well, then,' said Thomas, tearing up his ticket and instinctively looking for James Bower as they came out under the railway arch, 'I'll leave you here'; and he held out his hand in a rote gesture of good manners. The boy looked at it, and laughed, and out of a kind of spiteful mischief kissed Thomas on the mouth, noisily and not without compassion; then with a last hard, admonitory embrace slipped into the incurious crowd.

'Thomas!' said Anne with delight, gesturing to the friend she saw standing with a curious distracted look on the opposing

73

pavement by the station. Lunch had been a pleasure, and the pub nothing like the den of iniquity she'd imagined, though the table had been sticky and it had all smelt unpleasantly of smoke. She'd steeled her courage to say a silent grace before she ate, and been glad to explain to watchful Lorna why she'd done so, and even gladder to find herself quizzed over fish and chips and tea about Bethesda. 'How lovely,' Lorna Greene had said, acquiring a kind of avid look, as if Anne had been showing her jewels on her fingers, 'how lovely to have a faith, I do rather envy you, dear Anne: you remind me of my mother, who could recite whole psalms – and of course I'm really a terribly spiritual person, though I wouldn't say religious – you must let me come to church with you' – she'd yearned below the painted lids of her eyes – 'I have always felt there is something missing from my life, and out there, you know' – she looked with distaste over Anne's shoulder, where the bowed window of the Jackdaw and Crow gave a view of men and women streaming off the London train – 'out there' – she shuddered with a delicate motion of her blouse that let out puffs of scent, and suggested that briefly she had seen some tawdry thing.

So Anne had left the pub with gratitude, and the sensation that she'd pleased God and pleased herself: of course (she said) Lorna was welcome at Bethesda at any time, in fact there was to be a prayer meeting the following day. Then – upright among disconsolate crowds returning to serve out their sentences in offices and institutions – Anne had seen the unmistakable form of Thomas Hart in his suit of fawn linen, tearing up his platform ticket and frowning over some problem. He'll be thinking about the moon, thought Anne, he seems these days to have nothing else on his mind. 'Thomas!' she said, waving with pleasure and a curious sense of relief. 'Thomas!' But traffic intervened, and a fretful woman with a pram obscured the view, and when the way was clear again Anne had seen he'd gone. 'That was a friend of mine,' she explained, turning with apology to Lorna. 'In fact he comes to chapel, and you will meet him.'

'That man?' said Lorna, patting at her hair, fastening the plastic buttons on her coat. 'That tall man, with his back to you?'

'His name is Thomas Hart,' said Anne. 'He writes for the *Essex Chronicle.*'

'And he goes to your church? Dear me – I should have thought' – Lorna gave a curious delighted titter, which Anne could not decipher, and which was quickly concealed – 'but how terribly surprising! Well, we shall see' – she kissed the other woman with precision on the centre of each cheek – 'we shall see. God bless,' she said, seeming to have already acquired Bethesda's habits of speech as if by osmosis, and went tripping back towards the town on kitten heels that surely could not have been comfortable. Anne had stood for a moment in the shade of the Jackdaw and Crow, patting her cheek. She felt that Lorna had left on her the imprint of her babyish scent and dry expert kisses, and left also a sensation of flattered pleasure, but equally one of unease.

Grace Macaulay, leaving school the following day, thought she might go home by way of Potter's Field. Five times she'd met Nathan here, because they'd planned to meet, or because (she thought) it was providence their paths should cross at certain times on certain days. That they'd become friends seemed to her both natural and miraculous. From the minute she'd seen him blinking behind the hard dark ranks of Bethesda's pews, she'd felt he belonged to her: evidently God had ordained the whole business. So it was natural that he'd come to seek her out with his box of chocolates and his cigarettes, and it was natural that if his journey home from school intersected with hers they'd walk together, and sit for half an hour in Potter's Field with their backs to Bethesda, and that he'd teach her how to use deodorant and chewing gum to conceal the effects of a shared Silk Cut. But equally he seemed to have arrived out of a world whose laws and habits and even clothing were inscrutable and sometimes frightening. When he spoke about Southend United or *Emmerdale* or the glorious tragedy of Euro 96, she was ashamed to admit she grasped the significance of these words only vaguely and with effort; *I bet he drinks Carling Black Label,* he sometimes said inscrutably, or *Hasta la vista, baby,* and Grace would feel her own strangeness and isolation so keenly all colour would drain from the day. Often he had with him a Walkman and a pair of blue foam headphones he'd hold awkwardly to her ear and his, introducing her to music that unsettled and thrilled her, and set out to evoke sympathy for the devil from her Baptist soul. Occasionally she would seem to become the sole focus of his interest, and he'd interrogate her with the attention of a student making notes: why did she have to wear a hat on Sundays? Why did she never wear jeans? Why didn't she have a television? Was it true she'd never been to the cinema? When she answered, she said either it was because her father said so, or because God did; and as she answered it struck her that she was often unable to tell the difference.

Now she'd come to London Road: here was Bethesda, here was Potter's Field. She put herself between them on the pavement, where the chapel's iron railings terminated at a drooping wire fence. Two places of worship, she thought, turning from the chapel towards Potter's Field, looking with hope through the thicket of buddleia and nettle for Nathan's glinting head or the coloured patches on his jacket; but he was as absent from her as the east was from the west. So this was all for nothing, she thought, looking down at the costume she'd assembled – the black skirt trimmed with ribbon at the hem, the belt that had once been a curtain tassel, and a pendant of dripping silver bees – everything amounted to more or less nothing, unless Nathan saw it. How abject this was! Did women really assemble themselves out of the parts they thought most likely to be wanted? Was that love's requirement? If so, she'd have none of it.

Nothing now in the weeds and litter to interest her, and her whole life consisting of her own disappointment: helpless against the arrival of her bad temper, she kicked a crushed Red Stripe can at her feet. It struck a broken breezeblock and startled a pair of jays that lifted off for Lowlands with their noise of a football rattle. It seemed also to startle some other creature beyond the shrubs and bracken, back where a stripped hazel grew against the wall. The air was bright and clear, but all the same there arrived the sense that something dark and furtive had taken up residence in Potter's Field: it'll be the Lowlands ghost, she thought, nobody had loved her, either. She shivered, and wished Thomas were at hand. But now she saw that nearby a midden had accrued, of greasy paper packets and bottles and filthy scraps of cloth. What use would a ghost have for these? There was the movement again, and she saw it was a blue tarpaulin tilting downward like the sail of a sinking ship, with a leather satchel under it. Legs extended from the shelter, and she became conscious of the scent of an unwashed body that was peculiarly sweet. 'Hello?' she said. Silence in Potter's Field, and beyond the chapel wall. 'All right in there?' It struck her that perhaps she'd find some piteous vagrant, who'd look with gratitude and love at his benevolent visitor, all marvellous hair and kindness – 'I won't hurt you,' she said.

A man came out on hands and knees. He stood. He was extremely tall, and wore a scarlet coat, which he pulled about himself. The effect was majestic, and Grace felt the balance of power tilt in his favour; but feeling this was her land, she said, 'What are you doing here?'

The man said nothing. He shivered in his coat.

'Why are you shivering?' said Grace. 'It's spring – look: there are some daffodils – and it's not cold. Are you ill?' Was he perhaps deaf? This was unfortunate. 'Well? Are you ill?' He shook his head, then bent to assemble hazel twigs on a scorched pile of masonry. He tried to strike a flame. Grace watched. The endeavour was hopeless. She saw the wrecked thumb, and the swollen knuckles over which the skin was strained and white. Something disquieting, too, about the fingertips – she looked again – they were curiously soft and bulbous, their nails reduced to slivers: 'For goodness' sake,' she said, 'give me that.' She struck a quick flame. Pity made her impatient and cross. The fire took; the man, not seeming grateful, put a scorched trivet on it, and set a tin cup of water to boil.

'Do you need anything to eat?' she said. She felt herself to be gracious and kind. 'Shall I go to the shops?' The man looked at her with uncomprehending sadness, out of eyes as peculiarly vivid as Nathan's, then began to cry. This was appalling. 'Stop that,' she said, 'it never helps.' The water boiled. He made himself a thin black brew, and offered it to Grace with a gesture he evidently hoped would be refused. She did refuse. He drank.

'I'm Grace Macaulay.' Lightly she thumped her chest. 'I'm nearly eighteen. You?' Slowly the man shook his head. 'All right,' she said. 'You don't need to tell me. See that building over there?' She nodded at Bethesda. He looked, and began to cry again. 'It's called Bethesda,' she said. She recalled her Sunday School lessons. 'Bethesda was a pool in the New Testament. Sick people were taken to lie in the pool, and wait for angels to come and disturb the water, and heal them. I live there, more or less. It's my chapel.'

He looked quietly at Bethesda. 'You live there?' he said.

The jays returned to the hazel and set about berating Grace for her sins. 'Of course not,' she said. The fire had gone out. 'I live in an ordinary house.' Then it struck her that Christ, if happening by Aldleigh that day, would certainly expect her to give up her bed; but she didn't want this man of sorrows with his rank-smelling velvet in her room. This thought was painful: how hard it was to be good, when goodness really wasn't in her nature – and at any moment God might punish her, for example by taking Nathan away!

79

It was getting dark. Low in the north-west a pale blur appeared: it might have been the comet, it might have been a scrap of cloud. 'I think you should lie down. Are you safe here? No one can see you from the road.' The man stood, and his magnificent dereliction reminded Grace of images she'd once seen of elephants ransacked for their ivory stumbling hopelessly about, disgraced and severed from their tribe – 'I'm so sorry,' she said, and found to her astonishment that now she was also in tears. 'I really am ever so sorry.' She hoped he wouldn't hold out his hand, because it was ugly and broken and she didn't want to touch it; but he only bowed, and this was so deep and courtly a motion, and the velvet coat was so sumptuous and bright, that quickly she was laughing then, and bowing too: 'All right,' she said. 'I'd better go. I expect I'll see you again.' God, she felt, would approve of her kindness, but she ought not to have noticed the ugliness of the man's hands, still less recoiled from them. She held her goodness only lightly, and how easily she might drop and break it. The depth of her frown induced a headache. The comet was at her back. She went home.

That same evening the man in Potter's Field was woken by headlights from cars arriving beyond the wall. Watchful in his shelter, he saw Bethesda's door standing open, and heard music fading towards the traffic lights. Women and men solemnly progressed across the car park, and there was a kind of blood relation in their measured tread and grave smiles of greeting. He saw the girl who'd visited him go hastily in, looking from under the drooping brim of a velvet hat to the place where he was sitting, followed by a thin woman in a knitted cap, and a tall man with hair like a dandelion clock who looked about, as if at any moment some malefactor might steal his Bible. Then the last car came, and a woman stepped out, tottering because her pink skirt was too tight and her pink heels were too high. Stooping to the mirror of the car, she adjusted her pink hat; then she headed for the chapel with a constrained and ingratiating gait.

When she was gone, and the man was certain of his solitude, he came out from his shelter, stumbling because he was drunk. He cursed in his own language, and fell against Bethesda's wall, which gave beneath him as if the mortar were wet, and the builder lately gone on his lunch. The man painfully righted himself, and looked at the wall, which now bowed outward at the upper course of bricks. Compacted soil had shifted and broken open at the foundation, and cursing his own folly the man worked at it with his foot in hope of concealing his transgression. But as he worked, the soil seemed only more determined to make a breach and offer him a view. And there was a view, where the last course of bricks was disrupted by the hazel root – the man, exclaiming to himself, knelt with sounds less of curses than of invocations. He'd seen, animated by streetlight, a shining object, man-made and improbable, and insisting itself on him as if by an act of will. He brushed at the soil. This was difficult. He raised his hands, berated them, and began again. Soon it was possible to make out the corner of a metal box, buried by mistake or by design in the foundations of the wall, its shallow lid sealed with mud. He began to pull at it, but could find no purchase, and besides he was no match for the sullen Essex clay. Then one by one the lights on London Road went out, and the gleam in the soil receded. The man sighed, and stood, and returned to the tarpaulin and the square of carpet. He'd try again tomorrow: he'd do better.

Thomas Hart stood in the dismal kitchen at the *Essex Chronicle* making tea, and thinking of James Bower. The daily papers were scattered about, but Thomas saw nothing of strikes threatened by the Fire Brigades Union, or the race-hate leaflets that had done the rounds in Harlow; and it made no difference to him that the current prime minister was likely totting up the cost of removing his furniture from Downing Street: he was still in Lowlands, cloistered in fog, attending to the scent of a clean body inside a cheap coat. Abruptly it struck him there was something abject in the circuitous devotion of his thoughts, and he shook himself as a dog shakes off rain; then saw just beyond the limit of his vision a movement in the kitchen. He pictured Maria Văduva picking at pearl buttons on her black silk cuff, having followed him doggedly from Lower Bridge Road: *I wonder if you have a weakness*, she said, *for what you cannot reach?*

'Evidently,' said Thomas; then in another office someone turned the radio on, and idiot laughter did away with Maria and desire. Thomas gave himself an admonishing shake, and turning for the door was startled to find a silent girl standing at the kitchen entrance. The strip-light lent a sulphurous cast to her loose white clothes, and to a complexion marred by spots extending from her left cheek to her neck. She looked frightened.

'Good morning,' Thomas said. The kettle boiled. He poured it out. 'Perhaps you'd like a cup of tea?'

Steadily and with a kind of insolent fear she looked at him. Her pupils were blown to the rim of a pale iris, and she had the sour smell of an untended body.

'Have you come to see anyone in particular?'

She made a minute adjustment to the set of her head. Thomas took this to mean that she had, and that she'd found him.

'All right,' said Thomas. 'Why don't you come to my office, and tell me why you're here?' He turned away, and with untroubled attention put the pot and two cups on a tray, and carried this across the narrow hall to his office. Here he sat and surveyed the visitor. 'We'll give it a minute or two,' he said. 'Take any seat you like.'

She was perhaps twenty. Her foot was braced against the carpet, and her leg vibrated violently; she had the quality of an animal that might either bolt in fear, or spring at him.

'Perhaps you have a story for me,' he said, and pushed a cup towards her. A sluggish drop of blood was rising from the worst of her spots. 'I'm a writer, you see. For the newspaper. I expect that's why you've come.'

The girl scowled at the sharp note he'd struck, then took a notebook from the desk and tore out a sheet of paper. Silently she looked at him, then drew the symbol which had been painted on Bethesda's door, and on the wall and steps at Lowlands House.

'Ah,' said Thomas. 'I see. It was you. But what have you been doing at Lowlands?'

'I live there.'

'You ought to live elsewhere. The roof is unsafe. The damp is shocking. You could dissolve in it.'

'Nowhere is safe,' she said. 'You said so. I read it in the

83

paper. I saw your name. Bad omens, you said. Dark companions.'

'I see,' said Thomas. The symbol disassembled and remade itself, and took on the form of a comet moving down its orbit and traversed by a cross. 'Yes, I can see it now: this is all about Hale–Bopp.' Understanding amplified his unease. The greasy bird-print on the window flinched.

'I never heard of it before,' the girl said, trembling in her chair. 'Never thought about things like that – plenty to be scared of down here, isn't there, plenty of ways to hurt yourself – but it's in all the papers now, we've only got a few days left.'

'But there is nothing to be afraid of. It will come near us, that is all – it will pass between us and the sun at an immense distance –'

'Poisonous gases, you said, and pestilence – wars, and rumours of wars! Better to burn everything up now,' she said, reaching for her pocket, 'better to go before we all get sick and die.'

'That's only ever superstition,' said Thomas. 'It is just the fears of children, and people who think like children.' (But vaguely, as if it were a distant memory and not a newly arrived thought, it occurred to him that lately there'd been the sense of the world tilted a little further on its axis.)

With difficulty the girl pulled a handful of papers from her pocket, threw these on his desk, and rubbed her hands together with the motion of a fly. Thomas looked at the documents. They were foxed and buckled, and by the light of his desk lamp he made out familiar handwriting in familiar ink: *I do confess myself to myself: MV.*

'What's this? What are you doing with these? These are Maria Văduva's letters: you have stolen them.'

'I saw you,' she said. 'I was watching, I saw you with that man. I don't think you know what's coming. I don't think you have any idea at all. I think it's better to burn it all up –' Then she took a plastic lighter from her pocket, and set the paper on fire.

Thomas watched the ember and the thread of smoke with dumb surprise. 'What are you doing?' he said. 'What have you done?' Burning ash blew across the desk, and he patted at it; the fire had consumed itself, and the letter was gone to illegible air.

Now the girl's body was rigid and composed. 'Better to burn,' she said, looking at the muddy sky showing between the plastic slats of the blind. 'Better than all this waiting.' She stood, and the look she gave him then was frightening, because it was kind; and as she left he heard her making private incantations until her voice was consumed by the nearby radio.

Thomas sat for a long time watching the door. 'What's happening lately,' he said in a kind of exasperated despair, 'what are they putting in the water these days? And what a farce!' he said, afraid that in fact it had all been farcical: Maria Văduva and her maddened letters, the arrival of James Bower, the intimacy of derelict rooms in a derelict house. Outside a wind was getting up. It crossed the windowsill, and reached the ashes on the desk; carefully it disturbed a bit of paper that had come like Daniel unmarked out of the fire. The paper shifted by inches towards Thomas: 'Ah,' he said, 'thank you,' and picked it up. It was the quartered segment of a formless blot, contained within a circle inked with childish precision, letters inked at the rim; a remaining fragment of the signature MARIA VĂDUVA truncated by the paper's torn edge. 'Thank you,' Thomas said again, smiling at his own foolishness; and as he examined it the letters at the rim became larger – seemed actually to display themselves to him.

Then understanding came. It surprised him like joy; his body responded and summoned up the blood. The wind died back. Thomas turned and turned the document, and saw there not the formless scribbles of an unhappy woman, but the birthplace of stars. He picked up the phone.

James Bower had never troubled to imagine how Thomas Hart lived, but it struck him as he came to Lower Bridge Road the following day that it was all he might have expected. He was conscious of an interest that was more or less anthropological, as if the other man were the citizen of a province of which nobody else had ever heard. And how strange it was to acquire a friend at fifty, when life was already portioned out! Fondly his wife had taken to calling Thomas 'your ghost', saying after all she'd never seen him, and neither had their friends and acquaintances – in fact that she suspected her husband of roaming the grounds of Lowlands in the company of a spectre in brogues. And it was an odd business, wasn't it, thought James: no other man wrote letters when a call or an email would do, or invited friends to lunch on weekday afternoons. But since everything Thomas wore and said and did seemed strange, all this was no stranger than that he existed at all.

    Now James sat in a shadowy room on Lower Bridge Road, and was surprised by nothing. Lamps doubled their light on the polished surface of the sideboard and the table, and white tulips collapsed over the lip of a vase. Spring was strengthening in the streets, but the fire had been lit for the look of the thing, and the tiles that flanked the fire were embossed with yellow flowers that seemed on the verge of unfolding. There was no stereo or television visible, only books of every conceivable kind piled about, and on the further corner of the table an expensive laptop computer that struck James as vaguely malevolent, because it was so unlikely. Now and then a train departed Aldleigh for London and

86

rattled the knives and forks, and this would rouse James to a moment of troubling clarity; then quickly all the languid effects of the fragrant room and of Thomas's pleasant melodious voice would return. 'Tell me again,' he said. 'Tell me what you think it means.'

'It means Maria Văduva was not mad. Look,' said Thomas, handing James the scorched scrap of paper with the black blot on it. 'You see where she writes M42?'

'We've seen this before – a date, we thought, but written wrong –'

'She has done nothing wrong! I ought to have seen it sooner – it's all my fault: M42 refers to the Messier catalogue, which lists deep-sky objects discovered by the astronomer Charles Messier. Messier 42 is the Orion Nebula, which is visible even with binoculars in the middle of Orion's sword. Not demented scribbles by a woman disappointed in love: it is an image of a place where stars are being born!'

James looked again at the paper. 'Yes,' he said, 'I see it'; but this was a lie. The drawing in that bad light was as inscrutable as ever.

'You'll find it eventually,' said Thomas. 'Look –' With a gesture inconceivable in any other room, and from any other man, he lifted James's finger and described a pale curve in the centre of the circle. 'That is what they call Barnard's Loop,' he said.

James took his finger quickly from the paper, and paused before he spoke. Then, reverting to professional seeking after fact: 'So you think Maria Văduva was an astronomer – that this is what she meant, when she said she hunted by night?'

'An astronomer,' said Thomas, as proud a man as if he'd at that moment coined the word and conceived of the profession. 'Her drawings are of the stars, but we looked at them through cloud.' He moved to the kitchen, and a train departed Aldleigh for Liverpool Street and rattled the knives. James wondered if he ought to return to the museum, and get on with other business; but Thomas came in with warm bread, and goats' cheese softening in wax paper, and the languid effects of the afternoon returned.

'Three times now,' said James, eating what he was given, 'we've found lenses we thought must have come from spectacles. But perhaps she had a telescope?'

'Certainly,' said Thomas. He was pouring wine. 'She can't have seen Messier 42 in such detail with anything less than a six-inch objective lens.' He put the bottle down, and looked at James with one of his sudden apologetic smiles, as if caught out in small sins. 'You see,' he said, 'I am learning.'

'Messier,' said James. 'Thomas, do you remember how often she wrote of an M., who seems to have broken her heart – is this the man?'

Again, the apologetic smile. 'I'm afraid not – Charles Messier was born in the eighteenth century, and gone to the worms by Maria's day. He witnessed a Great Comet at the age of thirteen. This comet was visible by day to the naked eyes of the king and his courtiers, and the farmers nearby and the beasts of the field; and it's said that shortly after perihelion it developed six tails that could be seen above the dawn horizon like an opening fan.' He was speaking happily in the same long well-punctuated phrases in which he wrote, and the effect on James was the effect of the wine: he simply gave in. 'Charles fell in love,' said Thomas, 'and consecrated his life to the pursuit of comets. But the skies are full of distant blurred objects that might be taken for a comet, and like all astronomers he became prone to thinking he'd found what he loved, only to find he was mistaken. So he set about making a catalogue of every galaxy and nebula it was possible to view, and gave to airy nothing a local habitation and a number. Have more bread while it's warm enough to melt the butter.'

'So this place here is not smudged,' said James, examining the paper again. 'It is a cloud of light on a dark ground. But we still have no idea who M. might have been, or what happened to Maria. Where is her body? Where is her telescope? I've seen the inventories. There's no mention of it. We ought to go back, and look.'

'Yes,' said Thomas. 'We ought to go and look.'

'And you say she wasn't mad,' said James, considering historic charges against Maria Văduva in the light of fresh evidence. 'But didn't she say she saw the devil at her window, and wanted to go out to meet him?'

'Not the devil,' said Thomas, 'but Lucifer. You notice she saw him in the morning? In the Latin, Lucifer means "light bearer"; the equivalent in Greek would be Phosphorus, "the bringer of the dawn". So I think it is possible – are you sure you won't have more wine? – that what Maria saw was the planet Venus, which rises in the morning and is the dawn herald, and looks through even a decent telescope like an unfocused image of a pearl. And I wonder,' he said, clasping his hands behind his head, and sighing – 'I wonder if what her statue held was a telescope, and it's down there at the bottom of the lake.'

James noticed the pale blue of the well-pressed shirt, and the narrow belt where it was tucked – suddenly the room was suffocatingly small and warm, its furniture creeping towards him across the carpet, the rank scent of the cheese and the exhausted tulips stirring his stomach. He felt his view of the day abruptly alter, as if he'd been hurled against the further wall and forced to take a different view. He wanted to be in his office at the old town hall, he wanted to go home – his wife, he felt, would think fondly of them both: 'You ought to take him out into the street,' she'd say, 'and stop a stranger and say, "Do you see this man here, or is it only me?"'

Then Thomas returned to the table, and opened one of

the green notebooks stacked there. 'Let's examine our facts again. First, we know that Maria Văduva disappeared no earlier than August 1888, when the photograph was taken at Bethesda. Second, that she had a telescope, and made a number of astronomical drawings, and that this telescope and most of her drawings are missing. Third, that she had a friend, C., who lived in London, to whom she sometimes wrote. Fourth, that her heart was broken, by this M., who perhaps loved a woman named Veronica, though we can't possibly hope to identify him. I suppose,' said Thomas, frowning, 'Maria's husband wouldn't have liked that.'

James, laughing and relieved to be laughing, said, 'I am sure he wouldn't! Husbands,' he said self-mockingly, 'can be very conventional where their wives are concerned.' Here he received a look from Thomas so warmly complicit he was prompted to be brisk. 'I'll take this,' he said, putting the drawing in the file he'd brought, 'it will be safe with me: I'll see it photographed, and catalogued, and treated as treasure. And there'll be more, there is bound to be more – perhaps even a diary. A body, if we are lucky.'

'I almost hope,' said Thomas (he was gathering plates; he was not looking at James), 'we never come to the end of it, since that would be the end of the adventure – must you really go?'

'I must,' said James, 'or nothing will be done at Lowlands. I have to see to it we keep the house secure, before this woman burns it to the ground. Where is my coat? And is that the time, is it really?'

The fire in the grate ceded to ember. 'This is the time. Let's walk together to town.'

Thomas Hart, going down Lower Bridge Road with James at his side; Thomas lifting his face to the collapsing clouds. 'It was good of you to come,' he said. He did not say: please come back to me soon.

'My God,' said James (they were approaching the old town hall, and dolorous music came from nearby), 'is this your lot?' A group of men and women was standing by the war memorial. Last year's poppy wreath, wrecked by disrespect-ful weather, was rotting at the foot; the women and the men were singing. Thomas experienced that habitual longing for the sacred he never did shake off – there's the senior deacon (he thought this with love) and the pastor; there's Anne Macaulay in a new black hat. Then he saw, among the famil-iar faces with their familiar looks of patient piety, a woman in a full-skirted pink coat standing with her arm in Anne's. She was familiar with the queasy familiarity of something remem-bered from a dream. Her yellow hair resisted the wind that turned the pages of her hymn book, and as she sang she lowered her painted eyelids in pious sentiment. 'I've seen her before,' said Thomas, 'walking with Anne through Lowlands Park, and I wondered –' He could not have explained to James how bizarre it was to see Anne Macaulay attach her-self to a woman who might have been constructed like a mannequin to demonstrate every wicked thing Bethesda considered worldly. Her fine stockings strained over promin-ent ankle bones. The skirts of her coat blew open, and revealed the lower part of her thighs below a floral hem. 'There is a fountain filled with blood,' she sang, seeming on the verge of artificial tears, 'drawn from Immanuel's veins' – and beside her Anne Macaulay, flushing with pride or humiliated courage, extended her hand to a careless passer-by and gave him a gospel tract.

'Strange thing to be singing about,' said James, 'all that blood'; but he was inclined to watch, and receded into the lobby of a shoe shop. Thomas, discovering with shame that

91

he neither wanted to see or be seen, receded with him: 'I suppose they are my lot. I suppose they will always be.'

'*Behold, ye have sinned against the Lord*' – this was the pastor cautioning the man coming out of the newsagent's rolling a cigarette, the schoolboys hassling each other by the burger van – meanwhile Anne and the senior deacon gave out their tracts imploring Aldleigh to flee from the wrath to come.

'Still,' said James, looking at his watch, 'nobody here seems to mind – I suppose they've seen it before. Now I must go' – but he frowned, and moved out from the awning to take a clearer view. 'Did you see that? What's happening?'

Thomas saw the pastor flinch, feint left, and go on speaking; then there was the sound, distinct above the preacher and the crowd, of something striking the pavement. Looking in confusion for the source, Thomas saw – among the women with their shopping trolleys, and the girls swinging satchels from a single strap – a young woman standing some distance from the war memorial, holding a piece of cloth nailed to a length of wood pulled from a cargo pallet. This was a poorly made banner, already coming apart, and its message illegible. There was black paint on the wood, and on the woman's clothes; her narrow body shivered with purpose.

'Is that her?' said James. 'Is that the woman from Lowlands?'

'That's her,' said Thomas. She held the banner in her left hand, and with her right took small stones from her pocket and threw them at the war memorial with a bad aim.

'Mad as a hatter, poor thing,' said James, amused, 'now I really should go' – and meanwhile the woman in pink turned her back on Anne Macaulay and headed for the shelter of a phone box. Anne, valiant and uncertain, stood her ground. A stone landed by her shoe. She ignored it. Meanwhile people had begun to gather: 'You tell them, love,' said a man who nonetheless took a tract from the senior deacon with a nod of gratitude, 'you tell them!' – but in fact the woman told nobody anything, only went on standing in the ecstasy of terror summoned out of the comet, and herself, and all the anxieties of a creature that had never asked to be born. *'From that time,'* said the pastor, not looking up from his Bible, *'Jesus began to preach, and to say, "Repent, for the Kingdom of Heaven is at hand."'* He gestured to the cloud, which had taken on a greenish colour. The woman shook her banner, but had no more stones to throw. The pastor said nothing, and did nothing, and there was the impression of an old religion and a new one ranged against each other, battling for all the souls of Essex. The greenish cloud darkened, and shrieking schoolgirls ran for shelter; again Thomas heard the crack of small stones on hard places, and saw it had begun to hail, pelting saints and sinners and raising glittering drifts on the steps of the war memorial. The altered air roused the woman with the banner: she bent her head and with the lowing noise of an agitated bull charged towards the place where the pastor stood. But he was now attending so closely to the word of God, and the noise of the hail hissing on the pavements was so great, that he failed to notice – *'They brought unto him all sick people,'* he said, gravely intoning, *'and those which were possessed with devils, and those which were lunatic –'* Thomas, thinking he should avert an injury, stepped out of his hiding place towards the pastor, but at the last moment the woman altered her course and went running down the high street through the milling crowd, the banner showing overhead like a torn sail on a ship of fools. So relieved of his duty, and ashamed to be relieved, he returned to the shelter of the shoe shop: 'It isn't really anything to do with me,' he said, 'these open-air meetings aren't something I've ever done' – but found he was alone. James Bower had gone, returned to the life of which Thomas knew nothing, and hadn't been able to guess.

Late March, late afternoon: the Great Comet hanging unseen somewhat north of the sun. The yellowish plume of its dust tail curved with the curve of its orbit, and a jet of bluish gas streamed out as straight as if it comprehended perfectly the laws of Euclid. Meanwhile Grace Macaulay, having turned eighteen in the small hours, surveyed her mirror with pleasure. She'd made her dress herself, and it was red as the rope the harlot Rahab had hung out of her window; but her face was bare, since no daughter of Bethesda would ever paint her mouth or eyelids like Jezebel (who ended up eaten by dogs, all save the palms of her hands and the soles of her feet). Grace, feeling at that moment she'd exchange an eternity of rest for a tube of lipstick, bit her lips to bring up the blood, and fell into desolation. It was her eighteenth birthday, and all she had at hand was a walk down by the Blackwater with her only two friends, and tea with her peculiar family. Other girls on days like these held parties to which they wore jeans, and scraps of fabric that showed their breasts and collarbones; where they drank until they were sick, and danced to wordless music; where everything was animated by sex, the sin that seemed to her a kind of necessity towards which she was helplessly moving. Some girls she knew danced at nightclubs in cages (nobody could explain to her why), and grew thin (it was said) on cocaine – others had

94

terminated pregnancies they didn't want, or had tattooed moths or butterflies above their buttocks, and all this struck her as being both deplorable and glamorous, and the stuff of a life she'd never attain. But Grace had never danced, and always attended chapel with her head covered to make herself decent in the sight of God and men – I do want to be good, she thought, I do want to serve God, but what an effort it all is, and how tiring – though at least now it could be said she knew how to hold a cigarette, and draw on it without choking, because God had made Nathan break Bethesda's window.

She heard her aunt calling from the foot of the stairs, as if detecting through floorboards the direction of her niece's thoughts; so flushing with shame Grace ran down, tripping on her hem, and hearing stitches tear in the seams.

Anne Macaulay smiled at the scarlet dress with shy affection. 'They're here,' she said. 'They've come.' Grace kissed her aunt out of duty, and saw Thomas upright on a dining chair, and Nathan beside him seeming almost to vibrate with the effort of remaining in his seat. 'Hello,' he said. He wore his glasses, and these obscured the colour and clarity of his eyes and made him seem less remarkable, so that Grace felt the balance of power tip faintly in her favour. Laughing, she performed a curtsy, extending her small hand towards them.

'Happy birthday,' said Thomas, 'you wretched child.' He was holding a leather box, and this was promising. 'Is that for me?' she said.

'It is for you,' said Thomas, watching her discover a gold ring, dented and thin, and set with small stones. Grace felt that if she'd ever seen another woman wear it, she'd have stolen it right off her finger. 'That is the best thing I ever had,' she said, giving Thomas one of her hard burrowing hugs; then having forgotten Nathan in her pleasure she sat

95

cross-legged at her old friend's feet and leaned with thought-less affection against his knee.

'It cost very little,' said Thomas, fending off a troubled look from Anne, 'but I happened to see it in London and the man had no idea of its worth. The stones spell out the word DEAREST – diamond, emerald, amethyst, and so on – because that is what you are.' He delivered this tribute without embarrassment, then with diffident affection he patted Grace twice on the crown, as if she were a dog who'd pleased him.

'I didn't get you anything,' said Nathan, with the good cheer of a sinner already absolved, 'I forgot.'

Then Ronald Macaulay came in with holiness in the pleats of his trousers. The atmosphere thinned, as if the room had been elevated nearer heaven. 'Ah,' he said, 'Mr Hart: you're taking these two to Aldwinter, I understand? Very kind.' He didn't look at Nathan, whom he seemed to have accepted as he might have accepted a new piece of furniture he could tolerate but would never use. Then 'Journeying mercies,' said Ronald, and with gratitude returned to his room.

'It isn't any trouble,' said Thomas to Anne, who'd come in from the kitchen, 'I've wanted to go for some time, and write about it.'

'Have you told them?' said Anne. 'Does she know what you're taking her to see?'

'I haven't got any idea,' said Grace, turning and turning the ring. 'Nobody tells me anything; I'm always, always in the dark.'

'Come on, then,' said Nathan, shrugging off the house like a coat, 'let's go.' He looked down at Grace, and examined her dress as if he'd only just seen it. 'You'll get mud all over that,' he said. 'You're really an idiot, you know.'

They headed for the Essex coast, through industrial estates and shopping malls and plants for manufacturing farm machinery. In the passenger seat beside Thomas, Nathan searched for music never heard under Ronald Macaulay's roof, and behind him Grace attended devoutly to the lyrics, and equally devoutly to the movement of Nathan's shoulders, and the tender place at the nape of his neck. I've fallen in love, she thought, that is what has happened. It is a disaster. It cannot end well – there's no way out of this that won't cause me pain – then there was a kestrel over the verge, and Thomas was delighting at it. 'Look,' he said, slowing the car, 'the wind-hover.' The kestrel stooped, and Grace's heart stooped with it; she was conscious of being hurled into feeling against her will. The silk cord she wore as a belt became abruptly too tight, and it was difficult to draw breath; she untied it, and tied it again. 'Turn the radio off,' she said, 'turn it off, my head hurts.'

'Not long now,' said Thomas. Obedient Nathan turned the music off. They were passing through villages in which modern terraces were interposed between pink thatched cottages, and fields in which electricity pylons receded in ranks to a distant black point. Within minutes no more houses were in view, and it was bad weather on the Blackwater: slow brown river, marshes half-sunk. 'Here we are,' said Thomas. He'd brought them to a narrow road, terminating in fog that all day had been accruing in the ditches and hollows, and brought a muffling quiet. It's cold out here, thought Grace. Spring will never get this far.

'Anything could happen,' said Nathan, grinning and untroubled. 'A farmer might shoot us for frightening his pigs, and they'll have eaten our bodies by morning.'

They came out of the car and stood under a dripping oak. 'Thomas,' said Grace, 'did you get us lost?'

'Do you hear that?' said Thomas. 'A curlew, I think, since they say it sounds like singing underwater – let's go. Don't you trust me?'

They began to walk. The thickening fog opened to admit them and closed in their wake. Grace discovered that in fact she didn't trust Thomas, and didn't trust Nathan, and certainly didn't trust the steep slick verges underfoot. She tried to draw a deep consoling breath, and found she couldn't, and a rootless panic set in. Nathan was walking into the dissipating mist ahead – look at him, she thought, the size of him: fear and delight ran through her like an alternating current, and the ring slipped on a finger made thin by cold.

'Now look,' said Nathan, seeing nothing strange in all the world, 'look,' he said, 'the sun's coming out.' It was, and in the weak light he and Thomas were ordinary, and Grace was ashamed.

'Here we are,' said Thomas. He spread his arms. 'Here we are: Aldwinter, and the end of Essex.'

Through receding fog Grace saw they'd arrived on a deserted village green, where long grass ceded to mud in wet black tracts. A handful of Victorian houses mutely regarded each other; behind these, new white bungalows huddled against the soil.

'Well, happy birthday,' said Nathan. He pressed Grace with his shoulder. 'Do you think there's a pub? I bet he drinks,' he said, eyeing Thomas with his full eighteen years of worldly wisdom, 'I bet he can handle it.'

Grace surveyed the green. Mist disturbed the perspective: not possible to see how large the green was, or where it ended. Still – she stepped forward, and the obliging mist went with her – was it possible they were not after all alone? 'Can you see that?' she said.

'It's just fog,' said Nathan, 'it's all just a lot of nothing'; and Thomas, some distance away, wrote something in his notebook.

'How can't you see it?' said Grace, feeling her temper slip.

'How can you not see that?' She pointed to a place where the fog accumulated in the middle of the green, through which she made out a dark shape, high and irregular, with upper parts diminishing in mist, and a black mass spreading at the foot.

'Shit,' said Nathan. 'What's that?' He cupped his hands about his mouth and gave a kind of summoning yell.

'Stop that,' said Grace, her temper now out of her hands. She walked towards the high black thing. It was the sole fixed point in a disintegrating world, and its stillness seemed that of a savage creature keeping itself in check – 'Hello?' she said, thinking stupidly it was the man in Potter's Field, having taken off his scarlet coat and put a black one on, and grown incomprehensibly vast. 'Grace?' – this was Nathan, or it was Thomas: they were one thing, quickly approaching. The sun came out, and drew the black object ahead out of the occluded air: a dark mass, with dark limbs extending either side and curving downwards as if broken at the joints, and some pale hard protrusion pricking up out of it – so there's still giants in old Essex, Grace thought, doing away with deer to get horns for their crowns. 'I told you there was something there,' she said. The cord dropped from her waist into the mud, and she picked it up, and tied it again. 'Didn't I tell you? Didn't I say?'

'I'd hardly have driven you all this way,' said Thomas, 'if there'd been nothing here.'

'It's just a tree,' said Nathan. 'It's just some tree.' No mist now. Late sun suspended in its decline; all things visible. 'Just some tree,' said Grace, standing now at the foot of an immense oak dying of time or some other malady. Its trunk was split open, and its upper limbs were bare as bones; here and there the lower branches looped into the soil and out of it, and were dying off or coming into bud. All this was quite ordinary, and hardly worth the journey's trouble; but 'Look,' said Thomas, pleased with himself, 'do you see?'

Grace did see. Circling the trunk, in ranks two or three feet deep and lapped like the scales of a fish, were dozens of headstones removed from their graves. Some were wrecked by time and weather, their inscriptions overwritten by lichen and moss; others might have been propped there by the stonemason half an hour before. '*Called Home,*' said Grace, circuiting the oak in a daze, and reading aloud where she could, '*Gone to Glory, Forever With the Lord* – get down from there, you'll break something.'

Nathan, having jumped spring-heeled on to the shoulder of a broken angel, reached for a branch that cracked and complained. 'What do you want on your grave, then?' he said. 'What shall we write about you?' – the branch broke. He fell and righted himself, impervious to harm.

'You can bury me at sea,' said Grace. 'Oh look at this poor woman – *She Hath Done What She Could.* What a way to be remembered, that even your best was nothing much. But what is this, Thomas, why is it here – this dead tree, these dead forgotten people? What happened?' Her belt fell off again. She kicked it through mud, then tied it to a branch. It hung like a noose for a child.

'This is Traitor's Oak,' said Thomas, 'where Charles was said to have hidden from the law, though I doubt it, since Essex men and women were never really minded to kneel for the Crown.' He chose a branch for a bench, and disposed himself and his coat on it. 'This was a fishing village once, where they went down to the sea in ships and occupied their business in great waters, and what have you – past the green there was a quay, and in those days you'd see the oxblood sails of the old Thames barges going up the estuary with cargoes of oyster and grain, and a Saxon church with beasts carved on the pews.'

'Beasts?' said Grace. 'What kind?'

'I don't know. It's all gone now. The sea defences failed, back at the beginning of this century – so the tides came in too far, and they began to have trouble with the cemetery. The church warden would do his morning rounds and go picking seaweed from the headstones –'

'You're making this up. Nathan, truly, you can't believe a thing he says.'

'– sea kelp and bladderwrack and once a flapping mackerel, which he took home and grilled for his breakfast. Then one winter, as the Great War began, and artillery was heard thumping over the Channel –'

'This is all lies –'

'– there was a high tide on a stormy night, and two graves flooded and their coffins burst, and the next morning the congregation had two new members, strange and thin, who never sang a word.' Grace was laughing now, and she shoved Thomas with her animal affection. 'This began to happen with such awful regularity,' said Thomas placidly, 'that in due course the bodies were disinterred and buried again near Colchester where it keeps decently dry, and the headstones were put here to remember them by. Look carefully and you'll find the last citizen of Aldwinter was buried here in 1921, with some interesting markings on the headstone.'

'But why does nobody live here now?' said Nathan. 'Where's the church? Where did they all go?'

'Some still live here,' said Thomas, gesturing to houses and bungalows in which nothing and nobody moved, 'because they can't bear to leave. But there's no work, and nobody wants to insure buildings on land so prone to flood. The church burned down and inch by inch the coast eroded, and now the whole thing's underwater, though they say at low tide it's possible to see the remains of the tower and the nave, and hear the old bell ringing.'

'I don't believe you,' said Grace, with a contradictory grin; and Nathan, never still, gleamed with possibility.

'I'm going,' he said, 'I want to look – come on, Grace, don't you want to see if the tide's out? Don't you want to hear the bell?' He held out his hand. Grace looked at it, and her own hand lifted in response. Then she remembered her anger at the power he exerted over her happiness, and how unconsciously he exerted it; so she put her hands in her pockets, and shrugged, and delighted to see him flinch against this small refusal. 'All right,' she said.

Now the air was bright and clear, and the rim of Essex was nearer. Jackdaws were settling in Traitor's Oak, and down beyond the green there were curlews pacing in the shingle. 'I'll follow you,' said Grace. 'You go on.' So the woman and the man went down to the water, and Thomas Hart watched them go. Nobody spoke. Each was conscious of being absolutely solitary, and unsure of their destination.

Anne Macaulay was at home, wrapping gifts she'd bought for
Grace. The first of these was a gift of duty: a volume of
nineteenth-century sermons bound in oxblood leather,
chosen with care by Ronald and inscribed 'with love' in his
neat inexpressive hand. The second had required diligent
saving on Anne's part, and was a gold disc pendant engraved
with XARIS, which was Grace's name in the common Greek
and signified the undeserved favour of God. It was something beautiful and something good, leaving body and soul
equally accounted for; so with a sense of a task done well
Anne tied a narrow ribbon retrieved from a previous gift,
and inscribed a single kiss on a card. She was surprised by the
extent of her love for the girl, which had arrived late and
often felt inadequate; all day the house had felt incomplete in
her absence, its rooms too bare and too big. Lately her body
had longed for that small, cross child, with a sense of physical need she'd always imagined was reserved for women
who'd given birth: now the thought of one of those hard,
burrowing hugs restored something to the day.

Downstairs the bell was ringing, and Anne was brought
back to unease. This would be Lorna Greene, and not for the
life of her could Anne remember how she'd come to invite
the woman to her niece's party, only that perhaps it had
struck her suddenly what a poor affair it would be

otherwise – she took the gifts downstairs, and opened the door. 'Darling!' said Lorna, lifting her cheek for a kiss. Her yellow hair was set in glossy curls, and her powdery scent that was strangely like that of a baby; she was as small as Grace was small, but slight, so that in her presence Anne felt unformed and unwieldy. It was threatening rain. Anne quickly kissed her, and was kissed in return.

'Dear Anne,' the visitor said, going unasked down the hall and into the dining room, 'how pretty you've made it all.' She took in the best white tablecloth, the primroses on the windowsill, the balloons already exhaling Ronald's breath and drifting on their garden twine – 'And goodness,' she said, blinking, 'my word, look at that cake. I expect you did your best.'

'Thank you,' said Anne, who until that moment had indulged the sin of pride where the icing and the sugar roses were concerned.

'Not what you'd expect for an eighteenth birthday' – Lorna made adjustments to the cutlery, the folded napkins – 'but I'm sure she'll be pleased. Mr Macaulay,' she greeted the man who'd come in silently, carrying a Bible with his thumb marking a passage, 'your child has become a woman, and I am certain a virtuous one, with a price far above rubies.'

The rain was holding off. Outside, the silver birch was motionless, and the sky deepened and cleared. Then Anne, whose spirits had sunk with the balloons, saw the birch leap in passing headlights: that was Grace, she thought, and Thomas Hart, and the boy that broke the window. 'They're here,' she said, going gratefully to the door, but already it was open and here was Grace hurling in. She'd lost her coat, and the absurd silk rope she'd been wearing as a belt; she was flushed and hectic-looking, as if she'd acquired a disease from the Blackwater.

'Aunt Anne,' she said, 'there you are – we've found a man,

and brought him with us.' Sound then of a slammed door, and familiar voices – 'They're helping him now,' she said, 'they're coming.' She saw her father gravely waiting in the narrow hall, and quickly became sombre. 'I hope I haven't done something wrong, but we couldn't have left him there.'

'Gracious,' said Lorna, arriving beside Ronald Macaulay. 'Whatever have you been up to?' She moistened her lips with a delicate sharp tongue. Grace looked at her with something approaching contempt, which Lorna received with an unaltered smile, and another dart of her tongue.

Anne saw three men coming down the darkening drive. Here was Thomas Hart, upright and silent; here was Nathan, with his impatient onward gait. They had a stranger with them. He was a tall man, and thin, in a scarlet coat; and despite his drooping head he had a haughty look, like that of an emperor in the act of being deposed. He carried a satchel on his back. The other men drew him up the path.

'My goodness,' said Lorna as the men came with difficulty to the door. 'Do you think he is drunk?' She pressed a hand to her mouth, and her nails were hard and pink as shells.

Thomas looked placidly at her and with wary good manners said, 'Hello.'

'I found him,' said Grace, as if to say: *he belongs to me.* 'I found him living in Potter's Field. But we saw him walking on the verge miles out from Aldleigh and I recognised his coat, so we've brought him home.' Possibly she'd expected praise for this show of goodness. None came. 'Well,' she said, looking about for evidence she'd sinned, 'isn't it my birthday? Can't I do what I like?'

Anne said, 'Bring him in.' They did, and with difficulty sat him at the dining table. Roused by light, the man looked from face to face, and clutched the satchel. He spoke in long impassioned phrases that carried meaning through barriers of comprehension: he was grateful, they understood, but confused; he was tired, but neither sought nor required their pity. Meanwhile the Great Comet, buffeted by solar winds, traversed the window trailing incandescent dust. Nobody saw it.

'He likes coffee,' said Grace, patting the velvet shoulder, bringing up out of it the scent of an unwashed body, and of soil.

Lorna's mauve satin rustled. 'There are institutions better suited to vagrants and drunks,' she said. 'Hostels, for example, and charitable causes.'

Grace, with a level black look: 'He isn't drunk. He's tired. Anyone would be tired who'd walked so far for so long.' Again the cheap satin rustled. In a dark room, it would strike sparks.

Ronald Macaulay came forward with the look of a man incapable of an ungodly act. 'No, he is not drunk,' he said, 'though I'm not sure that I'd throw him out if he were.' He held out his hand. The stranger took it with astonishment; 'Thank you,' he said, and put his hands over his eyes. The satchel fell from his lap.

'He's probably going to cry,' said Grace, bringing coffee to the table; then since it was her habit to sit on the floor she curled at the stranger's feet. 'Look,' she said, putting a hand on his knee with competent softness that astonished Anne, since it seemed to have been acquired in the hours she'd been away, 'why don't you stay with us for a while. It's my birthday party, and I'm inviting you.' She butted against his leg in easy thoughtless affection. 'You can have something to eat, then we'll decide what to do.' Her dress was red and so was the stranger's spreading coat, and Anne had the impression of a courtier at the foot of an ailing king.

'Yes,' he said, 'thank you.' He fumbled with the coffee cup, and Anne saw with disquiet that his thumb seemed mis-placed and loose, and his fingertips unfinished. She was transfixed by sympathy so intimate and direct it struck her as a variety of love, and because of this became brisk: 'He should take his coat off or he won't feel the benefit.'

With her satin rustle and powdery infant's scent, Lorna made herself known, and came to stand beside Anne with an expectant smile and pert sideways tilt of the head. 'Oh, Mr Hart,' said Anne, 'you haven't met Miss Greene. Miss Greene, this is our friend, Mr Hart.' Thomas and the woman looked at each other with the bankrupt politeness of politicians, and Anne, oblivious to Lorna's expression of secretive pleasure, said, 'Ronald, perhaps you can give thanks, and we'll have something to eat?'

So Ronald, folding his hands, began to pray. Thomas Hart, not praying, now saw the diligent comet, and was the solitary witness. He saw, too, Anne frowning as she made her peti-tions to God; saw Lorna Greene raise and lower her pearly lids in a private assessment of the room and everyone in it. That acute attention reached Thomas, and remained there, and it seemed to him that she was making certain deductions that had never been made before in that room. There it was again, the perception of strangers – but this was not James Bower's smiling ease, it was a dreadful seeking-out, like the pricking of a witchfinder's pin. The man he was in London drew nearer and nearer, bringing other men in his wake: I'll be discovered, he thought, I will be known. He shivered, as if he stood under the shadow of the pulpit – now he saw Nathan in the corner, surveying Grace. Her badly made dress was slipping from her shoulder, her hands were folded in her lap; she frowned like her aunt as she followed the prayer. Nathan watched her with that same puzzled look that had come when she'd refused his hand in Aldwinter, and Thomas, understanding the boy had been inconvenienced by desire, both envied and pitied him.

'In Jesus name,' said Ronald, 'and for his sake: amen.'

'Amen,' said the stranger, and Ronald looked at him with solemn approval.

Grace and Anne together took the stranger's coat, and hung it in the hall, affecting not to notice the reek of the thing. Ronald directed him to a better chair: 'You'd be more comfortable here, I think. Now,' he said, 'perhaps we might give Grace her gifts.' But evidently this was the labour of women, and he receded from his daughter, and Anne came forward with the small present and the larger one, and said 'Happy birthday' with a faint flush of shyness, as if afraid she might be contradicted.

'Charles Haddon Spurgeon,' said Ronald as Grace opened the book. 'Now: grow in the root of all grace, which is faith.'

'Thank you,' said Grace, 'thank you' – she stroked the book, and was moved by it. Then quickly she turned to the smaller gift, and having always been alert to beauty opened the gilded box with indecent haste, and dropped it, so that it took a moment to retrieve the gold chain from the carpet. 'Oh,' she said, examining the disc, and being a child of Bethesda knowing biblical Greek when she saw it; 'oh, is that my name? Thank you, thank you.' She submitted to her aunt fastening the chain at the nape of her neck, and all the while beamed with uncontainable joy at everyone within view. 'Isn't it beautiful? Don't you think it's the best thing you ever saw?'

'Very nice,' said Lorna, flickering. 'Such a lovely birthday. Still,' she said, sighing and lowering her eyelids in sorrow, 'there is a peculiar smell in here, most unfortunate. And dear Grace, I wonder if perhaps you ought to change your clothes. Did you make that dress? I thought perhaps you might. How sweet. You've done ever so well. But you see: it's more or less falling off, and I am sure your father would like you to be decent. You won't mind my saying so. There's no side to me. I speak as I find.' She looked at Ronald with a pout of calculated prettiness, but discovered that he was attending to the stranger. 'Do we know his name?' he said. But they didn't, and nobody liked to ask.

'Lovely little thing, isn't she?' said Lorna, taking her avid blackbird's gaze to Nathan, and smoothing her satin skirt. 'I'm sure you've noticed.' She put a white hand on his sleeve: 'Men do notice these things, don't they?'

Nathan looked ashamed of her, and of himself, and of Grace, and of everyone in the small warm room. 'Never thought about it,' he said.

'Not much of a party, either' – Lorna sighed and let out gusts of her powdery scent – 'does she have no friends at all? Still, where two or three are gathered together, there is Christ, in the midst.'

Nathan glanced quickly at the door, as if the Redeemer might have arrived in a taxi, delayed by the traffic, and ready to insist on good behaviour.

Time passed. 'Happy birthday,' they sang, in the full harmony every good Baptist learns in the chapel pew, and Grace blew candles out, and the old foundling dined well on Anne Macaulay's bread and butter. Now the comet was departing the window, and Ronald, becoming playful, had turned the radio on, letting decorous music into the room. 'Quite the young lady now, isn't she, Mr Macaulay,' said Lorna to Ronald, cocking her head, as familiar as if she'd been at Grace Macaulay's cradle. 'Grace, dear,' she said, her well-modulated voice easily penetrating the air, 'now you are eighteen you must tell us what you intend to do with the life ahead of you. Your aunt tells me you're not an academic child; but perhaps you were born to marry and have babies. That would be only natural, really the most natural thing in the world.' She rolled a giddy hard eye at Nathan, who sank into the wallpaper. 'Only natural,' she said again, and there was a pause, and every creature in that room understood themselves to be biped animals enslaved by urges they could neither understand nor resist. 'Well,' said Lorna – she sighed, and smiled: it was all giving her pleasure – 'I'm sure your father only wants you to be happy.'

'Happy?' said Ronald, with the inflexion of a man trying out a foreign language. 'I've never given any thought to happiness. I only pray she becomes a servant of her Heavenly Father.'

'I think I want to be like Thomas,' said Grace. 'I don't mean writing, only that I want things to exist in the world because I existed to make them. It would make me happy to know that I left a mark.'

'And we think Mr Hart is happy, do we?' Lorna's voice was sweet as a robin's. The whole room surveyed Thomas, and doubted it.

'It's better to hope for contentment,' said Anne, 'than happiness.'

'Never emulate me, Grace,' said Thomas, laughing. 'I spend my life doing the only thing I have ever felt was worth doing, and because of this I wake each morning a failure, living in this gap between what I want to achieve and my capacity to achieve it. That's writing for you,' he said, 'nothing but spoiling things by touching them.'

'Then can't you stop trying?' said Nathan, looking at Thomas with the same bewildered expression with which he'd first entered Bethesda.

'I could,' said Thomas. 'Perhaps I will.'

Lorna meanwhile had come close to Ronald, so that her

hard fair head was at his shoulder. 'Oh Mr Macaulay,' she said, sighing, as if perceiving some sorrow in the offing, 'whatever are you going to do with her?' She murmured and flickered her eyes; but Ronald's attention was still on the stranger.

'I was thinking what we ought to do with him,' he said, taking in the vagrant's pleasure in the warm room, and the cake disintegrating on its plate. 'Providentially, this afternoon I prepared a sermon on the words of Christ when he said: *for as much as you do it to the least of my brethren, ye do it to me.*'

'The very least,' said Lorna. 'I wonder what he has in that bag? Stolen goods, I shouldn't wonder.' She came still nearer. Her satin skirt whispered as she moved. 'Did you see the state of his hands? I've seen such injuries before in drunks, and fighting men.'

Now Grace was showing the old man the ring on her finger – '*Dearest*, that's what it says, and that's me.'

'Grace,' said Ronald, in the admonitory voice he deployed in the pulpit; evidently he felt the evening should be brought to a close. But Thomas Hart was putting on his coat, and coming to speak to Ronald. 'I'll take him home with me,' he said. With deliberate bad manners he had his back to Lorna.

Grace looked quickly at him. 'Yes,' she said, 'you take him, and put him in your lovely house. Isn't it good of Thomas,' she said, and Ronald conceded that it was.

Lorna's face, which had altered as Thomas had supplanted her, reassembled itself into sweetness. She appeared now at Ronald's other side, and put her small hand in the crook of his elbow in a gesture that astonished him into silence. 'Yes,' she said, her gleaming eyelids lowering as she took in Thomas with her terrible assessing gaze – 'yes, I should think that will be very nice for you, Mr Hart,' she said. Her voice reached them all – the comet attended closely at the window; she patted rolls of hair that had been unmoved all night. 'You will like that, I expect' – she was smiling – 'I should think you rather like the company of men. What a treat: another man about the house!'

Anne Macaulay looked down at her cake, and didn't want the broken roses with her thumbprints on them. The vagrant was sleeping. Ronald, for whom the world was paved with sin, saw no hazard at his feet. 'Well,' he said, 'it's getting late.'

'What do you mean?' said Grace. With difficulty, because her feet were tangled in her skirts, she rose from the floor, and looked at Thomas, who was having difficulty with his gloves.

'This isn't something you ought to trouble yourself with' – Lorna looked steadily up at Ronald – 'but I would surely have thought' – the end of her sentence, not spoken, hung above the dining table. 'There's no side to me,' she said again, her small mauve body seeming to have grown smaller and more dense, and her greasy eyelids half-lowered. 'When the right-eous give way to the wicked,' she said, picking at something under her nail, 'it is like polluting a well.'

'Why are you even here?' said Grace, interposing herself between Thomas and the woman. 'You don't belong here – you don't belong with us at all.'

Lorna Greene shrugged, and the satin hissed in her arm-pits. 'If you read your Bible,' she said, 'you'll know that evil communication corrupts good manners –'

'What are you talking about?' said Grace, bewilderment amplifying her anger. 'If he is evil so am I, and so are you, and so are we all – just go away. Go away! None of us want you here.'

Lorna placidly drew her cuffs over her wrists. 'Such a pleasant evening,' she said, 'so delightful to take fellowship with you all. Dear Anne! It's getting late, and I rather think Grace has worn herself out, and become overexcited, as chil-dren so often do.'

But Anne saw painfully that the child she'd come to love was gone, and that now she was required to learn to love this stranger who'd come back from the Blackwater and taken her place. 'Must you go?' said Anne, doing nothing to forestall the woman moving to the door. 'Must you really go?'

'I must,' said Lorna, 'but so look forward to seeing you all again.' She kissed Anne, her lips rustling as her silk rustled, her yellow hair unmoved. 'God bless you,' she said, drifting through the open door, dispensing words meaningless in their repetition; and as she reached the doorstep she turned, and directed a last level look at the window, through which it was possible to see the vagrant standing in his scarlet coat, and raising his arms as if seeking an embrace.

'Tell me your name,' said Thomas Hart, 'since I have told you mine.' He'd left the party with the stranger, and taken him from there to Potter's Field. Here they'd untied the tarpaulin from the hazel, and rolled up the carpet underneath it, and all the while the jays had been remarking on the lateness of the hour. Then Thomas had taken the stranger home, and finding him biddable and childlike had put him in the bath, and washed him without difficulty or embarrassment. He'd wiped filth from his back and buttocks, and from his starved armpits; he'd discovered old wounds ulcerating on ankles damaged by bad boots, and doused these in boiled water in which he dissolved a teaspoon of Maldon salt; he'd clipped the hair back to the sunburned scalp, and found things living in the clippings, and put them in the kitchen bin. All this had caused the man to weep into the bathwater.

'When I was young,' said Thomas, pouring rose oil into a second change of water, 'the boys and men I knew began to get sick, one after the other. Nobody knew where the sickness came from, or what to call it, only that it came to men

113

like me. They became thin. There were black marks on their bodies, like the print on the fur of leopards, and a kind of white fungus grew in their mouths until it was difficult to eat – the newspapers called it the gay cancer, and preachers on street corners and in Bethesda's pulpit said we deserved it. Did we deserve it? I could tell you their names. I could tell you how they lived.' Grief Thomas thought long accommodated struck him violently, and before him passed the dispensing chemist, horn player, failed architect, teacher of Romance languages, plasterer, bad cyclist, schoolboy, exhausted proprietor of a Wanstead café, all in the end wanting a pillow between the knees for comfort lying down, and a small view of birds. 'A boy I knew died the week he should have taken his A levels, and his family hadn't wanted him saved – so it was left to his friends to do the work of his nurse and his mother, and I learned there really are such things as the death rattle, that death will eat a man like a pack of wolves in the night. After that I wasn't only ashamed of myself, I was afraid.'

The man in the bath submitted dumbly to the story and the water, and Thomas, divining in his silence neither censure nor incomprehension, said, 'Tell me, then – what do you think? Did he deserve to die at eighteen because he was homosexual? Do you think me evil – that I corrupt my friends by talking to them? Do you think God withholds destruction from the liar and the murderer but constructs a virus, in some celestial laboratory, to torment men like me – that my sin is greater than all the other sins that pass without notice? There is no sense in it, and they would have me think God a god of reason.' Thomas heard that he'd become plaintive, and felt ashamed of himself.

The stranger in the bath shook his head with such sorrow it took in the whole world. Then Thomas, having lifted him easily enough out of the water, dried the old body, and put lotion on cracked and swollen hands; then having given him pyjamas and put him in a chair beside the fire and the leaping marigolds he said, 'Now tell me your name.'

Pretending indifference to the stranger's refusal, Thomas went out to the kitchen. He heated milk with vanilla sugar in a copper pan, and brought it to the table in glasses. 'Whatever it is,' he said, 'and whoever you are, you needn't be ashamed. It wouldn't take much to bring anyone to where you've been. A bad landlord, say. A leg that broke and wouldn't set, too much trust in bad advice, a mortgage unattainable by half a per cent, and there we are: there I might be.' (Thomas in fact did not quite believe this, but wanted to be kind.)

The man reached for his glass of milk, then seeming to note his own hands for the first time flinched, scowled, and withdrew. 'I'm very tired,' he said. 'Can't you put me in a bed?' He reached for the satchel, which all evening he'd kept nearby, and his clumsy movements dislodged an empty bottle, followed by a packet wrapped in white cloth. Reaching after these he knocked his useless thumb against the chair; then cursed at length in his own language and reverted once again to tears.

'Let me,' said Thomas. He put the bottle and the parcel on the table. The parcel carried the sour sweetness of the vagrant's body, together with a note of turned soil. Thomas examined it. 'But this is a book,' he said.

'It is. You be careful.' The man examined the bottle, and when he found it empty swore again.

Thomas pulled at white cloth wrapping that came easily apart, and found a dark book bound in leather, with a broken spine. Lamplight picked out the title gilded on the cover, and Thomas, leaning forward, read the word aloud: '*Amintiri*,' he said, 'do I have it right?'; and in the corner of the room, certain shadows thickened in certain places, and took on the form of black skirts being shaken out: Maria Văduva was clearing her throat.

The stranger laughed in delighted contempt, and said the word three times with a cadence Thomas could never have predicted. 'This means memories, or perhaps you might say: recollections. It is Romanian, which is my own language. I found it by the place where I have slept, in a box which is broken up. It's been my company.' Reverently he opened the cover, and showed the title page that had resisted soil and time. He drew his finger down it: '*Jurnalul Stelelor al Maria Văduva,*' he said. 'You might translate this into English as: *The Star Diary of Maria Văduva.*'

Thomas made a wordless exclamation and spilled the last of his milk.

The stranger frowned. 'This is upsetting for you?'

'Forgive me,' said Thomas. 'It's just that these days it is all both absolutely surprising, and entirely to be expected.' (Maria – frowning spectre, companionable ghost – picked pearls from the hem of her skirt, and muttering returned to the shadows.)

'You expected this book – you know this woman.' Statement, not query.

'She's an old friend of mine.'

'But she is certainly dead.'

'She is certainly dead. But when, and why? It's a mystery.' Thomas was conscious of the sensation of an igniting flame in his stomach – Just you wait, James Bower! Just you see what I've got for you now! He leafed through the book: inscrutable diary entries made in a familiar untidy hand, star fields sketched in circles of black ink. 'Though perhaps now we've solved it, if you tell me what all this means.'

'Perhaps I will. But first give me a drink that is not milk. I'm not a child.'

'I'll give you whisky,' said Thomas, 'to help you sleep, but no more than this' – he poured a godly measure, and put the bottle back – 'then I'll tell you my mystery if you will tell me yours. Fair's fair.'

The stranger inclined his head, and Thomas felt he'd successfully petitioned a stubborn king. It was midnight. The comet had begun to rise again, and Maria Văduva in her chair by the window sat in pitying silence.

'Give me more to drink,' the stranger said. 'I ask not for pleasure, but for necessity. My name is Richard Dimitru Dines.' He held out his glass. 'I was a man of God once. More than that, Thomas. Too much will not be enough.'

Thomas, listening as the stranger spoke, began at first to write with the acquisitive interest of the writer; but after a minute or two put down his pen. That had been a trespass. The only moral thing was to listen, and bear witness to these bare facts: that Richard Dimitru Dines, whose mother and sisters had called him Dimi, had been a pastor in a church in Bucharest when such a thing was deemed enmity against the state; that officials had stood each Sunday on the church steps and taken a register of every member of the congregation, down to the newborn babies; that in time he'd been taken from his apartment and accused of sedition and treachery, and kept sixty feet under the city of his birth, in a silent jail where guards wore felt slippers to conceal their arrival at the cell door.

'Then they take you to a room,' said Dimi, whose body shook the chair he sat in, 'and in that room you see what is being done, and feel it carefully and exactly – but you cannot believe it, because to believe it would make you insane, like the men who carried it out are insane. They took such great pains with my hands.'

Thomas looked for the comet in the window, and couldn't find it.

'Now you are thinking,' said Dimi, 'that God abandoned me to the cell and the hammer, and so I abandoned him. But this is the truth, and it is not so easy to forgive: God was a very present help in trouble, and when trouble ended so also did the help. Eight years they dismantled me as a bad child dismantles a doll. Then the government fell and the West came East, and when I was brought up into daylight again I was blind for a week, because it was all brightness then, the cars too loud, the young people dancing to music in another language. I went back to the pulpit. Every week the congregation was smaller. You cannot serve God and Mammon, you see? I began to hate them. Also I did not sleep.'

He could not sleep, said the stranger, and this had been maddening: in the small hours he'd walk the streets wringing his hands as best he could, and find he'd arrived at the prison gates as a dog might return to a violent home. When he read his Bible the print bled and he could make no sense of it. When he prayed he felt only the sensation of knocking his forehead against a pane of glass. His small congregation drifted elsewhere: now the church was possibly a café, or a library, or a shop, and what difference did it make? 'Sometimes in a river you will see a branch,' he said, 'or thing thrown in that must go where the river goes. So I am washed up. So here I am.'

'But don't you think this is the way for us all?' said Thomas, concealing his pity. 'Though I never see a river – I see the motion of bodies in orbit, drawn by forces as bright as the sun, and other forces completely unseen. Perhaps you saw the chapel by Potter's Field and it drew you down your orbit – so perhaps you still feel the heat of the sun of God.'

'Perhaps,' said Dines. Then he looked at the other man as if he'd attained his pulpit again, and seen Thomas down in the pew. 'How is it for you?' he said. 'I think perhaps you are a man with his back to the sun.'

'My trouble,' said Thomas, 'is that I have two suns, and neither outshines the other. In Bethesda I'm the worst of sinners, and in London I'm the strangest of saints, and I am never comfortable anywhere. Now go to bed, old man, I'll help you up: there's time for my mystery tomorrow. Then I'll tell you about James Bower, and the knowledge of strangers, and how we hunt Maria Văduva down.'

Morning. No sun, no stars: the 6.23 to Liverpool Street rattling the windows in their frames, dawn seeping over Lower Bridge Road. Richard Dimitru Dines woke astonished to find a glass of water within reach, and drank this by bending and putting his mouth to the rim, because at such an early hour his hands were bad. The mattress and sheets were astounding to him, the sheepskin rug awaiting his feet was a miracle. Silence in the house. The radiators ticked. The pain receded. Soon he sat up against the pillow and sought out his companion in the broken book. So Maria Văduva regarded him from the foot of the bed, cleaning a lens with a soft pale cloth, and the hem of her skirt was thick with silver thread: *All day a warm wind blew*, she said, *so I went down to the place where the men were building and found them all gone* . . .

Lucifer comes every morning at dawn – arrives like a
lover at the window – so I go running out and can never
get near – it seems to me nothing but a photograph of a
pearl taken out of focus – then I think of M., and how
also I could come no nearer him than if he were
contained with the lens of the telescope – and I fall into
my old habits of love – which are humiliating to me –

Bad weather by night. Essex enclosed in cloud as in a
coffin – as I am enclosed in my petticoats of lawn, my silk
and garnets, my casings of wallpaper, tapestry, plaster and
brick! Late in the evening I read the *Iliad* – I think I
should have made as good a soldier as a sinner – I should
have stood on the battlements like Hector and faced the
spear of Achilles with a laugh behind my shield – let me
first do some great thing before I die, that shall be told
among men hereafter!

19 AUGUST

All day a warm wind blew. So I went down alone to the
place where the men were building and found them gone,
and the mortar drying on the bricks. What dour God
might consent to dwell in such a place? It is all hard and
grey and no beauty in it. As I stood men and women
came and sang their hymns on the lawn – their voices
were sweet, and I was moved against my conscience and
my disposition! – I hid behind the garden wall and heard
them pray for sinners. I think I would have been a sinner
had I ever had the chance –

Then a rare black glittering night that had me reeling as if
drunk – I turned my face to the sky and saw the Perseids
had begun and were piercing Orion and Cassiopeia –
filaments and spurs of light, and this light an absolute
untainted white – few at first – then in due course such
volleys I thought they might very well cut me where I
stood, so that poor John Bell would come to the terrace at
the appointed hour and find me in ribbons – and the
moon in its last quarter, drifting through the field of view,
like the sail of a ship bellied by strong winds –

C. asked me once why I put myself to such troubles – is it
for the pleasure of knowledge, she says, so that my name
will be known among men? I told her that it was, that
men ought never to think the skies are in their possession
for all that they parcel and barter the land – but I lied.
What do I care for the commendations of men? What
ought I to do with their respect? It is all done for one
man – so that I might bring down the stars and hurl them
at his door, so that he opens it for all the knocking!

Morning on Lower Bridge Road, the house taking in its solitary hour of sun: scent of good coffee, and of toast; scent of tulips sorrowing over the lip of their vase. Vagrant light passing over the diary with its broken spine, and arriving at the sheets of paper on which Dines was bringing Maria Văduva into English: *I would have been a sinner*, he'd written, *had I ever had the chance.*

'When I phoned to tell him,' said Thomas, 'I said he was welcome any time, and that the later he came, the more Maria he could read, since you were hard at work.' Dimitru put a hand on a stomach that swelled under borrowed clothes: a day or so in the company of Thomas Hart would fatten any man to contentment.

'We should give him something good to eat,' said the old man, having already acquired the comforts of a sitting tenant. Rising from his seat, he asked if by any chance there was yeast in the house, and flour, and fresh eggs; if Thomas could possibly find some jam. Thomas did have yeast. He had plum jam, and a dozen eggs; and so Dines, seated on a kitchen stool, directed Thomas to the manufacture of the pastries he'd liked best as a boy, which (he said) resembled the crown of the last Romanian king, who left his throne to wring the necks of chickens on a provincial farm. When all this was done, and the pastries were dredged in sugar and cooling on the rack, the men worked together in silence for a time among the books and papers and the planisphere; though Thomas found all his attention fixed on the pavement beyond the window, and his hopes resting on the sound of the garden gate.

Meanwhile James Bower, coming under the dripping railway bridge, stood at the corner of Lower Bridge Road and shivered. There was Thomas Hart, he thought, two hundred yards down there, concealed in that house arrested in time, with its curtains which were never drawn, and the purple acers coming into bud – there also was a further piece of Maria Văduva, disinterred from Potter's Field. He was conscious again of the two conflicting sensations that arose if he ever thought of Thomas. These ought to have cancelled each other out, but never did: the man intrigued and puzzled him equally, with his elegant demonstrations of friendship and his occasionally complicit-seeming smiles. If ever he put himself to the trouble of thinking what distinguished Thomas from other friends of his, he struck a hard place that prevented his going any further, because this would be difficult and inconvenient and if nothing else (here was the house in view) Thomas Hart redeemed him from boredom, which was his old besetting sin. 'We are pals,' he assured himself cheerfully, 'we are pals' – and there was Thomas coming to the door and seeming no more pleased than he ought to have been, if certainly no less.

'Now then, James,' he said, bringing him to a chair, 'I must introduce you to my good friend. This is Richard Dimitru Dines, though he says we should call him Dimi. Give me your coat and have one of these – Dimi says they're shaped like crowns, though I can't see it myself, can you? Then we'll show you what we've found.' The room was warm. Apples circled an orange on the table. Hyacinths bloomed out of banks of moss in bowls on the windowsill, and their perfume was that of a woman who'd left in a hurry.

'Welcome,' said the imperious vagrant, inclining his head, 'I am pleased to meet the friend of Thomas.' He wore a sweater of fine green wool, and slippers lined with sheepskin: he smelt of soap and whisky. With difficulty he lifted the plate of pastries, and James took one of these, and broke it. 'Thomas tells me,' he said, 'that you found the book in Potter's Field?'

'Yes. I found it.' (Impression here of pride: of having overseen the whole problem of Maria Văduva from the first.) 'I saw it shining in the mud. The wall was badly made, and moved, and there underneath I saw a metal box. A casket,' said Dimitru, selecting the word, and admiring it and himself, 'a casket as you might use for bones.'

'Yes,' said Thomas. 'We disturbed her grave. No wonder she haunts me now!' He nodded as if in greeting towards the corner of the room, where nobody sat, and certainly nobody raised a straight black brow.

James wiped sugar from his fingers. 'Well, then,' he said. 'Why don't you show me?'

So the diary was opened on a shallow cushion to preserve its damaged spine, and Dines, touching with reverence the gilded title, said, 'I have reached the summer of 1889. You see I have made a translation. I make quick work of it. I understand she was not a happy woman: she did not have the trick of happiness, as some do not have the trick, for example, of folding up their tongue.'

Carefully James Bower turned the pages of the diary, and unable to decipher the entries looked instead at the drawings interspersed throughout. 'How obvious it is,' he said, 'and how stupid we were not to have guessed. See here, Thomas, the phases of the moon – here a galaxy, I suppose, like water going down a plug –'

'Andromeda,' said Thomas: 'Messier 31, and our nearest neighbour, which they once called the Little Cloud –'

'And this is Romanian, then. I've never seen it,' said James, 'never met a Romanian. I would have thought it was Italian.' He attempted a word or two.

Dimitru laughed. He ate a pastry. 'I implore you,' he said, 'as much as you pity an old man: leave my language alone. Have my people not endured enough? Now you will ask me what I know of this woman. I should tell you that she is clever, as you see. I have said she is unhappy. Well, clever women are always unhappy. When she is not unhappy, she is all a kind of stupid joy. She is rich. She complains of her broken heart, but keeps it like a pet and wouldn't mend it if she could. My mouth is quite dry.' He rolled a bright eye at Thomas, who with a sigh, and indicating that here was a familiar transaction to which he submitted against his better judgement, reached for a bottle and poured the guest a measure. 'Out with it,' he said.

'Look here,' said Dimitru. 'See how the writing on this day is hurried. Did her hand shake? You see the ink. Perhaps the pen broke here. Thomas, give me more. Now I can tell you. This is what she has written: *I believe the big thing* – no, I will perhaps make an amendment – *I believe the great thing that I have longed for has happened at last* – then she speaks of love, and so on.' The glass was empty, the room was warm: he yawned immensely. 'Now I want to sleep.'

'A great thing she longed for,' said Thomas, 'and she speaks of love? This M. of hers, I suppose, come to Essex to tell her he was mistaken, that in fact he did love her, that he couldn't imagine what he'd been thinking – Dimi, are you tired of us already?'

James saw the old man's head drooping now, as if some essential mechanism had failed. 'Shall we let him sleep?' said Thomas, smiling with that curious complicit look, so that the warm room with its perfumed air became abruptly intimate. 'Shake him,' said James, 'go on, wake him up' – for a moment the men eyed the sleeping stranger, and the noises of the neighbourhood came in. A woman desperate with domestic irritation was shouting just beyond the window – 'Get back in here,' she said, 'just you get right back in here' – and this startled Dines awake. He looked bewildered around the room, seeming to make no sense of the men, the table with the notebooks on it, the woman shouting at the window. 'What have you done with me?' he said. 'What have you been doing?'

'Dimi,' said Thomas, 'it's all all right. Everything is all right, and has been for a long time.'

'Don't do it,' said the old man, 'please don't, don't let them again.' He huddled in the chair with his arms raised above his head, and Thomas came forward. 'Dimi,' he said. 'Come on, now. See this table, these chairs? See the sun trying to come in? It is spring in Essex. It's half past one in the afternoon. Stand up, stand with me' – his arms were under the old man's arms, bearing the weight – 'there's nothing to you, old man. There's nothing to you at all. I won't be long,' he said, turning to James at the door. 'I won't be long – will you wait for me?'

James Bower, waiting between empty chairs, felt uneasy in the absence of the other men. Every nearby object was too large and highly coloured, the scent of the tulips stagnant as that of a pond. He turned the pages of the notebook – '*Let me first do some great thing before I die,*' he read aloud; and oh yes, he thought, yes, me too! He looked about, expecting to find himself in company after all: Maria Văduva descending from the ceiling as if on ropes, deranged with all her unwanted love, pearl beads dropping from the hem of her skirt.

'Sorry about that,' said Thomas, returning to the room. 'He is never entirely here; he is always in part down there, and sometimes so far down he can't be reached. Don't go yet, will you? Don't go. The coffee is still hot.'

'He has worked hard on this,' said James, looking again at the notebook, 'and ought to be paid. But see how he stops just here, as if to taunt us!'

'He taunts us, and so does Maria. But all the same,' said Thomas, pushing the notebook away, 'more and more I understand what caused her to love the stars as much as she loved the man who didn't love her – see these apples, this orange? I try to teach myself interactions of the planetary orbits, and as soon as I grasp the mechanics it slips from my grasp. It is all so strange, so much more surprising than I knew – shall I tell you what I've learned about the moon?'

'Yes, please.'

'They say it once turned much faster on its axis, but the relation of forces between the earth and the moon made it slow down, and in the end the time it took the moon to make one full turn was the time it took to circuit the earth, and a lunar day was the same as a lunar year. They call this tidal lock, which is the influence of the earth and the moon on each other. We might say the sun rules the earth, and the earth rules the moon – but the moon isn't helpless, it has power too! So we have the tides, and even the ground rises up as the moon passes over: certainly one body is stronger, but the weaker one is not without effect. And I've been told the earth's rotation is also slowing down, so that eventually one side will eternally face the same side of the moon, and half the world will never see the moon at all – oh,' he said (James glanced at his watch, and noted the hour with a frown), 'I'm Scheherazade forestalling the executioner, and you have work to do.'

'I notice the moon these days,' said James Bower, 'and never did before. Yes, I should go; but we'll come back to this when Dimitru has finished his work, and we know what Maria found, and where she went. Then you'll get a book out of it, Thomas, you mark my words' – he was headed for the door – 'you'll get a book out of it, and your best work, and you can dedicate the thing to me.'

The following Sunday being Easter, every church in Essex prepared to celebrate the resurrection of the Son of God. In the cathedrals of Chelmsford and Brentwood, nervous choirs assembled in their stalls, and the clerestories made their hallelujahs ready; in the cold stone temple of St Peter-on-the-Wall, white tulips were cut for white vases on white altar cloths, and half a mile around the headland the white reactors of the Magnox nuclear power station had the look of empty tombs where giants had been buried.

Bethesda Chapel, the old dissenter, had no use for Easter. It rejected the sacred calendar with the vigour of Martin Luther slapping a communion wafer from the hand of a priest, and gave to Easter all the attention it gave to Christmas, which is to say: none at all. But it happened that this was also the day of the pastor's anniversary, and since he'd stood in that pulpit for thirty years, it was not quite an ordinary sabbath. 'There'll be a service of thanksgiving in the afternoon,' said Thomas, cleaning the red velvet coat with white spirit, 'and then we will have tea, and a service in the evening. You needn't come,' he added, mindful of the old man's shame and doubt, 'you can stay and keep Maria company.'

Dimitru said, 'I do not mind. But do you?'

Thomas attended to a button coming loose. 'If you think I'll be kept from the pew by that woman's malice, you are wrong. The more you send me away from the pew the more I want to sit in it, and the more I'm told to forsake the world the more worldly I become. So you see I don't expect ever to be a happy man – get up now, and put Maria down, or the sermon will have already begun.'

The two men found the chapel changed in the good spring weather. The coloured discs in the window were liquid and bright, and wind from the west agitated the air. Seagulls blown in from St Osyth and Walton-on-the-Naze went screaming over the roof; a fair was going on in Lowlands Park, and the blithe cheer of the waltzers could be heard above the old harmonium.

They were late. The milky chapel lights were shining on their iron chains. The pews were full, the godly having come from as far as Prittlewell and Aldwinter and Suffolk to be grateful for the preservation of the saints in general, and of the pastor in particular. As they entered some heads turned, and took in the familiar man and the unfamiliar one with brief impassive smiles, then went back to the pulpit. Dines sat clasping his satchel and surveying the chapel without apparent distress. Beside him, opening with rote piety his Bible and his hymn book, Thomas surveyed the women and girls with their heads decently covered in straw hats or dark felt cloches, and the dozen men and boys in their best black suits. There was Lorna in a thin white blouse that showed the hard elaborate casing of her underwear; there was the senior deacon going solemnly into the pulpit: '*Be perfect,*' he read, squinting at the lectern, '*be of good comfort, be of one mind, live in peace.*' The women had gone down early that morning to clean, raising dust that still came streaming from the gallery, and Thomas imagined it all to be astronomical, dispersed from the rings of Saturn and settling in the leaves of his hymn book. Suddenly he was struck by the obliterating knowledge of his smallness: but none of it matters one bit, he thought, leaning dazed against the back of his pew – how hard we try, and what are we but ants on a stone in a river going to the sea? Then they were on their feet, singing – '*Oh the deep deep love of Jesus, vast, unmeasured, boundless, free*' – and Thomas thought of other loves, which had been neither boundless nor free, but much nearer to hand than the love of God. He looked up to the gallery, and there was Grace Macaulay leaning on the ledge above the clock, in a dress of stiff pale blue fabric that buttoned to the neck and made her matronly. There too (Thomas was startled, and his exclamation was covered by the hymn) was Nathan, whose shirt and tie made him seem a boy lost in borrowed clothes. They were alone up there, in the box pews that could be fastened with a latch, where once when Thomas was young he'd found a note pushed between the seat and the arm of the pew – *Let him kiss me with the kisses of his mouth*, the note had read, and troubled him for weeks. Then the pastor was speaking, and everything under Bethesda's roof was pale, cool, serene – the walls that gave off the chill of brick and plaster, the vaulted ceiling and the moony lights, the cloth on the communion table, were all as still and white as if under a frost. Thomas saw the lights of the fair coming through the window behind the pulpit, and distantly he made out the bass of pop songs bizarre against the chapel quiet, and bells ringing as prizes were won and money was lost. 'To the glory of God,' said the pastor, 'amen'; then the harmonium drew a difficult breath for the last of the hymns, and Thomas Hart stood with the congregation. He turned to look up at the gallery again: Grace had put down her hymn book. Neither she nor Nathan stood as they ought to have done or sang as they ought to have sung, but leaned on the balcony, facing each

131

other and speaking quietly. Grace had taken off her hat. How could Thomas have explained to those going down to the fair, to the passengers in the cars idling at the traffic lights on London Road and the children peeling foil from their Easter eggs by the light of television screens, how indecent and defiant this was? She was a woman bareheaded in the house of God, and might as well have raised her skirt to her thighs – then with deliberate gestures he'd never seen before she piled up her hair and let it fall, and did it again. Ahead of him, three pews down, Lorna's white hat quivered. She turned, her nose moving like an animal scenting the air; she looked up, and saw Grace. She lowered and raised her gleaming eyelids, then looked carefully at Thomas, smiling her knowledge and her satisfaction. Then the hymn was over, and the harmonium's last note faded among the hanging lights. '*Now unto him who is able to keep you from falling,*' said the pastor, leaning on the lectern, '*and present you faultless before the presence of his glory with exceeding joy*' – and Thomas thought: the difficulty is that some of us would prefer to fall.

'Amen,' said the pastor.

'Amen,' said the congregation.

Thomas said, 'Amen.'

The worshippers came out of chapel darkness into ordinary light, and greeted each other in holy friendship saying what an encouragement the sermon had been, and wasn't it a blessing that spring weather had come; then they retreated to the dim cold hall behind the chapel, and took their places at trestle tables covered with white cloths. On each of these a silver tea urn stood. There were cups and saucers of a pale institutional green, and sandwiches of banana and stewed dates between slices of thin brown bread; there were sausage rolls releasing grease, and a kind of sweet iced tart nobody ever saw elsewhere, and which was as particular to Bethesda as the hymns and the harmonium. The air was fragrant with sugar and tea, and the congregation sang a grace that battled the noise of the fair. Thomas dispensed tea, and was the only man in Bethesda who'd ever think of doing so.

Dimitru meanwhile concealed his hands in the folds of his red coat, and told whoever would listen that yes, he was the man who'd lived for a time in Potter's Field, with jays and foxes for his neighbours – that in fact he was Romanian, and missed the city where he was born (nobody but Thomas saw him take imploring nips from a bottle concealed in the satchel with Maria).

Nearby Grace and Nathan wrote by turns on a piece of paper, laughing and hiding what they'd written. The Ten Commandments in forbidding black calligraphy hung behind them in immense oak frames (the Essex damp had got behind the glass, and blurred the ink so that deceit and adultery had become matters of debate); and on the tuneless piano in the corner a pretty child in a pink straw hat worked slowly at 'Abide With Me'.

Thomas poured tea with the dazed content of a man submitting to sedation, briefly forgetting the thorn in his flesh. Then the air altered; there was a powdery scent like that of a spoiled baby, the rustle of satin so cheap it could strike sparks – the tea urn was cold, and rivulets of water ran down it and blackened the tablecloth. Lorna Greene, her white hat fixed and quivering over her brow, was coming slowly through the tables, drawing Anne behind her and murmuring in whispers designed to penetrate the sleepy air in which old men dozed over cake. 'I'm only thinking of the child,' she was saying, 'I wouldn't for the world want you to worry, dear Anne, only you see' – she gestured to the empty places at their table – 'you see: she's gone, and the boy has gone with

133

her.' Into these words she poured every conceivable wickedness. Anne's face was unhappy. Thomas saw that Grace had
gone, and left her hat behind. 'Mr Macaulay,' said Lorna,
looking with ingratiating sorrow up at Ronald, 'Mr Macaulay,
I am afraid dear Grace has gone off. Perhaps she's gone down
to Vanity Fair, perhaps the boy tempted her to go. Really' –
she flirted through painted eyelashes, rebuking the sin she
invited – 'really I did think to myself: I'm surprised Mr
Macaulay has such a worldly young man under his roof!'

'They've just gone for a walk,' said Anne, 'it's such a beautiful day.' The girl at the piano fumbled the melody and
slammed the lid, and in the absence of the hymn they heard
the music from the waltzers.

'Perhaps we ought to look for her,' Lorna said, patting
Anne's arm with a gesture designed to arouse distress under
the guise of allaying it, 'perhaps Mr Macaulay –' Thomas
heard the screams of children and hawkers, and a volley of
drum and bass that seemed ludicrous against the tea urns,
the pristine tablecloths. 'Oh,' he said, 'she'll be all right' – but
as he said it something altered in the noise of the fair. A yell
of voices merged in warning lifted over the music, and
Thomas felt everything he'd eaten rise in his stomach: *peril*,
he thought, *peril*, the word tolling with a pain in his head. He
remembered these same people in this same hall, a baby
among them, her mother dead, acquiring him with her newborn oil-on-water eyes: 'I think she'll be all right,' he said,
and doubted it. There was the yell again, and Thomas experienced so sudden a contraction of worry in his heart that
without thought or explanation he began to run, and heard
behind him Anne's bewildered exclamation, and Dimitru
grunting in his sleep. He came out into the light, and went
stumbling up Bethesda's lawn to the line of silver birches;
but now the yell receded under the music and the children

134

laughing, and there was doubt again – it was just the noise of the crowd, and Lorna's whisper: no peril, no harm done.

Going through the silver birches he stood at the verge of Lowlands Park, and from this vantage saw crowds that milled between the fairground rides, and young men taking shots at plastic horses captive on their plastic roads, and wanted desperately to be among them. Behind him in Bethesda the same placid female faces were shaded by their sober hats, and the same grave men smiled cautiously behind their beards – but here was all the world, hectic and merry and heedless of their souls, if in fact they had any souls to heed: girls released from school uniform into constricting skirts or jeans, and prissy mothers tending to their prams; shirtless boys taunting larger men, and running for shelter; women as old as his mother would have been, half-cut on wine and yelling in censure or delight.

Thomas walked on through air thick with candyfloss, and here was a helter-skelter painted like a barber's pole, and a skeleton hanging by a noose from the painted roof of a painted house – here were children riding unicorns that bucked on the brass poles that pierced them, and the grass was littered with paper tickets. He felt unloosed – and was he really too old for the carousel, too old to ride a blue mat down the helter-skelter? Then again (he was recalled to himself by a noise nearby), where was that wretched child Grace, and where was that wretched boy? He stopped abruptly, as if at a signal, and heard again that same gathering yell. Peril, he thought, peril after all – two boys nearby halted, pointed upwards, and laughed without pleasure. He heard the noise of metal working against an obstruction, and turned with the boys to find a ride like a ship hanging inverted above the fair, its red steel sail an immense shovel poised above the grass. A dozen riders secured by bars were suspended upside down above the mechanism, which strained against itself with a shriek; a girl's hair fell streaming down towards the greased teeth of the parts. 'Something's got caught,' said one of the boys to Thomas, in the companionable way of strangers sharing disaster, 'something broke off and got caught.' Thomas found himself moving with the crowd towards the ride, until he could make out the sail's tip inches from the soil, and a man lying nearby. Here: quiet among the noise, and a man suffering in it, unzipped from thigh to knee. It was possible to see the astonishing brightness of the severed muscle, and the bone from which it had been separated as cleanly as if by a butcher preparing a joint; from time to time a hanging rider screamed for help, but in the reverent shock attending the man this seemed impertinent and nobody looked up.

The man was not quite conscious. His head was in the lap of a girl who sometimes patted his shoulder with useless affection. 'There it is, look,' said the boy to Thomas, with grave satisfaction, 'it broke clean off.' Thomas looked, and saw that a piece of the ship's sail had become somehow caught in the mechanism, and been flung out.

The crowd was intoxicated by disaster: a woman with arms full of plastic toys shouted, 'Put a belt round his leg or he'll bleed out right here while we watch!'; and how pleased she is, thought Thomas, in time it will be the defining feature of her character that she was here – then there was the siren of an ambulance, cutting the air with its pendulum swing. The baffled crowd began to move from side to side, taking Thomas with it. There was a moment when he felt himself lifted so that the toes of his shoes skimmed the damaged lawn; then the siren stopped, and this left a hollow place in which Thomas could make out the injured man's sorrowing moan.

Something gave in the mechanism of the ride, and with a

shriek the upturned ship swung down and came to rest. The violent movement raised draughts that blew paper tickets over the lawn, and the startled crowd dispersed. It threw Thomas out, and caused him to stumble backwards, grasping uselessly for purchase at the air. His heels slipped in the churned grass, and briefly it seemed he was airborne; then he stumbled again, and felt a blow to his hip. It came from behind, and was so direct and attentive a blow it occurred to him that he was being attacked, and had no means of defending himself. But there was no more violence, and the crowd was receding, and after a moment he discovered that he was sitting alone on the lawn, half-toppled against the steel generator that had wounded him with a surgeon's precise and disinterested assault. There was no pain yet; but with the clarity of prophecy he understood that some integral structure had been compromised and would never be right again.

Pop music came bumping from a nearby speaker, and Thomas fixed on the melody to quell the nausea setting in, trying to persuade himself it was a hymn. The yelling diminished. The injured man said nothing. Time passed, or seemed to. When eventually Thomas raised himself against the generator he found the crowd had thinned. The ambulance went quietly. A girl with blood on her dress ran briefly after it, realised her folly, and fell back. The sun was setting on the broken sail. Elsewhere rides still moved, and teenagers drifted aimlessly about: there was a furtive atmosphere, as if everyone was privately certain they were doing something wrong and afraid they'd be caught out.

Thomas went by inches through the fair. He was making for Bethesda, but it was difficult to order his steps. He'd forgotten Grace. He was certain something moved in his hip that was never intended to move, and it was this that made him vomit as he walked. Slowly he came to the edge of the fair, where lights were going on in caravans, and a folding chair had been put against an oak. Here Thomas sat among a litter of spent cigarettes, and was surprised by his own cry of pain. He judged the time by the declining sun: soon they'd start singing in Bethesda again – soon it would be dark, and he'd see the comet rise. Dazed contentment settled on him, and this was frightening – how easy it would be to succumb to this sinking sensation, and be taken for a discarded prop in a haunted house. 'Up you get, Thomas,' he said fondly to himself, and didn't.

Now: twilight. Pale things visible in the dim air; movements nearby in the oaks that fringed the park, as if cloth had been left hanging from a branch. Thomas went forward, raising pain almost ecstatic in its effects, so that minutes passed when the world consisted of nothing but sensation. When this receded the evening light was altered again, and the pale cloth was more plainly visible. 'Oh,' he said. 'Yes, I see.' Grace Macaulay in her ugly dress was leaning on an oak, pulling and releasing her skirt with odd thoughtless gestures while Nathan unbuttoned her from neck to waist. The buttons gave him trouble. He had an angry look. Grace laughed, then the dress opened like the case of a beetle: 'Come here,' she said. 'Come here.' Nathan had her by the shoulder, and swayed as if half-drunk; then his hand was inside the bodice and he made a sound like that of a man in pain. Grace laughed with a kind of tender mocking and Thomas saw with astonishment that the boy didn't know what he was doing. He pulled at the dress and there was Grace's shoulder and her breast, and Thomas saw the extraordinary pallor of her skin, on which coursed the single tributary of a vein. Then she was offering herself to the boy and her breast was in his mouth, and she bent and kissed him on the crown of his head, as if she pitied him this shock his flesh was heir to.

Thomas stood in a confusion of envy and unspent desire – it was never like that for me, he thought, and now I am old. With an animal instinct for refuge, he headed for Bethesda. After a time it occurred to him it might be easier to crawl than walk, and so he lowered himself to the ground, and encountered the sensation of his scalp lifting from his skull, and with it an immense release of pressure. In pain's delirium, Thomas saw that suddenly it was the hard light of noon. The last of the crowd, falling silent, was parting one by one to clear a path and let a man come dancing through: James Bower, his upturned face good to look at in the strange perpendicular light, and behind him Richard Dimitru Dines in his scarlet coat, pushing a shopping trolley that had rusted in the river. Maria Văduva was riding in it, grasping her shabby chariot and looking for the moon: 'The thing I longed for,' she was saying, 'has happened at last.'

'Wait for me,' said Thomas, 'I'm coming'; but they didn't wait, and he couldn't go. The noon light went out. Darkness came in like a blot from the edge of his view. James Bower dwindled to a pinprick, and so did the scarlet coat and the tilted shopping trolley. Thomas fell back. The Essex soil was soft and took him in.

Night, now. No cloud: first stars out. Then there it was, there it was: Hale–Bopp, the Great Comet of the age – radiant above the Lowlands pediment, and falling through Perseus like the last of the rebel angels.

In the meantime, and before the fall: Grace Macaulay went back to the chapel with Nathan, and found the congregation gone and all the windows shut. Ronald was waiting with her aunt by the doors, moving the heavy chapel keys from hand to hand, and clasping his Bible under his arm. Grace made hasty apologies: they'd taken a walk, she said, and time had run away with them. Then there was the sound of the gate, and of Lorna Greene going through it with her white hat on, having done what she'd set out to do. She paused to take them all in with a level look, before lowering her pearly eyelids and receding through the evening towards the town. 'Oh,' said Grace, understanding with perfect clarity: Lorna must have followed them to the fair, and seen their sin, and run to tell her father, whose white hair now more than ever had the look of a halo designating his virtuous state. Grace felt neither ashamed nor afraid, still having with her the scent of the loam under the oaks, and nature's indifference to sin. 'Go home,' she said to Nathan, feeling older than him by years, 'it's time we all went home.'

'Yes,' he said, blinking, 'all right,' and did as he was told. Grace watched him go, and this disrupted her calm with a flare of anger as intimate and particular as love. There he went, careless and at ease, and meanwhile her father was coming towards her, when after all it was Nathan that broke the window, not her! So she discovered that after all she was afraid, and that she was sore and felt a little sick. 'I'm sorry,' she said to her aunt, who wouldn't meet her eye – but it struck her that she was not sorry. She was afraid, it was true, and now there was the beginning of shame; but she was afraid of her father, and ashamed of having wounded her aunt. There it ended. She was not sorry, because she hadn't sinned.

Ronald, putting the chapel keys in his pocket, walked past his daughter. 'Get in the car, please,' he said, and obedient Grace sat behind her aunt, whose shoulders shook with the effort of retaining her tears. Nobody spoke as they drove home to the house on Beechwood Avenue, where new leaves were arriving on the silver birch, and Anne had already set out the breakfast things.

Ronald Macaulay, putting down his Bible and taking off his coat, spoke to Grace without looking at her: she was to go to the room where he slept alone in the bed he'd shared with his wife. Dumbly, and unable to summon the memory of Nathan's face, she obeyed her father. This room faced north. It was cold with a penetrating damp drawn up from the Essex clay, and Grace began to shiver. What remained of her calm dissipated. She'd wounded her aunt, she'd wounded her father, she had probably wounded God. Once in the pulpit a man had told her that no sin was a small sin, and every sin was a blow of the hammer on a nail in Christ's palm; so now she saw against the painted wall a good man's hand convulse against a length of wood. She thought of how quickly Nathan had left her, and the intimate anger returned, and this was shocking: nobody told her it was possible to love and be angry. There were two white pillows on the bed, and on one of these the impression of her father's head was full of shadows. Grace looked for a time at the second pillow and tried to imagine the colour of her mother's hair in the morning, and couldn't.

Ronald came into the room and sat on the bed and began to unlace his shoes. This took a very long time. His hair in the lamplight had a sickly yellowish look. He asked Grace if she knew that what she'd done was wrong, and again she lied and said she did. And did she understand, said Ronald, that she ought to be punished, since it was a father's duty to punish his children, and in so doing protect them from their wretched natures, and direct them to salvation? 'Go over there,' said Ronald. He looks frightened, thought Grace. 'Go over there,' said her father, who loved her: 'choose a belt.' There was a white cupboard in the room, where hung fastidiously ordered ranks of shirts and trousers, and several belts. 'You take one of those,' he said, 'you choose one,' and left the room. He crossed the hall to the bathroom, and locked the door, and Grace wondered what he was doing in there. The room was turning towards the moon. There were no cars on the street. She looked at the belts. She loved her father and she wanted to be good. She wondered if she ought to choose the heaviest of the belts, which would hurt the most severely, since she supposed she deserved it. But it hadn't felt like sinning, she wasn't sorry and she wouldn't lie – then she heard the slip of the bathroom lock. She looked at the belt she held. Its leather was cracked, its buckle was tarnished, it ought to be thrown away. She began to laugh: what the hell does he expect me to do? she thought. Do I hold out my hand – do I bend over like I did when I was a child, and he caught me out in a lie? Lights were on in the neighbours' houses, and she imagined someone looking in, and seeing a white-haired man solemnly beating a stooping woman, then returning the belt to the cupboard and going down to put the kettle on. It's ridiculous, she thought (she went on laughing), I won't do it, and how could he make me? Suddenly the faith of her childhood struck her as comical: the idea that hell boiled away under the tarmac and pavements of Beechwood Avenue, that if she put her ear to the carpet she'd hear the ringing of pitchforks forged on devils' anvils, the hissing of embers on penitent flesh – how ridiculous it was, how evidently only nightmares to frighten children!

So Ronald Macaulay, when he came in, had on his hands not a pliable reckless child to be drawn back from the brink of the pit, but a woman laughing beyond speech. Grace looked at her father, expecting to see all the old sorrow and censure, and here was the day's last shock: he was smiling. It was brief – it went – but she saw it. 'Never mind,' said Ronald. 'Never mind.' He put his hand on her shoulder, and it was there for a long time, and she wondered if he were praying. Then 'Go to bed, Grace,' he said. 'Lights out.'

Lights out in Aldleigh. Lights out in the bedrooms on Beechwood Avenue, where Grace Macaulay touches herself, and finds she's sore; where Anne Macaulay grieves to her worn chintz pillowcase. Lights out in Ronald Macaulay's study, where he sleeps with his forehead on his open Bible, absorbing the book of the prophet Isaiah through the frontal bone: *though your sins be as scarlet, they shall be white as snow.* Lights out on Ward H of Aldleigh General Hospital, where Thomas Hart is told he's a lucky man. Damage has certainly been done, but he'll escape the blade and stitches, if not a month or so of pain (in opiate dreams he encounters Maria Văduva standing in Bethesda's balcony, and filling the open baptistery with astronomical dust). Lights out in Potter's Field, the nesting jays mourning their solitary egg lost to a magpie that same afternoon, the buddleia cultivating cabbage whites, the hazel coming into bud so fast you'd almost hear it squeak.

On the verges of a slip road on the outskirts of town, Richard Dimitru Dines lights out for another territory. He's got a shopping trolley with him, and put Maria Văduva in it. Lights out in Vanity Fair, the false ship's sail cordoned and preserved for scrutiny, rats fat in the litter bins, the moon on the wane. Lights out in Lowlands House, the candle pinched out at the wick, no light but moonlight. Boards prised from a window, the small panes polished, Hale–Bopp making a transit, blown by the winds of the sun. Here a solitary figure sits with her thumb on the wheel of a plastic lighter making occasional flames, all the while repeating private incantations, of which a passing rat can make out not a single word.

'Thomas, who are you looking for?' Impatient Grace was repeating herself, since rain raised volleys against the window, and Thomas, dazed on pain and pain relief, seemed not to have heard. 'You keep looking over there in the corner but there's nobody here but me. Do the drugs they gave you make you see things?' She'd brought cheap roses secured with an elastic band, and their smooth green buds were splitting and showing pink frills in the slit.

Thomas had been home for days, and now sat bolstered by cushions, and tilting like a vessel holed below the waterline. Grace saw he'd been trying to work, since there were green notebooks near to hand; but the open screen of his computer was dark, and showed only his reflection distorted by a fingerprint. The house, thought Grace, was wounded with him. Flowers sagged in stagnant vases, and dust was accruing on the sideboard and lamps. Thomas himself was thinned out, as if he'd undertaken a forced march on hard ground, and not passed four days in bed. His shirt was untucked, and there was a stain on the collar that was curiously painful to Grace. How had it come about that she must now care for Thomas, when she had on her hands the question of her mortal body and immortal soul, and had no idea what to do with either?

'I'm sorry,' Thomas said, 'what did you say?' He looked

with a puzzled frown about the room as if something had been mislaid, but he couldn't think what.

'Never mind,' said Grace. 'Look: you ought to eat.' A sandwich curled uneaten on the table. The rain persisted. 'Tell me how you are. How long it will last?' She meant: how long before you come back to me?

'My hip isn't quite broken,' said Thomas, 'but something's gone wrong with the ligaments there and it hurts like hell. They had me on a ward with old men, and now I'm old too, I've caught time like a virus – did you see that?' He peered through to the kitchen in a fuddled way she disliked. 'Did you see that? Is anyone there?'

'He's gone, Thomas,' said Grace, thinking she'd like to shake Thomas back into the form of his old self. 'I told you: Dimitru has gone.'

'Yes,' said Thomas, sighing, 'and so has Maria. Tell me again what happened that day.'

'I wasn't there,' said Grace, 'because Nathan and I had gone for a walk.' She paused. Together they looked at the opening roses. 'My aunt told me that after you left the chapel, Dimitru woke up and looked for you. But you were gone, and he was frightened and angry, and a bottle fell out of his satchel and broke, and one of the children from Prittlewell cut her foot. Then Lorna interfered. She spoke to him, and only made it worse – he knocked the table over and all the cups and saucers broke, and Lorna said she was afraid he'd hurt her – that his hands were broken because he used them to fight.' She looked at Thomas. 'I hate her. I've never hated anyone before, and I like it – it feels like power, and I've never had any of that! My father said Dimi really ought to go, that it would be best. And he went. Nobody has seen him. I've looked for him in Potter's Field, I promise I looked, but he isn't there.'

'And he took Maria's diary with him.'

'Thomas, you're white. Haven't they given you what you need for the pain – don't those tablets work?'

'Did they look for it? Did anybody see it?'

'He left nothing behind. Does it matter so much?' But Thomas turned away and rubbed his face with his sleeve; and Grace was appalled to find him reverting to tears. She felt the weight of all the years already lived, and the weight of the years she'd not lived yet, and taken together they tired her out. 'Thomas,' she said, 'why do you go to Bethesda? Why do you stay?'

This startled him. Briefly the rain held off: blackbirds in the street, water on the windows in blots that shone like mercury. 'I stay,' he said, 'because I want to.'

'That isn't enough,' she said. 'Wanting something can't be a good enough reason to do it.'

'It can,' said Thomas. 'It is. You'll see.' A cushion slipped and caused him to tilt further; he grimaced, and his pallor spread. 'It aches,' he said, 'I doubt I'll ever be free of it. And I daresay it's over now,' he said. 'Dimi has gone, and taken Maria: so that's the end of the affair. No reason to haunt Lowlands now – no reason anyone might haunt me!' His despondency seemed to her so entirely out of proportion to the loss of some inscrutable documents retrieved from ruins that her pity ceded to irritation. 'Come on now, Thomas,' she said, brisk as her aunt sometimes was, 'come on. You'll find more letters, you'll work things out – or there'll be another mystery, there'll be another ghost.'

'No,' he said. 'There was nothing like that before – there'll be nothing like it again.'

'Oh,' said Grace. 'Yes, I see.' It struck her there were things she'd known for some time, but never looked at directly, and now they drifted into view. 'Thomas,' she said, 'is it Maria you think you've lost, or is it James?'

146

'You see, he hasn't phoned me,' said Thomas. 'He hasn't called. He only comes when I ask, and I only ask when there's news of Maria – so if Maria is gone, how can I ask him to come? I lost my faith,' said Thomas, 'I don't know where I've put it, and now my house is empty and I live alone.' Then the understanding that had been drifting into view arrived with such clarity Grace blinked at the brilliance: he is in love, she thought, he is actually in love with James Bower; and abruptly her native instinct to console poor Thomas Hart chilled in the shadow of Bethesda's pulpit. It is a man he loves, she thought: Thomas is a homosexual. She discovered that she'd shifted away from him, as if her body had been trained into distaste – he was a queer, a sodomite: the Bible (she'd been told) numbered men like him among the thieves and liars that would never see the kingdom of God. And this was her first and only friend, whose home she loved, whose food she ate, whose wisdom she prized – she found herself reverting to anger at Thomas, because he had inverted their natural order, and now she was required to understand and console him, when he had always been her comforter. 'Come on,' she said, 'you're being stupid. It's just an old diary. It's just a man.'

'Yes,' said Thomas, 'yes: just a man.' He was laughing, and for the life of her she couldn't understand what was funny. 'Yes,' he said, 'you're right, you wretched child! Put the kettle on, would you, I'm parched.'

How was it possible to accommodate the idea of his desperate sinful state against his old endearments, the familiar galley kitchen, the teacup she liked best that was chipped where she'd dropped it? Grace discovered that her distaste and her love existed simultaneously and to an equal degree, and that neither could cancel the other out. I'll make sense of it, she thought, and they say no sin is past redemption, but I don't know how to think of him now – and she glanced back at him, sitting a little more upright in his chair, with the familiar scent of sandalwood in the folds of his clothes.

Thomas reached for the pills that made it possible to pretend the pain was happening in another room. Perhaps it was also the drugs, he thought, looking hopelessly about, that caused the sensation of loneliness which was the first of his adult life: where had Maria gone, who looked over his shoulder as he wrote, and never gave him a moment's peace? Where was Richard Dimitru Dines, and what had James been doing while Thomas dozed with the old men in Ward H? But then here was Grace with the tray, frowning as if something in the kitchen had made her cross. Silently she poured the tea, and for a moment Thomas had the impression of looking at every version of Grace eventually to be seen in time – that she was eighteen, and twenty-eight, and a woman almost forty, and that one by one all these women were already lost. He drank the tea she'd poured, and then with effort set aside the loss of Maria and of James. 'Well then,' he said. 'What have you been up to? What were you doing, while I was laid up in bed? What's it been like, life as a documented adult? Do your knees ache? Is your hair going grey?'

'I've had three grey hairs since I was thirteen,' she said, with a frowning refusal to meet his eye, so that Thomas thought he must have wronged her, but couldn't think how. Then abruptly the frown cleared. 'Is that a blackbird, Thomas? Do they always sing like that, only I never noticed before?'

'They've always sounded just like that. So you see: you are changed.'

'Perhaps I am,' she said, looking at him with a kind of anguish. 'Thomas, I try and try to be good but I don't know how. I want to be free to think my own thoughts about what is good, and what is bad – sometimes I wonder what it would be like to wake up on a Sunday morning and have it be just another day – to wear make-up, and jeans, and go to parties, and not think every minute that I've made God angry, or been ashamed of the Gospel of Christ. Then I'm afraid that if I fail to be as good as I ought to be, or loved God as I ought to have done, then He'll take something away from me, and in the end I'll be unhappy, because I was never saved.'

Then I've failed you, thought Thomas: I have failed. He recalled again the day of her arrival at Bethesda, and the peculiar claim on him arriving out of the wicker basket. He'd resolved that day to keep a foot in the chapel door, and let a little of her spirit out and a little of the world in. And certainly he'd tried: at the age of seven, for example, she'd burned her hand on steam from the kettle, and wailed as Anne held her hand under the running tap and Thomas stood watchful nearby. Ronald Macaulay, coming distractedly in, had inspected the scalded palm. 'Does it hurt?' he'd said, and there'd been a moment when Thomas had been certain that stern sorrowing man would bend to kiss it better. But he'd become sterner and more sorrowing, and said to the child: 'You must remember that although this burning will end, there is a place where the fire is never quenched, and there is nobody to bring even a drop of water, and that is the wages of sin.' And Grace had received this dreadful sermon without surprise, because already her world contained the wormwood and the gall, boiling away below the Aldleigh pavements. But: 'Look what I found,' Thomas had said, coming forward as if for all the world he'd seen nothing odder than an ordinary father with an ordinary child, 'look what I found in my pocket!' – and he'd brought out a silver acorn charm and given it to her, and Grace had forgotten hell. So he did try, and he had gone on trying, but here she was: as fastened to Bethesda as the pulpit and the pews. He had failed.

'Grace, you aren't a child. You can leave Bethesda, if you like.'

'Can I? If I can, why can't you?'

'I leave it sometimes, and return sometimes – I think of myself as two men, and that suits me well enough, though it's tiring.'

'But why do you come back – do you believe in God? Do you believe in everything they tell you there?' She paused then, seeming to examine a thought and discard it. 'And besides,' she said, evidently unable to speak frankly, 'how will I know how to be good, if there is nobody to tell me?'

'Oh, goodness, what is it? Nobody can agree,' said Thomas, in whom pain relief had raised a nauseated giddy sensation. 'I scarcely agree with myself from one day to the next – sometimes I think goodness is something fixed and certain that we move towards as best we can, sometimes I think the nature of goodness shifts, which only makes it harder to obtain. But always I think it exists somehow alongside sin – that the two things never cancel each other out. Do you want to know the worst thing I ever heard?'

'No,' said Grace.

'It wasn't murder or adultery or deceit. I have always felt it's possible to do any one of those things, and perhaps be motivated by love – so then the sin is tempered by a kind of goodness. Surely the worst we can do is sin because it is sinful, and only because of that. Did you ever hear,' he said, 'about the ortolan?' Grace shook her head with its three grey hairs. 'It's a small brown bird,' said Thomas, 'and the only thing it's known for is suffering. Every year, as they migrate for winter, they're caught in great nets. Then they're caged in the dark, and in their despair and confusion gorge them-selves on grain, until they go blind and are too heavy to fly, and are thrown in vats of Armagnac to marinade and slowly drown. Then they're taken out dripping and roasted for seven and a half minutes exactly, and given to the diner, who holds the bird by the foot and tips back his head and puts the whole body in and eats it, spitting out the beak and bones. And the diner does all this with a white cloth draped over his head, because he is full of shame and must hide himself even from God. And the thing is,' said Thomas, deriving delight from the horror he caused, 'that there's no pleasure in it – no flavour that couldn't be obtained without such a parade of cruelty, just a mouth cut by shards of bone. It's the worst sin I ever heard,' he said, fancying himself for a moment in the pulpit, 'I think there must be other sins like this: that no matter how you examine it, and by what light, you'll find no goodness there. Keep it in mind,' he said, 'perhaps that's the best any of us can do: to never be so ashamed we must hide our faces not only from each other, but from God. How, I have no idea. You must work that out for yourself, either in the pew or out of it!'

'Thomas, what would I do without you?'

'Without me? I'm injured, not dying. Now leave me alone. I'm either going to sleep or be sick, and those are best done privately.'

Later that same day, Thomas pulled his body up the narrow stairs, and having slept for an hour or so woke to find the adamant blackbird singing. He listened. No footsteps in the kitchen, no sound of an old man surprising himself with laughter and putting the bottle down. But was there a rustle in the shelves, down among the poetry perhaps – was Maria Văduva coming up the stairs to slip letters under the door? A passing train shook him out of his self-pity: what was lost but his capacity to walk without aching, and a diary that was rotting away, in a language he couldn't read? Somewhere in Aldleigh James Bower was taking off his tie, and pouring himself a glass of wine – in fact (Thomas smiled at his own foolishness) there was Maria, look, there she was, having clambered out of the shopping trolley and abandoned Dimi on the Lowlands lawn, and wandered down Lower Bridge Road. She leaned against the doorframe admiring the rings on her fingers, and said: *For God's sake, Thomas Hart, for God's sake: isn't it all a question of orbits? Things go, things come. Something's bound to happen soon.*

The sun was going down.

ON COMING AND GOING

THOMAS HART *ESSEX CHRONICLE*,
20 APRIL 1997

I'm afraid I write this lying in bed. You see I am injured, and as I recover I've got nothing to do but write, and watch Hale–Bopp make its transit past my bedroom window. I've been timing it. It seems to me to go at more or less an inch an hour.

The night I was injured it was just the other side of the window in Ward H, and seemed so nearby I thought I could touch it, if only I could break the glass without bringing the nurses to tell their most difficult patient to behave. Of course, this was just a trick of the light, together with the things they gave me for the pain. Really it was always quite a distant comet, never any closer than 0.9 astronomical units, which is to say nine-tenths of the distance from the earth to the sun. Other comets come much closer to the earth – Comet Hyakutake, for example, came as close as 0.1 astronomical units – but they're often a fleeting presence, passing more or less without notice in bad weather. I suppose that's just like us: so dazzled by beauty we convince ourselves it's within reach.

Soon Hale–Bopp will cross into the southern hemisphere, and we'll never see it again. It passed the perihelion on April Fool's Day, and now it is coming to the end of the third week of a journey that will take 2,533 years. Already I suppose it's slowing down, and will only get slower until it begins its return to the sun – then picture it running with relief and joy, like a dog in sight of home.

I'll mourn Hale–Bopp, but be glad I ever saw it at all. Don't things go, and new things come? Lately I've been reading the diaries of a woman called Maria Văduva, who lived in Aldleigh's Lowlands House, and was always hoping to see something remarkable in the Essex skies (one day soon, I'll tell you all about her). She quotes from Homer's *Iliad* – 'Let me first do some great thing before I die, that shall be told among men hereafter' – and reminds me that every night, someone scans the sky over Maldon or New Mexico or Kiev, patient and hopeful and cold, waiting for some great thing.

153

Nathan, running full tilt through a monastery under scarlet banners, misjudged a flight of stairs and fell for the fourth time – 'God's sake,' he said, and threw away the controls that took him to imagined islands whenever he chose. Sometimes he found himself looking at his ordinary life with Grace Macaulay's eyes – what would she make of the television, the PlayStation, the three beer cans he'd emptied and crushed and left on the floor where he sat cross-legged all afternoon? Her house was so quiet the ticking clocks sounded like dripping taps, and subject to a thousand laws nobody ever explained – here there was laughter and argument and music forever spilling out of bedroom doors. His father rode bikes in bad weather, and could pick an egg out of boiling water without burning his hands – Grace's father had an undertaker's face. His own mother danced often, if badly – Grace had no mother, and her aunt certainly could never have danced. They lived with God, he thought, as if they had a lodger upstairs who'd bang on the floor with a broom if they ever made a noise.

Nathan found more beer, and drank it. He'd kept Grace secret from his friends, certain they'd find her ridiculous, or (this was worse) that they wouldn't. It occurred to him that she arrived as if from 1887: bewildered by his music; indifferent to the general election in which she was eligible to vote;

and appalled by the thought she might exchange her petticoats for jeans. She ought to have been priggish, but her stern morality was applied after a haphazard logic he couldn't fathom. She asked to be taught how to smoke, saying she couldn't for the life of her think of a Bible verse strictly forbidding it, but would never share his beer. She swore sometimes with pleasure, but said that blasphemy was a different matter, and that she'd never take the Lord's name in vain. When he thought of that half hour under the Lowlands oaks he was ashamed. There'd been other girls, of course there had – he was nineteen in November – but that had always been easy and sometimes funny and afterwards things had gone on more or less as before. With Grace it had all felt bewildering, every placement of his mouth and hand significant and doubtful and slow – there'd been the strangest sense that she was immense, that she'd had command of things.

He was confused by how she compelled him, that was half the trouble: she was too short, and he disliked the smell of the oils she used on her hair and skin. Her legs were sturdy and her hands were like a boy's, with unpainted nails bitten short, and she had no idea how to dress – but he was so acutely attuned to these deficiencies he had her memorised. She was the most alive person he'd ever met. The sight of her coming towards him roused a kind of animal alertness in his body, but he could never be certain whether that was the instinct of predator or prey.

He finished his drink. It was getting dark. Somewhere in his room, he thought, there was bound to be some weed. He found it. The curtains were closed, and the moonlight in the slit was cold, as if there'd been late snow. Inexpertly he rolled a joint, and thought with loving contempt of Grace's attempts to share his cigarettes, and refusal to admit they sickened her – then there was a noise at the door, and his sister was yelling for him; and oh, he said, that'll be Grace, that will be her. He ran down, misjudged the stairs, and fell for the fifth time.

Nick Carleton surveyed Thomas Hart. Should he remark on his gaunt, pale looks? Should he say: Thomas, it's gone half past seven, go home? He should not. Carleton was never certain of his authority's reach where Thomas was concerned. He looked instead at the documents spread on the desk and said, 'I'm afraid I'm not sure this is enough.' Lightly he touched the photograph of Maria Văduva standing by Bethesda's wall, and the green notebook with Dimitru's translation. 'I like these drawings,' he said, looking for stars in a smudged black blot, 'but nobody would be able to make them out. The whole story is unfinished. It lacks resolution. If only you hadn't lost the diary.'

'Well,' said Thomas, 'I am sorry.' He rubbed his hip with a distracted motion that had already become characteristic.

'What about your friend at the museum?' Carleton was leafing through the notebook. 'I like this,' he said. '*Let me first do some great thing before I die!*'

'In fact we spoke this morning on the phone,' said Thomas, with eagerness Carleton thought childish. 'He said there's bound to be more – between the floorboards, say, and in other rooms. Look, Carleton, where the translation ends – you see Maria met somebody, or saw her great thing. If we knew what –'

'But we don't know, and the diary is gone.' The editor aimed for a finality of tone, and achieved only rudeness. He flushed, tempering his voice. 'All the same,' he said.

'All the same.' Thomas reached for the drawings, and the motion disturbed something in his hip. Carleton saw him whiten, and submit to passing pain. 'Go home,' he said, rising from his seat. 'You ought to take time off. Oh!' He crossed quickly to the window, and moved aside the open slats of the blind. 'Thomas,' he said. 'Do you see that?'

'I'm a writer, young Nick: there's no time off. What are you looking at?'

'Don't you see it?' Carleton opened the blinds. 'What's happened to the moon? I think I must be going mad.'

Anne Macaulay, kept from Bethesda's weekly prayers by a bad cold in the head, went to bed early, and thought the light that night was strange, but closed the curtains all the same.

Ronald Macaulay, locking the chapel door when the prayer meeting was done, found himself in tears. He wiped his eyes and looked about, and located the moon. 'Do you see that?' he said, forgetting his solitude. 'Do you see that?' He held his Bible tightly.

James Bower came out of the Jackdaw and Crow, pleasantly a little drunk. He stumbled as he went, and this caused him to think of injury, and then of Thomas Hart. Really (he thought) he ought to visit. It would be fair to say he'd missed the other man. Now he was coming to London Road, and what a strange dark evening it was, given the spring – then he understood that in fact he was walking through smoke streaming downwind. Fragments of ash appeared on his sleeve and shoulders; an ember extinguished itself on his hand. He walked more quickly, and arrived at Bethesda where a man was standing by the iron gate. His stiff white hair showed like a nimbus in the gloom, and he had a displaced unworldly look that called Thomas Hart (again!) to mind. 'What's happening?' said James. 'There must be a fire' – but the man seemed untroubled by the smoke and embers, and was looking up past Bethesda's roof. 'What's up there,' said James, 'what are you looking at?' and instinctively looked with him. 'Oh,' he said, 'my God. My God.' The hair on his neck and forearms lifted as if in response to a static charge. Was this fear? He supposed so. But if he was afraid, why did he long to look, and go on looking?

'All right,' said Nathan, 'you don't have to stand there, you can come in.' Grace wore a white dress she'd evidently sewn from washed-thin linen sheets, gone grey at the uneven hem and pulled taut at the waist with a black scarf. A new pair of trainers showed absurdly when she walked. Nathan stepped aside, incited and embarrassed as he always was by this peculiar girl, who looked crosser than ever: 'I have to talk to you,' she said, trailing him up the stairs. 'So this is your room.' She looked with disapproving awe at the television, and the posters of famous women she could never have named – 'Where shall I sit?'

'Anywhere,' said Nathan. So here was the body that preoccupied him against his will, concealed somewhere in the folds of grubby cloth – here again the bewildering sense of attraction and repulsion she roused. And why had she come? Desperately he cast about for a defence against accusations he'd caused her to sin, with the outraged misery of an innocent man who sees the knotted rope.

She chose the floor at his feet, cross-legged and small; and with a nauseating shift of perspective the motion of her hair against her neck persuaded him there was never any girl as desirable as her. 'What's that smell?' she said.

'I've been smoking weed,' said Nathan, hoping to invite her playful censure; but she only nodded, and abruptly folded over herself, clasping her stomach with a groan. 'What's the matter? What have you done?'

'Just cramps,' she said, with defiant shame, 'my period has started'; and together they considered the implications of this, and were relieved. 'So that's all right,' she said, 'but I didn't come to tell you that. I want to talk about Thomas.' The pain had passed for now. She resumed her bemused assessment of his room.

'Ah! Why?' (The hangman stowed the noose.)

'I found out something, and don't know what to do, or how to feel.'

'What have you found out?'

'Why he won't be baptised. Why he goes away from Bethesda, why he lives alone. Why he goes to London, and what he does. Oh, and my stomach hurts.'

'Why don't you try this,' he said, lighting again the joint that had burned out in a saucer. 'My sister says it helps with cramp. But not so much,' he said, dreadfully moved by how obediently she took it, and with what concentration she drew in the smoke; 'just a bit more, then give it back. That's right. So what's the old man been up to?'

'Remember when we found him at Lowlands, that day the mist was everywhere and I didn't go to school?' She coughed three times; her eyes watered. 'Remember we found him with that other man?'

'Of course,' said Nathan, laughing with the mechanical levity arriving with the smoke.

'Thomas loves him,' said Grace, with enormous solemnity. Then 'I think I feel sick,' she said, and her wounding smile came without warning – 'I feel sick,' she said, 'isn't that funny?'

'It is funny,' said Nathan. 'Everything is, if you think about it. So Thomas is a poof,' he said cheerfully, and was startled by Grace reverting to her temper.

'Don't say that,' she said. 'Don't use the kind of words they say. Do you really think it's so bad of him? When I realised, I moved away as if I'd seen a spider on the wall – give me some more.' Again the concentrated attention on the joint, the choking cough, the quick helpless smile. 'First I was angry with myself for thinking badly of my friend, then angry with Bethesda for making me think badly at all, but in the end I was angry with him. He should have told me. People should be what they seem to be. If they're not, they're liars, even if they never lie!'

'It isn't bad exactly,' said Nathan. He saw how peculiar the light outside was, and turned away from the window. 'It isn't bad. It's just weird. I think they can do what they like as long as I don't have to see it.'

'They told me men like that were wicked. And I try and try to think Thomas is wicked, but I can't, it's like trying to write with my left hand. Do you think I should ask God to make me disgusted? I can't. I won't. Look at me. Nathan, look at me! How funny. I can't really see your face – can you see mine? Can you smell burning? Is it us? Have we burned down your house?' The thought delighted her.

'Only you,' said Nathan. 'And don't you ever brush your hair?'

'I can smell me too. I put rose oil on but I think I smell of blood – look: something strange is happening, something is happening out there –' She came quickly to her feet, stumbling inside her skirts and laughing, and reaching easily for his shoulder to steady herself. 'Look,' she said, 'stupid boy. Look at that. Look at the moon.'

In the offices of the *Essex Chronicle*, Thomas Hart came to the window with Carleton and saw the waxing moon rising in the east. 'Ah,' he said, with the inflexion of a cry of pain. He put his hand on his editor's shoulder. '*Let not your heart be troubled*,' he said, '*neither let it be afraid*'; but his own heart briefly failed him, because this was what caused James Bower and Ronald Macaulay to stand dumbfounded in Bethesda's car park, and what caused Grace to reach in appalled wonder for the boy beside her at the window: the moon's toppled crescent was a radiant, maddening blue. Thomas, casting about for how best to describe it, thought of the blue of gas flames and speedwell; of copper sulphate, broken Wedgwood plates, the old man's tarpaulin in Potter's Field. It was no good. No other blue would ever do. The moon was only as blue as itself.

'There'll be some explanation,' he said, looking instinctively for Maria Văduva (and yes, yes: there she was, assembled out of the thick evening air, perched on the windowsill three floors up and delivering the consolations of natural philosophy – *You must remember, Thomas, that light is altered by whatever stands in its path, and we are a part of all that we have met*).

Carleton said, 'It might be the end of the world.'

'It might,' said Thomas, 'but will not we fear, though the mountains be cast into the midst of the sea, and so on' – then cautiously, because his bad hip ached, he opened the window to its furthest extent, and leaned out. 'There, don't you smell it? Bonfires, blowing over the town.'

Carleton's phone rang. He took it, listened, put on his coat. 'It isn't as bad as all that,' he said. 'But Lowlands House is burning down.'

Grace ran. The fire, not visible from Nathan's window, was burning all the same on the television, and they'd been summoned downstairs to see it. 'Is that Lowlands?' they'd all exclaimed in delight and sadness. 'Is that the old house on fire?'

'Let's go,' Grace had said, 'let's go and watch'; and without thought or anxiety they'd run, laughing, half a mile to the Lowlands gates. Now they were crossing lawns still bruised by the Easter fair, and the weed's first giddy pleasure was gone, leaving a curious drowsy sense that everything was amplified: the clutching in her womb, the iron reek of her own blood, the transfigured moon. Increasingly the air had the warmth of summer. Nathan ran ahead, perpetually just beyond her reach. Then he halted, and she butted up hard against him and saw the old white house enclosed by old black beeches. The east wing was burning from basement to eaves. 'Oh no,' said Grace – a dreadful twist occurred in her abdomen, and at that moment the fire convulsed, causing the boards to split from their windows. Smoke plumed through shattered glass and formed a pall that rode the mild wind out to the fringes of the park.

'Is anybody in there?' said Nathan, blinking rapidly against the light. 'Is everybody safe?' Threads of people drifted in from every entrance to the park, looking about with troubled awe; the air was full of birds.

'Nothing but ghosts in there,' said Grace, 'and they'll survive' – then she saw a rim of white hair made coral by firelight, and knew this was her father. She began to burrow through the crowd with animal determination, and when she reached him was startled to discover she wanted to hold his hand – 'It's all right,' she said, having no idea who was consoling whom, 'it's going to be all right.' His cold grip tightened, and released her.

'Where are they,' a man beside her father said, 'why has nobody come?'; and Grace saw this was Thomas Hart's friend, who in that peculiar light had the adamant beauty of a dead stone king. 'Hello,' he said, with a frowning smile at Grace and Nathan, 'are you two always here?'

By unspoken consent they all drifted with the quiet crowd to the wire fence that kept the house from trespass: 'They can't do anything,' said Nathan, 'they can't stop it.' There was a rending noise, as if the house were a garment tearing at the seams, and this went on for some time, concluding in a thud that shook panicked birds out from nearby oaks. The smoke took on the look of morning mist igniting with first light. There were no sirens yet.

'Look how the flames make the shadows move,' said Grace, but her father's eyes were closed.

'Yes,' said James Bower, 'look' – there was the impression of worry joined with an ecstatic kind of interest, as if seeing something he'd longed for all his life – 'you'd think there was a party going on, and everyone was dancing.' The house was full of noises. Panes of glass burst on the terrace, and roof beams split and dropped; occasionally there was an almost-human cry of metal against metal.

'I can't believe it,' said Grace, 'I can't believe my eyes.' The pain in her stomach returned, with the sensation that something had actually become detached, and was turning and turning in there. 'Why won't it stop?' she said.

'In His name and for His sake we pray,' said Ronald, opening his eyes. 'Amen.' He looked at his daughter, he looked at the fire. 'Yes,' he said, 'you'd almost think somebody was running around inside.' The maddened moon was going down. Deer bolted for the forest from the copper beeches. Now: sirens.

'There's the sirens,' said Thomas, leaning on the stick he needed and despised, watching men at the Lowlands gate beckoning to fire engines turning in from London Road. He ought to have been in pain, but his interest in the moon decreased his capacity to suffer, and so he walked quickly with Nick Carleton towards the fire. Was that gas-flame colour fading, he thought, or was it that already it seemed the moon had always been blue?

'Hear that?' said Carleton, who'd thought to bring a Dictaphone for the sake of the front page, and held it at arm's length. 'Sounds like screaming.'

'That's just the fire,' said Thomas, 'now slow down' – a

gathering crowd kept them from the house. Bellowing importantly and without meaning, Carleton cut through, sometimes bringing his Dictaphone near a watching man or woman to record their distress; then Thomas saw white hair kindling above a solemnly bent head. 'There you are,' he said, 'there he is' – as if it were inevitable that Ronald Macaulay should be praying at the burning threshold, and that Grace in a curious white shroud should be standing with hands pressed to her abdomen and saying to Nathan, 'I think the hairs are burning on my cheeks.'

'Keep back,' said Thomas, with his old instinct for the preservation of Grace. 'You should keep back' – then he saw James Bower coming through smoke. 'Hello, James,' he said, taking in with pleasure the unshaved cheek, the hair which surely was a good inch longer than it had been before the fall.

'I just happened to be passing the church,' said James, 'and saw the fire. But how are you, Thomas, and should you be out?' He looked with compassion at the stick.

'I hardly feel a thing,' said Thomas, as if he could impose strength on himself by an act of will, and for the sake of James.

'We should go closer,' said Carleton, 'we ought to go and look' – but in fact it was James Bower who first walked towards the fire. 'Is it the metal beams,' he said, 'that hiss and sing like that?'

Now the engines had come nearby, and men made cumbersome by heavy yellow garments were drawing out a fire hose that bucked against the lawn and unleashed a bow of water. 'They'll put a stop to it,' said Thomas, 'they'll get it under control.' A wind was getting up, causing smoke to form in thick blots that obscured and revealed James in turn as he moved nearer to the house.

'Do you hear that?' said Grace. 'Do you hear something singing?'

'Just air escaping,' said Thomas, 'or an animal is hurt'; but he was helpless with ignorance. Beside the fire engines two men were bending now against unnatural draughts, and headed for steps down which tumbled blackened bits of brick. The door was gone, and in its place a sheet of fire made do for a curtain.

'They can't go in,' said James, calling back through smoke. 'If they go in, they won't come out.'

'Look,' said Grace, 'I didn't think a house could scream like that – somebody's in there, I told you so!' The men, bent double, entered the burning house through a breach in the wall, and the crowd produced a low harmonic moan of antici-pated sorrow.

'Shit,' said Nathan, 'fucking hell,' and Ronald Macaulay nodded as if these profanities were prayers. Unguessable minutes passed, then the men came back through the breach with a drooping figure. 'I told you,' said Grace, 'didn't I say?' They laid the figure on the grass. It did not move. Thomas was grateful he could make out no more than the white fabric of its clothes. Briefly it seemed all Essex held its breath in reverent silence; then the wet white bundle began to move, like animated cloth under an enchantment. It con-vulsed and lengthened, then was abruptly upright, showing weak haphazard limbs. The men, kneeling in their heavy suits, reeled in surprise, and the watching crowd moaned. The white figure, liberated for a moment, let out an eerie melodious shriek; then it bolted back into the fire. Briefly it was visible in the vacant doorway; then there was another rending noise, and the door's stone lintel broke in pieces on the threshold.

'Incredible,' said Carleton, leaving them to range among the crowd clasping the Dictaphone like a sacred icon, 'there's never been anything like this before.'

'*The Lord shall preserve thy going out,*' said Ronald, wringing his hands, '*and thy coming in —*'

'I think we're going to see somebody die,' said Nathan.

'Oh no, no,' said Thomas, seeing James Bower moving closer to the fire with the dogged slow step of a man in a trance. 'James. Don't. What can you do?'

The watching firemen, cautious and impassive, drew back and made adjustments to their clothing. A woman came forward, upright with authority, evidently saying they ought to be doing this, and doing that; meanwhile the men listened, and did nothing. The shadows were dancing in the house again, and grew substantial: it was possible to make out something dashing back and forth behind the bursting windows. 'Look,' said James, 'there they are.' The light struck his hair and the fibres of his clothes — he was rimmed with borrowed splendour: he is just like Maria, thought Thomas, always waiting for some great thing, and here it is. 'Here they are,' said James, and ran. Instinctively Thomas began to move, forgetting for a moment he was leaning on a stick, and stumbling hard against the uneven lawn now soaked with water running from the house. The pain he felt then was the pain of a new wound, and his shocked howl was concealed by the howl of the crowd.

'What's he doing?' said Grace. 'Why didn't you stop him? Why isn't anybody doing anything?'

The firemen on the steps, sealed now behind their visors, reached the broken lintel; but James had arrived at a window briefly free of flame, and scrambled over the cracked sill.

'Idiot,' said Nathan, with a kind of untroubled excitement, as if watching a fellow player make a bad move in a game.

'Do something,' said Grace, clasping her arms across her stomach.

'I can't move,' said Thomas, uncertain if it was pain that

fixed him where he stood, or a kind of calm that was like the beginning of death.

'I can,' said Nathan, 'I can go'; and this was said carelessly: he might have been sitting cross-legged on the bedroom floor in the light of the television screen, with several lives in hand – 'Yes, all right then,' he said, and began running with the easy power of his youth. Arcs of illuminated water ranged across the house, causing vents of steam that first obscured the view, then split to reveal the dying fire.

Thomas closed his eyes in resignation: it is preordained, he thought, it is the order of time – the rain falls on the just and the unjust, and God would have mercy on whom he would have mercy. Sirens again, and raised voices; Thomas opened his eyes. Grace Macaulay, on her knees beside him, clutched a bloodstained length of skirt in her fists, and prayed inaudibly with a child's passion. She is bargaining with God, thought Thomas, and no good ever comes of that – then there was an insistent pressure on his shoulder, and this was Ronald's hand. 'Shall we pray?' said Ronald, and with dumb obedience Thomas clasped his hands together. A murmur set up, and for a moment Thomas thought the crowd was praying with them – but 'There he is,' a nearby woman said, triumphant, 'there he is.' The blue moon had set. The roving arcs of water stripped dead leaves from the copper beeches. 'Look!' said the woman, now beside Thomas, pulling at his sleeve, and Thomas looked. Nathan was coming out from behind the house, slowed by shock and soaked clothing. His face was blurred by soot, and he held up his hands with the defeated gesture of a man under arrest. The firemen followed, and quickly all three were obscured by waiting officials and paramedics that moved with the purpose of a single machine. The pain in Thomas's hip was only the memory of pain. No other man came out.

Grace watched with an expression of triumph modified by fear. 'Amen,' she said. 'Amen.'

Dawn. Thin and early rain. The birds returning to the park, dismayed in the ruins; rats in the bracken doubled in number, every species of tenant now evicted from the house. Lowlands holding fast on the Essex clay: the west wing damaged, the east wing wrecked, the house confined by yellow plastic barriers that toppled on the lawns.

Mist in the fireplace, trespass in the ruins – Thomas Hart, sleepless with mourning and confusion, stood enclosed by the east wing's outer walls, from which the remnants of the upper floors dripped filthy water. Elsewhere men and women went about their business past the cordon, not seeing Thomas put his hand against wet walls retaining the night's warmth, or choosing not to see him out of pity. Was it here James took his last breath, thought Thomas – did he rest against this beam when his lungs failed, or that one? Where had his body gone, and what had they done with him? Thomas was struck by how peripheral he was, how much an afterthought: nobody would think to tell him that James Bower had died, and one day he'd limp through town and see a hearse and have no idea what it contained – I ought to have stayed to the end, he thought, recalling with shame how readily he'd succumbed to Ronald Macaulay's solemn insistence that it was all over, and best left to those in charge.

The house began to speak: he listened. He heard in the cracking plaster the voice of Maria Văduva at midnight, exclaiming over the sky; of John Bell alone in some other room lamenting over his wife. He heard the striking of the match that set the fire, and heard James Bower speaking in the hissing of water against brick. Then he heard himself crying readily and without shame, and discovered that sorrow

168

was as ecstatic as pain sometimes was, and as much a proof of life. Other proofs presented themselves, vivid in early light – a thin-tailed fox going untroubled to the lake, the Potter's Field jays breaking their fast on St Mark's flies swarming fat over the grass. The house was speaking again. Plaster had split from the brick in the heat, and revealed a flaw in the wall. Between the vacant fireplace and the door the mortar was more pale and the bricks more red: it had the look of a poorly matched patch sewn on a coat. The fire had caused this patch to unstitch itself, and gaps had appeared in the seam between the new brick and the old. *Look*, said the house, shifting on the soaking lawns: *look, I've got something to show you.*

'I didn't think it would still be standing,' said James Bower, speaking with Maria Văduva, with John Bell, with the groaning house: 'I didn't think it would still be here.' Something dropped on Thomas Hart's shoulder – irritably he shook it off – the pressure increased, became a clasp. 'Thomas,' said the voice, 'what are you doing? And what have you done to the wall?'

Slowly, because his bad hip ached, Thomas turned, and discovered James Bower holding his left arm in a sling against his breast, as if he'd been given something fragile he didn't particularly want. The remarkable face was made more remarkable by scorch-marks treated with a clear substance that ran like sluggish tears on to his collar. Thomas was astounded by a need for violence; how dare he, he thought, how dare he subject me to shock after shock, while all the while he wears that unaltered easy smile – 'I made it out,' said James (the easy smile in fact a little altered by the burn), 'I found a way out and brought the woman with me. I brought her out myself. I did it, she kept saying, it was me. They think she'll be all right, but she says she did it, and police are waiting in the hospital – don't look at me like that, Thomas, I'm all right. Though they tell me burns get worse as the shock wears off, and my knees were full of glass. So perhaps I am still in shock' – he looked about with interest, and took his hand from Thomas's shoulder – 'perhaps I should be at home, but I kept thinking of Maria Văduva and what she left behind.'

'I thought you were dead,' said Thomas. 'Why did you do it? Such a risk, and for a stranger?'

'I don't know – I can't explain it – only I thought: I can choose now not to be an ordinary man. But you'll never understand,' he said, shaking his head, wincing over his burns. 'You're content with your life. Why should I have to be content with mine?'

Impossible to explain, even to himself, what a peculiar kind of cruelty this was. 'I understand,' said Thomas, who understood only that his bad hip ached, and that the distance between them was impassable. Then there was a violent shearing sound that caused a woman on the terrace to exclaim in fright, and sent flies swarming in the fireplace – 'Look out!' said James, and the mismatched portion of the wall peeled back in a single piece, and dismantled into reddish bricks that lay distributed on the ruined wet floor. Thomas, silenced by surprise, experienced a tightening cold sensation on his scalp: the damage had revealed a shallow cavity, and the rising sun struck steel and glass. 'Oh!' said Thomas. 'There you are!' The need for violence of some kind had departed, and James Bower was at his side, smelling of soot and antiseptic. 'There it is,' said Thomas. He raised his hand in greeting, and laughed. 'Her telescope,' said James, so reverently that Thomas thought perhaps he too saw a tall black-browed woman in embellished clothes bending to the eyepiece, and exclaiming in delight. Together the men looked into the lens. The lens looked back. Hadn't it always been in the habit of seeking out light? It went on doing so.

Grace Macaulay stood alone in her father's shed. The faithless swifts had gone: it was the restless period between summer and autumn, when it was never possible to guess the weather, or dress correctly for it. All day and all night the sky was dull and uniform, and it seemed absurd to think there'd been a comet once, and a blue moon setting through stars.

The shed was warm, and fragrant with creosote; moss grew in soft green curds beside cracked panes of glass that rattled in the wind. Grace leaned against the workbench and looked down the garden to the illuminated house. She felt dislocated, as if it all had nothing to do with her, and it was impertinent to watch her father stooped over his Bible in the study, or her aunt coming to the bathroom in a thin towel dressing gown. Then she returned to the task of sorting through the pile of nuts and bolts ranged on the bench. Carefully she selected the heaviest of these, discarding washers dulled with rust that would stain her clothes. How many would she need? She had no idea. She'd never done this before; certainly she'd never do it again.

Low cloud brought an early dusk, and caused the house to shine more vividly at the garden's end: there was her aunt, moving to her own narrow room, where she'd put on the smartest of her blouses and her chapel hat; there was her father standing to relieve the scholar's ache in his back. And there also was a man, coming down the garden path with the step of someone acquainted with pain: 'Thomas!' she said, going quickly to the door. 'It's been a month. Where have you been? You abandoned me!' She withheld her embrace by way of punishment, and took frowning account of his long coat in pale wool, his shining shoes, the wicker basket he carried and the white cloth that covered it. The coat and the basket embarrassed her: could he not dress like other men, she thought, could he not use a plastic bag?

'What are you doing here so early?' she said, absently turning her ring. 'It isn't for another hour.'

'I've been in London,' said Thomas. He put the basket down. 'I have been about my business.'

'All you think about,' said Grace reprovingly, 'is that stupid telescope.' That Thomas and James Bower had discovered Maria Văduva's telescope in the aftermath of the Lowlands fire had pleased her at first, feeling Thomas's happiness was almost her own. Then she suspected she'd been supplanted first by a person and then by an object: now she'd gladly have seen the thing pushed into the lake, and the man after it. She understood that her irritation and envy was somehow also to do with Thomas being a homosexual, a word she found bizarre for its suggestion of a diagnosis. Sometimes out of a sense of duty she attempted to disapprove of Thomas; but she never could, and what was most confusing was that she never thought she should.

'That is true,' he said, 'I dream about it. Sometimes I think the lens still contains every star it ever saw. Now what are you doing?' He hung his coat on a nail.

'Aunt Anne made me a baptismal dress. She said if I do it, I'll make mistakes and it would come apart in the water. But I have to sew weights into the hem of the skirt, or it will billow up in the water and show my legs.'

'I'll help you,' said Thomas, who seemed livelier than she'd ever known him, despite the loss of Maria's diary and the pain in his hip. 'If you'll tell me how you are.'

A blackened seedpod of some kind had got in with the nuts and bolts, and Grace examined it. 'I'm all right,' she said.

'Then tell me how Nathan is.'

Grace felt herself colour with unhappiness and pride. 'He's got a job, and a car. Nothing about the fire hurt him – nothing ever does. Sometimes he's always calling me, sometimes he forgets me. He keeps saying I'm his friend, as if he's forgotten what we did – as if he doesn't know that I remember everything! But he's coming today,' she said. 'I told him weeks ago, and yesterday I phoned, and he said he'd come.'

'So you are to be baptised like John in the River Jordan, and Christ after him. Perhaps a dove will descend, or at least there'll be pigeons on Bethesda's roof! But you have more courage than I ever did, and certainly more faith.' Thomas found a washer furred with rust, and set it aside.

'I have to do it,' said Grace. She rolled the seedpod in her hands, and crushed it. 'I promised I would.'

'Two more here.' Thomas handed her a pair of heavy steel screws. 'Promised whom?'

Grace, leaning on the workbench, smelt again smoke drifting from the Lowlands fire, the blood seeping from her body, the weed that had made the night's events both amplified and muted. In that haze, the faith that all her life had been an exhausting obligation had been brought down to a single lucid certainty: that the God of Abraham and Isaac, at whose name every knee shall bow, happened also to be present in a small Essex town on a Wednesday evening, and out of the unfathomable sway of his power would attend to the prayers of a girl on her knees in the mud. 'Will you laugh at me?' she asked.

'I might,' said Thomas, and this caused Grace to smile,

and buffet him with her shoulder in her old way, and say, 'I promised God. That's the thing. I said: Bring him out of there, and I'll be good. Bring him safely out and then I'll be baptised, and I'll serve God all my days. Then there he was, walking out with his hands up, and not even his clothes were burned. I was so happy it was like being mad. Then I was afraid because I understood I was in debt to God and one day I'd have to clear my debt. And I should be baptised, because I do have faith, I do! And didn't God say that if you honour him, he will honour you, and doesn't he always keep his promises?'

Thomas was silent for a time. 'More bargaining,' he said. 'You look like a little witch, casting her spells with old iron. And I'm a poor backslider, Grace, but even I know this is pretty poor theology.'

'Perhaps I am a witch!' Then it struck her that this was blasphemous. 'But it isn't a spell,' she said, 'it's a prayer.'

'Grace,' said Thomas, speaking gently, 'do you really believe in all this?'

'I don't know! All these rules, Thomas, all the things I can't do – the hats I have to wear, the music I can't listen to – I've never been to the cinema. I've never danced and nobody will ever tell me how! But all the time' – lightly she thumped her breast – 'there's this thing in me that won't let me go. And doesn't it mean more, isn't it more amazing, to have faith against your better judgement?'

'It might be faith. But it might be fear, or love, or all those things, or none of them. You said to me once' – Thomas was looking with interest into a garden with nothing interesting in it – 'that you felt you ought to be good, or God would take away the things you loved.'

'So what?' said Grace, almost submitting to a childish desire to stamp her foot in her temper. 'So what? You think I'm doing this so God gives me Nathan?'

'I do think that. And haven't I known you all your life?' Now she had twenty pieces of steel to weigh her down in the baptistery. They were lined on the workbench, and began to shine: the sun was coming out.

'I haven't seen him in so long,' she said, 'and when I don't see him everything is dull and flat. But I asked him to come, and he said he would. He will, I trust he will.' She closed her eyes against Thomas; and when she opened them again, her aunt was coming quickly up the garden, carrying a white dress.

Shortly before four in the afternoon, as Bethesda's harmonium began to play for Grace, a violent wind dispersed the oppressive cloud that had enclosed Aldleigh all day. Thomas walked alone up London Road with the basket containing soft white rolls and apple cake made because Grace had asked him to do it. After her baptism, when her soaked clothes were exchanged for dry ones, they'd go together to the cold hall behind the chapel and have tea, where once an old man in a lavish coat had drunk himself into confusion. As Thomas walked, the beeches blazed where the low sun struck them, and the effect was of walking alone and unharmed through a forest fire.

Thomas thought of Anne coming to the shed with the baptismal dress, and of her cautious greeting: 'Oh,' she'd said, 'you're here,' conveying her sorrow that since the fire he'd been absent from the house of God. How could he explain that he'd exchanged the substance of things hoped for and the evidence of things not seen for James Bower, and a ten-inch reflecting telescope interred behind a wall?

It struck him that he'd never been so happy, but was wise enough to understand that his happiness consisted largely of hope. Their meeting in the ruin had been intimate and strange, and had sustained his spirit for days; but quickly they'd reverted to their easy pretence of being boys with a mystery on their hands. So they spoke only of where Maria Văduva had gone, and whether another casket of papers had been buried in the park; but all the while, Thomas attended minutely to every phrase and gesture, and worked at decoding them.

Meanwhile James Bower walked in fine weather with his wife, thinking with gratitude that he was briefly content with his lot. All day they'd been occupied with the administration of a shared life, and now accepted the beauty of the evening as an annual grace. The children would be all right in the end (she'd said, taking his hand), and if the oldest was quite a silent child it was not (he said, kissing the hand that held his) their fault, and likely wouldn't last. There was trouble with a bill or two, but that would resolve itself; and James was always tired (now she was laughing at him), but then he wasn't as young as he'd once been, and after all quite battle-scarred and not such a beauty these days.

They rounded a corner, and there was Bethesda on London Road, where James had once heard the harmonium, and seen Thomas Hart going quickly across the car park. Was it possible he heard that same melody again? Wind released beech leaves from their branches and raised eddies that made James think a devil was on the move; then 'Look!' his wife said. 'Look: isn't that your ghost?' The leaves abruptly dropped. 'It is,' she said.

It wasn't necessary for James to look up in order to see quite plainly the long coat of fine pale wool and highly polished shoes; the curious poise arising partly out of pain, and the old way of seeming to occupy an atmosphere that bemused and charmed his friends. But he did look: behold the man, behold the coat. He carried a basket, which gave him a queer feminine aspect, and he was standing very still. James felt oddly ashamed. It wasn't that he thought Thomas too strange a man to be introduced to his wife – wasn't he at all times courteous, and clever, and kind? – it was that they'd existed together on the margins, chaperoned by a woman who was dead.

'I think he looks wonderful,' she was saying, laughing as Thomas came nearer, and it struck James unpleasantly that he'd like to cross the road to avoid him. Now Thomas was shifting the basket from hand to hand as if it were heavy, and he was coming nearer. 'Introduce him to me,' said his wife, smoothing her hair, 'though perhaps he'll vanish and you'll see he really was a ghost after all – oh James, poor man. Don't look.' Thomas Hart was on his knees. The basket was in the gutter, and white things were scattered on the pavement and rolling under cars. Thomas fumbled with the dropped cloth; he gave a small frustrated cry audible above the traffic and harmonium. Then he stood with the care of an injured man, and came towards them, his coat blackened at the hem, the wicker basket frayed. He's embarrassed, thought James, that's why he looks so odd.

His wife, going forward with the unfailing kindness he loved, held out her hand. 'I promise,' she said, 'I didn't see a thing.'

Thomas showed her his palms, which were wet with mud from the gutter. 'I'm filthy,' he said, 'I'm afraid. James, good afternoon: you look well – you must have been to Lowlands without me. And this is –?' He gave James a look of enquiry, reserved and polite.

'This is Emily,' said James, 'this is my wife. Emily, this is Thomas.'

'Emily.' Thomas spoke as if he'd never heard the name before, and the syllables were giving him trouble. 'Your wife,' he said, and inclined his head in understanding. The harmonium struck up again.

'He often talks about you,' said James Bower's wife. 'In fact I've sometimes been jealous of what you two have been getting up to with your mysteries and your ghosts. So I'm glad to meet you,' she said, 'I'm glad to have met my rival. But listen, aren't you late?' They stood by Potter's Field, and heard the congregation singing: '*When sorrows like sea billows roll —*'

'I expect I got the time wrong,' said Thomas, 'I'm always making mistakes.' He moved away with a gesture of farewell, and a look not possible to decipher behind the hard glaze of his eyes. James took his wife's hand. He almost felt he was doing so for consolation. 'Goodbye,' he said; but already Thomas Hart was headed for Bethesda as if for a shore. 'I think I've heard that song before,' said James. *It is well, it is well with my soul.*

Thomas found the chapel altered. The communion table had been put by the harmonium, and the baptistery was open. The small deep cavity was tiled blue like a municipal swimming pool, and filled to the brim with water that had poured all day from copper taps. The water had been warmed by an iron heater clamped to the rim beside the steps, and this caused threads of steam to dissipate in the cool chapel air.

He found the pew that had been his since birth, and sat under the ten stilled moons bewildered by humiliation and loss. Emily, he thought, childishly despising the name, and the kindly smile, and the easy acceptance of her husband's hand; despising her hair, her clothes, the pavement where she'd stood. But what was lost, after all? Hope, that was it — the sensation of the world opening out with each encounter, of every word foretelling the next word, and the next, until — now that was all gone. Worse, everything that had been done and said was now absurd, and Thomas himself ridiculous. It has all been false pretences, thought Thomas, relieved to find anger arriving alongside loss: he knew what he was doing — wasn't he there, too? Now the congregation bent their heads in prayer, and how could Thomas join them? What prayer or praise could he rustle up now, with bruises coming up on his knees? The world consisted of nothing but the hard familiar pew. He looked at Grace, seated between her father and her aunt. She had a new hat on, and it drooped at the brim; there was defiance in the set of her shoulders under the loose white dress. This is all because of that boy, he thought, but he won't come, not if I know men, and I do. It would be better if he went away, because how can she stand it, when she's only a child?

The pastor came down from the pulpit. He put fisherman's waders on to protect his chapel suit from the water, and called Grace Macaulay to the lectern to give an account of her salvation. The atmosphere in the chapel was merry as she spoke of the helplessness of her eternal soul and surety of her salvation: a sheep was being gathered safely into the fold. But Thomas knew loss when he saw it, and that she cried less for her soul than for her body. Nothing but trouble, he thought, pouring anger on a careless boy: you've been nothing but trouble all along.

The pastor walked down into the water and held out his hand to Grace, who stood barefoot at the brim. I object, thought Thomas, I have a thousand just impediments! The pastor began to pray. Grace sighed, and frowned, and as she came forward caught her hem with her heel. There was the sound of tearing cloth, and of a handful of shining weights rattling down. With a humiliated exclamation of distress, Grace bent to pick up what she could, and Thomas heard the chapel door quietly open. He turned. Nathan was on the

179

threshold. His coloured clothes were violent against the cold pale walls; music came faintly through headphones clasped about his neck. He sought out Grace and couldn't find her. He took his glasses from his pocket, and looked again. There she was, in her absurd dress, kneeling at the rim of the water. You are late, thought Thomas, look, you've already caused her pain, and she'll just keep bearing it over and over again. Then the young man's gaze found his, and his expression altered: There you are, Thomas Hart! He smiled and came forward. Thomas shook his head with the slow deliberate motion of a threat: You aren't welcome, you're not wanted, you never were. The boy flinched as if struck, and briefly Thomas pitied his bewildered look, which was almost one of pain. Nathan saw Grace reach for the pastor's hand, and enter into the water with her back turned to the door. His bewilderment deepened, and possibly there was also a look of resignation. He nodded once at Thomas, and turned his back, and left.

The pastor spoke to Grace. She nodded: yes, she said. Yes. She smiled. Someone began to sing. One by one that solitary voice was joined until the pale vault of Bethesda's roof threw back the song. The water reached the child's waist and blackened her dress; then easily, as if they'd practised the steps of a holy dance, the pastor passed an arm around her back, and grasped her wrists where they were crossed at her breast. 'In the name of the Father,' he said (the chapel door banged shut), 'and of the Son, and of the Holy Ghost.' Then the roving sunlight struck the discs of yellow glass fixed in the windows by the pulpit, and refracting down at the ordained degree lit the surface of the water in the baptistery. So Grace Macaulay, turning with unmet hope towards the closing door, entered the shining pool not with the look of falling but of something headed for the sun, and the body of the sinner was lost to unmerited light.

PART TWO

2008

The Law of Equal Areas
in Equal Time

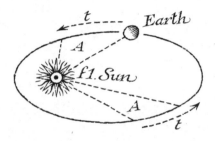

Fig. 2

It was October. The earth and all her passengers, listing to starboard, sailed through the wake of Halley's Comet, causing a meteor shower that was brighter and more lovely than Halley's last transit had been, the memory being better than the event.

October, then; and stars fell over the wet black verges of the A12, and the wet green lawns of the Colchester barracks; they fell over the Aldwinter tomb tree, and the housing estates in Chelmsford going up where poorhouses and leper colonies had been. Being fair-minded, they also fell on Aldleigh, and on a tall man coming down the high street with a satchel on his back. He wore the vestments of a Catholic priest, which suited him so well he might have grown them out of his own marrow: a white chasuble thrown up by his hasty long-legged gait, and a fringed stole dripping underneath; a cincture signalling continence and chastity, and a green amice embroidered with a cross from which gold thread came unstitched. Those who saw him noted the impression of power he gave, for all that he couldn't have been a day under seventy; they noted also the scent that followed him, which was of incense and whisky. Essex being a place of dissent, he received none of the deference that might have come his way in Norfolk, and certainly in Dublin or Nice; but a man leaving the Jackdaw and Crow was visited with ancestral memories of the confessional, and crossed himself without noticing he did it.

All change, thought this man in sorrow, passing the Aldleigh war memorial, which had lately been polished and regilded; all change, he thought, wondering where the butcher's had gone, with its sawdust floor and its chains in the door to keep bluebottles out. Where was the shoe shop with its striped awning, and why was it all so clean? Faintly he recalled potholes in the high street, and newsagents advertising cigarettes, and a café where once he'd been given bacon and eggs by a woman who certainly knew he was in no position to pay. A star fell on the roof of the old town hall, where two grey-haired men wearing green carnations kissed without shame on the steps, and ducked under confetti – where had the museum gone, and the man who'd sat in its offices? Now he came to the Alder, and it was all change there: the water cleansed according to certain municipal decrees, the drunken shopping trolleys absent from the bank. He watched the tidy river running, and drank from a bottle he kept in his pocket; then struck out for London Road. No change yet in Potter's Field, and no use found for the land: brambles dotted with unpicked berries blasted by weather, and a single censorious jay.

When he came to Bethesda he found it unaltered as the Northern Star. The chain was off the gate. It was the evening of the Lord's Day and the harmonium was playing. Against the austere chapel brick the old man's garments had the splendour of kings. He took a hymn book from the lobby table and went quickly in, and saw with gratitude the ten lights with their look of moons stalled in their orbit, the narrow windows with their meagre discs of coloured glass. But all the same, change in Bethesda too – where was Anne Macaulay? Where was her brother, with his look of having seen a sorrow that had passed the whole world by? And where was that child Grace, with her petticoats edged with lace; where was his friend? It was a congregation of strangers.

A man came down from the pulpit and stood beside the communion table, which had a white cloth on it. His beard was silver and square as a shovel, and the visitor recognised him with gratitude and relief: this was the deacon, not much changed, who'd once welcomed him in with a hand on his sleeve. *'For I have received of the Lord,'* said the deacon, *'that which also I delivered unto you, that the Lord Jesus the same night in which he was betrayed took bread.'* There were silver platters on the table, and cubes of cheap white bread on them; beyond the narrow windows squabbling cars blared their horns, and only the visitor heard it. Solemnly the deacon came down to the pews, and the silver plate was passed from hand to hand. *'This do,'* said the deacon, *'in remembrance of me.'* The bread was chewed in silence, and the body of Christ was broken again in Essex.

The visitor stood. He raised his arms in the moony light. 'Please,' he said, 'I must take bread with you also.' The congregation turned, and took in the Catholic vestments, the scent of whisky. 'Please,' the old man said. The deacon paused. He surveyed the visitor. Impossible to judge what calculations of manners and theology went concealed behind that beard; but after a time he went down the narrow aisle and offered the old man the plate. The visitor took bread, and ate it, and crossed himself; and this act, having as much to do with Bethesda's Protestant God as the slaughter of three black hens, caused a watchful child to gasp. *'After the same manner also,'* said the deacon placidly, *'he took the cup, saying, "This cup is the new testament in my blood."'* He poured thick liquid from a silver jug into a silver beaker, and was smiling privately. *'This do ye,'* he said, *'as oft as ye drink it, in remembrance of me.'* The cup was passed from hand to hand, and wiped at the rim between each supplicant; then the deacon put the tilted rim to the old man's mouth, so that he could drink without use of his hands. *'For as often as ye eat this bread,'* said the deacon, returning to the shadow of the pulpit, *'and drink this cup, ye do shew the Lord's death till he come.'*

The harmonium drew a breath and brought the matter to an end. The stranger spread his vestments out, and watched the chapel empty of men and women who passed his pew with wary courteous nods. The senior deacon, last to leave, took keys from his pocket and said, 'I know you. I'm certain I do. I trust you found the service a blessing.'

The visitor inclined his remarkable head.

'Ought I to call you Father?' said the deacon, who gestured at the gold cross unwinding on the stole (it was clear that under no circumstances would he call any man Father, no matter the length and whiteness of his robes).

'No need for that.' The visitor stood and with difficulty put his satchel on his back. 'I came looking for my friend,' he said, 'but he isn't here.' The deacon put the ten moons out. The stranger pursued him to the door. 'Please,' he said, 'could you tell me where he is?'

They came out to the car park, and a falling star briefly stitched a thread of light above the town. Solemnly the deacon locked the chapel doors; solemnly he put away the key. 'He's rather a man of the world, these days,' he said. 'You'll find him where he has always been: at home, on Lower Bridge Road.'

At home, on Lower Bridge Road: Thomas Hart, upright and contented at his dining table. Little change here; though the keen observer might think the painting over the mantelpiece has the look, does it not, of an Augustus John; that the sideboard sports no fewer than fifteen bits of gilded Moser glass. There is altogether a look of richness about the place, and about Thomas himself, who was buffeted by the winds of acclaim at the age of fifty-eight on the publication of his novel *The Horse and Rider* (dedicated *for J. B.: His Book*). Carleton, reading the novel as he walked home from work and late in the evening by lamplight, was pleased and startled to find the ambiguity he'd deplored in the early works of Thomas Hart replaced with a candour he admired, but which he could never reconcile with the nicely composed gentleman at his desk. Now and then, in Aldleigh or on Bishopsgate or in dentists' waiting rooms, Thomas encounters strangers part avid and part shy, and sometimes the brisk enquiry: 'Didn't you write that book – and didn't you win that prize?' Yes, he confesses: and nobody (he assures them) could be more surprised than he, for who wants the work of a dusty old Baptist, whose sentences run on for a page? Readers attend the readings he gives and queue beyond the door – often his hand is mutely squeezed, he's sometimes embraced and embraces in return. In some quarters he's believed too sentimental to be taken seriously, and fatally flawed by a tendency to think too kindly of his characters – but Thomas believes that any writer who thinks himself better than the products of his own imagination should seek out some more appropriate profession (such as dentistry, for example, or the construction of dry-stone walls).

He keeps up his column in the *Essex Chronicle*, to the bemusement of its younger staff. He remains a citizen of the empire of the moon, and has devoted the past ten years to acquiring a schoolboy's understanding of astronomy and physics: ask him about the easiest means to observe storms on the surface of the sun, for example, or how the spectrometer splits the white light of a star and reveals the fingerprints of God, and he becomes a talkative man. He has not dispensed with God, for all that this would be simple and convenient: sometimes on a Sunday morning his feet take him to Bethesda, and he doesn't object. He's rarely in London these days, and prefers his own company to that of other men (none of whom, after all, are James Bower). He is happy, except when he isn't; and the old wounds in his hip and heart still sometimes give him trouble.

Maria Văduva, made more or less incarnate, has become a sitting tenant. He does nothing to evict her. Often as he writes she reaches over his shoulder and puts her finger to the screen: *Come now, Thomas Hart*, she'll say, polishing a lens on the sleeve of her gown, *come on, you old deceiver, it wasn't like that at all*. She is the organising principle. Did Thomas love a man who did not love him? Well: so did she. Does his neck ache, what with all the looking at the moon? Hers will one day break. Can he think of Lowlands without sorrow? She hands him a handkerchief and it's already wet. 'One day,' he tells her, watching Orion walk over the railway bridge, 'I'll get to the bottom of this, you mark my words.' She doubts it.

So Thomas, upright at his dining table, emailed Grace Macaulay. A year had passed since last they met; but since she changed not at all in the first twenty-nine years of her life, he imagined this last one hadn't dislodged her black curls, her costumes of brocade and lace, her adamant affection and deplorable temper. *Come home, you wretched child*, he wrote, *it won't be long now —*

– it can't be long. Last week they brought in the hospital bed, and we put it where the dining table was, where every Sunday we ate tea at five o'clock and your father read from his Bible. Now I can hardly remember the room without it: the present comes in like a tide over the past.

Your father is a fine nurse. Did you ever see him boil an egg? Now he scrambles and poaches them to tempt her, and never burns the toast.

Every day she asks after you, and I'm running out of ways to lie. She is busy, I say. Or: she is in Paris. But you've never been to Paris and have no excuse for not being here. Come home, you wretched child! Do you think yourself no longer welcome, because you've dispensed with God? Do you think you will need to make a pretence of faith, for her sake? She will accept you as you are, and so will I – your father, I suspect, will not. But he always said you were a sinner, so what did he expect?

A train leaves Liverpool Street tomorrow at 5.03. I'll be waiting at the station. I'll take you home.

'Wretched child,' he said with a prick of anger he imagined must be like that of a father: amplified by love (his household ghost solidified against the window, obscuring a solitary star – *Nonetheless*, she said, speaking out of his own memory and guilt, *might you say you played your part in this, Thomas Hart?*).

'Leave me in peace, Maria' – but he smelt the water in Bethesda's baptistery and saw Nathan turned away at the door, and time had not passed as it ought to have done: there was Grace pulled out of the shining water, her face all hope and wanting. *All my love*, he wrote. Evening ceded gratefully to night. Stars fell on the railway bridge. Somebody was at the door.

*

Richard Dimitru Dines said, 'Hello,' and with difficulty put down his bag.

'Hello,' said Thomas. Ought he to say what a surprise it was, to see the old man on his doorstep dressed like a priest with a communion wafer in his pocket? Perhaps, but this would not be true. Things pass, and they return – 'Hello,' he said; and then (what use are manners, when you've washed a man in the bathtub, and picked lice from his hair?): 'I see you're drunk. You'd better come in. I'll put the kettle on.'

'It is true,' said Dines equably. 'I am drunk. I am also hungry, and would like to sit down, if you please.'

Thomas did please. He dislodged Maria from the arm-chair (she shook her black skirts, and seeped sulkily into the wall), and put Dines in it. 'It suits you,' he said, 'this ludicrous get-up, though I don't believe for a minute that you ought to be wearing it.'

'Ought I not?' Dines raised his arms, and lifted the wings of his chasuble: he looked angelic, if angels ever grew weary of their duties and consoled themselves with drink. 'No,' he said, 'I am not ordained exactly, but a man might be ordained by the Almighty as much as by a seminary. It is quite surprising to me that you doubt it.'

'Then tell me: are you a Catholic now?' said Thomas, not troubling to conceal his Baptist distaste.

'Why not!' said Dines. He raised his hands again, and Thomas saw that here time had been kind: the pitiful nubs at the nail beds were almost what they ought to be; the knuckles, if swollen, did not look as if the bone might at any moment erupt through the skin. The loose thumb, neither use nor ornament, had been removed, and a new scar marked the absence. 'Why not?' said Dines again. 'And I like to have these things on me, so that people look and say: There goes a man of God.'

Thomas, speaking from the kitchen, said, 'You've found your faith, I see, no doubt in the last place you looked.' He ground coffee; he unwrapped parkin from brown paper. 'You shouldn't drink so late,' he said, seeing Dines pull ecstatically at a bottle. 'Alcohol produces poor-quality sleep, and you look tired.'

'It is empty,' said Dines, and threw the bottle at the wall. Thomas, seeing the old man was not so blithe as he seemed, put buttered parkin on a gilded saucer, and gave it to him.

'I haven't found my faith,' said Dines between bites. 'I wonder where I put it?'

'But isn't this faith?' said Thomas, tugging at the fringed stole, noting that it could do with a clean. 'Doesn't an attempt at faith constitute faith itself? It's a dreadful thing to confuse faith with certainty.'

'You were yourself absent from the house of God today, were you not? And what is wrong with you – does something hurt you in your hip?'

'I had a fall,' said Thomas, 'and nothing has been right since. And these days I seek out my faith in other doctrines' – he gestured at a spectrograph nearby, and a four-inch reflecting telescope fitted with filters to aid in observations of the sun. 'I supplement God with physics, and understand each as well as the other. Which is to say: not in the least! But I find it magnificent, knowledge piled on knowledge, and the matter never closed – it's all no less strange and marvellous to me than the Resurrection, and it takes as much faith for me to believe it.'

In companionable silence they ate and drank; and Dines took off his stole and with it his priestly look. 'Where's that black-haired girl,' he said, 'who might have come from my country? Her pew was empty.'

'She lives in London. In Hackney, which she tells me these

days is quite fashionable, above a pizza shop. I wrote to her today and told her to come home. Her aunt is dying from a tumour in the stomach that was in her brain and bones before she knew she was ill.'

'And what then of your friend,' said Dimi, growing astute. 'What of your man, whose name was James?'

'Gone, I'm afraid. Gone from Aldleigh, from Essex, from me – gone in fact without saying he was going until after he was gone. Now I'm no fool, old man' – Thomas, smiling, heard on the stairs the movement of black skirts shedding pearl beads – 'is it possible that you didn't come here alone?'

The old man regarded him in silent mischief, then put his satchel on the table. 'The mystery is solved,' he said. With difficulty he brought out a file, and a black book that still retained, in its stitches and binding, fragments of the earth in Potter's Field.

'You still have her diary,' said Thomas, not with surprise, but satisfaction.

'I always have it with me, and the translation is complete: it has been the last work of my life to raise Maria like Lazarus from her grave. So I shall tell you again: the mystery is solved.'

'All solved?' said Thomas (and James, he thought: where are you now?). 'You know what she did, and where she went?'

'Not, I confess, solved entirely,' said Dines, 'but much is clear. For example' – he examined the diary, and found its last written page – 'you see that her final entry was on the seventeenth of June 1889. After that: nothing. I daresay this date means nothing to you, being English.'

'Nothing whatever.' Thomas bent to see words blotted by a woman in distress. He touched the page, and was surprised to find his hand unstained by ink.

Dines, speaking importantly as if from the pulpit, said, 'Maria Văduva Bell, on the seventeenth of June 1889, the same night on which we might think she disappeared, believed she discovered a comet. Let me read to you, Thomas, from the translation I have made. It was *a pearly smear*, she wrote, *extending fully two degrees from a nucleus — seeming to thicken and brighten as I watched* — she grows excited. *A comet — neither sought, nor expected* — now: you see she has a tendency to sentimentality, which we may forgive — *seen first by me*, she writes, *a woman now of Essex, whose heart was broken, but whose mind never was!*

Thomas said, 'A comet.'

'A comet,' said Dines.

'Have I always been blind to everything? Did I never see what was in front of my eyes?'

'It does surprise me,' said the old man in haughty reproof, 'that you did not think of it.'

'But where is it in the records? Is it a periodic comet — when is the return?' (Silently he pleaded with the celestial mechanic: God, let me see it — let me have that, at least!)

'That is not really the sort of thing I know,' said Dines, 'but certainly she made her observations and noted its position —'

'The right ascension and declination, yes,' said Thomas, 'that is the location of any point in the sky at any point in time, just as latitude and longitude —'

'But the document is gone. It is not there. Look.' Dines displayed the empty pages of the book.

'I must be clear on this.' It was midnight. Thomas was alert down to the last filament of his body. 'Maria Văduva Bell, having discovered a comet from the grounds of Lowlands House, disappeared that night or soon after, and did nothing whatever about it?'

Immense, triumphant, as if he himself had set the comet rolling down its orbit: 'Yes,' said Dines. 'Shall I tell you more?'

'Not yet,' said Thomas. He turned to the computer. 'First,

we should establish whether she did see a comet, or whether it was only her wanting that did it – you know it is possible to love in such a way that you command reality, that your sight cannot be trusted! If there was a comet, it would have been observed in this hemisphere, and there'll be a record. Nothing on the seventeenth of June 1889,' he said, frowning over the astronomical catalogues, 'but the following day in France, the astronomer Vincent du Lac identified a comet in Cassiopeia, which was first designated 1889 III (du Lac) and then, because I suppose nothing about comets can ever be straightforward, 330P/1889 L1 (du Lac) – might it be possible that in fact Văduva was the primary observer?'

'It might,' said Dimitru.

'I wish you wouldn't keep interrupting,' said Thomas. 'And – yes – it is a short-period comet – an estimated period of a hundred and seventeen to a hundred and eighteen years – so it is coming back to us: we need only wait ten years!' Thomas Hart, seated in his dining room with his deerskin slippers on, closed his eyes, and felt the charge of the comet's tail, and its streams of astronomical dust; he was untethered again from the earth, a dutiful citizen of celestial empires, and riding the solar winds. 'Well,' he said. 'Fuck me.'

'But ten years,' lamented the old man. 'We'll be dead by then, Thomas, we shall have obtained our reward. Now I've come a long way, and you must listen. Maria wrote often of a man she loved, who did not love her. Perhaps you remember.'

'I remember.'

'This man was indicated by the letter M. We may call this a clue. In due course I came across another. You recall how she speaks of Lucifer arriving at her window as if he were a lover?'

'That's no mystery. That is merely a reference to Venus, the morning and the evening star.'

'You are quite mistaken, Thomas, having no facility with the poets of any languages which are not your own. I, on the other hand, was in an instant transported to the classroom, and to the studies of Romanian literature, and in particular of Mihai Eminescu, the greatest of our poets, who conceived of Venus as Lucifer the Morning Star, who arrived at a woman's window and caused her to love him. Mihai. M. A great man, whom she loved, as I understand it, without hope and without return. You will also I am sure recall her envy of pretty Veronica. That is certainly Veronica Micle, who was the poet's lover. So' – he spread his hands; he was magnificent – 'you see the matter is solved.'

'Say his name again,' said Thomas, 'spell it for me'; he turned again to his computer, and there in a moment the poet was, drawn down through time and seated with them at the table. 'Yes,' said Thomas, 'yes, I see,' and looked with envy and admiration at the poet's full mouth and soft down-turned eyes, which seemed only softer against the firmness of his jaw. 'Poor Maria – it isn't fair,' he said, surprised by grief. 'It isn't fair that beauty secures love so easily, and often without meaning to.'

'I should tell you,' said Dines, 'that his face was better than his work. Still: do you see the date of his death? The fifteenth of June 1889 – two days before the comet came. He died in the sanatorium where doctors tormented him with mercury for his syphilis, and his dying hope was for a glass of milk. So Maria had the news – she did the great thing she hoped would bring her love – but already the source of love was gone.'

'But if Maria saw the comet on that date, it is hers: after all she did one great thing that should be told among men. It is hers, and not du Lac's – we owe a debt,' said Thomas, 'to truth. Perhaps she buried her observations back in Potter's Field – perhaps in the walls of Lowlands House – something must come right. Am I to give my readers nothing but long-ing and loss?'

'If I were her I should go home and take my papers with me. What is Essex, when there is Bucharest? Even now, with all that was done to it by ignorance and power, it is our Little Paris. So this is what we are going to do, Thomas. I will take Maria back to my country, and speak there with the librarians and the Eminescu scholars, who'll be kind to an old priest. And I will leave my translation with you, and you will look for her in Essex. Now my hands hurt. You should have put me to bed by now.'

Thomas returned the old man to his old room. He knelt at his feet and took off his boots with the quiet untroubled attention with which he'd once washed him in the bath, and dressed him in pyjamas that were too small. The tall broad body smelt as if it were failing, as all bodies fail in the end. 'Thank you,' said Dimitru. 'Please leave on the lights.'

Then sleepless Thomas sat up late in the company of Maria, and no stars fell.

Astounding night – my heart beats in my fingertips and
disturbs the pen! – still I must make my account – the
great thing I longed for has come to me at last!

These past days I have been sick – my head has ached –
indeed I vomited three times, which caused John Bell joy,
imagining we were to have a child, though thank God we
are not. So being sick I slept last night as a child might
sleep, having no thought of the hands of the clock – and
woke before dawn to a sky with no cloud in it, and no
pain or trouble in my mind or body. What then could I
do, being awake and strong as a boy, but go to my
telescope? John petitioned me with tears to remain
indoors, but it was good Essex weather, the sky having
the look of a black pool on which sunlight sometimes
played – so I made some observations of Jupiter, my
heart tender at the circling moons, and perfectly
comprehending their stupid loyalty –

Since the moon waxed bright above the south-west
horizon, I turned towards the darker portion of the sky,
and passed an hour slewing back and forth, released for a
time from the sorrow attending me on earth – then all at
once my heart and mind halted, as a loose dog might halt
at a high gate! It was a stop upon my soul! My eyes did
not stop – for they had seen a blur in Cassiopeia, faint as
a bird's breath might be in winter – and having also a
bluish look! I discovered that I was weeping, and could no
longer see, and could hardly have told the moon from
Jupiter for the heat and thickness of my tears – I wiped

197

my eyes on my sleeve and looked again, in terror that I
had knocked the eyepiece, and so lost my treasure as if I
were on board ship and had thrown it overboard – but
there, again: a pearly smear extending fully two degrees
from a nucleus, this nucleus also having a blurred look,
only seeming to thicken and brighten as I watched – a
comet, beyond doubt or confusion! – undiscovered,
unexpected, arriving in Essex out of the chilly vastness –
seen first by me, a woman whose heart was broken, but
whose mind could never be! I felt myself divide, as a cell
divides in its dogged pursuit of life – so that in part I was
dancing in Cassiopeia, and standing on its points with the
comet in my palm; and in part I was with M. in some
street in Bucharest, bringing him what I'd found as a dog
going to her master –

I will repeat my observations tomorrow – I will be sure
of what I've done – and have made meanwhile a
document, which I shall take to the Royal Astronomical
Society in London, that the matter may be examined and
corroborated. The injustice done to Maria Mitchell was
quickly restored – but who'd count on a woman's luck!

Dear James

When I took all these shameful letters out from where I hide them, I saw a year had passed since I last wrote your name. But all the same: I've had you in mind. Do you remember me – do you ever have me in mind?

And do you ever think of our old friend Maria? Well, I've got something to tell you: her diary has come back to me, and I have it with me here. Again and again I read the final page, and still I can hardly believe my eyes. All that time, here at my table and in Lowlands House with the mist coming in, we wondered who she was and what she saw – all that time, and now we know. James: it was a comet, and the comet's coming back. Shouldn't we have known? Shouldn't we have guessed?

So now I have a new task on my hands: I'll see to it Maria gets her name in the books of stars. I won't have her forgotten. There is a comet they call Miss Mitchell's after the woman who found it, but it would have been wrongly named for an Italian man had she not argued her case. Well, since our Maria cannot argue hers, I will argue for her.

(I paused just then to look up Miss Mitchell's Comet, and found it has a hyperbolic orbit. Do you know what that means? It means it has escaped the draw of the sun, and will never return. I want to say: how are you, James Bower, moving down that orbit of yours? Will I ever see you again?)

((But I will never post this letter. I'm no fool.))

THOMAS HART

ON FRAUNHOFER LINES

THOMAS HART *ESSEX CHRONICLE,*
12 NOVEMBER 2008

Imagine you wake from uneasy dreams to find light beaming from the soles of your feet and the palms of your hands. If you woke in a temper, I suppose the light might be red, and if you slept well, perhaps a peaceable green. Now I hear all my readers say: What strange notions you have, Thomas Hart! But bear with me: this isn't quite as absurd as it sounds. In fact, all your life you've been radiating electromagnetic waves, but since you never radiate the part of the spectrum that can be seen, we can tell nothing about you just by looking.

The stars are another matter. Look carefully, and you'll see their ancestry. Starlight and sunlight, split by a diffraction grating, display their own distinctive patterns of colour. I have always wanted to see this for myself, and recently bought an old spectrograph. It resembles two miniature telescopes mounted on a dais marked with numbers, and has been testing my poor skills and my patience for weeks. Then yesterday, just past noon, I finally saw the full spectrum of the sun projected on a sheet of paper pinned to the dining-room wall: a vivid rainbow flattened to a bar, the colours interrupted at intervals by narrow black bands, where there was no light or colour at all.

These absences of light are known as the Fraunhofer lines, and show where light has been absorbed by the matter it was passing through – and their placement allows us to determine the nature and composition of the matter present in the moment of its birth, in the nebula of formation: the fingerprints of God.

The strange thing is that when I first saw these lines I was almost afraid. Even a child knows the shape and colour of a rainbow, and I hated to see the rainbow broken on the wall like a shattered window. It was as if I'd been speaking to a friend I'd known all my life, who by a single word or action showed that in fact I knew nothing about them at all.

Imagine you are radiating light, I said. Well: perhaps you are – but I suspect you withhold it, too.

Grace Macaulay – in whose veins ran Essex rivers and Bible ink; in whose philosophy the devils of hell and the saints of Bethesda did battle with her reason and her nature – sat with her phone on the bare floor of a Hackney room and thought of Thomas Hart. *Come home*, he'd written, *you wretched child*, and I am wretched, she thought, and I think I'd like to go home.

She was twenty-nine, and ten years gone from the pew. That is to say: she was gone from her pew no more than Thomas was gone from his. It was true that she was no longer fastened there by guilt and love and obligation, but sometimes found herself back in the shadow of Bethesda's pulpit more or less out of habit, head covered by a borrowed hat and submitting to the consolation of the hymns. But the lucid certainty of her faith in the Lowlands fire now struck her as the last act of a child. Had she really believed that God – setting aside Albania and Afghanistan and continents of children dying under torn mosquito nets – would attend to a short-sighted reckless boy in Aldleigh? She had believed it, and had been willing to submit to baptism in her gratitude, but God after all had not been faithful and just (steam rose forever from the baptistery; the narrow door to the wide world never opened for Nathan).

She thought of the boy she'd loved with anger and sorrow

accommodated in the bare facts of her life, alongside the date of her birth and the size of her feet. That he hadn't come had betrayed her faith in God, and love, and the rewards of reaching after goodness. That afterwards Nathan had never thought to seek her out had aroused an implacable fury nothing like her childlike bursts of temper that so often ended in an embrace. All the same, in those past ten years she'd looked for him on the upper deck of buses and on station platforms and in the dreary offices where she worked, and never found him. Every year or so, with a painful opening in the chamber of her heart where he was kept, she opened social media profiles and constructed an idea of herself that seemed to her lovable; but she never found him, and he never found her.

The room was cold; it contained nothing of what Grace Macaulay loved. No absurd petticoats of lace and silk – no pendants, bangles, hair-combs and boots with laces replaced by ribbon. She had severed herself from herself. No scent of frankincense or lavender oil rising out of her hair and arms, only the penetrating smell of greasy dough rising perpetually up from the pizza place downstairs, diminishing her appetite. A pack of Silk Cut and a lighter were set beside a saucer on the windowsill where often she leaned out to shudder at the smoke, and watch the overground head for Croydon and Dalston. Her few clothes hung austerely on a rail, and a television overlooked the foot of the bed; she watched it indiscriminately and with confusion, trying to make Bethesda's child into an ordinary woman. And indeed she was ordinary, where certain essential matters were concerned – had not believed in hell since the day she'd laughed at the belt in her father's hand, devoutly hoped to one day see Thomas Hart with a man he loved on the steps of the registry office in the old town hall, was untroubled by the idea her ancestors had been stooped, and naked save for their own pelts. Each day she sent this ordinary woman out into the world, and passed more or less without notice, acquiring friends and lovers and colleagues; and what had at first been an anguished sense of her own strangeness had dwindled down to the discomfort of rough clothes worn over sunburn.

But *come home*, said Thomas; and now she heard – above the crowds headed for the station, the hungry customers converging on the pavements – the old harmonium and the sound of her aunt singing, and saw Bethesda's lights like moons against the rented wall. It suited her few friends to imagine she'd been subject to a thousand physical and spiritual abuses, and been thrown out of chapel doors that then were bolted against her. It was difficult to explain that her father and her aunt received her absence with sorrow tempered by their trust in the will of God. She would return to Bethesda, or she wouldn't, and really Grace herself had little to do with it: it all came down to predestination. Distance permitted her to view them clearly – her father's grief, and his sincere determination to serve his God; her aunt's shy diligent affection – and to love them better, and wish she could please them.

She looked again at her phone, which was busying itself with inconsequential messages: was she free tomorrow? Had she seen the news? What time on Friday? And there in the London noise was Thomas Hart, writing as if seated with sheets of ivory paper at his table on Lower Bridge Road: *come home*. She smiled, and smoothed her jeans as if they were yards of scarlet cotton over a rotting satin petticoat, and wrote:

Dear Thomas – all right. I'll come home tomorrow. Will you really meet me? Does she know I'm coming? And does she know I kept away because I can't believe this is happening and I don't want to see it?

I read your column online. I think you're the only person in the world who knows all my colours and I'm the only person who knows all yours! I still always want to tell you everything. Like this: last night I think I saw eternity. I often used to try and see it when I was little, because I knew that to die is to enter eternity, but I never could. I'd imagine a trapdoor opening under my grave, and something waiting underneath, but I could never picture time without end.

Then last night as I was almost sleeping I felt the strangest thing. Something was lifting up my bed, and it was tilting up at the foot, and I was sliding against the mattress towards the wall. I went on sliding and the wall was opening up to let me in and the bed was tilting and I was falling – but I understood that I was falling upward, and because of that I'd never stop, it would just go on and on.

What do you make of that?

See you soon –

G

I'll be there, of course. I'll take you to her. We'll surprise her with you.

It sounds to me like you are having visions – you are Julian of Aldleigh, you should sit all day in a white stone cell and weep with joy at the wounds of Christ. This is what I make of it: I'm quite an old man now, and will die before you. In that case my eternity will begin before yours – but if eternity has a beginning, how can it be infinite?

I think this is eternity, Grace Macaulay – I don't think it begins, I think it has begun. So this is eternity, we are taking part in it right now – I send this email in eternity, and I'll see you in eternity on platform 2.

THOMAS HART

Anne Macaulay, sick and tired, woke early after dreamless and unrestful sleep, and watched dawn illuminate the thin blue blanket on her knees, the paper kidney dish into which she'd vomited, the furred leaves of the African violets ranged in their saucers on the windowsill. The light also struck an orchid upright in a fluted white vessel, but could find no life in the plastic stem and petals. Dust settled on it. It would never die, thought Anne, and that was a loss. Briefly she inhaled the powdery scent deposited in the air the night before, when Lorna Greene had come in weeping, and kissed Anne with lips wet with tears, and said if only she'd heard sooner, if only she'd been told! Anne had received her embraces quietly, having no choice, and tried to be grateful for them. 'How long has it been, dear Anne,' Lorna had said, pushing violets aside to set her plastic orchid where it would best be seen from the street; 'how many years?' She spoke as if her absence had been forced on her by circumstance, when in fact she'd grown quickly tired of Bethesda, and in the intervening years been a Methodist, and a Unitarian, and briefly a spiritualist, and presently (so Anne wearily inferred from the new gold crucifix on its new gold chain) a Catholic. But Anne was too tired to bear a grudge, for all that there was so little distance left to bear them; so she'd succumbed to Lorna's scented presence, and her quick pats that had sometimes felt like smacks of reproach: 'Now whyever didn't you let me know sooner, whyever didn't you call? Silly dear Anne! Silly girl!'

Gratefully the light left the deathless orchid, and arrived at the table where every Sunday at 5 p.m. Anne had poured her pots of tea, and buttered the bread she made; so her memory populated the room, and there was Ronald bent over his Bible, and the old vagrant in his red velvet coat, and Lorna in her whispering cheap satin – there was Nathan with his arm in a sling, and there most vividly was Thomas Hart, unchanging and unchanged; 'Good morning,' she said, raising a hand to nobody, smiling at her own whimsy. Then the smile faltered: where was Grace, the child she loved because she'd been required to love her? She tried to account for time's transit, and could not – the girl might have gone just now into the kitchen, or might have been absent the whole span of her life. Bleakly Anne discovered that the only memory available to her was that of a toddler, bustling and plump and given to tempers, whose body had smelt of oats and oil; and the noise she made then was like the one she made in pain.

Ronald Macaulay came down the hall, holding the notebook in which he kept a record of the drugs he dispensed, and the intervals at which he dispensed them: she is in pain, he thought, and berated himself. He knocked on the door, and entered without waiting.

'Anne,' he said, 'is it happening again?'

'Where is she?' said Anne.

'Did you sleep?' He saw the thin green vomit in the dish; he saw the sweat that blotted the hospital pillow. The skin peeled from her fingernails, her palm was dry: what a disease this is, he thought, it grinds her bones to make its bread. Her coarse grey hair, thinned out to the down of a dandelion clock, was sticky on her neck. He poured water from a plastic jug into a plastic cup. How unfair it was that everything became ugly towards the end of life: the frame she'd used for walking when the disease had not yet done its worst; the hospital bed with its rails and rubber; even the blanket, pitifully thin, the depthless institutional blue of every ward he'd ever visited.

'Where is she?' said Anne. 'Why doesn't she come? Doesn't she know how things stand with me?'

Ronald in his later years had discovered that Bethesda's demands weren't always equal to life as he lived it. He ought to say: She may never come, and that will be all very well, if God wills it. But by this brute logic God had willed every malign thing that had ever occurred, and would ever occur, and so he set the virtue of kindness above that of truth, and sinned. 'She's coming,' he said. 'She isn't sure when – there's dreadful trouble with the trains, I heard that on the radio – but she'll be here soon. You must decide what to wear; she notices these things.' The blanket moved, and he saw the skin sloughed from her feet in little rags – she's slipping out of herself, he thought, she's going. He found among the litter of bottles and packets the lavender lotion Grace had sent with a hasty affectionate note. He rubbed this into Anne's feet, and the brittle tendons in the softening skin put him in mind of Rachel who had also died, and the balls of wool she'd held in her lap and pierced with knitting needles.

'Thank you. Have you always been this kind?'

'I don't think so,' said Ronald, 'but I can't remember.' This was true: life seemed always to have consisted of days meted out in portions of sleep, pain, sleep, the nurses' arrivals and departures, sleep, pain, sleep.

'I should have spoken up for that homeless man, Ronald,' Anne said. 'Do you remember him, and his red velvet coat? We shouldn't have sent him away. Did it matter that he was drunk, when he was made in the image of God? I've carried it all this time. I wish I could see him again, and ask him to forgive me. I'd like to put it down.'

'Even if you'd meant to cause harm,' said Ronald, pouring morphine into a plastic cup, 'it would all be washed away. Even if it had been like scarlet, it would now be white as snow.' She drank the sweet thick liquid, and licked the rim like a child wanting the last of her ice cream. 'Read to me,' she said. 'Read the bit I like best.' So he fetched the copy of *Pilgrim's Progress* in which ANNE MARGARET MACAULAY: HER BOOK was written on the title page in green and yellow pencil, and recalled having sat with her once in Sunday School, their feet in buckled shoes not able to reach the floor, awestruck by a magic lantern show in which Bunyan's Pilgrim did battle with the Giant Despair. 'I suppose I'll meet John Bunyan soon,' said Anne. 'Do you think he was as ugly as his picture?'

'I doubt anyone is ugly in heaven, or if they are we'll be unable to see it. Now you remember that Mr Valiant was called to cross the river, and he said to his friends, *I am going to my Father's —*'

'*I am going to my Father's*,' said Anne, who could not these days recall what day of the week it was, '*and though with great difficulty I am got hither, yet now I do not repent me of all the trouble I have been at to arrive where I am.*' She leaned across the high rail of her bed and tried to be sick, and could not.

'I'll leave you,' said Ronald. He kissed her on the cheek; he took away her book. Gratefully Anne felt drowsiness lop at her consciousness, and relieve the weight of guilt and sorrow. What remained had the persistence of a root, and this was the belief that she was not alone — that in fact she'd never been alone, because she was a child of God, and loved by him particularly, in all the particulars of her nature and her faults. She pulled the blanket to her breast. She was tired. Darkness came in from the periphery until the blanket was the whole of her view – and how marvellous it is, she thought, how remarkable, and it has simply been there on my lap all this time! Look how deep the blue is in the folds, look how the sun strikes it and makes the fibres burn – she lifted it to her cheek, and there'd never, not in all her life, been a sensation like it. She breathed it in, and there was scent of lavender and laundry powder and her own body wasting in the ugly bed; then beyond this, like a field seen through a gate, the smell of the lanolin that oiled the sheep's wool and the sweat of the farmer that sheared it – then last of all, in a base note of wet iron, the blood of the ewe that nursed the lamb in the hours it could hardly stand. This is a miracle, she thought, it is a miracle: if this were the last thing I ever saw, I'd go to my long home glad, I would take it with me to glory. It is well, it is well with my soul!

A change of weather. Rain blew up the Blackwater with companies of shrieking gulls; it came to Bethesda, and turned the slate roof blue. It came to Lowlands, and caused the lake to seep across the lawns – it came to Lower Bridge Road, where it rapped on the windows, wanting to be let in.

Richard Dimitru Dines had defrocked himself and descended to the ranks of the sinners; he wore a borrowed dressing gown. He spoke with the scent of toothpaste and whisky: 'So then. Your small friend is coming home.'

Thomas was in the kitchen, cooking eggs. 'She is coming home. It's a year since I saw her last, but really I find that nobody ever changes – that we all contain ourselves from the day we are born. I was up all night with Maria.' He cut butter from the dish. 'You have done good work, old man. It ought to be published. Perhaps I can see to that.' Careful to retain the softness of the eggs, he whisked the butter in. 'I feel more than ever that her papers cannot be lost; it can't have been her lot to love and not be loved, and then to be forgotten. Don't look at me like that, old man. This is not my story.' He distributed eggs on buttered toast.

'Soon this rain will blow itself out,' said Dines, as if he'd arranged the matter with meteorologists both mortal and divine, 'and you will take me to Lowlands House. I saw it once only from a distance, and it seemed to me it was haunted, as such places are. Once in the days of my degradation I saw a man walking there, looking at the moon. A man of sorrows, it seemed to me, and acquainted with grief –'

'I am not at all sorrowful. I never was. It was all just a trick of the light.'

'– and I could not have known that I would one day haunt his house, turning up like a bad coin!'

'You'll find Lowlands House as changed as I am unchanged. They've driven the ghosts out with a broom – they've washed the steps – I'm told there's to be a new glass case for Maria's telescope. I must say, Dimi: it would be mad to think we'll find a flagstone come loose, and her comet underneath it, melting into the mud.'

'But we are mad,' said Dines.

Meanwhile two men named Peter stood at the brink of Lowlands lake. Barriers behind them: also diggers, and articulated arms for dredging mud; sacks of concrete, and the means to mix it. Work could begin the following day, said the men, though it was in some ways a pity. 'Swam here once upon a time,' said Peter the elder, in whom sadness arrived like weather: 'fished in it. Pike size of a cow, couldn't land it.' He stirred the water with his boot. The rain-swelled lake inched diligently over the lawns.

211

'Did you ever see the ghost?' Peter the younger was prepared to believe whatever he was told.

'No. But I saw the graffiti, saw the fire. Was here that night – everyone was, you'd think it was the Easter fair. Didn't know anyone was in the house, of course. Wouldn't have watched if I did.' Together they turned to survey the house, which now had the uneven look of a man walking with a limp. The facade of the east wing, hollowed by fire, was buttressed with concrete and plate glass. Its roof was flat. It was accessible, air conditioned, spacious: no ghost would dare. The west wing and the centre portion, marvellously undamaged, had been restored. The ivy was gone from the plaster. The unblinded windows looked at the oaks. The oaks looked back. 'Funny thing,' said Peter the elder, 'could've sworn the moon was blue.' Then 'God's sake,' he said, 'who's this?' A priest was coming over the lawns with a rushing onward gait. A companion came in his wake, and this man had the careful tread of a man acquainted with pain. 'What have you been up to,' said Peter, 'got anything to confess?' – and the odd thing was the younger man did begin to feel he was in need of absolution, but couldn't think what he'd done.

The priest arrived. The rain had cleared. The sun struck Lowlands white as bones.

'What,' said the priest, 'is going on?' He raised his stole as he spoke, and it seemed to the workmen that it was indeed all a moral matter: the waiting diggers, the sacks of concrete, the barriers tipping in the reeds.

'Dredging,' confessed Peter the younger, wringing his hands. 'Improvements. It really isn't safe,' he said, 'it hasn't been for years. Last year someone got drunk and lay all night in the mud. He could have got Weil's disease!'

The man who was not a priest rubbed absently at his hip, and showed a courteous interest. 'Well,' he said. 'Did he?'

'Not that I know of. But it was possible.'

The man considered this with interest, and at length. 'It was among the probabilities, certainly,' he said. The cloud slipped.

'Tell me,' said the priest, 'did you find anything in the water deep down? Such as, for example, a sealed box of Romanian make, very fine? Perhaps in fact you discovered it in the foundations, when the work was done?'

'No,' said the men together, 'not a thing.' Then Peter the younger, responding to the atmosphere of holiness settling on the lake, said, 'They keep saying someone's down there, mind you. Nobody's seen anything. Nobody's heard anything. But someone quit last week: said he remembered the blue moon, didn't fancy being here when the dredgers went in.' The visitors were silent for a time, then spoke incomprehensibly between themselves. The priest was thirsty. He drank. He offered the bottle to his companion, who refused it, and thanked the men for their time with a fine hand pressed to the fine tweed of his suit. The men, vaguely enchanted, inclined their heads and watched them go.

'What was all that about?' said Peter the elder to Peter the younger. Jackdaws had gathered on the margins of the lake, and also sought an answer. The rain set in.

Five o'clock: Thomas sheltering from the solemn weather on platform 2. From this vantage it ought to have been possible to see Upper Bridge Road with its look of a dragon's spine, but rain obscured the view. It was rush hour. The arriving train pursued its own lights up the track. Thomas heard the ticking of the lines, and bags and bodies jostled through the doors — saw girls dressed for the city praising each other while men watched with indiscriminating eyes. Thomas also watched: he waited. A boy came last off the train, hurling down the platform and dropping a paper cup. Abruptly he slowed, as if remembering something unwelcome, and looked back with longing. How delightful he is, thought Thomas, with the old reflex of desire. He noted with pleasure the beautiful head revealed by black hair clipped to the scalp, and the hollow where the neck entered the skull; then the boy encountered rain, and pulled up the hood of his coat. His white face receded from admiration, and Thomas watched the boy come closer, and felt vaguely he'd been in some way tricked. Then there was a sudden reversal of perception that tilted the ground under his feet, and faintly repelled by himself and by the lovely head concealed in the hood, he said: 'You!'

'You did say,' said Grace Macaulay, putting back her hood in the station shelter. 'You did tell me I should come!'

Yes: I told you to come, but where have you gone? thought Thomas. She was altered beyond recognition. Where were her ribbons and skirts – where the soft brown arms, the cheap bracelets and rings, the silver bees dripping silver honey? She was thin. Tendons showed in the backs of her hands. She wore jeans, and boots that were too large and impeded her walk; her eyes retained something of their newborn oil-on-water shine. She had evidently shaved her head herself: a black tuft remained behind her ear. Did she have no friend to help?

'I did,' said Thomas, and discovered that at least her scent remained familiar: neither pleasant nor unpleasant, a little feral and rising out of her scalp.

'Have you been very cross with me?' – and there was his bad-tempered affectionate child, and Thomas with a relieved laugh said that yes, he had, but that that was all right: she was his dearest. So she hurled herself against him, and in her brief embrace he felt her shoulder blades flaring under her clothes, and the thought arrived, as if Maria had tapped him three times on the shoulder: she is unhappy, and it's all my fault.

'Let's go,' he said, holding his umbrella above them both. 'We have company. Richard Dimitru Dines has returned to Essex, and is sitting in my car.'

He discovered she still possessed the suddenly-arriving smile: 'Dimi!' she said. 'Remember I found him, Thomas? I saw him first!'

They came under the bridge, and there was the car in view. 'It's been a year,' said Grace, 'and it might have been ten – when did they paint the Jackdaw and Crow? Was the traffic always like this? Everything changes, and don't you think all change is loss? But you're not changed, despite your clothes,' she said, reaching for the old man in the back seat and conferring on him her acquisitive affection. 'Look at this' – she shook the stole with its goldwork cross – 'look at the work on this, and what have you done with your red velvet coat?'

'Where also is your shawl,' said Dines, 'and what have you done with your curls – change and decay in all around, I see!'

'Shall we go?' said Grace. 'I want to see her, and I'm afraid to see her, and how can both be true?'

'You can't expect only to feel one thing at a time,' said Thomas, 'though certainly it would be convenient. You can want to see her, and want not to see her, and neither cancels the other out: you are a woman, not an algebraic equation.'

'I can't bear it.'

'Well,' said Thomas, 'you will have to learn how.' Rain boiled on the pavements, and smeared the windows with the lights of stationary cars that confined each other on the roads. We are all thinking about Anne, thought Thomas – much to say, no time to say it. Impatient drivers leaned on their horns, and went nowhere. 'We'll go as soon as we can,' said Thomas.

Dear James

It's midnight. There's no moon, and Anne Macaulay is dead.

It was difficult to write that. Let me try again, and bear it better: Anne Macaulay is dead.

I'd planned to see her this afternoon. I'd planned to take Grace, who has been absent for so long, and old Dimitru who's come back to Aldleigh again. I'd imagined the surprise, and the pleasure I'd give – 'How good of you, Thomas,' my friend would say, 'how kind you are!' I wonder if we ever do kind things without thinking of the kind light we'll be standing in?

So we drove there through the vengeful rain; but as we came to Beechwood Avenue it seemed to wear itself out. There was that kind of brilliant sunshine that only comes after a storm, and already the road and pavements were dry. It was six o'clock: birds losing their minds in the silver birch, children coming out of doors. When Grace saw her father on the doorstep she ran to meet him, and when she put her head on his shoulder I saw him pat her like a dog.

Then we all went together into the room where Anne has lived these past three months. I saw the sun suspended in the window, and how the light made everything wonderful, everything – even the horrible bed, the rubber mattress, the pill-packets, tissues, incontinence pads, antiseptic wipes, teaspoons stained with tea. Anne wore a white cotton nightgown with plastic buttons that looked nothing like pearls, and stroked a thin blue blanket as if she'd never held anything so soft.

Grace looks these days like a half-starved boy, but Anne knew her without any trouble. 'Come here,' she said, 'come here,' and you'd think the wretched child had only been gone a few hours. So Grace climbed on to the bed and curled there and said nothing, and was never more like a little farmyard animal, and all the while Anne patted her and patted the blanket and looked at us all as if all the things she'd ever hoped for had been given substance. Her old shy smile was unchanged by pain – it came drifting up like something shining underwater: 'Thank you,' she said. 'Thank you.' That was the last thing she said to me, and I'm glad.

Dimi went forward then, and my memory dressed him in the old red velvet coat, and put birthday cake on the table and the Great Comet in the window. He held out his hands, and you'd think they'd healed overnight, you couldn't see the scars – 'Anne,' he said, 'Miss Macaulay.' I was afraid she wouldn't know him, but she did. She said only that she was sorry, and he said it was all right, and the river had gone under the bridge.

Then Anne looked at Ronald and there was her drifting smile again and she said, 'It was so heavy, and I've put it down.' Then there was an hour when she said nothing, and her hands were still on the blanket and sometimes she breathed quickly and sometimes not at all. Every now and then Ronald dipped cotton wool in water and used this to wet her lips, and I put my hand on hers and wondered what was passing through her mind – if she was thinking of her brother and her niece, who were bone of her bone and flesh of her flesh but each in their way so solitary – if she was thinking of her earlier life in the hills, and the life that waited on the other side of Jordan.

Then the angle of the sunlight altered, and suddenly every shadow was long and slanting on the wall. Anne roused herself as if she'd slept well, and looked at us one after the other with her old clear shy look; then she moved the blanket into the light and showed us the blue, and said, 'Isn't it all a miracle? Do you think there was ever any other life like this?' Then I suppose something essential somewhere failed, and Grace –

Thomas, whose bad hip ached, looked up from the letter that wouldn't be sent, and saw Maria Văduva in the empty armchair. Skirts three inches deep in Lowlands mud, eyes looking sternly out of the shadows: *Thomas Hart*, she said, *do you think I wasn't there – didn't you see me at the window? You old deceiver, you father of lies, it wasn't like that at all!*

'I wish you would leave me alone,' said Thomas, who'd persuaded himself absolutely, as he'd always been able to do, 'I wish you'd let me have a moment's peace. No,' he conceded, 'it wasn't like that. But all the world is composed of probabilities, and of all things this was the most probable, and the most right!'

Then black-browed Maria, righteous in death, spoke with the indignation of his conscience: *You never could bear to see things clearly, Thomas Hart. Look again.*

Look then, Thomas Hart: the car not ten yards from the station, windscreen smeared with the distorting rain; impatient Grace becoming bad-tempered, and raising her phone – 'Why aren't they moving, Thomas, for God's sake, we've been here half an hour, and my phone's out of charge, and why don't you ever have yours with you?' Above them on the railway arch another train departed, and further down the road a maddened driver got out and uselessly berated whatever was unfolding half a mile towards the town. Now the rain was coming in fat drops that rattled on the roof with a noise like shot, and Dines in the back seat had reached the last of his drink – 'Why are you keeping me down here,' he said, 'why are you doing this to me?' So Thomas turned and saw the old terror surfacing – 'Wait a little longer, Dimi,' he said; then in a car close by a passenger gave up hope, and throwing back the door struck the car where Dines sat, causing him to flinch and cry out. He fumbled with his seat belt, speaking rapidly to himself in Romanian, and clutching the satchel more or less fell out on to the pavement. 'I will not I think go with you,' he said; 'you will not make an old man sit so long. Let me go, Thomas, let me go, I'll find you in good time.' He slapped the car as if it were the flank of a horse: 'Now things are moving, and Anne is waiting, and you must go.' And the traffic was moving, and Anne was waiting, and there was so little time: 'We can find him again,' said Grace, 'we always find him somehow.'

Look again, Thomas: Grace Macaulay on the doorstep of her father's house. Lights out, bad weather. Grace, uncertain of herself and all the world, not knocking yet. Something altered in the look of the place, in the gone-over garden, the silver birch: something departed. Ronald coming out. Quick embraces, nothing said. Grace taken to the dining room. Ugly bed with nothing in it. Scent of lavender. Scent of vomit. Antiseptic. Tea. John Bunyan open on the table: *I am going to my Father's, and do not repent me of all the trouble I have been at to arrive at where I am.* Thin blue blanket on the floor. Ronald saying, 'It was only three hours ago, and they came for her so fast – did nobody else die today? Did they have nothing else to do?' Ronald bringing in a plastic bag: 'Let's clear up, let's get rid of it all, she doesn't need it now.' Thomas at the door, knocking once. Grace picking up the blanket, thinking:

doesn't look very warm, does it, I hope it was soft enough, she always did have trouble with her skin.

Later that same day, at the bell of last orders, two women left the Jackdaw and Crow, pausing at intervals to talk and kiss on soaked roads glossed by streetlight. They reached the shadow of the railway arch, and were there for a time against the wet brick – then 'Oh,' said one to the other, sobering abruptly, 'something isn't right.' In a long fuddled moment they sorted through what they saw: parked car, bollard, ticket booth, bin, all these in their proper places, unremarkable – then, between a van and the parking meter, a spread of white cloth, as if ready for plates, knives, glasses. Closer then, hands gripped now for courage: a booted foot turned out, and white cloth falling from a crooked knee – a fringed scarf with a gold cross unravelling, and at last a face propped against the kerb, a streetlight halo on the bald and marvellous head. It wasn't necessary to say that he was dead: because the eyes were open, sightless and wondering, fixed on the moonless sky.

How curious that none of this was frightening – that it was easy to hold his hand and remark that some damage had been done to him a long time ago. But it was all right now, they said to him – it was all right, it was all over now, and wasn't he a priest, wasn't he a man of God? They'd probably be waiting up there, probably put bunting on the pearly gates. Sirens then, and lights, and no efforts made to retrieve what was already gone; and nobody seeing in the gutter a black book with a broken spine dismantled by bad weather, the pages going one by one down the storm drain, and coming in time to the Alder and the Blackwater, so that by the morning of the following day, by the hour of Lucifer rising, Maria Văduva Bell was renewing over and over in the matter of the sea.

THE CLOUD OF UNKNOWING

THOMAS HART *ESSEX CHRONICLE*,
20 NOVEMBER 2008

I hope you'll forgive my recent absence. The fact is I've suffered a loss, and have been consoling myself not with religion, but with physics, reading about quantum mechanics and discovering it has all the strangeness of theology. It doesn't call laboratories to mind, but a mystical work on the nature of God they call *The Cloud of Unknowing*.

Let me try and explain. When I was taught about the atom, I drew in my exercise book a nucleus, and an electron orbiting it as the moon orbits the earth. As it turns out, my teachers were mistaken: we ought not to think of electrons orbiting the nucleus. This is because we don't know exactly where an electron is, only where it's most likely to be.

This has been demonstrated in an experiment that makes my head ache. First, I want you to imagine you drop two pebbles in a lake, causing two sets of waves to intersect. Where a peak meets peak, the peak is higher; where a trough meets trough, the trough is deeper. Where a peak meets a trough, the waves negate each other, and the water is flat. This is called wave interference, and it also happens to light: when light is shone through two slits, that same interference pattern appears in bands of light and shade against the opposing wall.

Now imagine that instead of shining light at a barrier perforated by two slits, you are firing electrons. You might imagine the electrons would pass through, making two patches like two pools of water under a leaky roof. Instead, something remarkable happens: a pattern begins to form that looks like the bands of wave interference: the electrons have behaved like a wave.

What is more astounding is this: if you fire the electrons one at a time, the wave interference pattern still happens. It is as if, while the electron has chosen to pass through the slit on the left, it has also passed through the slit on the right, interfering with itself. It seems to have taken into account all the possible outcomes of its own movement. This is why it's said that nobody can be certain where an electron is, until it is measured: it exists in a kind of cloud of probability.

Physicists bicker like sisters over the implications of the double-slit experiment. The simplest explanation, I suppose, is that we are mistaken in our understanding of it, and that quantum mechanics as it's proposed today may well be modified tomorrow. There is also a more astonishing explanation, though I daresay it's the most unlikely: that while we can only observe one outcome of all those probabilities, we cannot say that all the other outcomes are either real or unreal – that in fact there are infinite numbers of universes, constantly generated, taking into account the fulfilment of every probability, at any time. And since there is no means to disprove this preposterous-seeming theory, it has the lingering substance of a dream.

I'd thought the study of physics would be for me the study of certainties, but my hope has not been met: because of my wonder and the limits of my understanding, the study of matter is for me a question of faith – though it comforts me to think that where quantum at least is concerned, certainty isn't necessary for the world to function. So I'm baffled, but grateful for my wonder. In the fourteenth century the author of *The Cloud of Unknowing* wrote this: 'Whatever you do not know is dark to you, because you do not see it with your spiritual eyes.'

Dear Mr Hart

I'm writing to invite you to the formal opening of the New East Wing at Lowlands in December: please see attached. We've been so grateful for your help with the Văduva papers, and I hope you'll be pleased to see her telescope on permanent display.

Regards
Anna Fonseka
Essex Museum Services

Thank you for your invitation. I'd like very much to attend, and in fact recently came across some interesting new information regarding Maria Văduva. Would it be possible to bring a guest?

Best
T. Hart

How exciting. Delighted you can come. Do bring a guest. Best, A.

Dear James – I wonder if this email is still yours?

I'm writing to ask you to come back with me to Lowlands House. More than ten years since the fire, and at last they're putting Maria Văduva's telescope on display. I've attached an invitation to the opening. Won't you come with me, and be my guest? I have so much to tell you.

My regards to your wife and family.

Yours sincerely
T. Hart

Please note I have retired, and this account will not be monitored. I can be contacted on my personal address. J. Bower.

Ah – I always hoped I'd see you again! But since hope depends on doubt, I must have doubted it too. You won't see this. I suppose I can say what I please. But I never did, and wouldn't know where to begin.

T. H.

Please note I have retired, and this account will not be monitored. I can be contacted on my personal address. J. Bower.

Every day I think of things I want to tell you, and things I want to ask. Did your life become what you wanted it to be? Did anybody ever tell you why the moon was blue? And did you ever go to a bookshop and find a novel called *The Horse and Rider*, and see your initials there – did you understand it is your book?

T. H.

Please note I have retired, and this account will not be monitored. I can be contacted on my personal address.
J. Bower

ON THE NATURE OF BINARY STARS

THOMAS HART *ESSEX CHRONICLE*,
27 NOVEMBER 2008

It's taken me all my life to learn not to trust the sight of my own eyes, and it was the stars that taught me. They ask me to look, and look again, and be certain of what I've seen: I often think what trouble I could have saved myself if I'd learned this when I was young!

I was out the other night with my binoculars, taking a look at the Great Bear, and realised that what I'd taken to be a single star located in the 'handle' was in fact a pair. I can't say why this delighted me, only that I went home and passed the night learning what I could about the nature of binary stars.

In 1617 – the same year in which our old friend Kepler set out his laws on the motion of bodies in orbit – Galileo Galilei began to examine the pair of stars I saw. The larger star is Mizar, which comes from the Arabic meaning apron, or wrapping, and the second is Alcor. Together, they're known as 'the horse and his rider'. But Galileo, looking more closely than I ever did, discovered that Mizar itself consists of two stars fifteen arcseconds apart, and locked together in orbit around a common centre of mass.

Stars, like comets, are travellers. Sometimes a pair is formed as one star compels another towards it as they make their way through the galaxy; but it's more common to find binary pairs that were born like twins when immense clouds of gas and matter collapse in the act of creation.

Most stars, I'm told, are binary stars, and these pairs affect each other profoundly. One star might waylay another in space, but find in due course it suffers from this new proximity: it is possible for one star to draw matter from another in what they call mass transfer, growing larger and more bright at a dreadful cost to its companion. In this way the bodies of the stars are formed by the forces of attraction between them, and the closer the relation, the higher the risk.

If there cannot be equity, I wonder

if it's better to receive the greater proportion of love, or give it? I wish I knew. W. H. Auden, whose poem 'The More Loving One' considers the stars' indifference to the love of men, wrote this:

If equal affection cannot be
Let the more loving one be me.

Five days after Anne Macaulay died, the moon passed between the earth and the sun; and since by an absurd coincidence of celestial geometry the moon's disc slotted perfectly over that of the sun, it sealed in the light. At the time of total eclipse, animals and men in Novosibirsk and Kazakhstan and Northern Canada stood in the lunar shadow and saw starlight before noon, and in due course a corona surrounding the absent sun with the look of iron filings compelled by a round black magnet.

'They tell me the moon is slowly drifting away,' said Thomas. 'I wonder if there'll come a time when it will seem too small to cover the sun? In that case what a stroke of luck, that the age of humanity happens to be the age of eclipses.' He was walking with Grace in Lowlands Park. These were the early days of grief, when the death of Anne Macaulay was sometimes so improbable as to be forgotten, and sometimes the whole business of the day. Grace had woken that morning to find her old room so unaltered she'd thought she must be unaltered too, and it had been distressing to discover that in fact she had no hair, and that every tendon was visible on the back of her hand. For a time she'd watched the light traverse the wall, and highlight her possessions: the Romanian shawl she'd worn until the fringe was filthy, the books awarded each year at Sunday School (*To Grace Macaulay, for*

Attendance), the Bible with its pages folded and underlined – all as unchanged as Bethesda, and almost as persuasive. But she wasn't fooled. The alterations were absolute. The absence of her aunt did not exist only in the places where she ought to have been – in the empty bed, the tapestry armchair, the places on the kitchen floor where she'd worn the linoleum thin – it existed down to the last corner of the house. She was gone from the bathroom pipes, she was gone from the doormat, she was gone from the bone-handled knives she'd set out for Sunday tea. She was gone from the cushions, bookshelves and bathroom light-switch; from the African violets that were dying on the windowsill because nobody watered them. Only her father, in mourning all those years, went unchanged by loss.

'It will do you good to get out,' Thomas had said, arriving at Beechwood Avenue with flowers. 'Come with me to Lowlands – there's a partial eclipse in an hour, and no cloud'; and she'd felt her affection for him increase by the quantity of love her aunt no longer needed.

She said she wanted to go in to Lowlands the old way, as if she were a disobedient child again. So they'd walked past Potter's Field, where with a kind of stupid instinct she looked for Nathan; then down through Bethesda's car park and the line of silver birches that kept the chapel from the world. 'At least nothing here has changed,' she'd said, arriving at the margins of the park and deceiving herself – the altered wing of Lowlands House showed hard-edged against the copper beeches.

Now they stood some distance from the lake, where the dredging had paused, and the men were passing eclipse glasses and sheets of dark film from hand to hand. Beyond the lake, schoolchildren were lying on their backs, holding silver filters overhead. It was the last days of autumn, and the light was defiant on the lawns. All day the insolent moon had chased the sun, and had at last attained it. 'There'll be no totality here,' said Thomas, handing Grace a flimsy cardboard pair of glasses with lenses of black film, 'it will reach sixty-two per cent, and in ninety-six minutes it will be over – Look' – the schoolchildren gasped and cheered – 'it's begun.'

Seen through the solar filter, earth's near star was reduced to a coral disc clipped at the rim. This clipping never seemed to move, but each time Grace looked, the absence was larger.

'If you were to return to this spot in about fifty-four years,' said Thomas, 'you'd see this same eclipse, at this same time. And this is because of something called the Saros cycle, which repeats an eclipse every six and a half thousand days or so.' But the devastating sight of a damaged sun was invisible to the naked eye, and not yet affecting the daylight. The men by the lake lost faith, and returned to their tasks. The sound of diggers began again, and the children fought and rolled down a shallow incline.

But Grace, grateful to have been lifted out of Aldleigh, went on watching. 'I think I understand,' she said, 'how you fell in love with the moon. Is it nearly done?' She saw the sun half-gone, and briefly wondered if permanent damage had been done, and it could never regain its proper light.

'This is almost the end of the beginning,' said Thomas, 'hold on.' His bad hip ached: he rubbed it. Now perceptibly the late-autumn light was diminishing. Jackdaws lifted from a stand of oaks, interrogated the air, and settled. It was as if the entire afternoon had been excised from time, and abruptly it was six o'clock. 'It takes eight minutes for the light to reach us from the sun,' said Thomas. 'If it ever went out, darkness would spread out from it like a stain. And since no form of communication exceeds the speed of light, for those eight minutes we'd have no idea all life was coming to an end.'

Nearby a bewildered deer, drifting out from denser stands of oak on the margins of the park, looked mistrustfully at Thomas, and bolted. The children were clustered around a solitary adult, who made hopeless entreaties that went unheeded.

Grace, moved unbearably to remember Anne, felt the new shock of loss. 'It gives me the feeling,' she said, 'that nothing I ever do will matter. But at the same time, to be alive at all – to be with you in this park, at this moment – it's so strange and so unlikely!' She looked at Thomas – at the fair hair, neatly brushed, and gone greyer in her absence; at the well-cut coat and well-chosen shoes she recognised, surely, from back when she was young. 'You've been almost everything to me,' she said, with furious affection, 'because without you nobody would ever have told me what was the other side of the chapel door. And I used to be angry because you were all I had – but wouldn't it have been more likely that I never had you at all? Give me the glasses,' she said, 'let me have my turn.' The shadow was diminishing on the sun. The untimely evening receded.

'Have you been happy, Grace?'

'Of course I'm not happy! I'm not even sure I exist! I bargained with God, and I lost. What's left of me now? I don't know how to dress, or how to speak – I drink and smoke and sometimes go out dancing, but I remember every hymn I ever sang, and cry when I remember them. And I still pray, Thomas, I still look for the face of God, and think every day about how to be good. But what does that mean when there's no one to tell me how to do it – and besides, no one is watching?'

'Was it such a bad thing to lose Nathan?' said Thomas, examining the mending sun. 'You were just children – did it matter so much?'

'Don't you see what it taught me? It taught me how alone I am!' They'd drifted nearer the lake. The children had gone, full light was restored; the air was briny with the scent of water disrupted by the dredgers, and of black silt being drawn up. 'You must think me mad,' she said, 'to still love a boy I last saw ten years ago. But it doesn't make any difference, not to me.'

'No,' said Thomas. 'Distance separates you from him, and if the units of distance were miles and not years, nobody would think it strange – but would your life really have been so different, if he'd come that day?' On the lake's further shore an older man in a yellow jacket raised his hand in greeting: 'You, again?' he shouted. 'Where's that old priest of yours?' A wind was getting up, and bringing cloud.

'How does that man know you? – Oh, it would have made all the difference in the world.' Grace couldn't suppress the smile that came at the thought of Nathan at the chapel door. 'It would have kept God alive, and kept love alive – I'd have been content to stay in my pew if Nathan had sat with me! You don't believe me,' she said, seeing misery in Thomas, who for the first time in her life wouldn't meet her gaze. 'Not even you can understand! Are you all right, Thomas – does your bad hip hurt?'

'Stand there a minute, Grace, stop walking.' He was pale, and it occurred to her that perhaps he too was gravely and secretly ill, and she was about to sustain another loss. This brought the relief of her old temper: 'For God's sake what is it, Thomas, what's wrong with you?' Then he spoke, and it was difficult to hear above the sound of the dredgers, and the man in the yellow coat who was summoning other men from further round the lake. 'I can't hear you,' she said. 'Say it again.'

'He did come,' said Thomas. 'I think I should tell you that. It might help.'

'You're always trying to make things better for me,' she said, shaking her head. 'You just think it would all be easier for me. But I'm not a child now, Thomas, you can't always make things better.'

'He was five minutes late,' said Thomas, as if reciting lines committed to memory a long time ago. 'He wore that denim jacket that had got too small. He had his headphones on, and I could hear the music. He came in and saw you kneeling down, because your dress was torn, and he watched you, and he wanted to come in. But you'd already been so unhappy, Grace. You were just a child and already you were learning what it is to love and not be equal! So I sent him away.'

Grace was laughing. Was she really expected to believe that the sun had diminished and regained itself, that her aunt was dead, that Thomas on a whim had altered the course of her life? It was absurd – it defied all the natural laws. 'No,' she said, 'you couldn't. How could you do that?' She heard the old man in the yellow jacket shouting, and saw the arm of the dredger leaning over the lake as if yearning for the water. 'Why would you do it, when you were always my friend?' She shook her head, refuting the evidence of Thomas's pallor. 'Why? Why would you be so cruel?' She began with difficulty to move away from him through the sodden lawn at the spreading rim of the lake.

'I don't know,' he said – 'I didn't think it would matter. You were just a child, and children heal quickly, don't they? Come back from there,' he said, 'the water's dirty and deep.'

But her muddled disbelief was clearing, and in its place her old temper mercifully flared. 'Don't tell me what to do,' she said. 'Haven't you already destroyed my life? Look at me – look what you did – you killed God!' Thomas spoke again, but other men were shouting and the wind was painful in her ears – she thought of her room in London, with its bare walls that blackened with mould in winter, and the light of the television illuminating the narrow bed; that's my home, she thought, I will have to go back to that nothingness, and look for my own life. She was aware that she was shivering violently, and thought she must be cold, but her body seemed something she was tethered to and it was difficult to manipulate her feet against the mud. The thinning cloud allowed a pewter gloss to settle on the surface of the water; and where the dredger breached the lake, the light broke and mended. Thomas came towards her, and she was afraid that if she looked at him she'd find him as altered as Lowlands was altered – 'Leave me alone,' she said, and turned away too quickly. Her feet were slipping in the black silt, and the water was shining at her knees. 'Oh,' she said, 'I think someone needs to help me,' but couldn't think who that might be. The men were shouting, the silt sucked at her; there was a moment when she felt she could resist the water if she chose, but was too tired. Now there was an absurd slow fall which would go on forever, and her hands were full of a silken rotting substance and the hard stems of grasses, and something living that eluded her. Then a hand met hers, down in the enclosing water, and distinctly she felt the rocking motion of its greeting and rough grasp of its palm – so after all, she thought, wondering why it had become difficult to breathe, after all I am not entirely alone.

Peter the elder, for whom the sun held no interest, had been watching the man he recognised talking with the black-haired girl across the lake. Where was the old priest, he thought, and why did the girl insist on stumbling back towards the water: they ought to have put more barriers up, there would be hell to pay – but the men were calling him, and there was Peter the younger with his worrying look: 'Something's down there, it's got caught,' he said, gesturing to the toppled dredger straining audibly against the mud.

'There's all sorts down there, I shouldn't doubt,' said the older man, untroubled; then the dredging arm's reach exceeded its grasp, and the digger was impelled towards the water. A confused flurry of bodies eluded the arm, and gave out incomprehensible warnings and instructions; then 'Watch out!' he said, looking not towards the digger but yards distant on the further bank, where the black-haired girl was sinking as if she meant to do it. The dredging arm swung back and forth and raised a reek of rotting vegetation; then the girl was gone, and the man in the tweed coat was reaching for the place where she'd been.

'Stop!' said Peter the elder. 'This is an emergency! This is an emergency!' He left the toppled digger and ran towards the man, slipping as he skirted the lake and gathering others as he went. Someone cut the digger's engine, and in the ensuing silence he heard the man in the good tweed coat say, 'Is it all really my fault?'

'Step back, for God's sake, this is an emergency!' Peter pulled him from the rim of the water: 'Let them go in,' he said, 'best to let them do it.'

Other men went shouting and plunging through the reeds – 'Got her,' said Peter the younger, rearing up and coughing, 'got hold of her down here, got hold of something.'

'Is it my fault?' said the watching man, wringing his hands.

'Sometimes things just happen,' said Peter, 'sometimes it's all just mud and bad weather.'

'There we go,' the men were saying, in the soothing way of a mother comforting a child, 'there we go, we're all right now'; and together they pulled against the mud and reeds, seeming to strain against an immense weight. The watching man rubbed his hip. 'But she's only a little thing,' he said, 'she was always so small.'

Then there was a triumphant cry, and the men reeled back in the mud. 'Got her,' they were saying, 'got her safe and sound'; but Peter in fact saw two women lying speechless in the broken reeds. One surveyed the sky with unsighted eyes, and raised a stone skirt with a stone hand; the other clasped her with a choking grip, and rested her wet black head on an unyielding white shoulder. Her lower lip was split, her open palm was raw; jackdaws came and looked, and asked whatever was going on, and why. The mended sun came out.

'There you are, you see?' said Peter, but he was not able to say if the movements he saw were those of the black-haired girl stirring, or nothing but baffled creatures drawn up with the silt and leaving the folds of her clothes.

'Maria!' said the man at his side. 'There you are! There she is,' he said, turning to Peter and smiling with a curious relieved radiance, 'things pass, but don't they always return? Didn't I say?'

Later – when the girl had been taken home, and the stone woman given a tarpaulin shroud; when the men had exchanged their soaked clothes for dry ones and were talking it over in the Jackdaw and Crow – they all said how strange it was to see that radiant smile dissipate, and the man begin to cry with the adamant sorrow of a child. And it was equally impossible (they said, forgetting him soon after) to tell whether he cried with relief, or with loss.

Anne Macaulay was twelve days dead. They'd taken away the communion table, and put her small coffin in its place. This done in remembrance of her: a small spray of flowers on the bolted-down lid, a photograph propped beside it; the old harmonium exhaling its scent of the North Sea tides, the congregation packed in the pews. All the same: few tears, scant mourning. She'd gone to glory, she'd obtained her reward – and wasn't there peace in that valley where the lion lay down with the lamb? The congregation, biding time until they joined her there, raised the rafters with their hymn: '*Forever with the Lord! Amen: so let it be!*'

But Thomas Hart, who still feared death's sting, was grieving in his pew under the halted moons. Weak light shone on the brass plaque bolted to the coffin: ANNE MARGARET MACAULAY. So that varnished pine contained her flushed cheeks, walking shoes, prudence, preference for Yorkshire tea, shyness, cuttings of African violet, habit of testing the heat of the iron with spit, facility with mental arithmetic, dutiful affection, diligent faith. No other woman ever had her qualities, and none ever would again, and all that was particular about her was returning to the general matter of the earth. Thomas felt himself depleted by loss. James Bower, Anne, Grace – he numbered them off. Grace was three pews down, grazes on the stem of her neck visible under the brim of a borrowed hat, and was as lost to him as if she'd never been dredged with Maria out of the Lowlands lake. The thought occurred to Thomas that it might have been preferable to lose her to water than to anger: then he might have mourned the girl who'd loved him, and not been subject to withdrawal of that love. Then God forgive me, he thought, and it would have to make do for a prayer.

Brief noises in the lobby, where the undertakers in their high black hats were waiting; then the senior deacon stood in the pulpit. '*Behold,*' he said, '*I show you a mystery: we shall not all sleep, but we shall all be changed*' – and such change, thought Thomas, and wasn't it all his fault? Sometimes things just happen, the man by the lake had said, sometimes it's all just mud and bad weather; but it wasn't just that, Thomas had thought, I had a hand in the mud. In those years since Grace was baptised he'd persuaded himself that he'd disrupted the course of her life out of wisdom and love – that he'd sent Nathan away to preserve his small friend from the humiliation of inequitable desire. Noble Thomas Hart, with the judgement of Solomon, with the compassion of Christ, and so on! Now this self-deceit was no longer possible – it had been his own envy and sorrow that did it, he'd still been on his knees in the gutter, and James Bower had still been holding his wife's hand. And when Grace had come to her senses in the mud and reeds, Maria Văduva Bell submitting to her frantic embrace, it seemed she'd simply not seen him. She'd taken the hands and coats of strangers, and accepted their chastisement and care, and meanwhile Thomas had stood close by saying how sorry he was, and what a wretched child she'd always been, and her eyes had passed over him without interest or recognition.

'Push you, did he?' a young man had said, and there was a moment when Thomas had felt them all ranged against him, instinctively suspicious; but his evident shock had pleaded his innocence. 'No,' the older man had said, 'don't be daft. Just mud, just bad weather. I'll take her, shall I? Why don't I take her home?' So he'd taken Grace, who hadn't looked back when Thomas called. And meanwhile Maria Văduva Bell had raised an empty hand to her right eye, holding nothing, seeing nothing – 'She must have been looking for something,' said Peter the younger, 'and now she'll look forever.'

'That's all right,' said Thomas, 'she'd have wanted it that way.'

Now the senior deacon, speaking with the voice of the apostles, returned Thomas Hart to Bethesda: *'For the trumpet shall sound,'* he was saying, *'and the dead shall be raised incorruptible'* – and look, thought Thomas, there's the incorruptible dead, followed me down from Lower Bridge Road: Maria in her yards of funeral silk, seed pearls and Lowlands mud dripping from her hem, taking her seat beside him in the pew and putting a fond arm through his: *It is right to be unhappy*, she said. *Isn't the value of your love set by the heap of your sorrow? Now tell me, Thomas: who is that, sorrowing so noisily over there?*

Thomas heard weeping from the front, then a high wavering exhalation that penetrated the gospel descending from the pulpit, coming from a shining satin hat trembling with the performance of sorrow. Now and then the woman raised a useless scrap of handkerchief to her eyes, and withdrew it stained with mascara, and no tears: Lorna Greene, thought Thomas, discovering that his dislike and distrust were undiminished since he'd seen her last. She'd returned to Bethesda to display her piety and grief, and wouldn't wait until the closing hymn to do it – now she gave a gulping sob that caused the congregation to examine their open Bibles more closely in embarrassment. *'Though he were dead,'* said the deacon, admonishing such faithless grief, *'yet shall he live.'*

239

Soon the undertakers came up the aisle with their rehearsed solemnity to retrieve their possession, and Thomas looked up at the moony lights, refusing the evidence of the brass plaque: that Anne Macaulay would never again go briskly across the car park and greet him. He heard again that ludicrous choking sob, and saw Lorna Greene contrive to follow Ronald Macaulay, who followed the coffin out – then came Grace, shockingly slight, passing so close the scent in the creases of her clothes and skin reached him, and she had the blank uncomprehending look of a woman who hadn't even seen a stranger, had seen nothing at all. Thomas, whose consciousness refused the loss of Anne even as she was carried out on the shoulders of strangers, comprehended the loss of Grace absolutely: she'd left him as decisively as she'd claimed him under this same vaulted roof.

He was the last of the mourners, and encountered Ronald at the chapel door, who said what a lovely morning it was, as if briefly he'd forgotten that this wasn't an ordinary Sunday, with Anne already halfway home to put potatoes on for dinner.

'That went well,' said Thomas, 'didn't it?', and wondered what the years of his profession had ever taught him, if he couldn't locate one word of consolation. So he took Ronald by the elbow, and said how kind the undertakers had been, hadn't they, how professional. The two men walked together to the safety of the hall behind Bethesda, where time never passed, and never tried to: the white cloths on the trestle tables, the steel tea urns, the Ten Commandments bleeding ink behind their mottled glass, all resisted the ticking of the gallery clock.

Ronald paused for a moment on the threshold, and seemed inclined simply to turn and leave; but the congregation parted for him, and so he drifted half-smiling through, clasping and releasing the hands he was offered, and arriving in due course at a chair behind which stood Lorna Greene, her hat pierced by a pearl-headed pin. 'Sit down, dear Mr Macaulay,' she said, 'sit down,' and began to fuss over him in a penetrating whisper that affirmed to everyone present that of all who mourned Anne, she mourned most, and most generously. 'You will be hungry, I should think,' she said, with sugared solicitude, 'let me bring you something to eat' – then she saw Thomas, and arrested herself, pressing a hand to her satin breast, and saying, 'Dear me,' blinking rapidly, and shedding flakes of mascara on her gleaming cheek. 'Dear me,' she said with an embarrassed laugh, as if Thomas had transgressed every social and theological rule merely by coming forward with a cup of tea in his hand. 'You think it appropriate – even now, under these circumstances! – really I would have felt –' Then she amended her tone to something more solemn, and attended again to Ronald: 'I'm sure nobody could be more sorry than I am for your loss – though heaven has gained another saint' – here she concealed her crucifix in her palm, for consolation or to forestall Ronald's Calvinist distaste for the cross. Watchful Thomas was inclined to think it all false – but her cheek was gleaming, he thought, it was wet: after all she'd wept for Anne as sincerely as anyone had wept. Abruptly, and with unwelcome compassion for a woman he'd despised so cheerfully and for so long, he understood what loneliness had compelled Lorna to Bethesda's door, and to all the church doors after it – recognised, in fact, her capacity to modify herself to please her company. Wasn't he a different man to different men? It was among the least of her sins. 'Mr Hart,' she said, tears drying on collar and cheek, 'you won't remember me' – but I remember you, she conveyed with her blackbird's gaze.

'I do remember,' he said, 'of course I do'; and the warmth with which this assurance came out startled them both, so that briefly behind Lorna's hard glazed hair and lips and breasts it was possible to see a frightened and uncertain girl who all her life had tried only to make herself wanted. Then the girl was gone, and in her place a scented construction that put a hand on Ronald's shoulder and stooped to his ear and said: 'I'd rather understood from dear Anne that Mr Hart had left the chapel, and found somewhere better suited to his nature . . . still' – airily she looked at the trestle tables, the discreetly mournful sandwiches, the men and women now attending to her as if to the change in weather – 'still, your dear sister would hardly turn a sinner from the door! I hope I'm not rude. I speak as I find.'

'Sinner?' said Ronald, unable to pick any malefactor in particular out of the general mass; then he saw his daughter: 'Ah yes, Grace, there she is.'

Grace crossed the hall, her small body altered and seeming a tall gaunt thing rubbed down by life; her clothes were dark and ordinary, the neglected tuft of hair curling behind her ear, her swollen lip recalling her old babyish petulance. But she was not babyish, she was not petulant – lightly she touched her father's shoulder, and 'Yes,' she said, smiling at Lorna, holding out her hand, 'yes, I was surprised to see Mr Hart here' – she was horribly composed, her quick temper and pained joy gone – 'he never really belonged, did he?' She stood beside Lorna and patted her satin sleeve. 'Good afternoon,' she said smilingly to the senior deacon, the elderly sisters down from Colchester in their knitted hats, the restless children eating funeral cake, 'thank you for coming, my aunt would have been so pleased to see you here.'

Where have you gone, thought Thomas, where are you, unable to find his wretched child in these brittle social graces;

then the gaze that had avoided him so painfully took him in with a bright contemptuous assessment. 'You never belonged here,' she said, with Lorna's trick of speaking with sibilant quietness that reached the back of the hall.

'You aunt,' said Lorna mournfully, 'would have been so dreadfully shocked'; and gradually Thomas became aware that all the men and women were attending to her, listening frankly or affecting to speak among themselves.

'Shocked?' said Ronald, shaking his head, and frowning over the problem of Thomas.

'Didn't you see?' said Lorna. 'Didn't you wonder?'

'Grace,' said Thomas, 'do I deserve this?'

'I wish somebody would explain,' said Ronald, dwindling in his seat, his white hair thin as an infant's, 'I really don't have any idea' – but Lorna clasped his shoulder and stooped to his ear, and explained, and explained again, with distasteful precision it was not necessary for Thomas to hear, because he'd heard it so often elsewhere.

'Grace,' said Thomas, 'not now – not here'; and it seemed to him that out of some common understanding the men and women and children were receding from him, that he was alone on the thin brown carpet under the Ten Commandments bleeding ink – 'Grace!' he said, and could barely see her for the distance between them.

'All this time?' said Ronald.

'All this time!' – and this might have been Lorna, and it might have been Grace, so closely were the two women pressed together, so similar their voices; now Ronald was shaking his head in censure or confusion or both, and very lucidly, making her declaration, Grace Macaulay said, 'So you see, he never really did belong,' and turned away shrugging, as if she'd done nothing more than note the bad weather in the window.

I never did belong, thought Thomas, I never belonged anywhere, and was certain he saw comprehension arrive in one face after the other, and expressions alter from kindly grief into disquiet and distaste.

'But does it matter,' said Ronald, 'should we cast the first stone?' – and with astonishment Thomas saw that of all the mourners present it was Ronald who understood most, and was least troubled – 'Mr Hart,' he said, 'why don't you sit down?'

It does matter, thought Thomas, on whose tongue there was now the taste of a copper penny, whose bad hip ached – he saw his last link to Bethesda severed, and one by one every Grace he'd ever loved coming up to sever it. 'It's all right,' he said, feeling again the jealous clasp of a newborn fist around his finger, 'it's all right. It's true, I never did belong.'

'Look at that rain,' said Ronald, 'I hope they drive carefully'; and behind him the hearse moved slowly past the window.

'This is so pretty,' said Grace deceitfully, fiddling with a gilt bangle on Lorna's wrist, 'where did you get it?'; and it seemed to Thomas that he'd been erased from that moment and all the moments that preceded it, and that no pew or hymn book would retain the imprint of his hand. 'Well, then,' he said, 'I'll be going,' and encountered the untroubled nods of strangers; so the last he heard of Bethesda for some years after was not for example a hymn, or the apostle Paul rebuking him down through the centuries, but a false affectionate laugh from a child he'd loved: 'I couldn't possibly take it – well that's very kind of you! That's very kind!'

The small hours. Dawn slow-coming, rain gone, Aldleigh at uneasy rest. Silence in Lower Bridge Road, where Thomas Hart looked vainly behind closed curtains, under empty armchairs, for a black-haired frowning woman at hand to castigate and console, and found not one dropped pearl or inscrutable sketch. Thomas who was never lonely, who was once content – who balanced Christ and Eros so neatly on the points of his intellect – had become a man of sorrows and acquainted with grief. He was alone, he'd always been alone, the worms were fleeing from him through the soil – no old man at his table, no red velvet coat hanging in the hall; no cross affectionate child, no sombre congregation, no loving stranger's look of recognition, no household ghost: he was born in sin and shaped in iniquity and the lights had gone out on the moon. It struck him that there were no practical, ethical or religious reasons why he should be obliged to endure a life that might soon become intolerable. A sensible man could achieve that final thing easily enough, he thought – then rested his head on the table and submitted to such penetrating weariness of his body and spirit that he thought a fatal harm had been sustained – so he need only wait, and the end would find him.

Then something shifted under his cheek: a cheap green notebook, the stitches coming undone at the spine. Thomas raised his head, and looked at it. He looked at the dozens of these heaped on the table, astonished there were so many; looked at the silver laptop with the print of his own hand smearing the lid. Sighing, sitting up straighter, he looked at a handsome white hand loaded with rings, frilled with a black silk cuff; heard a familiar voice, half-admonitory and half-amused: *Get up, Thomas Hart*, said Maria Văduva, assembling herself at the table, *Get up. Haven't you got work to do?* And it was true, thought Thomas with despair, looking at the notebook. He'd tried out titles on the cover, then crossed out their decisive capitals as the writer's doubt set in – ON THE MOTION OF BODIES IN ORBIT. ENLIGHTENMENT. THE BAPTISTS????

Thomas opened the notebook up. *Monday*, he'd written: *late winter, bad weather*. Ten years or more, and he'd never finished the task he'd set himself, dissuaded and distracted by love and circumstance – what, would he go now, and leave his sentences unfinished and unrefined, his thoughts muddled and self-pitying? *Poor Thomas Hart*, they'd say, shaking their heads, *to think his last work was to have been his worst, and what kind of title was that!* The thought was more dreadful than the thought of his body discovered dirty and disarrayed – 'My God,' he said, not irreverent, 'my God – will I have to go on a little longer for the sake of a fucking book?'

Dawn broke. Light slipped under the railway bridge, and over the lip of the windowsill: it arrived at the carpet, the notebooks, the uneaten toast; it lit the opposing wall with Pentecostal fire. Thomas felt the matter of his body respond, helpless against the ordinary wonder of the world turning again and again to the nearest star – *Come on then*, said Maria, tapping the table, dissipating with the shadows. *Get on with it, Thomas Hart.*

Look here, James. Just one more thing: Maria Văduva's comet will return in the winter of 2017. Look up, won't you? Don't forget. T.H.

Please note I have retired, and this account will not be monitored. I can be contacted on my personal address. J. Bower.

And did I ever tell you about the laws of Kepler? The first describes how heavenly bodies orbit the sun, and that is the law of ellipses. The second law I've memorised as I used to memorise Bible verses when I was young: the semi-major axis sweeps out equal areas in equal time. This means that bodies in orbit move faster and faster as they near the heat of the sun, rushing like a man into his lover's arms. Then they move past their perihelion, the embrace is done, and they become listless and slow in the dark.

Lately it's seemed to me that you became a kind of sun – that since you've been gone I've moved through a world with no warmth in it. But my orbit is closed, and everything that passes will in its time return – so I imagine myself moving again towards some heat and light I can't make out – T.H.

I came to the office to collect some correspondence and found your messages. It would be good to see Lowlands again. I'll meet you there on December the tenth, if still convenient?

J. B.

Thomas walked to Lowlands in December, accompanied by all the probabilities: James Bower mocking, James Bower pitying, James Bower chastising – James offering his hand, and James withholding it; James the man Thomas had known, James a man he'd never known at all. Ahead on the illuminated path Maria Văduva fastened the lace at the neck of her gown: *Didn't I warn you, Thomas, didn't I say? Never think too well of any man, or you'll wreck your ship on their rocks!*

'You did,' said Thomas, 'and I have, but I'm not sure I mind.' Aldleigh in winter mimicked Bethesda's grey austerity. The pavements were pale with tracts of grit laid down before the frosts, and the parks stripped back to vacant beds; colour arrived only in litter blown up against garden fences, and the undecided traffic lights on London Road. I'm sixty-one years old, thought Thomas, and my bad hip aches, and my hands are like my father's hands, if I remember them correctly; but I polished my shoes and spent the morning in the barber's chair, as if I were thirty again and all London made available to me – and what do I hope for? *A clear night*, said Maria, *a good night for hunting*, and receded towards the lake. Thomas was alone. The house in the distance gleamed between the copper beeches, and moonlight struck the glass panels on the renovated wing.

Music arrived, and Thomas so disliked its thin tuneless

complaint that his mood altered, and he began also to dislike each last square foot of Lowlands Park, James Bower in all his iterations, and last and most of all himself – then 'Thomas Hart?' A woman of calculated beauty dressed in pleated silk and amber beads came down the steps with hands outstretched, grimacing at the music and tipping her head as if to indicate she too disliked all this unholy racket – 'Thomas Hart? Anna Fonseka. Thank you for coming. Are you warm enough? It's a lazy wind, as my mother would say, going clean through you to save itself time.'

'It looks wonderful,' said deceitful Thomas, surveying the new steps of York stone, the obstinate glass panels blotted with white marks to dissuade birds from harming themselves in flight. Beyond the glass were Christmas decorations, and ranks of cheap wine on trestle tables, and unremarkable people in unremarkable clothes moving aimlessly across the floor. Thomas longed for the splitting window seats, the obscenities and symbols painted on the peeling walls; and for James Bower, desirable beyond endurance under the lightless chandelier. He took a notebook from his pocket. 'Remind me,' he said, 'of the cost of the renovation, and the name of the funding bodies, and the date of opening again to the public.' Anna Fonseka gave her answers, then touching his shoulder with practised deferential gestures conducted him across the threshold. 'This is Thomas Hart,' she said, adroitly smiling to this person and that one, left hand in bondage to her amber beads, 'who was there when they pulled the statue from the lake – who found the telescope himself! I'll leave you here,' she said, having identified across the room some person of more importance; and becoming perceptibly still taller and more adroit left him in the company of Maria Văduva, rinsed of reeds and silt, and standing on a wooden plinth.

'Hello,' said Thomas, 'you look well.' His old friend's feet were bare, and her small high breasts were those of a girl; her head was a little larger than it ought to have been, and had a remote untroubled beauty in which it was not possible to discern her indignant sorrow. The right hand raised to the right eye looked absurd with nothing in it, and her stone skirts gave out the briny scent of the lake. Beside her, and just out of reach, her telescope was sealed in an immense vitrine of toughened glass that had a greenish cast. It reflected the oblivious men and women passing back and forth, so that it was difficult to see beyond these shining phantoms to the telescope itself. Coming closer, and leaving a handprint on the glass in a deliberate act of trespass, Thomas saw the renovations made to the optical tube and eyepiece, and engravings on brass fixtures from which the Essex mildew had been cleaned; but the objective lens had been left in place out of reverence for the passage of time, and was cracked across with a fissure that would break the moon like a plate.

Thomas turned his back and examined the room in which he'd once stood under a vacant chandelier while fog rolled in across the park. He felt himself enfolded in persistent time that had only ever seemed to pass – that everything that happened in Lowlands was still happening, and would always be happening: if I peel that new wallpaper back, I'll see a symbol with the paint still wet – if I look down I'll see a rat running with a severed tail. Here's Grace, and she smells of rose oil and borrowed cigarettes; here's Nathan leaping down the steps – the men are coming in to measure the hole in the roof, and I can smell James Bower's body in his winter coat. I'm Canute, he thought, amused, I'm holding off the tide of time. So he saw the unremarkable people in their evening clothes begin to ebb, and the Christmas lights grow dim with distance against receding walls. He could no longer make out the aimless conversation or the music: he was alone in Low-lands, and his bad hip ached. Then: he was not alone. A man was crossing the vacant floor towards him. The distance between them was so great this took an hour or two, and in that time Thomas felt no anxiety and no surprise: 'James,' he said, smiling with an uncompromised happiness he knew would be brief, and taking account of the ways in which the man was altered. The gilded hair had tarnished and thinned, and been expertly cut to conceal its thinness; the body was narrower at the shoulder and hip, or had always been so narrow. His coat was grey and fit him well; his shoes were cheap. He came nearer. Now it was possible to see how the skin drooped at the ears as if an essential stitch there had come undone, and that the old burns had healed in shining patches on his forehead. But these did nothing to conceal the careful sculpture of his skull, and if those copper eyes had tarnished it was with the green of verdigris; so Thomas was struck again by beauty. 'Hello,' he said again, and wondered if he ought to hold out his hand.

'Hello, Thomas!' They embraced efficiently. Then James folded his arms, and surveyed the statue and the vitrine with professional interest. 'They've done a good job,' he said, 'that can't have come cheap'; and for a time the men talked about the difficulties of securing sufficient funding for regional historical projects, and the inadequacy of the new parking arrangements; and all the while Maria Văduva stood at the window solemnly shaking her head, and Thomas noted that James had changed his aftershave, that his socks didn't quite match, that he'd grazed the back of his hand. Then 'A comet,' said James, with a more serious and more intimate look at Thomas, as if coming at last to the matter at hand, 'a comet, you said!'

'A comet, I said' – Thomas looked at the telescope as if he

might find, drifting behind the broken lens, particles of astronomical dust – 'a short-period comet, returning in the year 2017 or thereabouts. When Maria saw it they say it was distinctively blue, with a tail extending ten degrees at its highest magnitude – though perhaps this time we'll hardly pick it out of the sky. That would be my luck. But a comet, James – who would have thought it? Though in some ways I wonder if we ought to have done.'

'But what are you going to do about it,' said James, 'who are you going to tell?' He spoke with such serious attention that Thomas responded with equal seriousness, as if they'd been introduced moments before over cheap wine in cheap glasses: 'I'm told I must contact some official institution, but I have nothing to show but the diary of a woman who vanished and was driven mad by love, and a broken telescope.'

'What a pity,' said James, his seriousness deepening still further, 'how disappointing for you.' How funny this all is, Thomas thought: there was a time I'd rather have seen your face again than every comet in orbit together; and now you're here and I asked how the traffic was on the A12 – 'Are you laughing at me?' said James Bower. 'Have I misunderstood?'

Thomas felt laughter cede to an awful tenderness. 'Look,' he said, reaching for the other man's sleeve, 'let's go. I can't talk to you here.'

The room pressed in. Women danced with movements that made nonsense of music. The Christmas lights went out, and were coaxed on again. Nobody looked at Maria. 'Come on,' said Thomas, conscious of sounding imperious and perhaps angry.

'Ah,' said Anna Fonseka, arriving as if out of the vitrine, 'I've been looking for you' – but already Thomas was slipping out with James in his wake. He went more quickly than he ought to have done, and the other man found him biting his tongue to quell a complaint, and rubbing at his aching hip; 'Are you all right? I am sorry,' said James, 'I expect this is painful for you' – he flushed. It resembled shame.

'It isn't that,' said Thomas, 'it's an old pain. And in fact I should say sorry,' he said, 'writing to you the way I did. It was childish and ungracious – I find each year that I grow no older, no more wise: only that I cart the same old Thomas Hart about in a body showing signs of wear.'

'You didn't know I'd see your messages,' said James.

'It was improbable, but possible!'

'But I am sorry. I had no idea. I didn't understand how it was for you. I didn't know.'

'You see' – Thomas was gentle – 'I think you did know.' A full moon was rising. It was horribly large, and as yellow as streetlights.

'I am sorry. But I never meant you any harm – Thomas, why does the moon seem so big, and so low?'

'That is a perigee moon, moving through the nearer part of its orbit, and seeming larger because so near the horizon – but that's also a trick: it's just the same old moon. And I don't think you should be sorry,' said Thomas. 'Don't say you are, don't feel it. It's true you caused me pain. I think more pain than I ever knew before or since, and perhaps that means I'm a man who's led a happy life. But now I think the pain was a tax on riches. I'm grateful for it, I'm glad – how could I have written what I did without it? But it's strange, it seems to me almost a humiliation: after all this time I want to touch you, because I never did.'

'You never did,' said James. He was looking with fear at the lamenting moon. 'You never did. But do you want to, even now? You can' – he seemed to be leaning out of himself – 'I'm just here.' He breathed as if the air were thin. His lips were red. The buttons on his coat had come undone and he looked at Thomas with an elated will that had no desire in it. I know that look, thought Thomas, I've seen it before, when Lowlands was on fire. He always did want some kind of disaster to lift him out of his own life: I could have been a schoolgirl, I could have been a gambling debt.

'You think I pity you,' said James, 'but I don't, I never did.'

'I might have taken pity – I might have preferred that. But I am not a disaster. I'm a man.' I have refused him, thought Thomas, amazed at himself, I have refused him. The appalling moon was rising and pulling up the Essex earth, and Thomas rose with it. I did love you, he thought. I have loved you, I would have loved you, I do.

'Someone is coming,' said James. He was far below, inaudible, he was buttoning up his coat. 'I wonder if we'll see each other again?'

'Thomas Hart?' Anna Fonseka, her amber beads lost or removed, held out her hands. 'I was hoping you would say a word or two.'

'It isn't convenient,' said James, 'leave us alone'; and it was possibly the authority of his beauty, which time had made austere, that caused her to blink in surprise and recede obediently over the lawn. 'I don't suppose we'll meet again,' said James. 'There'll be no reason.'

'I suppose we won't,' said Thomas, and for now it was possible to think of this without pain. The music had finished in the house. Men and women were heading for their cars, stumbling sometimes against each other; a wind was getting up. 'Goodbye,' said Thomas Hart.

'Goodbye,' said James. 'It has been good to see you.' No handshake then, and no embrace; only a curious boyish salute as James walked away, and the brake lights of departing cars ignited the fabric of his coat. Possibly he spoke again, but somewhere a woman was noisily indulging her tears. 'Yes,' said Thomas, 'goodbye.' Distantly he felt a pain like that of the ache in his hip. It would recede; it would return. He turned his back to the house, and thought he could make out the silver birches, and Bethesda's sloping roof. The dreadful moon was on his left, the Pole Star pinned the night in place; Nick Carleton was in his office, and Grace Macaulay was on the London train – James Bower in the driver's seat was calling his wife, and over in Beechwood Avenue Ronald Macaulay was falling asleep. How astonishing, thought Thomas, and how terrible – how it all just goes on regardless! Darkness visible! Heaven in ordinary! The lights were going out in Lowlands House.

Dear James

You see I am back to my old habits now, of writing paper letters I won't send, because I don't need to send them. All the same I want to tell you what I've learned – what came to my full consciousness as slowly and with as much wonder and difficulty as the laws of physics. I have learned it was love that arrived with that first look of yours, and that first look of mine – it was love that caused the world to alter because it had you in it!

And this is also true, by virtue of predestination or fate or the mischief of time: I had already loved you all my life, as a condition of my immortal soul – and so in your way, you altered God.

But I won't have you think my heart was broken because it was a man I loved. My heart was broken because I am alive.

THOMAS HART

PART THREE

2017

The Law of Harmonies

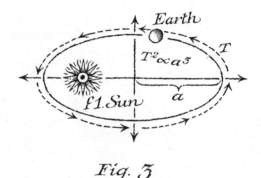

Fig. 3

A woman was leaving the asylum on midsummer morning. She went warily down steps leading to a gravel drive, observing her own feet with interest and care, as she might have watched children inclined to run into the road. The drive traversed a clipped and dying lawn between box hedges tended to by orderlies and patients; at the further end a taxi waited with an open door. The distance to the taxi figured to this woman as an unjust punishment. Her back ached, as did her hips; the early sun coaxed out spiteful insects to suck at the backs of her knees. Occasionally she paused to scrutinise the sky, as if expecting something up there beside the obstinate sun; then with a shrug either despondent or relieved she'd move slowly on.

She reached the taxi. It was difficult to get in. The manipulation of her body required care and strength: she gave it. The driver was untroubled by her appearance, or by her tongue's habit of slipping out: 'Lovely morning,' he said, and mutely she agreed that it was. He departed the hospital. The hospital departed her. He'd had a cousin in there once, he said, five years, that sort of thing ran in the family but had never come his way, touch wood. 'Came out a different man,' he said, 'but then who doesn't change in five years?' He was not unkind; but when she discovered him watching her in the rear-view mirror she was ashamed of her appearance and her unbiddable tongue.

'Been long, has it?' The driver wound the window down. 'Been a while since you were out?'

'I don't know,' she said, 'but I think so.' She examined the sky. She was afraid of nothing, and this was astounding: she'd been more or less afraid for twenty years. Aldleigh was approaching, and not much changed. These surely were the gates of Lowlands House – how could the old terror keep at bay, under such provocation? Schoolchildren waited at the gates in yellow vests; the lawns beyond the gate were striped and wet. Then very faintly – rising from the taxi footwell, the steering wheel, the driver's seat – she could smell smoke and water, and the tick of her heart halted. But that passed soon enough, and ordinary time took up its tick behind her ribs. 'Do you think,' she said, emboldened by courage, 'that you could take me to the town?'

'We can go where you please, love, no skin off my nose. Where d'you have in mind?'

The woman looked at her bag, which contained all that remained of her life. Toothbrush, sandals, two folded shirts that didn't fit; a paper bag containing medication she required and despised. A cheap book with a broken spine (*The Virago Book of Women's Life Writing*); and, making do for a book-mark, a new envelope containing an old one. 'Would it be all right,' she said, 'if you took me to the office of the *Essex Chronicle*?'

Thomas Hart had attained at last his threescore years and ten, and was sitting at his desk. Doubting, diligent, unchanging Thomas; clever old Thomas, the noted Thomas Hart. He went no more a-roving on the Strand and Bishopsgate, but there was no celestial border he didn't seek to cross, and he owned a telescope that would make Maria Văduva weep and break a lens. You mustn't think that doubting Thomas lacked in those days for sacraments: wasn't he a citizen of the empire of the moon, and a supplicant of its religions? So the sky at night offered him a liturgy, and he attended devoutly to the inscrutable beauty of its syllables and propositions: redshift, blueshift, and the proper motion of the stars; Ophiuchus, Andromeda and Perseus; zodiacal light and solar wind and the movement of bodies in orbit. Now and then he attempted the study of an A-level textbook on physics, which drove him almost to tears: what a stupid man it transpired he was, and had always been, to so fatally lack a facility with numbers and calculations, and never to have understood the nature of the electromagnetic spectrum! Occasionally it struck him that his love for the stars was no less a matter of faith than his remaining love for God; so his two faiths weren't opposed, but took up equal residence.

He'd lost perhaps half an inch in height, and gained

perhaps an inch in breadth; but generally speaking the years had glanced off him without damage, and he was as unaltered as Bethesda's pews. His office had more than ever the look of an Edwardian gentleman's salon, and nobody ever thought to dislodge him from it – besides, Nick Carleton had acquired a temper alongside an OBE for services to the regional press, having secured the future of the *Essex Chronicle* online against a year-on-year decline in print sales, and who'd risk the violence of his outrage by suggesting that Thomas Hart ought surely to retire? So Thomas remained known for his curious columns on the stars, his curious Romanian pastries that tasted of Turkish delight, his curious habit of rubbing at an aching hip. That he was a man of seventy surprised him every morning in the mirror, and he'd removed the clock from his bedside table, disliking the slicing tick that pared down the time remaining to a little stub.

Not much was going on in Aldleigh, those days. Essex, it seemed to him, would do well to recall its heritage of martyrs burned to the glory of God over faggots of green wood and sea-serpents plaguing the estuary, of gangsters shot in Land Rovers on icy country lanes and peasants revolting in the streets. Not much going on: so he occupied himself with the cheap green notebooks heaped high as ever on his desk, and the manuscript taken up and abandoned over twenty years that was now spread disconsolately among them. *Praise and Blame*, the title read, and suddenly this struck him as absurdly pompous – who do you think you are, Thomas Hart – Lev Nikolayevich Tolstoy, who died in a railway station on account of his bad chest, and could never sit comfortably on his heap of laurels? He crossed the title out, then heard with relief a single authoritative knock, followed by the arrival of Nick Carleton at the door.

'Thomas,' said the editor, 'you have a visitor again.' He

looked displeased, with the frank displeasure only safely afforded a friend.

'I can't help that,' said Thomas. 'I'm very famous, these days.'

'She tells me you've met before. Go in,' said Carleton, now speaking to somebody out of sight, 'go in, sit down.' He stood back to let a woman pass, and looked at the other man as if to say: what trouble are you causing now, Thomas Hart? He closed the door; he washed his hands of the matter.

The visitor came in with the self-possession of a person who understands they cannot pass without notice, and judges nobody for noticing. She was tall, and fat after a fashion that had caused her skin to take on the puffed and shining look of satin. Her face was broad at the cheekbones, and soft at the chin and neck, and here the skin was very white, and unmarked by any pore or blemish. She had a jackdaw's cautious, watchful, blue-eyed gaze, and her tongue roved over her lower lip as if there were something sweet on it. Thomas was startled to note that her clothes were shabby and cheap, since she had such a majestic look about her, and such a stately slow gait, that ermine and ribbons would have suited her better. He felt compelled by her, as if she possessed a gravitational field to which all lesser bodies would be subject, and came forward with hands outstretched to bring her to a seat.

'Thank you,' she said, and for a moment recovered her breath; then looked at him and 'Yes,' she said. 'Yes. It's me.'

Ought he to know her? He looked again at her hair, which had been badly cut, and had a pretty reddish look; he looked again at her worried, silken face. No bells rang. 'You see I meet so many people,' he said, 'and have no memory for faces.' He returned to his own seat, and was grateful for the expanse of desk between them: it was not that she caused him unease, only he was conscious of something very like a sustained note ringing out above the ordinary register. A jug of water was near at hand; he poured it.

'I've never been much good with time,' the woman said. She smoothed her cheap grey leggings as if they were silk. 'I suppose ten years, at least?'

'Ten years?' said Thomas. He examined them, and couldn't find her.

'I sat just here,' she said. 'I sat just where I am now, and burned a piece of paper. Look: I left a mark.' Thomas looked, and saw a dark blot on the desk.

'Oh!' said Thomas. 'No – not ten years. Twenty.' There, superimposed on his startling visitor, was the silent girl who'd sought him out, and burned Maria's letter to ashes; there too was the Lowlands fire, and the slumped and boneless figure on the terrace rising out of sodden clothes. He shifted in his chair, and put between them an additional inch of space.

'I'm sorry,' the woman said, her voice rising quickly to childish misery, as if he'd begun to berate her. She put her face in her hands, and shook with the effort of her sorrow: 'I shouldn't have done it. I don't know why I did, only I'd been waiting all my life for something to happen that would change me, and it never did. I think that man was hurt, I think he was burned – maybe even he died. I asked and asked, and nobody would tell me.'

'He did die,' said Thomas, 'but not for a long time, and not of his burns.' There was the sensation of a taut string behind his ribs being plucked once, and this was grief, and would pass.

'Ah,' she said, as if the news were painful. 'I am sorry. He was such a good-looking man. I remember that. And he seemed so young – what was it? What happened to him?'

I don't know, thought Thomas. I don't know, I don't know, I don't know. 'I think possibly cardiac arrest,' he said, taken over by a peculiar exhaustion caused not by events but by himself, 'or some inherited weakness that finally gave out. They say it was a quiet quick death while he was sleeping. I found out two years after. Nobody told me. Nobody knew they should.'

The sorrow he'd learned to contain overspilled in this stranger, who gave a single sharp sob as if the loss had been hers. 'I'm sorry,' she said. 'I'm very sorry.'

Thomas disliked and pitied her. 'Take my handkerchief,' he said. 'No: keep it. And have a glass of water.'

She drank. The remarkable skin was mottled, as if sorrow were a communicable disease. She put the water down. 'I expect you think I'm mad,' she said.

'Yes,' said Thomas, 'I do begin to think that. Though the nature of madness,' he said, 'depends really on the habits and conditions of the world we find ourselves in. They used to set madmen adrift on ships, which they called the ships of fools, and since there was no law or constitution on board to regulate the mind, how could any of the passengers be mad?'

The woman considered this — seemed briefly to thrill to it — then said, 'They told me I was not mad, only unwell. Poorly, they sometimes said, like I was a child being sick — they gave me names for it, and the names changed every few years. What they really meant was that I was mad, but it never seemed like madness to me. Didn't you put it in the paper, and didn't I read it? The comet was coming, and there was a dark companion, and a comet was always a bad omen!'

'But I meant nothing by it — I write all kinds of things. It wasn't important, I thought nothing of it at all.'

'Don't you think it matters, what you do and say? It always matters. Everything touches everything else. So I knew the comet was coming, and the dark companion, and I thought it wanted me. Every night I watched, and waited, and then there it was, but it was just a light. It brought nothing with it. It changed nothing. Everything was always going to be just the same. So I will make the change, I thought, I'll change everything, and I started the fire. You don't understand what it's like,' she said, 'to want something so much, and never have it, which is faith. Nobody ever does.'

'I understand,' he said. 'I do.'

Scornfully, eyes obtaining the facets of a gem: 'Go on then. Tell me what you believe, if you believe anything at all!' Her splendid body refused the confines of the chair, and the note struck in the room, seeming to emanate from her, rang in the high corners and against the window.

Could Thomas raise Bethesda on his desk and take it down again, to show her the tides of his faith? He could not. 'I believe,' he said with great care, 'that we move towards the good. That we're like ships who make their navigations, and drift towards a pilot light.' She was dubious. 'That is,' he said, 'I am not sure that we can help it – as if it really is the vessel that tends towards the light, whether the captain wants to or not. Now,' he said, becoming brisk, certain she'd sink this formless morality, 'don't you think you ought to tell me why you've come?'

The glint receded. She took on the look of a rightly chastised child. Slowly she opened her bag, and sourness rose from the contents. Thomas, with a pluck of recognition, saw a paperback as familiar to him as one of his own. 'I have that book,' he said. He felt peculiarly dazed. 'The diaries and letters of women who should never have been forgotten – an old man I once knew translated a diary, and I gave it to an editor, who published it' (now came the rustle of silk skirts behind him, and he refused to turn his head: can't you leave me alone for five minutes, Maria Văduva Bell?). 'Have you read it? The translator died. He died without my knowing, alone under the railway arch, and in the rain.'

'You can't know he was alone,' said the woman, 'unless you were there; in which case of course he wouldn't have been alone.' She looked at him with faint benevolent contempt. 'But yes,' she said, 'you are right, this book contains Maria Văduva's diary, and she lived at Lowlands House, and so did I.' She took an envelope from between the pages, and reached into it. Her smooth upholstered fingers were dexterous and quick. The room was resolutely quiet. 'Did you know I'd been in Lowlands for weeks before the comet came? Nobody saw me. Nobody knew or cared and nobody ever hurt me. There was a rat I loved, that had no tail – I saw the swifts come back in May and the white heads of their chicks up there in a row. And I was always finding things: broken glass and hairpins and torn-up bits of paper. The people who lived there hid things from each other. This was put between a mirror and a wall and I kept it with me, though I don't know who wrote it, or why.' Now she was holding a pale blue envelope, surveying it with a kind of wary attention, as if it were the drawing of a face she no longer loved. She put it on the table. 'Why don't you take the letter out?' she said, 'Why don't you look?'

Thomas took the letter out. He looked. He saw a folded sheet of paper, damaged by fire and water, the ink blooming in places. 'A letter sent from London,' he said to himself, to the various ghosts now drifting in and reading over his shoulder, 'and sent three days after Maria Văduva's diary ended.'

'Read it to me,' she said. 'I like to hear it.'

Obedient Thomas lifted the paper to the light. '*My beloved friend*,' he read:

'My beloved friend, you cannot ask this of me. It is not a
fair test of my affection! Do you think I (of all women!)

shall consign you to darkness for the sake of a man (of all
things!)? Have you not told me that a woman ought to live
by a brighter light than that dim and solitary candle! –
how angry I am – I will leave Foolish Street on foot and
walk to Essex and box your ears myself! Write at once
and assure me that you have regained your reason.
Meanwhile I absolutely rain pearls – and I am as ever your
devoted – C.'

'I never had a friend like that,' she said, 'did you?'

'I did once,' said Thomas. But what should he do with
this? It raised Maria, it raised James, and on they went as they
always had – vital, unterminated, coming at him over the
Lowlands lawns (it raised Grace Macaulay, in fact: he turned
his back). Abruptly he was tired. 'This is no use to me. It is
no further information. There is no address. The postmark
is hopelessly smudged. There is not even a name!'

His visitor shrugged, and this was a slow languorous raise
of her shoulders. 'Do with it as you like,' she said. 'Burn it,
for all I care.' With deliberate heavy grace she rose from the
chair. 'If I were you, I'd wonder what it was Maria asked this
woman to do, and whether she did it. But' – again, the luxuriant shrug – 'perhaps you are too old to trouble yourself.' She
was putting away the book, she was moving to the door.

Thomas went in her wake: 'It was good of you to come,'
he said, bringing out his old civilities, quelling the desire to
look back and see if she'd left scorch-marks on her seat. 'I
am glad to see that you are well, and grateful you brought
Maria back to my desk!' But he was not grateful, he was
not glad – a lancing pain went through his hip, and this
caused him to stumble, and rest on the slope of her shoulder, and the comfort of this sensation was appalling to
him. He righted himself, and received a final quick blue

look. 'Well,' she said, 'I am done, and it is finished. Good-bye, Thomas.'

Thomas said, 'Goodbye.'

Carefully now the woman walked through Aldleigh town. Tarmac softened on the heatstruck roads, and a steely haze was settling in potholes, and on the threshold of distant shops. How altered Aldleigh was. She'd never seen this bank before, or that café – had no recollection of the library, for example, or the war memorial; but possibly that was only the effect of the heat. Now and then she put her hand in her bag to feel for the envelope, and was puzzled by its absence. But that was all right – the last link was severed – the fear was gone.

She came to the Jackdaw and Crow: a woman came out of it. This woman was short as a boy, and plump, with a narrow back scooped deeply in above broad hips; her arms were bare to the sun, and the skin on them was radiant and dark. She wore a red dress seeming to disintegrate about her as she walked, or to be formed out of scraps with every step: it had a corseted bodice embroidered with stars, and a full skirt knotted to show white petticoats. Her sandals were cheap, and she was dirty between her toes. She'd contrived a little additional height out of black hair bundled above her brow and fastened with a pencil, and there was a white streak in it. It was not possible to make out her face, since she was bent to her phone, and intently considering what she saw – but it would be a marvellous face, no doubt about it: how I despise her, she thought, pinching the thin white skin of her fore-arm. What did women like her know of wanting change, and never finding it – of obtaining faith, and losing it – of carting about a body that ached in all weathers?

Now she was coming to the station, and the London train

269

was due; she was pressed on all sides by departing passengers. The shallow steps at her feet reeked of chicken bones taken by foxes, and of urine and spilled sweet drinks; she went up them with difficulty, and without fear. Up on the platform, the sun beat back from shining tracks and set up a pain in her head like the tolling of a bell. Lowlands drew her, as the north draws the compass needle – she drifted across the platform and saw it shining in the copper beeches, under the railway lines that sagged and ticked. No comet visible above the sloping roof, trailing its dark companion; no smoke unwinding from the window. A kind of weary ease settled on her. The white house between the copper beeches was impossibly near – it was nothing but an inch or so below the painted lip of the platform edge: look, the boards were down from the windows, the door between the white pillars was open, she could reach it if only she tried. She heard distant voices in the lower rooms, and these were calling her by name, they were calling her in; then there were trumpets sounding a welcome, and white banners hurled from the upper windows – so I am wanted after all, she thought, I am wanted! It was remarkable; it was what she had always expected. She ran forward.

Let's say the jays in Potter's Field, now in their seventh generation, were shaken from the branches of the hazel by a thud; let's say the rats in Lowlands Park paused briefly in their scavenging, and shrugged, and went on with vital business, as did the men in yellow jackets tending to the potholes on Station Road. Let's say Grace Macaulay, coming out of the pound shop into white perpendicular light, heard the bloodless mechanical wail that followed the thud, and thought perhaps a train had hit the buffers, or struck a deer wandered in from Lowlands Park. But she had no time to

270

spare on imagined disasters, and went briskly over the road to the Jackdaw and Crow where a woman watering hanging-baskets agreed with Grace that certainly it was much hotter than she would have liked, and that yes: she'd certainly heard that bang, but this was Aldleigh, and did anything ever happen here? No, said Grace, no, it never did; she walked under dripping baskets and delighted in the water, then went up an iron staircase fastened to the pub's external wall in case of fire. As she went up the world went down, and dwindled to something inconsequential at her feet: she had no stake whatever in the thud, the potholes in the street, the customers converging on the threshold of the pound shop. She covered her ears against sirens coming now down Station Road, and was home.

Grace had returned again to the town where she'd been born, and where she thought she'd likely die and then be burned or buried. The slow tide on which she'd drifted to London had simply turned and brought her back to Essex: it had all felt inevitable — it had all felt irresistible; she'd neither chosen nor refused her own life, only inhabited it as she inhabited her body. She'd liked London well enough, for its capacity to diminish her down to an anonymous working part in an immense machine, and because it was there she'd been tutored in the ordinary sins she might otherwise have practised and perfected in her teens. But relative poverty had driven her out, and it had never occurred to her to go any further than Essex, and the clay where she'd cultivated her soul. Now she lived in the attic of the Jackdaw and Crow, the pub she'd been raised to view with fear and suspicion as a den of alcohol-soaked iniquities. This attic had been abandoned the year Victoria died, and left to become a damp cavity certain (so drinkers said at last orders, looking up in pleasant terror) to be haunted. But since the present landlady was a woman who knew good business, it had been turned into a small home in the eaves, rented out to tenants in no position to mind that in winter their breath was visible even when the radiators trickled all night like digesting animals, and that in summer its several sloping windows gave the effect of a greenhouse. So Grace Macaulay, who all her life had barely had twopence to rub together, lived here alone in exchange for rent she often couldn't find, and one shift a week at the bar, where she poured her measures with the hectic cheer of a woman delighting in sin.

She came over the threshold with the gratitude of an animal returning to its burrow, and threw open windows tinted with the grime of passing trains and traffic. A weariness not in the least unwelcome overcame her, and demanded the submission of her spirit in her body. She undressed, and lay on the floor in the heat with her limbs arranged to prevent skin touching skin. Dimly she was conscious of flies at the window, and evidence of mice on the rug; of the scent of her cheap jasmine perfume that came in a tin, of butter going bad in the dish, of herself. Then: sleep.

Must we imagine Grace Macaulay happy? Regarding evidence for the prosecution, the court should be advised that she is only thirty-eight, and made of stern stuff as regards bone, musculature, immune system, and so on; is rarely seen to sneeze, or to complain of a bad head; that she has the kind of beauty undiminished by time, predicated not on youth but symmetry of bone, together with self-possession and colour and vitality. All children want to be ordinary, and she never was, and that had been difficult – but all adults want to be extraordinary, and now she amplifies her strangeness, delighting in her ignorance of worldly matters and her tendency to speak sometimes in a biblical cadence, telling men she meets that she was born in 1887 (this being the year they dug Bethesda's foundations) and meanwhile allowing her dress to slip from her shoulders. As to that: she has never loved a woman or a man as she loved Nathan, nor does she expect to; but is fluent in various love-languages, if always with the accent of a stranger. Her father is not dead yet. In his dotage he has become childlike, affectionate and easily teased: it's hardly possible to believe she feared him once, and smelt fire and brimstone in the seams of his clothes. She rises early in summer, and late in winter, and breakfasts on bad coffee from the pound shop and soft white rolls she bakes herself (and Anne Macaulay at her shoulder cautions her neither to under-prove the dough, nor over-bake it). She is servant to no master. She occupies her days with clothing – in the mending and embellishment of it for purposes theatrical and ecclesiastical, in ironing and starching it; even sometimes in constructing new garments out of old ones, and wearing them through Aldleigh in the knowledge that she is seen and admired and enviously mocked. Sometimes she is asked how she came to be doing such a thing, and did they teach her in London; but the truth is she has always done it, and she taught herself – her hands simply knew how to do it, it was as native as original sin. That it became her profession had really been a question of one garment after another – of favours extended and sought, of exasperated theatres in pantomime season desperate for another pair of hands. And her work these days is fine: she binds her seams in silk, her goldwork and embroidery would shame a bishop's cope. Her curls have come back, with their consoling animal scent; she eats and sings as she sews, and her softened body refuses jeans, and insists on petticoats and silk. Her fellow women she views with affectionate suspicion, with an anthropological interest: their willingness to suborn themselves to men and to the mechanics of reproduction strikes her as peculiar, but she generally wishes them well. She mourns Nathan when she remembers to mourn him, and wonders what she might have been if she hadn't lost him; but she knows who to blame for this loss. It is not herself, it isn't that she was incapable of securing Nathan's love: it was all the fault of Thomas Hart. She nurses her anger with intimate attention; when she sees him sometimes on Aldleigh High Street or on the station platform a prick of rage goes through her like a current, and she lives off this vital spark. Speaking of anger: Lorna Greene has gone to the genteel west, to Cheltenham possibly or Bath, and consequently is as good as dead. She loses her faith much as she sometimes loses a pair of dressmaking scissors, for example, or the lipstick she favours most; it turns up behind a sofa cushion, in the pocket of her winter coat. She attends Bethesda now and then, and there are even mornings when she comes near the mercy seat and prays with the sincerity of her childhood: *Thou art my hope, O Lord God, thou art my trust from my youth.* She is not certain of the condition of her immortal soul, but navigates as best she can towards the pilot light, the nature of which she hardly needs to know, only that it shines.

Might the court be persuaded to find her guilty of happiness, on such compelling evidence? Perhaps; but nonetheless steps forward, adjusting his horsehair, counsel for the defence. Grace Macaulay is poor, and only a rich fool thinks money can't buy happiness. In due course she imagines she'll inherit her father's house, but gives this little thought and scrapes by cash-in-hand. There have been winters she bathed out of water from the kettle poured into the plastic bowl in which she also washes dishes; there have been days when sometimes even bitter pound-shop coffee is beyond her means. Wherever she goes, she is alone. At the bar in the Jackdaw and Crow she is Bethesda's child, and deplores all their profanities; in her chapel pew she is a woman of the world, and deplores her sinful state. Often she tries to turn her *dearest* ring, forgetting it slipped off one afternoon and out of spite she refused to pick it up; often she thinks *I must tell Thomas*, forgetting that she can't and won't. That her body is ageing is a matter of horror: what (for example) has become of the skin on her breasts and her neck, and did she always bleed like this? She sleeps badly, in little fits and starts. She's prone to blisters, and to an infection in the finger that's pricked most often as she works. She can never find her needle when she wants one, though her rooms are full of needles. She has never been to Venice. She loved Nathan, and he did not love her; so at night on her bed she seeks him whom her soul loveth, she seeks him and she finds him not, and what have you. Does she try to be good? Certainly – but how exhausting and uncertain that is, when there is nobody to show her how – *O Lord God of my salvation, I have cried day and night before thee, my soul is full of troubles!* Case rests.

The judicious reader might well think neither prosecution nor defence have brought sufficient evidence before the court. Well, then. Grace Macaulay on the charge of happiness: case dismissed.

'Hear that?' said Nick Carleton, returning to Thomas that same afternoon with the avid look of an editor who scents a headline. 'Hear that? Man under a train, doubt there's much left: they'll be out there for hours with buckets and shovels. I've sent someone to take a look – but Thomas, you seem unwell: whatever did that woman say to you? Go on home, go on. The sun's out.'

The sun was out: light passed between the plastic slats of

the venetian blind, refracted through a glass of water, and arrived at the scorch-mark on the desk. Thomas passed his upturned hand between the scorch and the sun: 'Look at this,' he said, as if showing Carleton bright water cupped in his palm. 'Look – all those photons, born in the heart of the sun one hundred and seventy thousand years ago, and travelled eight and a half minutes for no task more serious than warming me up at my desk. Did I tell you there's a storm up there these days, and bad weather on the sun? In fact,' he said, spilling the sunlight and rising to his feet, 'perhaps I'll go and take a look.'

'Take a look, and write about it. Five hundred words,' said Carleton. 'Six, if the skies are clear.'

On clear nights, or nights when hope spoke louder than the weather forecast, Thomas these days would set up his telescope in the bare garden behind the house on Lower Bridge Road. Maria Văduva, baffled by its technologies, refused to learn the nature and utility of satellites and GPS, but admired the ten-inch objective lens, and directed him to Delphinus and Andromeda. Its shining barrel was surmounted by a camera, which scanned the stars to determine its position under the celestial sphere. Then Thomas – always with a boyish feeling that he was possibly doing something wrong – would take the control resembling an old-fashioned telephone on a spiral cord, and ask the telescope to find binary stars and galaxies and shining cities on the moon. There'd be a pause, and then a seeking whine as if the telescope yearned with Thomas to leave the earth; slowly it would turn and lift and fix its gaze on the desired object. There were nights it was all hopeless, the stars soon consumed by cloud; there were nights the seeing was good, and he resisted the cold that thudded in his aching hip, and sat for hours in the company of Maria: *Look, Thomas, see how the sky seems a black pool on which the sunlight plays?*

Now: the sun was out, and the telescope capped with silvered film to preserve the eyes. It was noon at midsummer, and the optical tube was almost perpendicular to the earth; so it was necessary for Thomas to crouch to the eyepiece to meet the near star. There they were, he thought, marvelling at the sight of solar storms: three sunspots drifting towards the eastern limb of the sun, with the look of drops of black ink dispersing in a pool of orange paint. 'Every eleven years,' he said to a disbelieving sparrow on the garden wall, 'the magnetic poles of the sun swap, and then a new cycle of activity and solar storms begins –' The sparrow departed with a dismissive shrug of its wing, and the sun slipped past the field of view, and Thomas was lonely: how he'd have liked Grace Macaulay to come quickly down the garden, willing to be amazed.

He abandoned the sun, and sat for a time in the shade, seeing the garden populated by the girl he'd loved in all her iterations – the bad-tempered infant prone to sudden bouts of joy, the black-haired bustling girl who brought him her troubles, the vengeful creature in a borrowed hat refusing to meet his gaze. There, too, was the unmistakable stranger he saw now and then coming out of the Jackdaw and Crow, or going with her old determined gait down the station platform: a small dark woman approaching forty in shabby opulent clothes with a white streak in her hair. How obdurate her anger was, and what a wretched waste it had all been. I gave up the freedom of my soul to stay in my pew and keep my foot in the door, he thought, and she betrayed me! A father's love for his own child is all very well, but essentially selfish. I loved her even though it was never my duty – oh I could knock her on to the railway track, I could chuck her in the river! But Maria was stooping to the telescope: *Then why are you crying, Thomas Hart?*

'Sometimes,' said Thomas, wiping his eyes, 'I have the strangest feeling that things happen not one after the other, but all at once. I felt it years ago, in Lowlands House, and here it is again. I can't explain it, only tell you that this afternoon I'm a young man in winter and someone's handed me a baby at a funeral – but also that I'm fifty, and the man I love is here and the sun is going down – and also that I'm older than I am now, and Grace is knocking at my door! Everything still happens within me – how else can I make sense of time? How else can I explain that I am lonely, and never lonely – that I despise my friend and I miss her – that James Bower causes me the worst pain I ever knew, and no pain at all?'

Come here would you, Thomas, lend me a hand. We've lost the sun.

DISORDERED TIME

THOMAS HART *ESSEX CHRONICLE*,
21 JUNE 2017

I wonder if you've ever shared my feeling that things happen not one after the other, but all at once? I expect it's just the folly of old age, but lately I've had a habit of saying to myself: Everything that will ever happen has happened, and is happening.

Many years ago (or tomorrow, or yesterday) I happened to see a palimpsest in the British Library. A fifteenth-century liturgy had been overwritten on parchments including a ninth-century gospel and a twelfth-century study of Plato; and to look at it was to hear a chorus of voices singing together in one place, but not from one time.

Now this is how the whole world seems to me. I've lived in Aldleigh all my life, and imagine I'll die here – so as I walk past the market square and the war memorial, or go through Lowlands Park towards the river, I experience the town not with this present self, but with all the selves I have contained, and will ever contain. Sometimes I meet myself on the stairs, and sometimes I see friends who died or left me in other ways – and my experience of them now consists of every experience of them I ever had. So you see, I've learned it's possible to despise and love a friend equally, in the same place and at the same time.

Since these days I look to physics just as I used to look to the scripture, and I find there a peculiar theory that appeals to me. This is the idea of the block universe, and is predicated on Einstein's theory of relativity: it conceives of the entirety of space and time existing together in a kind of three-dimensional cuboid. In this model there is no sequence of events unfurling on a timeline: it all occurs simultaneously, and our experience of it depends on how the block is sliced.

I doubt I've understood or explained it well, but all the same it does illuminate my life. If everything that will ever happen has happened, and is happening, at last I understand how it might be possible to fall in love at a glance, and know a stranger like a lover — perhaps already that love and all the events that followed were already unfolding elsewhere, and elsewhen. And I also understand how it might be possible to despise those who wronged us, and at the same time to feel at peace, which is perhaps the backwards echo of forgiveness we haven't yet seen. Now: my father was a preacher, and already I hear him chastise me from beyond the grave (or before it) — what comes of moral responsibility, Thomas, if the exercise of our will makes no difference to events — what would men and women do if they could shrug and say: It has all already happened!

I'll let the physicists and theologians argue over that, and look instead to T. S. Eliot. 'If all time is eternally present,' he wrote, 'all time is unredeemable.' Perhaps no matter how we conceive of it, time is unredeemable, and as soon as we do a thing, it's done. There was a time this would have made me sad. Now it refines every minute in my possession into something so precious I can't bear to throw it away.

On midsummer evening Ronald Macaulay laboured up the iron staircase at the Jackdaw and Crow, and Grace opened the attic door to let him in. 'Mr Hart gave me a lift,' said Ronald, kissing his daughter with his old dry kiss, 'but said he couldn't stay' (and down on Station Road Thomas Hart drove home, and wouldn't look up at the windows). Ronald vaguely understood that he saw little of Thomas these days, but out of confusion or self-preserving ignorance had failed to grasp that Thomas had departed Bethesda, and departed Grace. It was never clear what he'd understood as he sat wearily at his sister's funeral. Possibly he'd accepted Thomas's nature quite equably as a consequence of original sin, and no more shocking than a tendency to break the speed limit, for example, or to be rude when under strain. But it was equally possible that the idea a homosexual had occupied Bethesda's pews all those years had been so shocking he'd simply refused it, or that in the haze of grief it had all passed him by. Whatever the cause, he stood on the doorstep of heaven, a happy man prone to falling asleep in the day, and surprised when he woke to find he wasn't yet in glory.

'Come in,' said Grace. The declining sun illuminated the small kitchen in which she stood wiping her hands on a linen apron. She surveyed her father, who now roused in her a maternal worry that reversed the natural order: 'You look

281

thin,' she said. 'Whatever you've been eating, it hasn't been enough.' She brought him carefully into a room in which two sofas, broad and low as beds, regarded each other across a shipping trunk. Here too the sun had made its entrance, but nonetheless a dozen lamps shone in a dozen places (tell her she acquired her profligate habits of light from Thomas Hart, and she'd turn them off one by one). These had been retrieved from skips or thieved from provincial theatres, since Grace had never lost her magpie's habit, and thought whatever she found beautiful was hers by right. Lozenges of light were cast down on overlapping carpets, and up on walls hung (despite the landlady's edicts) with framed prints, and ugly oils in gilded frames, and various tapestries and garments that time had put beyond use, but not beauty. Plastic boxes were stacked against the further wall, interspersed with open baskets out of which spilled antique bodices and over-skirts and horsehair bustle-pads awaiting Grace's needle; a corkboard in hopeless disorder was covered with receipts, postcards, sketches, letters regarding unpaid council tax bills, and frail samples of fabric. A broken violin she had no idea how to play hung from a nail beside the door, and every-where rinsed jam jars were stuffed with cow parsley from the verges, and carnations bought half-dying from the market as it closed. There were few books, since Grace had never liked to read; but her childhood Bible was within reach of her sewing machine, as if she'd consulted Ruth or Esther for how best to finish a seam. Her visitors, looking about, often thought how like the woman herself it all was: suspended between the modern age and unplaceable time past, the laptop and mobile phone and television anachronistic, and the fading tapestries and linens in their proper place. It was so romantic, they said, so beautiful, admiring the fringed shawl that made do for a bedroom door, and sighing over the pearly shells she'd ranged on the kitchen windowsill; and thank you, she said – but really it was difficult to make do with what little she had, and humiliating to think she wasn't far off forty and could lose her home on the landlady's whim. On certain mornings in certain weathers the place had the disconsolate look of a tired child trying to be happy; but at these times Grace would see her own bare scalp lit by strip-lights in a Hackney room blackened at the skirting boards with damp, and persuade herself to be content.

Ronald sat with difficulty on a sofa that was draped in a quilt from which patched pieces were coming loose. Noises from the street sifted up, becoming indistinct under the eaves, and someone out there was singing Leonard Cohen. Grace put a white cloth on the trunk, and it was pressed with such care its creases produced a grid of shadows: 'My ship has come in, Dad,' she said. 'Last month I couldn't pay the council tax, and now I'm in the money! We're having crab, and prawns, and smoked salmon – so stay awake a bit longer, if you can.'

'Very good,' said Ronald vaguely, 'yes: very good. The Lord provides.'

'I have a new job,' said Grace, 'a good one' – she was bring-ing out a chipped porcelain dish, on which shellfish grappled with slices of lemon – 'it'll keep me gainfully employed for weeks.' She put the tray on the packing trunk beside a basket of her own white rolls, and gestured to a corner: 'Look at those boxes. They've been knocking down houses for flats in West London, and I suppose one of the houses must have been a tailor and cleaner once (here: take a napkin. Take this plate). Look what they found – all these furs and gowns and a man's coat with a box of matches in the pocket. Everything left behind and forgotten, sealed in paper with the old cam-phor balls rolling out, and bits of moth wing and dust, and the tickets still sewn on (shall I butter you some bread?). I've been given the best of them to restore, then off they'll go to film studios and theatre companies and thin eccentric women – it isn't difficult work,' she said, asserting professional pride, 'but I will do my best, and that's the rent until Christmas.'

'I'm sure you will,' said her father, with a sweet vagueness that exasperated Grace: Thomas, she thought, would have asked which garments in particular needed what work in particular, and asked to be shown them, and approved her answer in his reserved fashion. Well: it was his fault he'd no idea how she kept herself busy these days, and more fool him – 'Shall we say grace?' said Ronald, and closed his eyes. '*For these and all thy mercies, Lord, we give thee thanks*'; and Grace looked out over Aldleigh, and ate buttered bread.

When all remaining was a bowl of cherry-stones with scraps of red flesh attached, Ronald folded his hands over his stomach and said, 'Yes: very nice,' and slipped into sleep. The singer was still out there busking for tuition fees, and now Bob Dylan had arrived on the departing train – *let us pause in life's pleasures*, went the song, *and count its many tears*; but the passengers were heedless, and the evening swifts were screaming out to Lowlands Park. Now and then Ronald choked for breath, then returned to his childish sleep, and a skittish sound behind the skirting board was perhaps a rat inured to the poison Grace sometimes put down. The song went interminably on – *a pale drooping maiden toils her life away, with a worn heart whose better days are over* – and how good of him it was, thought Grace, to sing for me. Hard times, come again no more! Sweat formed between her shoulder blades and ran to her waist and settled there, and later, when the sun went down, the damp place on her clothing would make her cold.

There was nobody to speak to, and nothing she wanted to do – I am in my life, she thought, surprised by despair: this is my life, and I am in it! She had a vision then of her old room in her father's house, with the shadow of the silver birch swaying on the carpet, and the mottled mirror in which she'd examined her own body each night with troubled awe – saw again the narrow bed that had once tilted up at the foot and sent her falling forever upward, but never coming to an end. That's how it has always been for me, she thought, falling towards nothing – she pressed at a sore place on a pricked finger where infection had set in – soon enough I won't be a woman who doesn't have children, but a woman who didn't have children – soon nobody will see me, and there'll be no more surprises. But her self-pity these days was as sudden and brief as her temper always was, and there again was the rat going about its business, and distantly a train coming in from Colchester or London – she crossed to the cardboard boxes in the corner, and saw a frilled black cuff coming out between strips of packing tape with an imploring gesture: 'Yes,' she said, 'yes, I know: me too.'

She opened the box, and there was the smell she loved, because it marked out her own territory: camphor and cedar to repel moths, certain fungi that thrived in damp cloth, and what remained of the sweat and fragrance of dead women and men. Over on the sofa her father shifted and snorted, and the lamps were brightening against the dusk. Carefully she lifted out the dress. The black silk rasped against itself, and spoke. She listened. The narrow sleeves terminated in long cuffs fastened with mother-of-pearl buttons fixed with silver thread, and were set in stiff pleats at the shoulder. Grace marvelled at the craftsmanship, skilled and arduous as that of a stonemason – hours by daylight and gaslight, she thought, eyes and back perpetually sore – reverently she examined the high neck trimmed with rotting Belgian lace, and the immense skirt with a deep embellished hem. She took it to her workbench, and turned on a lamp that set the clock to noon. Again, that rasp of silk, which was as telling and particular as a voice – Grace bent to examine the needlework, and saw heavy silver thread couched down in whorls, here and there coming loose and recoiling against itself. Stitched among the whorls were so many seed pearls, in such a massed weight, the dress could only have been worn by a strong woman whose love for extravagance and style exceeded the desire for comfort. She passed a loving hand over the hem, and the dress complained: hair-fine silk threads disintegrated, and dozens of pearls dropped to the floor. 'I'm sorry,' said Grace, 'I didn't mean to hurt you' – she laid the dress down, and surveyed it from a distance with an expert's eye. Sewn between 1880 and 1890, she thought, judging by the set of those sleeves: the lace would need removing entirely, and she'd seek out another piece – this part just here (affectionately she passed a finger through a hole) could be patched and made good – the pearls and couched silver thread could be returned to their pattern, and that would be time-consuming, but it was all billable hours. And what after all was the pattern (a sleeve shifted; the silk spoke)? From that vantage it was possible to make out a sequence of ugly stiff-petalled flowers on absurd curved and leafless stems, and against such extraordinary workmanship this failure of skill and beauty was aggravating.

'Tomorrow,' said her father in his sleep, 'God willing' – and yes, thought Grace, I'll look again tomorrow. She moved away, and this caused her shadow to pass over the beaded hem, and alter the look of the flowers – 'Oh!' she said, with a curious tightening sensation on her scalp: not flowers, nothing like that – the stiff silk of the dress softened and spread, until it took over the room in a canopy, and the stitched whorls of silver began to turn with the look of water going down the sink; the pearls after all were not individual pricks of light forming lifeless flowers, but composed themselves into shining objects drifting down the hem, trailing curves of shining dust: 'Comets!' said Grace, laughing, almost convinced her bare feet were rising above the carpet, and her own body was in motion. 'It's comets,' she said again, seeing them clearly, drawn down their orbits by the sun, and interspersed with galaxies.

Her inertia dissipated. She was alert, as if responding to a high summoning note. Time collapsed – surely she stood ankle-deep in Lowlands mist; surely it was possible to put out her hand, and pluck the sleeve of a good tweed coat and say, 'Thomas, the strangest thing – do you remember Maria Văduva, do you remember I found her in the lake?'

'*Why art thou cast down, oh my soul?*' said Ronald, reciting psalms in his sleep, '*and why art thou disquieted in me?*' But Grace – disquieted but not cast down – was attending devoutly to the dress, and to a paper ticket fastened with a rough stitch to a bodice seam. She opened it. The looped pencil scrawl, preserved from light, was easily legible – the words spoke frankly down time: *C. S. / Foulis Street / for collection*. 'I see,' said Grace. 'Yes, I see.' The ticket dissipated, and in its place she saw a sheet of notepaper grown brittle at the fold: *to the only beloved inhabitant of Foolish Street* . . . 'Maria,' said Grace. 'There you are.' Thomas had hoped and hoped, she thought, and it occurred to her that she could phone him now as the sun went down, and begin again that schoolboy hunt for a vanished woman and her comet – 'Foulis Street, Thomas!' she said aloud, briefly inhabiting another possible world in which she was comfortable at his table. 'Don't you see? Maria's friend C. lived at Foulis Street, and she called it Foolish to tease her' – she felt an instinctive flare of pleasure and pride, and quickly suppressed it. No: he didn't deserve it.

287

Let him limp back and forth to the *Essex Chronicle*, to wherever he went these days, and have no idea Maria Văduva was in motion –

'Should I be going home soon?' said Ronald, coming to his feet, and smoothing what remained of his hair. 'Won't Anne be waiting for me?'

'Yes,' said Grace, 'she'll be waiting. But I don't think it'll be too long now.'

A LITTLE NIGHT MUSIC

THOMAS HART *ESSEX CHRONICLE*,
23 JUNE 2017

It's common knowledge, isn't it, that in space, no one can hear you scream? But I'm afraid the difficulty with knowledge (even the common sort!) is that it tends to open doors, not close them. And if you opened the right door and listened, you'd hear the earth singing.

I'll try and explain. Sound requires substance – you can hear nothing at all unless the air and its molecules are made to oscillate, creating sound waves like ripples in a cloth. When these ripples reach your eardrums, that membrane also begins to vibrate, and so you hear someone calling you, or music playing in another room.

Since space is more or less a vacuum, there's no cloth to shake. But you should never think that nobody is screaming just because you can't hear it. In fact the planets can never keep their peace – they are constantly radiating electromagnetic waves, and some of these are radio waves that fall outside the range of human hearing. It is possible to process these emissions, and show how they might sound if the matter of space could vibrate with the music, and make the music audible to us.

If you're curious – and really I think you ought to be! – you can find these melodies online, and listen to a little night music. I've taken to listening as I examine the planets with my telescope, and the effect is eerie and beautiful. When I hear Jupiter, I think of a Buddhist's singing bowl; when I hear Neptune I think of waves crashing on a pebble shore, while the wind blows through some abandoned structure yards away. Io, Jupiter's devoted little moon, sounds like an orchestra down in the pit, tuning its instruments before the curtain rises – and earth, of course, is singing too: with chirps and whistles like the calls of unfamiliar birds startled by the passage of a train.

Meanwhile the human body – constantly occupied in respiration and digestion – vibrates at very low frequencies. Your heart, for example, resonates at less than a single hertz, far below the beginning of the range of human hearing. I wonder if somewhere there is an animal capable of hearing all the quiet business undertaken in the chambers of my heart? *You are the music*, said T. S. Eliot, *while the music lasts.*

There was a change of weather. No rain yet, but clouds coming from Gwent and Gloucestershire on the western wind, and nights drawing imperceptibly in. A woman recently struck by a train was cremated two miles north of the station (it was said she'd wanted her ashes disposed of in Lowlands Park, but the authorities wouldn't have it). A white cat was missing on Lower Bridge Road. Since the seeing was bad for stars, insomniac Thomas took to looking for it in the small hours, walking off the ache in his hip, and reciting the Foolish Street letter: *you cannot ask this of me.*

Late on a Friday afternoon, Grace Macaulay walked down to Lowlands House. An inky bank of cloud was drawing over Essex, and in the dimming air the bindweed and buddleia in Potter's Field were luminous against the wall. She stood there for a time. Its neglect by now had become something noble, and not despondent – moss had taken hold on the piles of bricks, and all night it was noisy in the nettles and bracken. This is where I found Nathan, she thought, this is where I found Dimitru, and both of them have gone. Meanwhile there was Bethesda, implacable, unchanged, its grey roof seeping into grey cloud. She waited to encounter the operatic tides of sorrow and loss she once might have summoned up, and could only locate a placid fondness for the smooth clear pane of glass that replaced the window a careless boy had broken. Inevitably she thought of Thomas Hart, and there was her old temper after all, in a vivifying flare – all week she'd removed and restitched pearls from the hem of the black gown, and the pad of her thumb was calloused with pricks: now she rubbed the callous with a vengeful smirk she might have thought unpleasant if she could have seen it.

Then she went through the screen of silver birches behind Bethesda, and struck out for Lowlands Park. Summer had thickened the hedges at the boundary, and these resisted her entry and tore her skirt – she came through to the clearing, and saw lawns rising faintly to the house that stood unpleasantly white against the sky. A wind was getting up and the oaks shivered. She walked on. The lawns had not been cut: it was like wading. The lake was on her left, altered beyond her recognition: it had been dug out deep and square, and was bordered by pale slabs of York stone, and four black iron benches with sea-serpents forming curved arms. A high yew hedge bounded it on three sides, and enclosed the sky with mathematical exactitude. Maria Văduva, clean and empty-handed, stood at the eastern end in the breach in the yews, looking forever at the house.

Vaguely Grace thought of a story she heard once about a girl who bruised her shaved scalp on a statue as they pulled her from dirty water – but that has nothing to do with me, she thought, despising that girl with her shorn head and her temper. She came near the house, and made out careless people on the terrace watching the weather come in, and lights on in the new glass wing where Maria's telescope went unused. Now the air all around her was peculiar, and uniform darkness was coming overhead like an early dusk. She went on walking, conscious of a nervous pricking sensation, and had no idea whether it came from her, or was imposed on her by the unsettled weather. Rain began. It struck the nape of her neck with a volley of blows, and soon the soaking air caused the house and the copper beeches to blur and dissipate – everything was composed of water, and so was she; it was all a gathering wave that at any minute would break, and her own matter would be forever indistinguishable from that of the lawns, the oaks, the Lowlands brick and plaster – wind pleated the rain, and her unaccountable nerves gave way to hysteric pleasure in the wind and water. So she went through it revelling, watching men and women go running from the terrace, laughing and shaking out their clothes. Her own dress was soaked, as if she'd just come out of the baptistery, and she stumbled once in tangled cloth and paused to right herself.

It was because of this she failed to see an old man until he was close by. He was stooped, hesitant, reliant on a walking stick; he'd never outrun that bad weather. He tracked across the lawns from the margins of the park, and Grace – whose own body had never much betrayed her – found pity and irritation moved her equally. It was inconvenient, this trespasser on her solitude, and probably he'd be all right on his own. That cautious walk called Thomas Hart to mind; but in fact this man was not as tall as Thomas, and nothing like as old, nor were his clothes so fine. Now the long grass and irregular ground was giving him trouble, and it occurred to her that she ought to be good; so she went towards him with her hand held out.

The Potter's Field jays, aggrieved by rain, flew over with their horrible cries, and this startled the man. He looked up. The jays were gone. He saw Grace. He stopped abruptly, which appeared to cause him pain; he made a sound as if choking on his own discomfort. He was looking at her with a furtive downward tilt of his head, and this was curiously intimate, and not quite a stranger's look – then he set his stick hard in the wet lawn and turned his back.

How shocking it was, to have offered her hand out of kindness, and to have been rejected – a bleak sensation settled on her that was not proportionate to a stranger's departure, or even to the cooling rain now causing her to shiver. Grace felt she might cry, and this too was an irritation and a shock: was she really so prone to loneliness and sorrow, after all these years, with a grey streak in her hair? Two children, thin and uncannily alike, were darting about aimless and quick as insects, going into the rain and out of it with delight; they came near the man and laughed at him and mimicked his pained walk – I hope they fall and hurt themselves, she thought, I hope nobody comes when they cry.

There was an interruption in the rain. Briefly the air was clear, and in this pause Grace heard children shrieking, and jackdaws squabbling in the oaks; distantly a train drawing out of the station, and a man's shocked cry, more familiar than it ought to have been. Her body returned shock for shock. A pulse set up in her ears. Now the man was supine in the grass, his stick was out of reach. His jacket, black with water, was spread out: he was on his back. Twice he raised himself then fell. The rain set in again. Grace moved towards him. She tripped in mud and righted herself: she was a quick strong animal. She reached the man, who turned away from her. His hair was fair and rather long: it obscured his face. Grace went down on her haunches in the mud. She took his wrist: he took it back. 'You're being stupid!' she said. She felt she'd like to hit him. She also felt she'd like to sink down with him. He made the choked noises of a man who has been taught not to cry. Jackdaws flew over: What's all this? they said. What's going on, and why? Lowlands House looked out of the copper beeches, untroubled and unsurprised.

'You can't just lie here,' said Grace. 'If you do, I'll lie here too. Why won't you look at me?' His hair could do with a cut, she thought.

He turned his head a little. He wore glasses to which the rain adhered in shining blots that blinded him. He took them off. There was a kind of splitting sensation, as if her consciousness had run ahead and reached an understanding, while her body lagged behind in the mud – 'Just fucking get up!' she said. I'll hit him, she thought, I really will.

He said, 'I can't.' He raised himself on his elbows. 'You can see that I can't.' He fell back, and gestured to his left leg. 'It doesn't work properly,' he said, 'and my back is bad.' He looked at her. The rain came down. He went on looking, not blinking away the water. He let out his breath, and resigned himself to the mud.

Grace took account of his face. It was thin. Possibly it would be fair to say that it was gaunt; that the cheeks had sunk more than they ought to have done, that he was too pale, with a waxen poreless look. Still she found him beautiful. She raised her hands. His eyes were very blue, and more thickly lashed than hers. 'No,' she said.

'I tried to get away,' he said. 'I did try.'

'Nathan.' It was not a query. 'I've been looking for you,' she said, 'I've been looking for you all my life.' She wanted to touch him and didn't know how. Her hands were in her lap. But they wanted him and were compelled: she thumped him twice on the shoulder. 'All my life!' she said.

'Get me up,' he said, blinking rapidly. He's angry with me, she thought, and was grateful, because that was a kind of intimacy, and all she had for now. 'Get my stick,' he said. She reached for the ugly metal tube in the grass. It was wet, and slipped. She dropped it. He swore. She gave it to him: she wanted to hit him again. 'You'll have to help me,' he said.

'Left side.' It struck her that this was all ordinary to him – the fall, the humiliation, and the need. His pallor reached his lips. He sat up, braced against his stick; then he raised his left arm and she burrowed under it, and took his weight. With a hard sharp cry, he was standing.

His hand shook on the stick. He said, 'One minute.' Sixty obedient seconds counted silently. Idiot thoughts: were there streaks of make-up on her face? Was her hair dank and unlovely, would he like the look of her? 'Come on then,' he said. He manoeuvred his body as if it were a vehicle he didn't trust and had never been taught to drive. The rain was receding, but not the cloud. She was alert to him in all the particulars: the soaked jeans, the dragging foot, the shirt tucked in at the beltless waist, the smell of soap and mud, the marvellous implausible fact of his weight. 'All my life!' she said.

'Yes,' he said. 'Yes, I know.'

'Nathan,' she said.

'Yes,' he said. 'Grace.'

They'd come to the terrace. Windows once blinded by boards now looked placidly out over the lawns. The children, done with play, stood watchful by the door.

'You're heavy,' Grace said. They came to a table, and Nathan put his body in a chair. His hands shook on his cane; he let out a cry, and was white. He asked for something to drink, and Grace went to fetch it. She had the giddy sensation of a woman on a high ledge. It was all unbelievable – it was all inevitable. She brought tea and water on a tray, and found him occupied in pressing pills out of their packets; he took them with the look of a man underwater waiting to come up for breath. His eyes were closed. Privately she examined his face, and found the boy she'd loved.

The sun was out. It hardened against the glass. Nathan

opened his eyes, and examined the tea in his cup. The waxen pallor was receding. 'What a coincidence. There you are.'

'Here I am,' she said, 'gone round my orbit again. I looked for you everywhere, and never found you. Where have you been, Nathan, where did you go?'

'Kent.' There was the easy untroubled smile she remembered.

'As far as that! Those children are watching us. Look.'

'At that age everything is interesting.' His shallow quick breaths were gone. 'My daughter,' he said, softening still further, 'is just the same.'

Grace looked at her tea. Dust had settled on it, and the hair of a stranger. I had him to myself for half an hour, she thought, for only half an hour. 'Nathan,' she said, 'tell me what happened to you' (and she was in love with the jacket drying on the back of his chair, the empty pill-packet on the table, the hairs on his wrist, the glasses he wiped with a napkin).

'When I was twenty-five,' he said, 'I crashed the car. It wasn't so bad. Nothing broken, just always a threat of being hurt, like living with a dog that sometimes bites. Then two years ago I fell while walking and two discs here, just here' – he patted himself, was rueful, offered her a smile – 'ruptured. I was thirty-six and that was the last day I was young.'

Grace, whose own body had spared her suffering, whose head never ached, was bewildered. 'That's all?' she said. 'You fell?'

'That's all. I lay on a mattress on the floor and counted the minutes until I could be drugged again. I would have killed myself,' he said, 'only the drugs were kept out of reach. Then they operated on me, and something went wrong. Quite a common thing, and not so bad, but the nerve was damaged, and now my foot won't work. You don't need to cry.'

'I do.' Horribly it occurred to her that perhaps she wept

because in fact she did not want this real Nathan, in his compromised flesh. Was this what she'd waited for? Had she bartered her soul for a gaunt man with a wife and child and a dragging foot?

'This has been a bad day,' he said, 'you've seen me at my worst'; and this was so evidently said to reassure her, and so like his old easy kindness, that yes, yes: it was all she'd waited for. There was a moment when he took her in. His eyes are on me, she thought, I can feel them moving on my arms and neck, and I wonder how I'll have disappointed him.

'Tell me why you're here,' she said. 'Why come so far from Kent?'

'A death in the family,' he said. He was not done looking at her. This look was new: intent, assessing, seeming almost amused. 'My grandfather. Funerals and paperwork and probate.'

'I am sorry. We should never have grown up!'

'I'm not sure we have. I'm not sure we can.' Then he said, 'And you? Are you still' – with a gesture he indicated the Bibles and baptistery, the prayers before eating, the drooping chapel hats.

Instinctively she looked out across the lawns to the silver birches, and Bethesda behind them with its iron gates unlocked. 'Sometimes I think I am, because I can't help it. But I don't believe what I believed when I was a child' – though even as she said it, she was uncertain if it was true.

'And what did you believe?'

He has acquired authority, she thought, I can't resist that. 'I believed I was elect – that I belonged to God. That I'd be forgiven everything I ever did.'

'Then what do you believe now?'

She laughed, and saw his responding gleam, and was grateful. 'If I wake up convinced there's no God,' she said, 'I'll find him by lunchtime. But if I go to bed and pray for the salvation of my soul, I'll know I've got no soul to save by breakfast.' The children had come in from the garden, and dripped between the tables, looking at Grace. A plaintive woman rapped on the glass. They ignored her. 'I did come, you know,' said Nathan, with sudden force. 'I came to the church. You were standing at the front in strange white clothes; then something happened and you were down on your knees.'

'I know.'

'Thomas saw me and sent me away.'

'Yes: I know he did.'

'And I was glad he sent me away. I'd always been afraid of you, your father, the things you said and how you said them – there wasn't anyone like you then, there hasn't been anything like you since. I didn't understand what you were doing. I didn't know why you wanted to do it. I thought you wanted to be normal – I thought you wanted to be like me.'

It occurred to her then that she could say: I bargained with God, I gave him my soul, and thought you would be my reward. But she was ashamed of her childish theology, and ashamed to have lost her bargain; and how diminishing, she thought, how absolutely debased I would be, if this man with a whole life elsewhere knew I'd set such a high price on his love! So she was silent, and perhaps a little sullen, and the silence seemed to cause his withdrawal. The intimacy of his attention was gone, as if it were an object he'd removed from the table and put in his pocket; he put his glasses on, and with polite interest asked what she did with herself these days, and what had become of her family. Her aunt was dead, she said, but her father was not; and desperately she wanted to give an account of the hospital bed in the dining room, the thin blue blanket on the floor.

'And what about your friend, Thomas?'

'Oh,' said Grace, with elaborate vagueness she doubted he believed, 'I think he's about. But I don't see him. It was so strange, wasn't it, it was so unnatural that he wanted to spend time with children.' There briefly was that acute assessing look – whatever happened, Grace Macaulay? What did you do? – and Grace flushed at her slander.

Then again there was his withdrawal behind ease: 'You know,' he said, looking at the telescope in the vitrine, the wipe-clean tables on the swept-clean floor, 'I haven't been here since the fire. Twenty years – I thought it might be difficult, but the truth is I hardly remember it – or if I do remember, it's as if it was all something somebody told me about another boy. Tell me, did you ever find out what happened to that woman? Maria, that was her name – remember how we came in here before the fire, when the windows were boarded up and there were no lights, and dead insects everywhere, and old bits of paper falling off the table and getting lost'– he looked about the bright clean room as if hoping to find dust settling on furniture, and a rat crossing the floor.

'Strange you should ask – she comes back again and again, like a kind of ghost: sometimes I almost wish she'd leave us alone. They say she discovered a comet. They say it's coming back this winter – can you believe that?' And there's more, she wanted to say: I think I have something of hers at home, I think my hands must smell of her clothes. But she was afraid he'd tire of her.

'Yes,' he said, 'I can believe it. I could believe anything of you' – but his smile was charming, easy, costing him nothing; there again was the suspicion he spoke to her as he might have spoken to friends of his daughter, with a fondness that was instinctive and not particular.

Still: for lack of nourishment she feasted her spirit on

crumbs. 'Now I live over the Jackdaw and Crow,' she said, smiling and lifting her hair from her neck, 'and sometimes do shifts at the bar. So I spend my life in the den of iniquity my father would never go in!'

But Nathan was looking at his watch. 'I'm very sorry,' he said, 'I can't miss my train, I must go. Forgive me?'

No I won't forgive you, she thought, I will not. Her temper arrived, quick and ungovernable: how dare he dismiss her? 'Nathan,' she said, 'there are no offices here, no solicitors – there's no reason for you to come to Lowlands at all. So what were you doing here – were you just passing the time?'

He stood without apparent pain. 'Whenever I'm in Aldleigh,' he said, 'I come here, and I look for you.' He was buttoning himself up, he was moving away. The mud was dry on their clothes. An absurd gap was opening out between what they ought to have been, and what they were. He was holding his stick: 'I'll walk to the station,' he said, 'but slowly. Will you go that way?'

Ten minutes of small talk! She'd rather have nothing at all. 'I'll stay here,' she said, 'I haven't finished my tea.' Together they looked at the mug, and the pale skin forming in it.

'Give me your number,' he said, 'and I'll give you mine.'

Grace was obedient. The balances of power were in his favour. 'We would never have had any trouble,' she said, taking out her phone, 'if we'd had these in our day.' There was a polite exchange of laughter. Nobody watching, thought Grace, would have any idea where his mouth had been.

'Well then,' he said. He put down his stick, and raised his arms.

'Well then,' she said. He embraced her, and this was unmannered and ungentle: Christ, she thought, he'll break a rib. She returned to her seat. 'Go on then,' she said, 'go home.' Her tea was thick and cold: she drank it. He stood aimless, looking at the blinded telescope as if it might afford a view of wisdom; then with a kind of resigned and hopeless shrug he left.

Later that same evening, half-drunk on the sofa with her bare feet on the packing trunk, Grace tended to a galaxy coming unstitched on the black silk dress, and discovered that her fingers were trembling and unequal to the task. This is like fear, she thought, it's as if I'm afraid for my life – and in fact she was afraid for her life, which she had created out of whatever leftovers she had to hand, and which she sometimes loved. It was small, strange, curtailed and poor, but every day made new by the beauty she detected in torn table linen, dying stems of forecourt carnations, silk ribbons sold for a pound in charity-shop baskets: she was free to think as she liked, to say what she liked, to do as she pleased – sometimes on the Lord's Day she would attend Bethesda's morning service and cry in the last verse of the last hymn, briefly feeling the presence of the Son of God, then all night pour double measures at the Jackdaw and Crow, where nobody implored her to consider the condition of her soul. But Nathan had sat with her an hour, that was all, and already she was dissatisfied with her own life, and jealously constructing his out of the scraps she had to hand – who was it opened the door for him when he went home? Who took his coat, and asked after his back – whose face did he see in his child's face? Bitterly she pictured a happy woman, clever and competent and kind – she pricked her finger, and was glad she did it.

Thomas would understand, she thought, with horrible loyalty, Thomas would know – she finished her glass of bad wine. Briefly it occurred to her that she could call him – that if ever a man left his number unchanged in years it would certainly be Thomas Hart.

She pierced a comet with her needle, and for a time scrolled aimlessly through her phone. She arrived in time at the *Essex Chronicle*: a fatal crash on the A12, a woman shot dead in Billericay, never any good news. And Thomas Hart would no doubt have written something recently – his little sermons, she thought, his godless parables – she saw the title 'Disordered Time', and rolled her eyes. How like him, to think he had the authority! *I wonder if you've ever shared my feeling,* she read, *that things happen not one after the other, but all at once?* Yes, Thomas, she thought, I have, I do. So she read on, and experienced an instinctive softening against the determination of her dislike: his voice was in the room, accentless and precise and kind – 'So you see,' he said, explaining himself, 'I've learned it's possible to despise and love a friend equally, in the same place and at the same time.'

Grace put down her phone, put down the dress: there was an extraordinary pain behind her left breast, and her hands shook as if she suffered a disorder of the nerves. She doubled over and embraced herself, because there was nobody else to do it. 'It's such a shame,' she said childishly over and over, 'it's just such an awful shame.'

Comet 1899 III du Lac, not truthfully named, is five months from perihelion. It is crossing the orbit of Jupiter. Obedient to Kepler's stern and perfect laws, the semi-major axis of its orbit sweeps out equal areas in equal time, which is to say: it's only going to get faster. It is excited. Already its hard cold carapace is thrilling to the sun, and sublimating into gas; it has acquired a little atmosphere, and particles of dust are drawn out from the comet's faint gravitational field. It's seen by certain diligent observers in the southern hemisphere, whose twelve-inch telescopes pick out something blurry in the constellation of the wolf; but no naked eye has any hope until the earth has drifted a little further down its orbit.

Meanwhile in Aldleigh: summer contains autumn, which contains winter. There's the suggestion of burning in the beeches on London Road, and the verges of the A12 are blacker than they ever were. Ronald Macaulay recedes through the years and has not yet reached childhood, but often mistakes his daughter for his wife, though in fact Grace resembles Rachel no more than a changeling might.

The cat is still missing on Lower Bridge Road. Thomas goes up and down the lanes at night, looking for a fleet-foot scrap of white coming out from under a car. As he walks he composes phrases for his book on the motion of bodies in orbit, commits them to memory, and goes home to type them up – and everything that will ever happen has happened (he thinks), and is happening. Still he cannot bring the book to its conclusion – it is all question, and no answer. What can he say to his readers but 'I wonder'?

Grace Macaulay is late for her shifts at the Jackdaw and Crow: she's rude to the landlady who's rude in return. She cannot concentrate. She pricks herself and bleeds into the hem of the Foulis Street skirt, eats sometimes too little and sometimes too much. She's up on a high ledge and nobody can bring her down. 'Give me your number,' he'd said, 'and I'll give you mine'; and after the tormenting decency of two days' silence he'd illuminated the phone on her pillow: *How are you?* Now they communicate most days and never plan to meet. Her phone runs out of charge by noon. She watches the screen for a sign. It illuminates: let it be him, let it be him! It is often him (it is more often her). How are things? Is it raining where you are? Saw this and thought of you. This wasted leaf. This sunlit gull when nothing else was lit at all. These bits of broken glass. That song. This one. And this one. Did you read this article? Did you know Maria Văduva's diary has been published in a book? In text he is not civil and kindly, but has a means of speech as easeful and merry as he always was. He is ready with a printed kiss. He rarely mentions home. She conceives of him as solitary, speechless, on a hard-backed chair in an empty room, waiting for her to come glittering in through the window. Then he does mention home – he mentions his daughter, he implies a wife, and never names either – and this brings a grieving splitting sensation: there's a whole life there she cannot see and will never occupy – a series of loves and languages all incomprehensible to her, she is absolutely peripheral, bolted-on, and the bolts are coming loose.

She stands in the pound-shop aisles and bursts into tears: if he died nobody would tell her, why would they, she wouldn't know for days. And why does he never name the mother of his child, who presumably nursed him when things were bad, pressed pills out of their packets when he needed them most, washed him, held his body when it was pliant with sleep, saw the stitches dissolving in his spine? Sometimes at midnight when her collarbone is slick with sweat she'll send an idle message and watch for a reply and meanwhile touch herself and think: would he touch me like this? And will he? Time (said Thomas Hart) is not what we take it to be, and everything that will ever happen has happened, and is happening. All my life, she thinks. And here we are. Thomas grows larger in her consciousness: he felt what I feel, he knows what I know. Occasionally it occurs to her that now forgiveness might be possible. After all (her phone ignites again with Nathan's name) her life was perhaps not destroyed in the baptistery, only altered –

On the second evening in August, Thomas abandoned his manuscript with a cry of disgust – at his imagination, vocabulary, wisdom, phrases, capacity for characterisation, and in fact the whole absurd enterprise of literature – and went through to the galley kitchen. There was bad news on the radio, and nothing worth his attention in the fridge and cupboards; he could neither read nor write, and the lens of his telescope had acquired a film of dust. The pain in his hip set up with the insistent spite it generally reserved for winter, and this was the effect of boredom: there was nothing else to occupy his mind. So it was a relief to hear someone knocking at the door, with the impolite demanding knock of a man in trouble, or instigating it – something to do with the lost cat, he thought, going quickly down the hall, or Nick Carleton needs me for a story – he opened the door, and the humid air of the evening entered the house like a breath.

'No,' said Thomas to the diligent sparrow on the garden wall, 'no, this can't be right' – it was all just collapsing time, he said to himself, some kind of echo: certainly that could not be Grace Macaulay standing on the garden path. But the image didn't dissipate into memory as it ought to have done, only insisted on being seen: Grace, changed and unchanged, dressed in loose white clothes that left her arms bare and carrying a woman dressed in black. This other woman was so thin and frail her body had more or less disintegrated within the sleeves and bodice, and there was an unpleasant moment when her right arm disarticulated and swung impossibly loose from the shoulder.

'Hello,' said Grace, and this caused an abrupt alteration in perspective: Thomas saw with relief that the dress was empty.

'What are you doing here?' he said, surprise and unease sharpening his words to needless points. How difficult it was not to say: That looks heavy, you wretched child – come in, sit down. But then there was the vision of her hard eyes evading his, and her fond hand on Lorna's wrist: You don't belong with us at all.

'I don't need to come in. I just wanted to show you something. You ought to see it. Look' – she spread out the skirt – 'do you see this? What do you see?' Something detached from the hem, and rattled on to the path.

Thomas, shrugging, said he saw nothing but an old dress that needed mending; but this was untrue, and behind him in the hall there was a movement, and a remonstrating voice: *Look again, Thomas Hart.*

'Look again,' said Grace, with a stern authority acquired in their years of estrangement. He looked. The loop of the skirt resolved itself into an orbit down which a shining series of comets moved, and moved so insistently and with such brilliance that night fell, and Thomas saw in a celestial parade the comets Halley, Hale–Bopp, Hyakutake, McNaught. It was impossible to suppress a cry of surprise and pleasure, or ignore the quick responding gleam in his visitor's eyes. 'There,' she said. 'You do see it.'

'Where did you get that – what have you been doing?'

'Never mind that' – this was a deliberate closing of her door – 'but I have it. No it's best you don't touch it, the silk is very old – but I wanted you to see this.' Cautiously, as if approaching an old unreliable dog, she came forward and handed him a folded square of rough paper. 'That's the dry-cleaner's ticket. Open it.'

Thomas did as he was told: '*C. S.*,' he read. '*Foulis Street / for collection.*'

'Not Foolish Street,' said Grace, with deliberate patience, as if she saw before her an old man grasping vaguely at fact. 'That was only their joke: it was Foulis Street, which is a road in Kensington – and this was her friend C., and I suppose Maria gave her this dress.' She folded the skirt, she extinguished the comets. 'That was all I came to say. Keep the ticket.' Now she was going, and there was the familiar headlong gait, the black hair glossy at the roots and tied with frayed ribbon – there too, he thought, her temper, her thieving, her ungovernable joy.

Let her go, Thomas, he said to himself, bending to pick up seed pearls from the path. Have you learned nothing, all these years? Let these forces move her as they must, and bring her back in good order.

My dear James (that's what you are now, no less than you ever were: dear, and mine)

It's been nine years since I saw you last, and ten since I last wrote. And three years, two months and fifteen days have gone since you were found (so they tell me) on the bedroom floor, and I had no idea – saw no unfamiliar shadow on the moon, felt no rupture in the air: only went about my ordinary day, while the heart that had no room for me gave up its various ghosts. But this evening I think you're no more distant from me in death than you ever were – closer, even, since there's nobody now to say: he is not yours. He is not dear.

James, do you miss Aldleigh? It's autumn here. Mists are coming up the banks of the Alder and nearly reach the high street. No swifts now. Blackberries on the verges are dropping sugar on the bones of deer. Orion has come back as he always does, and the children have gone back to their schools. There were storms on the sun, and they've blown themselves out. Now when my bad hip aches, I feel an echo of the pain in my good hip, in the joints of my knees – my heart sometimes feels like it's failing and every month my hair is thinner. I don't need much sleep these days. Sometimes I go out and think I hear the whole world ticking.

James, won't you help me? I'm in a bad way. I understand now what they mean by writer's block: I have on my hands the book that I think will be my last, but if I go to it my hands shake and I find all language and courage and beauty and truth have deserted me. This book is too much myself – it asks too much of me. I cannot even write my columns. I have nothing to say. And it is not only a block to writing – it is a block to living – I feel a kind of lifelessness take over my body as if I have a disease of the nerves. I don't like to cook, and when I cook I don't like to eat – books bore or confuse me – I can't even see the cities on the moon. I count loss after loss and mourn what I still have, because I'll lose that soon enough. Even Maria Văduva is fading from me – she thins out, she doesn't speak to me, I see a shimmer by the window or a shadow in the hall but nothing ever comes of it. You made me so unhappy, but it never brought me to a standstill – it sent me to the page. This is a kind of nothing. All I've done lately that was worth doing was find a lost cat on Lower Bridge Road and take her to her owner – but she was lost again the following week, and so it all begins again.

And how I miss my old friend, my wretched child. I thought I got on very well without that responsibility I never asked for, but she came to my door the other day and time folded in and knocked me over like a wave – there she was, with Maria Văduva in her arms – and love moved my body three steps down the path. Am I never to be free of those troublesome women – am I never to be free of my hope for freedom? And do you think I should forgive, and ask forgiveness?

I have with me now a paper ticket. I've unfolded it and folded it once too often, and it's cracked like a plate across the seam. But still the words are so clear I think if I listen well enough I'd hear the writer put their pencil down – *C. S. / Foulis Street / for collection*. I wish you were with me now – I wish I could explain it to you, and see your face illuminate with pleasure and be the face of the

boy I never knew and would certainly have loved if I
had . . .

What should I do now, James? I've seen Foulis Street on
the London map, I know the look of the houses – I could
go there now and look through each letter box, and see if
comet-light comes out. But after all this time I have no
name and no house number, and what would I be but an
old fool limping back to Liverpool Street empty-handed
and alone, on streets paved with all the men and boys I
was once, and loved once?

It's absurd, this chase of mine – it's always been absurd –
it's three months to perihelion and Comet du Lac is
headed for the sun. Perhaps it's better I lay down my arms
and leave the field of battle where I only ever lost –
perhaps it's better to live with hope than disappointment:
to greet the comet and think with melancholy of what
might have been, and not endure the pain of failure?

So here I sit, and can do none other: Thomas Hart, an idle
man, for whom life has exhausted all surprises –

Thomas Hart, preparing to sign his name, was disturbed by
motion at his elbow – by the scent of fragrance and flesh in
a black silk gown too heavy to be worn with comfort; by the
rattle of seed pearls dropping from the hem. *But Thomas*, said
Maria Văduva, summoned out of the privation of his spirit,
frowning and insubstantial at his elbow, *but Thomas: you forget
the principles of proper motion! Don't you understand you cannot help
but move? Besides* – retrieved from the folds of her skirt: a
volume of Tennyson, cracked at the spine, the pages folded
disgracefully down – *that which we are, we are! Made weak by time*

and fate, I'll allow you that — doesn't your bad hip ache? Don't you wake too early, and sleep too late? But it's only a Tuesday in September, it's hardly half past ten — aren't we strong in will, Thomas Hart, don't the valves of our hearts open and close in good order — don't we keep the lenses of our telescopes preserved at all times from fingerprints and dust? Come now, Thomas. What is there to do but to strive, and seek, and find, and not to yield?

ON THE PROPER MOTION OF THE STARS

THOMAS HART *ESSEX CHRONICLE*,
13 SEPTEMBER 2017

I want you to imagine you're standing by the River Alder, looking at an oak tree on the further bank. Behind this oak are other trees: three willows to the left of it, and three willows to the right. Now imagine you walk a little while along the riverbank, and look again at the oak. It has moved, or seems to have moved – now there are only two willows to the left, but four willows to the right. They call this effect parallax, and better astronomers than I'll ever be use this principle to judge the proper motion of the stars.

Proper motion is nothing like the movement we think we see as the stars turn west over Essex. This is all just the illusion of perspective, as the earth spins inside the celestial sphere. We like to reassure ourselves that although the stars appear to move, they're fixed in place – so we have something to pin ourselves on. But I'm afraid this is not at all the case. Nothing in all the universe is fixed, and everything is changing: stars have their own proper motion, and even the Pole Star is adrift.

Generally speaking, stars are so distant that their travel through space appears to us agonisingly slow, detected only over the course of tens of thousands of years. But some stars are quite nearby, and we can live long enough to see them move just a little: Barnard's Star, for example, has drifted some distance in the seventy years of my lifetime.

Now come back to the Alder with me. It's a cold clear night and we're standing together on the bank. Overhead there's the whole black dome of the sky, and every star is out. Imagine also that time is racing by: that for us each hour is ten thousand years. So as we stand there watching, the oaks and willows quickly become immense, die back, reseed, and grow again – and overhead the stars are dancing in their proper motion: Orion throwing his spear, Delphinus leaping out of an infinite sea.

I have found the proper motion of the stars a comfort. It reminds me that we are all in motion, and we're never unchanged. Often it seems we stand still and lonely, absolutely solitary on the turning world. But all the same: we move.

Thomas, don't think I forgive you. I don't and can't and never will. I only write now like this because if I call or email you'll reply, and I won't have you asking how I am or telling me how to be good. But I've got something to tell you and then we don't ever have to speak again. That will be that.

I'm coming home from London where I took back the clothes they gave me to mend. I didn't want to give away the comet dress, so I stole pearls from the hem and I'll wear them until they fall off (there, you see: a sinner). But Maria followed me. Did you see her leave? She was wearing the dress and I heard pearls rolling under the trains on the Tube where the mice were running. And because of this I thought of Foolish Street. I thought of the ticket on the dress, and C., and the comet. I thought of you. I'm angry with you but I was never angry with Maria, and I thought I felt her hand in mine. So we went to Foulis Street.

It is a wide street and there are thirty-two houses behind iron railings with bay trees by the doors. I walked up and down and Maria was walking with me, but told me nothing. The houses are big and white as wedding cakes, and since nobody could be so rich and not be wicked, I knew they wouldn't be kind to a stranger in a home-made dress. It was all a waste of time, and my feet hurt, and I wanted to go home, but Maria wouldn't let me. She reminded me of a man I knew once who told me that every census they ever took was kept in the archives at Kew, and that if C. had lived at Foulis Street I'd find her name in the books. That must have been Maria, mustn't it? You know I've never been clever enough to think of something like that. So there was Maria dragging me back to the Tube and suddenly I was at the National Archives, thinking how much it looks like a prison, as if they're afraid all the dead names will break out and take over London.

Well, this is what I found out. On 5 April 1891 there was a census, and a man took down the names of every person who lived in Foulis Street that day. They let me see the copies, and I took them to a table by the window and read carefully because the handwriting was worse than mine, worse even than Maria's. And I am angry with you and I don't want to talk to you but it was like you were there, too. I had Maria reading over my left shoulder and you reading over my right, and I have the phrases memorised like I used to memorise scripture – look, I can write it out for you now: *The Undermentioned Houses are Situated within the Boundaries* . . .

Three women whose names might be C. S. lived at Foulis Street in 1891. Of course this is two years after Maria disappeared and it may mean nothing at all. But I wrote it all down and I'm going to put this through your door when I get off the train. You can do what you like with it. It isn't my comet, it isn't my mystery. It never was.

GRACE

Signing her name with a plastic pen that leaked, Grace had a vision of Thomas at home in the house she'd loved. This was so vivid it overlaid the outskirts of London as they scudded past – she saw the Persian carpet, and the precious Moser glass; smelt lilacs stuffed into translucent jugs, and those curious Romanian pastries thickly dusted with sugar. This did not diminish her anger, only amplified it: he took this from me too, she thought, returning gratefully to vengeance, he took my other home.

The train was not quite full. Shenfield arrived and receded: the sun was declining over Essex. She folded away the letter and the census copies – yes, she thought, I won't have Thomas tell me to be good – besides how can I be good, where Nathan is concerned? She summoned up the man she loved, composing him of the ardent boy under the Lowlands oaks, the man in the mud, the civil stranger drinking tea – he'd always contained it all, she thought, it had all been in the hand that broke Bethesda's window. At Chelmsford she read over and over their correspondence, which had neither the easy fondness of childhood, nor the compressed diffidence of when they'd last met, but a new way of speaking possible because it was disembodied – *I think I need you to keep me alive*, he'd said one Tuesday afternoon as she ironed the cuffs of a dead woman's nightdress; *yours sincerely*, she'd sometimes say, and *yes*, he'd say, *yours*.

Now the train was entering the evening. Waning moon rising, impetuous stars out first – quickly she wrote: *Clear night there? Look for the Great Bear later. Binary star in his tail. Two stars locked together because they can't help it.*

Nothing came. No light, no evidence of the filament that joined this hard seat in this rattling carriage and wherever Nathan sat with his good kind wife seeing to dinner nearby, his daughter bent over her homework. How fragile it all was,

317

how almost non-existent: whatever was between them was unlatched from life, insubstantial as bored thought – abruptly she was weary of the train, of Nathan, of her self: she leaned against the window and dozed.

She was woken by a change of air. It came like spring. She couldn't account for it, only discovered that she was upright in her seat, untired and frowning, casting about for the cause. In front of her, a drab thin girl in grey, occupied with a drab thin book, looked up from the pages with a rabbit's dumb vigilance. The train was departing a station. The strip-lights overhead were replicated in the windows and cast unkind light on the upturned faces of the passengers. The thin girl put down her book. A compartment door was opened and slammed. A man came down the aisle. Those facing him looked up, and went on looking. Grace turned and saw him, and was inclined to laugh: this man was young, and immense. Thick reddish hair at the crown of his head almost brushed the strip-lights; his shoulders would have cast shade for two men. He wore a white shirt unable to contain the span of his chest and the bulk of his upper arms; the sleeves were rolled to the elbow, and showed burnished skin. The world bent to accommodate him: he insisted on being admired. His face, impassive, was that of a lesser god. The thin girl flushed, and returned to her book. Grace felt her body respond, and this was a delight – she was only an animal, she could hardly be blamed.

The young man sat beside the blushing girl, and opposite Grace. His curved thighs were spread on the seat. His hair blazed. The girl shifted away from him with nervous care. Grace laughed, and covered her laugh; the young man, surveying the carriage, caught her in the field of his view, and flicked a bright black gaze over her body. Well: let him. It was a pleasure to see and be seen. Restlessly she looked at her phone. No light, no sign. Her mood, dependent now on the whims of Nathan's affection, began to sour.

'Tickets please' – and the inspector was coming down the aisle, expertly riding the carriage, looking from side to side. 'Any tickets from Ingatestone, please.' Tickets were retrieved, shown. The ticket inspector – whose belly strained his belt; whose clipped moustache was grey – arrived at the young man's seat and stood behind him. 'Ticket, please,' he said. He surveyed the young man's back, the hard curved thigh splayed out across the aisle. 'Any new tickets?' he said, and wiped his moustache. The indifferent back did not move; the young man was looking at his phone. Now the atmosphere was charged, as if before a lightning strike. A woman in a purple coat leaned forward in her seat, avid for another look. 'Sir,' said the inspector, sharpening his voice, hooking his thumbs in his belt. 'Your ticket.' Still: nothing. The beautiful passenger examined his nails. The thin girl, astounded by such marvellous disobedience, put down her book. The inspector, seeming diminished in size, looked at his watch as if time's mechanism might take pity and hurry him on. He went a little further down the aisle, turned to face the passenger and blinked rapidly, as he might have blinked at the beam of a torch. 'Don't ignore me, young man,' he said, reaching after the tone of an exasperated teacher whose fondness for his pupils had been tested, and not getting there. 'A penalty fare will apply.' He put his hand on the shoulder of the offender, who looked up, and with a shrugging smiling gesture brushed back a lock of hair and revealed a hearing aid. On that superb body, it had the look of augmentation, not correction; but nonetheless the inspector coloured, softened, became helpless. 'I'm sorry, sir,' he said, 'I didn't realise.' He repeated himself, with overloud and careful diction: 'I am sorry.'

'It's OK,' said the lesser god, 'that's OK.' He was

untroubled; he signed as he spoke. He reached in his pocket, and came up empty-handed, then rolled his eyes at the inspector, who'd taken on a fatherly watchful look: all right, son, you've got all the time in the world. The young man took out his wallet and hooked a finger in each compartment. Nothing. The passengers looked on, their early worship amplified and made tender by their sympathy: nobody wished him ill. Now the young man was searching under his seat, and compelling the passengers to watch the articulation of muscles not concealed by his shirt – with a furious movement he raised himself, and spread his hands in hopeless apology. 'Sorry!' he said. 'I just don't know what's happened.'

All eyes on the inspector, all bodies awaiting the spark – let him be, let him get home, give him anything he wants! The inspector was jovial. He clasped his hands. Where was sir getting off? Colchester. Oh that was all right. The barriers would be up this time of day, on account of sheer weight of passengers. Speed things up, you know? The lesser god nodded down from his great height. He knew: of course he knew. 'Just go through' – with tentative reverence the ticket inspector put his hand on the sloping shoulder, and left it there a moment – 'you'll be all right.'

'Good, that's good. Thanks.' A thumbs-up, done with shy majesty. All well: justice in carriage B, and mercy on the tracks. The inspector, sensing his passengers' approval, basked his way down to the buffet car. The woman in the purple coat was licking her lips; the drab girl smiled into her drab book. The young man seemed oddly to dwindle down, as if releasing the other passengers from his thrall. Interest receded from him. Grace looked at her phone: still no Nathan, still no light. Then she saw the young man lean towards the girl beside him. She flushed, and raised her book as a barrier. But he wanted to speak: he put his finger in the spine of her book, and lowered it. The girl gasped at the enormity of this transgression, and the radiant face. The young man whispered, 'Never had a ticket, did I?' He grinned immensely; his teeth were white and small. 'Didn't even have a ticket!'

Then, having handed her the burden of his guilt, he rolled his shoulders and looked out at the small town coming down the line – park, lake, floodlit cricket pitch, bus station, shoe shops, Essex bringing down its shutters for the night. The train slowed and halted. The young man stood, and after all was not so immense, nor so beautiful: possibly that had all been a trick of the light. He grinned down at the girl. He grinned down at Grace, who smiled complicitly – her desire was occupied elsewhere, but she was willing to concede her body had wanted his. She watched him leave the train, and quickly cross the platform as mortal passengers parted at his speed and power; saw him come up short against the ticket barriers, which were after all not open. He paused. The train was ticking on the tracks; the lights of the station struck radiant off his shoulders, the crown of his head. With no apparent effort and no backward look, he vaulted over the barrier and was gone down the narrow stairs.

Grace Macaulay, who all her life had tried to be good – who tried even when she had no idea what constituted goodness, or where to find it – felt a peculiar kind of exhilarated distress. Such a small transgression, she thought, such an infinitesimal sin, I ought not to have noticed – but imagine it, only imagine it: knowing what is good, and simply choosing not to do it! Again she felt the sensation of standing on a high ledge from which she could see the world – again that dizzied feeling of capacity, that fear her feet would slip. She looked for Nathan, she looked at her phone. Nothing. No light.

The following day – early morning; good clear weather – Nick Carleton left his miserable office and went as he often did to speak to Thomas Hart. The offices now were half what they were, and the desks bafflingly more or less paperless. Worst of all was the penetrating quiet, when once there'd been the invigorating clamour of ringing phones ignored or snatched exultantly off the hook, of keyboards pecked at long into night, and occasionally (he fondly thought) of something thrown against a wall. His staff these days were young, diligent, poorly dressed, and kind; they lived with their parents, they filed copy from their phones, they didn't drink, they couldn't spell nor did they need to. So Carleton made his way to Thomas with a grateful sensation, as if they were the last of a lonely species of which only a single pair remained.

At the furthest end of the corridor, where the high windows overlooked Aldleigh and were occasionally blotted with the imprint of birds, the door was ajar, and the departing light was diffuse as that of a gas lamp. Music also departed with the light, and it was the melancholy kind Thomas favoured these days. Troubled at the sound, Carleton reflected that in fact all had not been well with Thomas lately – he stayed too late at his desk, and wrote too little for the terms of his employment; it was no longer possible to rouse his elegant irritation by insisting for example that he stop using the world *whilst*, or confine himself to one biblical quotation a year. Even the fineness of his clothes had faltered these last few weeks (once there'd been the suggestion of a coffee stain on his cuff, which Carleton had ignored as he would have ignored nakedness), and it evidently had been some time since he'd seen his barber – in fact there'd sometimes been the sense that the strange machine that constituted Thomas Hart was winding down.

Then Carleton heard the music pause, and begin again in a kind of wild dance that stirred him without his consent. 'What now,' he said to himself, 'what now?' – he went in, and discovered the Thomas of time past: upright, fastidious, self-contained, a silk handkerchief in pale green folded in the breast pocket of a sports coat in charcoal linen, the overlong hair not yet cut, but at any rate glossed and ordered by a comb. 'Hello,' said the editor, coming warily towards the desk: this abrupt reversion was as troubling as the slow decline.

'Young Nick,' said Thomas, reverting to old endearments and adjusting a silver cufflink, 'I was thinking of coming to see you. I have news. Sit.'

Carleton sat. 'Turn that off, would you? It makes my head ache.'

Gravely and with good humour Thomas turned the music off. Silence in the office and the corridor; silence on the river, the railway, the market square: 'You'd think,' said Thomas, 'that nothing is happening. But it is all happening, Carleton – it has always been happening: look at this.' Spread on the desk, beside the cheap green notebooks that had accrued in a drift against the window, were three pages torn from a lined notepad, and untidily written over in a leaking pen. Thomas moved these aside with what looked very like contempt, and instead passed Carleton a sheet of paper on which an old document of some kind had been photocopied.

'*The Undermentioned Houses*,' read Carleton, turning the paper over as if hoping to find something more interesting on the reverse. 'What is this?'

'That is a record of every human soul that lived at Foulis Street in London on a certain night in April 1891. That is the echo of a footstep that has followed me for twenty years, Carleton – that is the sound of hope!'

'Thomas. I am tired – talk sense: is this about that wretched woman?'

'If you mean Maria Văduva Bell, late of Lowlands House – astronomer, Romanian, unquiet spirit and friend – then yes: it is about that wretched woman, and that wretched child. Grace Macaulay – oh, never mind her – give me that. Look: you see these names underlined?'

Carleton, if tired, nonetheless drew from Thomas Hart a little of the energy that struck sparks from the finger that traced the page. 'All right,' he said, native instinct for a story surfacing, 'let me look.' He looked. The document showed a page from what he slowly understood to be the last census of the nineteenth century, taken at Foulis Street in London in 1891. Three names were underlined, and a note had been written on a blank part of the page:

THREE POSSIBILITIES AT FOULIS STREET??
(Women / names with C. S. / married.)
At no. 3: Christina Susannah Lord, 78. Too old?
At no. 17: Cora Seaborne, 24. Michael Seaborne (father?), 51
At no. 29: Clementine Louisa Stanton Yates, 23 (a husband, Eric Stanton Yates, 41)

'I see,' said Carleton, who did begin to see (in fact: was there possibly the suggestion of moving cloth in the corner of the office, where lately Thomas had installed a coffee machine?). 'You are looking for her friend.'

'I'm looking for her comet!' said Thomas. 'It is shut up in one of these houses, waiting to be let out! We know Maria gave her papers to her friend. We know her friend lived at Foulis Street. We know she was young, and married. Now she must be one of these women.'

'But the census was taken two years after Maria disappeared –'

'Never mind that. Luck must eventually be on my side, for God's sake. She must be one of these. Not Miss Lord, I think, she was too old. Cora Seaborne I suspect was some clever spinster who lived with her father. Clementine on the other hand lived to see a hundred and two, and her son was elected Fellow of the Royal Astronomical Society shortly after the war, and that has promise.'

'Cora Seaborne,' said Carleton (and out of the corner – displacing the silk skirt, the coffee machine – there came the scent of a receding tide, and perhaps of oyster shells). 'That's a good name.'

'I've waited twenty years,' said Thomas, 'for this story to come to an end. Now at last we're getting there, and just as time is running out – Comet du Lac is coming and already visible to better telescopes than mine.'

'I have every faith. But meanwhile: you owe me three columns.' Carleton summoned his authority with effort. 'You may be a grand old man of letters, you may be the jewel in our crown, but if you will take your salary –'

Thomas put his documents away. 'Yes,' he said, 'yes – only I don't have a single thought in my head but Maria.'

'You will think of something. Five hundred words, and six

if they come to mind. And less quantum, Thomas, more Essex. Our readers are ordinary men.'

'There are no ordinary men,' said Thomas.

'Get out of Aldleigh. Head out Maldon way. Take a Thames barge up the estuary, eat an oyster. Do something about Aldwinter. See what they're digging up in Colchester these days.'

Thomas surveyed his superior. 'If you like,' he said, with an immense and deliberate grace, 'I could do the Aldwinter Knots.'

'The Aldwinter Knots? They say it's a strange business, that.' Carleton considered the strange business, and liked it. 'Go on, then. Make it a feature. And careful you don't get in trouble: they're a right lawless lot, out there on the Blackwater.'

Towards the end of September, the sun crossed the celestial equator, and briefly the opposed forces of night and day were more or less equal in Essex. A waxing crescent moon rose early in this lovers' truce, and it was a low tide in Aldwinter, where a quick brown fox came running out of the bracken on hind legs. It stopped and turned its avid face from side to side, then gulped and screamed and bolted. Other foxes followed – also hares, deer, a wretched badger with a torn pelt; a flightless blind owl and a slot-eyed goat. They were all singing. Pause: nothing for a time, no lame or headlong beast, then a rabbit came running with its white scut hanging by a thread, and screaming as it sang. Thomas Hart watched from his vantage near the tomb tree, where chapel pews and plastic chairs had been put out in ordered ranks, and sank each half hour a little deeper in the grass: Aldwinter was briefly inhabited again. Women and men had come down from Maldon and Colchester and Billericay, and from such far places such as Suffolk and Norfolk and Kent; and since it was the day of the Aldwinter Knots, all those attending had tied on their wrist or around their neck a bit of string, or ribbon, or whatever had come to hand.

Sheaves of wheat kept back from harvest had been stacked between the headstones that lapped the tomb tree, and twisted corn dollies tied with red ribbon were put here and there, and fell off, and were quickly put back. The split oak had not yet disposed of its leaves, which blazed and rattled in occasional wind; two dead branches white as stag horns rose from the crown. Summer seemed loath to leave the green, which still had its share of clover and loosethrift in the grass, and in the hedges the dog-roses bloomed a little later than was decent. Thomas opened his notebook: *Two hundred in attendance*, he wrote, *and a fine day. Autumn hardly dares come in. The air is full of salt.*

The singing came nearer, sometimes unlovely and sometimes harmonious, punctuated often by a wordless screech from a panicked fox or hare. A great fish of some kind, slim as a serpent, came up behind a pair of deer and deliberately made them stumble; then it went on, shedding aluminium scales. *Whilst it is said*, wrote Thomas (having Carleton in mind), *that this is an ancient Essex rite marking the autumn equinox, I have my doubts, since it was never mentioned when I was young.* The fish slipped nearer. Thomas wrote *KNOTS?*, and underlined it three times. He considered the length of garden twine tied tight round the wrist of the man seated at his left. *Knots*, he wrote, *were of great interest to the Saxons, whose bones are perhaps stacked three deep under Aldwinter —*

'I heard it was all made up,' the man next to him said, surveying a deer that danced itself frenzied and left rags of its own pelt on the looping bramble. 'I heard it's only been going twenty years.'

'I'm sure it is,' said Thomas, 'this ritual and every other – made up, elaborated, misheard, remembered, amplified – does it matter? Everything begins somewhere.'

'I knew you'd say that,' the man said, with shy unwarranted sweetness. 'I knew you'd say something like that.' Thomas, receiving the sweetness with confusion and pleasure, turned to look at this stranger. A walking stick was propped against his right knee, and Thomas felt his own hip ache in companionship.

Briefly the singers paused, then up from the Blackwater Estuary a split skein of geese headed elsewhere for winter, and Thomas looked at the man again. He encountered a curious clicking sensation behind his ribs, as if a key had been turned in a lock. He knew that fair hair, left to grow too long, that astounding blue gaze. 'Oh!' said Thomas. 'Nathan,' he said, 'there you are!' – as if all morning he'd been looking for the boy who'd leaped easily among the headstones and never been able to keep still. There he was – and with a kind of grief Thomas saw the man's left foot turned faintly in; saw his thinness, and how the clean-shaven cheek had sunk under the broad high bones of his face, and knew pain when he saw it.

'Here I am,' said Nathan, holding out his hand; 'Mr Hart. Thomas. I'd have known you anywhere. I think you and Grace must be the only people in the world who never change.'

It was not quite noon. High in the earth's atmosphere the light refracted through ice crystals in obedience to certain laws, and described a perfect geometric circle round the sun, solid and unbroken as a city wall. 'Do you see that?' said Thomas, dismissing Grace, and the echo of her name in the vestibules of his heart. 'They call it a sundog, or a parhelion, if you prefer the proper term.' I wonder if Grace can see it, he thought, I wonder if there's a sundog over Aldleigh. So he could not dismiss her after all, and the past few days had required an effort of will not to mount the iron staircase at the Jackdaw and Crow, and summon his wretched child and say: look here, the comet is coming – twelve weeks until I see it with my own two eyes. But the vision of her hand on Lorna's wrist revisited him, and brought with it the completion of a lifetime's shame – and there too was the other shame, of his cruelty as she knelt by the baptistery. Now he was conscious of a bright assessing look from the man at his side: compelled as if in a confessional Thomas said, 'I haven't seen her lately. I'm not one for the chapel pew these days. Tell me, is she well?'

The other man was quiet. The sundog brightened. Then 'I've only seen her once in twenty years,' he said, 'and she was just the same, and it made me think I was, too. She's coming here,' he said, with a curious secretive look, as if admitting a sin without guilt. 'She told me she'd never been, and would meet me by the oak' – he took his phone out of his pocket and passed a thumb over the screen as if caressing a living thing – 'she's on her way. Do you have to go' – instinctively and with a sound of refusal Thomas was rising from his chair – 'do you really have to go? Wasn't she your friend?'

This was the frank simplicity Thomas had known, and it was charming to see the boy retained in the man. But how could he explain, given the appeal of that blue gaze now turned on him, that he and Grace had disgraced each other, and disgraced themselves? 'You see,' said Thomas, patting the pocket where his notebook was folded in two, 'I must go and take a look at what's going on over there, or I'll have nothing to write.'

'But look: there she is,' said Nathan, with more wonder

than he'd summoned for the tomb tree, the animals dismantling themselves, the shining loop around the sun. 'There she is,' he said again, and there she was, no better than she ought to be and coming through the crowd. She glittered. The equinoctial light was wonderful on her white dress, her bent brown neck. The dress was plain as a shift, though she'd done some elaborate beaded pleating on the sleeves, and the bodice was cut to show the bonework of her clavicle and shoulder blades, and the deep scoop of her lower back. Her skin retained summer; she'd picked at a horsefly bite and lifted the scab. Already her dress was dirty: coffee on the skirt, mud on the sleeve. The horsefly bite was bleeding. She had more than ever the look of a woman who belonged nowhere, and in no time. Immense irregular pearls drew down the lobes of her ears, and a few seed pearls were threaded on a length of silk around her wrist. Her mouth was blotted red, as if she'd painted her lips, regretted her sin, and rubbed her shame on the back of her hand.

Nathan stood. The walking stick dropped to the grass. Grace, blinded to Thomas by desire or vengeance or both, held out her arms. Nathan entered them, bending to do it, and it struck Thomas that the motions of their bodies had little to do with thought. 'Do you remember,' said Grace, drawing away, 'do you remember my birthday, and the oak coming out of the fog?'

'I remember,' said Nathan. This was kindly and politely done; he'd stepped carefully back, and put distance between them. 'It was a good day,' he said, and sat down with a helpless noise that seemed to signal not the body's weakness, but rather its terrible capacity.

'Then we went home,' said Grace, 'and there was Dimi on the road to Aldleigh in his velvet coat. He died,' she said, lightly touching Nathan's shoulder as she sat, oblivious to

Thomas near at hand. 'He died, and we didn't find out for months.'

Now the animals had gathered around the tomb tree, and looked out at the crowd with identical vacant eyes. At a signal their tuneless hectic singing resolved itself into a sweet and repetitious melody: '*Western wind,*' they sang, '*when wilt thou blow? The small rain down can rain.*' Thomas saw Nathan shift in his seat, and put an inch of further distance between himself and Grace; saw, too, her look of bewildered hurt that arrived and was quickly concealed. There again was the echo, ringing against partitions raised against her, of his old instinct to protect and console: 'But he isn't dead,' he said, 'not really – whenever anyone reads Maria Văduva's diaries they hear Dimi, too.'

If he'd hoped for some kind of softening, none came – 'What are you even doing here anyway,' said Grace, turning her hurt on Thomas. Overhead the parhelion brightened and hardened. At opposed sides of the circle, where three and nine might be marked on the face of a clock, two vivid lights appeared and faintly showed the colours of the spectrum.

'Thomas says that's a sundog,' said Nathan, and Grace's anger faltered against the gentle admonition in his voice – 'Just sit down, Thomas,' she said. 'Where are you going? Can't you just sit down?'

'Maria Văduva,' said Nathan. 'Every now and then I'd remember that name – when I was late for work, or waiting for a prescription – and wonder about you.'

'Yes,' said Grace, glittering, eager – she leaned briefly against him – 'yes, me too.'

Nathan, upright in his chair, cultivated stillness that was uneasy because it was against his nature. And what will happen, thought Thomas, if he doesn't keep himself in check? Pain, I suppose. The green was full of women and men in morris costumes carrying wooden batons; others had put on party clothes. Someone nearby had set up a stall of Pyefleet oysters and shucked them without doing herself damage. Everywhere on the oak bits of string or lengths of rope had been tied on branches, and anyone might think the grass was full of infant snakes. The animals were huddled beside the tree. A drum struck up. The vacant eyes of the deer and foxes were intent on something out of sight. From somewhere there came a high plaintive note that dislodged the jackdaws from the oak; then again there was the drum, and the animals put up their limbs and plucked away their faces. Masks of papers were thrown on the grass; the heads of anxious children now appeared, seeking families out.

'Isn't it strange,' said Grace, speaking to Nathan or to Thomas or to nobody, her right hand on her left breast, 'I feel the drum more than I hear it.'

Yes, thought Thomas, receiving her old look of thunder-struck joy with a responding joy of his own, yes: it's like all Essex has a pulse – it is life, life, eternal life!

The beat quickened. The children clapped with a clever erratic beat, and sang words so ancient as to be nonsensical. It was noon. Men on the margins were setting up tables with kegs of beer, and the morris men tied ribbons to their knees. One by one the crowd joined in the song as if they knew it, and in due course it seemed to Thomas that he knew it, too – had always known it, had heard it at his mother's breast. He began to sing, and so did Grace, because Bethesda had given them the habit of song – but Nathan sat upright, politely smiling, interested and untroubled, his stick sinking into the grass.

A creature shook its torn white scut and moved between the lapping headstones to tie a ribbon to the tree, and wept when the ribbon unwound and dropped. Then more children came, knotting their scarves and bits of string: it looked as if the oak had been taken over by some parasitic vegetation that would strip its leaves by dusk. The crowd swayed and clapped, and there was the scent of beer spilled by the trestle tables, and of the tide on the Blackwater turning. The parhelion crowned the oak with silver. Three suns shone.

Now there was only wordless music, piped and drummed, and men and women going up with bits of thread and ribbon, careful of the headstones and the sheaves of wheat. A young man carrying rope came close by where they sat: he was immense, with curling reddish hair; he'd taken off his shirt, and the hair on his body was also reddish and grew thick towards the navel, so that he had the look of an upright animal. Thomas was inclined to laugh in delight and derision at how monstrously handsome he was; then 'You!' said Grace, with an inflexion of satisfaction and chastisement that affected Nathan, who flinched in his chair as if struck. 'It's you,' said Grace, laughing, and seeming for a moment to forget the man at her side; 'It's you,' she said again, and caught his eye with an imperious gesture. He paused, and shifted the rope on his shoulder, and gave her such a long assessing look that Thomas flushed as if he'd been caught out spying. 'I know him,' said Grace, smiling now at Nathan, and watching with open pleasure as the young man moved on, hurled his rope over a high branch, and laughed as a nearby girl wound the rope three times around her waist. The exchange had caused Grace's eyes to bloom, as if something had entered her bloodstream; meanwhile Nathan inhabited his own body as if afraid he'd break it. Anything might happen, thought Thomas, there's no doctrine or government here – and what is there for an old man to do, but cause mischief? 'Let's drink,' he said, 'let's get something to drink.'

333

'I can't,' said Nathan, 'not really, not with the painkillers they give me – and I have to drive home.'

'Go on,' said Grace, putting her hand on his thigh and quickly removing it, 'go on'; and very briefly there passed between her and Thomas a complicit look that stirred him unbearably. From a nearby trestle table he bought dark beer in plastic cups that spilled easily as he handed them out; and there was a moment when all three drank to slake their various thirsts.

'But what does it all mean?' said Nathan. 'Why do they do it?' Wool and ribbon was streaming from the oak like Spanish moss, and musicians in absurd clothes were bringing instruments out of black cases left open in the grass. The drums pulsed on.

'What do you want it to mean?' said Grace. 'What do you want?' Her bloomed eyes took him in; and it was possible to see the boy Thomas had known looking down at her, amused and puzzled by his strange companion, and restless with life. 'I don't know,' he said, smiling, shaking his head, 'how should I know?'

The wind changed. Low pale cloud blew up from the estuary and put the sundog out. The Aldwinter sky took on the pearly look of an upturned oyster shell.

'I want to do it,' said Grace, done with her drink. 'I want to tie something – I want to tie myself up and leave myself behind.' She'd left her seat, and was drifting nearer the tree. 'How can we go until we've done it? We'll bring ourselves bad luck.'

Slowly Nathan followed her, leaving his stick in the grass. His weak foot dragged and lifted. The crowd at the foot of the oak was thinning out, and here and there children stood between headstones, reaching for the lower branches.

'I don't have anything,' said Grace, lamenting, 'I have nothing to tie. I could tear my dress, I could do that.

Oh – there you are again,' she said, laughing and glittering at the immense red-haired boy whose rope now hung like a pole from a branch. Nathan halted nearby; he watched. He surveyed the boy with a baffled expression of envy, awe, contempt. The red-haired boy took the end of the rope in his fist, and shook it wordlessly at Grace. 'Come on then,' he said, 'come here, you'; and Grace went forward with her skirt in her hands: 'But I know I can't trust you,' she said, 'I know you can't be trusted.' He offered her the rope and she took it. The crowd nearby was dancing, and their movements were deliberate and slow because they'd tied themselves together about the wrists or waist or sometimes, foolishly, the knees. The boy pressed his wrists together, and offered them to Grace, who – with a child's diligent, obedient frown – tied them with the rope. Then dancers came by, and for a time obscured the view: old men and young ones, half-drunk or drunk entirely; girls clasped together and turning in stately circles; old lovers quick-stepping in practised concourse. Dazed by beer and music, Thomas saw all the threads that bound them in varieties of human bondage – knots made of habit, blood, resentment, desire offered and withdrawn, love met and not met, all tying and untying as he watched. Bleakly it struck him that in all Aldwinter only he and Nathan were alone. With pity amplified by the remembrance of desire, he came near the younger man, and put his hand in his pocket, hoping to find a bit of string to join their ruined bodies. Then the dancers parted, and Thomas saw Grace standing small and dark beside the boy, whose shoulders covered half the span of the oak's trunk. She leaned indolent against a marble headstone, and idly tugged at the rope fastened round the boy's hands, as she might have tugged at a dog's lead: 'Come here, then,' she said, as if she had some particular sin and punishment in mind.

'What's happening?' said Nathan. He gripped his right hand with his left. 'What are they doing?'

'They're just playing,' said Thomas. The drums beat on. Rooks began to gather on the green. Grace under the oak was immense, glittering, her white dress showing plainly in the diminishing light. The boy seemed to have dwindled, become humble; now and then Grace threw a black look out at Nathan, assessing his distance, his manner, the composition of the air between them. Nathan had become rigid, and the long line of his throat was hard and beating with the drums; he doesn't like this, thought Thomas, he can't bear it, the power has shifted, after all this time. Laughing, Grace gave a sudden pull on the rope and the boy stumbled forward with a grunt, and his body covered hers against the headstone, which rocked between the roots of the oak. 'Look at them,' said two women going slowly past with white ribbon round their necks. 'Would you look at those two. Anything goes!' Grace was concealed by the boy's immense body, but there was the impression of intent unseen movements made out of sight – 'Stop it,' said Nathan, quietly seeming to implore himself. 'Stop it!' he said again, now taking in the crowd, the drums, the aimless children, the declining sun – 'Get off her!' he said, going as quickly as he could, which was not quick. He reached the boy, and wrenched at his shoulder. 'What are you doing?' he said. 'Get off her!' How pitiful, thought Thomas in a daze, how absurd: you can't impose your manners out here, with everything tending to the mutinous sea.

The boy turned and looked with surprise, and no rancour. He smiled, shrugged, drifted away; was claimed elsewhere by acquisitive women. Grace leaned smiling against the headstone. Her breasts and neck were wrapped with rope: she gave the impression of a hangman's having done a poor job, and gone off to seek another profession. 'Look what you've done!' said Nathan. He was cruel as a father. 'Look what you've done to yourself!' But Grace would not shrug off the rope as she decently should, and Nathan, chastising her with words not audible to Thomas, fumbled with the rope; then Grace shook herself free like a dog, and leaned against the headstone as if exhausted.

The rooks on the green rose in a dense black mass and settled in the oak to roost. 'Get up,' said Nathan, and she did. Her sleeve was torn. She bowed her head in mute humility; then surveyed the headstone, and saw how it shifted now in the roots of the oak.

'What have I done this time?' she said. She rocked it. 'Look what I've done. I didn't mean to.'

'It's all right,' said Nathan. 'It isn't that bad. Anyway she's dead.' Thoughtlessly he took her hand. Grace accepted it. Thomas saw against the coming dusk two careless creatures, suspended forever between childhood and maturity and as innocent and sinful as the day they were born: I did love you, he thought. I have loved you.

Softly Grace began to pet the headstone like a living thing. It was a slab of marble, thickly mossed; it listed away from the oak towards the estuary, as if it wanted the water. Grace traced the lettering. Not dark yet. Small fires on the green. She spoke to Nathan, who stooped with her to read. She burrowed against him with an impulse of affection and pleasure. It seemed to Thomas that even to watch them was a trespass, and nobody, he thought, a bit of old string in his hand, nobody on earth was ever as solitary as me. But Grace was beckoning him, and this was extraordinary, and Nathan was raising his arm: 'Thomas!' they were saying. 'Thomas Hart! Come here!'

Thomas walked forward through Aldwinter as it was, and

had been, and would be – 'There,' said Grace. 'There, you see?' She stood aside. Thomas was at the headstone. It was difficult to read by firelight. The face of a fox grinned out of the grass. Then it seemed to Thomas that letters formed themselves because he wanted them – that he summoned them up as he watched:

CORA SEABORNE FGS

1867 – 1921

FRIEND AND MOTHER

'Look closer,' said Grace. High tide on the Blackwater, sea-frets on Aldwinter Green: 'Look!' she said. Thomas stooped to the work of the stonemason, and with his forefinger traced in the marble an ammonite fossil, coiled like the horn of a ram. Beside it, dim and unmistakable in the astronomical twilight, he saw a comet with a curved and double tail: hankering after light, but impounded in the stone.

'Take me to Bethesda,' said Grace Macaulay after dark. Nathan, dazed by beer and pain relief, and persuaded to leave his car until morning for the sake of the law, sat upright and civil beside her in the back seat. Thomas placidly regarded them both in the rear-view mirror, and thought of Cora Seaborne.

'Take me to chapel,' said Grace, glittering at him.

'I am taking you home,' said Thomas.

'Isn't that what I said?' – another look: only you understand what I mean, Thomas Hart.

The Blackwater receded behind them; so too did the fires set on Aldwinter Green, the morris men, the pulsing drum. Ordinary Essex came quickly into view: rush hour on the outskirts of Colchester, cheap planes fleeing Stansted; oaks going over, and cars dying on bricks outside freshly painted front doors. 'Don't you want to see it again?' said Grace. 'Don't you ever wonder who sits in your pew?'

'Cora Seaborne, friend and mother,' said Thomas. 'FGS. So then she was a Fellow of the Geological Society. And dead at fifty-four, which seems to me now no age whatever. And a comet on the headstone,' he said, with as much pleasure as if du Lac had just then crossed the ecliptic, and come into view above the A12's dual carriageway, 'which settles the matter, to my mind. What we must do is this: establish what happened when the Aldwinter graves were disinterred, and whether this Seaborne woman had descendants who kept her papers and correspondence. I doubt she was very important,' he said, experiencing at that moment, and for no evident reason, a bolt of pain in his hip, 'I doubt she'll have troubled the history books, even if she ought to have done.'

'Please take us to chapel, Thomas,' Grace said, 'please' – not enough room in her heart these days for the dead – 'that was all downright ungodly, back there, and I'd like to go and sit in a pew.'

'I'm not sure it's godliness you have in mind,' said Thomas; then the car struck a pothole, and Nathan cried out in his seat: 'I'm sorry,' said Grace, as if she herself had damaged both the tarmac and his spine, 'I'm sorry, love' – the endearment passed without notice.

'It will be locked,' said Thomas. He wanted only to be at home in the shadow of the railway bridge, with his cheap green notebooks to hand, drafting a letter to some council official: *I wonder if you might direct me to some documents* – 'It will be locked,' he said, 'and I have a book to finish' (they were coming to Aldleigh now, and he heard above the engine the old harmonium playing, and the cadence of the prayers).

'Look,' said Grace, 'there it is, there's Bethesda, like it's sailing towards us down the road.'

'There it is,' said Thomas, and found himself nodding as if at an acquaintance: there was the austere chapel, huddled in the car park beside Potter's Field, all as it had ever been. The traffic lights on London Road were red; so they waited where James Bower had waited, and saw what he had seen.

'What time's the last train?' said Nathan, with the civility of a man who had duties at home – who had never, for example, unravelled rope from the breasts of a woman who toppled a headstone; whose throat never beat with the drums. 'I've work tomorrow, I ought to get back, my phone is out of charge.'

'It was good for you,' said Grace. 'It was good to step out of your life and into mine – go in, Thomas,' she said. 'Look, here we are.' Thomas saw Bethesda's gates standing open, and the bay tree flourishing in its small black bed; and briefly a muddle of resentment and affection left him speechless.

'Go in,' said Grace, 'please go in.' Helpless against forces he could hardly make out, Thomas turned through the iron gates; and 'Somebody's there,' said Grace, 'somebody's cleaning the pews.' A dark and busy thing went by the mottled glass of the window. There was no music.

'I used to play there all the time,' said Nathan, looking at the vacant plot beside the chapel. 'I used to watch you all going in. Do you never go now, Thomas?' he said, with his old frank interest. 'Have you both abandoned it all?'

'It isn't that,' said Grace, 'you don't understand, that's like asking if we've abandoned our bones.'

'I'm not a man of that faith in particular,' said Thomas,

'and haven't been in almost ten years. It was made clear to me then that a man like me was not welcome, and never could be welcome.' (A brief glance at Grace; briefly, her shame.) Thomas cut the engine, and released himself from his seat: 'But I'm still a man of faith, I think.' An image in mind: small ships, and the pilot light hazy on the dock. 'Often when I wonder what it is I believe, and how I can go on believing it, I always come down to this: that wanting God is God himself. He exists in the stars not because he made them on the fourth day, but because we have the inclination to look up, and wonder.'

'Yes,' said Nathan, 'I see, or hope I do' – he was leaning on the wall and looking over Potter's Field. A slow smile came. 'I remember my red coat,' he said, 'and how I broke the window. Sometimes I think I have no memory from that year that doesn't have you in it.' Grace came to lean beside him on the wall, and very slightly he moved his body away.

Thomas meanwhile was at the threshold, standing on that same bristled mat. How extraordinary it was that Anne Macaulay would never again come through the lobby with her hymn book in her hands; that Dimi would never again drink from his bottle on the last pew by the door. Who played the harmonium now? Who handed round the silver communion plates? He looked back to Potter's Field, and saw Grace put her head on Nathan's shoulder, not with her old hard nudge of love, but with a kind of acquiescent shame. Then she saw Thomas going in, and followed him. Nathan followed her. The green bay tree was flourishing. The lobby doors opened, and a woman came out, and greeted Grace – it had been a long time, hadn't it, yes, and they'd missed her: was her father well? Yes, said Grace, quite well, praise God; and might they stay a while, for old times' sake, and lock up after they were gone?

So Grace in triumph shook the iron chapel keys, and the obedient men followed her in. The loop of time enclosed them: here as ever the halted moons drifted under the pitched white roof, and the green walls were as ever cold to the touch; here the tulip of the pulpit still bloomed against the wall. Maria Văduva was standing by the communion table, this do in remembrance of me; there was broken glass in the aisle. The cleaning woman had raised dust that rose on draughts of air, and Thomas saw it depart through open windows and go streaming over Essex to the upper atmosphere, becoming blown in due course by solar winds into the tail of Comet du Lac.

Grace, not speaking, touched her old pew, which was stained with oil from her palms and the palms of generations of believers before her – she touched the closed harmonium, and stood for a time by the place where she'd been baptised. Tail lights were blotted in the narrow windows. Aldleigh passed them by. 'You were standing there,' said Nathan, 'where you are now, and your dress was white that day, too.' He had a curious dreamlike look. His competent fatherly manner was gone, and the old teasing levity came up like something unloosed from the bottom of a lake: 'You looked ridiculous, in fact,' he said, 'but then you always did.'

'The whole time,' she said, 'in every hymn and every verse I tried to think of my salvation, but was waiting for you to come in.'

'I did,' he said. Together the children turned to Thomas, and regarded him.

It was difficult for Thomas to see Grace's small white body pressed against Nathan, whose stick was on the communion table; to see his bewildered grateful look. So he turned to the harmonium and pressed without skill at the pedals and keys, and an old thread of an old hymn went up with the sea air in the pipes.

'It was here they taught me I ought to be good,' said Grace. 'But isn't love goodness, and wasn't I good for waiting all this time, and didn't I see you first?' She was laughing – it was all a game, having no significance at all.

It was hard for Nathan to stand so long without his stick. He stepped back, but stumbled; so he took hold of her dress at the hip, and held it. 'I ought to go,' he said. 'Does anyone know when the last train leaves?'

'I should have brought string,' Grace said. 'I should have brought rope, I'd tie you to me. You see?' she said, and shook her skirt where he held it. 'You don't want to let me go.'

Thomas would have prayed for them both if he could. No use, he thought: I can't put my hand out, and stop a body in orbit, not when my bad hip aches – 'That was it,' he said. He stood. 'That was the last train. Didn't you hear it go?' Grace heard nothing. Two hands now at her hips, the stick dropped by the baptistery; again a helpless quick embrace, and a sound that might have been pain, and the small strong body burrowing hard against the man it wanted. Thomas Hart was not seen and not wanted. He left his pew again.

Grace Macaulay, no better than she ought to be, stood fastened against the man she loved and wouldn't let him go. Soon this also caused him pain, and Grace heard the little cry, and pitied him, and because of this desired him more. 'We can't stay here,' she said. 'Why don't you come with me?'

'What else can I do?' he said. No answer. Lights out in Bethesda; fires dying on Aldwinter Green.

They walked slowly and without speaking past Potter's Field, and on down the high street with the Alder running on their right; and all the while Grace had the helpless sensation

343

of an object dumbly submitting to the laws of motion. She said nothing, because anything that came to mind seemed to her ridiculous: did you know, Nathan, that you can know what it is to be good, and simply choose not to do it? Sometimes he spoke in the civil way of a colleague remarking on the weather — how warm it was, how Aldleigh was altered these days; and was it always so busy at the Jackdaw and Crow? Then she'd encounter an intent assessing look, bewildered and half-amused, and have no breath left in her.

It was difficult for him to climb the iron stairs. She gave no help. He would have refused it if she had. She unlocked the door, and locked it behind them; and after this there was a time of inconsequential conversation, embarrassed by themselves and by each other, feeling how inconvenient it was, how humiliating, to be tethered to bodies that insisted on all this: yes it was cold up here in the winter, yes sometimes she was woken by the trains. 'So this is where you sleep,' he said, as if it were all marvellous, 'this is where you sit, when we speak at night.' Stolen lamps lit, baskets of cloth spilling on the carpet; the white cloth on the shipping trunk, her unmade bed and the smell of her body in it. He looked angry and unhappy. He took his jacket off. He put his hand on the buckle of his belt and it was appalling to discover how the gesture unmade her. Carefully he sat on the bed and she undressed and knelt at his feet, and smiled as she did it: see how abject I am — see how I'm brought to my knees by pity and want? She took off his shoes and socks, and then the submission was his; but it struck her that another woman knew how best to help him, and she was overtaken by sorrow. Why don't you go away, she thought, why don't you just go away and leave me alone; but she had his weak foot in her lap and was touching the callouses there, and loving them, and loving the limp that made them.

'Stand up,' he said. She did. She put her right hand on her stomach where it was soft, and he tugged it away quite harshly: 'Let me look.' When he'd done looking, he lay down. 'Come up here,' he said, 'come over me, I have to look, I have to see everything,' and now she was biddable again, and knelt above him, and this seemed to humiliate and elevate her equally. She pressed her palms to the wall, and sometimes her forehead, and occasionally the noises she made seemed to her those of a lunatic, and at these times she would raise herself from his mouth in a kind of ecstatic despair. But he always seemed to anticipate the withdrawal and bring her down, grasping her hips with extraordinary compensatory strength; and later, when he was able to speak, he said, 'Does this hurt? Am I hurting you?' – because his movements after all weren't gentle, and caused her the curious cleaving pain that sometimes came when she'd gone a long time without; and 'Yes it hurts,' she said, 'will you do it again?' So it went unbearably on. All those little deaths (her mouth was fastened to a mark on his shoulder; she was set on obtaining every part of the body she'd desired for so long), all those little deaths – but this is annihilation, it will kill me, there'll be nothing left. So after all that time – after the years of loss and envy and coincidence, and all those terrible negotiations of holiness and wanting – it all came down to this: mutually assured destruction, and streetlight hardening on the bedroom wall.

Subject: Aldwinter Tomb Tree
9 October 2017

Dear Dr Syed

I'm writing in my capacity as a journalist for the *Essex Chronicle.* We're hoping to publish an article on the headstones relocated from the Aldwinter church cemetery to the oak on the village green. It's my understanding that the bodies were reinterred in the municipal cemetery in Colchester in 1952 following the North Sea flood, and I'm looking for any documents relating to the removal, which may possibly be kept by the Essex Museum Services. I am particularly interested in the headstone of Cora Seaborne, 1867–1921.

I'd be so grateful if you could give me any information on this matter.

Best – Thomas Hart

Re: Aldwinter Tomb Tree
14 November 2017

Dear Thomas

Do forgive the delay. I hope you'll be pleased to hear that we've uncovered some information regarding the Seaborne grave which may be of use. A number of objects were removed from Aldwinter during the 1952 disinterment, and where possible returned to the families of the deceased. An item was discovered intact in the

Seaborne grave, and this was donated to the museum by her surviving relative in 1965.

The item in question was a small and quite elaborate lead box of Eastern European make, possibly designed to protect its contents from damp. A note made at the time of acquisition in 1965 lists the following:

A/1952.65.CS 1: A Book of Common Prayer, containing –

1(a). A letter dated 26 April 1915 (from a Rev. Ransome, chaplain of the Essex Yeomanry stationed at Ypres)

1(b). A blue square of fabric, possibly a handkerchief

A/1952.65.CS 2: A large trilobite fossil of exceptional quality

A/1952.65.CS 3: Four documents in a leather case

The box is on permanent display in Chelmsford, and the trilobite was acquired by the Natural History Museum in London. The fabric together with the prayer book and its letter have unfortunately been lost. However, it appears from administrative records that in March 1997 my predecessor James Bower requisitioned a number of documents relating to Aldwinter, including the remaining Seaborne papers. To my knowledge they have since been held in storage at the Aldleigh Museum. I've alerted my colleagues there that you'll be in touch, and I'm sure they'll be pleased to help you. Look forward to the article. Good luck!

S. S.

Dear James – will you let me write just one more letter, one more time? I can't have your last sight of me being that of a self-pitying old man stagnating in his little life.

I'm sitting at the table where once you and I would eat and talk and raise Maria from the dead. The moon comes under the railway bridge, bad music comes from next door. It's midnight. Grace Macaulay is sleeping in an armchair nearby, worn out by her own misery. Sometimes she talks in her sleep but I can't make it out.

She came to the house again this afternoon. I knew her knock. Who else ever hurled themselves at my door? I opened it and her anger came in like wind – 'You did it again, didn't you?' she was saying. 'You sent him away again.' James, did you ever think yourself guilty, because somebody said you were? For a moment I thought: yes, yes, I must have done – I did, and I'm sorry! Then her anger dissipated and my wretched child arrived down time: small, dark, all love and fury, seeping into tears. 'Come in,' I said, and she did, and for a moment I was not a complicated man: my friend was in my house again.

She went through the hall and into this room as if she owned the lamps, the sideboard, the rug, the plates and forks in the kitchen, the lunar telescope on the windowsill, and sat where she is sleeping now – 'Did you?' she said. 'Did you send him away?'

'No,' I said. 'Not this time.'

We were quiet for a long time, or so it seemed to me: I suppose we each considered what the other had betrayed.

I saw her hand on Lorna's wrist, and saw her diminish the battle of my nature against my soul into something small and furtive and cheap – but more clearly and with more pain I saw Nathan at Bethesda's door, and that look of bewildered relief when I turned him away. I had been responsible for her pain then, and I was responsible for her pain now; and it was like that first day in Bethesda, with the infant stranger in the wicker basket and a new obligation in my heart. 'What happened, Grace?' I said. 'What did you do?'

She asked for something to drink, and I gave it to her. Then she told me that briefly and after all those years Nathan had been her lover – one night, in her room over the Jackdaw and Crow, after the Aldwinter Knots. He was changed absolutely from the last time, she said, and he was absolutely the same – it had been an appalling surprise to find him at Lowlands, it had been inevitable. But he had a wife and a daughter – his life was sealed up, there was no way in. 'And at first,' she said, 'I persuaded myself I could have him, and still be good. I said to myself: to love a body and the soul it contains, and never touch it, not once – that would be a crime against love, it would be a lie! But then I understood there was another way – that I could know how to be good, and choose not to do it. Only you will understand how frightening that was, how it was like being given a power I'd never asked for and didn't know how to use!'

Now, she suffers. He's gone away from her, she says, that kind of drifting a woman feels more than she sees. 'It's like he was holding my hand,' she said, 'and let it go one finger at a time until I was clutching at air.'

I knew that look she had. I knew how bewildering it is to love and know your love goes unmet and unmatched. It's the law of harmonies, I thought, it is all as Kepler said, and this is what we have in common: our bodies moved by forces not possible to resist. Then she said, 'He is gone again, and now I'll be as sad as you.'

I was angry with her then. What need did I ever have for her pity? What need have I ever had for anyone's pity? I'm a man who lived, as all men must live: that is all.

So I told her this: that it's true that I've only rarely been happy, and perhaps more often been sad. But I have been content. I have lived. I have felt everything available to me: I've been faithless, devout, indifferent, ardent, diligent and careless; full of hope and disappointment, bewildered by time and fate or comforted by providence – and all of it ticking through me while the pendulum of my life loses amplitude by the hour.

All the while she sat crying in her childish way. And I wanted to console the child I'd loved, and so I told her this: that in the ordinary way we love because we're loved, and give more or less what we're given. But to love without return is more strange and more wonderful, and not the humiliating thing I'd once taken it to be. To give love without receiving it is to understand we are made in the image of God – because the love of God is immense and indiscriminate and can never be returned to the same degree. Go on loving when your love is unreturned, I said, and you are just a little lower than the angels.

She cried harder then. 'You ruined my life,' she said. 'I don't forgive you, and I never will.'

'Well,' I said, 'you ruined mine. I would have left Bethesda when I was young, I would have been free – then there you were, and because of you I took my shame to the pulpit every week, and because of you I left the comfort the pulpit sometimes gave me. And I don't forgive you,' I said, 'nobody was ever as cruel to me as you.'

I wish I could say: James, we forgave each other in the end. I wish I could say: she put her head on my shoulder and I welcomed it and we laughed and said all was well. But in fact we were quiet for a long time, and we heard a television laughing over the road and the train leaving for Liverpool Street, and then she said, 'Do you think we can love each other and never ever forgive?'

I didn't know, I said. But I thought we ought to try.

THOMAS HART

As Thomas walked through the town the following afternoon, he found his attention turning not to Grace, or Maria, but to Nathan. Poor man, he thought, poor boy, picturing again the walking stick in the grass, the dragging foot, the remarkable eyes uncompromised by time and pain. Poor man, never forgetting that strange girl in her strange clothes, while the world turned and brought him before he knew it into employment, and mortgages obtained and renewed; a child who doubtless loved her father, and whose mother was doubtless sensible and kind (there, again and as ever on London Road in autumn, James Bower was carelessly kissing his wife). Then in due course pain, and the clock ticking, and Bethesda best remembered as a dream – but the trouble was that while you cannot re-enter a dream, the trains went from Kent to Essex via London Bridge on the hour every hour – poor Nathan! Poor boy!

He passed the war memorial and came to the old town hall. Here Aldleigh Museum, defunded and dispirited, occupied dingy quarters accessible only two afternoons a week, and Boudicca had been disarticulated by careless men. Nonetheless Thomas felt a movement in his heart like that of a compass needle seeking north, as if James Bower might still be at his desk, filling in those thin pink requisition forms, having in his hands the solution to a problem he'd not yet foreseen. Or possibly he was only now arriving, coming up behind him and reaching out his hand. Oh it is possible, thought Thomas, it is among the probabilities – perhaps James Bower lives on undiminished in some thread of time running parallel to mine. And in fact he heard footsteps, certainly he heard them, and certainly no stranger would come so close – everything was happening, and time was never what he'd taken it to be! His breath was quick and shallow with the folly of his hope: he turned, and (this was absurd; it was improbable) found a familiar man walking in his wake, and looking at him now with a long-lashed intimate gaze: 'Hello,' he said.

'Hello,' said Thomas, and briefly he felt his scalp flense from his skull; then reason returned, and his breath slowed. 'My God,' he said, lapsing into laughter, 'is Essex so small? Can none of us escape each other?'

'In one of your columns,' said Nathan, untroubled and unsurprised, 'you'd say this is all to do with gravitational fields and orbits.' He was dressed in a dark suit of some cheap cloth that was cut too large, and the effect was diminishing: he seemed a schoolboy not yet grown into his uniform.

'I expect I would. But what are you doing here, Nathan?'

Nathan gestured to an anonymous building nearby, and explained it had been necessary to see a solicitor about a will, blinked rapidly behind his glasses as if ashamed to have been caught transgressing. 'I'm sorry,' he said, and there was the impression that if he listed his causes for apology they might very well be there all week. How young he is, thought Thomas, softening suddenly, how young they both will always be: standing outside Lowlands with their stolen cigarettes, peering in between the broken boards, as innocent as the day they were born and no better than they ought to be – 'Tell me,' he said, 'are you busy?'

353

'No, not any more, and my train isn't for an hour' – he had a half-shamed, half-hopeful look, like that of a dog.

'No,' said Thomas, as gently as he could. 'No, it isn't Grace. But I want you to come with me – I've hunted Maria's comet all these years, and weren't you there at the beginning? Don't you think you should see the end?'

It seemed to Thomas that the other man was relieved and despairing in equal measure: 'Yes please,' he said, with his old merry willingness to take part in whatever was at hand. So the two men walked together favouring the parts of their bodies that ached, Thomas explaining that possibly – and after all this time! – what he'd wanted most to find had been in Aldleigh, but they'd never thought to look.

'It should seem strange,' said Nathan, 'it should be unbelievable. But these days I just think: of course.' The museum entrance was relegated now to the side of the town hall, its door blotted with torn posters and bolted against curious passers-by.

'Look,' said Thomas, raising mischief in himself, 'look, light coming under the door, dust on the doorstep – the comet's in there, waiting.'

They knocked once. A woman came out; and really, thought Thomas, she was hardly more than a child. She surveyed the troubled weather, then brought them into the dim hall with courtesy he suspected owed more to his age than his reputation. Dr Syed was on leave, she said, leading them down corridors in which artificial lights flickered in fly-clotted fittings, and most of the doors were locked, but everything was ready. They passed a larger room in which display cases were kept polished and in good order, but nobody looked at their contents. 'Here we are,' said the young woman, with an indulgent smile at Thomas, and a more speculative one at Nathan, 'would you like tea?'

'Thank you,' said Nathan, who'd taken off his glasses. 'You are kind.'

'Go in,' she said, flushing against his blue gaze. 'Do go in.' Shyly she directed them to an open door. Faint light came over the threshold containing sifting particles of dust.

Thomas went in, and looked cautiously about as if anticipating pain. Weak lights overhead hardly brightened the air, and a scent like that of leaf-mould in autumn came out of the carpet. The ceiling was soiled with mould. The Essex coat of arms had lost a seax, and furniture no longer in use had been draped in sheets that shifted in the draughts. Only a handsome desk with a gilded leather surface remained uncovered, and a pair of plastic chairs set nearby. A desk lamp with a harsh white bulb illuminated a cardboard box from which a plastic label was coming unstuck. A bit of paper was taped to it: F.A.O. THOMAS HART.

'What is it,' said Nathan, 'what have you seen – are you all right?' He came quickly forward, and put his arm around the older man with such competent strength that Thomas realised with shame he'd been swaying where he stood, weakened to stupidity by the desk with its tea-stains, the dust that sifted in the morning light, the broken coat of arms – 'I'm all right,' he said, and would have liked to shrug off the enclosing arm out of pride, but couldn't – in fact could not see Nathan at all, or the boxes stacked against the wall and the shifting sheets: the room contained nothing but James Bower.

Nathan said, 'Sit down,' and put the other man in a chair, then greeted the young woman arriving with tea on a tray: yes, they were fine, thank you – no, they needed nothing more. Thomas looked at the tray, and at the green teacups on green saucers, and all the valour with which he'd configured his loss into an act of grace dissipated, and he felt again that he knelt in the gutter on London Road, choked with confusion and shame. There was silence for a time, and the sensation, encountered as if from a great distance, of Nathan patting his back with a diffident uncertain affection that only amplified his loneliness. Then slowly Thomas became aware of movement in the margins of the room, among the disconsolate sheets and cheap stacked chairs, and looking up discovered his household ghost, pulling a pearl from her hem in a temper: *What are you doing here, Thomas Hart? Can you not let the matter rest at my feet, where my heart is?*

'You see, I have never been alone,' said Thomas, 'not really.' Then 'Thank you,' he said, taking the green cup Nathan offered. He took a notebook from his pocket, and put it beside the cardboard box. The blinds tapped the windows. Distantly down the corridor the young woman was speaking on the phone. 'The difficulty is,' said Thomas, 'that if what I've been looking for is here, it is all at an end. What would be left for me then? What would I have to move me?'

Maria Văduva was coming to the desk, and there were seed pearls on the floor; and there was a woman with her whose fingernails were full of Essex clay: *Get on with it*, they said, *get on with it*, and rapped the table three times. So obedient Thomas moved the lamp to get a clearer view, and took out from the box a file containing documents. The first of these was a requisition slip, pink fading from the paper, requesting the transfer of a number of items from Chelmsford to Aldleigh, for cataloguing and possible display. *James Bower*, it was signed, *March 1997*; and with a kind of ecstatic misery Thomas saw the day of his arrival at the office, and the familiar stranger seated at his desk.

'Thomas,' said Nathan, 'are you sure you aren't ill?'

'I'm sure. Stand back. Let me have light.' A letter then,

typed and corrected in a minute and fastidious hand, dated 1965:

> I am not certain of the full significance of this box and its contents, but it seems to me that my mother must have erred in her actions, as she was sometimes inclined to do. Therefore I give them to your care.

FRANCIS SEABORNE

'But there's no box,' said Nathan. 'What box, Thomas, and where?'

'It would be a lead box,' said Thomas, 'of Romanian make. They keep it in the Chelmsford Museum, but there's nothing in it.' Carefully he took out a leather document case, greased black by the hands that had held it, and marked with a gilded monogram: *C. S.* This is the end, he thought, it is finished: I'd rather burn it and throw the ashes in the river! But the women were watching from the corner of the room, and Nathan was holding his breath; and isn't the loop of your orbit closed, Thomas Hart? Doesn't your end encounter your beginning? Time's getting on, Thomas, the light is ticking on the wall —

Maria Văduva Bell
Lowlands, Essex
JUNE 1889

Beloved Cora – my child – this is the last you will have of
me – I shall never write to you again! It is not that I
intend my body to die – though perhaps it might, now
that my blood is become nothing but salt water – it is only
that my spirits have at last deserted me –

I have received news from Bucharest – and it has blighted
me, as one sometimes finds a solitary tree in the wood
struck dead as bones – the man I love is dead. He is
already in the ground – so my light is gone! I cannot see
the stars – or I will not – and what we will not see has no
form or being! I have blinded my telescope – what use do
I have for it now? I was to have a comet in my name – I
was to outlast myself – but all I ever saw, I saw for him –
it was his comet, and never mine – it was all done only
that I might make myself worthy of his admiration and
his love. How very like a dog I have been, rooting in the
sky for a stick to bring her master!

I struck a match. I put it to the paper containing my
observations. But I find I cannot burn it – I burned my
finger first – so I give them to you. You may take pleasure
in them, out of your fondness for knowledge – and I give
you my comet dress, which once I said I should be buried
in – but what use do I have now for the stars, even dead
stars made of pearls –

You have said you love me. Very well – I will test your
love, as a musician tests her instrument! – if you love me,

you will allow the manner of my grief! When this comet is falsely named for its false discoverer you will keep your silence – and when you die, you will inter the comet with you – so the depth of my love may be measured by the height of what I have lost: they will say what a love that was, that she loved him more than her comet and more than her own name!

And my Cora, let me tell you this before I go – you set too much store on loving and on being loved – this is a hopeless cause! Do you think the act of loving secures love's return? It does not! It cannot! You must learn to prize your mind above your heart – you must seek out your comet where you can, and wonder at it – whether it is above your head, or under your feet! For my sake, do some great thing that will told among men hereafter!

And forgive your friend –

MARIA

11.12 p.m. 17 June 1889

At Lowlands House, Aldleigh, in Essex

Right Ascension 0h42m30 / Declination 58° 45' 12

Object in Cassiopeia having bright nucleus and double tail
extending four degrees north-east, of bluish colour

MARIA VĂDUVA BELL

'What will you do now?' said Nathan. They were coming out of the town hall arm in arm, neither man certain who wanted help or who gave it. 'Cora Seaborne did what her friend asked – will you?' The pewter sky had acquired a polish in their absence, and Aldleigh was contemplating closing for the night. Here and there early Christmas decorations pricked the streets with implausible lights, and the wind had worn itself out; behind them the girl was locking the museum, and singing out of tune.

'If Maria wanted her secrets kept,' said Thomas, averting his gaze from the woman who walked beside him in forbidding silence, 'she ought to have known better than to confide in a writer, for whom the whole world is nothing but a store of sentences. I'll write this evening to the International Astronomical Union in Paris, and request an inquiry of some kind: less than a month to perihelion, and no hope of seeing the comet properly named by then – but it never leaves without beginning its return, and isn't there always time, after time? But look,' he said, speaking now with the authority of his years, 'I want a word with you.'

Nathan, flushing, was again the boy who'd broken Bethesda's window: he had a look of equal guilt and mischief, knowing that he deserved to be chastised, and not much minding. 'I know,' he said. 'She talks so easily about love, she always did!

But how can she know what she means? If she ever loved me that was twenty years ago, and we were children. I am a different man – an ordinary man, I have a whole life! And I was never what she imagined. I can hardly myself remember the boy she knew. Thomas, I love my wife. I love my child. Do you think Grace alters that? It doesn't. It never could.'

'I don't understand it all,' said Thomas. 'I've wondered all my life what I owe to love. There was a time I felt that because I loved a man, he was in my debt – that he'd made me love him, and so he owed me his love in return. And now he is dead, and I can never receive even a part of what I gave! But the world turned and I came to believe that all we owe to love is humility and gratitude that we were ever loved at all. You think it's humble to say it cannot be real – that she's mistaken, since you're not free. But that's a kind of pride. Real humility is submitting with wonder and gratitude to being loved – real wisdom is understanding how amazing it is, how improbable and really absurd, that she was summoned out of nothing as we all were, and happens to breathe this air when you breathe it, and see this world when you see it, and that out of all her billions of fellow travellers it is your word she waits for as she sits alone in her room! Well: that's a responsibility and probably a terrible one, and I can't help you with it. You must work out your own salvation with fear and trembling, and let me work out mine.'

Overhead a canopy of cloud had split from east to west; and at the further end of Aldleigh – over the newsagent's and shoe shops and the man in old boots clearing dead leaves from the gutter – bands of shining coral deepened and hardened as they watched, and the effect was of walking towards seams of quartz that traversed a quarry wall. The sun was setting: for now.

N, Thomas told me how you met in the street. He said you were with him when he found Maria's comet. I can't believe it's been in Aldleigh all this time. But I can believe it. It seems right somehow. I am glad you were with him. I wish I'd been there too – G.

But won't you love me, Nathan? Won't you let me love you? Isn't this as terrible for you as it is terrible for me? Don't I love you and haven't I loved you all my life? Don't I need you to keep me alive, and don't you need me?

Come here, Nathan. Come here. Meet me at Lowlands when the comet comes. We'll watch it and I'll put my head on your shoulder and I won't speak. I won't say I love you, I promise, I won't say a word.

Just come.

Shortly before the perihelion of comet du Lac, Thomas Hart sat surveying an image cut from a magazine with the attention of a pious man turning to his scripture. It had come that morning in the post marked with an almost imperceptibly small kiss from Grace, and a note that said yes, she'd come to Lowlands tomorrow, she'd take a look at his wretched comet; and that she'd seen this thing, and thought of him.

Thomas conceded to himself that he couldn't fully understand the image, only comprehend its beauty and trust in its significance. It was (said the accompanying text) a map of the galaxy Supercluster Laniakea, this meaning 'immeasurable heaven': radio emissions from the near universe distilled into a gold cloud drifting against a ground of blue, speckled with white dots seeming to move as particles of water might move in mist. The shape of this cloud was the shape of a human heart, and it was marked all over with shining filaments that coursed out from the centre with the look of capillaries carrying vital blood. These white dots were drifting galaxies, and these shining filaments their flow towards the centre of mass; and on the edge – set like a city on the mouth of a river – there was the Milky Way, there was home. A red dot marked the place, labelled as a map might be in Aldleigh's municipal car park: YOU ARE HERE. Thomas rested his head on the table, and his hand on the image. The gold heart was beating against his palm: you are here, you are here, you are here.

Then roused by himself, or by his diligent ghost, or by the passage of the London train, Thomas poured cardamom coffee and attended to the remaining post. Charitable causes, admonitions from readers, despatches from utility companies, all were set aside with noises of boredom or disgust; then last of all, in a thin blue envelope, a letter postmarked Paris. Thomas looked at it with the sensation of a man in the dock looking the jury in the eye: here it was, verdict of disinterested strangers on whose whim the outcome of twenty years' hope and despondency depended. Quickly there came the sensation of distracted grief he always encountered at the end of a task: the manuscript was nearly done, the comet was at his doorstep; all that mattered was coming to an end – what to do then, with the brief time remaining? The glass was falling hour by hour, but wouldn't fall forever – *Get on with it*, said Maria Văduva, settling herself on the windowsill, boots two inches deep in Essex mud.

'Get out of my light,' said Thomas. Lifting the letter to the window, he encountered the baroque translated sentences first with frank amusement, then in due course with delight:

Dear Mr Hart

The International Astronomical Union places much emphasis on a felicitous collaboration between nations, institutions, and individuals of both the professional and amateur kind.

Thus we were pleased to hear from you regarding comet 330P/1889 (du Lac). Having surveyed the evidence, and examined the comet's orbit and position in the year of its discovery, we consider it a probability that Maria Văduva Bell, of Aldleigh in Essex, first identified the object on 17 June 1889 at 11.12 p.m. in the region of Cassiopeia. It is the policy of the Union to name a comet after a maximum of two primary observers, and it is therefore our proposition that the comet should now take the designation 330P/1889 (Văduva–du Lac). We regret that this resolution arrives too late for the present perihelion, but trust you will be satisfied with this outcome.

Amitiés sincères

PROFESSOR DAVID LANE

Thomas put the letter down, and looked for a time at the opposing wall. The glass was falling hour by hour, and now had fallen further – he rested his head on the table, and with confusion and shame felt the arrival of tears. He'd anticipated joy and satisfaction: what came was a sense of loss. What now, Thomas Hart? What will you do with your remaining time?

Up you get, Thomas, said Maria Văduva, standing at the window, having knocked over his coffee in a temper: *gone ten in the morning, and work to be done*. Gone ten in the morning, and work to be done, and meanwhile Grace Macaulay mourned in her cold room under the eaves. Thomas, thinking of her sorrow, felt the old movement in his heart, and what came to mind was an infant in Bethesda, carried in a basket like a suitcase to the door. He'd entered then into a contract from which he'd never be set free, the terms of his employment set and circumscribed by love, and now it demanded he should act. Maria sought out his eye, and nodded once: *Do what you must, Thomas Hart.*

Nathan – did Grace tell you the comet is coming? Perihelion
tomorrow. Now: humour an old man. Come to Lowlands 8 p.m.
They promise clear skies – and didn't you help me find it? Isn't it
almost yours? T. H.

Shamefully swift, a response:

Thank you. Not sure if free, will check, hope to see you there – N.

You are not free, thought Thomas, and you never were. More
coffee then, and toast with too much butter, and another
note (Maria left him to his business):

Dear Nick

I am writing to resign from my position at the *Essex
Chronicle* with sadness, and with immediate effect. You
will smile now, and you will say to yourself: Thomas, it is
not before time.

Please see attached my last column. I hope it will give you
pleasure.

God bless you and keep you!

THOMAS HART

He felt again the dreadful peace that threatened to leave him
motionless at his table; but it occurred to him that nights
these days were cold, and that Grace would expect him to
bring something to eat. So he shook his own body as if free-
ing it of dust, and went out into the kitchen where he
decanted milk into a blue-banded bowl, and crumbled in a

cake of fresh yeast. There was the scent not of new loaves, but of champagne. Then Anne Macaulay was coming down the hall, arriving out of the shadow of the coat-stand and sewing a plastic pearl button on her nightdress: 'Give it a pinch of sugar,' she said, 'give it a helping hand.' So a pinch of sugar for the yeast to fatten on, and Thomas, not surprised by her arrival, waited by the window. It was not yet dark, but already a canopy of cloud was drawing over from the west and putting out his hopes. 'No clear skies yet, I see,' said Anne, examining the yeast, 'but possibly tomorrow: have faith.'

'It is currently in the constellation of Perseus,' said Thomas, 'turning and turning as it comes. You remember Hale–Bopp, you remember the Great Comet of 1997, and the girl who set the fire? There was never another like it, not in all the years since, and I won't live to see Halley again – so I must pin all my hopes on this.'

He cut cold butter into a bowl of sifted flour and Maldon salt; and 'Yes,' said Anne. 'I remember. You'll be wanting to rub lightly, Mr Hart: fingertips only, remembering at all times that heat is the enemy of good pastry.' In with the foaming milk, with the yolk of four large eggs and a teaspoon of Madagascan vanilla – 'Turning and turning through Perseus,' said Thomas, 'coming at a thousand miles an hour; and as I understand it space opening out around it – bending, if you like: a fine net being pulled aside.' No answer: Anne Macaulay had begun to thin out, to drift towards the door – she never did approve of his fascination with the matter of the stars. Now Thomas formed the dough, and kneaded it; he rolled it to the thickness of an old pound coin, and folded it around fragments of Turkish delight, as he was taught by a man who was taught by his mother.

The oven was ready. Powdered sugar waited in a bowl. It

was the time of astronomical twilight, and there was darkness on Lower Bridge Road. Thomas moved across his kitchen, and fancifully it occurred to him that the motion of his body displaced the universe — that it slipped aside to accommodate him; that it might be said that he was no less significant, and certainly no more, than a comet dispensing its days of ordinary grace. The gold heart was beating on the table. You are here, Thomas Hart. Here you are.

THE MOON ON THE WATER

THOMAS HART *ESSEX CHRONICLE*,
12 DECEMBER 2017

In the twenty years since I began this column, I've written many pieces on the stars, and the few principles of physics that have fallen within my limited capacity, and which I hardly began to understand. I never wrote as an expert, but as an amateur; and since an amateur is one who loves his subject, that's what I remain – I only hope I've been forgiven where I've erred.

Since this is my last column, I'm returning to the moon because I loved it first and best. Some weeks ago, I happened to be walking late at night after a day of rain when there were puddles in the streets, and I found as I walked that at certain times, when the position of the puddle and the angle of the light were judicious, the moon would arrive at my feet.

I looked for a long time at these commonplace reflections, and found them wonderful. They were not the moon, and not the water, but a third and separate thing: the moon-on-the-water, born like a child of the relation between the two.

Now: I've heard it said that at the first sip from the glass of the natural sciences you will become an atheist – then at the bottom of the glass, God will be waiting for you.

Some claim these are the words of the physicist Werner Heisenberg, and some say he never said any such thing – but it charmed me enough to seek him out on the shelves, and find as ever that my wonder and my comprehension did battle, and left me reeling. It seems to me that Heisenberg proposes this: that although the electron is certainly real, nothing we can say of its location now can do any more than say where it might probably be in the future. It is a mysterious thing, not quite existing separate from any other thing, and coming most fully into being at the moment of connection.

I wonder in that case if the world and everything in it – you, me, the moon and the water – consists not of solitary beings, but rather out of how each thing relates to another, so that in the end it is only out of connection that the whole world is made.

Dear reader: I'm grateful that you've been my companion all these years – that we have existed together on this page. I must leave you now, but as it happens a comet is coming in as I am going out: Văduva–du Lac, discovered in 1889 by Maria Văduva Bell of Lowlands House in Aldleigh, on a clear Essex night. If ever I gave you a moment's interest or pleasure, will you do this for me? Go out. Look up. Experience with me this act of grace which is common to us all. You cannot earn or command it: it is a gift, and it will be wonderful because of your wonder. Look up, with me, won't you? Look up – and at the moment of our looking there'll be this one marvellous thing, shining in time, under common grace: the comet-in-us.

Perihelion

Now: perihelion. Comet 330P/1889 Văduva–du Lac has crossed the ecliptic plane; it will rise in the east in the region of Pisces, tumbling head over heels in its haste. In the observatories of Paris and Kielder and Pulkovo, its apparent magnitude is judged to be -1: give it a clear night and a day or two, and it will outdo the Great Comet of 1997 and all the attending marvels and disasters.

Aldleigh is waiting with the patience of the saints. It has no choice. Tinsel in the pound shop, blowsy in the narrow aisles; white lights strung on yews and privet hedges winking out when the battery goes. Choirs rehearsing in town halls and sitting rooms and small cathedral naves: glory to God in the highest, and on earth no great expectation of peace. Ronald Macaulay is sleeping in slippers embroidered *R. M.*, to remind him of his own name – to assert that yes, here he is, here he has been: a man for whom no natural love could match his love for heaven. Children are coming home to Aldleigh on the London train, watching their own vast lamplit faces scud over Stratford, Shenfield, Chelmsford: we are giants in the land, they think, we could occupy the towns – and meanwhile their parents, nursing lifelong headaches, tot up the costs of the day. Frost is paling the banks of the Alder, where smashed plates and dented wedding rings wash up in shopping trolleys full of silt; and in the basement of the old town hall Boudicca's dismantled breasts are pricked sore by holly wreaths.

The tills are ringing in the Jackdaw and Crow, where schoolgirls and women and men are by turns angry or peaceable and never conscious of the cause; they make one body heaving over to the bar, drawing breath and singing they wish it could be Christmas every day. Prayers holy and idle and sometimes profane rise like sparrows from bungalows and offices where the tinsel is already coming loose: my God, look at that and Christ, you frightened me and Lord, make me good (but not yet)! Snowdrops are coming up on the grave containing all that could die of Anne Margaret Macaulay, and she communicates in the litter blowing back and forth between the headstones: oh I did live, Thomas Hart, and I do, but I rather think the harmonium never really was in tune. Lovers are lying down in Potter's Field and can't believe they found each other, can't believe their luck. It's quick and hard on account of the cold but never mind that, never mind the admonishing jays in the bare trees on the margin, it's done and dusted and the night can get on with its business: be swift my soul to answer him, be jubilant my feet! Southend United is two–nil down and the hero born of woman crushed the serpent with his heel; the barrels are empty at the Jackdaw and Crow and Thomas almost thinks that his Redeemer lives. The Bible is open in Bethesda's pulpit and the broken pane of glass is coming loose; so the wind gets in and turns through Genesis and Exodus and the Song of Songs: Bless the Lord oh my soul and forget not all His benefits, and meanwhile half a mile away the *Essex Chronicle* is going to the press.

Gone eight in the evening. Thomas Hart is seated on an iron bench beside the Lowlands lake, and he's cold in his good winter coat. The air's hardening to frost in shining particles that punish the cyclamen come up round the roots of the Aldwinter oak. Stars appear and disappear in banks of

373

cloud tethered like lost continents off the far horizon, but overhead it's clear. Thomas looks out east to the breach in the yews, but no sign yet.

Nathan is here. Nathan was early, and has cut himself while shaving. He sits mute beside Thomas with his hands on his cane and his body trembles sometimes with pain, or December, or anticipation. 'She'll come,' says Thomas, 'she'll come,' but in fact moment by moment he grows uncertain – might it be better if she stays in her room by the three-bar fire with her dressing gown on, might it be better if she has her pride? He attends to the basket he put down between his feet; he brings out white cloth napkins, a tin of pastries wrapped in paper, white rolls that drop flour on his coat. The body of the man at his side is all alertness, all expectancy and poise: 'Thomas, is that it?' he says. 'Is it here?'

It is here. It is risen. It drifts above the pricking skyline, and emerges in the darkening sky like something rising to the surface of deep water. Thomas stands. The tin drops from his lap and opens and lets loose the scent of roses. 'Oh, look,' says Thomas with joy indivisible from loss. 'Look.' His eyes are latched to it as if by hooks: he is in pain. By slow degrees the sky darkens, and the comet brightens against it, and however will I do it justice, thinks Thomas, coming up hard against his incapacity, and the hopeless falling-short of language – it's a searchlight beam, it's a pearl crushed to a smear, it's the night worn thin and the Shekhinah glory coming through – it isn't like any of these and no use trying for a phrase.

Nathan stands and he's steady and silent on his feet – he reaches for Thomas, and finds him: 'I didn't know what to expect,' he says, gripping Thomas hard enough to hurt, 'I never did.' The comet, ecstatic in the company of the sun after its time of solitude, begins to show its double tail: here's the gas-jet, blue as the moon once was, here's the sunlit dust stream blown by solar winds and curved like the blade of a seax on the Essex coat of arms; it is indifferent to every kind of doctrine and legislation, and its universal light is neither sacred nor profane.

Movement now beyond the lake, in the breach between the high black yews, and Nathan makes a sound that's very like that of his pain: here's Grace Macaulay in a red velvet coat, coming quickly like an animal only wanting one thing, with a whole company in her wake. They come through the breach, they assemble by the lake – every soul Thomas has ever loved: here's Anne Macaulay in her cotton nightdress, marvelling over the thin blue blanket in her arms: *It is well, it is well with my soul.* Here's James Bower meeting his eye with affection and shame: I did know, I did know, I did. Here's Richard Dimitru Dines half-cut on whisky with his satchel on his back, and his arm round the senior deacon, whose beard is blacker than ever; here's Maria Văduva Bell and she's got Cora Seaborne with her: 'Darling child,' she is saying, 'let them never dissuade you from your course,' and all the pearls have gone from the hem of her gown. Here's Grace Macaulay in a scarlet coat, scent of rose oil rising from her arms, giving out her uncontainable joy, coming first to her enemy and friend; there's her butt of affection so like that of an animal; how immense love is, thinks Thomas, how surprising, to go on unforgiving and undiminished. Now she is gone, she is going to her lover, and her body is hard against his: they're matter dispersed by time and circumstance, assembled for this moment according to the natural laws.

'You are here,' says Thomas, surveying the company, 'you are here.' It is uncontainable, he cannot stand it: the comet is only going to rise, and equally dispense its pearly light on love offered and met and refused and mistaken, the law of

375

harmonies unfailingly in operation on the human heart. He hears the ticking of his watch, and music drifting down from Lowlands House: everything that would ever happen had happened, and was happening, and the heavens were declaring the glory of God. He hears all the dogs of Essex barking, and all the trains departing all the towns – hears time's first speech, and last recorded syllable – sees the early constellations dancing, and earth's near star put out: it is all one engine of perpetual motion, driven by God or fate or unmotivated time, turning over and over through gain and loss and gain, every part of it remarkable, essential to the whole. How absolutely improbable it is, he thinks, standing amazed between the comet and the water, what a miracle that I am here at all – that out of matter I was made, to stand here with a button missing on my coat, heart broken by nothing but illuminated dust!

What now then, Thomas Hart, at the light of perihelion? What creed and consolation can you rustle up for your friends, now all of your notebooks are filled?

Perhaps this is the wonder, Thomas, and this is the whole of the law: you are here. You are here. You are here.

Acknowledgements

Thank you to my parents, who raised me in the light of God and science together.

Thank you to Robert Perry, who has listened so long and so patiently.

Thank you to all my family and friends, whose patience and affection for me must have been sorely tested during the many years I have worked on this book. I can never repay their kindness.

Thank you to Jenny Hewson, Hannah Westland, Katherine Nintzel, Suzanne Dean, Sarah-Jane Forder and Graeme Hall. Rarely has a novelist had more cause to be grateful to their agent and editors for their wisdom and skill – without them this book would be less than half what it is, and its writer less than a quarter. Thank you to all at Jonathan Cape for their work to bring this story to its readers.

Thank you to Kate Devlin, Chris Gribble, Mark Haddon, Sarah Hall, Caoilinn Hughes and Louisa Yates for reading early pages when I most needed readers. Thank you to Gladstone's Library for being again a place of refuge.

Thank you to Dorian Jessu for assistance with Romanian. Thank you to Marilyn Sher and Adam Sheppard for assistance with keeping me more or less in one piece.

Thank you to David Butler, Paul Behrens and Nathan Yanasak for their help with matters of physics and the stars. David, my father, raised me with an eye to the telescope and taught me the laws of Kepler, and in doing so enlarged my mind and my life; Paul kindly made me think more clearly and with pleasure. I am especially grateful to Nathan, who gave of his time and expertise with extraordinary generosity: I have quoted directly from him where tidal lock is concerned. Carlo Rovelli's writing has been vital to this book and to me. Where the novel errs in the matter of physics, the errors are entirely Thomas Hart's, or mine.

Thank you to S. G., for the orbits. This is his book.

Permissions

READ ON FOR AN
EXCLUSIVE ESSAY

Friendship

SARAH PERRY

When recently asked what I thought my novels held in common, a few things came to mind. I'm eternally fascinated and bewildered by matters of faith and science, for example, and generally to be found up to my knees in East Anglian mud, or peering through river mist at some distant troubling figure.

But now I wonder if these things are incidental, and what really preoccupies me is a kind of taxonomy of love – as if I'm poking away at every kind of intimacy and attachment and desire, for all the world as if I wore a white coat, and could weigh out love, and identify it, and preserve it in a bottle of formaldehyde.

Being constitutionally inclined to mischief, I'm most drawn to kinds of love ordinarily greeted with a degree of confusion or suspicion, or – even better! – hardly greeted at all. So friendship in particular preoccupies me, perhaps because it has fallen from favour as worthy of the kind of serious artistic attention given to romantic or familial love, and I like to be out of style.

It's fascinating – and possibly a little sad – to look back over centuries of Western literature and correspondence, and see what's been lost where the treatment of friendship is concerned. The French essayist Michel de Montaigne, grief-struck by the death of his friend Étienne, could only explain the depth of his attachment by reverting to a kind of existential cry: 'If you press me to say why I loved him, I can say no more than because he was he, and because I was I.' Meanwhile, it's often forgotten that when Tennyson wrote "tis better to have loved and lost than never to have loved at all', he grieved not the death of a lover, but of Hallam, his friend.

When such passionate affection is expressed, the question of whether the relationship was romantic will be raised; but just as we cannot say Tennyson loved Hallam as a lover, we equally can't say that he didn't – and besides, it's hardly the case that erotic feeling makes it necessary to lift love out of its little bottle labelled 'Friendship', and into a larger jar.

Perhaps Tennyson's love for Hallam strikes modern sensibilities as suspiciously romantic because the habit of speaking lovingly to friends has been lost. But the poet Keats wrote to the painter Hayden, 'I have that sort of fire in my heart that would sacrifice everything I have for your service . . . I open my heart to you'; and when George Eliot received the gift of a hand-carved book-slide from a young woman who admired her work, they entered into a friendship so intimate that Eliot began to sign her letters 'from your loving MOTHER'. Helen Keller and Mark Twain adored each other so much that he once wrote, 'I suppose there is nothing like it in heaven; and not likely to be, until we get there and show off.' Meanwhile, Ellen Nussey was so possessively attached to her friend Charlotte Brontë that she withdrew from all contact when Brontë announced her engagement; and for the rest of their lives, the husband and the friend were bitterly at odds.

Writing *Enlightenment*, I found myself again in my white lab coat, engaged in a taxonomy of love. I looked closely at faith, and understood it to be a kind of love; I wrote about the love of learning, which can be as exhilarating and transformative as faith. There is erotic love in this novel, and unrequited love, and love acquired more or less by mistake; and perhaps most significantly there is a friendship between an older man and a girl.

My old inclination to mischief came over me when I first conceived of the friendship between Thomas Hart and Grace Macaulay. For reasons only too evident, any attachment of a man to a child that is no relation of his is likely to be met with confusion at best, and suspicion at worst. Readers raised on a diet of novels in which the abuse and exploitation of children is heavily foreshadowed (and sometimes lingered over) might perhaps have expected Thomas to reveal himself to be in some way monstrous, and Grace herself a vehicle for trauma. Who can blame them? Perhaps the most famous love of a man for a child is that of Lewis Carroll for Alice Liddell, the girl who inspired *Alice's Adventures in Wonderland*, and twenty-first-century commentators have enjoyed taking a dim view. Carroll adored the real Alice, and said so often and openly; he photographed her obsessively; he asked her for a lock of hair; he wrote that he saw no reason why little girls' bodies should ever be covered up. On such evidence one can hear the judge bring down the gavel. But Carroll adored all children, perhaps because his own childhood, said Virginia Woolf, was 'lodged in him whole and entire'; and thinking the bodies of children exempt from the shame of nakedness is perhaps a sign of too much innocence, not too little. Besides, Victorians were so given to seeking locks of hair from each other that it is not at all surprising they had such a fashion for hats.

Still, Carroll can never be quite free from the narrowed gaze of readers, who after all have been given precious few models of friendships between men and children in fiction. There is the wrenching, tender, fatherly attachment depicted in Michelle Magorian's *Goodnight Mr Tom*, and the decades-long and mutually irritated friendship between Adrian Mole and Bert in Sue Townsend's series of comic masterpieces; but generally speaking adults are depicted as exploiting the innocence and malleability of childhood, as with *The Go-Between*, or *Great Expectations*.

So it has delighted me to confound expectations, and instead propose a friendship based not on the mechanics of age and identity, but rather on something as simple as it is strange, which is at the heart of all great friendships in literature and life: that Thomas was Thomas, and Grace was Grace, and nobody else would do.

—Sarah Perry, 2024

About the Author

Sarah Perry is the internationally bestselling author of the novels *Melmoth*, *The Essex Serpent* and *After Me Comes the Flood*, and the non-fiction book *Essex Girls*. She is a winner of the Waterstones Book of the Year Award and has been nominated for the Women's Prize, the Folio Prize and the Costa Novel Award. She is a fellow of the Royal Society of Literature and has a PhD in Creative Writing.